Other books by
James R. Beller

The Soul of St. Louis
The Collegiate Baptist History Workbook
Sacred Betrayal: The Coming Destruction of the Baptist People
America From Sea to Shining Sea (1ˢᵗ grade history text)
Baptist Heritage Learn and Color

Visit baptistchristianworldview.com or
21tnt.com/pfp

AMERICA IN CRIMSON RED

The Baptist History of America

James R. Beller

Quoted material in this book has been copied exactly from its
original source. All mistakes and
misspellings have been retained.

Also, scriptures quoted are from the *Authorized Version* and need
no earthly permission to be used.

ISBN
978-0-9668766-3-5

For further information write:
Prairie Fire Press
3705 Telegraph Road
Arnold, Missouri 63010

Visit
Baptist Truth and Testimony of the 21st Century
www.21tnt.com
www.baptistchristianworldview.com

To Max Q. Hardy.

Without his help this book would not be a reality.

ACKNOWLEDGMENTS

The search for Baptist history is at times a frustrating process. I would like to express my appreciation to these friends who aided along the trail:

First and foremost, my gratitude to Jesus for His amazing grace.

I thank my sweet and patient wife Vickie, not only for her constant encouragement, but also for her research, typing and typesetting skills.

My gratitude to the following library and archive professionals we worked with across the country:

Karen Sundland and Stuart Campbell, Samuel Colgate Historical Library, Rochester, New York;

Dr. Mark Brown, Curator; Timothy Engels, Manuscripts; Martha Mitchell, Archivist; at the John Hay Library, Brown University, Providence, Rhode Island;

Tricia Feeleg, Reference Librarian Boston Public Library, Boston, Massachusetts;

Richard Stattler, Associate Library Director, Manuscripts Curator; Meredith Paine Sorozan, Associate Library Director and Reference Librarian; Julia Wilczynski and Robyn Flynn, staff; at the Rhode Island Historical Society, Providence, Rhode Island;

Elsie Fisher, Librarian; Dee Day, Assistant Librarian, and Kenette Harder, Reference Librarian at William Jewell College, Liberty, Mo.;

Angela N. Stiffler, Archival Director at the Partee Center for Baptist Historical Studies, William Jewell College, Liberty, Missouri;

Julia Bradford, Assistant to the Director of the N. C. Baptist Historical Collection, Personal Collections Section and the University Archives at the Z. Smith Reynolds Library at Wake Forest University, Winston-Salem, North Carolina;

Fred Anderson, Director, and Darlene Slater, Research Assistant, at the Virginia Baptist Historical Society, Richmond, Virginia.

My thanks to these George Washington scholars: Willard Sterne Randall, Visiting Professor of the Humanities, Chaplain College, Burlington, Vermont; Dr. Clair Keller (retired), Iowa State University; Dr. Stuart Leibiger, LaSalle University, Philadelphia, Pennsylvania.

My gratitude to Vickie Beller, Mary Mann, and Shirley Goad for selected typing of resources; and to Vickie Beller, Mary Mann, Shirley Goad, Jane Palczynski, Mary Kathryn Hardy and Patricia Dlubac for their help in proof reading.

A note of thanks to Dr. James Sightler for his insight on the Overmountain men, John Leland, and the Bill of Rights.

My gratitude to Dr. David L. Cummins for his passion and work in preserving Baptist heritage, and for his timely advice and encouragement.

My gratitude to Bro. Jeffrey Faggart, pastor of Harvest Baptist Church and director of the Baptist History Preservation Society. Thank you friend, for taking me to see the remains of our history, and introducing to me our forgotten heritage. "Mine eye affecteth mine heart..." Lamentations 3:51.

My gratitude to Dr. William P. Grady for convincing me to write this book next.

My gratitude to Rev. Dan Clubb for believing in his friend's burden.

A note of thanks to the people of the Arnold Baptist Tabernacle for their prayers and patience; and to that first group of financial backers of Prairie Fire Press: Edward and Michelle McCarter, Terry and Linda Bohnert, Robert and Melanie Black and Patricia Dlubac.

Thank you, Jeremy, Nicole, Zackary and Katherine for being patient with the avalanche of books, papers and endless nights of typing, not to mention nights away from Dad. May God "visit this vine" for your sakes.

In Memory of

American Missionary Pastor John Kelley, martyred while attempting to help found a New Testament Baptist Church in Baghdad, Iraq, February 14, 2004.

TABLE OF CONTENTS

PREFACE

Baptist History is a subject with which every member of the Baptist faith ought to be familiar. The contributions, which the Baptists made to the founding of our nation and to religious history, are extremely significant, yet they are often overlooked or ignored. Though there have been many volumes written about the Baptists, it has been many years since an in depth study of the Baptists in America has been presented. Sadly, during those intervening years, there have been some who have chosen to forsake the name, character, and principles of the Baptists. Consequently, there is an urgent need for our people to be stirred to remembrance.

America in Crimson Red accurately chronicles the rise of the Baptists and their struggle for religious liberty. It is evident that the author has spent much time in researching many credible documents and histories of a bygone era. He has collated the facts of history with unusual insight and candor. The result is an excellent treatise that is a must read for every Baptist. The reader can expect to gain a good working knowledge from the following narrative and will be rewarded with a greater appreciation for the labour, sacrifice, and courage of the many Baptists who stood firmly upon scriptural principles despite severe persecution.

The best way of preserving our history is to acquaint ourselves with the stories of the past. Then our history will become a personal heritage to be lived before a future generation. It is our belief that those who read this book will be strengthened in their faith.

Pastor Jeff Faggart
Harvest Baptist Church
Baptist History Preservation Society

FOREWORD

Samuel Butler opined, "God cannot alter the past, but historians can." That statement is surely proven in many American history textbooks that are set before the youth in America's public school systems in this twenty-first century. One cannot read so-called modern historical accounts of America without the realization that historians have distorted and obliterated our past that they might shape and control our future. Tragically, these "historians" have followed the three steps necessary to re-write history. They have put the "spin" on our history by omitting some records of vital truth, adding ingredients to make history politically correct, and altering the true accounts to further their own ends. The media and academia have merged in this all too successful revision of our history. Our once proud Constitutional Republic has been portrayed as a mere democracy. Our Bible-laced past has been brought into doubt, distorted and finally denied. Our honored heroes of the past have been re-evaluated without any historical evidence and made to appear as reckless, godless men of ill repute.

How pleased I have been to discover that James Beller has taken upon himself the task of researching and restating historical truth in his latest book, *America in Crimson Red*. As he has researched ancient archives, Pastor Beller has discovered the long-forgotten role played by Bible-believing Baptists in the early days of our republic. This volume will cause every American reader to hold his or her head high and honor our revered past. Believing that this tome deserves a large audience, I am pleased to write this recommendation. Those who read this book will discover long-forgotten details of our history, and hopefully, many youth in America will as a result of this volume, be enabled to serve God with unfeigned fervency.

David L. Cummins
Deputation Director
Baptist World Mission Decatur, Alabama

INTRODUCTION

N o historian is able to give facts alone. I say the "historian" cannot hide his heart, for if he does he becomes the reason the reader is disinterested. I cannot divorce myself from the fervor of our historic testimony. I pray you will feel the same.

I knew what *I* wanted from the experience of our five years of research. I wanted the testimony of our forefathers to transform my own life. I wanted to thirst for God like them, to preach with fervency like them, and for God to use me in like fashion. I also wanted to search for our distinctives and discover how our people maintained them through the years.

The knowledge of our heritage has changed our church. We have dedicated ourselves in our own small way to birthing churches. I have more desire to continue to preach to the lost and birth new works than at any time in my entire ministry. So my purpose was to fire my own soul and help my church gain a greater vision for the lost. From that, emerged the absolute *necessity* of preserving the testimony and distinctives of our forgotten forefathers.

America is a Baptist nation. Her principles are altogether Baptist and her heritage is imbued with Baptist ideals, courage and blood. She is governed by Baptist polity, ingrained with the higher plane of soul-liberty and under girded by a hidden, yet profound Baptist history.

Our reader must not dismiss this seemingly outlandish premise. Historians have been rewriting for the last 50 years and honest and forthright commentators have slipped on plain issues while sitting on the toadstools of the obvious.

To recognize that historic America is indeed Christian is somewhat like admitting that fire is hot. Those who argue against that premise are guilty of dishonesty and do not deserve a hearing. Verily, a junior high student with access to a public library can come to the realization of America's Christian heritage. However, the outrageous premise of America being a *Baptist* nation is harder to accept; yet one of the aims of this book will be to enlighten you on this truth and stir up your mind.

The *baptized believers* have always been the embarrassing remnant of those who are called *Christian*. The so-called *re-baptizers* ("Anabaptist"—a name of scorn) go back to the New Testament and Acts 19:2-5.

A baptism that was not upon a profession of faith in Christ was *no baptism* and our "Anabaptist" forefathers were not *re-baptizers*. They were *baptized believers*. They have been known by various derisive names through the years, and in most cases their tormentors and accusers named them.

The first case of this in ancient history was the "Donatists." They suffered persecution by Augustine and the "Catholics" in the middle of the 4th century. They practiced baptism for believers and demanded that the bishop who baptized should also be a believer.

Baptist faith and theology has historical roots not in the "Holy Roman Catholic and Apostolic Church," but in the independent congregations of the first three centuries following the resurrection of Christ. Those separate churches birthed from Asia minor and spread to Syria where the Paulicians flourished; Southern France, from whence the Albigenses sprang; the Alpine regions and their valleys, where the blood of the Waldenses flowed; and into the British Islands, where the evangelist Patrick baptized over 100,000 converts **by immersion.** But Europe and Asia from A. D. 50 to 1600 is not the subject of this volume.

Our narrative focuses on America between 1620 and 1905. What will be presented to you is the astounding story of how a band of disfranchised and banished believers went from "the sewer of New England" to become the most influential voice in the foundation of the greatest republic in the history of mankind.

I know of no historian, secular or Christian, who seems willing to discuss the enemy of souls and our *adversary*, the devil. Ignoring his devices is unwise. His device of diversion is one of his greatest weapons. When Baptist origins in America are discussed, we are usually pointed to Roger Williams. Williams was indeed a great man but as we shall discover, he was not our founder. We have been diverted from our truly great American pioneer pastor, Dr. John Clarke. This diversion has continued throughout American history. This is just one error in history which this narrative seeks to uncover and correct.

Every American should be aware of the testimony of Isaac Backus, Shubal Stearns, Samuel Harris, James Ireland, Daniel Marshall, John Gano, Thomas Baldwin and Isaac McCoy. Perhaps you have read of Silas Mercer, James Furman or John Leland. But what of Obadiah Holmes, who was beaten on the streets of Boston for visiting and holding an unauthorized church service; or John Weatherford, whose wrists and hands were lacerated while he preached from a Virginia jail; or John Waller, who was incarcerated several times for preaching without a license; or James Ireland, whose family was poisoned in retribution for his pointed preaching?

What a pity this generation has forgotten about the real history of America, and has neglected even the resting-places of the most influential of early American patriots. Blame must be placed upon the shoulders of the last generation of historians, educators and preachers who failed to raise memorials to our departed servants of Christ.

The recording of progress of the Baptists in American history began with the preservation of *the Diary of John Comer*, circa. 1730. Comer began to gather materials for a comprehensive history of all of the colonies. However, God called John Comer home early in his life. His materials landed in the hands of John Callender, his successor at the Baptist Church at Newport, Rhode Island.

Callender delivered as a discourse, and printed the first written history of the Baptists of America in 1734. His focus was primarily on Rhode Island.

Arguably, the greatest American Baptist historian was the incomparable Isaac Backus. Backus obtained the papers of Comer and Callender. He diligently gathered the testimonies of our suffering ancestors. Backus published his *Church History of New England* in 1804 and gave the triumphant details of the Baptist struggle in Puritan New England. Our nation is eternally indebted to Elder Backus for gathering the tremendous archive known collectively as *the Backus Papers*. Much of these papers have yet to be examined by sympathetic eyes.

David Benedict was the next widely read historian and was one of the first to tie the American *baptized believers* to their European forefathers. His *History of the Baptist Denomination* was published in 1813 and was a catalyst for the advancement of church planting and missions in this country.

The diligent William Cathcart gave us the fabulous *Baptist Encyclopedia*. It contains hundreds of short biographies and historical narratives so valuable in understanding our heritage. The *Encyclopedia* was published in 1883.

In 1887, Thomas Armitage gave a thorough view of the Baptists in his *History of the Baptists, traced by their Vital Principles and Practices* and provided a historic bridge into the 20th century. His work complimented Cathcart.

The last widely read Baptist historian in America was Henry Vedder. Vedder was heavily influenced by the theories of Dr. William Whitsitt of the late 19th century. Vedder incomprehensibly could not find *immersion* as a sure point of distinction within the ranks of the *baptized believers*. We shall discover the source of his error.

The most passionate of all Baptist historians in America was Robert B. Semple. Writing in 1810, his view of the great grace and rapid spread of the "Separate" Baptists stirred a multitude of hearts in his definitive, *History of the Rise and Progress of the Baptists of Virginia*. His account of the powerful revival that transformed the south still burns. It is with the spirit and passion of Semple that hopefully, *America in Crimson Red* is penned. For what good is history if after you have been told the truth, it motivates you to do nothing.

For this narrative, I have used the standard sources listed above. I have also given some attention to the Brown University scholar, William McLoughlin, whose work on the Backus Papers was helpful. McLoughlin attempted to make observations on the lives of early American Baptists through 20th century sociological lenses, something I believe to be a mistake. But we are grateful for his sorting of many facts contained in the Backus Papers.

On several trips to New England and the eastern seaboard I have attempted to find and record those things from our heritage which have been ignored, glossed over or misrepresented. The journeys included digging in archives, old periodicals and wherever our gracious God led me. I have found that if an old warrior for God was considered controversial, it was usually because he was right. If some flaming evangel was considered eccentric, it usually meant he was consecrated beyond what the critics would consider normal.

I approached the records assuming that those who recorded our heritage were sincerely moved by the spectacle they observed. I do not explain away what was recorded. The actions of God's servants continually inspire all of us to strive for that which He has ordained *us* to do. When I read about the Apostle Paul and the mighty wonderful works that God wrought through him, I believe it, and long and pray for God to use me also. Don't you? And if you do not, why bother to read the Bible or narratives such as this unless your aim is to criticize, pick, and explain away the power of God. May Almighty God confound you in your purposes!

Let us not be doomed to repeat the folly of ignorance of our heritage and theology of which the Baptists of 1800-1850 were guilty. Let us not repeat the error of our early 20ᵗʰ century brethren who nearly buried our heritage. Can our churches and our colleges survive without their true roots? History has proven they cannot. Moreover, let us not be satisfied to have a religion of mediocrity with no burden, no tears, no passion, and no true holiness.

I contend there were 12 outstanding men in the forming of our nation. On this list of 12, only four were politicians. Eight were preachers. Six of the eight preachers were Baptist preachers. They were—in the correct order of their influence—Shubal Stearns, Samuel Harriss, George Whitefield, John Clarke, Roger Williams, Jonathan Edwards, George Washington, Isaac Backus, Thomas Jefferson, James Madison, John Leland, and Patrick Henry.

Lest this assertion astound some, let me direct the critic to the pages of this narrative where concrete proof will be given, although to some it will seem only as solid as last winter's snow. The politicians on the list you already know. The preachers—you really ought to meet. We will begin in a boat on the Connecticut River.

James R. Beller
Arnold, Missouri

Teach me old man, what my young heart doth not know, and make me want to live out my days in splendid struggle for a cause.
—J. R. B.

Timeline of Events in New England from the Landing of the Pilgrims to the Dismissal of Henry Dunster

1620 Pilgrims land at Plymouth Rock

1628 Beginning of large migration from England to New England

1630 Massachusetts Bay Colony founded

1631 Roger Williams arrives in Massachusetts

1636 Williams banished from Massachusetts

1637 Dr. John Clarke arrives in Massachusetts

1637 Clarke and the *Opinionists* banished from Massachusetts. His church meets in the winter wilderness of New Hampshire.

1638 Portsmouth Compact. The beginning of the Baptist church on Aquetneck Island, the first in America

1639 "Church" founded and disbanded by Roger Williams in Providence, R. I.

1644 The Beating of Thomas Painter

1651 The Beating of Obadiah Holmes, the death of John Hazel

1653 Henry Dunster, first president of Harvard, refuses to bring his child to infant "baptism." He is forced to resign.

CHAPTER ONE
The Hand of Kind Providence

*As Williams earnestly laboured to promote the establishment of full
liberty of conscience in this country, they bent all their power
against him.*—Isaac Backus

There was a universal apostasy of the whole Church of England.—
John Robinson

The small vessel snaked its way up the Connecticut. It was cold and
a storm had brought rain most of the day. It was dusk now and
dangerous.

For several years there had been skirmishes between the natives of
Massachusetts, Connecticut and Rhode Island and the English settlers.
Already there were brutal ambushes and counter bloodletting. It simply
could not continue.

John Oldham was bushwhacked, murdered by warriors of the Pequots. Rumors were that Sassacus, the great Sagamore of the Pequot
nation wanted all English settlers out of Massachusetts. Sassacus needed
the Narragansetts and the Mohegans to help him.

That was the reason the ghostly boat brought a banished preacher to
the rendezvous point on the Connecticut River. It was 1636.[1]

As his craft slid onto the shore on the outskirts of what would one
day become New Haven, Connecticut, the Narragansetts stood on shore
to greet him. Mr. Williams was no stranger to them. His knowledge of
their culture and command of their language was a plus, but his respect
for them and yes, his love for their souls multiplied his effectiveness in
negotiating with them.

Strange now, how the Boston court needed the very man they had
banished. But as Joseph of old was jettisoned from his brethren for the
purposes of later redemption, Roger Williams now stood as a mediator.
He was brokering protection for the very group of people whom just a
few months previous were wishing he was 2,000 sea miles away.

The most venerated of America's Baptist historians, Isaac Backus recalled this unjust turn of events by writing, "And what would the English have done, if they had sent Williams out of the country as they intended? But a *kind Providence* prevented it."[2]

Williams had arrived in Boston in February 1631, and five short years after his arrival, his enemies exercised his banishment. In January of 1636, overcoming their design to ferry him back to England, he escaped out of their hand into the New England mist. For what was left for him in England anyway? One brother, Robert, was in England. His other brother Sydrack, a turkey merchant, had little contact with him in years. He had a sister, Katherine, who had just married the Anglican clergyman John Davies and was quite settled.[3] His father and mother, James and Alice, were deceased. Old England held no attraction, and for Roger Williams the canoe on the Connecticut was just a part of his *call.*

On this lonely trip through the terror of the Pequot nation were memories of St. Sepulcher's church and of King James and Edward Coke. There were memories of Old England and Captain John Smith. Oh yes, Captain Smith, who came to St. Sepulcher with that Indian maiden, Pocahontas. It was all so exciting, so cavalier. Yet, even in those days Williams could sense some injustice, something awry. He was evolving into a non-conformist in a Church of England home. Williams began at the tender age of *twelve* to side with the Puritans and the Separates of London. This was to the chagrin of his father whose strenuous disagreements caused him to reveal later that he was "persecuted, even from his own house."[4]

*   *   *

Roger Williams was born in the city of London, England, sometime near the year 1599. For a man destined to major on the details of life's absolutes, it is odd that the date of his birth is an uncertainty.

All biographers are certain that he lived in London, attended St. Sepulcher's church and won a scholarship to Cambridge. He studied languages, theology and the classics and became quite adept at stenography and short hand.

His office skills were profound at an early age and came to the attention of Sir Edward Coke, the famous juror of England who prosecuted Sir Walter Raleigh and later the members of the infamous Gunpowder Plot.[5] Williams became the equivalent of an office manager for Coke and recorded procedures for him in the myriad of court dates and duties of the most famous lawyer of his day. This brought him into contact with the elite band of dissidents whose collective voice was beginning to be heard from on high.[6]

So it was in the 1620's, that Mr. Williams' association with the Separatist leaders of England built definite principles into his young mind. His Separatist views were nurtured by the independent thinking of Coke and other men opposed to King Charles I. Contrary to modern historical rewrite,[7] his views were not a New England evolution of thought. They were definitely Old England. It is evident that this group of non-conformists wanted nothing less than the right to worship as a separate church, independent of the compromise and unregenerate state of the Church of England.

Astute readers of history must now see the difference between the Separatists and the Puritans, for it will be important when we wade onto the shores of our blossoming America. The Separatists believed the Church of England to be apostate and were trying to establish independent congregations apart from their mother church. The Puritans were seeking to purify the Church of England from within without breaking away from the communion of their mother. Both views would pose a problem for the *baptized believers* in America.[8]

Upon leaving Cambridge, Mr. Williams was assigned the duty of personal chaplain to Sir William Masham and his Lady Joan. Both were Puritan sympathizers leaning toward Separatism.

The Separatist wing of the Church of England had given birth to two brave churches—the Scrooby congregation and the Gainsborough congregation. Both churches migrated to Amsterdam, Holland, in search of liberty. For the Scrooby flock, under the pastoral care of John Robinson and Richard Clifton, Amsterdam was a bit too much liberty. They chose to migrate to Leyden, Holland. The Gainsborough congregation had as their pastor, John Smythe and his assistant Thomas Hellwys. In a short time, the Mennonite element of Amsterdam had a doctrinal effect on Smythe and Hellwys. Some historians believe Smythe first performed baptism upon himself[9] and then upon the rest of his congregation. Amidst great confusion and in the wake of Smythe's death, the Gainsborough church split and Thomas Hellwys, with the flock, retraced his tracks back to England. This church supposedly became the first "General" Baptist church in England, officially organized in 1611. However, evidence shows that Baptists were in England much earlier.

The Scrooby congregation stayed together in Leyden and determined to go to yet another country to worship God in peace. This they did in 1620. Over 100 of them sailed upon a small vessel across the raging Atlantic. We know them as the Pilgrim Fathers and their vessel was the *Mayflower*.

That was all exciting news to the Mashams as a young Roger Williams came to be their personal chaplain. At last there could be a place within England's jurisdiction where one could be a Separatist and be free to exercise the tender dictates of conscience.

The kind hand of Providence was evident in many other events. Williams' biographer, James Ernst, informs us that Lady Joan Masham had a niece, Jane Whalley, with whom Mr. Williams fell in love.[10] But his upbringing was not of nobility and he was passed over, losing the first battle of intellect and emotion in his young life. So instead, he fancied a common servant of the Masham's named Mary Barnard. He fell in love with her and they married in December of 1629. Mary began a whirlwind life with her firebrand husband and stood faithfully by his side for over 40 years. In her youth she could have never imagined the ride her young heart would endure.

Now Mr. Williams' wheels were turning quickly and in correspondence he spoke of a "call to New England."[11] We assume he was referring to the only church in Boston. The Boston churchmen were impressed with his résumé. After all, they knew him personally and were pleased with his scholarship, courage, and independence. They were impressed by his relationship with the Puritan leaders in Old England and the direction he was heading. They were impressed until he arrived. Williams became impassioned with the possibilities of freedom and separation from the chains of the *standing order*, away from the pressure of England's *black hats*.

He and Mary boarded the good ship *Lyon* in early December of 1630 and sailed for the shores of the New World. 66 days later, February 5, 1631, the *Lyon* arrived at Nantasket near the harbor of Boston. Even the length of the cruise could not dampen the enthusiasm of the young Separatist preacher. He was now in the New World, a new environment devoid of the religious bigotry that poisoned his mother country. It was a once-in-history chance to forge a new country with new principles. Only Roger Williams and a handful of others would understand the irresistible force of it.

Those "guys" in the *black hats*[12] were ruling in New England. Boston in the 1630's was ruled by a court of 25-30 deputies chosen from the membership of the Congregational Church. Immediately the hypocrisy in Boston was evident to Roger Williams. The shame of the Puritans demanding toleration in England and then denying toleration in the "New" England was at first aberrant and then intolerable for Williams' equitable mind to accept.

The Boston Court was a *church court*. True, it was separated from the Church of England by the ocean and by its structure. The *standing order* in America was independent of England—it was the "independent" Congregational. But the Boston Court was a *church court with a perfect marriage between the church and the magistrates*. This was the same pain against conscience that was despised in mother England. The Separatists of the Church of England saw their mother as corrupt, and only separation from her would bring purity to God's people. This position put the Separatists on a one-way course to religious and cultural disaster.

While they were in Old England the men of the Boston court were philosophical allies of Mr. Williams. Williams debated the duties of man to God, and man to man in depth in those years. He also made his dissatisfaction with the "Book of Common Prayer" quite plain.

During the early years of the 20th century, new evidence came from the publication of Williams' writings, and from records in England, which gave a new perspective on the relationship between New England's most important men.

With Archbishop Laud[13] bearing down on the Puritans, it became apparent that many of the preachers would face jail, banishment or death. Out of this agony came the dream of the Massachusetts Bay Colony. With the Separatist "Pilgrims" sailing to the New World in 1620, these "Puritans" were also anxious to start anew. If the church could be reformed, so be it; if not, perhaps sailing to the New World would be a solution. In 1629, the Puritans met with the Earl of Lincoln in Sempringham, Lincolnshire, to discuss their options, and at this meeting the Massachusetts Bay Colony was born.

During this time, while exercising his duties as chaplain to Sir William Masham, Roger Williams had become closely acquainted with Thomas Hooker. Williams and Hooker went by carriage together to meet with another young preacher destined for fame in the New World—John Cotton. From Cotton's church in England's old Boston, the three traveled together to attend the famous meeting in Sempringham. What happened on the journey is an open window to understanding early American history. Ernst tells us:

> The famous meeting brought together a goodly company of godly men at Sempringham. Even the Bishop of Lincoln aided his brethren to escape the persecutions of Laud's party. They discussed the plans for settling, financing, and governing the projected colony, and talked a great deal of Indian conversion. Here Mr. Williams met his future New England persecutors—all seeking an escape for "tender consciences."
>
> During their ride to and from Sempringham, the three men of God carried on a lively discussion about theology and church reform, making the trip a memorable one. "Possibly, Master Cotton may call to mind that the discusser," recounts Mr. Williams, "riding with himself and one other person of precious memory, Master Hooker, to and from Sempringham, presented his arguments from Scripture why he durst not join with them in their use of Common Prayer."[14]

Looking back now, how is it that John Winthrop could write that Mr. Williams "hath broached NEW and DANGEROUS opinions against the authority of the magistrates?" His opinions were neither new nor dangerous.

Mr. Williams went to accept the call to be "teacher" among whom he was led to believe were Separatists; however, the Church at Boston was not what it appeared to be. Separatist in name only, the church continued to tether a relationship with the apostate Church of England. The preacher could not bring himself to compromise and officiate their services. For all of his convictions, our Separatist firebrand was labeled "divinely mad."[15]

He soon moved south to Plymouth and then north to Salem to preach the Gospel at Salem church, but the *black hats* were watching from ivory towers.

A nation was forming around these men, although the plan of God was still invisible to them. Over 21,000 new Englishmen streamed into Massachusetts Bay from 1628 to 1643. Some decisions had to be made about these points of doctrine and law. Unfortunately for Roger Williams, things were not going to go his way. Fortunately for the rising republic, Williams was not going to give up on his ideas...ever. In recalling his declination of the Boston pulpit Williams wrote: "I conscientiously refused and withdrew to Plymouth, because I durst not officiate to an unseparated people."[16]

On April 28, 1634, King Charles I gave a commission to Archbishop Laud and eleven others to revoke all the charters which had been given to the new colonies, so new laws and new constitutions were made. In the wake of the imposition of the dirty dozen, governors were displaced, laws rewritten and for the first time, permission was granted that tithes be imposed on the population for support of the clergy. These laws were enacted along with fines, imprisonment or the death penalty implemented to enforce the tyranny.

The Oath of a Freeman

After a short sojourn in Plymouth, Mr. Williams assumed preaching duties at Salem, Massachusetts. In March of 1635, the Boston court passed an ordinance requiring all men aged 16 and older to take "*the Oath of a Freeman.*" [17] On the surface, this appeared to be a good idea, to break from the dominance of England, and declare oneself "free." However, the oath was not only a declaration of freedom from English dominion, but also a swearing of allegiance to the new *standing order*. The oath made one swear to abide by the laws of New England in both civil and religious matters. One had to be a member of the Congregational Church. And how did one become a member of the Congregational Church? He was initiated at the time of his infant baptism.

Let us now understand that here, in America, on our shores, such a thing existed. We are too far removed to remember, and for over 100 years our historians have not bothered to remind us. The church-state marriage in Massachusetts remained in place for over 160 years—past the time of the American Revolution. The results of this Euro-dominating civil government were devastating. Homes were stolen, property taken, and banishments were effected. There were beatings and imprisonments, whippings and hangings—a spectacle in *crimson red*.

Roger Williams preached against taking the oath and was called before the Boston court April 30, 1635, but he "refused to retract what he had done."[18]

The Law of Patents

The oath is not all Williams spoke out against. He went on record as the first settler to recognize the terrible injustice of the so-called *law of patents*. It was arrogantly believed that a "Christian" King could lay claim to any lands "discovered" by "Christian" explorers. This *divine right* made Central and South America Spanish lands, subjugating the native population to the terrors of Pizzaro. It made North America French, Dutch, Spanish and English lands. The "divinely mad" preacher of Salem had the audacity to proclaim that the natives owned the land and that they ought to be fairly compensated for its worth.

As far as the form of civil government, Williams was ahead of his contemporaries. As to his belief in the responsibility of the governors to the governed, he was a universe ahead. He was brilliant in his criticism of the doctrine of *patents*:

> The sin of the *patents*, Mr. Williams says, lay heavy on his mind, especially that part of which Christian kings were invested with a right, by virtue of their Christianity, to take and give away the land and countries of other men.[19]

Williams' rejection of *patents* gained his first rebuke from John Cotton. As David Benedict tells us:

[Williams] was most thoroughly convinced that the untutored savages were lords of the soil on which the God of nature had planted them, and therefore took the utmost care, that none of the inhabitants of this infant colony should occupy the least part of it until it was fairly purchased of the aboriginal proprietors.[20]

The Puritans fancied themselves as founders of a "New Israel," not just New England, but of a Christian theocracy, a theocracy based on their brand of Christianity. The *baptized believers*, who were constantly finding themselves at odds with the enforcement of the "first table," knew they would be in trouble (again) in this brave new world of Congregational theocracy. They rightly argued that this system would be nothing but a new antichrist reign. The only difference would be the substitution of the tyranny of the reformed in the place of the tyranny of the papacy. And they had the Anabaptists of Switzerland and Germany as historic proof that this would happen.

Williams was keenly aware of this and protested *patents* to John Cotton. The Puritans were carefully incensed. They turned to the very thing that originally caused their flight to "New Israel"–persecution. Backus wrote:

What human heart, can be unaffected with the thought, that a people, who had been sorely persecuted in their own country, so as to flee three thousand miles into a wilderness for religious liberty, yet should have that imposing temper cleaving so fast to them, as not to be willing to let a godly minister, who testified against it, stay even in any neighboring part of this wilderness, but moved them to attempt to take him by force, to send him back into the land of their persecutors![21]

Enforcement of the First Table of the Law

If speaking out against *the oath* and preaching against *the law of patents* were not enough, Mr. Williams lit the match on his stack of dynamite by speaking out against the enforcement of *the first table of the law*. The *standing order* believed the state had a duty to enforce the first part of the Ten Commandments, that is–man's responsibility to God. In layman's terms, Williams and other Separates did not believe any citizen should be punished by law enforcement if they chose not to serve God. Punishment for the violation of the "first table" meant imprisonment, banishment, confiscation of property, or even death. Some examples from European history of the violation of the "first table" were: Sabbath breaking, holding conventicles (unauthorized church services), and refusing infant baptism. The number one declaration of blasphemy and rebellion against the "first table" was REBAPTISM, usually resulting in certain *death* at the hands of the executioner.

Historically, first table enforcement was standard operating procedure for the *standing order*. The Donatists of the fourth century argued with the infamous Augustine over the magistrates enforcing religious law. Augustine won the argument and used the magistrates to kill the Donatists. Pope Innocent III used the enforcement of the first table to kill the Waldenses and Albigenses of the 13th and 14th centuries. John Calvin used the enforcement of the first table to burn the heretic Servetus. The reformer Zwingli used the enforcement of the first table to drown the Anabaptists of Switzerland. The reformers of England used the enforcement of the first table to burn Joan Boucher and the Welsh Baptist Edward Wightman. Several hundred thousand more dissenters, Quakers and Baptists in Europe were executed in the same fashion. Holy Mother Catholic Church introduced the enforcement of the first table. Her "daughters" of the reformation continued the practice. Roger Williams, from his pulpit in Salem, went on record to oppose this violation of conscience.

The Land for Preacher Deal

After his public stand, the court at Boston called for the removal of Williams from his pulpit. Their first order was to fire the preacher, however, this command went unheeded. What followed remains one of the most fascinating portions of untold American History.

At this point dear reader, the author would like to direct your attention to a map of Massachusetts and the area north of present day Boston. You will likely see just north of Boston the suburb town of Salem. Looking due east you will find one of the most beautiful shoreline beaches in America—Marbleneck.

The Boston court was aware that the original town environs of Salem included that gorgeous beach at Marbleneck. After calling the entire town of Salem to a meeting, the court asked them to either surrender their preacher or lose the beach. Being true and loyal Americans they elected to keep the beach and lose their preacher.[23]

To this day, there is something strange and creepy about Salem. When the author was researching in New England, we purposely stayed out of Salem for the night. The city of Salem was the site of the infamous witch trials and the author believes the violation of Psalm 105:15, *"touch not mine anointed, and do my prophets no harm"* has repeatedly brought reproach to the town.

The court moved swiftly to remove Roger Williams. There was even talk of execution, but Winthrop opposed such measures at the time. Deportation seemed to be the best answer. And so it was, that Roger Williams was banished from Massachusetts in September of 1636.

Are there any surprised souls when it is revealed that Mr. Williams did not report to be banished? When the exile did not show up for his personal escort across the seas, the Boston court began a manhunt to bring in the dangerous firebrand. But "Joseph" escaped with his coat left behind. He had been gone three days when his journey led him to a crossroads named Rehoboth in the extreme west of Plymouth jurisdiction. He found some solace among Pilgrim sympathizers, token evidences of their Separatist feelings. But Governor Winslow of Plymouth suggested that the "madman" go west beyond Seekonk, into Rhode Island, the "sewer of New England."[22]

There is a river inlet that flows into the Narragansett Bay that at that time separated the Plymouth colony from the American wilderness. This land, west of Seekonk, was Narragansett Indian land. Our exile knew he had to make contact with the Sachems and negotiate a land deal. However, this was not a difficult thing for Roger Williams. The firebrand knew the "savages" were men who responded to respect and honesty. So in the cold of November 1636, Williams crossed his "Jordan" and sought out his new friends. He did not have to search long for them, for as his canoe reached the western bank a voice cried out in Indian accent, "Whattcheer?!" It was the voice of a Narragansett familiar with the English greeting of charity. Williams testified:

I testify and declare in the holy presence of God, that when at my first coming into these parts I obtained the lands of Secunk of Osamaquin, (Massasoit) the then chief Sachem on that side, the Governor of Plymouth, Mr. Winslow, wrote to me, in the name of their government, their claim of Secunk to be in their jurisdiction, as also their advice to remove but over the river unto this side, where now by God's merciful providence we are, and then I should be out of their claim, and be as free as themselves, and loving neighbors together.[23]

The question of the hour was could the land be purchased? The answer from Massasoit and his friends was yes. So Roger Williams and his wife, two little children and eleven of his followers migrated to the land north of the Narragansett Bay on the banks of the Seekonk River. After fourteen weeks on the run as a fugitive, Williams founded a colony. He called it *Providence*.

*   *   *

Roger Williams recorded years later that he was grateful for a chance to bless those in Boston who had cursed him. And while Boston was reluctant to ask the madman for help, their scalps were dependent upon his good relationship with the leader of the Narragansetts. So, after a long journey paddling against the elements of the early winter, a thankful Roger Williams now stood in the tent of Miantenimo. This great sachem of the Narragansetts had been at war with the Pequots and their fierce leader, Sassacus, for many years. As early as 1631 the Narragansetts under Miantenimo urged the English to colonize Connecticut to thwart the cruelty of Sassacus. This fear had been realized. And now Roger Williams, the first missionary to the Indians (ahead of John Eliot), the first European to publish a primer on the Native American languages, the first statesman to defend Native American land rights, and the first "American" to be banished for religious convictions, began to urge his sachem friend to come to Boston for a meeting to unite with the Mohegans. The Boston court needed native unity to defend them against the 17th century New England version of Attila the Hun.

Williams succeeded in his mission. The Naragansetts and the Mohegans united under Miantenimo and Uncas. The evil forces of Sassacus were sacked at Mystic fort in Stonington, Connecticut, on May 26, 1627. Sassacus fled west to the Mohawks who promptly beheaded him and sent word to Boston that the wicked Sagamore of the west was dead.[24] And New England had peace—for a while.

In the next 150 years her towns would run *crimson red* in the American struggle to find her identity and shake off the consequences of the blood of the innocents.

For all of the success of Mr. Williams in the Pequot war, Mr. Winthrop sought to have his ban lifted. But alas, to no avail. We have no record of Roger Williams ever returning to the land he saved from whence he was exiled.

Two years after the stunning success of their founder, in August of 1638, the people of Providence Plantation approved the first public document establishing government without interference in religious matters. It was the first of a series of American political documents promulgating government by the consent of the governed and *liberty of conscience*. It was visionary for its time. Notice the simplicity:

> Providence compact.[25]
> We whose names are underwritten, being desirous to inhabit in the town of Providence, do promise to submit ourselves in active or passive obedience to all such orders or agreements as shall be made for public good of the body in an orderly way, by the major consent of the present inhabitants, matter of families, incorporated together into a township, and such others whom they shall admit unto the same, *only in civil things.*[26]

The men who signed the Providence Compact were Stukely Westcoat, William Arnold, Thomas James, Robert Cole, John Greene, John Throckmorton, William Harris, William Carpenter, Thomas Olney, Francis Weston, Richard Waterman, and Ezekiel Holliman.

After the signing of the Providence Compact, the men of Providence moved to form a church. Since they had been excommunicated, they believed that a new church ought to be formed on Baptist principles. So Mr. Holliman baptized Roger Williams and Mr. Williams baptized the other candidates for membership. As Isaac Backus expressed it, "now we are come to an event that had made much noise in the world:"[27] the baptism of Roger Williams and the church in Providence. According to Governor Winthrop, this baptism took place in March, 1639 with Ezekiel Holliman baptizing Roger Williams who in turn baptized Holliman and "some ten more."[28]

Some have guessed that Winthrop may have been mistaken in his reporting of the incident.[29] The *standing order* historian of that era says that Williams led the group "into anabaptism, and then to antibaptism and familism, and now finally into no church at all."[30] That was not entirely true.[31] It is evident that what was left of the little Baptist experiment carried on with a restructuring taking place a few years following. Some may argue the issue until Jesus comes back.

The truly sad concrete fact is that Williams renounced his baptism a few months later.[32] The firebrand could not find a scriptural warrant for an unbaptized person baptizing anyone. His solution to this dilemma was to wait for an installment of new "apostles" to correct the corruption in the church.[33]

Williams became a "seeker." This way of life was designated to those who were caught in the midst of being "Separatists," yet not finding a legitimate "establishment."

The modern critics of Roger Williams are quick to call him "tragic, self-righteous, impossible, arrogant, judgmental."[34] Is this a true representation of him?

Marshall and Manuel commented:

From the moment [Williams] stepped off the boat, he brought anguish to the hearts of all who came to know him. Because to know him was to like him, no matter how impossible were the tenets he insisted upon. And they *were* impossible.

Williams insistence upon absolute purity in the Church, beyond all normal extremes, grew out of his own personal obsession with having to be right—in doctrine, in conduct, in church associations—in short, in every area of life. This need to be right colored everything he did or thought; indeed, it drove him in one untenable position after another. For the alternative—facing up to one's self-righteousness and repenting of it on a continuing basis—was more than he could bring himself to accept.[35]

Friends, here is Marshall and Manuel's definition of the "Liberty of Conscience:"

> "Nobody is going to tell me what I should do or believe." Taken out of balance and pursued to its extremes (which is where Williams, ever the purist, invariably pursued everything), it becomes a license to disregard all authority with which we do not happen to agree at the time.[36]

While modern historical rewriters[*] bring Mr. Williams to shame, his contemporaries were fond of him but hated his views. However, Williams' attitude was clothed in forgiveness, as documented by obscure court proceedings discovered almost 300 years after his death. A brother, Robert Williams, took an inheritance belonging to Mr. Williams and his brother Sydrack. Sydrack sued for compensation, but Roger frankly forgave Robert.[37] In fact, Mr. Williams never exposed Robert and his brother rose to some prominence in Providence and Newport.

Over 350 years have passed since the banishment of Mr. Williams and the founding of Rhode Island colony. Historians are still trying to sort out the details and come to their proper conclusions. Our Mr. Williams has been beloved and hated, venerated and dismissed. Secular historians minimize his influence for fear of a Christian recension in American history. Christian historians discredit him for fear that a Baptist flavoring in the mix of our American heritage will emerge. And Baptist historians are quick to point out his flaws, for Williams did not remain a Baptist and perhaps brought an invalid baptism upon his little flock.

However, if what we mean by being "American" is freedom, *liberty of conscience*, the right to worship God as we deem correct—yet without coercion or interference by the government; then Roger Williams was the first "American." An army of others would soon follow.

The author concludes that Roger Williams was one of the greatest American statesmen our colonies ever produced. He was a visionary in the affairs of government and proved himself a Christian gentleman at

---

[*] For more on the defamation of Roger Williams by Peter Marshall and David Manuel, see Appendix A.

every opportunity. But in all reality, he was not a very good *Baptist*. We ought to forgive him.

What can we discover about the church Mr. Williams founded? If we are to believe John Callender,[38] the most ancient of Baptist historians in our country, then the first church on American soil founded upon Baptist principles was *not* the one in Providence formed by Roger Williams and then disbanded. The distinction of being the first Baptist church in America should belong to another congregation.

As for our voyage of discovery, the events of Boston, Salem, and Providence set the stage for the theological battle that would birth the American republic.

Dr. John Clarke

CHAPTER TWO
Banned in Boston

*Though they (the Lutherans and the Calvinists) were precious shin-
ing lights in their times, yet God has not revealed His whole will to
them. And were they now living, they would be as ready and willing
to embrace further light, as that they had received.*—John Robinson

*But what followed among them may be a warning to all after ages,
against confounding church and state together in their government.
For disputes and divisions about grace and works, between their
chief rulers and ministers, came on in Boston, and spread through
all the country to a great degree.*[1]—Isaac Backus

When the Scrooby congregation landed at Plymouth Bay on
November 9, 1620, they were without their original spiritual
leader. John Robinson had elected to stay in Leyden, Holland,
with the remainder of his flock. It was William Brewster who made the
journey with them, 101 souls sailing for the Hudson River in England's
vast Virginia.

They did not make it to the Hudson, but landed providentially several hundred miles to the north in a beautiful bay inside of Cape Cod.

The hand of God was good to these Separatists for they could have
easily landed a few miles to the north or south and suffered annihilation
at the hands of hostile natives. The land herself was the Pilgrims worst
enemy in that first winter separated from mother England by the cold
green waters of the Atlantic Ocean.

It was in those waters that the Pilgrims met their first terror. Before
the Mayflower landed at the famous Plymouth Rock, she was anchored
in the bay while her genteel ladies waded out into the water to wash
their husband's clothes. Incredibly, some caught their death of cold and
contracted severe flu. During the terrible winter that engulfed them—
they perished.

Of that first party of pilgrims that journeyed to the New World,
over half of them perished in the first 12 months.

The journey of the Pilgrim fathers was a search for religious liberty. The Scrooby congregation had sued for a patent in the New World and for liberty of conscience. The patent was secured from the English government, but there was no written agreement as to their separation from the Church of England. So then, even without the guarantees of total liberty, they came to North America believing the distance would allow them to worship without the liturgy and false forms of the Anglican Church.[2] Freedom, for them, would come with a heavy price. Liberty for all would come 150 years later.

The Pilgrims[3] were not as the Puritans,[*] who opposed the liturgy, ceremonies and parts of the constitution and discipline. Nor were they of the same mind as the Presbyterians in old England who primarily opposed the ceremonies. They were independents—"Separatists" who wanted a clean break, "seeking to lay aside the liturgy and all ceremonies together."[4] They were helped by God's providence. No honest examiner of their history can deny that profound fact. Time and space does not allow us the luxury of giving the Pilgrim story in great detail. But the providential hand of God in helping these early Americans is a stunning study in the supernatural.

Their intentions were to bring a contingent of Pilgrims, a crew of hired "adventurers," a military leader (Myles Standish), and an extra ship, the *Speedwell*. But the *Speedwell* was full of holes and even a last ditch effort to patch her ended in failure. But that setback did not discourage them, the cargo was loaded onto the *Mayflower*, and after a weeping farewell, they sailed for New England.

Half of the crew was merchantmen, and thus the Pilgrims nearly drove their worldly crew insane with their fervent prayers and psalm singing. A Christian who wins souls knows that his good testimony can drive a lost man spiritually insane, and our Pilgrims were bent on giving their shipmates something to think about. One such crewman had enough of it and took to calling the floating churchgoers "pukes." Perhaps the cause was their music, or maybe it was the testimonies, but more probably it was the seasickness. Anyway, all criticism of the stock-

---

[*] John Callender, pastor of the Baptist church at Newport, wrote the first Rhode Island historical narrative. He delivered it as an address in 1739. He identified three definite parties in Old England at the time of the first great Puritan immigration to the New World: The Puritans, Presbyterians and Independents (or Separatists).

ing and buckled bunch ceased when that shipmate went overboard—*permanently*.

In 66 days, the *Mayflower* finally reached land. She came along Cape Cod on November 9, 1620. Some have speculated that the *Mayflower* missed her landing place on purpose, but as time would soon tell, the purposes were of God. As the crew and passengers cautiously took a few days to carve out shelter, they were amazed at the absence of natives and the obvious evidence of a previous settlement. The land had been cleared and the area had plenty of fresh water springs. There was something else too, stashes of corn and grain. It was not until they met their Indian friends and benefactors, Samoset, Squanto and Massasoit that they learned of the mysterious disease that had wiped out the warlike tribe that inhabited the bay before their arrival.

With the help of benevolent natives, the Pilgrims survived and then thrived. Elder Brewster lived to pastor his flock for over 24 years. God began to prosper them, and by 1629 their number increased to over 300. With these winds of encouragement, the Puritans of Old England took heart and so began the immigration to the New World.[5]

*   *   *

The English were interested in the areas to the north of the Pilgrims, for there was definite concern about French designs for the area. The possibility of colonization and the mysteries of what the land might yield lay heavy upon the English mind. So in 1629 after eight years of Pilgrim isolation, Charles I granted the Massachusetts charter for a Puritan exodus to "New Israel."

So mighty and wonderful was the hand of God in allowing a despot like Charles I and his murdering, harassing Bishop Laud to encourage the flight to the New World. Laud burned Edward Wightman,[6] the Welsh Baptist, at Smithfield in 1612 and with him a number known only to God, met their sorrowful, yet triumphant ends. Whether the Puritans from the Church of England cared for these pitiful people derisively called *Anabaptists* cannot be discerned; however, the pressure from the throne and the Archbishop of Canterbury on the Puritans to abandon their reforms was becoming too much to endure. Removing to New

England seemed the logical will of God—so they took to the seas and sailed to the New World.

As the Pilgrims of Plymouth and the Puritans of Massachusetts ran on in years they began to blend into a new *standing order*, although Plymouth never really embraced the tyranny that her brothers to the north would.

The Pilgrims and the Puritans were destined to run into the *real crucible of New England*: baptismal legitimacy. As Joseph Hall, Anglican bishop, had said to John Robinson, Pilgrim pastor:

> Either you must go forward to Anabaptism, or come back to us. If we be a True Church you must return, if we be not you must re-baptize. If our baptism be good then is our Constitution good.[7]

In 100 years his prediction was fulfilled.

We are past the time when American school children are taught the true story of the Puritans of New England. A real understanding of our republic must begin with an understanding of these pioneering Englishmen who came seeking a better country. The author hates to bring bad light upon the Puritans especially in the current economy of hatred and bigotry toward Christians of all sects in 21st century America. However, truth is more important than white wash. Although none could question their character and dependence upon God, nevertheless, the Puritans have a horrific record concerning the *baptized believers*. The Puritans came to American shores to escape the brutality and persecuting arm of the notorious Church of England henchman—William Laud. And with freedom theirs, the reformed children of Rome were faced with the same question that dogged Luther and Calvin: Where does the authority of "the Church" begin and end? Would the New World have a feudal government and religious establishment, or civil government and religious liberty? Sadly our Puritan forefathers chose the former for New England. John Callender alluded that these first Americans were incapable of "mutual forbearance"[8] and their religious intolerance would last into the 19th century.

But before all of those bad things happened, the Pilgrims must be saluted at Plymouth Rock. All Americans should be aware that in the infancy of our struggling country, the Pilgrims of Plymouth produced our first independent document of self-rule: the Mayflower compact.[9] The document is inseparable from the conduct and character of the pioneers who penned its words. It was drawn inside the bowels of the *Mayflower*, and it was the first document of separation from mother England.[10]

The nobility of that gorgeous bay at Plymouth is well kept. Its components of Christianity have been removed, a phenomenon we shall see repeated as we continue our narrative, but it is still an awesome experience to visit. The focal point is "Plymouth Rock," and a fence and platform have been constructed around it. The two times the author has been to visit that place, large numbers of vacationers have been seen leaning upon the rails and looking at the rock. Some throw coins for good luck; others stare at it either admiringly or incredulously.

Now, however, the author would like to invite the attention of the reader to another rock, not as well known, but perhaps more important to our posterity. It is found 45 miles southwest of Plymouth in the northeast neck of the Isle of Rhodes, in a little park off the beaten path. The location is at old Portsmouth and the rock marks the spot where the banished believers from Boston drew up the first written government document declaring the liberty of conscious for all of its citizens. A plaque on the rock records the document:

Portsmouth Compact
We whose names are underwritten, do here solemnly, in the presence of Jehovah, incorporate ourselves into a body politic, and as He shall help, will submit our persons, lives and estates, unto our Lord Jesus Christ, the King of kings, and Lord of lords, and to all those perfect and most absolute laws of his, given us in His holy word of truth, to be guided and judged thereby.
signed by:
William Coddington, John Clarke, William Hutchinson, John Coggshall, William Aspinwall, Thomas Savage, William Dyre, William Freeborne, Philip Sherman, John Walker, Richard Carter, William Baulstone, Edward Hutchinson, Edward Hutchinson Junior, Samuel Wilbore, John Sanford, John Porter, Henry Bull.

The document, written on the Isle of Rhodes and signed on March 7, 1638, was a singular point in the conception *of the land of liberty.* An idea was being incubated that would give birth to something called the Constitution and the Bill of Rights.

The chief architect of this concise and powerful piece of political history was Dr. John Clarke, beloved physician and banished believer from Boston. Until this time, there were four great settlements in New England: Plymouth, 1620; Massachusetts Bay, 1630; Hartford, 1635, and Providence, 1636. Dr. Clarke was about to participate in the fifth.

John Clarke's first sight of Boston from his sailing vessel was of excitement and marked anticipation. Boston needed a physician and he needed to be needed. As his baggage went over and he lumbered onto the dock the sweet smells of New England filled the air. Born in Suffolk, England, in 1609 and educated in London, Clarke became a practicing physician. He arrived in Boston in November 1637 with Separatist tendencies. Like Roger Williams before him, there was something about reaching the New World—all tyranny was out of place.

And there was a lot to do. Sickness was in the air and Dr. Clarke[11] wasted no time in ministering to the growing population. Upon his arrival he found the city of Boston in an upheaval over religion.

Clarke was used to controversy. He was a part of that brave contingency that began to resist the tyranny of the King and the will of the magistrates to chain the conscience. Talk of separation and *liberty* had his support. He may have been aware of the future implications of a *constitution*; his genius certainly would indicate he knew where he was standing in the crossroads of history.

Not unlike the physician-missionaries that would launch from the new American nation 175 years later, the skills of a doctor opened many doors for John Clarke, and pain drew him and commanded his attention. Perhaps that is why the pain of injustice arrested his soul as the plight of dissidents in Boston unfolded before his eyes. Since the inception of the colony, Massachusetts Bay was considered an experiment in government. She was to be a "Holy Commonwealth," John Winthrop's "City upon a Hill." Even though the hard lessons of Europe during the dark ages proved otherwise, the New England Way was hoping to make people conform to the image of the church.

And the church was *reformed*, it was *Calvinistic*. Clarke knew that, however, not all the tenets of Calvinism made scriptural sense to him, and he was not alone in his sentiments. That was not essential, until the rumble over the decrees and order of salvation and assurance of salvation lit up the blue skies over Massachusetts.

John Clarke did not know that Roger Williams had been banished until he arrived. It is hard to tell just what he had been told that November when he disembarked and went looking for lodging, but when he went to church an even stranger series of events was unfolding.

Williams had been banished, his struggling colony at Providence was nearly two years old. This turn of events led to the paranoid "Magistrates law" of 1636 forbidding citizens to be members of churches which were not pre-approved by the magistrates.[12]

The best Boston had going for it was John Cotton, the hero of the dissidents in Old England. The fabled John Cotton had been censured by the arrogant Bishop Laud in Old Boston. But he had such a following of Puritans from mother England that many, including Mr. Wheelwright, Mr. Hutchinson and Mr. Dyer, sailed to the New World to be under his ministry. John Clarke knew all of these things, and it was a thrilling opportunity to come to Boston and help in this experimental colonization. But as he made his acquaintances and began to do his duties, church affairs marred the happy atmosphere.

John Wheelwright was assisting the Boston Congregational Church by preaching at Braintree. He was filled with the zeal his mentor John Cotton had given him concerning salvation and the precious work of the Holy Spirit. He preached on the convicting power of the Holy Spirit and that a man can have assurance of salvation based on the word of God. John Cotton's belief fell along those lines, putting Mr. Wheelwright in a good position, as Mr. Cotton was the undisputed spiritual leader of all of New England. Cotton, concerned about the dead orthodoxy so typical of the Church of England, gave credence to *experimental religion* as it was preached in the conventiciles of England and Scotland

and believed that "lively faith in Christ" was a prerequisite for salvation. But as Dr. Clarke soon discovered, this was not acceptable doctrine to some.

Mr. Winthrop, the former governor[13] was blowing up a tempest that Wheelwright was violating the "decrees" of God. In all probability, Wheelwright did not even realize he was getting himself in trouble, not at first, with the majority of the people agreeing and being blessed. This brand of experimental, lively, and personal religion was getting a label: *Opinionist.*

Further entangled in this Calvinist chaos was the fabled politician Henry Vane. Vane had emigrated from England in 1635 and saw nothing wrong with the *Opinionists.*[14] [15] On the same day, John "City upon a Hill" Winthrop was elected deputy Governor and Thomas Dudley an assistant. These three became a "Standing council," and claimed their election "for life." Just five days later, on May 30, 1636, the "Standing council" enacted its first order. They asked the constable of Salem to warn its inhabitants that they may not meet together for unauthorized church meetings. The order stated they must "conform themselves to the laws and orders of this government, or else let them be assured that we shall by God's assistance take some such strict and speedy course for the reformation of these disorders."[16]

Well, no one knew exactly what "the laws and orders" were. So the general court passed an act to make a "draught of laws agreeable," and present it to "the next general court."[17] That meant that it would take a year to sort out the "opinions."

What happened in the next 12 months became a kind of a Calvinist *brouhaha,* which John Clarke encountered when he stepped off the boat. The Court itself became divided with deputies disputing and fighting over the best evidences of salvation. On December 31, 1636, John Cotton, teacher at First Congregational Church, Boston, publicly debated the Rev. Mr. John Wilson, the pastor of First Congregational Church, Boston. The same day, Henry Vane, Governor of Massachusetts, and John Winthrop, Deputy Governor of Massachusetts, debated in the same church. Debate was going on all over the colony and many of the people met in their homes on the Lord's Day to discuss the opinions of the *Opinionists.* 50 years after the controversy, Cotton Mather wrote about the theological battle:

The question was, by what evidence, must a man proceed, in taking to himself the comforts of his justification? The bigger part of the country laid the first one main stress of our comfortable evidence, on our sanctification; but the *Opinionists* were for another sort of evidence, as their chief, namely the Spirit of God, by a powerful application of a promise, begetting in us, and revealing to us, a powerful assurance of our being justified.[18]

It is nearly unfathomable that these reformed people were arguing over how you can know you are saved. Yet, the debate was concerning "the order of things in our union to our Lord Jesus Christ."[19] As it got uglier, the *Opinionists* were labeled "Antinomians" or those "without law." This was because they expounded the covenant of grace and their enemies believed them to be teaching license. Those on the other side were labeled "Legalists," or under the covenant of works. Both labels were distortion, but the "Legalists" were soon identified as *Orthodox* and it became obvious that they were going to win—even if John Cotton was *not* on their side.

The most obnoxious turn of events occurred as the house meetings held across the area were condemned. And the best way for the *Orthodox* to stigmatize these home Bible studies was to find a fiend among them. They found the fiend in Anne Hutchinson.

There is no evidence to suggest that Mrs. Hutchinson was all that unique to the controversy other than the fact that she was bright, attractive and articulate. She was conducting a ladies meeting in her home with her husband's approval. They were held primarily in support of John Cotton the Hutchinson's hero and mentor. The Hutchinsons, Coddingtons, Aspinwalls, and Dyers came to Massachusetts seeking a better country with a free preacher.[20] Not many, including Dr. John Clarke looked upon these Sunday afternoon meetings as a thing of rebellion. The truth is that there were many such meetings in and around Boston during this swirling time, but Mrs. Hutchinson received the sharpest criticism and was made an example by the court. She was accused of "having a masculine spirit," "denying the resurrection," and "threatening a subversion of the peaceable order in Government."[21] The opponents of the *Opinionists* made Mrs. Hutchinson look like Jezebel for the sake of "the City upon a Hill."

John Wheelwright entered the fray. Anne Hutchinson was sister to Wheelwright's wife and he did not appreciate the attack on his family. So on the fast day on January 19, 1637, he preached what some believe to be "the most momentous sermon ever preached from the American pulpit."[22] The sermon was *The Covenant of Grace* and it defended the *Opinionists* and accused the present magistrates and government officials of quite possibly being "the enemies of Christ."[23]

Like a deer staring into headlights, Wheelwright was now a target; and oh, the intrigue that wormed its way into Boston. If Winthrop and the *Orthodox* were going to prevail, they had a problem. They wanted Wheelwright banished and called for his removal on March 9, 1637. But public opinion was not on their side. Wheelwright's court date for dismissal was delayed until September 26, 1637. That gave the *Orthodox* on the court time to remove the *Opinionist* Henry Vane as governor and set John Cotton straight.

The removal of Vane was accomplished on May 17, 1637, when after a cauldron of public debate John Winthrop[24] was elected governor. With that, the wheels began to turn on Wheelwright. The first law the governor and the new spring deputies of the court enacted was an ordinance against keeping anyone in your home as a guest for a period of more than three weeks. This almost got rid of an outraged John Cotton, who threatened to move out of Boston because of it.

Remember that the court gave itself a year to find out what its own set of opinions would be. Now with Vane gone, Wheelwright called on the carpet, and unauthorized church meetings illegal, a *synod* was called. The court of deputies called for this. It was to be a religious council separate from the court.

The synod commenced on the 30th of August 1637, in Newtown. In three weeks, the synod condemned *80 errors*. On every point, it was a victory for the *Orthodox*. Most of the errors were errors, but in most cases the *Opinionists* were not guilty of them; therefore, the synod succeeded in creating enemies out of nothing. It became clear that the simple defense of your position could be construed as *sedition* in the mind of the Boston Court. Callender wrote, "How shall we excuse the Protestants, nay how shall we justify the Puritans themselves, if it be seditious to oppose any religious opinions we think are false or erroneous when the major part of the Society happens to think otherwise."[25]

In the end they wasted a good amount of time fighting over the decrees of Calvin, but God in His sovereignty meant it for good.

With all events converging, a strange thing happened on the way to the Wheelwright banishment. On September 26, 1637, when Mr. Wheelwright appeared for the charge of sedition, he was dismissed "until sent for by the court."[26] Amazingly the court "dissolved" itself so that a new court could be elected, not in Boston, but in Newtown. And now the *Opinionists* knew the curtain was coming down.

Never before had the deputies been elected three times in a year. They were dutifully elected every spring and fall. Now there was to be a second fall election. Protests were scrambled, complaints lodged, and a petition against the proceedings was drawn up but no such petition was allowed. Sometime in October, a new Court of Deputies was elected which suited the designs of Governor Winthrop and the "Standing council." When the new Court convened on November 2, 1637, it passed sentence on John Wheelwright for sedition and disturbance of the peace. He was disfranchised[27] and banished, "having fourteen days to settle his affairs."[28] John Coggshall was disfranchised; and William Aspinwall was disfranchised (for signing the petition), and banished, his banishment to be in effect by the end of the month of November. And Mrs. Ann Hutchinson[29] was banished.

Our reader may sense the hostility and possibility of a future onslaught of armed rebellion and apparently the Boston—now Newtown—court thought so too. Not only did they disfranchise at least 15 men they disarmed—took the weapons—of 76 others.

As all the events from 1635 to 1637 were laid out on the table for Dr. John Clarke to see, he did what real men do—act. Clarke saw a real conflict coming. Perhaps his skills as a physician had quickly won the *Opinionists*' respect, or perhaps they had known him for years in Old England, we do not know from the record. But whatever the reason, John Clarke assumed the reigns of leadership of the banished, disarmed and disfranchised brethren and became the Moses of Aquetneck Island.

Dr. Clarke suggested that they move for the sake of peace. So before blood was shed, he led a group of 18 families to New Hampshire in the winter of 1637-38 to avoid the heat of the Boston controversy.

Their banishment in the winter of 1637-38 of necessity made them a church in the wilderness. Although there is no written record, such devout people would have formed themselves into a church in 1637. They certainly would have not waited until "about 1644," as some have erroneously stated.

But the cold of the New Hampshire winter influenced them to move again and by sailing vessel they went on a journey they hoped would lead them to Delaware, yet they did not plant their feet in that place. On their journey around Cape Cod, they sailed into the Narragansett Bay to lodge with an understanding and kind Roger Williams. It was during that time of repose and reflection that Mr. Williams convinced the band of believers to look at the beautiful garden of the Island of Aquetneck. It was spring of 1638.

The banished believers from Boston received assurance from Plymouth that the island was out of both Pilgrim and Puritan jurisdiction. And so through the communicative skills of Roger Williams, they purchased Aquetneck from the Indian Sachems Caunannicus and Miantinomu, and promptly renamed their paradise "The Isle of Rhodes." And there on the north neck of the Island, 150 miles southwest from Boston, was signed the first governmental document protecting religious *opinion*—the Portsmouth Compact.

Meanwhile, a wounded John Cotton was deciding he did not want to be known as an *Opinionist*, so he began to backpedal.

In 1638, with the opposition gone, Massachusetts acted swiftly to enact a compulsory tax to pay for support of religious ministers of the *standing order*. The general population, who was a part of the church by law, had no vote in the tax and dissidents who remained in the colony had no voice in choosing the ministers. This marked an epoch in America, it

was the first instance of TAXATION WITHOUT REPRESENTA-
TION.

The First Baptist Church in America

Not long after the company of believers signed the compact at
Portsmouth, some of them migrated to the south end of the Island and
founded the city of Newport. Those pioneers were meeting as a church
under the leadership of Dr. John Clarke.

John Callender, in his *Historical Discourse of Rhode Island*, tells us of
the circumstances:

> The people who came to Rhode-Island, who were Puritans of the
> highest Form, had desired and depended on the Assistance of Mr.
> Wheelwright, a famous Congregational Minister aforementioned. But
> he chose to go to Long-Island, where he continued some Years. In the
> mean Time Mr. John Clarke, who was a Man of Letters, carried on a
> publick Worship at the first coming.[30]

Which means they had church services in 1638. This was simply a
carrying over what they had begun in the New Hampshire wilderness
the previous winter.

The Baptist church at Newport was gathered "about the year
1644"[31] according to Isaac Backus. But would it be reasonable to believe
these folks would have no church from the time of their banishment in
the winter of 1637 to the time of the Portsmouth compact, until 1644?
In fact, there is no contradiction in Backus' assessment, for indeed the
church was not the Baptist Church *at Newport* until 1644.

John Winthrop mentions a church on Aquetneck as early as 1639.[32]
John Callender said they had worship immediately in 1638. Ironically,
some that credit the church at Providence as being the first in America
point out that a better model and mother of churches began with John
Clarke and the Newport church. The Providence "church" disbanded in
1638; in fact, John Callender testified that Williams never formed it:

> I find some Reasons to suspect, that Mr. Williams did not form a
> Church of the Anabaptists, and that he never join'd with the Baptist
> Church there. Only, that he allowed them to be nearest the Scripture

Rule, and true primitive Practice, as to the Mode and Subject of Baptism. But that he himself waited for new Apostles, etc. The most ancient inhabitants now alive, some of them above eighty Years old, who personally knew Mr. Williams, and were well acquainted with many of the original Settlers, never heard that Mr. Williams formed the Baptist Church there, but always understood that Mr. Browne, Mr. Wickenden, Mr. Dexter, Mr. Olney, Mr. Tillingast, etc, were the first Founders of that Church.[33]

If Callender is correct then the first Baptist church in Providence began in 1639. Which means the Baptist church in Newport, meeting in the wilderness in 1637, was the first Baptist church in America. This witness is typical of the *baptized believers* throughout history. The beliefs, zeal and *crimson red* testimony on the part of John Clarke and his pioneering flock would confirm it.[34]

At various times in the life of Dr. Clarke he was called upon to state his beliefs. He left behind a statement of faith that leaves no doubt about his belief in the Bible, the blood atonement, man's sinful and impotent conditions, and the work of grace in the hearts of those receiving Christ as Saviour. His theology was scripturally sound with a fervent zeal for souls.[*]

We cannot trace all of America's Baptist history to Newport or Providence.[35] Nor can we, according to some opinions, trace it to Swansea, Massachusetts; the Welsh Tract in Delaware; or Philadelphia, Pennsylvania. As we shall see, revival and the spread of Baptist distinctives would be a multi-pronged work of the Holy Ghost.

John Clarke's vision and duty to call must not go unnoticed by our generation. He is the ultimate underrated figure of the political and religious history of our nation. James W. Willmarth, in completing the editing of *The Diary of John Comer*, said of Clarke:

> More than any other man, he is entitled to be called the Founder of the Baptist Denomination in America. His large participation in the public and political affairs of the infant colony was rendered necessary

---

[*] John Clarke's confession may be found in Appendix C.

by imperative circumstances...his fame has not equaled his merits. It is to be hoped that future historians will do him fuller justice.[36]

John Callender would write that the disputes leading to the founding of Rhode Island were purely doctrinal over the assurance of salvation.[37] The dispute would continue concerning *experimental religion*—the insistence of being "born again." It was a controversy that would come to dominate the American mind in the ensuing generation. When Jonathan Edwards and George Whitefield appeared on the New England landscape 100 years later, the controversy erupted into a volcano of self-examination, fervency and... awakening.

CHAPTER THREE
The Devil's Post

I hope none will be so blind and ignorant as to set their posts...to the devil's post, their whipping-post or gallows, over which professors and talkers of God have hauled lambs and followers of Christ, and in which they crop their ears, and banish, whip and hang them in their blind zeal.[1]
—Samuel Gorton, founder of Warwick, Rhode Island.

With his head spinning, Henry Vane took the long journey home to mother England. Left behind was a large knot of difficulties in New England that he could not untangle. He knew in reality it was probably not his fault, but his dreams of liberty and living out his days under the fabulous John Cotton were gone. Old England needed Vane terribly. England was struggling for her religious and civil identity, and a level head like Vane's might help unravel her confusion.

He had served the Massachusetts Bay well. In his relatively short career, he had presided over the colony during the dangerous Pequot war in 1636, and saw a rush of new settlers swell the population of Boston to over 3,000, but the Calvinist controversy shook him and he felt led to leave. The collusion on the part of his *Orthodox* friends in the *Opinionist* affair left him dazed but not defeated. Sir Henry Vane left New England still friends with both John Cotton and Roger Williams. He did not think he would see either again. As usual, God had other plans.

In New England, Thomas Painter was tending to his business. He was one of those eager immigrants, fleeing for conscious sake and opportunity. He began a business in Boston and opened a small mercantile. His work brought him into contact with those *Opinionists* in Boston that had not yet been banished or scattered; those who were not only separating from the Church of England as the *standing order*, but were re-examining the baptism of mother England.

With the publication of the *Authorized Version* under King James and the advancement of printing, the Bible was getting out among the public. Crates with the written word of God began arriving for sale and distribution throughout the growing British Empire. For the colonists, the arrival of the word of God was imperative. For the first time in history, the population of a nation was preparing for lift-off with the written word of God readily available to guide the launch.

The Bible was being read and studied by churchmen and dissenters alike. The dissent resulting from the study of the Bible was producing the problems described in the previous chapter. A larger dissent resulting from the study of the Bible produced the problems we shall unravel in this chapter. The New England crucible over infant baptism was in the pollination stage and the Bible was the pollinator. So it was that Thomas Painter came to embrace both the Saviour and the principles of believer's baptism.

In 1644, the time came for the infant baptism of the Painter baby, and Mr. Painter weighed the consequences of refusing the christening. He forbade his wife to take the child to First Church and Pastor Wilson for infant baptism. Later he was arrested and hauled before the Court of Deputies at Boston. Thomas Painter refused to consent to their baptism and with a brave voice called infant baptism "an antichristian ordinance."[2]

As a result they led him to the whipping post where a morbid audience saw him receive 20 lashes, which he received "without flinching"[3] claiming a "Divine help to support him."

From his tower in Boston, John Winthrop wrote in his journal: "Anabaptism increased and spread in the country, which occasioned the magistrates at the last court to draw an order for banishing such as continued obstinate after due conviction."[4]

Here is how that law read in part, dated November 13, 1644:

Forasmuch as experience has plentifully & often proved that since the first arising of **the Anabaptists**, about a hundred years since, they have been **the incendiaries** of commonwealths & the infectors of persons in main matters of religion, and **the troublers** of churches in all places where they have been...It is ordered & agreed, that if any person or

persons within this jurisdiction shall either openly condemn or oppose the baptizing of infants...or authority to ...punish the outward
breaches of the first table, ...shall be **sentenced to banishment**.[5]

As more emigrants came, some of the finest of preachers arrived
looking for liberty. Hanserd Knollys graced the colonies in the spring of
1638 hoping to preach the gospel as a Puritan minister of the Congregational Church. He was in Boston three weeks trying to garden[6] to put
some food on his table when constables, the "guardians of supralapsarianism," approached him about his *antinomian* ideas. The only way the
authorities could have known of his tendencies *toward experimental religion* would have been if the "doctrine inspectors" had done a covert in-
terrogation. One might imagine the conversation with the new man on
the block: "And how are ye?" and, "they say ye preach" and, "what do ye
say of grace against werks?"

Knollys wanted no part of hair splitting over Calvin and soon set
out for Delaware where he preached the Gospel for four years. Wales
was invading the Delaware colony and a good number of Welsh Baptists
began to influence him.

Receiving word that his father had died, Knollys returned to England in 1641. There he embraced Baptist principles and began pastoring
a church in London. In a matter of a few years his congregation grew to
over 1,000. Knollys baptized the renowned Henry Jessy and died in
1691 at the age of 93.

Hanserd Knollys was only in America for a short time, but his influence was lasting. He certainly made an impression on John Winthrop,
who called him "a weak minister" and complained of Knollys "slander-
ing the government" and "holding familistical opinions."[7] The friends
of Hanserd Knollys can only shake their heads in disbelief at such dia-
tribes.

In the same period of time, Samuel Gorton espoused truly strange
things and prompted the Boston Court of Deputies to spring into action, not only for banishment, but for death to his followers. Gorton
also came to Rhode Island and founded the town of Warwick in April
of 1644.

The First Congregational Church of Boston was founded in 1630 and sat on the south side of State Street at the corner of Devonshire. State Street ended there, forming a kind of city square with the Market Place* in the square just west of the church. The first "teaching elder" of the church was John Wilson.

Wilson was born in Windsor, England, in 1588 and was one of the "first comers" to the Massachusetts Bay Colony. He was chosen pastor or "ruling elder" at First Church in 1632 and was soon joined by John Cotton, who became the new "teaching elder." Thus they began a spiritual relationship in the church in which they disagreed as much as they agreed about things.

The Reverend John Wilson had a residence across from the church just north and east of the Market Place. The Reverend Mr. Wilson could view from his front porch, the center of Boston, the Market Place, and the north lawn of the First Church of Boston. It was a quaint and busy, but not too crowded, business square. On the north lawn, visible from the Reverend Wilson's front porch stood the ominous whipping post.

*   *   *

Obadiah Holmes migrated to Massachusetts Bay in 1638 just after the Calvinist *brouhaha*. He was born in Reddish, near Manchester England around 1615. At the tender age of 23 he experienced a "spiritual awakening."[8]

England was a confusion of religious faces in Holmes' young lifetime. As a boy working on his father's farm, the majority of the inhabitants practiced Puritanism under James I. As a teen, the crown returned to rigid Anglicanism under Charles I. In 1628 Charles appointed William Laud as Bishop of London. Laud then became the Archbishop of Canterbury or religious head of the Church of England in 1633. Laud had a vendetta against the Puritans and fought them, banished them, and discredited them all the years of his "ministry."

Holmes took to wretchedness and carousing, living to "do the most wickedness."[9] His mother's illness and ensuing death settled him down

---

* The Old Town House would not be built until 1657.

enough to fall in love and marry. His bride was Catherine Hyde, and they were married at the Collegiate Church of Manchester, England, on November 20, 1630.

Things were far from settled as Laud pressed hard for the "Book of Common Prayer," and burned dissidents and Baptists by the bushel. Laud put the bookseller Thomas Smith behind bars for peddling Puritan propaganda in 1638. As a result, a great many Englishmen wanted to go to New England, to America, to be free, to be Puritan. With this Obadiah Holmes agreed, and soon he and Catherine sailed for Massachusetts colony.

They settled in Salem but things did not work out for the Holmes family there. Perhaps he went to a church without the magistrates approval, or perhaps he dared to have someone stay as a guest in his home for longer than three weeks, or perhaps he had *opinions*. Whatever the reason, Obadiah Holmes moved to Seekonk where the Holy Spirit was waiting for him.

Roger Williams and the colonies at Providence, Portsmouth, and Newport had fears of the designs of Massachusetts. Early in 1644, Williams set sail for England. He could not leave directly from Boston, so he traveled west into Long Island.

An Indian uprising met him there. The Dutch had fallen upon women and children of the Algonquin tribe, and vengeance was being exacted for their innocent blood. The Indians raided settler's homes and burned the pioneer bungalows. They killed Anne Hutchinson and her children who were guilty only of trying to find solace on the beautiful isle. They had moved there after the untimely death of William.

In this situation the indescribable powers of Williams in negotiation with the natives again resulted in a peaceful solution for the Dutch. Thus he was ultimately enabled to sail for Britain.

There was a parliamentary uprising that met him there. A war was on in England between the King and Parliament, but when Mr. Williams went to petition for incorporation of the colonies of Rhode Island, he was met with a familiar face—the venerable Henry Vane.

Vane had returned to England to serve his country in troubled times. He had become a respected member of the Parliament. And now eight years after Williams had helped Vane in Massachusetts, Mr. Williams was vying for a turnabout.

Vane did not disappoint him. On March 14, 1644, a distracted Parliament of England gave the colony of Rhode Island full power and authority to rule themselves. The charter for the *Incorporation of Providence Plantations* was signed.

That would have been the entire story except for a minor detail that took on gargantuan proportions. While Roger Williams was in England in 1644, he published his treatise against the Massachusetts government, *The Bloody Tenet of Persecution*. The publication sprinted through the British domain and shocked the Puritan world.

Roger Williams exposed the practice of legalized persecution and the enforcement of religious laws of the first table as error. A flame of religious and civil liberty ignited the world for an entire generation.

John Cotton was incensed in Boston and wrote an answer to Williams entitled, *The Bloody Tenet Washed and Made White in the Blood of the Lamb*. Williams responded by writing *The Bloody Tenet Yet More Bloody*. The books had to be sent to England to be printed for as of yet, there was no printing press in America.

In Williams' main argument he contended, "tares are anti-Christians" or "false Christians" and, as in Matthew 13: 30, 38, "Let both grow together until the harvest."

Cotton answered and defended the actions of Massachusetts by writing:

> It is not the will of Christ that anti-Christ be tolerated...for God will put it into the hearts of faithful princes in fullness of time to hate the whore...to burn her flesh with fire according to Rev. 17:16-17.

Whereupon Williams responded, "The rejection of the whore will not be by ordinance but by Providence." In other words, God Himself will destroy antichrist. We have no part in it. John Cotton did not have an answer for this.[10]

An invasion of books came to New England from the mother country and most nauseating to the *standing order* were pamphlets against infant baptism and for the liberty of conscience.

At this point in our narrative, it becomes necessary to introduce to you our second set of *black hats*. As Massachusetts had its house of "Deputies" (known for the most part as the Boston Court), so then all of New England held to a loose confederation of "Commissioners" which met periodically. Plymouth and Boston (Massachusetts); and Hartford and New Haven (Connecticut) were represented; Rhode Island was not. The commissioners referred to themselves as the "United Colonies."

On September 9, 1646, this set of *black hats* meeting at New Haven enacted this:

> That none be admitted as members of the body of Christ, but such as hold forth effectual calling, and thereby union with Christ the head; and that those whom Christ hath received, and enter by an express covenant to observe the laws and duties of that spiritual corporation; that baptism, the seal of the covenant, be administered only to such members and their immediate seed; that Anabaptism, Familism, Antinomianism, and generally all errors of like nature, which oppose, undermine and slight the Scriptures may be duly and seasonably suppressed.[11]

They also condemned "any carnal liberty under a deceitful color of liberty of conscience."[12] But, as Isaac Backus observed, "the commissioners from Plymouth did not concur with this act." The Pilgrims of Plymouth were ahead of their brethren the Puritans. The Holy Spirit was beginning to establish the fact that this new nation was *not* England, Europe or Rome. This was going to be God's *golden cup*.

At this time, the Baptists of Old England were getting their theological house in order. In 1644, the Particular (Calvinist) Baptists signed a confession of faith that broadcast to the world that they were orthodox concerning the grace of God for salvation. They maintained that immersion of believers was the only scriptural mode of baptism. *The London Confession of Faith* for the Baptists put into motion a similar declaration by the Presbyterians, famous and forever known as *The Westminster Confession of Faith*. These confessions were published at a time of great turmoil in mother England and had a calming effect upon the enemies of the dissidents.

So the Congregationalists of New England, the *standing order*, met in a synod in Cambridge in June of 1647 and August of 1648 to discuss the future of the Holy Commonwealth and United Colonies. The synod officially adopted a congregational form of church government and a confession of faith similar to Westminster. The adoption of these forms and catechisms became known as the Cambridge Platform.[13]

With Rhode Island excluded from these meetings, it became apparent that there was a need for the colonies at Providence, Newport and Warwick to unite into a government. They met and elected a President and assistants in May of 1647.

*   *   *

Seekonk is directly east of Providence across the inlet of the Narragansett Bay just beyond the Runnins Rivulet. In the mid 1640's a migration of emigrants from England and Massachusetts had increased the population of the township to approximately 300 settlers. It was spread over a wide area and encompassed Rehoboth.

Down the bay the Baptist "society" on Aquetneck, under the pastoral care of Dr. John Clarke, received a breath of fresh air with the arrival of Mark Lucar, a *baptized believer* from London. He arrived sometime in 1648.[14] Lucar was a member of John Spilsbury's church. Spilsbury was a pioneer among the Particular Baptists of England, a church formed in 1633. Mr. Lucar brought with him a soul-winning zeal that was contagious and a love for God that made him courageous. Courage was needed as Dr. Clarke and his newfound missionary friend planned a preaching campaign into Seekonk and Rehoboth. In early 1649, they led a group of soul conscious Christians from the Baptist Church at Newport, from the island, up the bay and into Seekonk. They met with breath-taking success.

There at Seekonk, Obadiah Holmes was struggling. He managed to get into a scrap with the *standing order* pastor, Mr. Samuel Newman. According to his pastor, Holmes had taken a false oath in court. When Holmes sued for slander, Newman admitted speaking against Holmes on hearsay evidence.

But another problem further soured Holmes on his *standing order* church in Seekonk. It was a matter of the authority of the pastor in voting matters. Holmes thought a charge brought against another brother was unjust and judgment against that brother was levied when a small number of the membership was present. But, kind reader, that was really not the issue. Obadiah Holmes was going through a spiritual crisis. A spiritual crisis predicted by Joseph Hall and a spiritual crisis being acted out all across the colonies: What about baptism? Was baptism legitimate for infants? What were you scripturally, if you were a baptized person but not a believer?

Being a short trip to Providence, and in Plymouth jurisdiction and not Boston, he began to ponder these questions. But there was simply no place of remonstrance and no other place to go to church. Then Holmes, in his own inimitable way, established a "separate" church. Nearly 100 years before the "Separates" began their break from the *standing order*, Obadiah Holmes established a "separate" Congregational Church in Seekonk. This courageous act shook *up the standing order* and earned him the reputation of being "the arrantest rogue and rascal"[15] in that part of burgeoning America.

When John Clarke arrived, Obadiah Holmes was ready for the truth of the scriptures concerning the new birth and believer's baptism. As part of a sweet revival in Seekonk, Obadiah Holmes received the assurance of his salvation and was baptized by Dr. John Clarke early in 1649.

If there were any doubts on the part of the reader as to Dr. Clarke's view of preaching the gospel and his willingness to offer Christ to the lost, let Roger Williams describe the 1649 revival for you in his letter to a horrified John Winthrop:

> At Seekonk a great many have lately concurred with Mr. John Clarke and our Providence men about the point of a new Baptism, and the manner by dipping; and Mr. John Clarke hath been there lately (and Mr. Lucar) and hath dipped them. I believe their practice comes

nearer the first practice of our great Founder Christ Jesus; than other practices of religion do.[16]

June of 1650 came into full bloom and so did Holmes' accusers. A petition was presented to the Plymouth court accusing him of setting up an irregular church meeting. It declared that "all such schismatical activity should cease."[17] They were to "desist, and neither to ordain officers, nor to baptize, nor to break bread, nor yet to meet upon the first day of the week." The pressure was put on three men: Holmes, Joseph Torrey and William Carpenter. In the end, Mr. Carpenter backed down from his stance; but no threats could stop Holmes and his friend Torrey.

Thus it was that, on October 2, 1650, Obadiah Holmes and nine other brave souls were charged with "continuing a meeting contrary to the order of the court."[18] It is not clear what constituted the penalty for the sins of these malcontents, but what is clear is that they did not stay in Rehoboth. What else is clear is that Boston was irritated that Plymouth allowed such **incendiaries** to escape without full punishment.[19] Not just corporal punishment, but *capital* punishment.

Solace was found for the "Plymouth Ten" in Aquetneck, the Island of Rhodes, where a heart-felt welcome greeted them in Newport.

Peace reigned for them as they took in the teaching of their pastor, John Clarke, and dreamed of bringing the gospel to the whole of the United Colonies. The Plymouth Ten included Edward Smith and wife, Obadiah Holmes, Joseph Torrey and wife, James Mann and wife, William Deuell and wife and "Loyal" John Hazel.[20]

At this point we pause to introduce to you the malignity of historical re-write. So-called historians, pretend that the ethical character of our forefathers was overrated. They attempt to make our forefathers of the same diseased morality as themselves. They fancy that modern morals are no worse than the morals of those who sacrificed all for the sake of conscience. The heroes of chapter three were stalwart and true men. They were to embark on a journey that will set in motion a shift in the religious and political direction of America.

In the last 350 years, the incidents of July-September 1651, in Massachusetts have been examined and dissected by the *blind persons* of academia.

One attempt has been made to make the pastoral visit we are about to narrate a political move, set to stir the people of Rhode Island against Massachusetts.[21] Supposedly the actions of Dr. John Clarke and Obadiah Holmes would have blocked an attempt by the Massachusetts Bay Colony to annex Rhode Island.[22] That of course, is nonsense. The Massachusetts Bay Colony had no desire to be united with the "sewer of New England."

Sometime in the summer of 1651 Newport Baptist Church received from the aged William Witter a request of visitation so that he might hear the word of God.[23] It would require navigation to the mainland and to Lynn in the Massachusetts jurisdiction. Not only was the trip dangerous and expensive, the propositions of traveling anywhere close to Boston could mean imprisonment for the missionaries. Clarke knew well the violence of the Boston Court. The visit would cause a crisis with the law. But, leaving our present generation an example of apostolic leadership (Acts 5:29—*Then Peter and the other apostles answered and said, we ought to obey God rather than men.*) Clarke and his men were willing to pay the price. In July Dr. Clarke, Obadiah Holmes and a layman, John Crandall, journeyed into Massachusetts's territory.

They arrived in Lynn on Saturday evening and having enjoyed fellowship with William Witter, they prayed and decided to stay over until the Lord's Day and have service. News in Lynn spread fast and quickly, a warrant for the arrest of the strangers was delivered to the constable:

> By virtue hereof, you are required to go to the house of William Witter, and to search from house to house for certain erroneous persons, being strangers, and them to apprehend, and in safe custody to keep, and to-morrow morning at eight o'clock to bring before me.
> Robert Bridges.[24]

The next day July 20, 1651, as the good doctor proceeded to have church in the Witter home, folks began to show up at the door. First one, then another came until four or five were in attendance at the impromptu meeting. Predictably, the constables came to break up their meeting. Dr. Clarke asked that he might continue, but the constables would have none of that. So the "strangers," Clarke, Holmes and Witter were placed in the "ordinary" or jailhouse.

They were soon escorted from the "ordinary" to the *standing order* meeting-house where church was in session. Dr. Clarke protested and said, "We shall be constrained to declare ourselves that we cannot hold Communion with them."[25] But the constable would have none of that, and they were taken into the church.

They entered, saluted, and sat down with their hats on. This action indicated to the entire congregation that the visitors were not in agreement with the church. Mr. Bridges commanded the constable to knock off their hats. This was in keeping with protocol. They were registering a complaint; the church was protesting their protest.

It was from William Witter that the Lynn church had experienced marked protest in the past. Witter had been arrested in 1646 and testified that "infant baptism was the 'badge of the whore.'"[26] Oh yes, the church was familiar with him.

Now, as the service was ending, it was incumbent for Dr. John Clarke to speak. He arose and said to the stunned audience, "I desire, as a stranger, if I may, to propose a few things to this Congregation, hoping, in the proposal thereof, I shall commend myself to your Consciences to be guided by that wisdom that is from above, which being pure, is also peaceable, gentle, and easy to be intreated."[27] He was commanded to be silent. This was the beginning of Dr. John Clarke's attempt to defend Baptist doctrine in Massachusetts. He would say much when allowed and his eloquence would be answered by a telling silence.

From "church" the threesome was led back to jail where they spent an uncomfortable night. Somehow they managed to be loosed[28] the next day for a period of time.

They returned to Witter's and had the Lord's Supper with him. When they reappeared at the Lynn Court the deputies were flabbergasted and signed a **mittimus** and handed them over to the Boston Court. They were charged as follows:

> For being at a Private Meeting at Lin, upon the Lord's Day, exercising among themselves; for offensively disturbing the peace of the Congregation at their coming into the Publique Meeting; for saying and manifesting that the church of Lin was not constituted according to

the order of our Lord, &c.; for such other things as shall be alleged against them concerning their seducing and drawing aside of others after their erroneous judgments and practices, and for suspition of having their hands in the rebaptizing of one, or more, among us.[29]

On Tuesday, July 22, 1651, Holmes, Clarke and Crandall were taken to Boston so that they might appear before their adversaries. The members of that 1651 version of the *black hats* included a newly elected Governor, John Endicott; Deputy Governor, Thomas Dudley; Richard Bellingham, William Hibbins; and among others, Increase Nowel.

To the Court of Boston, these three citizens of Rhode Island were diseased.[30] They had defied and denigrated the Massachusetts system of civil and ecclesiastical government set down by the newly approved Cambridge Platform. On Wednesday, July 31, in the heat of a summer day, things intensified in the courtroom. The Court of Deputies was present along with the pastor of the Congregational Church, Rev. John Wilson. There was no trial, just a reading of their allegations and a commencement with the sentencing. Clarke was fined 20 pounds, or be "well whipt;" Holmes 30 pounds or be "well whipt;" and Crandall five pounds, or be "well whipt." Something in their demeanor must have miffed the governor. To the trio, Governor Endicott said, "You are Anabaptists."

Clarke answered, "I am neither an Anabaptist nor a Pedobaptist nor a Catabaptist."[31]

"You deny infant baptism," replied Endicott, and gaining anger as he progressed said, "You deserve **to die**! I will not have such *trash* brought into our jurisdiction."

The good governor railed on, "You go up and down, and secretly insinuate into those that are weak, but you cannot maintain it before our ministers. You may try and dispute with them."[32]

Before Dr. Clarke could say he would like to dispute, the constables began to usher them out of the room. The emotion of this whole scene ran heated with its actors. Then the *hated* Obadiah Holmes announced to the courtroom, "I bless God I am counted worthy to suffer for the name of Jesus."

When these words were uttered, the most Reverend John Wilson could no longer contain himself and struck Holmes across the face saying, "The *curse* of God goe with thee!"[33]

Sitting in the jail, John Clarke took his next course of action. Mr. Endicott had challenged him to dispute with his ministers. On Thursday, Clarke pleaded to his captors[34] saying, "I readily accept [a dispute] and therefore desire you would appoint the time when, and the person with whom, in that public place where I was condemned, I might with freedom dispute."[35]

At first Clarke was encouraged that indeed, a disputation was going to occur within the next week. But when the ministers of the churches in the Boston area conferred the following Monday, they sensed another *brouhaha* in the making. They did not like the idea of a dispute with such a one as John Clarke. So the ministers brought Clarke before them to stand, after the manner of the Sanhedrin.

Sensing it may be his only opportunity to speak the truth in love, John Clarke came to the meeting ready to give vindication for the growing number of *baptized believers* in the commonwealth. To the Sanhedrin, Clarke said:

> You say the Court condemned me for matter of fact and practice. Be it so. I say that matter of fact and practice was but the manifestation of my judgment and conscience. If the faith and order which I profess do stand by the word of God, then the faith and order which you profess must needs fall to the ground. I would draw up the faith and order which I hold...in three or four conclusions, which conclusions I will stand by and defend, until he whom you shall appoint shall by the word of God remove me from them.[36]

Surprisingly the group of ministers agreed to the dispute and so John Clarke drew up his conclusions for their scrutiny. In essence, Dr. Clarke's conclusions or points of doctrine were:

> 1. I testify that Jesus of Nazareth, whom God hath raised from the dead, is made Lord and Christ; this Jesus I say is Christ; in English, the anointed one hath a name above every name; he is the anointed Priest, none to or with him in point of atonement; the anointed

Prophet, none to him in point of institution; the anointed King, who is gone unto his Father for his glorious kingdom, and shall ere long return again;

2. Baptism is by immersion for believers only.

3. Prophesying and gifts are for every believer.

4. No believer may infringe upon the liberty of another, or by force "smite his fellow servant." [37]

Clarke's points of doctrine affirmed what the ministerial circle had feared: John Clarke was an articulate and formidable defender of Baptist principles.

John Clarke never got the opportunity to defend these principles in an open dispute, for unknown to him "someone" paid his fine and he was released. Crandall was released also, leaving only the "rascal" Holmes in custody.

Our common sense should tell us why Obadiah Holmes was singled out for a more heavy-handed taste of Puritan medicine. He refused infant baptism, took his *standing order* minister to task, started a separate congregation in Seekonk and then the unthinkable—was baptized as a believer by the hated Newport Church. Moreover, he was not a practitioner of quiet remonstrance.

From July until September 1651, Obadiah Holmes remained imprisoned. His pastor John Clarke had returned to Newport along with John Crandall and immediately faced a problem affecting all of Rhode Island which our readers will hear of in a few pages. But Obadiah Holmes was not alone in Massachusetts because "loyal" John Hazel came to Boston to stand by his old friend and pastor.

Finally, the day of the execution of his sentence was announced and a larger than usual crowd gathered for the macabre entertainment. Obadiah Holmes wrote an account of his sufferings, which was sent to the Baptist churches in London. This account was published there in a short history entitled *Ille Newes from New England*, written by John Clarke. Here is the account from the Devil's post from Obadiah Holmes:

> I desired to speak a few words, but Mr. Nowel answered, It is not
> now a time to speak; whereupon I took leave, and said, Men, breth-

ren, fathers and countrymen, I beseech you to give me leave to speak a few words, and the rather because here are many spectators to see me punished, and I am to seal with my blood, if God give strength, that which I hold and practice in reference to the word of God, and the testimony of Jesus. That which I have to lay in brief is this, although I am disputant, yet seeing I am to seal with my blood what I hold, I am ready to defend by the word, and to dispute that point with any that shall come forth to withstand it.

Mr. Nowel answered, now was not time to dispute; then said I, I desire to give an account of the faith and order which I hold, and this desired three times; but in comes Mr. Flint, and saith to the executioner, Fellow, do thine office, for this fellow would but make a long speech to delude the people; so I being resolved to speak, told the people, that which I am to suffer for is the word of God, and testimony of Jesus Christ.

No, saith Mr. Nowel, it is for your error, and going about to seduce the people; to which I replied, Not for error, for in all the time of my imprisonment, wherein I was left alone, by brethren being gone, which of all your ministers came to convince me of error? And when upon the Governor's words, a motion was made for a public dispute, and often renewed upon fair terms, and desired by hundreds, what was the reason it was not granted? Mr. Nowel told me, it was his fault who went away and would not dispute; but this the writing will clear at large.

Still Mr. Flint calls to the man to do his office; so before, and in the time of his pulling off my clothes, I continued speaking, telling them that I had so learned that for all Boston I would not give my body into their hands thus to be bruised upon another account, yet upon this I would not give the hundredth part of a "wampum peague," to free it out of their hands; and that I made as much conscience of unbuttoning one button, as I did of paying the thirty pounds in reference thereunto. I told them moreover, that the Lord having manifested his love towards me, in giving me repentance towards God, and faith in Christ, and so to be baptized in water by a messenger of Jesus, in the name of the Father, Son, and Holy Spirit, wherein I have fellowship with him in his death, burial and resurrection, I am now come to be baptized in afflictions by yours hands, that so I may have further fellowship with my Lord, and am not ashamed of his sufferings, for by his stripes am I healed.

And as the man began to lay the strokes upon my back, I said to the people, though my flesh should fail, and my spirit should fail, yet God

would not fail; so it pleased the Lord to come in, and to fill my heart
and tongue as a vessel full; and with an audible voice I break forth,
crying the Lord not to lay this sin to their charge, and telling the people that now I found he did not fail me, and therefore now I should
trust him forever who failed me not; for in truth, as the strokes fell
upon me, I had such a spiritual manifestation of God's presence, as I
never had before, and the outward pain was so removed from me,
that I could well bear it, yea, and in a manner felt it not, although it
was grievous, as the spectators said, the man striking with all his
strength, spitting in his hand three times, with a three corded whip,
giving me therewith thirty strokes.

When he had loosed me from the post, having joyfulness in my
heart, and cheerfulness in my countenance, as the spectators observed,
I told the magistrates, **you have struck me as with roses**; and said
moreover, although the Lord hath made it easy to me, yet I pray God
it may not be laid to your charge.[38]

Obadiah Holmes sentence was 10 less stripes than the maximum
and 40 lashes were considered a death sentence. His sentence was the
same punishment given to those guilty of adultery, rape and counterfeiting.[39]

From all accounts, the beating was an attempt to kill Holmes. From
the crowd came protests and exclamations of outrage. No less than 13
warrants were issued for the arrest of citizens that called for the punishment to stop.[40]

In the aftermath, a certain sweetness overtook the carnage, again
Holmes in his own words:

After this many came to me, rejoicing to see the power of the Lord
manifested in weak flesh; but sinful flesh takes occasion hereby to
bring others into trouble, informs the magistrates hereof, and so two
more are apprehended as for contempt of authority, their names are
John Hazel and John Spur, who came indeed and did shake me by the
hand, but did use no words of contempt or reproach unto any. No
man can prove that the first spake anything; and for the second, he
only said, Blessed be the Lord; yet these two, for taking me by the
hand, and thus saying, after I had received my punishment, were sentenced to pay forty shillings, or to be whipt. Both were resolved
against paying their fine: nevertheless, after one or two days impris-

onment, one paid John Spur's fine, and he was released; and after six
or seven days imprisonment of brother Hazel, even the day when he
should have suffered, another paid his, and so he escaped, and the
next day went to visit a friend about six miles from Boston.

When I was come to the prison, it blessed God to stir up the heart
of an old acquaintance of mine, who with much tenderness, like the
good Samaritan, poured oil into my wounds, and plastered my sores;
but there was present information given what was done, and inquiry
made who was the surgeon, and it was commonly reported he should
be sent for: but what was done, I yet know not.

Now thus it hath pleased the Father of mercies to dispose of the
matter, that my bonds and imprisonment have been no hindrance to
the gospel; for before my return, some submitted to the Lord, and
were baptized, and divers were put up on the way of inquiry; and now
being advised to make my escape by night, because it was reported that
there were warrants forth for me, I departed; and the next day after,
while I was on my journey, the constable came to search at my house
where I lodged; so I escaped their hands, and by the good hand of my
heavenly Father brought home again to my near relations, my wife and
eight children, the brethren of our town and Providence having taken
pains to meet me four miles in the woods, where we rejoiced together
in the Lord.

Thus have I given you, as briefly as I can, a true relation of things;
wherefore, my brethren, rejoice with me in the Lord, and give all glory
to him, for he is worthy, to whom be praised forevermore, to whom I
commit you, and put up my earnest prayers for you, that by my late
experience, who trusted in God and have not been deceived, you may
trust in him perfectly; wherefore, my dear beloved brethren, trust in
the Lord, and you shall not be ashamed nor confound.

So I rest, yours in the bond of Christ, Obadiah Holmes.[41]

John Spur later testified that he was saved at the beating of Obadiah
Holmes, saying, "I, John Spur, being present, it did take such an impression in my spirit to trust in God, and to walk according to the light that
God had communicated to me, and not to fear what man could do unto
me." But "Loyal" John Hazel never made it back to Newport. Ten days
after leaving Boston, he died from complications stemming from his
imprisonment.

When the above account was published in London in 1652, Sir
Richard Saltonstall, member of the British parliament and at one time a

black hat from Boston, wrote his brethren a protest letter in reaction to the Holmes' beating. John Cotton pleaded innocent of any wrong doing, calling Holmes and other dissidents "profane persons." That was one of the last acts of John Cotton, for he passed from this life on December 23, 1652. He left the Devil's post in the hands of Mr. Wilson.

Yes, the Reverend John Wilson observed history from his front porch like a balcony over a dramatic stage. The *black hat's* "Platform" seemed to be working, but someone else was watching the drama through different eyes, just across the Charles River.

CHAPTER FOUR
A Yankee Defector in Harvard Yards

The Lord keep us from being bewitched with the whore's cup, lest
whilst we seem to detest and reject her with open face of
profession, we do not bring her in by the back door
of toleration.–John Cotton.

Joshua Glover was the rector at Sutton Church in Surrey England. He was a talented printer and gained the attention of the Puritans of England for his gifts. The quills of the Puritan resistance needed Mr. Glover. Indeed, tidal waves of tracts and pamphlets printed in Holland were invading England and "polluting" the minds of her choice pulpiteers and students. Now in the 1630's, Anglican England had "succeeded in forcing the Dutch government to interfere with the printers who had been producing books 'unsafe' for England."[1] The Anglicans were trying to keep Puritan, Separatist and especially Anabaptist literature out of the country. As New England settlements had taken the place of Holland as a land of reprieve from Episcopal tyranny, now New England would become a place for the printing of protest against that tyranny.

Needing a printing press to propagate those sentiments, Mr. Glover sailed for the New World in June of 1638. He never made it. But his wife and his printing press did.

*   *   *

Henry Dunster was born in England about the year 1612. His formal education was received at Cambridge, England where he cultivated a friendship with men such as John Milton, Ralph Cudworth and Jeremy Taylor. He began his ministry as an Episcopalian priest, but like so many before him, he yearned to be loosed from the chains of liturgy and episcopacy and he became a Puritan. Single and full of hope for a better life in Puritan New England, Dunster arrived in Boston in 1640.

Henry Dunster was an extraordinary scholar of the Oriental languages. The historians of that era agree on his tremendous ability in the Greek, Hebrew and Latin language.

The General Court at Boston had appropriated 400 pounds to establish a college at Cambridge in 1636. This college became the first of its kind in North America—Harvard. As Providence would have it, the well-educated and brilliant Mr. Dunster was asked to become president of this institution on the 27th of August 1640. Mr. Dunster never really wanted to be a college president. He wanted to teach, but the sovereignty of God intervened in that plan.

"Pleasant lines" fell upon our fair-haired boy after becoming president of Harvard. Mr. Dunster became enchanted with Elisabeth Glover, the wife of the Reverend Joshua Glover, our deceased printing professional. Dunster married Elisabeth in 1640.

As things always progressed quickly in the colonies, Elisabeth Dunster died in 1642. So it was that Mr. Dunster inherited five children from Joshua and Elisabeth, along with a farm, a house, some furniture, and in the basement of the house—the only printing press in the American colonies.

A new charter for Harvard in 1642 was obtained by his diligent work and he financed several buildings including the president's house. Truth be told, he was also responsible for the construction of these buildings, getting physical help from the students themselves.[2] He was constantly trying to help the college, having also "contributed at a time of the utmost need one hundred acres of land towards its support."[3]

Captain Johnson, finishing his history of New England in 1652, said of Henry Dunster, "Mr. Henry Dunstar [sic] is now president of the college, fitted from the Lord for the work, and by those that have skill that way, reported to be an able proficient, both in the Hebrew, Greek and Latin languages, and orthodox preacher of the truths of Christ, and very powerful through his blessing, to move the affections."[4]

Henry Dunster became proprietor of the printing press by the hand of God. Papers and booklets printed on it would first marvel and then shake its proprietor. He had overseen the printing of the *Oath of a Freeman*, the *Bay Psalm Book*, and numerous other books and pamphlets. Providentially, he viewed the *Bloody Tenet of Persecution* by Roger Williams and the account of the beating of Obadiah Holmes. The events across the Charles River in Boston proper caused a shock to the young academic world of Harvard and declared a testimony in *crimson red* affecting the formation of our native land.

For ten years the young preacher and scholar held his position and prospered in his purposes and remarried. But soon, as study so often demonstrated in those days, Mr. Dunster began to wonder about the mode of baptism and the prerequisites for baptism as set down by the Cambridge Platform. He knew that the Westminster Assembly, in session from 1643 to 1649 was disturbed by the controversy of "dipping." In fact, those Presbyterian "divines" decided that "it was lawful and sufficient to besprinkle," by a vote of 25 for "besprinkling" and 24 for "DIPPING."[5] His sharp mind was becoming overgrown with the weeds of baptismal regeneration for he knew that if the grace of God was the only remedy for sin, then baptismal regeneration could not be correct. And if baptismal regeneration was not correct, then what was the purpose of infant baptism?

The entire town of Boston was exasperated at William Witter's public repudiation of infant sprinkling, and Witter was not the only dissident. Add to his testimony the sufferings of John Clarke, Obadiah Holmes, John Crandall, and as we shall soon discover, Thomas Gould at Boston. All of this sagacious testimony had a telling effect on Master Dunster. However, the most powerful tool in bringing Dunster to Baptist principles was the word of God.

It is a fairly well known fact that the Pilgrim fathers brought with them the Geneva Bible to America in 1620. A version from the Protestant reformation, the Geneva Bible carried a lot of clout against the apostate Church of Rome and gave credence to independency in the margin notes. The King James or Authorized Version was first printed in 1611 and came over to the American colonies by the hand of John Winthrop in 1630.[6]

In a few years, the Geneva was replaced by the avalanche acceptance of the King James Bible. A steady stream of the Authorized Version came into the New World.[7] The study of this Bible, though authorized by an Anglican King and supported with notes about the Common Book of Prayer from the Church of England, was beginning to turn a generation away from a corrupt baptism to a baptism of life and liberty in Jesus Christ.

So with all of these influences, it came to pass that Henry Dunster rejected infant baptism in favor of believer's baptism. In 1653, following the lead of Thomas Gould, he refused to present his fourth child, Jonathan, for infant baptism. He then plainly preached against infant baptism in the Cambridge church. This no doubt was as popular as throwing needles in a balloon factory.

With immediate urgency, the *standing order* attempted to plaster the latest crack in the wall. Jonathan Mitchel, pastor of the *standing order* church in Cambridge, came to Henry Dunster to try and convince him of his error in opposing infant baptism, but Mr. Dunster nearly convinced Mitchel to renounce infant baptism.[8] It had such a stunning effect on Mitchel that he labored incessantly for the rest of his life to prove Dunster wrong. The result of Mitchel's effort was a treatise found in his own biography, which began a sort of gossipy outlook on those who opposed infant baptism for many years to come. In Mitchel's estimation, those who opposed infant baptism were quite simply "of the devil." Like the infamous tag of "madman" placed on Roger Williams, it was a description of the *baptized believers* that was hard to shake.[9]

Thus ended the career of Henry Dunster as president of Harvard. It was hard for the Boston Court to give up such a gifted and consecrated servant, but the Puritans could not endure someone whom as Cotton Mather said, "fell into the briers of anti-pedobaptism."[10] After he was indicted by the grand jury for disturbing the ordinance of infant baptism in the Cambridge church, Dunster was sentenced to a public admonition and compelled to resign the office of the presidency.

> No man ever questioned his talents, learning, exemplary fidelity, and usefulness. Dunster deserves all this from the historian of Harvard. He was as noble a servant as ever followed Christ in times when truth demanded painful sacrifices. It is singular that such a man should become a Baptist. Brought up under other influences, having everything earthly to lose and nothing to gain, a profound scholar capable of weighing the merits of the controversy, nothing but the force of truth can account for his adoption of our sentiments.[11]

Mr. Dunster was sued a few years later. The children of his deceased wife Elizabeth were not kind in their attacks. They sued him for the house, the farm, the china, and the barn. They sued him for everything and they got it all,[12] except his liberty.

Both early accounts of New England History, one by Captain Mason and the other by Governor Winthrop testify that the Mohawks, Mohegans and Narragansett Indians were grateful for the defeat of the Pequots and the wicked Sagamore, Sassacus. The result of the war of 1636-37 was no less than the destruction of the Pequot nation and the opening of Connecticut to more English colonization.

Connecticut began in 1636 with the moving of the *standing order* church in Dorchester, Massachusetts to Connecticut and the planting of Windsor. Richard Mather had come to Dorchester, Massachusetts in 1636 to start a church, but upon examination of the people he found them to base their salvation upon "dreams and ravishes of the Spirit by fits." However, Mather and company were satisfied with their progress and within a year, the church was planted at Dorchester.[13]

Thomas Hooker and Samuel Stone settled Hartford, Connecticut in 1636.[14]

Mr. John Haynes was the governor of Massachusetts in 1635 when Roger Williams was banished. He moved to Hartford in the early colonization of Connecticut. There he said to Roger Williams, "I am now under a cloud, and my brother Hooker with the Bay, as you have been; we have removed from them thus far, and yet they are not satisfied."[15] In the beginning, Connecticut under Hooker was a more mild government than Boston, but later that would change.

Thomas Hooker was "more noble" on infant baptism in the words of Backus, for he allowed "only the infants of communicants or active members to be 'baptized.'" His insistence on this point began an acute controversy that would bother the colonies until the revolution.[16]

The controversy was the doctrine that allowed unregenerate parents to bring their children to the _standing order_ church for infant baptism. Connecticut was the culprit in the propagation of the **half-way covenant**, to which her founder, Thomas Hooker, was opposed. Connecticut promoted it when all common sense said no. Connecticut promoted it when the best of her native sons preached against it. Connecticut promoted it and her sons and daughters paid a high price for it.

The colony of New Haven began in 1638. This became the seat of learning for Connecticut. Yale College began in 1701 and eventually moved educational operations to New Haven in 1716.

With two great establishments for intellectual exercises, Harvard and Yale, great thinkers were beginning to deal with the _real crucible of New England_:

> If the citizens of New England were "baptized" shortly after birth, just what were they scripturally until they were born again?
>
> _If you acknowledged experimental religion, or the necessity of the new birth, then you were an unregenerate church member from the time of your baptism until your conversion—and there was certainly no scriptural warrant for that._
>
> If you rejected _experimental religion_ with no necessity of a new birth, then the baptized infant was already in Christ and had no need of conversion.
>
> In addition, if you were a baptized member of the church but showed no token evidence of salvation, should your infants be brought to baptism?

To answer these questions, conventions and synods were held. Endless questions were submitted and inadequate answers followed. The synod of 1657 and 1659 answered nothing. The **half-way covenant** was presented as a solution to the problem of backslidden or unregenerate parents who desired their children to be baptized into the membership of the _standing order_ church. The covenant was partially accepted in 1662 but was not at all universal—except in Connecticut. This acceptance allowed persons in "half-way" churches to bring their children to baptism, who were not fit to come to the Lord's Supper themselves. And how could anything but disaster follow?

Although the age of the Holy Commonwealth was a meager 20 years, histories of its epic epochs began to spring up. Mitchel's history in 1653, Captain Johnson's in 1654, Mr. Morton's *New England Memorial* in 1669. None of these mentioned Mr. Dunster's beliefs in a respectable light and none of them contained any reference to Obadiah Holmes—at all. The Baptists were summarily dismissed as "diseased," "incendiaries," "madmen," "insane," "cowards" and other adjectives. There were even adjectives invented to describe them such as Captain Johnson's "toleratorists."[17]

*   *   *

Down in Newport, Dr. John Clarke had a wounded bear on his hands. While the doctor and his brave friends were taking a beating on Boston Square, the governor of Providence Plantations had gone to England and practically had himself crowned King of the Islands. William Coddington, leaving on the heels of the great revival at Seekonk and sensing the weakness of a confused Parliament, did his best impersonation of Charles I and somehow convinced the good lords of London to proclaim him Governor—for life—of Rhode Island.

This attack from the rear guard resulted in an emergency team rescue that would take 12 years off the life of the most important man in New England, Dr. John Clarke.

In 1651, Newport, Providence, Portsmouth and Warwick chose John Clarke and Roger Williams to go to England to regain their charter. The progress was slow due to the confusion of the continuing revolution and reformation in the mother country. King Charles I was deposed, and executed. Oliver Cromwell became the Lord Protector and then dissolved Parliament. In October of 1652, Clarke and Williams managed to obtain an order for their colony to unite again under their former charter, but this was temporary. Williams returned in 1653 with a shipment of books he had published in England, and left Clarke to continue negotiations. For 11 years the Dr. Clarke wrestled with the crown over the fate of Rhode Island, and perhaps, America.

The removal and dissolving of charters of the colonies by mother England was one of the seeds of the American Revolution. But time would reveal the break had to be both political and religious.

*   *   *

When we left Henry Dunster he was out of a job and out of his inheritance. He had left the Boston area to settle in Plymouth colony. Sometime in 1655, he came back to the city to visit in the home of a troubled Bostonian named Thomas Gould.[18]

Gould was a member of the first Congregational church in Boston and was one of the many in the colony weighing the issues of church membership, regeneration and infant baptism. Henry Dunster, after suffering for his opposition to the practice of infant baptism, began communicating to Gould his convictions concerning the subject. We do not have a record of how long he stayed at the Gould home, but what he shared with Thomas must have had an effect upon his heart, for sometime in that fateful year of 1655, Gould began voicing his doubts about the validity of infant baptism.

Events were put into further motion when Thomas Gould refused to take his daughter to receive her infant baptism at the hands of Zechariah Symmes, the pastor of the church at Charlestown. In December of 1655, he was summoned to a meeting at the church to discuss his delinquency.

This latest edition of the Sanhedrin began with Pastor Symmes announcing to the church that Mr. Gould refused to answer a letter requesting him to come for discussion. According to Symmes, Mr. Gould refused to come and would appoint no time. Immediately Thomas Gould began to defend himself and said, "There was no such word in the letter, for me to appoint the day."

In an instant Symmes was on his feet, and reminiscent of the infamous sweathouse meeting that condemned Clarke, Holmes and Crandall, declared, "You do lie." After two exchanges of accusation and denial, Thomas Wilder stood and testified to the church that Thomas Gould was telling the truth for he had read the church letter himself.

Wilder was rebuked and asked to produce the letter. By the grace of God, he reached into his pocket and pulled it out. How did it get there? Henry Dunster had given it to him. The letter was served to Gould while Dunster was a guest in his home.[19] At that time Gould, Wilder, and Master Dunster read the letter. Mr. Dunster had the presence of mind to give the letter back to Wilder for safekeeping. Being a veteran of previous Sanhedrins, no doubt Dunster knew Thomas Gould would need it. The letter was in Wilder's pocket for eight or nine weeks! Wilder had put on an extra pair of "breeches" that morning because of the cold, found the letter in his pocket, and brought it along.[20]

Things sort of disintegrated at the Sanhedrin after that.

Symmes asked, "Why did you not bring your child to baptism?"

Gould answered, "I did not see any rule of Christ for it."

So Mr. Symmes began the tired John Calvin argument: Since infants were circumcised under the Old Testament covenant, then children ought to be baptized in the New Testament. Mr. Gould answered, "God gave a strict command in the law for circumcision of children; but we have no command in the gospel, nor example, for the baptizing of children."

The next week Gould endured another grilling, this time at the home of Richard Russell. Here Symmes spoke and postured from prepared notes and demanded that Gould keep to the arguments that he was currently proposing. To this, Thomas Gould answered, "I thought the church had met together to answer my scruples, and to satisfy my conscience by a rule of God, and not for me to answer your writing."

Gould later wrote: "We spent four or five hours speaking to many things to and again; but so hot, both sides, that we quickly forgot and went from the arguments that were written."[21]

Thus began an ordeal such as had never been seen in America. For the next several years, the first Congregational church in Charlestown tried to convince Gould of his errors. Mr. Gould protested as dissenters did, by walking out during infant baptism, or turning his back while a christening was conducted. He was threatened with beatings, spent time in jail, and threatened with excommunication. But with all of this to endure, in his mind the most heartbreaking censure of all was to be denied the Lord's Supper. In retrospect, we sense we are observing the life of a very unusual man. There was no public flogging for Thomas Gould, though his disobedient ways could have earned him one. There was no excommunication, and no banishment. Perhaps Gould's testimony alone was a deterrent for tyranny, or perhaps a post-Obadiah Holmes Boston had become squeamish about excessive punitive measures. The Quakers, however, were not as fortunate.

On October 20, 1659, William Robinson, Marmaduke Stevenson, and Mary Dyre were condemned to die, for returning to Massachusetts after they were banished. Knowing that they would be put to death simply for returning to the colony, the two men were hanged on the 27th of October, 1659. Mary stood at the foot of the hanging tree and watched as her fellow Quakers were executed under the tender care of John Wilson. There was a delay with fair Mary, because not everybody wanted her dead. She was strikingly beautiful and had suffered extreme persecution and slander at the hands and pens of the *black hats*. Ever since she and her husband William escaped with the Wheelwrights to Rhode Island, Mary was a subject of scorn. She was said to have given birth to a "monster," a "hideous thing" according to the ridiculous account of Cotton Mather.[22] Of course this was construed as judgment upon her for befriending William and Anne Hutchinson, the banished believers who went out to the Island of Rhodes.

So, by delay, Mary was allowed to escape to Rhode Island once again. But her conscience bothered her that she should be given preferential treatment. So she returned to Boston against the better wishes of her husband. With a pleading letter of mercy from William Dyer in his hand, Governor John Endicott condemned her to death. From the gallows Mary said, "Nay, I cannot save my life; for in obedience to the will of the Lord God I came, and in His will I abide faithful to the death."[23] She was hung June 1, 1660 and buried somewhere on the common. William Leddra, followed her to the hanging tree for dissident beliefs March 14, 1661.[24] 100 years later Isaac Backus wrote, "And from hence we may see, that the use of force in religious affairs is a bloody practice."[25]

1662 provided another religious farce on the stage of English politics. The Act of Uniformity, the so-called "Clarendon Code," provided that all clergymen, college fellows, and schoolmasters had to accept the new anti-Puritan revisions to the Book of Common Prayer. In essence, England turned 2,000 Gospel preachers out of their pulpits under pain of prison, persecution or premature death. It is believed by many to be the saddest day in the history of Britain.[26] But it proved to be a boost to American liberty.

Dr. John Clarke returned to America in 1663, in the months after the Act of Uniformity. Dr. Clarke secured, "from Charles II, that remarkable document which was held as fundamental law in Rhode Island till 1842."[27] It was the powerful Rhode Island Charter[28] and it said in part: "No person within the said colony, at anytime hereafter shall be otherwise molested, punished, disquieted or called in question for any differences of opinion on matters of religion."[29]

The Act of Uniformity did some very bad things for all of the British Empire including destroying some of the best men in England. The friend of Roger Williams and Rhode Island, the friend of the Opinionists and Dr. Clarke, Sir Henry Vane was beheaded in England in 1663 for his loyalty to the dissidents. In the wake of such tragedy we must remember that "all things work together for good" and the Act of Uniformity did at least one good thing for the colonies: It brought John Miles to Massachusetts.

John Miles, in 1663 founded the Church of Christ (Baptist) at Rehoboth, Massachusetts. This church was the 4th church of the baptized believers in America.

After being fined by the town of Rehoboth for unauthorized meetings the church moved a small distance and became known as the Swanzey Church in 1663. It's first roster of members were: John Miles, elder, James Brown, Nicholas Tanner, Joseph Carpenter, John Butterworth, Eldad Kingsley, and Benjamin Alby.

An invasion of Wales came to pass. Samuel Johnes, South Wales, sailed to Pennepeck, Pennsylania in 1683. Thomas Griffith followed to Pennepeck in 1701 and then proceeded to found the Welsh Tract Baptist Church in present day Delaware. Griffith's church became a powerful mother of churches throughout the colonies. Nathaniel Jenkens arrived from Wales in 1701 also and settled a church in Jersey. Hugh

Davis came from South Wales to Chester County, Pennsylvania in 1710. Abel Morgan, of great influence, settled in Philadelphia from Wales in 1711.

Concerning Miles, Thomas Armitage wrote:

> So far as is known Miles was the first Welsh Baptist minister who ever crossed the Atlantic. He was born in 1621, at Newton, (England) near the junction of the historic rivers, Olchon and Escle. He matriculated at Brasenose College, Oxford, March 11th, 1636, and is on record as "a minister of the Gospel" in 1649, in which year he formed the first Strict Communion Church at Ilston, near Swanzea, Wales, now Swansea. His love of truth, his art in organization, together with his perseverance and courage, soon made him a leader in the denomination; and in 1651 we find him representing the Welsh Baptists at the Minister's Meeting in London. Persecution soon selected him as one of its first victims, and when the cruel Act of Uniformity, 1662, affected two thousand ministers, and opened all sorts of new sufferings to God's servants, he, with a large number of his Church, removed to America, carrying their Church records with them, which are still preserved. They settled at Wannomoiset, then...called Swansea, ten miles [east] from Providence.[30]

The 20th century Brown University historian William G. McLoughlin[31] summarized the planting of the first Baptist church in Boston, Massachusetts as simply a "memorable effort in sectarian piety and civil disobedience."[32] But he was off base. There were *generational* repercussions resulting from that monumental church plant.

In our present day preachers shy away from birthing churches for fear of opposition or dread of the heavy work. It is the sincere prayer of the author that some young men reading the following account might be set on fire to birth churches in our dying America.

Knowing the religious and political cauldron of Boston in the mid-17th century might make the curious reader believe that no church comprised of *baptized believers* could *ever* be organized in Boston. But "with men these things are impossible, but with God all things are possible." Mark 10:27.

The first four Baptist churches in America were 1. The First Baptist Church, Newport, Rhode Island, 1637; 2. The First Baptist Church, Providence, Rhode Island 1639; 3. Second Baptist Church, Newport, Rhode Island, 1656 and 4. The First Baptist Church, Swansea, Massachusetts, 1663. A group of brave Americans now proceeded to plant the 5th such church.

Thomas Gould received encouragement from the Act of Uniformity. In November of 1663, emigrants from England came to Boston. Richard Goodale and his wife, members of William Kiffin's Baptist church in London; William Turner, fresh from military service under Oliver Cromwell and Rober Lambert arrived. Turner and Lambert were members of Mr. Stead's Baptist church in Dartmouth, England. A small group of believers began meeting in secrecy in Charlestown sometime in the early 1660's.

When this was noised abroad, the Charlestown Congregational church called Gould and his wife Mary along with Thomas Osburne before them for yet another tribunal. On November 18, 1663 the *standing order* church accused Mary of Quakerism. This was a grave accusation designed to strike fear in the heart of Thomas and Mary. They were well aware that another Mary was mercilessly hung three years earlier at Boston common for the same offense.

Surprisingly, at this point, Gould was simply censured.[33] This indicated forces, moving in the background, were turning the hearts of Massachusetts to a more tolerant attitude. After all, good people were dead, productive people were no longer allowed in the commonwealth. Additionally, Roger Williams's books were read as contraband and John Cotton's arguments against Williams were weak. Sympathy for the determined *baptized believers* in New England was gaining momentum.

On May 28, 1665, a very courageous group of believers officially began the Baptist church in Boston. They followed the Lord in believer's baptism and signed a covenant agreement organizing into a church. The members were: Thomas Gould, Thomas Osburne, Edward Drinker, John George, Richard Goodale, William Turner, Robert Lambert, Mary Goodale, and Mary Newell.[34] Notwithstanding all of the gains in the attitude of the Massachusetts' authorities, the dispute over First Baptist Church Boston, was far from over. The importance of these events to the future of our America will be demonstrated.

As the antichrist is credited with "wearing out the saints of God" in Daniel 7:25, the Boston Baptists were subjugated to a relentless attacks of the *standing order* to disrupt their worship. The tactics of *the adversary* were in full force as Gould and his flock were dragged (sometimes literally) before countless councils and courts. In Boston, a new scornful identification was given to the *baptized believers*: "antipedobaptist."

In August of 1665, Richard Russell called on the constable of Charlestown to go looking for these dangerous people.[35] Making no attempt to cloak themselves, they were discovered and the small congregation was summoned to the Court of Assistants in September. In an attempt to establish their credibility the Boston Baptists published their confession of faith for the Court of Assistants. This had nearly no effect. However, the *baptized believers* continued to defy the *standing order* and have services.

Since the Court of Assistants could not convince Gould and his members of their evil ways against the state, on October 11, the General Court of Deputies stepped in, and everyone knew what the *black hats* would do.

Thomas Gould, William Turner, Thomas Osburne, Edward Drinker, and John George, were sentenced thus:

> This court doth account themselves bound to God, his truth and his churches here planted, to bear their testimony, and do therefore sentence the said Thomas Gould, William Turner, Thomas Osburne, Edward Drinker and John George, such of them as are freemen, to be **disfranchised**, and all of them, upon conviction before any one magistrate or Court, of their further proceedings herein, to be **committed to prison** until the General Court shall take further order with them.[36]

Disfranchised.

This is the third time in our narrative we have seen this sentence. The punishment for this sentence was a fiscal banishment where the guilty party was forbidden to buy or sell in the common markets of the colony.

This brings to mind the financial policy of antichrist when his enemies will not be allowed to buy or sell (see Revelation 13:17) without his mark. Little wonder some of the brethren took to calling infant baptism "the badge of the whore."

Their ultimate punishment was going to be imprisonment if they continued to meet. The Baptist church sent this answer to the *black hats*:

> For our Gathering together and practice we have already given in our Grounds which we Judge were according to Scripture.
>
> Secondly Wee humbly consider the Patent Gives us leave for soe doeing, as his Majesty hath explained in his letter to the general Court saying that the principal end and foundation of that Charter was and is the freedom and liberty of conscience.[37]
>
> Thirdly, Wee consider the Law of the Colony doth not deny it to us, though with some Provisoes added which soe farr as wee failed of Attending unto wee humbly crave Pardon or Submit to the Penalty of the Law therein.[38]

This petition was met with thunderous silence, but the Baptist church continued to meet anyway. This time Gould, Osburne and George were set before the Middlesex County Court at Cambridge on April 17, 1666 and fined four pounds for "neglect of worship," and for "holding a religious meeting contrary to law."[39] They were fined 20lbs. apiece for contempt of court and when the church refused to pay their fines, they were summarily put into prison.

At this point, with their preacher and leaders in prison, the hunted and hated church removed itself to an island in Boston Bay named "Noodles Island."* They knew to stay in Cambridge, Charlestown, or Boston proper would have meant imprisonment.

The preacher and his two loyal friends now had another meeting with the General Court of Boston. The Court of Assistants was recommending to the General Court of Deputies that the "Noodles Island Gang" be banished. But the Assistants did not get all of what they wanted. The fines of the three were upheld, but the Deputies of the

---

* Now East Boston. The name "Noodles" is alternately spelled "Noddles" (probably the correct spelling) and "Noodles" on old maps of the area.

General Court, the *black hats*, surprisingly, were *not* for banishment at this time. They must have sensed what was about to happen.

The men were released from prison. How they got out of prison, no one seems to know, but since this is the third time we have reported this phenomenon in our narrative we must assume that it was as the Apostle Peter of old. (See Acts 12:5-7)

Gould, Osburne and Mrs. Newell were again fined in April of 1667. Gould declined to pay the fine and had a levy placed upon his property. Gould was brought several more times before the county court for failure to attend church, and one time winning an acquittal by a jury! The court immediately reversed that acquittal.[40] Now it would all come down to the infamous "Great Baptist Debate" of 1668.

The Governor and "Council" challenged Thomas Gould, John Farnum and Thomas Osburne to a debate, "of the grounds for their practice."[41] The association of Governor and "Council" appointed six *standing order* preachers. They were: John Allen, Thomas Cobbett, John Higginson, Samuel Danforth, the nervous Jonathan Mitchel (whom Dunster shook) and Thomas Shepard, Jr. for the purpose of "reducing of the said persons from the error of their way, and their return to the Lord and the communion of his people from whence they are fallen."[42]

Thomas Gould was elated. It was a chance to voice his beliefs and preach the gospel.

*   *   *

Governor Bellingham[43] was a respectable successor to John Winthrop. Holding the office several times from 1644 to the time of his death, he was re-elected governor of the Massachusetts colony soon after Winthrop's death. He is well known as a character in the classic novel, *The Scarlet Letter*, by Nathaniel Hawthorne. With as much or more zeal as Winthrop, he was determined to rid the colony of poisoned and paralyzing opinions. Bellingham had a sister, Anne (Bellingham) Hibbins who was one of the unfortunate women burned as a witch in the Salem Witch Trials.

As far back as 1642, Bellingham wrote:

We have had some experience here of some of their undertakings, who have lately come amongst us, and have made public defiance against magistracie, ministrie, churches, & church covenants, &c. as antichristian; secretly also sowing the seeds of Familisme, and Anabaptistrie, to the infection of some, and danger of others, so we are not willing to joyne with them in any league or confederacie at all, but rather that you would consider & advise with us how we may avoyd them, and keep ours from being infected by them.[44]

So with great pride of purpose Bellingham presided with his "Council" or Court of Assistants over the great Baptist debate, which began April 14, 1668.

All of New England was there. Dr. John Clarke sent Hilcox, Torrey and Hubbard to assist their brethren in the debate, but it became quite clear that none of them were going to be allowed to speak. The *standing order* stuck to a rigid game plan and basically demanded an answer to this:

Whether it be justifiable by the word of God for these persons and their company to depart from the communion of these churches, and to set up an assembly here in the way of Anabaptism.[45]

Ah, but this, friends, was an unlearned question and not the real issue. The issue was not "departing from communion." The issue for the Baptist church at Boston was MAY WE HAVE CHURCH WITHOUT YOUR APPROVAL?

It may be remembered that Thomas Gould never wanted to break fellowship, but the battle over baptism was about to force him to do so. In this debate, as recorded by Thomas Danforth and preserved in the Massachusetts Historical Society Archives, John Crandall and Benanual Bowers, two Boston Baptists, argued that the Puritan churches were so corrupt as to be null and void. This, of course, was correct, and in 40 years the Separate Baptists would repeat it loud and often. But at this particular moment of time, some of the other Baptists did not know how to say it. In light of all they had suffered, they certainly should not be criticized for the oversight.

In any event, the *standing order* was not about to let anybody speak from Clarke's Rhode Island crowd.

Even when Thomas Gould set forth unanswerable arguments against infant baptism, the *standing order* evaded the issue, and of course, declared themselves the victors.

The most telling exchange in the debate came when Thomas Gould eloquently explained: "Christ dwelleth in no temple but in the heart of the believer."

Whereupon Mr. Shepard answered by quoting, "I will dwell in <u>them</u>, therefore it is not true, that He dwelleth only in a particular believer."[46] And with that, the armies for *experimental religion* and against *experimental religion* began to line up.

With the "Noodles Island gang" back in prison, the *standing order* preachers passed their judgment against the Baptists. They were: "an enemy in the habitation of the Lord; an anti-New England in New England. If this assembly be tolerated, where shall we stop?" Therefore on May 7, 1668, the General Court of Deputies took the advice of the most reverend fathers and banished Thomas Gould, William Turner and John Farnum, Sr. They were put in prison to await their escort out of Massachusetts.

When the news of their imprisonment reached England, a letter was sent to the Boston Court by Robert Mascall. He wrote, "How do you cast a reproach upon us who are congregational in England, and furnish our adversaries with weapons against us! We pray that God would open your eyes, and persuade the hearts of your magistrates, that they may no more smite their fellow servants, nor thus greatly injure us their brethren and that they may not thus dishonor the name of God."[47]

While they awaited the forced exile of their leaders, the Boston Baptist church on Noodle's Island continued to meet. The aged and venerable Obadiah Holmes preached to them from time to time refreshing their souls with his words and example.[48] Then in a stunning turn of events, the General Court of Deputies received a petition signed by 66 of the Bay's most outstanding citizens asking for the release of the three men. The mortified Court did absolutely nothing about the petition except take note of who signed it. The three lay in prison for six more months. In the meantime, Farnum recanted and returned to Increase Mather's church.

Apparently out of pity, the Court granted a three-day release for Gould and Turner and like John Clarke before him, as soon as he was released he organized a church service. He was discovered and in the confusion of arresting 15 offending church attendees, Gould made his escape. Out into the night he fled until he came upon some transportation to Noodles Island. A fortunate William Turner also escaped and met him there.

For five years, Thomas Gould held forth the word of God on Noodles Island, preaching to whomsoever would take the trip across the watercourse to hear him. Souls were saved and lives were touched on that remote oasis of freedom in Massachusetts Bay. One dark night, William Turner made the mistake of rowing back to the mainland. He was immediately arrested, but somehow he made his escape to military immortality, as we shall discover.

The hand of God began to move. In May of 1669, shortly after declaring that "Separation, Anabaptism, Korahism, and not subjecting to the authority of synods," were the chief sins among the people of Massachusetts,[49] the right Reverend Dr. John Wilson, pastor of the first Congregational church, passed from this life hopefully into the next. The Boston church, the first *standing order* church established in New England, chose the controversial John Davenport of Connecticut as his replacement. Immediately the battle over the **half-way covenant** ignited. The first Congregational church of Boston split and the "South Church" came into being. Then, unexpectedly, the governor who wanted the Baptists buried was buried himself. Bellingham died in 1673. This brought the more tolerant John Leverette into power. These two acts of God eventually brought an end to the Noodle's Island occupation.

Elsewhere, in 1671, the seventh day Baptist church sprang from the Newport Church. It was the third Baptist church birthed from Dr. Clarke's congregation, and the sixth church of the *baptized believers* in America. During this time, 1669-1680, the grand jury of Boston brought indictments against no less than nine Baptist congregations. Churches sprang up in Woburn, Concord, Cambridge, Newbury, Malden, Reading and Billerica.[50] Bellingham's response was to import the English punishment of the "ducking-stool." A derisive punishment aimed at the *baptized believers*:

Whereas there is no expresse punishment by any law hitherto established affixed to the evill practise of sundry persons by exorbitancy of
the tonge in rayling and scolding, it is therefore ordered, that all such
persons convicted, before any Court or magistrate that hath proper
cognizance of the cause for rayling or scolding, shall be gagged or sett
in a ducking stoole & dipt ouer head & eares three times in some
convenient place of fresh or salt water as the Court or magistrate shall
judge meete.[51]

In response to the permanent exit of Wilson and Governor Bellingham, the brave Baptist flock returned to Boston in the summer of 1674.
They began meeting in the house of Symond Lynde.[52]

In the midst of a tremendous struggle for liberty and the souls of
men, Thomas Gould died on October 27, 1675. His nation should
honour him, but does not know who he is. It must have been a lonely
funeral dirge that fall as the exiled saint of Noodles Island was laid to
rest in an inconspicuous grave at the conclusion of an inconspicuous
church service. Gould's entrance however into the pearly white city was
not inconspicuous.

In January of 1678, the Boston Baptist Church, now under the
temporary care of John Miles, started to build a building in the city hidden from their oppressors. The land belonged to Phillip Squire and Ellis
Callender. Their permanent new pastor, John Russell, was ordained in
Boston July 28, 1679 and the new church met in their stealth building
for the first time on February 15, 1679. On cue, in May, the *black hats*
came in full force. They passed a law condemning the structure.

Unbelievably, tidings from Old England and King Charles II informed the authorities to leave the Baptist church alone, and when this
miraculous piece of correspondence was made public, the emboldened
Boston Baptists met in their building. They were surprised when their
leaders were once again jailed, and THE HOUSE OF GOD WAS
NAILED SHUT IN MARCH 1680.

Apparently the *black hats* had been victorious. They had won in the
face of negative public opinion and they had successfully waited for the
death of the popular Thomas Gould. They had put up with the latest
sightings of the venerable rascal Obadiah Holmes, and now they had

successfully **nailed shut** the door to the renegade church house. In a day or two total victory would be theirs when the whole church would stand trial in contempt of the Boston Court.

No one knows who told the chief officers of the court but word soon spread that the nailed doors had been opened, and worse, the church of the *baptized believers* had gathered there again. So it was that God's people met in Boston in the church house until May of 1680 when the WHOLE CHURCH was summoned to appear before the Boston Court. War weary and knowing that no good would come of their court date, the church did not even bother to attend the summons.[53]

The Baptist church of Boston petitioned the court for the right to meet and worship late in 1680 and waited for an answer of mercy from a group of men who were their avowed archenemies. Almost as an afterthought, **the church was granted permission by the court to meet as a CHURCH in February of 1681!** The sufferings and good testimony of 50 years by noble saints finally paid off. What a triumph! From the portals of glory, **Thomas Gould must have been cheering.**

The blood of the innocents came calling from the ground in New England. It came in the form of the awful war of King Phillip.

In 1673, the English held Miantianimo prisoner at Boston. They meekly gave him up to Uncas,[54] who had him dispatched by tomahawk. The English, allowing this to happen, produced in the Indians a deep resentment.[55] Through the years, many other outrages fueled the fire for the coming war. The letters of Roger Williams could not longer calm the anger of the Indians of New England. They could no longer be convinced that their people throughout the colonies would be treated with the same respect given them by Providence Plantations.

The plot thickened when a friend named John Sassaman betrayed King Phillip, the son of the acclaimed Massasoit. Sassaman was a Narragansett Indian who was trained in English culture. In his attempts to please the Massachusetts government, Sassaman discovered the plan of King Phillip to arouse the Indians of New England to drive the English from their lands. After Sassaman revealed Phillip's plan to the government in Boston, he was murdered at Middleborough by agents of King Phillip. When those "hit men" were arrested and executed by the English at Plymouth, King Phillip's War came on with a vengeance.

Their final defeat required an army of 1,000 able bodied men under the command of General Winslow and a little known banished Baptist—William Turner.

The first skirmishes brought Rehoboth and Seekonk to a smoldering ruin, as the Indians drove through southwest Massachusetts and into mainland Rhode Island. John Miles and his congregation left their church and town in flames and Miles headed north to tend to Thomas Gould's exiled church at Noodle's Island.

The Indians then built a fortification in the north parts of Massachusetts and dug in for a defensive battle, but were defeated on December 19, 1676 in a blinding snowstorm.

They rallied, and in a great January thaw, they battled on through New England and by the end of March burned Groton, Warwich and then Providence to the ground. This resulted in the loss of all the records of Providence church and environs.

The burning of Rehoboth, Seekonk and Providence brought William Turner and his Baptist brigade into the fray. They gathered themselves to defend Rhode Island, and providentially delivered the "United Colonies" which Rhode Island had not even been allowed to join.

Turner's company drove King Phillip's men on though Northhampton, Massachusetts on March 14, 1676. But ambushes were a constant threat and numbers of the Rhode Islanders lost their lives.

The Indians were encouraged by their successes, and encamped at the Great Falls[*] above Deerfield, Massachusetts, making plans to march on Boston. On May 18, 1676, an attack force led by William Turner completely surprised the army of King Phillip. The tribes were stunned and scattered. Turner lost his life in the battle.

---

[*] Now named Turner Falls.

The war ended when Phillip was killed at Mt. Hope on Aug 12, 1676. The results of this conflict were a virtual destruction of the Indians in Massachusetts both physically and spiritually. John Eliot, the second missionary to the Indians behind Roger Williams, had gathered 12 societies of "praying Indians" but after the war nearly none were left and no society survived. Only on Cape Cod and the islands, such as Martha's Vineyard, did the Indians survive and keep their testimony. The correct model for reaching them seemed to be through the Mayhews of the 1650's who left their ministry on Martha's Vineyard to Peter Folger. Folger later formed a Baptist church from their converts.[56]

*　　*　　*

In 1681 a group of Baptists were gathered in Kittery, Maine on the Piscataqua River in the southwest part of the district. These were first in communion with the church in Boston under Pastor Hull. William Screven was their pastor. But their enemies broke them up and many of their people were scattered through out New England. Screven, with a handful of his followers, made a pilgrimage to Somerton, South Carolina in 1683 and then to Charleston, South Carolina in 1693. In that place was the first stand of the *baptized believers* in the south.

The passing of the Patriarchs

Thomas Hooker called home on July 7, 1647.

Henry Dunster died February 27, 1659.

Thomas Gould on October 27, 1675.

John Winthrop Jr., friend of Roger Williams, died 1676.

John Clarke had stayed in England to secure a charter to thwart Coddington and secure from the mother religious and civil liberty. He returned from Britain in 1664 with the Rhode Island Charter, having now penned two of the most important documents in the forging of our nation. He was reimbursed somewhat for his expenses and was promised a reward for his work. He was never rewarded on this side of the river as he went to his heavenly reward on April 20, 1676.[57]

On the West facade of the capitol building in Providence, Rhode Island are inscribed these words,

> THAT IT IS MUCH ON THEIR HEARTS (IF THEY MAY BE PERMITTED) TO HOLD FORTH A LIVELY EX-PERIMENT, THAT A MOST FLOURISHING CIVIL STATE MAY STAND AND BEST BE MAINTAINED AND THAT AMONG OUR ENGLISH SUBJECTS, WITH A FULL LIBERTY IN RELIGIOUS CONCERNMENTS– John Clarke

Before there was a John Gill, John Dagg, A. H. Strong, or J. P. Boice, there was John Clarke. The Baptists never needed any greater depth nor understanding of theology.

John Russell, pastor of First Baptist Boston, serving after Thomas Gould, died December 21, 1680.

Thomas Olney, First Baptist, Providence died 1682.

Obadiah Holmes, who took Dr. Clarke's place as pastor of the Baptist church in Newport, served in that capacity for six years. He died on October 15, 1682, "his sufferings having made a lasting effect upon the lives on many."

John Miles, First Baptist Swanzey, Massachusetts, died on February 3, 1683.

Roger Williams, seeker, died in April 1683.[58]

*   *   *

While the sun was setting on Congregationalism a dawn of bright shining light was rising in Philadelphia. Founded by Quakers but over-run by the invasion of Wales, Philadelphia became a lighthouse of liberty. Seventy-five years before our fathers declared their liberty from

England, our grandfathers established an association of churches who determined to spread the gospel of liberty to the growing population and vast wilderness. The Philadelphia church age was about to begin.

The Puritans were dying and their children, following the lead of a backslidden Connecticut, would embrace the **half-way covenant**, while the Philadelphia Baptists would go all the way with God. Four key men[59] arose as our America headed into the 18th century. We shall discover our first key man in chapter five.

CHAPTER FIVE
New England Lost

*God grant, that as we increase in numbers and riches, we may not
increase in sin and wickedness, but that we may rather be lead, by
the divine goodness to reform whatever may have been amiss or
wanting among us.* [1]
—John Callender

*And to the angel of the church in Philadelphia write; These things
saith he that is holy, he that is true, he that hath the key of David, he
that openeth, and no man shutteth; and shutteth, and no man openeth; I know thy works: behold, I have set before thee an open door, and
no man can shut it: for thou hast a little strength, and hast kept my
word, and hast not denied my name.*—Revelation 3:7-8

*I had vehement longings of soul after God and Christ, and after more
holiness, where with my heart seemed to be full and ready to break.*
—Jonathan Edwards.

America became a republic which based its policies on belief. From
1662 to 1740 the belief system of the United Colonies would
undergo two fundamental changes. A British tyrant named Andros transported one change to her. The other was self-inflicted tyranny
in the form of the Saybrook Platform. These changes would force the
mindset of the population to change from tyranny to liberty and pave
the way for the most extraordinary figure in American history. As the
persecuted colonial *baptized believers* had preached the high plane of liberty and free conscience for the first 60 years of New England history,
the *standing order* was about to receive from personal experience the importance of the message.

The *evil* Sir Edmund Andros, the ultimate *black hat*, arrived in New
England in December of 1686. He came on commission of King James
II to govern New York and all of New England. Thus he arrived, and
became an important catalyst for the case of liberty in the American religious revolution. Mass confusion occurred in 1684 as the charter of

Massachusetts, under the influence of Andros, was vacated. In essence, the English Council dethroned the Boston Court. Then, incredibly, all colonial charters were forfeited from the Carolinas to New England. It was declared that all lands belonged to the king. New titles were now necessary and needed to be purchased. Roger Williams' denunciation of the "Divine Right of Kings" now echoed from his lonely Rhode Island grave. England had in effect, swept away 45 years of the history, blood, sweat and financial investment of the colonists.

In 1687 King James II set forth his "Declaration for the Liberty of Conscience." However, the *evil* Sir Edmund Andros threatened the *standing order* with nails on church doors and guards to prevent them from entering their own places of worship without due payment to the new government. One could almost hear the *baptized believers* quoting Galatians 6:7—"Be not deceived; God is not mocked: for whatsoever a man soweth, that shall he also reap."

Increase Mather[2] made a mad dash to England to get the *evil* Andros off of his back, and Massachusetts was given a new charter dated October 7, 1691. Maine and Plymouth were united with them. It may be suggested that the reason for the revocations and vacating of charters under Andros was due to a nervous Old England not wanting too much independence in her American colonies. It was true that as the first generation of settlers began to die off, the attachment to the mother country began ebbing away.

The new charter however, while giving the right to govern back to the colony of Massachusetts, ultimately was a killer of Congregationalism. Under it, "the whole power of choosing and supporting religious ministers was put into the hands of the voter in each town, who acted therein without any religious qualification in themselves. Formerly the church had governed the world, but now the world was to govern the church about religious matters."[3] The people of the town were then taxed to support the elected minister of the *standing order*.

Congregationalism, then for all practical purposes, became a mixed marriage of church and state in New England. Instead of independent congregations, the county government had the final say in seating preachers of the Gospel. In one of the last acts of the venerable Increase Mather, the **old** *standing order* preacher came out against the **new** *standing order* and warned that it went against the tenets of Congregationalism. From 1691 until *after the Revolutionary War*, the new charter was law in Massachusetts, Connecticut and Maine. Scenes of heartache, thievery and bloodshed followed. In the ensuing years, no one quite knew what to do if a church elected a pastor and the town decided not to vote him in. The result was the invention of councils.

Increase Mather obtained an exemption from these town ministerial approval laws for the town of Boston—The Act of Toleration of 1693. But the rest of Massachusetts and Connecticut suffered. Yes, it was TAXATION WITHOUT REPRESENTATION, the second such instance in American history. Yet, how many uninformed Americans realize this original outrage was a religious tax.

Mather ironically, found himself on the same philosophical side with the hated Baptists. To his credit he began to regard them in a better light. Ellis Callender had become pastor of the Boston Baptist church in 1708. When his son Elisha became the pastor in 1718, the aged Increase Mather and his son Cotton, those venerated *standing order* preachers, actually assisted in his ordination. Things seemed better for our besieged Baptists until Dr. Cotton Mather later reversed himself and lashed out against them which case we shall soon discover.

Samuel Torry, minister of Weymouth, preaching in Boston on May 16, 1683 said, "There is already a great death upon religion, little more left than a name to live; the things which remain are ready to die, and we are in great danger of dying together with it; this is one of the most awakening and humbling considerations of our present state and condition. Oh, the many deadly symptoms, symptoms of death that are upon our religion!"[4]

Salem Witch Trials

A sad chapter in American history occurred in 1692—The confusion about witchcraft. A certain blood fever was demonstrated in the confusion over witchcraft in Salem, Massachusetts. There is not room to narrate the odd proceedings but suffice it to say that the *baptized believers* of New England had no part in the destruction of those 20 people, who in a matter of four months were executed.

In reaction to the deaths of the so-called witches, Michael Wigglesworths solemn words written to Increase Mather are important to note:

> I fear (among our many other provocations) that God hath a Controversy with us about what was done in the time of the Witchcraft. I fear that **innocent blood hath been shed**; and that many have had their hands defiled therewith. I believe our Godly Judges did act Conscientiously, according to what they did apprehend then to be sufficient Proof: But since that, have not the Devil's impostures appeared? and that most of the Complainers and Accusers were acted by him in giving their testimonies. Be it then that it . . . was done ignorantly. Paul, a Pharisee, persecuted the church of God, shed the blood of God's saints, and yet obtained mercy, because he did it in ignorance; but how doth he bewail it, and shame himself for it before God and men afterwards.[5]

*　　*　　*

In 1700, Solomon Stoddard declared that the Christian Church was **national**, and that all baptized persons, who were not openly scandalous, ought to come to the Lord's Supper, "though they know themselves to be in a natural condition." So lost people were now invited to the Lord's table. This unwise declaration by Solomon has gone down in history as the **half-way covenant**. Individual churches had approved the practice of baptizing and welcoming the unregenerate to communion as early as 1663. The Charlestown, Massachusetts church, as our reader may recall, approved the practice in the midst of its swirling controversy with Thomas Gould.

In 1707, Stoddard erroneously declared, "That a minister who knows himself unregenerate may nevertheless lawfully administer baptism and the Lord's Supper."[6] This was Augustinian/Calvinist doctrine taken to its absurdity. Only evil can be the result when the so-called "sacraments" are given powers to bestow grace.

The **half-way covenant** made it unnecessary to experience the new birth. Yet, how may one know he is saved? How may one know he is converted?—Is it not by experiencing the conviction of the Holy Spirit, turning to Christ with a heart of repentance and being born again? This was (and still is) the heart of *experimental religion*. John Clarke had led a banished group of Americans to exile over it.

The Episcopalians believed Solomon Stoddard's idea of a national church, and began a campaign to make their version of Catholicism the national church. They succeeded in becoming the *standing order* in Virginia and Georgia. Amid all of this taxing and pulverizing the opposition, the *baptized believers* could only stand back and watch the world spin with anxious eyes. The **Saybrook Platform**, complete with Presbyterian overtones and the **half-way covenant**, became the standard confession of faith for New England in 1708.[7] Shortly before his death in 1715, Increase Mather published a book in which he condemned the new Saybrook Platform scheme, knowing that it would destroy Congregationalism.

Notably, the ministers of New England presented legislative measures in 1715 to make the scheme of ministerial taxes mandatory for all counties. They did not get all they wanted, but got permission for a grand jury to prosecute every town or district who neglected to support their *standing order* minister.

*   *   *

At Norwich, Connecticut, the Congregational minister, John Woodward busied himself attempting to install the Saybrook Platform. The articles of Saybrook gave permission to dissent, but the minister at Norwich at that time, John Woodward, read the act without mentioning the part about permission. Joseph Backus and Richard Bushnell were opposed to the whole scheme. They had been delegates to the Saybrook Synod, but when they returned home they were not allowed to give their dissent. When no other recourse was possible, they withdrew and held church by themselves. Several others from Norwich joined them and they met for three months—and then were expelled from the Norwich church. This was the beginning of the *Separate* movement. The church later reunited when Woodward was ousted. The Saybrook Platform was then rejected and the Cambridge Platform reinstated at Norwich.

Although the acceptance of the Saybrook Platform was supported by the writings of Solomon Stoddard, its actual author was James Pierrepont, the *standing order* preacher of the New Haven Congregational church. In 1703, Solomon Stoddard witnessed the birth of a grand child, Jonathan, son of his daughter, Esther who had married pastor Timothy Edwards. In 1710, James Pierrepont witnessed the birth of a daughter, Sarah. In 1727, Jonathan Edwards and Sarah Pierrepont were married.

Valentine Wightman and the first Baptist church in Connecticut

In 1704 a certain group of dissenters petitioned the "Hounorable Court Setting at New Haven" saying:

> We differ from you in some Poynts of Religeon but yett we desier to live Pesable and quietly with our Neighbors . . . that since it has Pleased the Almity God to putt it into the hart of our grasious Queen to grant us dissenters proclamated liberty of Conscience . . . and we understand that your laws requiers us to Petition to you for the Settling of our Meeting. . . do beseech of you that you would not deny us herein. . . that our meeting might be stated and held at Will Starks in New London.[8]

This was to release the church from the shackle placed on it by the Connecticut government. For charges had been filed:

> To the Sheriff of New London County. . . or to the Constable of Groton, Greeting: . . . Petition that Sheriff summon and give notice to the aforesaid Valentine Wightman and his said wife. . . that they appear before Richard Christopher. . . to answer the charges and be dealt with as the Law directs. 25 Nov. 1707.[9]

All charges were dropped on June 4, 1708, when it was proved that Valentine Wightman and the Baptist church at Groton was complying with the Connecticut Act of Toleration.

Perhaps it was due to the long suffering of the first Baptist church of Boston, or to the changing of the guard of the *standing order*, but most certainly by the hand of God the Baptist church at Groton, Connecticut was allowed to form. It was the first Baptist church established in the land of the Saybrook Platform. Its founder was of Baptist pedigree, Valentine Wightman, who was a direct descendent of Edward Wightman, the last *baptized believer* burned in England.

Valentine was a continuation of the Rhode Island blessing to New England. He was born in North Kingston, Rhode Island in 1681. On February 10, 1702, he married Susannah Holmes, the granddaughter of Obadiah Holmes and the great-granddaughter of Roger Williams.[10]

He continued his ministry at Groton for more than 42 years, and died June 9, 1747, aged 66 years. Valentine's son, Timothy Wightman, filled the pulpit for a period of more than 40 years, succeeding his father in his pastoral office. Timothy's son, John Gano Wightman, pastored the church for another 40 years. The Wightmans pastored in Groton for over 125 years!

How out of place would Valentine and his sons be in modern America with the average tenure of a Baptist preacher being under three years. The outlook of the author of this book was changed while studying the life of Valentine and visiting his final resting-place. Oh God! Evermore send us more Wightman families!

The Open Door: The Philadelphia Association

Historians try with every given opportunity to trace American Baptist roots to Roger Williams and the First Baptist Church of Providence. The truth is that the First Church of Providence under Williams birthed no children. She passed her baptism down to no one. Baptism in America has its roots in three basic streams: English, Welsh and German ancestry. American mother churches are too numerous to pinpoint one great grandmother. However, the Baptists of America do have a place where they first steadied their ship, got their bearing, and sailed off to save souls. That place was Philadelphia.

Elias Keach arrived in Pennsylvania in 1686. He was the son of the celebrated Benjamin Keach of England, one of the most prominent Baptists of his day. Elias was only 19 when he stepped into the new world and fancied himself quite a preacher.

He lobbied for an opportunity to preach to a gathering at Pennepek. Using his pedigree and promoting himself as a "young London divine,"[11] Elias dressed in black garb and clerical collar, drummed up a crowd and began to speak. He was barely into his discourse when the power of God fell upon the meeting. The first person to fall under conviction was Keach himself. He paused in his delivery and weeping, abandoned the meeting. Keach made his way to Cold Spring, Bucks County, Pennsylvania on the Delaware River to confer with the venerable white-haired Thomas Dungan.

Dungan, an ancient Baptist preacher, had migrated from Rhode Island to Cold Spring in 1684, and gathered a Baptist church there.[12] He had come from Ireland to Newport, because of the persecution of the Baptists under Charles II. The church, as Armitage puts it, "lived at a dying rate" and passed out of existence in 1702. But before it "died," it brought forth life in Elias Keach whom Thomas Dungan brought to Christ and baptized.

This began a work among the Baptists west of the Connecticut River. The end result of the work became the heart, soul and doctrine of the *baptized believers* through the time of the Revolution. A great door was opened, and the warmth of Wales passed through it, bringing to America a missionary zeal and love for God that is still resonating.

Cold Spring paved the way for the revival at Pennepeck and Elias Keach. Pennepek was the place in Pennsylvania from which the first churches of the first association of Baptists in America were birthed. Pennepeck church was formed from these four groups:

> From Wales...
> By the good providence of God, there came certain persons out of Radnorshire, in Wales, over into tills Province of Pennsylvania, and settled in the township of Dublin, in the County of Philadelphia, namely, John Eaton, George Eaton and Jane, his wife, Samuel Jones and Sarah Eaton, who had all been baptized upon con-

fession of faith, and received into the communion of the Church
of Christ meeting in the parishes of Llandewi and Nantmel, in
Radnorshire.[13]

From Ireland...
John Baker, who had been baptized, and a member of a congregation of *baptized believers* in Kilkenny.[14]

From England...
In the year 1687 there came one Samuel Vans out of England,
and settled near the aforesaid township and went under the de-
nomination of a Baptist, and was so taken to be.' These, with
Sarah Eaton, 'Joseph Ashton and Jane, his wife, William Fisher,
John Watts' and Rev. Elias Keach, formed the Church. [15]

Converts from Pennsylvania...
Ashton and his wife, with Fisher and Watts, had been baptized
by Keach at Pennepek, November, 1687. [16]

In the month of January, 1688, the church at Pennepek was organized.

Keach became a powerful evangelist, pastoring the Pennepek church
and preaching the Gospel all around the Philadelphia area. He preached
the Gospel in "Trenton, Philadelphia, Middletown, Cohansey, Salem
and many other places, and baptized his converts into the fellowship of
the Church at Pennepek, so that all the Baptists of New Jersey and
Pennsylvania were connected with that body, except the little band at
Cold Spring."[17]

After a time, these branch churches or chapels of Pennepek under
Elias Keach began to meet twice a year for public preaching and exhortation. "Morgan Edwards tells us that twice a year, May and October,
they held 'General Meetings' for preaching and the Lord's Supper, at
Salem in the spring and at Dublin or Burlington in the autumn, for the
accommodation of distant members and the spread of the Gospel, until
separate Churches were formed in several places."[18]

Elias Keach returned to London in 1689 where he began a work for
God, baptizing 130 in a nine month span. He died in 1701 being only
34 years of age. His influence in young America was felt in the power

and ingenuity of the work that he left behind, manifesting itself in the Philadelphia Association. Thomas Armitage wrote:

> "The Pennepek Church, after some contentions, built its first meeting-house in 1707, on ground presented by Rev. Samuel Jones, who became one of its early pastors; for many years it was the center of denominational operations west of the Connecticut River, and from its labors sprang the Philadelphia Association, in 1707. It was natural that the several Baptist companies formed in different communities by this church should soon take steps for the organization of new churches in their several localities, and this was first done in New Jersey, in Middletown in 1688, Piscataqua in 1689, and Cohansey in 1690."[19]

The Philadelphia Association was formed of the five following churches: Pennepeck, Middletown, Piscataqua, Cahansey and Welsh Tract.[20] As the Baptist historian William Cathcart said, "Formed on the twenty seventh day of the seventh month on the seventh day of the week," the Philadelphia Association began its work. The purpose of this first Baptist Association was declared on numerous occasions: **It was established for communication and unity of doctrine**. The early Baptist associations had no intention to control or manipulate the churches. All churches were independent and the thought of a hierarchy among them was contemptible.

The influence of the Welsh Baptists on the Philadelphia Association was great. Abel Morgan immigrated to America in 1711 and brought with him the fire and earnestness of the preaching and singing of Wales. His nephew, also named Abel Morgan, would reveal the Welsh mind.

In 1742 the association adopted the Philadelphia Confession of Faith. The confession was based on the London Baptist Confession of Faith of 1689, with some differences in the practice of the Lord's Supper.[21] Benjamin Franklin printed the confession in 1743 for the general public. This brought about a good sense of unity among the Baptists who for so many years had to struggle just to survive. Now there was hope that there would be some settling of doctrine and practice. Those that adhered to the confession came to be known as "Regular" Baptists.

Nearly all of the pioneer Baptist associations of America adopted the Philadelphia Confession of Faith.

Armitage again, writing in the year 1887, noted the importance of the Philadelphia Association:

> Humanly speaking, we can distinctly trace the causes of our denominational growth from the beginning of the century to the opening of the Revolutionary War. In the churches west of the Connecticut there was an active missionary spirit. At first the New England Baptists partook somewhat of the conservatism of their Congregational brethren, but in the Churches planted chiefly by the Welsh in New Jersey and Pennsylvania, South Carolina and Virginia, the missionary spirit was vigorous and aggressive. As from a central fortress they sent out their little bands; here a missionary and there a handful of colonists, who penetrated farther into the wilderness, and extended the frontiers of the denomination.[22]

The Philadelphia Association grew to contain 53 churches in its membership by 1791.

Back in New England in the year 1702, there were no less than four histories chronicling the rise of the marvelous Massachusetts Bay colony, informing the world of the mighty hand of God upon the Puritans. There was Mitchel, Johnson, Hutchinson, and Morton who attempted to give the facts of the religious and political progress of New England. In those four narratives not a single word of recommendation is given to the Baptists. Not a word about other dissenters is given except contempt. Some of the *baptized believers* were growing weary of the pompous parade of self-promotion of their enemies. But even with the advance of those four Puritan histories, the greatest and grandest of the Congregational histories was published in 1702. Still quoted often by historians three centuries later, *Magnalia Christi Americana* was released.

Doctor Cotton Mather *wrote Magnalia* in honour of the *standing or-der*. It was a monotonous volume full of pomp and circumstance. Its publication hit the *baptized believers* like a cheap shot in an alley fight.

There can be no doubt that Dr. Mather influenced Dr. Daniel Neal of England. Neal finished his *History of the Puritans* in 1732. It received wide distribution, earned fame and respect for its author and became for England the standard non-Catholic history text of the 18ᵗʰ century. According to Baptist historian Thomas Crosby, Dr. Neal had promised his book would give a fair account of the English Baptists. Large amounts of materials were sent to him documenting the troubles and persecution of the English Baptists. However, when his history was pub-lished the obvious disdain for the "Anabaptists" came through without a veil.[23] Neal basically ignored the evidence and material set before him. As Neal became the standard in England, so Cotton Mather's *Magnalia* became the standard Christian history of America.

In America, Mather had made no promises to the *baptized believers*, and he made no effort to paint them in a favorable hue. *Magnalia* was a triumph for the Pedobaptists in every way. It would be some time before the Baptists of America, struggling to exist, would have someone write on their behalf.

*   *   *

About this time, a Boston group of *standing order* ministers decided to spy out Rhode Island's liberty and wrote to the Governor of the col-ony in 1721 informing him of their intention of coming to plant Con-gregational Churches. Jonathan Sprague answered them in a letter ac-knowledging their liberty to do so, but reminded the Massachusetts "di-vines" of their history of persecution. The facts set down by Sprague's letter became a public point of discussion. The *standing order* denied all of Sprague's charges and answered with a spirited attack on his charac-ter. It was one of the first attempts at rewriting history in the infant years of our country. Here is Sprague's reply to the *standing order* rewrite:

> Why do you strive to persuade the rising generation, that you never persecuted nor hurt the Baptists? Did you not barbarously scourge Mr. Obadiah Holmes, and imprison John Hazel of Rehoboth, who died

and came not home? And did you not barbarously scourge Mr. Baker, in Cambridge, the chief mate of a London ship? Where also you imprisoned Mr. Thomas Gould, John Russell, Benjamin Sweetser, and many others, and fined them fifty pounds a man. And did you not take away a part of said Sweetser's land, to pay his fine, and conveyed it to Solomon Phipps, the Deputy-Governor Danforth's son-in-law, who after by the hand of God ran distracted, dying suddenly, saying he was bewitched? And did you not nail up the Baptist meeting-house doors, and fine Mr. John Miles, Mr. James Brown, and Mr. Nicholas Tanner? Surely I can fill sheets of paper with the sufferings of the Baptists, as well as others, within your precincts; but what I have mentioned shall suffice for the present. Jonathan Sprague, 1721.[24]

After the printing of *Magnalia*, it became apparent the Baptists needed a history of their own. The struggle for an accurate portrayal of American Baptist history began with the birth of John Comer on August 1, 1704.

Born in Boston, Comer's stepfather stole his educational savings fund when he was just ten years of age. At the age of 14 he studied under Zechariah Fitch to learn the "glover trade." Fitch was not much pleased with the boy for he said, "I see you won't do for me, for you read too much."[25]

From August to November, 1721, while a student at Yale, John Comer was in travail of his soul over his salvation, even moving to Cambridge for fear of the small pox epidemic. As Providence would have it, the family with whom he was lodging contracted the disease. Those circumstances led to his conversion to Christ. Comer wrote:

> Aug 1, 1721, Being this day seventeen yeas old, I set it apart as a day of solemn fasting and supplication in my chamber, to humble my soul before the Lord; to bewail the sins of my youth and of my nature which is the woeful spring of all actual transgressions. I bemoaned myself before the Lord in secret, and between each prayer I spent the time in close examination and in reading Mr. Vincent's book, entitled Christ's certain and sudden appearance to judgment.[26]

After his salvation, John Comer came under conviction about the *real crucible of New England* by reading the book, *Treatise on Baptism*,[27] by Joseph Stennett.[28] This *real crucible of New England* was increasingly being debated: if an infant is baptized and converted in older years, what scriptural term describes the unregenerate person in the intervening years? Indeed, the debate about baptism would drive a new generation of Americans into a deeper dependency on God.

The passages that brought John Comer to conviction about baptism by immersion for believers only were Acts 8, Matthew 3, and Romans 6. He wrote:

> After serious and mature deliberation and earnest prayer to the Lord, I found the churches not so fully in order in the point of Baptism as they should be, tho I valued them as the Spouse of Christ and would willingly maintain my communion with them.
>
> But to take up such a cross in my early days, when I had not one relative in the world of that mind, was exceeding difficult, so that I feared to let my mind in this case be known to any one soul, and being newly admitted into full communion with the church in Cambridge, I feared it would be hurtful to the churches and displeasing to God.[29]

Comer was baptized on January 31, 1725 by Elisha Callender at the first Baptist Church of Boston. From there he went to Swansea, Massachusetts and in May of 1725, began preaching duties. By November of 1725 he accepted a call to the Newport First Baptist Church (Dr. John Clarke's church). He assumed pastoral and preaching duties under William Peckom.

He was a single man when he assumed the pulpit at the famous Newport Church, but soon fell in love with Sarah Rogers. Sarah was a survivor of a church split caused by Daniel White, a split in which her own father had left to form another church in Newport. So Sarah was one of 18 members left in the legendary church when John Comer came to pastor. He and Sarah were married January 20, 1726.

Mr. Comer was not able to stay at the Newport church for an extended time. Within three years he became convinced of validity of the ordinance of "laying on of hands." Comer believed it was an ordinance of the church and should be practiced. He preached a message on the subject November 17, 1728,[30] and a great controversy ensued. He was dismissed on January 8, 1729. That night, his daughter Sarah was born.

The very next day Comer was received by the Second Baptist Church at Newport and received the "laying on of hands" by Daniel Wightman. Wightman was a cousin to Valentine Wightman and a Six-Principle Baptist. The second Baptist church in Newport was pastored by James Clarke, nephew of Dr. John Clarke. The Six-Principled Baptists were advocates of "laying on of hands" but were also much too "Arminian"[31] for Mr. Comer. But he was grateful for their hospitality and love for souls.

Eventually, John Comer became the pastor of the Baptist Church in Rehoboth, Massachusetts on January 20, 1732. Rehoboth church was a church plant from the First Baptist Church of Swansey, Massachusetts and their pastor Ephraim Wheaton.[32] John Comer now entered into the most important work of his life. As the account of Cotton Mather's *Magnalia* was repeated, quoted and used against the *baptized believers*, Comer began an ardent effort to preserve the true record of his new-found heritage. On page 92 and 93 of Comer's diary, he speaks of his desire to communicate with Henry Loveall to gain information on the churches in "the Jerseys." He began his gatherings in October of 1729.

He wrote to Thomas Symonds, a pastor in South Carolina, for information on November 5, 1729. He wrote to Chowan in North Carolina on November 7, 1729. He wrote to Paul Palmer, in North Carolina November 30, 1729. He wrote to Nicolas Eyres in New York on December 5, 1729. In March of 1731 he traveled south in search of the Baptists in New Jersey and Pennsylvania. He arrived in Philadelphia and had designs to go to the Jerseys for research.

Comer recorded two Seventh-Day Baptist churches in New England making the number of churches of the *baptized believers* in that part of the country 18 total. No one knew the number elsewhere, and he was trying to remedy that by his own research.

In 1732 Comer reported that "According to my best knowledge that there were 26 Baptist churches in America under their several divisions and about 2,110 communicants, reckoning from North Carolina to Boston."[33]

On June 28, 1731, Comer was reconciled to his old church, the First Baptist of Newport. He was not called back as pastor. Instead, his friend John Callender became the pastor on Sept 20, 1731.

Cathcart wrote of Comer:

> Mr. Comer was the most remarkable young man in the Baptist history
> of New England, and his early death was a calamity to the churches in
> that section of that country, suffering at the time so severely from Pu-
> ritan persecutions and needing so much his unusual talents and ac-
> quirements.[34]

John Comer's controversy with the Newport First Church was settled in 1733. There was forgiveness and tender mercy and agreement to
disagree and finally Mr. Comer felt free enough to move on. He did not
know that he had but few days left to serve. He settled in Rehoboth,
Massachusetts and with the help of Ephraim Wheaton, he established a
Baptist Church. In just a short time he saw a large number of people
come to Christ.

Mr. Comer was diligently working on a compilation of historical
documents regarding the plight and the trials of the pioneer *baptized
believers* in New England. Our Lord did not allow him to finish. He died
May 23, 1734 from consumption. His work fell into the hands of his
good friend John Callender. Sadly, only a few of Comer's writings ever
reached the capable pens of Morgan Edwards, Isaac Backus, or David
Benedict. His materials and remains were pilfered and vandalized and
the documents stolen.[35] Only his diary remained intact.

*   *   *

The argument for *experimental religion*, first voiced in Boston by John
Clarke, was about to be tested.

Emerging from the darkness of the early 18th century came an incisive mind with a daring pen. Ironically, the mind and pen came from
the family of Solomon Stoddard. Stoddard, the sage among the ministers of the *standing order*, had opinions that carried a lot of clout. His
opinion concerning the **half-way covenant** elevated that false doctrine to
orthodoxy in the early days of the 18th century. No Baptist historian, not
John Comer, Isaac Backus, Morgan Edwards, or David Benedict could
explain Stoddard's affection for this destructive doctrine. Yet as Mr.
Stoddard pressed on with this, New England spiraled into an apathetic

and lifeless spirituality which resulted in the judgment of God. The correction of this error arguably led to the ultimate unification of the American nation. And the leadership for the solution was provided from Stoddard's own descendents.

Within the bounds of providence, God gave Solomon Stoddard a lovely daughter whom he named Esther. In time Esther met and married a greatly blessed preacher, Timothy Edwards. Their only son, Jonathan would pastor the Stoddard church in Northampton and began a journey to correct the wrongs of Grandfather Solomon and the Saybrook Platform. Edwards is our first of four key men. It is the author's contention that none of America's history, sacred or secular, can be fully understood without a good understanding of Jonathan Edwards.

Though Edwards was not a Baptist, his influence on the *baptized believers* was deep and lasting. The English Baptist historian, Thomas Crosby mentions him with great respect. The first American Baptist historian, Isaac Backus, credits him with the opening fires of the Great Awakening by declaring, "As to real reformation, one instrument of it deserves particular notice, namely, Mr. Jonathan Edwards."[36] Alvah Hovey, who gave us the biography of Isaac Backus, said that Edwards "did much to spread and strengthen the desire for revival." [37]

Jonathan Edwards was born in Windsor, Connecticut on October 5, 1703. His father was a preacher, a believer in *experimental religion* and a witness to great revivals.

Edwards was one of the first students and graduates of Yale, completing his course of study in 1727. In those days of deep study Edwards came to realize the mistakes of his grandfather. For years he was suspect of the **half-way covenant**, but since that doctrine had become synonymous with his beloved grandfather we may imagine his dilemma in opposing it. Nothing but love and respect towards the memory of Stoddard was in his heart and his honourable constitution was resistant to show criticism of his mother's father. Still, without doubt, the belief system had to be corrected.

Since 1704 the "sacrament" of baptism "from that time was viewed as a converting ordinance."[38] The dulling effect of this on *experimental religion* was brutal. Churches began to die. Between 1718 and 1727, Mr. Stoddard's church as well as all of New England experienced in his own words, "a far more degenerate time among his people, particularly among the young than ever before."[39]

February 15, 1727, the 24-year-old Edwards became Pastor of Northampton Congregational church. Grandfather Solomon Stoddard was still alive and when Jonathan became pastor, Stoddard remained in the church.

Edwards began to prepare two discourses weekly after his ordination in 1727 and entered into a time of intense study. In this time frame he devoted large amounts of his time to study. He desired to be a theologian, but God would make of him an unusual combination of theologian and revivalist.

He spent 13 hours a day in his study. This was for two purposes: First, to make himself available to those that needed him and secondly, for extensive study.

He kept a rigorous office schedule and made himself easily available to those in distress of soul, where they were treated with "all desirable tenderness, kindness and familiarity."[40]

The church had experienced a dry spell due to the half-way covenant. The church was lax and lethargic. When Edwards came to the pulpit an immediate change began to take place. In a few weeks, 20 adults came under conviction and were saved.

Physically, he was frail and he knew it. He worked on his health. He paid close attention to his diet, even to the point of noting what foods affected his body and mind. But most obviously he WALKED WITH GOD.

When we study his life from a 21st century viewpoint we may tend to forget that all of the towns in New England in the 18th century had compulsory church attendance. The pressure of door-to-door soul winning and canvassing was not as great. People came to church out of necessity, but that made the possibility of a dead church greater. The difficulties of pastoring such a group of people is hard to understand.

In July 28 of 1728, Edwards married Sarah Pierrepont, the daughter of James Pierrepont, the aforementioned celebrated "tutor" of Yale and staunch supporter of grandfather Stoddard's position on the **half-way covenant**. Pierrepont was the *standing order* preacher of the New Haven Congregational church. He was the actual author of the "Saybrook Platform." Complications set in when Edwards came to reject and then publicly oppose Saybrook.

Sarah Edwards was born Jan. 9, 1710. "She was a young lady of uncommon beauty. The native powers of her mind were of a superior order; In her manners she was gentle and courteous, amiable in her behaviour, and the law of kindness appeared to govern all her conversation and conduct. She was also a rare example of early piety; having exhibited the life and power of religion, and that in a remarkable manner, when only five years of age."[41]

Mr. Edwards talents came to the attention of his peers when in Boston, in July of 1731 he preached *God Glorified in Man's Dependence*. This was published as a written discourse not long afterward.

The Great Awakening commenced in 1734. The events of the early defining moments of this tremendous event were recorded in Jonathan Edward's *Narrative of Surprising Conversions*. The roots of the Great Awakening were in Edwards and his church: "There began a better attitude and 'a disposition to yield to advice in the young.'"[42] Mr. Edwards was concerned about the lax attitude toward Sunday services. Not absences, but inattention. He preached on it and the next evening a large number came to his home wanting to do something about it. He challenged his people to warn their families... But to the surprise of everyone, the young people were already discussing their mediocrity and repenting of their complacency. God began to move in their midst.

A small revival stir occurred from there to the little village of Pascommuck. That began a stirring across Massachusetts and New England. Jonathan Edwards preached his epic sermon *Sinners in the Hands of an Angry God* in the parish church of Enfield, Connecticut July 8, 1741. The Great Awakening was under way.

The reason Baptists owe so much to Edwards is for his stand on *experimental religion* and his support of George Whitefield, whom we shall meet in chapter six.

Jonathan Edwards exercised, slept very little and ate very little.

He used investigation and argument in his works and prospered under long constrained applications of study. He lived by a great schedule and self watch, and he was a man of self-denial. A great principle found in Edward's life: The force of habitual duties creates a change of habit. He said, "When at any time I have a sense of any divine thing, then I seek to turn it in my thoughts to a practical improvement."

We cannot make revival happen but we can pray, work, and apply our talents—and perhaps sense it's approaching fragrance. Jonathan Edwards certainly did.

*   *   *

What is the ground of thy Controversy?

The great Boston fire occurred in 1711. In 1721, a small pox epidemic hit Boston, and over 1,000 people were killed in one year. The first inoculation was introduced at that time. The ancient Increase Mather died in 1723. He was 86 years of age.

On October 29, 1727 an earthquake—"Tis the most remarkable earthquake ever known in New England."[43] Isaac Backus wrote, "at ten in the evening, came on the greatest earthquake that had then been known in this country, and great numbers were awakened thereby."

Comer said, "This year (1727) proved troublesome to the state of this Colony, which was in a distressing condition. There never was so many supporters of the State taken away in one year as in this remarkable year. It looks like a sad token of God's displeasure."[44]

1728 started with no better prospects. On January 17, 1728, Comer wrote, "This night Mary Dye went and drowned herself as the Jewry [jury] gave it; but most concluded she was murthered by her husband. One of her arms was broke and on that arm appeared ten black and blue stripes."[45] Cotton Mather died on February 13, 1728 at the age of 65. Deborah Brinman, was killed by lightning at Narraganset on May 31st, 1728.[46] A child drowned at Connanicut on August 23rd 1728, and on April 7, 1728, five more citizens drowned in a sailing incident.[47]

In May of 1728 an exemption was made for Baptists and Quakers for relief from ministerial taxes IF they lived less than five miles from their place of worship. Backus likened this to the pharaoh allowing the Israelites to worship but not to worship too far away. In the awful year 1729, 28 baptized believers went to jail in Bristol, Massachusetts for refusing to pay the Congregational ministers.

What did Comer see on October 2-3, 1728? From a mind looking for answers he vividly described the Northern Lights:

> This morning about an hour before day, being in bed and awake, observing an very uncommon light I got up and finding it in the North, upon steady viewing at bottom of the horizon there appeared a thick vapour, and above it a redness like unto fire, and in the middle a hundred or more spears pointing upwards, extending towards the zenith. The whole body of the appearance had a slow motion towards the east, the whole face of the south was lighted as by the moon, which then had been set about three hours.[48]

John Comer reported an example of an unregenerate preacher named Joseph O'Hara. An Episcopalian, Mr. O'Hara was ousted literally from his pulpit on November 3, 1728 by "an extraordinary gust of wind" which blew both he and a large window out into the street. O'Hara was later jailed for theft.[49]

More tragedy for the small colony was recorded on December 8, 1728, as woman was found dead in Dyre's swamp. Four more drowned off Hog Island on December 21, 1728. Solomon Stoddard died on February 11, 1729. And yet another man drowned on the 17th of March, 1729.[50]

Then Comer recorded this bit of unpublished American history: "A number of Baptists, Churchmen, and Quakers, in all 30 persons, belonging to the township of Rehoboth, (Mass), were committed to Bristol jail, by reason of their refusing to pay the ministers' rate. The measles brought into town and spread. Same day. March 3, 1729."[51]

He reported five more dead with their funerals in one day in October of 1729. Comer wrote, "the voice of sudden death" warns us, "be ye also ready."[52] On October 22, 1729, the small pox was _again_ reported in Boston. It was brought to Massachusetts on an Irish vessel, from which 19 fell victim and were cast into the sea.

On November 5, 1729, the light came back. Mr. Comer identifies it on January 4, 1730 when he says he saw the "Aurora borealis, in the north."[53]

Lastly, on October 22, 1730 Comer wrote:

This evening between six and seven of the clock came on **the most terrifying awful and amazing Northern light as ever was beheld in New England as I can learn.** There was at the bottom of the horizon a very great brightness and over it an amazing red bow extending from North to East like a dreadful fire and many fiery spears, and the East was wonderfully lighted and some part of the appearance continued many hours and people were extremely terrified. Words can't express the awfulness of it. **What God is about to do is only known to Himself.**"

After seeing strange lights in the sky four times in three years, reporting numerous drownings and suicides, unjust jailings and hangings, a measles outbreak, the small pox epidemics in Boston, July heat, August lightning, a September hurricane, and the October earthquake, John Comer wrote:

The interest of Christ in the Baptist churches looks very dark at this time; the harvest is great, but the labourers are few. Oh that the Lord of the harvest would furnish and send forth into his harvest! I mourn over the churches. Lord show us, **what is the ground of thy controversie?**" [54]

*   *   *

On March 24, 1738, John Callender delivered his historic discourse on the history of Rhode Island. It was the first answer to Cotton Mather's ill treatment of the *baptized believers* in *Magnalia*. Callender said, "Jesus Christ is King in His own Kingdom and that no others had authority over His subjects in the affairs of conscience and eternal salvation."[55]

In language that brings "Japheth" to mind, Callender observed, "New England promised a great addition to the trade and riches and power of the Kingdom [of Great Britain], and greatly enlarged its territory."[56] With that observation, Callender warned, "God grant, that as we increase in numbers and riches, we may not increase in sin and wickedness, but that we may rather be lead, by the divine goodness to reform whatever may have been amiss or wanting among us."

*   *   *

The Six Principle Baptists[57] petitioned the Connecticut government for relief from the ministry tax. This was done in September of 1729:

> To the Honorurable General Assembly of the Colony of Connecticut, to be convened at New Haven on the second Thursday of October next. The humble memorial of the General Association of the Baptist churches, convened at Northkingston, on the 6th day of September, a.d. 1729, humbly showeth, That your Honours; Petitioners having sundry Brethren of their Communion dwelling up and down in your Colony, they therefore do hereby humbly crave that an Act of assembly may be passed to free them from paying any taxes to any ministry except their own, and from building any meeting-houses except for their own use, humbly hoping your Honours will consider they are utterly unable to maintain their own way of worship and to pay taxes also to the Presbyterians, and that the gracious act of indulgence together with the reasonableness of our request will be motive sufficient to move ye Honours to grant the request of your Honours; humble Memorialists. Sighned in the name and by the order of the said Association, this 8th day of September, A.D. 1729, by Richard Sweet, Valentine Wightman, Samuel Fisk, John Comer, Pardon Tillinghast....elders, John Wightman, James King, Benjamin Herendeen, Timothy Peckham, Joseph Holmes, Ebenezeer Cook, George Gardner, Thomas Durke, Ebenezer Graves, James Bates, John Tillinghast, Joseph Sanford, Samuel Weight [58]

*   *   *

A typical day was ending for Jonathan Edwards. Just before quenching the lamp on his desk, he wrote in his journal, "We have long been in a strange stupor; the influences of the Spirit of God upon the heart have been but little felt, and the nature of them but little taught."

New England was very much now like a ship that had lost her way. The destitute attitudes of the churches of New England from the Boston Fire of 1711 to the year 1735 were bringing a certain "fearful looking for judgment." Dryness had set in. Orthodoxy prevailed without spiritual power and the "letter killeth" without the breath of God.

A great evangelist of that era said, "The churches are asleep—only a loud voice can wake them out of it."[59] And so we shall meet our second key man. The great and effectual door of America was destined to become double, and a loud voice on the calendar of God's providence was about to declare them open.

George Whitefield

CHAPTER SIX
The Great Awakening

If the began apostasy should proceed as fast, the next thirty years, as it has done these last, surely it will come to that in New England, that the most conscientious people therein will think themselves concerned to gather churches out of churches.[1]
—Increase Mather predicting
the rise of the "Separates."

My being so long in ye country has given me an opportunity to make my observations on man from ye highest to ye lowest, and I have hardly met a man that rightly understands what a soul is, much less its faculties.[2]
—Howell Harris

I cannot but marvel to see how soon the children will forget the sword that drove their fathers into this land, and take hold of it as a jewel, and kill their grandchildren therewith. O that men could see how far this is from Christ's rule!
—Solomon Paine

As Benedict Arnold assembled his men in preparation for his assault on Quebec in 1775, he carried with him pieces of stolen white cloth. The cloths had been given to each commanding officer as tokens of good luck in the impending battle.[3] They were strips of cloth from the funeral gown of George Whitefield, the great evangelist of the Great Awakening. Arnold had taken them from Whitefield's coffin in his crypt at the Old South Church in Newburyport, Massachusetts. It happened in 1775, five years after the death of the American Elijah.

This Benedict was the sixth Benedict Arnold of New England. This one no one wants to claim for obvious reasons, but unlike the first three Benedicts, he was born in Connecticut. His great, great, great, great grandfather was a Benedict Arnold, but that Benedict was an original Rhode Islander, a pilgrim to Providence Plantations with Roger Williams and the first governor of the breakaway colony. And as sure as liberty birthed in Rhode Island, treason had a foothold in Connecticut and we shall see how those two ideas collided somewhere north of Boston.

Benedict Arnold VI was born in January 14, 1741 in Norwich, Connecticut. He was the second son of Benedict Arnold IV. His older brother, Benedict V, died in infancy. Benedict VI's father had migrated to Connecticut in 1730 in search of better opportunities. He began as a cooper, but longed for a more exciting, more lucrative life. He found that life when he married Hannah Waterman King. Hannah was the widow of a Norwich tradesman named Absolom King. King was lost at sea during one of his dangerous and daring ocean crossings. Benedict IV took over the business of Absolom and became a prosperous merchant and an excellent sailor. His navigational abilities earned him the nickname "Captain Arnold."

All did not remain well for the Arnolds in Norwich, however. Norwich had become a great inland port located up the Thames River in Connecticut, far enough inland to allow brisk trade with the farmers and craftsmen who had settled into the interior. But with the onslaught of the trade wars with Spain and France in 1744-1748 the American colonies, including Norwich, suffered severe setbacks in trade. According to some writers, the effects of the trade wars, coupled with the harsh realities of life (which included the deaths of four of six children) may have driven Captain Arnold to bitterness and hard drinking.

Central to the life of the Arnolds and central to our narrative was their church, the Congregational Church of Norwich. Their pastor was Benjamin Lord. The Great Awakening was about to descend on Norwich and Mr. Lord's reaction to it would affect two families pivotal in American history.

Benedict Arnold VI received infant sprinkling by the hand of Benjamin Lord in January of 1741. The salvation of her son was tantamount in Hannah's life as evidenced by existing letters written by her hand, recorded by James Martin:

> Each of the surviving letters by Hannah, five of which she addressed to young Benedict, stressed the need to "let your first concern be to make your peace with God, as it is of all concerns of the greatest impor-

tance." Hannah worried continuously about her son's spiritual state and repeatedly reminded him, "My dear, make the Lord your dwelling place and try and trust His care. We have a very uncertain stay in this world, and it stands us all in hand to see that we have an interest in Christ, without which we must be eternally miserable."[4]

Sadly, there is no evidence that Benedict Arnold ever received salvation "experimentally" and was born again.

When the Great Awakening came to Connecticut, the number of converts presenting themselves for membership in the Norwich church reached a total of 62 for 1742 alone. That was more than the total number of converts for the previous ten years. Among those born again were Captain Arnold and Hannah.[5]

The Great Awakening had begun in Northampton, Massachusetts under the leadership of Jonathan Edwards and was extended throughout the colonies. Among the Congregationalists, those that embraced the revival became known as the "New Lights," and those that rejected the revival began to be known as the "Old Lights." In the middle colonies the hand of God was evident upon the Dutch Reformed evangelist Theodorus Frelinghuysen and the Presbyterians William Tennent and son Gilbert. Soon the Presbyterian camp in America split into two definite groups: the "Old Sides" who were opposed to the itinerants and the revival and the "New Sides" who embraced the revival and most of what came with it. The Baptists, in the beginning of the Awakening had no traveling patriarchal itinerant. They were struggling for existence against persecution and bloodshed, however, as we shall see, the Baptists became the greatest beneficiaries of the great revival.

*   *   *

Elizabeth Backus and her children were also members of the Norwich Congregational church. The Backus family had a history of deep involvement in the church. Even though Norwich was in Connecticut, the birthplace of the Saybrook Platform, the town was very much settled on the Massachusetts Cambridge Platform. We must remember Cambridge had no **half-way covenant**, and Saybrook featured it.

In 1708 the Saybrook Platform was adopted by the churches of Connecticut.[6]

The previous chapter gave details on the beginning of the "Separate" movement in Norwich. But Joseph Backus was dead now and John Woodward was gone. The church had reunited under the Cambridge Platform. However, 30 years later Benjamin Lord reinstated the Saybrook Platform at Norwich. When the Great Awakening hit, things became intense.

*   *   *

George Whitefield was born at Gloucester, England in the year 1714. He was afflicted with measles as a child, which left him cross-eyed. Whitefield's early life, according to his own account, was a time of "lying, filthy talking, and foolish jesting, and that he was a sabbath-breaker, a theater-goer, a card-player, and a romance reader." All this, he says, went on till he was 15 years old. He entered Oxford as a servitor at Pembroke at the age of 18.

Whitefield's life was changed at Oxford. He came to a saving knowledge of Christ and was soundly converted. He spent time visiting the city prison, reading to the prisoners, and trying to do some good.

He became acquainted with John and Charles Wesley, and a little band of like-minded young men, including James Hervey, later a great English writer. This group of students founded the "Holy Club" at Oxford. They were later nicknamed "Methodists" for their strict "method" of living.

Whitefield privately studied Thomas Kempis, and Castanuza's *Spiritual Combat*, Scougal's *Life of God in the Soul of Man*, Law's *Serious Call*, Baxter's *Call to the Unconverted*, Alleine's *Alarm to Unconverted Sinners*, and Matthew Henry's *Commentary*. He began a vigorous habit of self-denial. He says in his Journal, "I always chose the worst sort of food. I fasted twice a week. My apparel was mean. I thought it unbecoming a penitent to have his hair powdered. I wore woolen gloves, a patched gown, and dirty shoes; and though I was convinced that the kingdom of God did not consist in meat and drink, yet I resolutely persisted in these voluntary acts of self-denial, because I found in them great promotion of the spiritual life."

"Above all," he says, "my mind being now more opened and en-larged, I began to read the Holy Scriptures upon my knees, laying aside all other books, and praying over, if possible, every line and word. This provided meat indeed and drink indeed to my soul. I daily received fresh life, light, and power from above. I got more true knowledge from reading the Book of God in one month than I could ever have acquired from all the writings of men."[7] Of all of those involved in the "Holy Club" Whitefield had the best grasp on *experimental religion* and the grace of God given in salvation.

He was ordained by Bishop Benson of Gloucester in 1736.

At this early juncture in his life Mr. Whitefield established a list of convictions for each day which he believed would establish his fellow-ship with God and benefit his quest for holiness and sincerity. He would judge himself each day by asking:

Have I:

1. Been fervent in private prayer?
2. Used stated hours of prayer?
3. Used ejaculation (short communicative prayers) every hour?
4. After or before every deliberate conversation or action, considered how it might tend to God's glory?
5. After any pleasure, immediately given thanks?
6. Planned business for the day?
7. Been simple and recollected in everything?
8. Been zealous in undertaking and active in doing what good I could?
9. Been meek, cheerful, affable in everything I said or did?
10. Been proud, vain, unchaste, or enviable of others?
11. Recollected in eating and drinking? Thankful? Temperate in sleep?
12. Taken time for giving thanks according to Law's (William Law) rules?
13. Been diligent in studies?
14. Thought or spoken unkindly of anyone?
15. Confessed all sins?

Here is Mr. Whitefield's own description of his first sermon preached:

> Last Sunday, in the afternoon, I preached my first sermon in the church of St. Mary-le-Crypt, where I was baptized, and also first received the sacrament of the Lord's Supper. Curiosity, as you may easily guess, drew a large congregation together upon this occasion. The sight at first a little awed me. But I was comforted with a heartfelt sense of the divine presence, and soon found the unspeakable advantage of having been accustomed to public speaking when a boy at school, and of exhorting the prisoners and poor people at their private houses while at the university. By these means I was kept from being daunted overmuch. As I proceeded I perceived the fire kindled, till at last, though so young and amidst a crowd of those who knew me in my childish days, I trust I was enabled to speak with some degree of gospel authority. Some few mocked, but most seemed for the present struck; and I have since heard that a complaint was made to the bishop that I drove fifteen mad the first sermon! The worthy prelate wished that the madness might not be forgotten before next Sunday.

His preaching startled England. His style and pathos were unique. His delivery was loud and gripping. It was his intense walk with God and passion for souls that came through to his hearers. It is abundantly evident that the mighty power of God fell upon him and his listeners were convicted, converted and helped.

After a short but important ministry of two months in the town of Dummer, Whitefield took the responsibility of the care of an Orphan House, which had been set up near Savannah by the Wesleys, for the children of colonists. He sailed for America in the latter part of 1737, and continued there about a year. The needs of this Orphan House occupied him much for the remainder of his life. Some question to this day the wisdom of Whitefield's involvement in it, but it is the opinion of the author that God used that ministry and need and Whitefield's loyal obligation (partly due to his loyalty to the Wesleys) to keep him in America for large portions of time.

Whitefield returned from Georgia to England in 1738. His voyage across the Atlantic took nearly a year due to what we believe was a direct attempt on his life by satanic forces. He found a storm of controversy about himself and the majority of the clergy of the Church of England now in opposition to his ways, means and doctrine. The greatest criticism was his insistence on regeneration, or the new birth. The number of pulpits to which he had access rapidly diminished. Churches and ministers were filled with indignation at a man who declared fully the atonement of Christ and the work of the Holy Ghost, and began to denounce him openly.

At this time, Mr. Whitefield came under the influence of two forgotten men in the history of revival: Griffith Jones and Howell Harris. Although Jones was nearing the end of his ministry, his influence was great. He was called "the morning star of the revival." Jones was ordained an Anglican priest in 1709 and immediately began to cry against the sins of the ministers of the Church of England. Of Jones' preaching it is written:

> Every feature, nerve and part of him were intensely animated. When he came to the application he seemed to summon up all his remaining force; he gave way to a superior burst of religious vehemence, and, like a flaming meteor, bore down all before him. No wonder that his hearers wept. No wonder that he was so successful in the conversion of sinners, when it was the Divine Spirit that made the Word effectual.[8]

Griffith Jones was one of the first thunderheads in the storm of revival that would sweep England and America from 1730-1745.

Howell Harris was an itinerate evangelist who brought Wales to its knees in the beginning years of the Great Awakening. Harris was enrolled in St. Mary's Hall, Oxford, preparing for the ministry, but grew disillusioned with the backslidden condition of the professors and students. He withdrew from college and commenced his work as a "reader" and "exhorter" in Wales. Since it was against the law to hold unauthorized church services, Howell Harris organized societies and pioneered the preaching of the gospel in the open air. His house meetings drew huge crowds and his tremendous compassion drew huge crowds. Jones, Howell, and Whitefield made a great effect on the Baptists, for they well understood the ramifications of preaching without a license. This also explains the Baptist affection for Whitefield when he arrived in America. Howell Harris described his own preaching in this fashion:

A strong necessity is laid upon me, that I could not rest, but must go to the utmost of my ability to exhort I could not meet or travel with anybody, rich or poor, young or old, without speaking to them concerning their souls,. I went during the festive season from house to house in our parish, and the parishes of Llangors and Llangasty, until persecution became too hot. I was absolutely hard and ignorant with regard to the reasons of religion; I was drawn onwards by the love I had experienced, as a blind man is led, and therefore I could not take notice of anything in my way.

My food and drink was praising my God. A fire was kindled in my soul and I was clothed with power, and made altogether dead to earthly things. I could have spoken to the King were he within my reach – such power and authority did I feel in my soul over every spirit...I lifted up my voice with authority, and fear and terror would be seen on all faces. I went to the Talgarth fairs, denouncing the swearers and cursers without fear or favour.

At first I knew nothing at all, but God opened my mouth (full of ignorance), filling it with terrors and threatenings. I was given a commission to rend and break sinners in the most dreadful manner. I thundered greatly, denouncing the gentry, the carnal clergy and everybody.[9]

It is easy to see how both these men influenced the young George Whitefield. Denied many pulpits, Whitefield would take to the fields and these two Welsh evangelists would show him the way. Both Harris and Jones were basically unwanted in the Church of England, although they did not advocate separation from the church.

Ryle described Whitefield's first attempt at field preaching:

His first attempt to do this was among the colliers at Kingswood near Bristol, in February, 1739. After much prayer he one day went to Hannam Mount, and standing upon a hill began to preach to about a hundred colliers upon Matthew 5:1-3. The thing soon became known. The number of hearers rapidly increased, till the congregation amounted to many thousands. His own account of the behaviour of these neglected colliers, who had never been in a church in their lives, is deeply affecting. "Having," he writes to a friend, "no righteousness of their own to renounce, they were glad to hear of a Jesus who was a friend to publicans, and came not to call the righteous but sinners to repentance."

The first discovery of their being affected was the sight of the white gutters made by their tears, which plentifully fell down their black cheeks as they came out of their coal-pits. Hundreds of them were soon brought under deep conviction, which, as the event proved, happily ended in a sound and thorough conversion. The change was visible to all, though numbers chose to impute it to anything rather than the finger of God. As the scene was quite new, it often occasioned many inward conflicts. Sometimes, when twenty thousand people were before me, I had not in my own apprehension a word to say either to God or them. But I was never totally deserted, and frequently (for to deny it would be lying against God) was so assisted that I knew by happy experience what our Lord meant by saying, "Out of his belly shall flow rivers of living water." The open firmament above me, the prospect of the adjacent fields, with the sight of thousands, some in coaches, some on horseback, and some in the trees, and at times all affected and in tears, was almost too much for, and quite overcame me.[10]

On April 27, 1739 Whitefield began open-air preaching in London. He had gone to Islington to preach for Mr. Stonehouse. He was forbidden to preach in the church building because he lacked a license from the diocese. So he preached in the churchyard.

He recorded in his diary, "God was pleased to assist me in preaching, and so wonderfully to affect the hearers, that I believe we could have gone singing hymns to prison. Let not the adversaries say, I have thrust myself out of their synagogues. No, they have thrust me out."

On Sunday, April 29th, he recorded: "I preached in Moorfields to an exceeding great multitude. Being weakened by my morning's preaching, I refreshed myself in the afternoon by a little sleep, and at five went and preached at Kennington Common, about two miles from London, when no less that thirty thousand people were supposed to be present."

Other places he preached in the open air were: Hackney Fields, Mary-le-bonne Fields, May Fair, Smithfield, Blackheath, and Moorfields.

His opportunities to preach for the ministers of the Church of England nearly ceased. But the common people heard him gladly. He was instrumental in creating great growth for his own denomination.

In Whitsuntide week after preaching in Moorfields, he received 1,000 letters from people under conviction of their sin and brought 350 persons into Anglican communion. In 34 years it is conservatively estimated that he preached publicly 18,000 times.

*　　*　　*

On October 30, 1739 Whitefield arrived in America for the second time. After serving in Georgia and establishing a benevolent fund for the orphanage at Savannah, he had returned to astonishing success in England. Now he was returning to shore up the ministry in Georgia and preach the gospel wherever the Holy Ghost would grant him permission.

He landed in Lewistown, Delaware with the express purpose of going to Philadelphia. In nine days of preaching, the town was turned upside down and the wrath of the clergy came wildly upon him. He set out on horseback to New York where he met an anxious Gilbert Tennent, whose Presbyterians had split over the awakening into "New Sides" and "Old Sides." The "New Sides" were in favor of the revival and Mr. Tennent emerged as the leader of the "New Sides."

Mr. Whitefield immediately went to obtain permission from Mr. Vessey, the commissary of the Church of England in New York, but Vessey had already sent a scathing rebuke and refusal for Whitefield to grace the Anglican Church of New York. Instead, he took to the fields. An anonymous eyewitness sent this letter to the *New England Journal*:

> When Mr. Whitefield came to the place before designed, which was a little eminence of the side of a hill, he stood still and beckoned with his hand, and dispos'd the multitude upon the descent, before and on either side of him. He then prayed most excellently...The assembly soon appeared to be divided into two companies...The one were collected round the minister, and were very serious and attentive. The other had placed themselves in the skirts of the assembly, and spent most of their time in giggling, scoffing, talking and laughing...Towards the last prayer the whole assembly appeared more united, and all became hush'd and still; a solemn awe and reverence appeared in the faces of most, and a mighty energy attended the Word. I heard and

felt something astonishing, but I confess, I was not at the time, fully rid of my scruples.[11]

Once there, he was invited to the Wall Street Presbyterian Church. He then returned to Philadelphia where he caught the attention of Benjamin Franklin. Franklin remarked on the marvelous change in the people of Philadelphia after Whitefield had preached:

> It was wonderful to see the change soon made in the manners of our inhabitants, From being thoughtless or indifferent about religion, it seems as if all the world were growing religious, so that one could not walk thro' the town in an evening without hearing psalms sung in different families of every street.[12]

Franklin was tremendously impressed with Mr. Whitefield's ability. "He had a loud and clear voice," Franklin said, and documented the fact that he could be heard from a distance of one mile.[13] Mr. Franklin became a friend to Mr. Whitefield, even printing his sermons, but Franklin never claimed to have received Christ as his Saviour.

In late November 1739, Mr. Whitefield preached his last sermon of that tour in Philadelphia to a crowd of 10,000 solemn hearers. They knew he was to leave their city and wept for their great sorrow in parting with him. Whitefield set out to see the rest of America on horseback heading south in the direction of Georgia and the orphanage. Over 200 horsemen followed him out along the road. During the first 100 miles he stopped often to preach. His journal recorded the results:

> **Chester**, Thursday, Nov. 29. I preached to about five thousand people from a balcony. It being court-day, the Justices sent word that they would defer their meeting till mine was over.

> **Wilmington**, Friday, Nov. 30. Preached at noon and again at three in the afternoon. Received several fresh invitations to preach at various places, but was obliged to refuse them all. Oh, that I had 100 tongues and lives, they should all be employed for my dear Lord Jesus.

> **Newcastle**, Saturday, Dec. 1. Preached to about 2,000 from a balcony, but did not speak with so much freedom and power as usual, God be-

ing pleased to humble my soul by inward visitations and bodily indis-
position. Lay on the bed after sermon, which much refreshed me.

Whiteclay Creek, Sunday, Dec 2. The weather was rainy, but upwards
of 10,000 people were assembled. It surprised me to see such a number of horses. There were several hundreds of them. I preached from a
tent erected for me by Mr. William Tennent. I continued my discourse for an hour and a half, after which we went into a log-house
near by, took a morsel of bread and warmed ourselves. I preached a
second time from the same place. My body was weak.[14]

Of the Whiteclay Creek meeting, Benjamin Franklin reported over
3,000 horsemen alone as part of the huge crowd.

In the fall of 1740, Mr. Whitefield made his first preaching tour of
New England. He landed at Newport, Rhode Island Sunday September
14, 1740. The minister of the Church of England in Newport was Mr.
James Honeyman, and he was less than sweet on receiving Mr. Whitefield into his church to preach. In a letter Honeyman said:

Last Sunday arrived here from South Carolina, the noisie Mr. Whitefield. [He] desired leave to preach in my Church, if I denied him, the
Old Teacher had strongly invited him to the Meeting-House, and he
would accept of it. At last I complied...I shall endeavour to correct his
mistakes and evince a just distinction betwixt Christianity and enthusiasm.[15]

He stayed but four days in Rhode Island and made his way to Boston. A meeting was arranged with the ministers of the established
Church of England. Whitefield was questioned on his acceptance of the
Presbyterian Gilbert Tennent. He was questioned about his speaking
with the Baptists. In his conversation with the commissary of Boston on
that September day in 1740, Mr. Whitefield voiced *the real crucible of
New England*:

WHITEFIELD: "If every child was really born again in baptism,
then every baptized infant would be saved."
DR. CUTLER: "And so they are."
WHITEFIELD: "How do you prove that?"

DR. CUTLER: "Because the Rubric says 'that all infants dying after baptism before they have committed actual sin, are undoubtedly
saved.'"

WHITEFIELD: "What text of Scripture was there to prove it?"

DR. CUTLER: "Here, said he (holding a Prayer Book in his
hand), the church says so."[16]

After this discussion with the Boston Church of England officials,
Mr. Whitefield's American association with his mother denomination
for all practical purposes, ceased, though he never separated from his
orders from England.

It was during this first tour of New England that Mr. Whitefield
met with Jonathan Edwards in Northampton, Massachusetts.

Some credit Jonathan Edwards with convincing Whitefield at this
time of the more defining tenets of Calvinism, but there really is no evidence of that scenario. What Whitefield believed may have been termed
"Calvinism,"[17] but his actions were fervent regarding the offer of salvation to a lost and dying world.

Concerning Calvinism, Whitefield wrote, "My doctrines I had from
Jesus Christ and His Apostles, I was taught them of God. I embrace the
Calvinistic scheme, not because Calvin, but Jesus Christ has taught it to
me."[18]

In a 1739 letter to Hervey, his friend, fellow laborer and confidant,
Whitefield voiced his theological sentiments:

> The doctrines of our election, and free justification in Christ Jesus are
> daily more and more pressed upon my heart. They fill my soul with a
> holy fire and afford me great confidence in God my Saviour.
>
> I hope they shall catch fire from each other, and that there will be a
> holy emulation amongst us, who shall most debase man and exalt the
> Lord Jesus. Nothing but the doctrines of the Reformation can do this.
> All others leave freewill in man and make him, in part at least, a Sav-
> iour to himself. My soul, come not thou near the secret of those who
> teach such things...I know Christ is all in all. Man is nothing: he hath
> a free will to go to hell, but none to go to heaven, till God worketh in
> him to will and to do of His good pleasure.
>
> Oh the excellency of the doctrine of election and of the saints' final
> perseverance! I am persuaded, till a man comes to believe and feel
> these important truths, he cannot come out of himself, but when con-

vinced of these, and assured of their application to his own heart, he then walks by faith indeed! Love, not fear, constrains him to obedience.[19]

The above statements could rightly be termed Calvinism, but consider Whitefield's fiery words in a letter sent to Howell Harris at about the same time:

Put them in mind of the freeness and eternity of God's electing love, and be instant with them to lay hold of the perfect righteousness of Jesus Christ by faith, Talk to them, oh, talk to them, even till midnight, of the riches of His all-sufficient grace. Tell them, oh, tell them, what He has done for their souls and how earnestly He is now interceding for them in Heaven. Shew them, in the map of the Word, the kingdoms of the upper world, and the transcendent glories of them; and assure them all shall be theirs if they believe on Jesus Christ with their whole hearts.

Press them to believe on Him immediately! Intersperse prayers with your exhortations, and thereby call down fire from Heaven, even the fire of the Holy Ghost—to soften, sweeten and refine, and melt them into love.

Speak every time, my dear brother, as if it was your last. Weep out, if possible, every argument, and as it were, compel them to cry 'Behold, how he loveth us!'[20]

It is little wonder that scholars, historians and interested persons argue over Whitefield's theology to this day. When laying the above letters side-by-side, Calvin-styled "election" is overrun by Arminian-styled preaching.

Dallimore summed up Whitefield's theology by stating:

Though he sometimes used the word *Calvinism*, he did not give great place to it. He made much more of the fact that the views he held were those he had discovered in the Bible and he more frequently referred to them as the doctrines of grace.[21]

The greatest benefit of the Whitefield-Edwards meeting was their discussion and agreement on *experimental religion*. They were also in complete agreement on the horrific state of religion in the pulpits of the American colonies.

Whitefield had said, "Many, perhaps most, that preach, I fear, do not experimentally know Christ," and "Are not unconverted ministers the bane of the Christian Church?"[22]

Gilbert Tennent had said, "They are blind who see not this to be the case of the body of the clergy of this generation." Mr. Porter of Bridgefield had said,

> No sooner do these light, airy, fashionable young men, who evidently deny, oppose, and banter, both publicly and privately, the great soul-humbling and Christ exacting doctrines of the Gospel, and ridicule *experimental religion* as enthusiasm, and resolve Christian experiences into an over-heated imagination and disordered brain, I say, no sooner do these young men come forth from the feet of Gamaliel into the world, and begin to exercise their gifts, but they are at once invited to preach and settle in the ministry; and there are ministers and churches enough that will ordain them, notwithstanding the testimony which the serious bear against it. He is willfully blind that does not see it![23]

Men like Chauncy and Benjamin Lord preferred the "Old Light" way of accepting "educated men, if orthodox in doctrine and regular in their lives" into pulpits to preach the gospel. But this "form of Godliness, but denying the power thereof" was something from which the Separates began to understand they must "turn away." A current close examination of most major Protestant denominations will reveal this same powerless doctrine. No evidence of the "new birth" is required for membership or sacred service.

When the "New Lights" took public stands on the unregenerate state of the ministers of America, the foxes were tied at their tails, set on fire and released throughout all America. Vicious opposition was the result. Isaac Backus, writing about the opposition to Whitefield and the Great Awakening said, "But a great majority of the ministers and rulers through the land disliked this work, and exerted all their powers against it."[24] Jonathan Edwards preached a sermon at New Haven in September 1741 speaking in favor of the awakening and giving scriptural reasons for it being authentic. This message, *Marks of a True Work of God*, greatly influenced the general population but not the majority of *standing order* ministers. It was published in 1742 in America, as well as England.[25]

Jonathan Edwards now faced the pelting scorn of the unregenerate church crowd. He wrote, "Owning the covenant, degenerated into a matter of mere form and ceremony...they do it for their credit's sake, that their children may be baptized."[26] Edwards faced opposition, but he knew that he held in his hand a canister of theological sure shot, and when he discharged it, it scattered a thousand spiritually dead ministers and sent them scrambling to regroup.

In an attempt to thwart Whitefield, the Guilford resolutions of October 1741, made any preacher guilty of disorderly conduct for preaching out of his parish.[27]

*   *   *

Back in Boston, Charles Chauncy was troubled. Chauncy was the minister of the Congregational church at Boston, and he was advocating change. With John Cotton long gone to his reward and John Wilson off into eternity, the infamous Chauncy was very busy opposing everything about the Great Awakening. He was annoyed at Whitefield's insistence that he, the minister, should be "born again."[28] He was dismayed at Jonathan Edward's approval of Whitefield. Chauncy was the forerunner of all that became bad about Congregationalism and liberal Protestantism. He was the forerunner of American liberal unbelief. He denied essential doctrine and was the first of many unbelievers occupying pulpits and mouthing their devilish ideas about doctrine. There can be no doubt that the soon approach of Unitarianism and Universalism was given swift access to the Congregational Church because of the presence of lost men in her pulpits. Chauncy and his minions never deserved a hearing or any dialogue, or any consideration, and *should* have been urged to be converted.

Chauncy answered Whitefield's contention that "unconverted ministers were the bane of the church" by saying, "Conversion does not appear to be alike necessary for ministers in their public capacity as officers of the church, as it is in their private capacity."[29]

Chauncy was concerned about Whitefield and Edwards, but Elisha Paine also badgered him.

*   *   *

Elisha Paine has been rightly called the father of the Congregational "Separates." Paine was a lawyer who witnessed the injustice of prosecuting gospel preachers for preaching outside their parishes. God used this to call him into the ministry and so he began a dangerous life of itinerant preaching across New England. He was jailed, offered an ordination by the "Old Light" ministers, released, and jailed again.

In October of 1744, Paine preached in the courtyard of the jailhouse at Windham to crowds so large that the jailer was forced to release him. It culminated in the establishment of Separate churches—not Baptist (as of yet) but Separate. All the ministers of Windham County, though they wrote a condemnation letter against these separate churches, could not keep the hungry crowds away.

Connecticut actually passed a law against the Great Awakening forbidding any preaching unless first approved by the minister of the local parish. This leads us back to Mr. Benjamin Lord and the church at Norwich, Connecticut; Captain and Hannah Arnold, and Elizabeth Backus.

*   *   *

From his study in Norwich, Benjamin Lord just could not accept *experimental religion*. Although he was grateful for the new membership in his church, he was not grateful for the intense revival atmosphere that came with it. Many of the church folk had been saved, but Mr. Lord was re-installing the Saybrook Platform complete with the half-way covenant and the Great Awakening was stalling his plans for installation.

Captain Arnold and Hannah were born again at this time and so was Elizabeth Backus. Her son, Isaac, who was running from God, finally came to a saving knowledge of Christ.

Thus begins our discovery of the third key man in our narrative. Isaac Backus at age 17, was converted after hearing Eleazar Wheelock, the founder of Dartmouth. It was August of 1741. Of his salvation Backus wrote, "I perceived I could never make myself better, should I live ever so long. Divine justice appeared clear in my condemnation, and I saw that God had a right to do with me as He would."[30]

Trumbull, the first historian of Connecticut revealed:

> It does not appear that ministers in general, at that time, made any particular inquiry of those whom they admitted to communion, with respect to their internal feeling and exercises. The Stoddardean opinion generally prevailed, that unregenerate men could consistently covenant with God, and when moral in their lives, had a right to sealing ordinances.[31]

The "Stoddardean opinion," of course, was the "Old Light" opinion that "educated men, if orthodox in doctrine and regular in their lives" could be ministers of the Gospel.

At Norwich under Mr. Lord, Isaac Backus said, "The nature of conversion and of the soul's walk with God, the teaching of the Divine Spirit and the substance of *experimental religion* were not clearly held forth; and that many things were publicly and from the pulpit assailed, which my soul well knew to be the work of God."[32] Mr. Lord publicly complained about "lowly preaching," that is, preaching by uneducated men. Of course that would be any "Separate" and especially any Baptist.[33]

For the above reasons, Isaac Backus did not join his own church in Norwich, Connecticut. The Rev. Mr. Lord "obtained a major vote to admit members into the church without so much as a written account of any change of heart." Backus finally joined because he longed to receive the Lord's Supper.

It was obvious now that a separation was coming. The Arnolds turned their backs on the "New Lights" and began to oppose them with Benjamin Lord.

The son of the Captain and Hannah, Benedict Arnold, was a mere 4 years old at the time of the Separatist controversy, but some writers make the battle over *experimental religion* a watershed in his life.[34]

One thing is certain, Benedict Arnold rejected the God of the Bible and would have nothing to do with salvation through Christ.

*   *   *

At the beginning of the Revolution, Benedict Arnold led American troops into some of their first battles with the British. In 1775, General Washington gave the young commander permission to assemble an army of 1,000 New Englanders for an early assault on Quebec. Arnold assembled his men at Newburyport, Massachusetts in September of 1775. The troops were congregated for a church service at the Old South Presbyterian Church, the church in which the American Elijah had been laid to rest five years earlier.

After the religious service, Benedict Arnold wanted something. He requested of the sexton of the church to see the crypt of Whitefield. He and Daniel Morgan, along with their chaplain, descended into the cellar and to the crypt beneath the pulpit. Incredibly, Arnold then had the coffin forced open. More incredibly, He reached into the coffin and removed the collars from Whitefield's neck and wrists. He cut the cloths and handed them to Morgan and a few other of his officers and re-emerged to march his troops to the mouth of the Kennebec River.

There can only be one interpretation of this incident seeing it came from the hands of a man in contempt of the religion that George Whitefield lived and preached. This verse comes to mind:

> **Touch not mine anointed**, and do my prophets no harm.
> Psalm 105:15

The campaign of Benedict Arnold to Quebec that winter of 1775 was a disaster. Starting with 1,000 men, the army attempted to float some distance up the Kennebec, but the bad weather caused some of their flotilla to sink and they were forced to march and carry their vessels for much of the way. Over 400 men were lost BEFORE THEY EVER ENGAGED THE ENEMY. When they finally reached Quebec, they attempted to storm the fortress and a blinding blizzard forced them to surrender. Benedict Arnold was shot in the leg. But he escaped to fight again, and go down in flames on infamy's stage with treason in his heart.

In 1745 Isaac Backus and many other persons withdrew from the *standing order* and began to hold meetings as "Separate" churches. They were hungry for truth and true religion and not a form, and obedience to 2 Corinthians 6:14-18 was their motivation.

All over the country, "Separate" churches were springing up. The *standing order* scrambled to enforce a 1742 law in Connecticut forbidding churches from "settling ministers" who were not Yale, or Harvard or Foreign educated.[35] This was done to try to counter the large number of unordained "exhorters" who were engaged in preaching the gospel all over New England.

The "Separates" argued that the office of the Gospel ministry may be exercised by men who did not hold a formal education. This made good sense, since there is not scripture warrant for the necessity of higher education, the only stipulation in scripture being those laid out by the Apostle Paul in I Timothy 3, II Timothy 2 and Titus 1. But even Jonathan Edwards wrote opposing the idea of an uneducated preacher or pastor. The problem was the rapid increase of converts and the growth of "Separatist" ideals. The establishment of new churches, especially Baptist churches, called for a goodly number of new preachers. Still, reason and scriptural precedent was for the internal call of God, whether or not the formal education was available. In fact, as Whitefield had pointed out, formal education may even be a hindrance to the Gospel preacher. Backus wrote: "In our colleges many learn corrupt principles, not only about what makes a minister, but also about what makes a Christian."[36]

Isaac Backus was called of God to preach the gospel in September of 1746. He gave a testimony of this call in his 1753 published sermon, *Discourse on the Nature and Necessity of an Internal Call to preach the everlasting Gospel.* If it is an *internal call,* then it must be in the life of a regenerate person. If it is an *internal call*, then a corrupted church form does not produce it.

This was not to say that Isaac Backus rejected the local church, he wrote:

> A converted person, has an internal right to all the privileges of the Christian church, yet has no external right to them, till he is openly received as a member; so a person who is called to preach has no right to act in duties peculiar to an officer of the church, till he is publicly set apart there in. Praying, exhorting, and preaching, though duties to be performed in the church, are not so confined to it, that they may not rightly be performed where there is no church at all. But only those who have a visible standing in the church can administer *special* ordinances or act in cases of discipline, for these are things peculiar to a visible church.[37]

Backus did not have a visible church to administer special ordinances in the beginning of his ministry and violated the 1742 law against lowly preachers. For five years he preached as an itinerant evangelist until the year 1748 when he gathered a "Separate" church in Middleborough, Massachusetts.

Here is a partial list of "Separate" preachers who came out of the *standing order* churches in New England from 1745 to 1751:

John Hovey, Mansfield, October 1745; Solomon Paine was ordained at Canterbury, September 10, 1745; Thomas Stevens at Plainfield, September 11, 1745; Thomas Dennison at Norwich Farms, October 29, 1745; Jedidiah Hide at Norwich Town, October 30, 1745; Matthew Smith at Stonington, December 10, 1745; John Fuller at Lyme, December 25, 1745; Joseph Snow at Providence, February 12, 1747; Samuel Wadsworth at Killingly, June 3, 1747; Paul Park at Preston, July 15, 1747; Elihu Marsh, at Windham, October 7, 1747; Ebenezer Frothingham at Weathersfield, October 28, 1747; Nathanael Shepard in Attleborough, January 20, 1748; Isaac Backus at Bridgewater, April 13, 1748; John Paine at Rehoboth, August 3, 1748; William Carpenter at Norton, September 7, 1748; John Blunt at Sturbridge, September 28, 1748; Ebenezer Mack at Lyme, January 12, 1749; Joshua Nickerson at Harwich, February 23, 1749; Samuel Hide at Bridgewater, May 11, 1749; John Palmer at Windham, May 17, 1749; Samuel

Hovey at Mendon, May 31, 1749; Samuel Drown at Coventry, October 11, 1749; Stephen Babcock at Westerly, April 4, 1750; Joseph Hastings at Suffield, April 17, 1750; Nathanael Ewer at Barnstable, May 10, 1750; Joshua Morse at New-London, May 17, 1750; Jonathan Hide at Brookline, January 17, 1751; Ezekiel Cole at Sutton, January 31, 1751; Ebenezer Wadsworth at Grafton, March 20, 1751; Shubael Stearns at Tolland, March 20, 1751; Nathanael Draper at Cambridge, April 24, 1751; Peter Werden at Warwick, May 17, 1751.

Immediately the "Separate" bodies began to suffer. They were looked upon with the same contempt as the Baptists. To name just one instance of the contempt in Connecticut concerned congregational minister Philemon Robbins. Robbins was pressured to say that he broke the law of God because he went to a Baptist meeting-house to preach the gospel. In 1747, he was deposed from preaching the gospel. Robbins wrote a narrative of his experiences.[38] The people of the "Separate" church at Norwich were fined to support Benjamin Lord and his church and when they refused, 40 persons both men and women were imprisoned in a single year.

Isaac Backus was informed of a tax levied against him in support of the *standing order* minister of Middleborough. He refused to pay it. On February 6, 1749 an officer seized him. Upon that tragic scene a friend came who stopped the imprisonment and paid Mr. Backus' tax. But this action would repeat itself many times. The church of Canterbury, for 15 years, had its people imprisoned, property stolen, and church harassed simply because they did not want to support a minister they did not choose.[39] "To these were added the imprisonment of Mr. Frothingham five months, Mr. John Paine eleven months, and Mr. Palmer four months all at Hartford, for preaching without the consent of parish ministers. And three gentlemen, only for being members and deacons in these separate churches, were, at different times, expelled out of their legislature, namely, Captain Obadiah Johnson, of Caanterbury, Captain Thomas Stevens, of Plainfield, and Captain Nathan Jewet, of Lyme."[40] All this occurred in Connecticut. Even the great Jonathan Edwards was not spared Connecticut injustice. He was voted out of his church by the "parish committee" by one vote and removed on June 22, 1750. His insistence on conversion as a prerequisite for communion was his downfall at Northampton.

Massachusetts was also guilty of tyranny at this juncture in history. Peter Thacker, minister, passed away in 1744 having seen his church, the Congregational Church at Middleborough, grow during the Great Awakening to over 340 communicants. The parish committee (which was the county legislature under the Saybrook Platform), worked against the congregation in calling another pastor. (Oh, the intrigue when the church is mixed in with the state.) The parish committee called another man and sent him to the church. Middleborough church refused to hear him and withdrew to examine the man of their choice. But the parish committee, in a general election, rejected the wishes of the church. So then, the church called for a council of five other churches to settle the matter and they ordained the church's choice of pastor. But the parish committee went ahead and ordained the man of their choosing, occupied the meeting-house and taxed the people for support of a preacher they did not choose. Yes, it was TAXATION WITHOUT REPRESENTATION.

*   *   *

Isaac Backus received this letter from an imprisoned "Separate" jailed for refusing to pay the ministerial tax:

I have heard something of the trials among you of late, and I was grieved till I had strength to give up the case to God, and leave my burden there. And now I would tell you something of our trial...Samuel lay in prison twenty days. October 15, the collector came to our house, and took me away to prison about nine o'clock, in a dark rainy night. Brother Hill and Sabin were brought there next night. We lay in prison thirteen days, and then were set at liberty, by what means I know not. Whilst I was there, a great many people came to see me; and some said one thing and some another. O, the innumerable snares and temptations that beset me, more than I ever thought of before! But, O the condescension of Heaven! Though I was bound when I was cast into this furnace, yet was I loosed, and found Jesus in the midst of the furnace with me. O, then I could give up my name, estate, family, life and breath, freely to God. Now the prison looked like a palace to me. I could bless God for all the laughs and scoffs made at me. O the love that flowed out to all mankind! Then I could forgive, as I would desire to be forgiven, and love my neighbor as myself. Deacon Griswold was put in prison the 8th of October, and yesterday old brother Grover... [They] are in pursuit of others; all which calls for humiliation. This church hath appointed the 13th of November to be spent in prayer and fasting on that account. I do remember my love to you and your wife, and the dear children of God with you, begging your prayers for us in such a day of trial. We are all in tolerable health, expecting to see you.

These from your loving **mother, Elizabeth Backus.**

On his third tour of America and his second of New England, George Whitefield was only 29 years of age. He was physically exhausted, having made five Atlantic crossings in five years and preaching nearly non-stop in that period of time. He landed at York in New Hampshire (present day Maine) on October 26, 1744, this time accompanied by his wife, Elizabeth. Within a week of almost non-stop preaching he collapsed and lay apparently dying. In anticipation of the evening service, Mr. Whitefield rose up, and said to the doctor, "by the help of God I will go and preach and then come home and die."

Whitefield did arise and preach and then began to face the most dramatic conflict of his ministry in America. The opposition came from two sources: Thomas Clapp of Yale College, and the President and Professors of Harvard. There is not sufficient room in our narrative to dig into the details of the Yale-Harvard Clapp flap, but Harvard's *Testimony from the President and Professors, Tutors and Hebrew Instructor of Harvard College, against the Reverend Mr. George Whitefield and his Conduct* and Mr. Whitefield's answer are valuable to our knowledge of the rise of the *baptized believers.*

Back in 1712, the ministers of Connecticut, at their general association, recommended that a candidate for the ministry should be required to give satisfaction of his skill in the Hebrew, Greek, and Latin tongues.

If you were the devil and you knew that liberal and higher education was a prerequisite to preach the Gospel, what would you attack? Whitefield understood this and the apathy and apostasy at Harvard and Yale became subjects of his sermons.

In summary, the Harvard Testimony had five major complaints. Whitefield was: 1. An enthusiast, depending upon dreams and impulses from God for his direction in life; 2. He was uncharitable, seeing he charged Yale and Harvard as being places of spiritual darkness; 3. He was a deluder for he did not itemize his expenses at the Georgia orphanage; 4. Whitefield's extemporaneous preaching and itinerating were unscriptural practices and 5. He intended to root out all the ministers in America and replace them with foreigners.

In answer to these charges Whitefield was swift and effective. He admitted he made statements as a younger man that were extreme and immature. He did not however, deny the statements about the darkness of the colleges and quoted the then present president of Harvard, Edward Holyoke, from a chapel message in which Holyoke decried the college as "decayed." Whitefield then pointed out that those to whom he gives account of the orphanage were "fully satisfied" with his records, but pledged to be even more detailed. Finally, his defense of his own preaching and itinerate ministry was marked once again by quoting Holyoke who says: "Those two pious and valuable men of God, [that is Whitefield and Tennent] have been greatly instrumental in the hands of God, in reviving this blessed work, and many no doubt have been savingly converted." His answer did much to remove criticism and enhance his ministry,[41] even though the colleges still scorned him. It is refreshing to see once again, that human hands cannot stop the work of the Holy Ghost. The great revival rolled on accomplishing that which God in His will intended. A nation was galvanizing and the country that the American Elijah was uniting would become the greatest force for salvation the world has ever known.

*   *   *

Now Isaac Backus faced the real *crucible of New England*. He undoubtedly knew of Able Morgan, nephew of the Welsh immigrant and a product of Welsh Tract church. Morgan was the pastor of the Baptist church in Middletown, New Jersey. He had debated with Samuel Finley, the President of Princeton, over the subject of infant baptism. Abel Morgan had left the Presbyterian Finley nearly speechless with his masterpiece of Bible doctrine, *The Baptism of Believers Maintained and the mode of it by Immersion Vindicated*. Benjamin Franklin published this pamphlet in 1746.[42]

The "Separates" just north of New Jersey struggled to find their true identity from 1745 to 1760. They were in the same search for the true meaning of baptism. They were now settled in the fact that only those who were regenerated by the Spirit of God could rightly be called "Abraham's seed," and "heirs according to the promise." But their theology did not mix well with infant baptism. Through their communications and seemingly endless numbers of councils and conferences, the "Separates" began to accept believer's baptism as viable.

Among the first in the church at Middleborough to embrace believer's baptism was Ebenezer Hinds and Jonathan Woods. Backus studied and prayed with them over the matter. His first impression was that infant baptism was valid. His second impression was that baptism could be for believers only. He then preached in favor of believer's baptism only. He then recanted that stand and retreated in confusion about the matter and in his confusion he confused his entire church.

Backus then posed a question to himself that had been the *real crucible of New England* from 1620 until his present day:

> *Where, and in what relation to the church of God do those stand who have been baptized and yet are <u>not</u> believers?*[43]

Backus knew that in the Bible there was some delay in the baptism of believers. Most were baptized immediately after being "savingly converted." In the first three centuries of Christian history those believers who awaited baptism were called "catechumens." This was not a Bible word, but a word that at least described a saint of God not yet baptized. Mr. Backus knew that no incident of baptism before conversion ever took place in the Bible. It was always *belief first*, then baptism. So what were these baptized yet unbelieving people? They were certainly not church members, and certainly not "heirs according to the promise."

After two years these thoughts and further study caused Isaac Backus to seek believer's baptism. Elder Benjamin Pierce of Warwick, Rhode Island immersed him along with six members of his church on August 22, 1751.

Oh, the battle that came upon Isaac Backus now. His "Separate" church censured him. The other "Separate" ministers doubted him. He went to Norwich where his mother brought him comfort and encouragement. She attended the church that separated from Mr. Lord, but even her new pastor Mr. Hide doubted Mr. Backus. He was entering that dark tunnel of suffering now. We should learn from Backus, who gave up his standing, his career, and even his dignity to do right, to do the revealed will of God for his life. How many pull out of the "dark tunnel" before light breaks upon their faces.

No less than four councils were held among the "Separates" concerning Backus and his beliefs about baptism. In the end Isaac Backus won the battle and remained the pastor of the "Separate" church at Middleborough. It was determined among the Separates that infant baptism and believer's baptism could co-exist in the same church.

Time would prove that theory wrong because now quarreling among the "Separates" over who should receive the Lord's Supper began. It was simply unavoidable. Rather than slow our narrative down to a crawl our reader need only understand that infant baptism and believer's baptism could not possibly exist in the same church. The result of such a system was mixed communion with Pedobaptists and *baptized believers* trying to sit at the Lord's table in a state of discord. Isaac Backus had tried to maintain unity, but eventually realized that baptism was so vital that disagreement over it would always bring about a break in communion.[44]

In the end Backus wrote:

> I was constrained to give in that we ought not to receive any to the Lord's table who have not been baptized according to the gospel rule. I was brought to see that we had made Christians our rule, instead of the Word of God; for His Word requires a credible confession of saving faith, in order to baptism; and if we come to the Holy Supper with any who were only sprinkled in infancy, we commune with unbaptized persons.[45]

On January 16, 1756, the Baptist Church at Middleborough, Massachusetts was founded by Isaac Backus and his congregation of "Separate Baptists." **In his spiritual journey, leading to the founding of the Baptist Church in Middleborough, Isaac Backus represented a microcosm of the American mind, with baptism being the single most important intellectual debate before the Revolution.**

Isaac Backus was sharp, independent, and pious. He wanted what was real in religion. He rejected the establishment or status quo and struck out on his own seeking the truth and finding kindred spirits. He rejoiced in newfound truth, stood for it, and then suffered and paid a price for it. His courage ultimately led him to triumph in it. He is the quintessential citizen of *Baptist Nation.*

*   *   *

The "New Lights" were left in a vacuum as their Baptist breakaway brethren rode off into the sunset and saved the country. The number of "Separates" who became "Separate Baptists" was astounding. Many of the "Separates" passed through *the real crucible of New England* and became Baptist. As C. C. Goen wrote, the Separate Congregationalists were the "nurseries of Baptists."[46] Here is a partial list of the "Separate" Congregational preachers who became Baptist from 1745 to 1760:

> Matthew Smith of Stonington, Elihu Marsh, of Windham, Isaac Backus of Bridgewater, William Carpenter of Norton, John Blunt of Sturbridge, Ebenezer Mack of Lyme, Samuel Hovey of Mendon, Samuel Drown of Coventry, Stephen Babcock of Westerly, Joseph Hastings of Suffield, Joshua Morse of New-London, Shubael Stearns of Tolland, Nathanael Draper of Cambridge, and Peter Werden of Warwick.[47]

When Mr. Whitefield became aware that so many of his converts had become Baptists, he was reported to have said, "*All my chickens have turned into ducks.*"[48] *Baptist Nation* was in the toddler stage and the *standing order* was sensing it.

What was left of the "Separate" Congregationalists eventually went back home to their mother church and lost their luster and their zeal for *experimental religion.* Although they eventually planned a union with the Presbyterians in the beginning of the 19ᵗʰ century, it never came to pass. The Congregational Church became an evolving, changing body, whose ministers were the first in America to apostatize. The Unitarians nearly overran their denomination and much of the denomination eventually embraced Universalism and ceased to invite sinners to Christ. While the 19ᵗʰ century brought several great Congregational evangelists to the forefront, such as Edwin Payson Hammond, and Dwight L. Moody, the denomination eventually devolved into the apostate United Church of Christ.[49]

*   *   *

By the grace of God, imprisonment for religious reasons was eventually terminated in Norwich and Canterbury. Canterbury repented of their oppressions and in 1771 dismissed their "parish committee" minister and declared liberty for their county. More liberty was to come. The mentality of the "Separates" gave rise to the idea that independence was possible. The stunning successes of the "Separate Baptists" testified to Americans that independence was superior.

Sometime in 1757, a group of itinerant preaches ran swiftly through New Bern, North Carolina, stirring up the pioneers and denouncing the sins of the woodsmen. The Anglican clergy thought for sure that a band of Methodists had descended from New England, probably under the direction of Mr. Whitefield himself. The clergy petitioned the English "Society for the Propagation of the Gospel" to stop these "strolling preachers from New England." The society replied they did not send these men and Mr. Whitefield said they certainly were not "Methodists." If that was the case, then who were these preachers and where did they come from? We will discover this and meet our fourth key man in chapter seven.

*   *   *

Before we leave our present chapter let us visit with the American Elijah in the moments just before he was ushered into heaven.

In Southold a solitary resting-place, the home of Thomas Fanning,[50] had gone through numerous changes of hands. Through it all, a piece of history remained. A room in the home where George Whitefield lodged had a token left behind of his gracious visit. He had taken a diamond pin and etched a phrase in the windowpane, a phrase that remains to this day: "One thing is Needful."

All true saints of God who have a love for poor lost souls thrill to read of Whitefield's exploits. But we must remember, yea, we cannot forget that which made him such an irresistible force for God—"One thing is Needful." It is in the area of consecration and devotion that Whitefield most arrests the attention and imagination of our souls. Our hearts should contemplate this about the American Elijah as he rode from Portsmouth, New Hampshire to Newburyport, Massachusetts on that fateful weekend in September of 1770.

Whitefield arose early from his place of lodging in Portsmouth, on September 29. He mounted his horse and made for Newburyport. But he was stopped in Exeter, New Hampshire where a crowd beseeched him to preach. This he did from a makeshift platform built for him in a field. He preached from 2 Corinthians 13:5 for nearly two hours. It was to be nearly his last sermon.

He intended to retire early for the night and went to the parsonage of Jonathan Parsons, the pastor of the Old South Presbyterian Church in Newburyport. Parsons was a great friend and supporter of Whitefield throughout the days of the Great Awakening. In a scene repeated nearly every day of his ministry, a large crowd began to gather outside the home of Mr. Parsons. The day was ending and September 30, 1770 began with Whitefield once again preaching. Let us allow Arnold Dallimore to relate the next series of events:

> But by the time the street in front of the house had filled with people, and as he began to make his way up the stairs, several of them were at the door, begging him preach. Unwilling, despite his weariness, to

forego any opportunity to declare the Gospel, he responded to the request and stood on the landing, halfway up the stairs, candle in hand, preaching Christ. He was soon greatly alive to his subject and becoming heedless of time he continued to speak, till finally, the candle flickered, burned itself out and died away.[51]

As the candle burned itself and died so did the American Elijah flicker and catch his last breath that night. He labored to breathe through the night but this bout with asthma would bring him to his Saviour whom he had served so fervently.

He had not intended to speak to the crowd gathered at the door of Jonathan Parsons' home, nor did he intend to speak before the huge crowd gathered at Exeter, but then, as always, he felt an obligation to speak for God. As he mounted the platform at Exeter, a bystander said to him, "Sir, you are more fit to go to bed than to preach."

Whitefield replied, "True, sir," and then prayed as he had prayed twenty-seven years earlier in York, Maine, "Lord Jesus, I am weary in thy work, but not of thy work. If I have not yet finished my course, let me go and speak for thee once more in the fields, seal thy truth, and come home and die."

We now know that which Whitefield said in reply had become a catch phrase with him, the phrase about speaking and then "going home to die;" but this time he paused, and then uttered the most telling phrase of his life, "I die to be with Him."

1701   CHURCH OF ENGLAND ESTABLISHED IN N. CAROLINA

1707   PHILADELPHIA ASSOCIATION FOUNDED

1751   CHARLESTON, S. CAROLINA ASSOCIATION FOUNDED.

1751   THOMAS AND GARRARD BEGAN THEIR MINISTRY IN VA.

1753   JERSEY SETTLEMENT BAPTIST CHURCH FOUNDED

1754   DANIEL MARSHALL ENDS HIS MISSION TO THE MOHAWKS AND MOVES TO OPECKTON COUNTY, VA.

1754   SHUBAL STEARNS AND COMPANY ARRIVE IN OPECKTON COUNTY VIRGINIA.

1755   NOVEMBER 22, STEARNS AND HIS PIONEER CHURCH, FOUND SANDY CREEK SEPARATE BAPTIST CHURCH.

1756   TIDENCE LANE (AT SANDY CREEK), ELNATHAN DAVIS (AT SANDY CREEK), JAMES READ (AT GRASSY CREEK), AND PHILIP MULKEY (AT SANDY CREEK), CONVERTED.

1756   REGULAR BAPTISTS REFUSE TO ASSIST SHUBAL STEARNS IN THE ORDINATION OF DANIEL MARSHALL.

1758   HARRISS CONVERTED. BAPTIZED BY MARSHALL

1758   JANUARY, FIRST CAMP (ASSOCIATIONAL) MEETING OF THE SEPARATES AT SANDY CREEK

1758   SANDY CREEK, NORTH CAROLINA ASSOCIATION FOUNDED, THIRD BAPTIST ASSOCIATION IN AMERICA.

1760   FIRST SEPARATE BAPTIST CHURCH FORMED IN VA.

1762   DAVID THOMAS (REGULAR BAPTIST) FOUNDS BROAD RUN BAPTIST CHURCH IN VIRGINIA

1765   JANUARY, HARRISS PREACHES IN PITTSYLVANIA CONTROVERSY BETWEEN THE SEPARATES AND REGULARS INTENSIFIES.

1766   HARRISS AND READ TEAM IN VIRGINIA.

1766   CONGAREE CHURCH ESTABLISHED IN S. CAROLINA

1767   JOHN WALLER BAPTIZED BY JAMES READ.

1767   NOV. UPPER SPOTSYLVANIA BAPTIST CHURCH, FOUNDED.

1768   WALLER, CRAIG AND CHILDS IMPRISONED IN FREDERICKSBURG, VA.

1769   KEHUKEE (REGULAR) BAPTIST ASSOC. OF NORTH CAROLINA FORMED.

CHAPTER SEVEN
God's Power out of North Carolina

*The hearts of the people being touched by a heavenly flame could no
longer relish the dry parish service conducted for the most part as
they thought, by a set of graceless mercenaries.*—Robert B. Semple,
on the ministry of Sandy Creek Baptist Church

*I make bold to say that these Separate Baptists have proved to be
the most remarkable body of Christians America has known.*[1]
—George Washington Paschal

A great revival was about to begin in the south. It was clearly the
greatest revival in American history. No one could have foreseen
the scope of it. No one could have possibly predicted that it
would involve the hated, hunted *Baptists*. Few of the historians of the
present generation pay attention to it, and even fewer give it the credit
or respect it richly deserves. It involved an obscure New England Congregationalist, awakened under the preaching of George Whitefield,
who became a "Separate" Baptist in Tolland, Connecticut. His name
was Shubal Stearns. He is our fourth key man. Before we meet this most
important American pioneer, background on the first of the *baptized
believers* in the southern provinces is in order.

*   *   *

A foothold for the *baptized believers* was carved in the south, in
South Carolina, just before the Great Awakening. It was a small niche
started by emigrants from the persecuted Baptist church in Boston,
Massachusetts who migrated first to Kittery, Maine and then south.
They landed their hopes in the harbor of Charleston, South Carolina.
These brave souls were led by William Screven and began their stand for
Christ in 1683. The second Baptist church in South Carolina was Ash-
ley River founded in 1736.

The famous Welsh Neck Baptist church, part of the Philadelphia Association was founded in 1738. They planted a church on the Pee Dee River in South Carolina. A church was planted at Euhaw in 1746. The Pee Dee branch planted a church north, in the Yadkin River valley area in the central part of North Carolina which they called "the Jersey Settlement."

All of these were "Particular" Baptist* in their sentiments. They soon became known as "Regular" Baptist churches, following closely the Philadelphia Confession of Faith.

Charleston, South Carolina became the base for the second Baptist association in America, appropriately named the Charleston Association, founded in October of 1751. The Charleston Association was in close fellowship with the Philadelphia Association, which as we have noted, was founded in 1707.

*　　*　　*

Turning now to the early years of **Virginia**, we find Robert Nordin arriving from England in 1714. He and Thomas White were ordained in London, and sailed together to serve God in Virginia. However, Mr. White died en route. Robert Nordin did arrive and after a sufficient time of labor, gathered a church at Burley, in the county of Isle of Wight.[2] This was the first Baptist church in Virginia. John Comer also mentions a church in the county of Surry in Virginia, during this same time frame.

Between the years 1743 and 1755, three more Baptist churches were constituted in Virginia: Opeckon (Millcreek), Smith's Creek and Ketocton. All three were "General" Baptist and came from Maryland.

Preacher Nordin died in 1725 and Richard Jones came from England to be the pastor of the church. He was still there when the Separate Baptists began preaching in Virginia in 1755.[3]

In 1751, the Philadelphia Association appointed David Thomas and John Garrard missionaries to Virginia. Thomas had been tutored at the Hopewell Academy, the institution that eventually became Brown Col-

---

* That is, they believed in "particular" or "limited" atonement. Their ties were with the Philadelphia Association.

lege. In those days, Hopewell was in New Jersey and the chief instructor was Isaac Eaton. Thomas[4] was ordained at age eighteen and entered the ministry in Virginia in 1751.

David Thomas' preaching in Virginia was met with jeers and persecution, but the Lord blessed with great numbers turning to Christ. Through him, the first few churches in northern Virginia were established. Thomas became a legendary figure, his testimony being that of a battered saint standing against the religious bigotry of the Episcopalian *standing order*. He founded the Broad Run Baptist church in 1762.

John Garrard[5] came to Virginia in 1754 and founded the Mill Creek Baptist church in Opeckton County. He quickly succeeded in planting the Ketockton Baptist church as well.

Garrard and Thomas became co-laborers in evangelism as Regular Baptist ministers when the Separate Baptist revival began. Verily, they became somewhat dazed in the whirlwind of Separate Baptist zeal.

*   *   *

We now turn our attention to the earliest years of **Baptist churches in North Carolina.**

The first Baptist Church in North Carolina was gathered in 1727 in Chowan County about 10 miles north of Edenton.[6] It was gathered by the General Baptist evangelist Paul Palmer.[7]

The General Baptists of North Carolina had a great ministry in North Carolina. They began under the leadership and work of Paul Palmer. These General Baptist churches[8] in North Carolina were formed between 1727 and 1755: Chowan (1727), Pasquotank (Shiloh) (1736), Kehukee (1742), Tar River Falls (1744), Fishing Creek (1745), Lower Fishing Creek (1748) Tar River (1749), Great Cohara (1749), Redbanks, Tosneot (1756), Bear Creek (1756), and Swifts-Creek.

Despite this great beginning, the General Baptists of North Carolina were made nearly extinct by the ministry of Benjamin Miller and P. P. Van Horn who toured North Carolina between 1755 and 1756. Miller and Van Horn were sent as agents by the Philadelphia Association to correct the errors of the General Baptists. In that one-year span the Philadelphia duo reconstituted the majority of the General Baptist churches into "Particular" Baptist churches, until only three General

Baptist churches remained.[9] After that, as in other places in the colonies, the Particular Baptists began to refer to themselves as "Regular."[10]

Thus the General Baptist churches in North Carolina were transformed. Nearly all the above named churches were reconstituted as Particular (Regular) Baptist. There was now a third wave coming.

To sum up the pioneering efforts of the Baptists of the south to the year 1755, we find: four churches in South Carolina and the Charleston Association; six churches in Virginia and no Baptist associations; and twelve churches in North Carolina with no associations. There were no Baptist churches in Georgia. In just 20 years, all of that would drastically change.

George Whitefield himself lamented the absence of ministers in the province of North Carolina and expressed a desire that God would send forth a John the Baptist to preach and baptize in the wilderness.[11] Such was the state of religion in the south before Shubal Stearns, providentially prepared by the Holy Spirit, arrived at his place in American history.

North Carolina had a population of approximately 100,000 souls in 1755. Most had emigrated from Virginia, Pennsylvania, and New England.[12]

The Quakers came to Cane Creek in central North Carolina in the mid 1750's. The Moravians settled on the Yadkin River near present day Winston-Salem on a 100,000-acre tract of land they named "Wachovia." To the south and east of them, Gaelic speaking Scots and Irish Presbyterians settled in small groups. Central North Carolina, was at that time, filling with English speaking frontiersmen from the Mid-Atlantic States and New England.

In 1755, three forest paths traversed the province of North Carolina. The Settlers Road, also known as the Great Wagon Road, ran from north to south all the way from Pennsylvania to South Carolina. Secondly, what eventually became known as the Boone Trail, ran west from Wilmington to the Yadkin settlements. Thirdly, the Trading Path, came from southeastern Virginia (Norfolk) to the Waxhaw country.

Those three trails converged on a little notch in the wilderness of North Carolina by the waters of Sandy Creek. That spot, which is nearly remote today, was in the days of the Separate Baptist revival a national crossroads between north and south.

Just to the west of that crossroad, Tidence Lane had migrated to the Yadkin River area of North Carolina. Sometime before 1755, he left his parents and his brother Dutton in southern Virginia in Pittsylvania county. Tidence was homesteading, trying to carve out a living with his wife Esther by farming, hunting and fishing.

News had traveled to the central west settlements about an extraordinary preacher who was demolishing the sins of the backcountry and seeing the settlers converted at an astonishing rate. There was a groundswell of opposition to the preacher already for he was a Baptist and had taken to immersing his converts in Sandy Creek. Some of the men of the backcountry and piedmont areas of North Carolina, with their Church of England heritage, began to swear oaths to *never* become a Baptist.[13]

Still, Tidence had a desire to hear this preacher, for even with the criticisms of his loud voice and gestures, he believed seeing Mr. Stearns might be interesting at least. So he rode out, having no idea of how life would change for his entire family. Tidence Lane later testified:

> When the fame of Mr. Stearns' preaching had reached the Atkin, (Yadkin River) where I lived, I felt a curiosity to go and hear him. Upon my arrival I saw a venerable old man sitting under a peach-tree with a book in his hand and the people gathering about him. He fixed his eyes upon me immediately, which made me feel in such a manner as I have never felt before. I turned to quit the place but could not proceed far. I walked about, sometimes catching his eyes as I walked. My uneasiness increased and it became intolerable. I went up to him thinking that a salutation and shaking hands would relieve me: but it happened otherwise. I began to think that he had an evil eye and ought to be shunned; but shunning him I could no more effect than a bird can shun a rattlesnake when it fixes its eyes upon it. When he be-

gan to preach my perturbations increased so that nature could no longer support them and I sunk to the ground.[14]

History is buried at Sandy Creek, beneath endless winters, summer heat, and the leaves of two centuries of autumn. We thank our Heavenly Father that such history can be resurrected, for there on those sleepy hillsides the settlers witnessed quite possibly, the greatest outpouring of the Holy Ghost on a group of believers since the day of Pentecost.

Shubal Stearns was a New Englander, born in Boston, Massachusetts, January 28, 1706. His father was Shubael, as he spelled it, and his mother was Rebecca Larriford. Shubal Stearns, the son, like so many other New England men, was caught in the Holy freight train of the Great Awakening. Both he and his future brother-in-law and fabulous assistant in revival Daniel Marshall, were converted during Mr. Whitefield's 1745 tour of Connecticut.[15] He and his wife, parents, sisters and brothers were immersed by Wait Palmer in Stonington, Connecticut in March of 1751. He was ordained on March 20, 1751 by Wait Palmer and Joshua Morse. In 1755 the Lord began to move upon this group of Connecticut Baptists.

Stearns married Sarah Johnson, of whom very little is known. She served with him faithfully over the mountains and through the wilderness. While they had no children, the number of spiritual children birthed from their ministry would grow to an uncountable sum.

Throughout his life Shubal Stearns' driving force was a sure calling of God. Robert B. Semple described Stearns call to preach the gospel to the southern and western provinces:

> Mr. Stearns and most of the Separates had strong faith in the immediate teachings of the spirit. They believed that to those who sought him earnestly, God often gave evident tokens of his will. Mr. Stearns, listening to some of these instructions of Heaven, conceived himself called upon by the Almighty to move far to the westward, to execute a great and extensive work.[16]

Constrained by that call, Shubal and Sarah Stearns, with his parents Shubael and Rebecca Stearns; his brothers, Peter Stearns and Ebenezer Stearns and their wives; Joseph Breed and wife; Enis Stimson and wife;

and Jonathan Polk and wife began the journey south. They first landed in northern Virginia. Semple relating:

> Stearns first went to Opeckton, Berkley Co. Va. were he met with the church under the care of John Garrard. He met with his brother-in-law, Daniel Marshall, in that place. Marshall united with Stearns from there, forming a team that would rival the apostle Paul and Barnabas. Shubal Stearns provided the leadership and organizational skills, Daniel Marshall became the tireless labourer.[17]

At Opeckton, Stearns united with his brother-law-law, Daniel Marshall.

This introduces the testimony of the meticulous Daniel Marshall, who, without apology, ought to be remembered as one of the greatest missionaries of the 18th century. Marshall was born in Windsor, Connecticut in 1706. He no doubt received infant sprinkling in the same church with Jonathan Edwards as they were both from Windsor and nearly the same age. He served as a deacon in the First Congregational church of Windsor for 20 years. He had a son named Daniel from his first wife, Hannah.

Mr. Marshall was 38 years of age in 1745 when he heard George Whitefield preach the gospel.[18] This began a reinvestigation of his priorities and an examination of the doctrines of the Saybrook Platform so accepted in Connecticut. During the next three years, Mr. Marshall came to reject the half-way covenant and infant baptism and embrace *experimental religion* and believer's baptism.

Evidence shows that Mr. Marshall offended the church at Windsor by "preaching the Baptist doctrines."[19] This would indicate that by 1748 Marshall was leaning towards the Separate Baptists, albeit, not yet baptized. Evidently, Daniel Marshall's entire family was affected by his preaching. Eunice, sister of Daniel Marshall was jailed for "exhorting and preaching."[20] In any event, what followed was Marshall's unofficial banishment and excommunication.

The attitude of the established church at Windsor was evident. Marshall's wife Hannah grew ill and died. The church, which he had served faithfully for over 20 years, completely forsook him during his grief.[21] About 1748 Daniel Marshall married Martha Stearns, sister of Shubal Stearns.

A Baptist meeting-house was built in 1750 in Windsor.[22] It is significant that it stood near the Marshall home.

After his marriage to Martha, and believing that the end of time was near, Marshall migrated up the Susquehanna River into Pennsylvania. Perhaps with the ministry of David Brainard in mind, they went to the Mohawks and endeavored to bring them to Christ.

But the intrigue and suffering of the French and Indian War caused Daniel and Martha to move south to Opeckon, Virginia to what is present day Winchester. There they united with Martha's brother, Shubal.[23] Daniel and Martha Marshall finally received believer's baptism by the hand of Samuel Heaton at the Mill Creek church in 1754.[24] Mr. Heaton could not have imagined what this 45-year-old convert was going to accomplish with the rest of his life. At that time also, Joseph and Pricilla Breed were baptized.

The evidences of the Spirit of God in mighty power attended the Separate Baptists in Opeckton and a revival ensued. With the revival, accusations of the "disorderly" way it was being conducted spread.[25]

This apparently worried the orderly folk at the Philadelphia Association who sent an informant,[26] Benjamin Miller. But instead of being critical of Shubal Stearns and Daniel and Martha Marshall, Miller was impressed and genuinely moved by the meetings. In fact, Miller highly valued Daniel Marshall and his wife and said he "would take gold for them."[27]

On June 13, 1755, while laboring in northern Virginia, a still restless Shubal Stearns received a letter from some friends in North Carolina. It proved to be his "Macedonian call:"[28]

> The work of God was great, in preaching to an ignorant people, who had little or no preaching for an hundred miles, and no established meeting. But now the people were so eager to hear, that they would come forty miles each way, when they could have opportunity to hear a sermon.[29]

This report[30] burned in the heart of Shubal Stearns.

Leaving Opeckton in the summer of 1755, the group of sixteen believers, now with Daniel Marshall and his family included, journeyed southwest down the Shenandoah Valley. They crossed east across the Blue Ridge into North Carolina where they found their permanent home at the crossroads by Sandy Creek. William Lumpkin in *Baptist Inroads in the South*, wrote the choosing of Sandy Creek "may have been providential." This statement by Lumpkin "may have been" the undisputed understatement of all time.[31]

The Separate Baptist pilgrims built a meeting-house immediately and began to hold church services. A little village sprang up around them as they built pioneer cabins, hunted, and broke up the ground to farm.* They formed themselves into an independent Baptist church on November 22, 1755, with Shubal Stearns as their pastor or elder, as they termed it. Daniel Marshall and Joseph Breed were identified as exhorters or assistants. As we consider the leading that Stearns had and the vision that God laid upon his heart, it is not difficult to see his need for those exhorters or assistants. Indeed, God would send more than these.

They were "Separate" Baptists, but preferred to be called "New Lights."[32] They shamelessly wanted to associate themselves with the work of the Great Awakening, and as Robert B. Semple wrote, "into them was none admitted, who did not profess vital religion." However— as was always the case with the *baptized believers*—the nickname given them by their enemies stuck to them: *Separate Baptists*.

Shubal Stearns had no formal degree, but had a brilliant mind and was greatly gifted in organizational skills. He was highly intelligent and a planner, planter, and tireless worker. After yielding to his heavenly vision, (see Acts 26:19) he prepared his work and made it fit for the field (see Proverbs 24:27). He envisioned a work force to quickly plant a large number of churches. There can be no doubt God had revealed to Him a great plan for the work that needed to be done. In the history of God's believing people, God always laid the need of the hour at the feet of those who were willing. He then enabled them to meet the need. Would to God, He would raise up the willing to meet the desperate needs of

---

* Sandy Creek was originally in Orange County, which became Randolph County, which became Guilford County.

our present dreadful hour! Of Shubal Stearns, Isaac Backus wrote, "his soul was red with zeal to carry light into these dark parts."[33]

The most noteworthy gift in the life of Shubal Stearns was his **voice**. Described by several eyewitnesses to his ministry as "enchantment," Shubal Stearns used his voice to bring men to an earnest examination of themselves before God. Morgan Edwards described it:

> His voice was musical and strong, which he managed in such a manner as to make soft impressions on the heart, and fetch tears in the eyes in a mechanical way; and anon, to shake the very nerves and throw the animal system into tumults and perturbations. All the Separate ministers copy after him in tones of voice and action of body; and some few exceed him. His character was indisputably good, both as a man, a Christian and a preacher.[34]

Indeed, the preachers who surrendered to the call of God under the ministry of Shubal Stearns, took on similar characteristics. Semple again, describing the Separate Baptists:

> But the manner of preaching was, if possible, much more novel than their doctrines. The Separates in New England had acquired a very warm and pathetic address, accompanied by strong gestures and a singular tone of voice. Being often deeply affected themselves while preaching, correspondent affections were felt by their pious hearers, which were frequently expressed by tears, trembling, shouts and acclamations.[35]

The scene described above is nothing less than the roots of the OLD TIME RELIGION, so identified with Bible believing Baptists. The description we have of Stearns' voice and preaching habits bring to mind the admonitions to Ezekiel to "strike the thigh," and "stamp the foot" and "lift up your voice like a trumpet." George Whitefield no doubt influenced his pathos, and his earnestness and fearlessness were telltale evidences of Whitefield's influence. If George Whitefield was the American Elijah, then Shubal Stearns was his Appalachian *Elisha*, following in his footsteps, wearing his mantle and affecting the lives of thousands. We believe that about Stearns and more, for he could also be rightly called "the Apostle Paul of the Backcountry." He and his followers took up the banner of *experimental religion*.[36] Semple wrote:

> The doctrine of Mr. Stearns and his party was consequently quite strange. To be born again, appeared... as absurd as it did to the Jewish doctor, when he asked, if he must enter the second time into his mother's womb and be born again. Having always supposed that religion consisted in nothing more than the practice of its outward duties, they could not comprehend how it should be necessary to feel conviction and conversion.[37]

In this aspect, Stearns resembled Jonathan Edwards, George Whitefield and most significantly, John Clarke in his insistence on *experimental religion*. But the results of his ministry were all Holy Ghost phenomena. The Holy Ghost was doing something that a mere man could neither start nor finish. We hope our generation will desire to unlock the secrets of the success of this meteoric leader. What we discover about him ought to inflame our hearts and stir our minds to more consecrated service.

Stearns certainly stirred the attention of that generation of pioneers. Arguably, he became the most influential man of the emerging culture of the south. What we recognize as the manners, morals and style of Southern living began in the Sandy Creek Separate Baptist revival, and when we think of the "Bible-belt" we should in reality think of it as "the Separate Baptist belt." David L. Cummins wrote of this view:

> The often used term 'Bible Belt' was coined by H. L. Mencken in the 1920s to describe areas of the nation dominated by belief in the literal authenticity of the Bible and accompanying puritanical mores. He did not give the term a specific location, but he did associate it with rural areas of the Midwest and, especially, the "Baptist back-waters of the South." He used the term in derision. When one reads of the exploits of the Separate or New Light Baptists and realizes that their field of service was indeed in what might be described as the "Baptist back-waters of the South," even Mr. Mencken would have to concur that the "Bible Belt" was actually the "Separate Baptist Belt." Any honest historian would then have to admit that the Great Awakening was not a figment of imagination or the invention of a fanciful annalist.[38]

Stearns and his preachers took to the fields and towns. For them, religion was real, hell was real, Jesus was real, and you needed to be born again. Shubal Stearns and the band of preachers that followed him were a different stripe from which colonial Americans were accustomed. They were loud in their preaching and urgent in their prayers. They were deliberate in their diction. Even their appearance was different. Gone were the clerical robes, braided hair and powdered wigs. Their hair was cut short,[39] of all things, and they did not give the air of aristocracy. It was like Whitefield without the wig; Whitefield without the Anglican chains; Whitefield without infant baptism. It was just what the American frontier needed.

Not long after the conversion of Tidence Lane, by the banks of the Slow River in the central western part of the North Carolina colony, a young woodsman named Elnathan Davis, an emigrant from Maryland, heard that the New England preacher Shubal Stearns, was coming into the area. Stearns was to baptize the giant John Steward. Since the preacher was widely known as "but a little man," Davis figured the baptism to be a sure calamity and worth the ride to the site for sheer entertainment. What he did not expect was the overwhelming presence of God when he came to view the spectacle. Morgan Edwards wrote:

> He had heard that one John Steward, being a very big man, and Shubal Stearns of small stature, he concluded there would be some diversion if not drowning; therefore he gathered about 8 or 10 of his companions in wickedness and went to the spot. Shubal Stearns came and began to preach; Elnathan went to hear him while his companions stood at a distance. He was no sooner among the crowd but he perceived some of the people tremble as if in a fit of the ague; he felt and examined them in order to find if it was not a dissimulation; meanwhile one man, leaned on his shoulder, weeping bitterly; Elnathan, perceiving had wet his new white coat, pushed him off, and ran to his companions who were sitting on a log, at a distance; when he came one said, "Well, Elnathan, what do you think now of these d_____ people?"

He replied, "There is a trembling and crying spirit among them; but whether it be the spirit of God or the devil I kno't know; if it be the devil, the devil go with them; for I will never more venture my self among them." He did not keep his promise long, however.

He stood a while in that resolution; but the enchantment of Shubal Stearns voice drew him to the crowd once more. He had not been long there before the trembling seized him also; he attempted to withdraw; but his strength and his understanding confounded, he, with many others, sunk to the ground. When he came to himself he found nothing in him but dread and anxiety, bordering on horror. He continued in this situation some days, and then found relief by faith in Christ. Immediately he began to preach conversion work, raw as he was, and scanty as his knowledge must have been.[40]

Shubal Stearns baptized Elnathan Davis[41] in May of 1764.

The Lord added to the church daily quite literally, and more men surrendered to God's call to preach the Gospel. As the Separate Baptist ministry of Stearns and Marshall worked north a meeting was conducted at Grassy Creek, North Carolina. James Read was saved at the visit of David Marshall to Grassy Creek in 1756. Shubal Stearns baptized him.[42] A church was established there within the first year with James Read pastoring. Read was an unusual man, who was gifted to preach, but illiterate. Immediately after his salvation and call, his wife began to tutor him to read so that he might study the word of God. He became a great student, pastor, and evangelist.

God added more laborers to the church at Sandy Creek. Sometime in 1756, John Newton joined with the group of Separate Baptists. Newton was born in Kent County, Pennsylvania on August 7, 1732, and was baptized by Isaac Potts in Southampton County, Virginia. After answering the call to preach, he was ordained pastor of the Black River Baptist church in Duplin County, North Carolina March 7, 1757. From his charge at Black River, John Newton preached the Gospel over the Virginia border in Halifax County, Virginia. His most illustrious convert was Phillip Mulkey. Morgan Edwards recorded this testimony from Mulkey:

One night as I was going home from the house where I had been playing the fiddle to dancers, a hideous specter presented itself before me just as I opened the door; the effect was, fainting, and continuing as dead for the space of about 10 minutes, as the people about me report the matter; when I recovered, I found an uncommon dread on my spirits, from an apprehension that the shocking figure, I had seen was the Devil and that he would have me. I mounted my horse and went homewards. My fears had so disordered my understanding that I fancied the first tree I came to bowed its head to strike at me, which made me start from it. Happening to look up, I fancied that the stars cast a frowning and malignant aspect upon me. When I came home I went to bed and endeavored to conceal the matter from my wife; but I could not be, for thenceforth I could neither eat, nor sleep nor rest for some days; but continued to roar out, "I am damned! I shall soon be in hell!"

Meanwhile a benighted stranger (this was John Newton) came to my house to read a chapter (53rd of Isaiah) and prayed; and thereby turned my thoughts to Christ and salvation by him, for the first time. The novelty of this matter, and the possibility it introduced, that my sins had been laid on Christ and that God had stricken and smitten Christ for them affected me in such a manner as exceeds description. I found an inclination to adore the stranger, and to question whether he was an angel or man? The next day he departed, and as he was going this thought came in my mind, "There is Lot going out of Sodom! As soon as he disappears fire will come down and burn me and mine!?"[43]

Mulkey was converted and joined the ranks of preachers out of Sandy Creek.

Shubal Stearns baptized William and Joseph Murphy in 1757. Joseph Murphy, being possessed of a strong mind, ready wit, and a heart for God; became a very useful and much respected preacher throughout an extensive circle of churches. William took the Gospel all the way across the mighty Mississippi.

Abbott's Creek

A group of infant churches began to gather from the converts. The first Separate Baptist church plant in North Carolina from Sandy Creek was 30 miles due west at Abbott's Creek. James Younger was an unordained Baptist preacher who emigrated from the Welsh neck church in Pennsylvania and settled at Abbot's Creek. Younger heard about Sandy

Creek Baptist Church and went to Shubal Stearns to request a preacher to come and establish a church at their settlement.[44] He fetched Daniel Marshall to preach for them. A little further west from there was the Jersey Settlement church. It may be wondered why Younger's group did not unite with Jersey,[45] but be that as it may, Daniel Marshall helped gather them with tremendous energy and success. An independent Baptist church now needed to be constituted.

This newly constituted church needed an ordained pastor. Daniel Marshall was the logical choice, but was not ordained. Shubal Stearns desired another ordained preacher to aid him in the ordination, but none could be found. Benjamin Miller, who had great affection for the Marshalls, left the Yadkin area in January of 1756. None other could be found. So Elder Stearns and Brother Marshall ventured down the Yadkin River to the Pee Dee Church in South Carolina to ask Pastor Joshua Edwards for assistance in the ordination. Joshua Edwards was a "Regular" Baptist and had heard of the "irregular" way in which the Separate Baptists conducted themselves. Therefore, he refused to assist due to the "noise and confusion" in the Separate Baptist church services.[46] Finally, the friendly Henry Ledbetter, pastor of the Baptist Church at Lynch's River, South Carolina, agreed to assist in the ordination of Daniel Marshall. He may have been friendly because he also was brother-in-law to Daniel Marshall. Some modern historians doubt this, but the author tends to doubt the modern historians.[47] The refusal to ordain Marshall by the Regular Baptists fueled animosity between the two groups that would last 30 years. Finally, the Abbott's Creek church had a pastor.[*]

Grassy Creek

Grassy Creek was the next church plant.

In 1756 Daniel Marshal left Abbott's Creek to preach meetings in Grassy Creek, just south of the Virginia-North Carolina border. James

---

[*] Sandy Creek Baptist church observed nine ordinances: baptism, the Lord's supper, the love feast, laying on of hands, the washing of feet, anointing of the sick, the right hand of fellowship, the kiss of charity, and devoting children. Abbott's Creek embraced this scheme. The keeping of the ordinances varied with every new church they constituted.

Read was converted there. Read was later baptized by Shubal Stearns and eventually became the pastor of the second church plant out of Sandy Creek: Grassy Creek. From this strategic location, James Read was responsible for much work for God northward into Virginia.

Sandy Creek Baptist Church now established a pattern. According to Robert Devin, the author of *the History of the Grassy Creek Baptist Church*, Sandy Creek would birth a church in this manner: Members would journey to a needy area and "sit as a church" under the preaching of a man of God.[48] They would "sit"* to encourage the work, bring people, and win converts. Then a preacher would be ordained and another work begun. This work went on continuously with several missions occurring simultaneously.[49]

Deep River

Deep River Baptist church was constituted in 1757. It was the third church plant from Sandy Creek. It's location was probably at the "Falls of Lockville" in Chatham County, east of Sandy Creek.[50] In October of 1757, Philip Mulkey was ordained to pastor the Deep River church, becoming the third ordained preacher of the Separate Baptist order.

In 1760, Deep River broke into two churches. Phillip Mulkey took the majority of the church to Fairforest in South Carolina and Joseph Murphy took the remaining part of Deep River Church to the Yadkin River. Murphy constituted the Little River Church there. By 1763 Little River had grown to over 500 members. Joseph Murphy left in 1769 to begin a church at Shallow Fords on the west side of the Yadkin, not far from the Movavian settlements.

From Deep River two new preachers, Nathaniel Powell and James Turner, went to the North Carolina-South Carolina border and formed the Lockwood's Folly Baptist Church.[51] Lockwood's Folly church came from a group of fishermen who emigrated from Cape May, New Jersey and settled close to the mouth of the Cape Fear River.

---

* This would not necessarily be the same "sitters" at the same infant church every week.

Shubal Stearns and Daniel Marshall began to travel extensively. By the end of the first year, (1755-1756) Stearns and Marshall turned their attention east and preached the Gospel all the way to the North Carolina seaboard. During the first eastern North Carolinian seaboard campaign, their enemies began to refer to them as the "Enthusiastical Sect."

They seemed to be omnipresent in North Carolina. They were in Jones, Johnston, Onslow, Duplin, New Hanover and Brunswick counties. Their Anglican opponents thought they were Methodists, an accusation that George Whitefield categorically denied.[52] It was Stearns himself, the "Apostle Paul of the Backcountry," with his Barnabas, Daniel Marshall, whom Governor Dobbs and the Right Reverend Mr. Reed called "strolling preachers from New England."[53]

By the end of 1756, the established Church of England (Anglican/Episcopalian) in North Carolina had grown quite nervous about the "strollers." Even though the General Baptists had been in the state since 1727 and the Regular Baptist takeover had occurred from 1751 to 1755, no protests were made against the Baptists until Stearns, Marshall, and their converts began to preach far and wide with power.

Somewhere along the trail God raised up Ezekiel Hunter. G. W. Paschal wrote, "of Elder Ezekiel Hunter there is little other record."[54] Yet from such records that we have we conclude that Hunter was an extraordinary man. Ezekial Hunter is an illustration of the innumerable company of God's servants of whom we know so little. He canvassed Duplin, Sampson, New Hanover, and Carteret and brought them to Jesus, with little fanfare of his exploits.[55] Yet, we know the results of his preaching and pastoring put the Anglican Church in jeopardy in Onslow County. Indeed, the Anglican minister, Alexander Stewart said that Onslow was "the seat of enthusiasm in this Province."[56]

The records show that almost *the whole population of Onslow County became Baptist.* The Right Reverend Ebenezer Stewart of Bath, was aghast about this turn of events and wrote to the Society for the Propagation of the Gospel in London, begging for reinforcements to stop the bleeding from the mass conversion of the Church of England into Ezekial Hunter's New River Baptist church.

McCauley said, "The churchmen (Anglican/Episcopalian) made war on schism (the Baptists) with so much vigor that they had little leisure to make war on vice."[57] Within four years, the situation with the Church of England had grown so grave that one of their parsons complained, "Last winter," (1760-61), says Reverend Alexander Stewart of Bath, "I went as far southerly as New River into Onslow County, the present seat of Enthusiasm in this Province; where having preached twice, *the few remaining Episcopals there were very thankful to me*." He also called for more missionaries to Onslow to counteract the work of the "Enthusiasts."[58] Ezekiel Hunter died in 1773.[59]

Not only were "churchmen" coming to Christ during the 1755-1756 revival, but also imminent Catholics and Quakers. John Dillahunty, a refugee from Maryland married a Quaker wife, Hannah Neal. Being excommunicated by both religious bodies, they came to their pioneer home in the New Bern, North Carolina vicinity sometime around 1755. Dillahunty was the sheriff there and when Whitefield preached along the North Carolina coast in February of 1755, Dillahunty grew concerned about his soul. He was ready when the "Apostle Paul of the Backcountry" and his helper Daniel Marshall came to New Bern the following year. Hannah was converted and then John. They were baptized by Philip Mulkey and became a part of the Trent River Church.[60]

The years 1755-1757 proved to be banner years for the Separate Baptist revival. Just as great was 1758. One example of God's power was made manifest in the younger brother of Tidence Lane, Dutton. Morgan Edwards wrote of Dutton's summertime conversion of 1758:

> As he was returning from hunting with the game and his rifle in his hands he fancied that the saw the devil, standing in the way before him; upon which he stopped, meditating on what to do; to go on (he thought) was daring; and to fly, cowardly; firing at him, he judged, would be in vain; therefore he turned on one side and took another path; when he came between him and home he fancied the devil was pursing him, but dared not to look back; he quickened his pace, till he came near the house; then bolted the door, and fell down with rifle and game and all, on the floor. After continuing in this situation for a

while he came to himself, but never got rid of the fear till he was plucked as a brand out of the burning.[61]

Dutton Lane like others before him, began to preach immediately. He became a part of a team that saw the conversion of the most influential of all their fellow preachers. In 1758 Daniel Marshall, William and Joseph Murphy, and Dutton Lane traveled to Virginia. They gathered a crowd near Allen's Creek, on the road from Booker's Ferry on the Staunton River to Pittsylvania Court house. In this meeting, a strapping Virginian militia commander was next to join the Separate Baptist tidal wave and destined to lead it to its finest hour in Virginia. Samuel Harriss' conversion was recorded by the Virginia historian James B. Taylor:

> It is said that when engaged in the army, in the discharge of his official duties, he providentially found an opportunity of hearing the gospel by Joseph and William Murphy, who had appointed a meeting at a house near Allen's Creek, on the road leading from Booker's Ferry, on Staunton, to Pittsylvania Court-house. As the people were collecting, Colonel Harriss rode up, splendidly attired in his military habit. "What is to be done here, gentlemen?," said Harriss. "Preaching, Colonel." "Who is to preach?" "The Murphy boys, sir." "I believe I will stop and hear them." He dismounted.
>
> The house was small, and in one corner stood a loom, behind which the colonel seated himself. The Lord's eye was upon him, and the truth became effectual in deepening his convictions. Such was his agony of mind that at the close of the meeting his sword and other parts of his regimentals were found scattered around him.[62] His conversion was brought to pass in an unusual manner; it began with a deep seriousness without his knowing why or wherefore; conversation and reading, directed his attention to the cause; pressed with this conviction he ventured to attend the ministry of the Baptists; his distress increased; and his heart was ready to burst. Once as the people rose from prayer, the Colonel was observed to continue on his knees, with his head and his hands hanging down the other side of the bench; some of the people went to his relief, and found he was senseless as in a fit; when he came to himself he smiled, and brake out in an ecstasy of joy, crying, "Glory! Glory! Glory! etc..."[63]

Some time after this, Daniel Marshall baptized him.

Harriss began preaching the gospel immediately. His preaching quickly brought John Weatherford under distress of soul. Soon Weatherford was converted, and about the year 1761, he also began to preach the Gospel. He was one of the first evangelists to assist in setting the Virginia hills on fire for God. Weatherford was to providentially leave his own testimony in *crimson red* as we shall discover in chapter ten.

*   *   *

Shubal Stearns vision of a great and extensive work in the western parts was coming to fruition. In just 18 months, God had wrought a great work. Semple wrote:

> In process of time some of the natives became converts, and bowed obedience to the Redeemer's scepter. These, uniting their labors with the chosen band, a powerful and extensive work broke out. From 16, Sandy Creek Church soon swelled to 606 members; so mightily grew the work of God![64]

By the end of 1758, three fully constituted churches were in existence from the Sandy Creek church with over 900 members, with the following branches and their pastors:[65] Little River, Montgomery County–Joseph Breed; Grassy Creek, Grandville County–James Read; Southwest, Lenoir County–Charles Markland; Black River, Duplin County–John Newton; New River, Onslow County–Ezekial Hunter; Lockwood's Folly, Brunswick County–Nathaniel Powell, James Turner.

There was something else in the vision of Shubal Stearns that was born in 1758–the association *camp meeting*. As we shall detail in chapter eight of our narrative, Shubal Stearns and Daniel Marshall stirred the hearts of the wilderness to attend a meeting of the Separate Baptists. The purpose of the meeting was nothing less than a full throttled awakening. The attendants where instructed to come and "camp." Indeed it was actually called a *camp meeting*.[66] Many historians mistakenly credit the Presbyterians and James McGready with the invention of the camp meeting during the Great Revival of the West in 1800, but the record clearly points 42 years earlier to the "Apostle Paul of the Backcountry" and his army of converts.

Lockwood's Folly

A little company of Baptists formed at Cape May at what became known as "Lockwoods Folly." They began in 1712. They connected with the Philadelphia Association and were called "poor families of fisherman" by the Anglican Mr. MacDowell. Somehow they came into fellowship with Stearns and Marshall and began to call themselves "New Light Baptists."[67]

In 1762 Ezekial Hunter went to Lockwood's Folly to baptize and made the church a branch of his New River congregation. He later preached extensively in Bladen County at White Swamp and Brunswick County at Livingston Creek in 1765. Ezekial Hunter pastored both New River and Lockwood's folly until 1773 when James Turner became pastor but Turner died soon after. Lockwood's Folly was the last of the list of Separate Baptist Churches mentioned by Morgan Edwards and Robert Semple.

Hunter's New River Baptist Church established the Southwest Baptist Church under Charles Markland in October of 1760. Markland joined the revolution at the outbreak of the War and the church all but disappeared when he marched off to offer his life for our liberty. What remained of Southwest Church merged with the Baptist church at Trent, North Carolina after the revolution.[68]

*   *   *

Here are the churches started during the years 1755 and 1771 in the Separate Baptist revival:

These churches were started in **NORTH CAROLINA**
1- Sandy Creek: 1755, Shubal Stearns
2- Abbott's Creek: 1756, Daniel Marshall
3- Grassy Creek : 1756, James Read
4- Deep River: 1757 Joseph Murphy, Phillip Mulkey

5- New River: 1758, Ezekiel Hunter

6- Little River: 1759, Joseph Murphy

> Little River grew to 500 members in 3 years.
> Little River had four branch churches in ten years: Little River 2, Rocky River, Jones Creek, Mountain Creek.

The eastern N.C. churches: Great Cohara, Hillsboro, New Bern—1757-1761

8-Black River: 1760, John Newton

10- Trent: 1761, James McDaniel

11- Southwest: 1762, Charles Markland

12-Haw River: 1764, Elnathan Davis

> Haw River from 1765 to 1772 grew to five branches in 7 years:
> Deep River 2, Rocky River 2, Tick Creek, Collins mount, Caraway Creek.

Lockwood's Folly: 1772 Nathaniel Powell, James Turner, Ezekial Hunter

Shallow Fords: 1768, Joseph Murphy

These churches were started in **SOUTH CAROLINA**

9-Fairforest: 1760, Philip Mulkey

Congaree: 1766, Joseph Rees

Stephens Creek: 1766, Daniel Marshall

These churches were started in **VIRGINIA**

7- Dan River: 1759, Dutton Lane

1765 the thrust into Va. begins

Upper Spotsylvania Church: 1767, Lewis Craig

Staughton River (Blackwater): 1768, William Murphy

Lower Spotsylvania: 1769, John Waller, Jeremiah Walker

Fall Creek: 1769, Samuel Harriss

Goochland: 1771, William Webber

In the present chapter of our narrative the great commission has been vividly illustrated. May we be courageously inflamed to do the same.

Into Virginia the Separate Baptist revival spread. Immediately, in 1759, an Anglican minister in Lunenburg warned: "In Halifax, one Samuel Harriss, formerly Burgess for that County, and one William Murphy have raised and propagated a most shocking delusion, which threatens the entire subversion of true religion in these parts, unless the principle persons concerned in that delusion are apprehended or otherwise restrained."[69]

In August of 1760, Daniel Marshall formed a church at Dan River, Virginia River after the baptism of 42 converts. This was the first Separate Baptist Church in Virginia.[70] Dutton Lane became the pastor.

In January of 1765, Allen Wyley, a baptized convert of the Regular Baptist pioneer preacher David Thomas, became curious to hear a Separate Baptist preach the word of God. He journeyed to Pittsylvania to seek such a preacher and providentially landed in a meeting held by the incomparable Samuel Harriss. Harriss had been preaching throughout Virginia for five years with a long list of converts which included John Weatherford, Anderson Moffett, and Lewis and Elijah Craig. At this point in his ministry, Harriss was being compared to George Whitefield. His preaching ability was aimed straight for the heart. Semple tells us "perhaps even Whitefield did not surpass him in this." Some described him, when exhorting at great meetings, as "pouring forth streams of celestial lightning from his eyes, which, whithersoever he turned his face, would strike down hundreds at once."[71] Allen Wyley led Harriss back to Culpeper where he preached in his home. The first meeting went well, but the next day an angry crowd met them with whips. Captain Ball and his gang came and said, "You shall not preach here."

A Virginia convert, Jeremiah Minor, replied, "But we shall."

The parish parson had stirred the Anglicans against the Baptist converts. The Baptists, being a rough bunch and having a converted Virginia colonel as their spiritual leader, saw the opportunity to knock
some spiritual sense into the Episcopalians and a riot broke out. Harriss
escaped the brawl and headed to Orange County and stayed that night
in the home of Elijah Craig. Lewis Craig was left to guard the door.
Ball's gang came and broke down the door. Pandemonium and confusion ended the day and Harriss preached the following day in a barn
owned by Elijah Craig.

This introduces us to the Craig brothers, Lewis, Elijah and Joseph.
All three became Separate Baptist preachers and all faced persecution.
The most influential in the author's opinion was Lewis. John Taylor
wrote of him:

> Mr. Craig became awakened, perhaps as early as 1765, by the preach-
> ing of Col. Samuel Harriss. Mr. Craig's great pressure of guilt induced
> him to follow the preachers from one meeting to another, and when
> preaching ended, he would rise up in tears, and loudly exclaim that he
> was a justly condemned sinner, and with a loud voice warn the people
> to fly from the wrath to come, and except they were born again, with
> himself they should all go to hell together; while under his exhorta-
> tion, the people would weep and cry aloud for mercy. In this manner,
> his ministry began before himself had hope of conversion, and after
> relief came to him, he went on preaching a considerable time before
> he was baptized, no administrator being near, many being converted
> under his labours. When he was baptized, a church was constituted at
> once, in Spotsylvania, Virginia, and Mr. Craig soon ordained as their
> pastor.[72]

*   *   *

Back in North Carolina, James Read was restless. He ate little and
slept less. Tossing and turning upon his bed he was heard to cry in his
sleep, "Oh Virginia, Virginia, Virginia!" God would soon call him there.

In 1766 Samuel Harriss headed into Orange County with Allen
Wyley. Scores were brought to Christ. His converts gathered together
under the Regular Baptist David Thomas. But Thomas unwisely began
to criticize the Separate Baptists. Thomas' preaching was much more

subdued and laced with the Augustinian/Calvinistic tendencies of the reformed. The converts of Orange County began to call for Colonel Harriss to baptize them. But he was unable to baptize them for he was not yet ordained. So Harriss rode with Elijah Craig and two other young preachers sixty miles into North Carolina to fulfill the dreams of James Read.

Read was one of only three ordained Separate Baptists in the south and was preparing to travel to Virginia in response to his vivid dreams when Harriss came looking for him. In the months and years to come they saturated the state of Virginia with the Gospel.

The two returned immediately to Orange County, Virginia and encountered a large crowd waiting for them near the homestead of Elijah Craig. They preached with great power. In the crowd were the Regular Baptist preachers David Thomas and John Garrard. In the ensuing days, Read, Thomas and Garrard worked on a plan to unite for a great campaign together in those parts. It was a grand plan, one that no doubt would have resulted in the salvation of many. However, the people, remembering the criticisms of David Thomas, literally called for Harriss and Read over Thomas and Garrard.

The revival in Orange County continued with huge crowds listening with rapt attention to Samuel Harriss and James Read and a small remnant attending the services of David Thomas and John Garrard. All of it was an embarrassment to Thomas and Garrard and the rift between the Regular and Separate Baptists, which had begun when the Regular Baptists refused to ordain Daniel Marshall, now widened.

From Orange, Colonel Harriss and James Read pressed into Caroline, Hanover and Goochland counties. The Holy Ghost confirmed their labour with converts.

From 1766 to 1770, Harriss and Read visited the area between the James and the Rappahannock with tremendous blessing. On one occasion, 75 adults were baptized in a sparsely populated area. On another occasion 200 adults were immersed. As Semple wrote:

> It was not uncommon at their great meetings for many hundreds of men to camp on the ground, in order to be present the next day. The night meetings, thro' the great work of God, continued very late; the ministers would scarcely have an opportunity to sleep; sometimes the

floor would be covered with persons, struck down under conviction for sin.[73]

So powerful were these meetings that men would travel over 100 miles on horseback to attend.

Sometime in 1767, Lewis Craig was arrested for "keeping unlawful conventicles" and "worshipping God contrary to the laws of the land." The jury withdrew with the intention of giving perhaps another hearing and retired for refreshment which Craig himself provided. While the men were enjoying the drinks,[74] Lewis Craig said, "Gentlemen, I thank you, for your attention to me, when I was about this court yard, in all kind of vanity, folly and vice, you took no notice of me; but when I have forsaken all those vices, and warn men to forsake and repent of their sins, you bring me to the bar as a transgressor, how is all this?"[75]

Back in the courtroom, Craig finished his defense by saying, "I forgive my persecuting enemies, and shall take joyfully the spoiling of my goods."[76]

On the jury at Craig's hearing was John Waller. This was "Swearing Jack" Waller, given the name to distinguish him from the crowd of other Wallers in that part of the country. "Swearing Jack" was a notorious sinner, a mocker, a gambler and a profane person. He was a leader of lost men who was referred to as the "devil's adjutant." But God was doing that remarkable thing of conviction in his heart and at the testimony of Lewis Craig, "Swearing Jack" Waller felt the calling of a loving God to a lost sinner. Soon after, he was converted and baptized by James Read.[77]

*   *   *

With the Baptist revival burning bright, the Anglican/Episcopal *standing order* of Virginia moved violently against it. At the first appearance of the Separate Baptists no attempt was made to throttle them, but when the advancement of souls became an avalanche, the religious establishment had to move to crush it.

In the words of Robert Semple:

There was an established religion: the Nebuchadnezzars of the age, required all men to bow down to their golden image: these Hebrew children refused, and were cast into the burning fiery furnace of persecution: the Son of God walked with them there, to the utter dismay of their enemies. The decree finally went forth, that none should be any more forced, to worship the golden image.[78]

The Episcopalian battle plan to silence the Separate Baptist revival was largely executed by enforcing the Virginia statute prohibiting "disturbing of the peace." Armed with this weapon, on June 4, 1768, the sheriff of Spotsylvania County apprehended James Childs and Lewis Craig. They also rounded up John Waller for preaching in the home of Henry Goodloe.[79] Waller had already reached a kind of legendary status.

When the trio was brought before the court, the accusation against them became a famous saying in Virginia as the court was informed:

> May it please your worships, these men are great disturbers of the peace, for they cannot meet a man upon the road, but they must ram a text of scripture down his throat.[80]

It reminds the author of present day Laodocian Christians who express contempt for believers who make it a habit to canvass door to door with the gospel or hand out tracts on a regular basis. Indeed, the accusation against Childs, Craig and Waller serves to convict the spiritually dead churches of today.

In court, John Waller defended them. They were fined and commanded to cease preaching in Spotsylvania for a year plus one day. With this they refused to comply. So they were escorted to the gaol, chained and paraded through the streets, no doubt with the intention to embarrass them. However, the intention backfired as the three prisoners sang as they walked,

> Broad is the road that leads to death,
> And thousands walk together there;
> But wisdom shows a narrow path,
> With here and there a traveler.
>
> Deny thyself and take thy cross,
> Is the Redeemer's great command;

Nature must count her gold but dross
If she would gain this heavenly land.

The fearful soul that tires and faints,
And walks the ways of God no more,
Is but esteemed almost a saint,
And makes his own destruction sure.

Lord, let not all my hopes be vain,
Create my heart entirely new,
Which hypocrites could ne'er attain
Which false apostates never knew.

The early summer air caught their enchanting serenade and a crowd gathered and began to express their outrage. Lewis Craig's little brother, Joseph was in the crowd. Joseph, overwhelmed with the procession shouted out: "Arise, ye dead, and come to judgment!" With that, some in the audience fainted.[81] The revival was fanned with the persecution.

Unfortunately for Virginia[82] persecution was repeated often from 1768 right up until the Revolutionary War. The imprisonment of Baptist preachers would spring Patrick Henry into the public fray over liberty and bring Thomas Jefferson to believe the Baptist ideal of soul liberty.

Around the 4th of July in 1768 and after spending four weeks in the Fredericksburg jail, Lewis Craig was released and went to Williamsburg to attempt to secure a release for the others. The deputy-governor of Virginia, John Blair, sent this letter to the attorney for the King of England concerning Craig and his Baptist companions:

> SIR, I lately received a letter, signed by a good number of worthy gentlemen, who are not here, complaining of the Baptists; the particulars of their misbehaviour are not told any further than their running into private houses and making dissentions. I am told, they administer the Sacrament of the Lord's Supper, near the manner we do, and, differ in nothing from our church, but in that of Baptism, and their renewing the ancient discipline; by which, they have reformed some sinners, and brought them to be truly penitent. If this be their behaviour, it were to be wished, we had some of it among us. -John Blair. July 16, 1768.[83]

Waller and the others continued in jail 43 days. While in prison, they constantly preached through the grates. The mob without used every exertion to prevent the people from hearing, but to little purpose. Many heard indeed, "upon whom the word was in power and demonstration."[84]

After their release, the trio pursued the lost in Spotsylvania with abandon. Semple says, "Day and night, and indeed almost every day and night, they held meetings in their own and the adjacent neighborhoods. The spread of the gospel, and of Baptist principles, was equal to all their exertions; insomuch, that in very few sections of Virginia, did the Baptist cause appear more formidable to its enemies, and more consoling to its friends, than in Spotsylvania."[85]

On December 2, 1769, the Lower Spotsylvania Church was constituted. On December 4, 1769, Blue Run Baptist Church was founded and Elijah Craig ordained pastor. In November 1770, Lewis Craig was ordained pastor of the Upper Spotsylvania Baptist Church. This church would later accomplish one of the greatest acts of faith in the history of Christianity.

Semple informs us that Samuel Harriss strongly influenced Lewis and Elijah Craig, John Waller, James Childs and John Burrus. They were "anointed by an ardent desire for the advancement of the masters kingdom."[86]

Goochland was the next to be affected. John Waller baptized William Webber and Joseph Anthony. Joseph Anthony and Reuben Ford saw revival while preaching together throughout Virginia.

Then the revival came to Amelia County. William Mullin was converted when he heard the gospel in 1769. He came to Middlesex and brought his brother John and brother-in-law James Greenwood to a saving knowledge of Christ. In November of 1770, the revival visited Middlesex under the preaching of John Waller and John Burrus. Here "Swearing Jack" left his innocent blood *crimson red* in the soil of Virginia as a magistrate attempted to pull him off a stage from which he was preaching. Someone threw a rock and hit a bystander barely missing Waller's head.[87]

James Greenwood began to preach. A great number believed and awaited the constitution of a church and scriptural baptism.[88]

In the meantime, the Holy Spirit was bringing about more work south of the James River. The "Murphy boys" William and Joseph, part of the first group of preachers called directly under the ministry of Shubal Stearns, were teaming with the nearly omnipresent Samuel Harriss. They were preaching to serious crowds in the Richmond area.

Robert Stockton was among those whom God called into the ministry at that time. The counties of Halifax, Charlotte, Lunenburg and Mecklenburg heard the gospel from Samuel Harriss, James Read, Jeremiah Walker, John Williams, John King, James Shelburne and Henry Lester.[89] From their labours, the Nottoway Baptist Church was formed with Jeremiah Walker as pastor. From this sprang the Middle District Association.

*   *   *

In December of 1770, William Webber and Joseph Anthony passed over the James River and into the land of Chesterfield, Virginia and "turned the population to 'madness' with their preaching."[90.] Within a few weeks they were put into prison and remained until March of 1771. Semple relates:

> While in prison, they did much execution, by preaching through the grates; many people attended their ministry, and many professed faith, by virtue of the labors of these, the Lord's persecuted servants. This was the beginning of God's work in the county of Chesterfield; no county ever extended its opposition and persecution to the Baptists farther than this, and yet, in few counties, have Baptist principles prevailed more extensively, than in Chesterfield.[91]

After the success in Chesterfield, William Webber joined forces with John Waller and in August of 1771, they turned their attention to Middlesex. Webber narrowly escaped being clubbed to death when a sympathizer grabbed the sheriff's stick as he was drawing back to strike.

William Webber, John Waller, James Greenwood and Robert Ware were then imprisoned.

The ground at Middlesex caught the *crimson red* blood of the innocents also as Thomas Waford was severely injured while receiving a whipping. On August 10, 1771, Waford was released and the next day being Sunday, brought the *baptized believers* and other interested persons to the prison courtyard to hear the imprisoned preachers:

> Many of their friends came to see them, and were admitted into the prison; James Greenwood preached to them. They gave notice that they would preach every Wednesday and Sunday; many came to hear them, insomuch, that their enemies began to be enraged, and would frequently beat a drum, while they were preaching.[92]

They had their day in court with the Virginia version of the *black hats* once again sternly ordering them not to preach in Middlesex County. Once again they refused to cooperate and were sentenced to an indeterminate time of prison. Semple wrote: "The persecutors found that the imprisonment of the preachers, tended rather to the furtherance of the gospel. The preaching seemed to have double weight when coming from the jail; many viewed it with superstitious reverence."[93]

Anger at the Separate Baptists was widespread, as Semple observed:

> The rage of the persecutors had in no wise abated; they seemed, sometimes, to strive to treat the Baptists and their worship with as much rudeness and indecency as was possible. They often insulted the preacher in time of service, and would ride into the water, and make sport, when they administered Baptism; they frequently fabricated and spread, the most groundless reports, which were injurious to the characters of the Baptists.[94]

*   *   *

Into South Carolina the Separate Baptist revival spread. Deep River, North Carolina broke up in 1760 and most followed Phillip Mulkey to Little River in South Carolina. In 1762, it removed to Fairforest, South Carolina. In that location, they became a great church planting work. In

1765, John Newton immigrated to South Carolina. According to the historian G. W. Paschal, Newton was ordained twice[95]—in 1757 and 1768. The second time was at Congaree Baptist Church in South Carolina along with Joseph Reese by the Regular Baptists Oliver Hart and Evan Pugh. That ordination led to some problems at Sandy Creek.

After ten years of nearly constant preaching, Shubal Stearns was enjoying some of the fruit of his labor. Despite the fact that Stearns ministry was so effective, we do not have a single publication of anything he preached. We have no journal, no notes, and no thoughts of his as he experienced this great outpouring of God's power. Every historian of that era testified of his gifts and the overwhelming wave of revival that emerged from his church and the association he founded. Yet, we only have a handful of witnesses that bothered to record any details of this important juncture in American and Baptist history. The author will offer his weak effort of explanation of this puzzling peculiarity in the pages that follow. It is our opinion that schools, towns, counties and institutions be named for Stearns. Yet he remains in obscurity, and the reasons for his obscurity are as deeply mysterious as any enigma of history. The reliable William Cathcart, Baptist historian of the late nineteenth century gave this opinion:

> Few men ever enjoyed more of the Spirit's presence in the closet and in preaching the Gospel. Had he been a Romish priest, with as flattering a record of service to the church of the popes, long since he would have been canonized, and declared the 'Patron Saint' of North Carolina. . . and stately churches would have been dedicated to the holy and blessed St. Shubal Stearns, the apostle of North Carolina and the adjacent states.[96]

There was not a place in North Carolina where Stearns had not preached; there was hardly a hamlet in which he did not see some token evidence of the Holy Spirit at work. This beauty would somehow be turned into ashes in just a short period of time. Just before those heart-wrenching events would become a reality, Stearns wrote to Isaac Backus:

> The Lord carries on His work gloriously, in sundry places in this province, and in Virginia, and in South Carolina. Not long since, I attended a meeting on Hoy River, about thirty miles from hence. About seven hundred souls attended the meeting, which held six days. We received twenty-four persons by a satisfactory declaration of grace, and eighteen of them were baptized. **The power of God was wonderful.**[97]

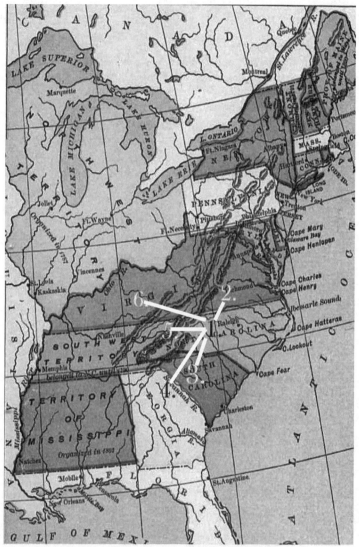

The advance of the Separate Baptists:
1. Sandy Creek, N.C.   2. Dan River, Va.   3. Fairforest, S. C.
4. Kiokee, Ga.   5. Buffalo Ridge, Tn.   6. Gilbert's Creek, Ky.

A TIMETABLE OF EVENTS IN THE SEPARATE BAPTIST CRUCIBLE

1768   FEBRUARY, THE SEPARATE BAPTISTS JOHN NEWTON AND JOSEPH REESE ARE ORDAINED BY THE REGULAR BAPTISTS OLIVER HART AND EVAN PUGH IN SOUTH CAROLINA

1768   JUNE, FORMAL COMMENCEMENT OF LEGAL PERSECUTION AGAINST THE SEPARATE BAPTISTS BY THE VIRGINIA COURTS

1768   CONFRONTATION AT HILLSBOROUGH, NORTH CAROL-INA, SAMUEL HARRISS PREACHES TO *THE REGULATORS* AND IS JAILED.

1768   OCTOBER, NEWTON AND REESE "CENSURED" BY THE SANDY CREEK BAPTIST ASSOCIATION

1769   *REGULATOR* CONTROVERSY HEATED INTO ARMED ACTION IN NORTH CAROLINA

1769   SHUBAL STEARNS ATTEMPTS TO BRING A RESOLUTION IN THE SANDY CREEK ASSOCIATIONAL MEETING, CON-DEMNING ARMED REBELLION AGAINST THE COLONIAL GOVERNMENT OF NORTH CAROLINA

1770   SANDY CREEK ASSOCIATION DIVIDES INTO THREE SEPARATE ASSOCIATIONS: SANDY CREEK, RAPID-ANN (VIRGINIA) AND CONGAREE (SOUTH CAROLINA)

1771   MAY 16, THE BATTLE OF ALAMANCE—THE COLONIAL MILITIA ROUTS *THE REGULATORS* AT ALAMANCE CREEK JUST EAST OF SANDY CREEK

1771   NOVEMBER 20, THE DEATH OF SHUBAL STEARNS

1771-2   MASSIVE EXODUS AND MIGRATION OF THE BAPTISTS FROM NORTH CAROLINA

CHAPTER EIGHT
A Corn of Wheat
The Church of England's War Against the Baptists

*We must either deny all influence to the preaching of democratic
and individualistic ideas in religion, or we must admit that the
preaching of Stearns and his follow laborers quickened the spirit of
democracy among their hearers and emboldened them to make that
resistance to oppression which resulted in the Regulator movement.*[1]
—George Washington Paschal

In the fall of 1769, somewhere in the woods between the tidewater of
Virginia and the mountains of Appalachia, a group of mounted
preachers stopped their ride and settled camp for the evening. They
were on the trail between Carter's Creek and the Blue Ridge and were
heading for a chance to glimpse the near legendary sight of Shubal
Stearns, the leader of the greatest revival in American history.

These preachers were old "Regular" Baptists who had gathered at
Smith's Creek and were determined to attend the associational meeting
of the Sandy Creek Separate Baptists and hear the "Apostle Paul of the
Backcountry." They carried with them a request from the Ketockton
"Regular" Baptist Association to consider a union between the Separates
and the Regulars.[2]

The preachers were overtaken on their journey by a young buck, a
novice, from the new Baptist society at Smith's Creek named James Ireland. Ireland had been awakened and became convinced of the Baptist
way by a series of meetings and debates involving his own Episcopalian
parson and the Separate Baptist "incendiary," John Picket.[3] Ireland began to preach the gospel. He had heard the Baptist preachers of the Ketockton (Regular) Baptist Association were planning to visit the famed
Sandy Creek Association to petition for a union with the Separate Baptists and their firebrand association. Those Regular Baptists were aware
that "Jamey" intended to tag along so they hurriedly saddled up and
rode southwest without him.

James Ireland wanted Shubal Stearns to baptize him and perhaps even ordain him to the gospel ministry. Reckoning this was his best opportunity, Ireland made a mad dash across a back road through Culpeper county riding his horse out from under him in an effort to catch up with the caravan. He over took them in the woods somewhere west of the James River.

The desire of the young man both amused and impressed the old preachers. There in the dark of the forest, as was their custom, the traveling preachers prepared to have a church service by the campfire. They prodded "Jamey" to stand and preach. It was a kind of initiation for the young man. The venerable Nathaniel Saunders stood and introduced James Ireland to the small audience around the campfire[4] which included the battle-worn John Garrard and Richard Major.[5] Saunders then stepped a foot or two away and stared into the face of the preacher-boy and said, "Preach Jamey."[6]

If intimidation was his intention, Jamey did not fade from it, for he preached with great pathos and surprising elocution. So impressive was Ireland that his malefactor faded into the tiny congregation and sat giving attendance to the young man's discourse. Not only did Ireland pass the test of bearing, the older preachers called on him to preach repeatedly on their journey. It would not be the last testing of James Ireland.

Their small company continued the drive to Sandy Creek.

For 16 years 1755-1771, Shubal Stearns held forth as the undisputed leader of the greatest revival in American History. Perhaps the fruit from the revival made it the greatest revival in any history. Morgan Edwards wrote in 1772, "I believe a preternatural and invisible hand works in the assemblies of the Separate Baptists bearing down the human mind, as was the case in primitive churches."[7]

Humanly speaking, we may attempt to explain the rapid growth of the Separate Baptists by noting pockets of disfranchised people, quite possibly rejects from the shifting of the Regular Baptist re-constitution who longed to hear preaching. At best this was just a core base that was coupled with an astonishing number of converts from the population (which was growing exponentially). Soon the idea of an association of these new churches seemed fit for the backcountry. Robert Baylor Semple wrote that Shubal Stearns "conceived that an association composed of delegates from all would have a tendency to impart stability, regularity and uniformity to the whole."[8] A preliminary meeting was set for January of 1758.

Although Stearns and Marshall had only been in North Carolina for two full years the interest in the meeting was overwhelming. At the preliminary meeting it was decided that the Sandy Creek Baptist Association would gather in June. Word spread like a brush fire throughout North Carolina, Virginia and South Carolina, and when the meeting was convened an astounding number of pioneers came from hundreds of miles.[*]

The participants turned the associational meeting into an encampment. Thus in 1758, the era of the "camp-meeting" in America began at Sandy Creek, though few today would give proper credit to them for its invention. The fame of its power spread from the Appalachians through the piedmont and to the coast. Its rich testimony engulfed the East Coast from Georgia to Pennsylvania.

As we might expect from this group of unusual people, the Sandy Creek Baptist association was unique. It was not like the other two existing Baptist associations, Philadelphia and Charleston. It was not an organizational meeting of a denomination, or a group of "bishops" dominating the churches. It was, to put it simply, a revival meeting. The frontier needed it and embraced it![9] Semple wrote:

> Thro' these meetings, the gospel was carried into many new places, where the fame of the Baptists had previously spread; for great crowds attending from distant parts, mostly though curiosity, many became enamoured with these extraordinary people, and petitioned the association to send preachers into their neighborhoods. These petitions

---

[*] From that point, the association would commence every year on the second Sunday of October.

were readily granted, and the preachers as readily complied with the appointments.[10]

When assembled, their chief employment was preaching, exhortation, singing, and conversing about their various exertions in the Redeemer's service, and the attendant success. **These things so enflamed the hearts of the ministers, that they would leave the association, with a zeal and courage, which no obstacles could impede.**[11]

James Read wrote the only known narrative of that first Sandy Creek associational meeting:

At our first association we continued together three or four days; great crowds of people attended, mostly through curiosity. The great power of God was among us; the preaching every day seemed to be attended with God's blessing. We carried on our association with sweet decorum and fellowship to the end. Then we took our leave of one another with many solemn charges from our reverend old father, Shubal Stearns, to stand fast unto the end.[12]

Skip the **modern** associational meeting—Give us *revival* and may the Spirit of God fall on God's men!

For the next twelve years many men of God made the yearly trip in October to meet together and hear the impassioned preaching of Shubal Stearns and his "preacher boys." Many had their "countenances sharpened" and their hearts touched with the fire and power of God. The unity and power of the association was unprecedented.[13]

From 1755-1769 indescribable good had been done in North Carolina, Virginia and South Carolina; but for Sandy Creek itself, it had come at a high price. The church, though still strong had lost its core families to the pioneering of church plants throughout the south.

*   *   *

All we may do is imagine the thoughts of Shubal Stearns as he rode alone coming back from a preaching engagement on September 7, 1769. His sweet and fervent sister Martha was gone. She and her missionary-husband Daniel Marshall were about to depart from Stephen's Creek in South Carolina to journey to Georgia, where they would weave the very cultural fabric of the south. Shubal's parents were now in Heaven. He and his wife Sarah, though childless, had witnessed the push of their *spiritual* children in all directions with the best of them, into Virginia. And in Virginia, terrible news was coming nearly every day about the persecution that was raging. But the power of God was apparent, especially in the life of Samuel Harriss. The rest of Elder Stearns' family was gone also, traveling as a church with Phillip Mulkey to Fairforest in South Carolina, where once again revival birthed a large number of churches. Only Tidence Lane, the first notable convert of the Yadkin settlements was still there, faithful at Sandy Creek.

In the midst of these losses, social problems were multiplying in North Carolina. Rebellion was on the horizon, maybe even a national revolution. There was no precedent for the American Baptists in such a social and political chaos. Elder Stearns' only frame of reference was the pacifistic sects of Europe or the aberrant militants from Munster, Germany. Nearby, the Moravians were peaceful, but would defend their families if they were forced. He had done what the Lord had directed him to do and as a result, a large number of North Carolinians were *baptized believers* with no small respect for his opinions.

As Stearns rode, a thunderstorm broke out over the hills. He dismounted from his horse and in front of him he saw something he interpreted as some kind of sign or message from God:

The time was September 7, 1769, memorable for a great storm. As he was ascending a hill on his way home he observed in the horizon a white heap like snow; upon his drawing near he perceived the heap to stand suspended in the air 15 or 20 feet above the ground. Presently it fell to the ground and divided itself into three parts; the greatest part moved northward; a less towards the south; and the third, which was less than either but much brighter, remained on the spot where the whole fell; as his eyes followed that which went northward, it vanished; he turned to look at the other, and found they also had disappeared. While the old man pondered what the phantom the division, and motions of it meant, this thought struck him: 'The bright heap is our religious interest; which will divide and spread north and south, but chiefly northward; while a small part remains at Sandy-creek.' Time has proved these interpretations to be just; for in Virginia (which is to the north of Sandy-creek) the interest prevails more than in the Carolinas and Georgia.[14]

The Separate Baptists were of the Obadiah Holmes stripe. They were the embodiment of John Clarke and company. Therefore, they were on a collision course with the established church. As Robert Baylor Semple wrote, "Their success was so great, that numbers of the parish clergy, who were opposed to the revival, were apprehensive that they should be deserted by all their hearers."[15] In fact, those successes began to carry political implications. Because North Carolina was as most American colonies, wedded to a religious establishment, the threat of a religious surge independent of the Anglican/Episcopal hierarchy could only mean an eventual political schism. So the Separate Baptist revival began a political slide toward independence which turned into an avalanche in North Carolina known as *the War of the Regulators*.

*   *   *

The War of *the Regulators* was a war against the Baptists of central and western North Carolina. This disturbing truth is debated in some circles today, but it was an open fact to the historian George Washington Paschal in 1930.[16] Paschal, who wrote while employed at Wake Forest College in Winston-Salem, flatly titled one of his chapters, "The War Against the Baptists" in his definitive, *History of the North Carolina Baptists*. This work was published in 1930. Then, as if Paschal were shouting, "IN CASE YOU DID NOT HEAR ME THE FIRST TIME, THE WAR OF THE REGULATORS WAS A WAR AGAINST THE BAPTISTS," he published *The History of the North Carolina Baptists, Volume 2*. He re-iterated his findings from volume one. This work was finished in 1955. No doubt Paschal is now an embarrassment to the Wake Forest "Demon Deacons" who are no longer associated with the Baptists.

Paschal begins his findings on *the Regulators* by introducing the "Society for the Propagation of the Gospel in America." This organization should have been named, the "Society to Insure that the Episcopal Church Should Rule," and Paschal points to the work of this "society" as the beginning of troubles leading to the controversy and "War" of *the Regulators*. It is an undisputed fact that for 66 years the Episcopal Church attempted national supremacy through the work of the "society" within the colonies. They managed to succeed in establishing themselves in Georgia, Virginia and North Carolina. It meant suffering for the *baptized believers*.

The War of the Regulators

Law had established the Church of England in North Carolina in 1701 upon motion of Dr. Thomas Bray of the English Society for the Propagation of the Gospel, but it was weak in North Carolina. By the end of the proprietary period of the colony in 1729, not one Anglican minister could be found there.[17] By 1760, there were just five.

There were three sets of taxes levied prior to the War of *the Regulators*. A property tax, and two poll taxes, which were punitive in nature. One of the poll taxes was for general sale of goods; the other was **the hated parish tax** in support of the Anglican/Episcopalian church.

The Schism Act was passed in English Parliament in 1714, and was supposed to have been repealed in 1718. However, no schoolmaster was to teach without license from the Bishop of London. Even though this was an abolished English law, two successive governors, Dobbs and Tryon, enforced it out of obedience to the instructions of the Bishop of London. This impeded the progress and education of the Baptists and other Dissenters.[18] No place of higher learning could be administered except by the ministers of the Church of England. This was done so that it could be said that the Baptists were "obstinately illiterate, and grossly ignorant."

The Marriage Act of 1741 gave the Church of England exclusive rights to perform marriages. The implication was clear: To be anything but Anglican meant you were not entitled to basic liberty.

In 1755 just as the awakening of the Separate Baptists began, **poll and religious (vestry) taxes** were imposed upon North Carolinians. It was TAXATION WITHOUT REPRESENTATION, as was the ministerial taxes in Massachusetts. And here in the backwoods of the American frontier, the revolutionary movement really began.

Perhaps most disconcerting from the backcountry in Georgia to Pennsylvania was "The Proclamation of 1763." The Proclamation established a boundary that prohibited the migration of settlers west into the mountains. This proclamation was so heinous to the people that Thomas Jefferson referred to it directly in the Declaration of Independence. Jefferson indicted King George III saying, "He has endeavored to prevent the population of these states; for that purpose obstructing the laws for naturalization of foreigners; refusing to pass others to encourage their migration hither, and raising the conditions of new appropriations of lands."

Rowan County violently opposed the vestry (religious) tax. Most dissenters were decidedly Baptist. Their converts began to pluck the strings of resonating liberty. Their fervor promoted the British and Anglican governor to refer scornfully to the Separate Baptists as "Superior New Lights from New England."[19]

The Sandy Creek Baptist Association formed in 1758. In September of that same year, a so-called "mob" of at least 700 pre-revolution patriots, formed near Jersey Baptist Church to protest **the Marriage Act**. With some levity, we could muse that this was the birth of the first "mob" in American history. Only this "mob" existed for good. The Bethabara Diary of the Moravian settlement recorded the event on September 23, 1758:

> The 'mob', about 700 strong, had formulated its demands into certain articles. One article demanded that the Vestries should be abolished and that each denomination should pay its own ministers.[20]

As the colonial records show, the government in the province of North Carolina was more than a little worried at this turn of events. The Separate Baptists now began to take on the inevitable nicknames given to nearly all our Baptist forefathers. They were referred to as "strollers," by the right reverend Mr. Reed, and were immediately labeled as "Anabaptists" to connect them with the so-called "heretics" of Europe, and England. The Anglican Church of England in North Carolina took to calling the Separate Baptists "the Enthusiasts." Once again, they must have actually been *enthusiastic* about their salvation.

The right Rev. Mr. Reed said these preachers gave him a good deal of trouble. There was a right Rev. Mr. Smith who came from the Society for the Propagation of the Gospel to "curb (if possible) an Enthusiastic sect which call themselves Anabaptists* which is numerous and was daily increasing in this parish."[21] The right Rev. Mr. Smith soon found that curbing was not possible.

We know what Shubal Stearns was preaching by what his enemy the right Rev. Mr. Reed said in 1761, that the Separate Baptists were "preaching up the inexpediency of human learning and the practice of moral virtue, and the great expediency of dreams, visions and immediate revelations."[22] By this we can determine that the Separate Baptists were being maligned for the same reason as the "Opinionists" of Massachusetts (see chapter two), for their belief in *experimental religion*, that is, the necessity of the new birth.

Reed went on to say "the Enthusiasticals" were **"obstinately illiterate, and grossly ignorant."**[23] (You were warned they would do that!) They certainly were not ignorant of the human condition and the tremendous spiritual needs of the people of North Carolina.

Not everyone hated or disregarded the Separate Baptists. Notice what the right Rev. Mr. Michael Smith said: "I find that these preachers have been of great service to me."[24] There was a right reverend Mr. Barlett to whom the Baptists of Lockwood's Folly had graciously allowed access to their meeting-house for Episcopalian services.[25] The Moravians, who came to the Piedmont of North Carolina from central Europe in search of religious liberty, had great admiration and respect for them. These Moravians had settled near present day Winston-Salem in a tract of North Carolinian wilderness they named "Wachovia." After establishing the cities of Bethania, Bethabara and Salem, the Moravians began to enlist the services of the Separate Baptist preachers from the Sandy Creek Association. Shubal Stearns, Daniel Marshall and the Murphy boys were just a few miles due east of Wachovia and the great Moravian preacher Solle` often invited them to preach, especially William and Joseph Murphy, and Samuel Harris. Solle' wrote in his diary:

---

* They did *not* call themselves Anabaptists.

Mr. Harriss, a well-known Baptist of Virginia, visited here to acquaint himself with our doctrine and constitution and to talk with us. We hope that this may be for his good and the good of those to whom he preaches, for **at this time the Baptists are the only ones in the country who go far and wide preaching and caring for souls.**[26]

However, in the eastern part of North Carolina the inevitable battle over infant baptism came to the forefront. The one thing the Anglicans had going for them was the control exercised by their clergy in the practice of sprinkling infants. Tracts were written in defense of infant "baptism" by the Episcopalians in the eastern seaboard. The right reverend Mr. Reed wrote: "I do affirm they (the Separate Baptists) sprung from the seed which he (Whitefield) first planted in New England and the difference of soil may perhaps have caused such an alteration in the fruit that he may be ashamed of it." When Mr. Whitefield heard of this criticism of his ministry, he affirmed his belief in infant sprinkling and declared himself a minister of the Church of England.[27]

Eventually and surprisingly, the Anglican/Episcopalians admitted that **immersion was really the proper mode of baptism**. The colonial records confirm the Anglican admission, and their attempts to head off the Baptist onslaught by immersing adults themselves![28]

It didn't work.

The Baptists were first called "strollers" by Governor Dobbs in 1756[29] and were accused of immorality. Dobbs died on March 28, 1765 and a strong advocate arose for the Anglican/Episcopalians: William Tryon. During his tenure, Dobbs had attempted to get promised aid to the Anglican clergy. Tryon stepped up the effort. The new governor began to grow in his hatred for the "strolling" preachers. He made the demolition of the dissenters one of his main objects... perhaps his *main* object.[30]

To establish his object and intentions, and vent his anger against the Baptists, Tryon went to work enforcing **the Vestry Act**. Although approved in 1755, the Vestry Act was not widely enforced. Since there was no stipulation in the law on how the tax would be collected, Tryon himself took on that duty. In addition, Tryon shockingly took on the duty of installing the ministers of the Church of England. He immediately called for clerical reinforcements into western North Carolina. Overnight, he became a "bishop" to North Carolina as the Bishop of London gave him authority to rule the newly recruited Anglican priests that would be sent to the Province. He became the sole proprietor of religion, appointing clergyman and disciplining any who opposed him. His opposition toward the dissidents, especially the Separate Baptists, became an obsession.

* * *

Events concerning the *War of the Regulators* now began to accelerate towards a collision. In 1766, the people were taxed to build a palace for Tryon the tyrant. Edmund Fanning entered the stage of these events. He was the judge of the Superior court. When Fanning attempted to collect the taxes for the "palace," he was met with stiff opposition. In the minds of the men of the backwoods, there was no difference between the tactics of Tryon, Fanning, and King George III with his the stamp act. Indeed, there was no difference. Taxation was (and still is) a legal form of robbery when abused. The British government of North Carolina allowed no form of compromise or relief. No appeal or public petition was heard and the natives now grew angrier at each passing season. The Palace cost 15,000 pounds of British silver.

Through it all, the Separate Baptists, especially in the central and western counties of Tryon's Anglican paradise, continued to grow.

Turning the Presbyterians against the Baptists

Governor Tryon, sensing a rivalry, began to pit the Presbyterians against the Baptists. There was bad blood anyway—according to the Colonial Records.[31] There is a 1766 letter describing the rivalry by stating: "their rancor is surprising."[32] Indeed there was a rivalry for the souls of the pioneers, as Woodmason wrote:

> The most zealous among the Sects to propagate their notions and form establishments are the Anabaptists. When the Church of England was established in Carolina the Presbyterians made great struggle but finding themselves too weak they determined to effect that by cunning (The principles they work by for they are all males) which

strength could not effect. Wherefore as Parish churches were built along the Sea coast they built a set of Meeting-Houses quite back be-hind in the interior parts, Imitating the French—who making a chain of Forts from Canada to Louisiana endeavored to circumscribe the English & prevent the extension of their trade. So did the Presbyteri-ans with our Church. If they could not suppress they would cramp the progress of the Liturgy and church establish—and accordingly did erect meeting-houses aforesaid. None of the Church opposed them and the Almighty by taking these people in their craft have suffered them to fall into the net they spread for others. For the Anabaptists of Penn-sylvania resolving themselves into a body and determined to settle their principles in every vacant quarter began to establish meeting-houses also on the borders. And by their address and assiduity have wormed the Presbyterians out of all their strongholds and drove them away. So that the Baptists are now the most numerous and formida-ble body of people which the church has to encounter with in the in-terior and back parts of the Province and the antipathy the two sects bear each other is astonishing.[33]

The Presbyterians were given the right to marry by Tryon, but their previous marriages were called "fraudulent & illegal" in the so-called preamble of 1766.[34]

History has revealed that Tryon's "kindness" toward the Presbyteri-ans was a smokescreen. The right reverend Mr. Reed, then a close asso-ciate of Tryon wrote to the Society for the Propagation of the Gospel:

> In explanation of why the bill in favor of the Presbyterians had been allowed to pass: 'Upon the fate of these, other Bills were dependent, and it was good policy to keep the Dissenters (Presbyterians) in as good humour as possible at such a critical juncture.[35]

Whatever false affection Tryon had for the "Dissenters,"* he held not even feigned affection for the Baptists, referring to them as "rascally fellows."[36]

Tryon continued to play "the Presbyterian card," even recruiting the support of Presbyterians ministers Hugh McAlden, James Creswell,

---

* The Presbyterians were referred to as "dissenters." The Baptists were not even considered worthy of that name.

Henry Patillo and David Caldwell.[37] And when the governor began to enlist an army for battle against the spreading heresy of Baptist principles, these Presbyterian ministers sent a letter to the Presbyterian inhabitants of North Carolina. The letter urged them to side with Tyron, in an effort "to prevent the *infection* spreading among the people of our charge."[38]

Governor Tryon then began to build a military force comprised mainly of recruits from Presbyterian districts. Incredibly, he marched his force to Wachovia in an effort to turn the Moravians against the Baptist and Quaker settlements. He then went west of the Yadkin and succeeded in stirring up the Presbyterian counties against what he called a "faction of Quakers and Baptists." He plainly stated his battle with the "mob" was against a faction of the Quakers & Baptists. Since the Quakers would not bear arms, the obvious threat in his mind was the Baptist threat.

In 1768, the "mob" became known as **the Regulators** and Governor Tryon repeatedly referred to **the Regulators** as being Baptist.[39] Historical evidence shows that no Baptist community sent soldiers to the aid of Tryon.[40] In 1768, Tryon could not get the militia of Orange County, a Baptist stronghold, to fight against *the Regulators*. The population by this time, was predominantly Baptist in that part of North Carolina.[41]

On April 13, 1768 a letter from Governor Tryon was sent to *the Regulators*, promising "his service would not be wanting to redress any real grievances."[42] However, that promise proved to be disingenuous. The governor, knowing that according to *Regulator Advertisement No. 9* [43] many of *the Regulators* were indeed Baptist,[44] declared: "the Baptists were **the avowed enemies of mother church** and **enemies to society** and a **scandal to common sense.**"[45]

Violence and Intimidation

In the spring of 1768, the horse of a *Regulator* was confiscated for back taxes. News of this action spread like a brush fire and soon a crowd assembled at the Hillsboro courthouse in the county of Rowan. *The Regulators* overpowered the sheriffs and took the horse back. Shots were fired into the home of Edmund Fanning. Governor Tryon mobilized his troops. Troops arriving in Hillsboro arrested Herman Husbands and William Butler. After this incident a small number of Baptist people began to pack their families and head over the mountains into the Holston River area of what would become Tennessee.

The next logical step had to be armed resistance. This was the thing all the governments of the colonies feared. Disarming was a tactic used against dissenters since the Puritans took the weapons of the "opinionists" in 1635. Considering the wilderness savvy of the population, disarming would have been impossible.

Extortion and fraud agitated the pioneers. The sheriffs were defrauding the population. An investigation in 1768 showed an excess of 64,000 pounds collected and still the provincial debt was unpaid. *The Regulators* wanted an account of that defrauded money. They did not receive an accounting. Along with that grievance, the registration of deeds became an avenue of extortion for the registrars. In some cases, they charged four times the amount allotted by law.[46] In fact, Edmund Fanning, the right hand man of William Tryon was convicted of extortion in 1768.

Because of the successful organization of the Regulators, laws against peaceful assembly were enacted. George W. Paschal, rightly judging another misstep in history, wrote:

> And Tryon by numerous proclamations sought to rob the oppressed of the right of assembling so as to formulate their grievances, while Samuel Johnston and others who followed his lead, as a fitting consummation of the invasion of the rights of the people, passed that bloody Act making it a felony for the wronged farmers of Orange to hold or to have held such assemblies. And yet the bust of the same Samuel Johnston is set in a niche of our State Capitol.[47]

The province of North Carolina was basically being operated by an old-boy network of cliques and clubs with, of all things, the Masonic union. Indeed, Edmund Fanning "boasted that their union (Masonic) was so strong and widespread in the county that the common people were powerless to elect other officers.[48] Two petitions were brought before the provincial Assembly of 1769, one from Anson County, and the other from Rowan and Orange. The petitions asked for a reform in the vestry taxes, marriage laws and tax collection. These petitions were ignored.[49] What happened next was a hinge upon which the souls of thousands hung.

James Ireland was anxious to be baptized by Shubal Stearns. At the beginning of this chapter, we left him with that small sojourning set of Regular Baptists, making their way to the 1769 meeting of Sandy Creek Association.

The year 1769 proved to be controversial for the association. The previous year, Sandy Creek Association had its very first brush with disunity over the ordination of John Newton and Joseph Reese. Newton and Reese were censured by the Sandy Creek Association for receiving ordination by the "Regular" Baptists in South Carolina in 1768. [50] But this year, things unraveled, and got complicated. As badly as Ireland desired baptism and ordination by the "Apostle Paul of the Backcountry," a sea of troubles would prevent it. *The Regulator* movement was in full debate and division among the Baptists was the result.

The Regulators were growing restless while their demands for reform in the government of North Carolina were being ignored. In some cases they themselves became overbearing, demanding allegiance and forcing men to join their ranks.

The undisputed leader of the North Carolina backcountry was none other than Shubal Stearns, the Separate Baptist preacher. We last left him in our narrative in a thunderstorm, with the rain pelting him and the Lord speaking once again to his heart.

The Yadkin valley had more Baptist people in it than anywhere else in the colonies. In reality, it was the center of Baptist strength in the entire world. What would be the judgment of Shubal Stearns' on the matter of *the Regulators?*

In this controversy, Stearns tried to remain neutral. There really was no precedent on what a Baptist leader in America should do. His knowledge of the ancient Baptists must have been scant. The known records of the actions of the *baptized believers* in Europe placed them in a position of so-called "pacifism," not drawing the sword. Refusing to "draw the sword" on the part of the persecuted *baptized believers* was a natural stance, seeing their military duties would have made them march and destroy their own families as heretics. His nearest neighbors were not pacifists; the Moravians would defend their families if needed. So then, stopping short of the Presbyterian support of Governor Tryon, Stearns tried to keep the men of Sandy Creek from bearing arms against the government by bringing a resolution to the association that placed a ban on armed rebellion against the government of North Carolina. He may have simply been trying to rely on Romans 12:18 as the best course of action.

There is no record of the total number of persons present at Sandy Creek Association in October of 1769, but the attendance was probably several thousand. By now, the power of the associational meeting was legendary for social and spiritual reasons.

The association at Sandy Creek had become a part of the society of the backwoods. It was the largest of any social or political meeting anywhere in the colonies. It was a place of reunion, fellowship, enthusiasm, and affection and in the wake of preaching—it was a place of profound conviction.

No doubt unscrupulous men also viewed the meeting as a business opportunity and rowdies also enjoyed the atmosphere. Eventually, all pioneer camp meetings and associations had to enlist the help of county law officers to encourage order. No doubt into the mix at Sandy Creek in 1769 was a multitude of curiosity seekers, ne'er-do-wells and, if the reports coming from the eyewitnesses of frontier baptism are true, the mix also included bitter enemies. In 1769, as we shall see, the most renegade of *the Regulators*, also were present.

October 11, 1769, the first day, was a joyous day for the Virginians. Their beloved "apostle," the venerable Samuel Harriss, was ordained at the Sandy Creek meeting-house.

As was their custom, the day began and ended with preaching and the indescribable call of God on the heart of the lost. Revival more often than not followed and ran well into the evening. The business meeting itself with the delegates took place apparently in the early afternoons.

The next day was marked by controversy as the Virginia Regular Baptists of the Ketockton Association brought their petition for union to the meeting. These men, John Garrard, Richard Majors and Nathaniel Saunders, were fresh from their long ride with the young James Ireland. Their letter of proposition for union said:

> Beloved in our Lord Jesus Christ: The bearers of this letter can acquaint you with the design of writing it. Their errand is peace, and their business is reconciliation between us, if there is any difference subsisting. If we are all Christians, all Baptists, all New-lights, why are we divided? Must the little appellative names, Regular and Separate, break the golden band of charity, and set the sons and daughters of Zion at variance. 'Behold, how good and how pleasant it is for brethren to dwell together in unity,' but how band and how bitter it is, for them to live asunder in discord. —To indulge ourselves in prejudice, is surely a disorder; and to quarrel about nothing, is irregularity with a witness. O! Our dear brethren, endeavor to prevent this calamity for the future.[51]

After a lengthy discussion, this proposition was rejected.

That the Ketockton "Regulars" wanted union with the "Separates" of Sandy Creek is an amazing thing seeing just a few years earlier, the Separates were unjustly dismissed as being "disorderly." As it turns out, the record suggests strongly that the Ketockton Regulars were more in agreement with the fire and zeal of the Separates than the majority of their orthodox, and in some cases, *dying*, Regular Baptist brethren. Their main reason for union may have been the same as James Ireland, who went to be baptized and ordained by Shubal Stearns with these thoughts, "We wished to know which of the two bodies, Regulars or Separates had the warmest preachers and the most fire among them; we determined in favor of the latter." [52]

Their purposes were disappointed. The offer of union was rejected, for the Separates were concerned about certain points of doctrine and dress standards they feared would be compromised.[53]

Sandy Creek Association was enormous, spreading over three states and becoming nearly impossible to keep organized, yet the Ketockton

Regulars desired to be a part of it. However, with the ordination of Samuel Harriss, their intentions would be fulfilled in another way. Again, as was custom, the second day at the association began and ended with preaching and once again, with the indescribable call of God on the hearts of the people.

The third day of the 1769 meeting of the Sandy Creek Baptist Association brought heartache to the "Apostle Paul of the Backcountry." He knew something must be said about the Regulators. He believed their grievances to be just. But he could not be in favor of armed rebellion against the colonial government in North Carolina. Since all evidence points to Elder Stearns as the moderator of the meeting,* the following resolution was probably his desire:

> The resolve of the Baptist-association, held at Sandy-creek the second Saturday in October, 1769, "If any of our members shall take up arms against the legal authority or aid and/or abet them that do so, he shall be excommunicated etc."[54]

One would suppose that news traveled at the speed of light at a meeting of such magnitude and however it happened, after the resolution to reject armed action against the state was laid on the table, the meeting-house was invaded by one of the leaders of the Regulators, followed by an undetermined number of those loyal to the cause of Regulation. Morgan Edwards wrote of this:

> When this was known abroad, one of the four chiefs of the regulators with an armed company broke into the assembly and demanded if there were such a resolve entered into by the association. The answer was evasive; for they were in bodily fear."[55] [56]

The author cannot agree with Morgan Edward's assessment that Shubal Stearns was in bodily fear. The preacher had faced many mobs of angry men who had hurled outrageous threats and venom at him for many years. One man with a small group of thugs was not going to faze him. The author cannot agree with Edward's assessment that the answer was evasive. What we want to know from Edwards is "What did Shubal

---

* No official moderator was ever elected while Shubal Stearns was alive.

Stearns tell those men?" In sorrow, we must report that there is no record. Only Morgan Edward's opinion offers us insight. We must note that Morgan Edwards was a Welsh Baptist, immigrating to America in 1761. He was a Loyalist, siding with the British during the American Revolution. Most of his "materials" were never published. The materials that were published suffered for want of purchasers quite possibly because of his political sentiments, which were made well known during and after the Revolution.

In any event, nothing more was accomplished at the meeting after the incident with the Regulator chiefs except to announce that the 1770 meeting would be held at Grassy Creek.

In the course of the next 12 months tensions in North Carolina intensified. Moreover, with Samuel Harriss ordained, the Separate Baptists in Virginia began to ordain preachers on their own, with James Ireland the first to receive ordination from Samuel Harriss. Even in the face of grave dangers from within and without, the Separate Baptists continued to grow in the next twelve months.

As the 1770 Sandy Creek associational meeting approached, great excitement mixed with anxiety fell upon the Separate Baptists. The Regulator problem was about to explode in bloodshed, and anger against the government, mingled with desire to obey the Lord was no doubt a confusion, which seemed to have no remedy. The Regulators had exposed much corruption and when Governor Tryon did nothing, the Regulators now took matters into their own hands. Another attack by the Regulators at the court at Hillsboro was begun in September of 1770, bringing the western Baptist counties of North Carolina to the brink of war against Tryon's Presbyterian troops.

To add to the anxiety, as the attendees of the 1770 Sandy Creek Baptist Association began their ride to Grassy Creek, they were informed of the death of George Whitefield, the evangelist who unwittingly began the "New Light" Separate revival among them, and to whom so many of them, including Shubal Stearns, had given great honor, credit and respect. One so great among them would also come to his end, within thirteen months.

The 1770 meeting of the Sandy Creek Baptist Association was of immense historical significance. Elijah Craig, who was present at the meeting, left this account:

> The Separate Baptist Association met again in 1770 at Grassy Creek meeting-house, N. Carolina. The churches had now become numerous, there being a considerable number in each of the three states. It had been usual with them, to do nothing in associations but by unanimity. If in any measure proposed, there was single dissentient; they labored first by arguments to come to unanimous agreement; when arguments failed, they resorted to frequent prayer, in which all joined. When both these failed, they sometimes appointed the next day for fasting and prayer, and to strive to bring all, to be of one mind. At this session, they split in their first business: Nothing could be done on the first day. They appointed the next for fasting and prayer. They met and labored the whole day, until an hour by sun in the afternoon, and could do nothing, not even appoint a Moderator. The third day was appointed for the same purpose, and to be observed in the same way. They met early, and continued together until three o'clock in the afternoon, without having accomplished any thing. A proposal was then made, that the association should be divided into three districts, that is, one in each state. To this there was a unanimous consent at once.[57]

The churches in North Carolina kept the name Sandy Creek, while the churches in South Carolina took the name Congaree, and the churches in Virginia adopted the name Rapid-ann.[*]

Thus came an end to the unity of the "Separate" Baptists directly under Shubal Stearns. As it happened, the vision of the thunderstorm came abundantly true. The proof of this is verifiable history.

Moreover, it is evident from the record and the remains of history that several measurable results came from the division at Sandy Creek. First, the association itself lost its unanimity. Second, Shubal Stearns lost much of his immediate influence. Third, 1500 Baptist families fled North Carolina to settle in Virginia, Kentucky, and especially Tennes-

---

[*] Rapid-ann Association soon changed its name to the General Association of Separate Baptists.

see. Fourth and most importantly, the Separate Baptists scrambled over the Alleghenies to bring revival to the American frontier.

By 1770, Governor William Tryon had established 18 Anglican priests in the 32 parishes of North Carolina. For this he was beloved by the Anglican/Episcopalian hierarchy. His hatred for the Separate Baptists was about to find closure.

It came to pass that *the Regulators* marched to Hillsboro court in September of 1770. A letter, signed by 174 Regulators and addressed to Judge Richard Henderson stated:

> We have labored honestly for our bread and studied to defraud no man, nor live on the spoils of other men's labors, nor snatched the bread out of other man's hands. Our only crime with which they can charge us is virtue in the very highest degree, namely, to risk our all to **save our country** from rapine and slavery in our detecting of practices which the law allows to be worse than robbery...To sum up the whole matter of our petition in a few words, it is namely, that we may obtain unprejudiced juries; that all extortionate officers, lawyers and clerks may be brought to fair trials.[58]

"Fair trials" was the last thing Governor Tryon wanted. He wanted those people, *the enemies of Mother church*, out—and he moved to make it happen.

The promise made by Tryon, back in April of 1768, to "redress any real grievances" was now shown to be hollow. A bill to overturn the hated **Marriage Act** was summarily dismissed in January of 1771. The Baptists were basically affirmed to be non-citizens, with no power to marry and no real birth evidence, due to their rejection of infant baptism.

By the spring of 1771, political disorder had spread over the entire province. Fifteen counties were in protest. An encampment of *Regulators* situated themselves on the Yadkin River just west of Salisbury in March of 1771. When they were assured relief from royal arbitrators, the majority of the 500 men who camped there went home. However, Tryon rejected the compromises reached by his own advisors and ordered out the provincial militia. His intent was to kill, humiliate and scatter the Baptists whom he believed to be his worst enemies. The truth is that he was haply fighting against God, for he could not understand that the power he was wrestling against was God's power. For the Lord had transformed his Anglican province, filled with "graceless mercenaries," into a garden filled with regenerate persons. The revival had turned his backwoods into a Bible-believing bastion of the Baptist faith and an incubator for the stunning Baptist revival that would eventually engulf the entire south.

Governor Tryon issued a mandate to be read throughout the province demanding *the Regulators* to submit to his authority or be called traitors. Forces for both sides began to amass at Alamance Creek, west of Hillsboro. On May 16, 1771, around two thousand Regulators faced nearly the same number of colonial militia in what many consider **the first battle of the American Revolution**. It was a tentative battle that lasted but two hours. In all, eighteen men were killed, nine *Regulators* and nine militiamen. But *the Regulators* were routed from their place and scattered over the hills. William Edwards Fitch wrote:

> At the "Battle of Alamance" was kindled the flame, though small in the beginning, that eventually, Vesuvius-like, spread with the rapidity of a wild forest fire, until the oppressed of the thirteen colonies were aflame with righteous indignation and unitedly determined to throw off forever the YOKE of British oppression. The incidents of extortion from 1765 to 1771 were fraught with such momentous consequences upon the destinies of civilization throughout the world that we can never tire in contemplating the instrumentalities by which, under Divine guidance, the liberty and independence of the Colonists were effected. The "War of the Regulators" has taught mankind that oppression, misrule, and extortion under any government tends to weaken and ultimately destroy the power of the oppressor; and that a people united in the cause of freedom and their inalienable rights are invincible by those who would enslave them.[59]

The Battle of Alamance was over but the war on the Baptists was not. Governor Tryon, impassioned with victory and with a large number of new recruits, now set his face west and began the only religious cleansing campaign in American history. Reminiscent of European troops marching against the *hated* Vaudois, (Waldensians) Tryon marched southwest toward the Sandy Creek Baptist church in search of the ring-leaders of *the Regulators* and hoping to terrorize the Baptist settlements.[60]

Tryon encamped at Sandy Creek in the summer of 1771. His personal headquarters was located on the farm of Benjamin Merrill, a known Baptist and *Regulator* leader from the Jersey Settlement church. Merrill was captured, convicted as a traitor and hung publicly. He was then cut in pieces—quartered—and his body scattered. Of Merrill, Morgan Edwards made this debatable observation, "One of the seven Baptists was executed; and he (Benjamin Merrill) at the point of death did not justify his conduct, but bitterly condemned it."[61]

However, as Paschal points out, "this was not so according to the *Boston Gazette* of August 12, 1771, 'Merrill died in the most heroic manner, his children being around him at the place of his execution. He declared that HE DIED AT PEACE WITH HIS MAKER AND IN THE CAUSE OF HIS OPPRESSED COUNTRYMEN.'"[62] Others would soon suffer similar deaths. In all, 6,409 North Carolinians were forced to say an oath of allegiance to the British provincial government. This is a large number, but the estimated number of people west of Wake County and east of the mountains who were active in the Regulator movement exceeded 50,000.[63]

John Gano is given credit in some circles as being the encouraging factor in the assembling of *the Regulators*, however the "boss" of the "mob" according to Governor Tryon was Joseph Murphy. Murphy, as we have seen, was one of Stearns' preachers, and one of the famed "Murphy boys." Since 1769, Murphy was pastor at Shallows Ford on the west side of the Yadkin very near the Moravian settlements. Beginning with 32 members, the church had grown to a membership of 185 in three years.[64]

Tryon wanted Joseph Murphy's head in a charger. Murphy was so hated by Tryon that he put a bounty on him. But the rugged preacher proved too elusive for capture. Some have speculated he hid in a cave on the property of Squire and Sarah Boone, the parents of Daniel Boone. The Boones were members of Murphy's church at Shallows Ford.

By the month of May, Governor Tryon was finished. He had succeeded at intimidating the Baptist settlements while Granville, Brunswick and Cumberland Counties (where the Presbyterians had the majority) were not invaded by Tryon's army. Although Tryon won the battle of Alamance against *the Regulators*, in the end, he lost the war against the Baptists. In June of 1771, William Tryon went to New York to become governor of that province. There he met with his ultimate enemies: George Washington and the Continental Army.

The blood of Baptist people on the field of fire at Alamance most certainly made a difference for the cause of liberty. Just five years after, at the North Carolinian Constituted Congress at Halifax, North Carolina, the first two considerations were: abolishing Episcopalian vestry and marriage acts, and giving all ministers of all denominations the legal authority to marry.

It must be remembered that after the War of *the Regulators*, most of the Baptist churches were decimated. Morgan Edwards, who toured the area just two years after Alamance, stated, "their grievances must have been real, for within a few months after Alamance, 1500 families quitted the province." It happened at Shallows Ford, where Joseph Murphy had seen such great revival. 1772 now reduced the church, which had grown to 185 in three short years, to 48.

Four months after the Battle of Alamance, the mother church at Sandy Creek, as well as many of the rest of her children, had a mass exodus. From a zenith of over 900 members and a steady stream of church planting successes, the church of the "Apostle Paul of the Backcountry" was reduced to 13 members. Those saints were gone into South Carolina and Georgia where they would participate in the great awakening of the "old" south. They had also gone **over** the **mountains** into the future land of Tennessee, where they would wait patiently for the coming of Tidence Lane, and an opportunity to fight for their liberty.

So then dear readers, the question begs to be asked? Why the demise of Sandy Creek Baptist Church?* And why did the association itself not survive?

On November 20, 1771, Shubal Stearns died. He was buried just down the trail between the meeting-house where he preached and the creek in which he buried several thousand pioneers in believer's baptism. For whatever reason, he is not remembered nor revered in the conscious of America's *baptized believers.* Yet, the legacy of his ministry was so mighty that Morgan Edwards wrote of it:

> **From this Zion went forth the word, and great was the company of them who published it: it, in 17 years, has spread branches westward as far as the great river Mississippi; southward as far as Georgia; eastward to the sea and Chesapeake bay; and northward to the waters of Potomac.**[65]

All of our generation should now repeat the story.

A scriptural reason may offer the best understanding for obscurity of Shubal Stearns. He that demonstrated the most mercy in the Bible rarely received any in return. The Apostle Paul understood this. The "Apostle Paul of the Backcountry" could expect no better treatment than his scriptural counterpoint.

Paul wrote in 2 Timothy 1:15:

*"This thou knowest, that **all** they which are in Asia be **turned away from me.**"*

---

* The church remains in name as two: Sandy Creek Baptist Church, (Southern Baptist) and Sandy Creek Primitive Baptist Church.

Most profoundly, the life of our loving Saviour, Jesus Christ, vividly illustrates the truth that the Apostle Paul of the Scriptures and the "Apostle Paul of the Backcountry" demonstrated in their lives:

> Verily, verily, I say unto you, Except a corn of wheat fall into the ground and die, it abideth alone: but if it die, it bringeth forth much fruit.—John 12:24

Elder Isaac Backus

BAPTIST ASSOCIATIONS IN AMERICA TO THE TIME OF THE REVOLUTIONARY WAR

THE PHILADELPHIA ASSOCIATION, PENNSYLVANIA, 1707
THE CHARLESTON ASSOCIATION, SOUTH CAROLINA, 1751
THE SANDY CREEK ASSOCIATION, NORTH CAROLINA, 1758
THE KEHUKEE ASSOCIATION, NORTH CAROLINA, 1765
THE KETOCTON ASSOCIATION, VIRGINIA, 1766
THE WARREN ASSOCIATION, RHODE ISLAND, 1767
THE CONGAREE ASSOCIATION, SOUTH CAROLINA, 1771
THE GENERAL ASSOCIATION OF SEPARATE BAPTISTS OF VA., 1771
THE STONINGTON ASSOCIATION, CONNECTICUT, 1772
THE RED STONE ASSOCIATION, PENNSYLVANIA, 1776
THE NEW HAMPSHIRE ASSOCIATION, 1776

IN 1700, THERE WERE 14 BAPTIST CHURCHES IN ALL AMERICA. IN 1740, NO MORE THAN SIX BAPTIST CHURCHES EXISTED IN ALL OF NEW ENGLAND, BUT BY 1800 THERE WERE AT LEAST 325 CHURCES REPRESENTING OVER 25,000 PERSONS.

DURING THE GREAT AWAKENING (1735-1750) THE NUMBER OF BAPTIST CHURCHES IN NEW ENGLAND
INCREASED IN THIS FASHION:
MASSACHUSETTS: FROM SIX TO 30 CHURCHES
CONNECTICUT: FROM FOUR TO 12 CHURCHES
RHODE ISLAND: FROM 11 TO 36 CHURCHES
THERE WERE OTHER CHURCHES PIONEERED IN NEW HAMPSHIRE, VERMONT AND MAINE.

CHAPTER NINE
Who Hath Believed our Report?

And is there one man among us, who would be willing to be compelled to support any teacher that he never chose? Yet this is the natural consequence of allowing any men to support teachers by the sword of the magistrate. And this practice has caused the effusion of blood, among all nations, more than any other means in the world. And the combination of rulers and teachers herein, I believe is the beast and false prophet, which will finally be cast into the burning lake.[1]
—Isaac Backus

While the Separate Baptists and Shubal Stearns were experiencing a monumental revival in the south, a northern religious revolution was paving the path to religious liberty. This truth of liberty was riding a wave generated by the venerable Isaac Backus.

According to Backus, there were two ideas that produced the tremendous growth of the Baptist churches in America. First, saving faith is necessary to give any soul a true right to communion in the church of Christ. Second, since saving faith is necessary, the half-way covenant is false and infant baptism "expires."

These principles became self-evident and the *baptized believers* began to win the spiritual and philosophical battle over infant baptism. The things that followed were liberty, opportunity, revival and enormous growth. The principles of liberty and *experimental religion* became the mindset of the nation. It is regrettable that this dynamic of American history has been banished to the "sewer of New England" or stranded on "Noodles Island." The author reminds his readers that forty-five years before Backus began his ministry, Increase Mather had predicted a breakaway movement from the *standing order*.[2] Now in the wake of the ministry of George Whitefield, this prophecy would be fulfilled in New England and Isaac Backus would lead the way.

*   *   *

Tyranny did not die with the success of the noble experiment of Rhode Island. No, although the Revolution was percolating in the background, the sons of John Clarke, Obadiah Holmes, John Crandall and Valentine Wightman were still trying to find a way to survive persecution at the hands of their American brothers. The tyranny of the colonial states was shocking and virtually unknown to most Americans of today.

Isaac Backus was called of God to chronicle the events of 1725-1806. His papers number in the thousands, and no one has ever completely studied and given the full thrust of their meaning. His diaries, journals, and reports of the sufferings of our Baptist patriot forefathers are priceless memorials for us to emulate AND to use as warnings for the impending rise of antichrist.

Some of you holding this book may well doubt what you are about to read. No matter, God knoweth, I speak the truth and lie not. Backus wrote, "Our Lord assured the Jews, that all the blood which had been shed by former persecutors, whom they imitated, should be required of them. The blood that was shed at Boston, an hundred and forty years ago, brought the greatest reproach upon New-England, of anything that was ever done."[3]

The prejudices and hatred for the Baptists in New England had a long history as our reader may recall the 1644 law in Massachusetts that declared, "the Anabaptists [were] the incendiaries, infectors of persons, the troublers of churches."[4]

In 1666, our aforementioned hero of Noodles Island, Thomas Gould, was imprisoned repeatedly and fined fifty pounds. Gould's associates, John Russell and Nicholas Turner, along with Benjamin Sweetster, John Miles, and James Brown, were also fined fifty pounds a man. Land was taken from Sweetster.[5]

Remember that the charter of Massachusetts was revoked in 1684 and the Congregational standing order was forced to re-think its mindset of persecution. Cotton Mather was forced to sail to England to secure liberty. So the Baptists had relief for a short period of time. William ascended to the throne after James and granted a new charter to Massachusetts in 1691 and our Baptist forefathers in Massachusetts had rest for about fifty years, but those in Connecticut did not. As we have seen, that time was bloodied by the execution of 20 so-called witches, some of who were Baptists and falsely accused.

Then the General Court at Boston began to require every town to support an "orthodox" minister and punishment was prescribed for any that would refuse, and the tyranny that followed created blight on the history of New England. When fourteen persons were rounded up and sent to prison in Bristol, Massachusetts in 1718, for refusing to pay the minister in Freetown, Massachusetts, the fight for religious liberty began in earnest.

In May, 1723, Philip Tabor, a Baptist preacher, was imprisoned along with *three tax assessors*, whose only apparent crime was neglecting to tell the Baptist people of their jurisdiction that they owed tithes. We know that those tithes were to pay for a preacher that did not minister to them. Such strange doings are appalling in our minds today, but our New England Pedobaptist friends were just beginning.

The whip of Massachusetts laid open the back of John Bolles and seven other people of Norwich, Connecticut in July of 1725. One of those "severely whipped"[6] was a woman heavy with child. By 1728, an exemption was made for Baptists and Quakers but the law could not exempt them if their church was more than five miles from their residence! This was the five-mile rule, imported from England, the same rule that put the famous John Bunyan in jail. From this point on, the exemption expired and changed every few years, with changes in 1729, 1734, 1740 and 1747.[7]

*   *   *

In March 1729, the Rehoboth, Massachusetts authorities imprisoned twenty-eight Baptists, two Quakers, and two Episcopalians in the Bristol jail for refusing to pay the parish ministers' tax.

In Isaac Backus' home state of Connecticut, church/state tyranny also prevailed. As far back as 1709, Richard Bushnell and Joseph Backus had withdrawn from the parish church at Norwich because of the awful half-way covenant, and as in Massachusetts, every town in Connecticut was required to support an orthodox minister. The penalties included indictment by the grand jury, fines, beatings and jail time. Even the itinerant preaching of George Whitefield could not keep Connecticut from passing a law forbidding any minister preaching in the parish of another without consent.

We have already documented the behavior of the Connecticut government in those days toward the "Separate" Congregationalists, those stirred by the Great Awakening. Those imprisoned included Backus' brother and mother. If the pressure on Backus as a Separate Congregationalist was great, the pressure on him became greater after he was immersed and became a Separate Baptist. On April 14, 1748, Isaac Backus baptized his first convert, Phebe Leach.

As we approach the time of the Revolution, persecution against the Baptists in New England intensified rather than lessened.

In 1749, Ebenezer Moulton of Brimfield immersed John Blount, the *standing order* minister! 62 members of his church at Sturbridge followed their pastor as he followed Christ, and were also immersed. From 1749 to 1751, Sturbridge, Massachusetts was a place of violent persecution. Five of the Sturbridge Baptists were arrested and imprisoned in the Worcester jail, their property seized for the minister's tax.[8] Baptist churches were required to turn in written exemption papers for relief from ministerial taxes. These were called "certificates." At Sturbridge in 1749, even though the Baptists turned in their "certificates," the people of the church were still taxed to support the *standing order* minister. They refused to pay and were jailed for it. What followed was a crash course in theft and larceny. County officials took property, livestock and various other items of value as payment for their "taxes." Abraham Bloss was imprisoned twice at Sturbridge, once in 1750 and 1753 for 40 days.

Among those baptized at Sturbridge by Ebenezer Moulton was Jeremiah Barstow. Barstow had been converted the year before and was imprisoned in the Worcester jail after inciting a near riot outside a *standing order* meeting-house for preaching to a crowd of Congregationalists.[9] He now spent 12 days in jail at Sturbridge for refusing the ministerial rates. He was not finished with his protest. Barstow attended the ordination of a *standing order* minister in Brookfield, Massachusetts and after mounting his horse, he announced to the dispersing crowd that a

Baptist preacher would be in town that evening to hold meetings. The Sturbridge Congregationalists, no doubt piqued at having to pay their preacher and meeting-house dues without the help of the Baptists, decided Barstow's boldness was better bottled-up and fell upon him with clubs. With peace officers looking on approvingly, the mob tried to pull Barstow off of his horse. That failed, and only encouraged the 23 year-old preacher to begin an exhortation. For the next half an hour, Barstow preached while the mob beat him with clubs.[10]

But the growth of the Baptist churches moved forward, although it had its harsh critics. As Backus wrote:

> Many had asserted that the Baptist principles always came in at the tail of a reformation, when the life of religion was gone, and people were for settling down upon the bare letter of Scripture. For a dozen years, [in New England] this argument was much harped upon, until it was silenced in these parts by clear evidence to the contrary.[11]

In 1753 an addition to the exemption act of 1747 was more oppressive than any previous. This addition ordered the "Anabaptists" to register their names on the assessor's list and also provide a "certificate," signed by thier minister and two "principle" members of the church. In addition, the minister of the Baptist church could only be considered legitimate if he had a certificate from THREE OTHER Baptist churches stating that he was indeed, "conscientiously" an "Anabaptist" minister. This incredible paper chase is an illustration of one of Satan's most useful weapons: *Wearing out the saints of God.* Surely, present day believers can look for more paper chases the closer we get to the reign of antichrist. The addition of 1753 was intended to kill the New Light revival and squelch the transformation of the Separate Congregationalists into Baptists.

The main problem with the addition to the exemption in 1753 was that the *baptized believers* did not believe they were ***Ana-***baptists. They "conscientiously" believed themselves to be *Baptists*, not ***RE-***Baptists. The entire theological argument of our Baptist forefathers was that baptism of an unconverted person was NO baptism. The outrageous demand of the Congregationalists to get the Baptists to disregard their own doctrine and heritage makes the heart sick. However, what the enemies of believer's baptism could not get the Baptists to do in the 18th century, we look on in disbelief as the Baptists of our present generation do *voluntarily*.

John Proctor, a member of the Second Baptist Church in Boston, was commissioned to go to England to draw a remonstrance against the 1753 addition to the exemption act. However, he did such a masterful job of defending Baptist principles before the General Assembly at Boston, that someone made a motion to arrest him and the signers of the remonstrance on the spot. Governor Shirley stopped that sentiment and appointed a committee to meet with the Baptists.

Our venerable Backus informs us about the founding of two other Baptist churches in his own town of Middleborough, Massachusetts between 1758 and 1762. During those years a drought had blighted some parts of New England; but in those parts where the Baptists were having revival, the rain fell and stopped the mouths of the critics.

One such place was at Ipswich, where the "Separate" Congregationalist had Mr. Cleaveland as their preacher. Noah Alden, who had been baptized by Shubal Stearns, came through Ipswich preaching. The attendance was slim, but in the congregation was a young rowdy named Biel Ledoyt. Ledoyt[12] was greatly convicted of his sin and was converted in March of 1764. Soon, his wicked friends made an attempt to convert him back to the world. They met him at a school one evening but in the course of their efforts a revival of religion broke out instead. Backus wrote, "Who could help rejoicing, to see a large number of young people turned from lying vanities, to an earnest engagement in religion."

The *standing order* discouraged that group of converts fearing their zeal and especially their desire to receive believer's baptism. So they formed their own Baptist church in Ipswich in 1766 with Biel Ledoyt himself ordained as their pastor.

*   *   *

John Adams, founding father, was born in 1735 in Braintree, Massachusetts and christened by the Rev. John Hancock* at the Braintree parish church. His parents were simple town dwellers, and his father owned a small farm. They lived in the quiet quaintness of the *standing order*.[13]

Adams' parents, like most New Englanders, were devout and had a desire for their son John to become a minister of the Gospel. He was a brilliant child who was often bored by formal education and extremely bookish. He went off to Harvard College at the ripe age of 15 and received his degree in 1754. College was a blur for him; he marked his time by more independent study and debated strenuously with his classmates about religion and theology. When he graduated he became a schoolmaster at Worcester.

He took a liking to the parish minister at Worcester, Thaddeus Maccarty. He had lively discussions with Maccarty while he contemplated pursuing medicine, law, or the ministry. He reasoned that the ministry would require his mind to be too rigidly set.[14] Adams returned to Braintree in 1758, where he began a career as an attorney. It was there that he began to experiment with the greatest passion of his life—politics. While there is plenty of information concerning his first passion and vivid interest in religion,[15] we never read of John truly trusting Christ, and there is no record of him ever being converted. In truth, whatever we may think of him, ignorance of the religious state of affairs in Massachusetts could not be a description of him.

* * *

James Manning received his education at New Jersey College, now known as Princeton, graduating in the year 1762. Manning felt an immediate need to establish a college for the education of Baptist preachers and to provide a place of education where liberty of conscience prevailed. The college he envisioned was already forming. Brown College elected him as president in 1765. Seven men received the first academic degrees on September 7, 1769. Manning later became the principle in-

---

* This is not the John Hancock of patriot fame.

strument of the establishment of the Warren Baptist Association in 1767.

Among Mr. Manning's innumerable letters, he alludes to "unreasonable opposition made against [the college] by Pedobaptists."[16] This opposition was keenly felt in all of New England, not only against Brown College, but also against Baptist preachers, property and persons.

John Gano married James Manning's sister. Gano, not unlike Samuel Harriss, seemed to be everywhere. We find him as an extremely young man under the tutelage of Isaac Eaton at Hopewell Academy. As a very young man, he was on a mission to North Carolina, where he met and warmed the heart of Shubal Stearns and the Separate Baptists at Sandy Creek. While still a relatively young man, Gano settled as the pastor of the Baptist church in New York and became a trustee of Brown. He baptized his friend, Hezekiah Smith. When the Revolutionary War began, he would lead the charge of the *baptized believers* in the cause of liberty.

Hezekiah Smith, was a fellow student with James Manning and came to New England preaching, in the spring of 1764. He was well received, even by the *standing order* churches, including Jonathan Parsons at Newburyport, Massachusetts where Smith preached to 4,000 persons![17] A group of Baptists in Haverhill called Hezekiah Smith to pastor them. When this was noised abroad, his former Pedobaptist "friends" turned decidedly against him. After hearing the Pedobaptist ministers, Flagg and Tucker, preach against him and his church, Smith wrote, "[I] expected to have more stones thrown into my chamber that night, after the ministers had reflected so much upon myself and the people who had separated from them."[18]

A revival began at the new Baptist church at Haverhill where Hezekiah Smith began his ministry. So heavy was the number of *standing order* converts that it was decided that a book needed to be published against the Baptist threat. The responsibility for publishing the anti–Baptist diatribe, known as *Dickinson's Dialogue*, rested upon Benedict Arnold's pastor, Benjamin Lord. Lord wrote the preface of the New England print of *the Dialogue*:

It seems people do not think in reason what a sinful, God-provoking and soul-destroying evil it is to break over God's institutions. First be wavering, unsettled, not steadfast in any right principles, nor in the covenant in which their infant baptism declares them to; and then *break covenant*, and separate themselves, as being in their own esteem holier and better than others. It is hid from them, that evil men and seducers wax worse and worse. It is hid from them, or rather they will not see, that they have fell into the way of Cain.[19]

Massachusetts would soon get their revenge on Hezekiah Smith and Haverhill. In May of 1765, the Baptist church at Haverhill was heavily taxed by the parish assessors to pay not only the Congregational ministers salary but also to pay for a new meeting-house.

This outrageous event was in fact typical, but not willing to tolerate it, the church moved to rectify the situation. However, the County Court seized property from one of the more prominent members for the tax. It became impossible to retrieve either the land or the money it was worth due to delays and judgments. The Haverhill incident had national repercussions. It was discussed in Philadelphia and elsewhere but no relief was found for the Baptists or Hezekiah Smith. Smith took the pelting scorn of the *standing order*, with insects thrown on him, stones thrown through his bedroom window, and threatening letters tacked to his door. When he preached at Bradford, the sheriff came out to stop him along with a group ready to riot, but when Smith began to preach, the evil element of the crowd melted away.

The Haverhill assessors had a penchant for cruelty to widows in direct violation of scripture. Martha Kimball, a widow, was arrested in the dead of winter, leaving three small children at home. She finally paid the tax after being transported several miles from her home, walking back in the snow. Mary Corliss refused to pay her tax to the *standing order* church, and had her cattle stolen for payment. She said, "I was oppressed in a province where there is a universal cry for LIBERTY!"[20]

The pernicious attitude toward Baptists was everywhere accepted and universal. In 1767 the reverend Mr. Fish, in reference to the Baptists refusing to christen their infants, wrote, "They little think as I charitably believe, how far they join with the gates of hell, in opposing the church of Christ, by laying waste the nursery out of which his vineyard is supplied."[21]

The Episcopalians of Georgia, North Carolina and Virginia were pushing for Church of England establishment among all the colonies. As vividly illustrated in chapter eight, the Anglican/Episcopalians were pushing for total control of the religious affairs of the colonists, thereby keeping them tied spiritually to mother England. Their blatant exercises in control called for the best guns in the Congregational arsenal. When the infamous Dr. Charles Chauncy, wrote vehemently against the establishment of the Anglican/Episcopal church, his *standing order* Congregational friends publicly thanked him for stating their views. But hypocritically and typically, Chauncy argued for maintaining the *standing order* of Congregationalism in Massachusetts, opposing any dissenters, especially the Baptists. This insanity both puzzled and angered Isaac Backus.*

Despite the setbacks, another window opened as the first Baptist church in Vermont was formed in Shaftsbury in 1768.

* * *

Having rejected the half-way covenant, Chileab Smith fully sided with the New Lights and was born again during the Great Awakening. For this he was mockingly told to move west and seek out Jonathan Edwards, but he settled his family westerly in the new county of Hampshire. He founded the town of Ashfield in 1751 and stayed during the dangerous days of the French and Indian War, even maintaining a defensive outpost. Through his own study and teaching, many of the people of Ashfield were converted. In the process of time, Chileab's family received Christ and his son Ebenezer was called into the ministry. The congregation embraced believer's baptism and in 1761 they constituted a Baptist church with Ebenezer Smith as their pastor.

---

*Backus' problem with Charles Chauncy was altogether doctrinal. In 1782 Chauncy turned to universalism saying, "the fire of hell would purge away the sins of all the race of Adam, so that they would be all saved, after ages of ages." The pamphlet he wrote was actually called "Purgatory." See Backus' *Abridgement*, P. 205.

The majority act of the town embracing him should have made Ebenezer Smith the privileged first minister according to Massachusetts law. However, as the town grew, so did the wishes of the *standing order*, which moved into Ashfield in large numbers. In 1765, when they filed to be incorporated the State Assembly *renamed* the town! Incredibly, taxes were levied against the Baptists for the purpose of building a meeting-house for the Congregational church. The people of the Baptist church were additionally taxed to support the Congregational preacher, a tax which they courageously resisted. Two of the tax assessors recognized the Baptist Ebenezer Smith as the first settled minister.[22] However, the third assessor brought charges against the other two and won in court. The Congregationalists of Hampshire County, Massachusetts then ordained Jacob Sherwin and gave him the privilege of being the first minister of the town.

At this point the Baptists of Ashfield did something that plowed into the soil and planted some more of the seeds of the Revolution. On May 25, 1768, rejecting the prejudices of the exemption application, they brought a memorial petition to the statewide General Assembly at Boston asking for relief on the grounds of **liberty**. The petition read in part:

> We are brought under distressful circumstances, which, we think, cry aloud for some pity to be shown our ability, and have yearly our money taken away from us, or our land sold at an out-cry to support their worship. We pray therefore...**free us and our lands** from paying any more towards the maintenance of the minister, or finishing the meeting-house, of a society we do not belong unto, we being willing to pay our Province tax and all others, except the above mentioned.

The reaction to the above petition was most obnoxious. The session of the Assembly, under the direction of Colonel Israel Williams, enacted a new tax law for Ashfield, which took the power of taxation out the hands of the inhabitants and placed into the hands of "proprietors." The "proprietors" were owners of huge tracts of land in Hampshire County. By contrast, the "inhabitants" were those who owned 50 acres or less. As Backus stated, "This was done under the same influence which has since involved the nation in blood and confusion."[23]

This same Assembly, that had resolved to send letters to the rest of the colonies, requesting a union to fight against TAXATION WITHOUT REPRESENTATION, voted to enact the same tyranny on its own people. Or was it that they did not believe the Baptists to be a part of "we the people?" The Assembly dissolved after passing the oppressive law.

The religious state of affairs in Massachusetts now came to the doorstep of John Adams, who had begun his legal career in earnest.

In 1765, Adams began to publish a series of newspaper essays entitled, "Dissertation on Canon and Feudal Law." The news of the Stamp Act became public before he had finished his essays. Therefore, Adams used his final essay as a forum to attack the Stamp Act. The town of Braintree selected John Adams to write a protest against the Stamp Act. John hesitated but was assured by his cousin, Sam Adams, that it would bring him some notoriety in Boston. John was less sure. In his diary he poured out his anguish. John complained that to become a successful lawyer, he first had to deal with poverty with few friends to help him, and now the Stamp Act conspired to ruin his law practice.

But the protest of John Adams did bring him some notoriety. Samuel Adams invited John to attend the meetings of the Caucus Club. The Caucus Club was a political organization in which Deacon Adams was a member. John was impressed with the meeting as well as the smoky room, which was filled with future revolutionaries.

On February 22, 1766, the British House of Commons repealed the Stamp Act. It took three months for the news to reach Boston. The repeal of the Stamp Act reduced much of the anti-parliament fever in Boston. Adams was able to return to his law practice and his budding political career. In 1769 Adams won his first notable case. He succeeded in having charges of wine smuggling dropped against a notable client. Who was Adam's client? It was none other than the richest man in Boston, John Hancock.

Nathaniel Green, pastor of the Baptist church at Leicester and Charlton, was arrested in 1769 for refusing to pay civil taxes. He brought suit against the assessor at Leicester, Seth Washburn. Green claimed exemption as the "settled" minister. John Adams argued against Green claiming he was not a legitimate Baptist since he was not in fellowship with a certain Calvinistic association. Adams lost that case but the temporary victory for the Baptists did nothing to alleviate the tyranny.

On March 5, 1770, both Adams' career and America's direction changed in an instant. Three men were killed and eight were wounded in the square by the townhouse in Boston. They were part of an angry mob that threatened and shoved at a small group of British soldiers. The event was known as the Boston "Massacre" and the blood spilt on the square mingled with the forgotten faded bloodstains of Obadiah Holmes.

* * *

Ebenezer Smith, the Baptist pastor at Ashfield, received no notice that his land was sold. 20 acres went to his enemy, Elijah Wells, and to add insult the land included his home and the burial ground of the Baptist people he pastored. To add further insult the land was sold for a mere *thirty-five shillings*. It was part of the April 4, 1770, sale of 398 acres owned by the Baptists of Ashfield. It was sold for payment of their delinquent ministerial taxes. Wells wasted no time. He claimed his land within 24 hours of the sale and uprooted the apple orchard, cutting the trees to pieces. When news of the cruelty was made public, especially the travesty of the graveyard, a public meeting was held to change the survey.

At the meeting Mr. Elijah Wells made a mock sermon, making fun of the "enthusiastic" tone of the Baptists.[24] Such was the fruit of the 1768 judgment of the Assembly. For several years, the Assembly was petitioned for relief, but to no avail.

When it became obvious that the oppressive judgment of 1768 was not going to be reversed the Baptists of Boston, in an act of extraordinary courage, took out an ad in the *Boston Evening Post*. On August 20, 1770 they asked for written testimonials of all acts of oppression or persecution toward them be written and presented to the Warren Baptist Association in a meeting to be held in September.

*　*　*

John Adams was called upon to defend Captain Preston, the leader of the regiment involved in the Boston "Massacre." The trial began on September 7, and mainly because of Adams brilliant defense, Preston was cleared of all charges. Immediately the trial for the soldiers began. The prejudices against these young men were more than overwhelming, yet Adams defended them with unmatched skill. In his closing arguments for their defense Adams said, "We find in the rules laid down by the greatest English judges...we are to look upon it as more beneficial that many guilty persons should escape unpunished than one innocent person should suffer. The reason is because **it is of more importance to the community that innocence should be protected than it is that guilt should be punished.**"[25]

*　*　*

When the meeting of the Warren Baptist Association was held at Bellingham on September 11, 1770, a resolution was passed stating that if no relief from Massachusetts could be found concerning ministerial taxes, then the Baptists of New England would petition the King of England for help. That resolution moved the politicians in Boston to urge the Baptists to instead draw up another memorial and have it signed by the preachers of Baptist churches at Boston and Haverhill. This they did and it was delivered to the Assembly at Cambridge in October of 1770.

Now the battle shifted to the ground of public opinion and the *Boston Evening Post* of October 29 published an opinion stating that the "Baptists had complained without ANY JUST REASON AT ALL."

But the Baptist committee, appointed at Bellingham had received written testimonies from these places: one from Ashfield, two from Princeton, two from Berwick, one from Douglass, one from Colchester (New Hampshire), and three from Enfield (Connecticut). They appointed Elder John Davis of the Second Baptist church of Boston, to answer the article that appeared in the Evening Post. He answered in the *Massachusetts Gazette* of December 27, citing the actions of Massachusetts concerning Ashfield. John Davis wrote the article and signed after his name: A BAPTIST.[26]

The persecuting spirit of the *standing order* was alive and well as evidenced in a letter answering Elder Davis that appeared in the *Boston Evening Post* of January 7, 1771:

> There is a little upstart gentleman, [Davis] lately settled in town, who calls himself A BAPTIST; and the youth discovers a most insufferable arrogance and self-sufficiency...I very much suspect, that he is one of those deluded young men, who are employed to defame and blacken the colonies, and this town and province in particular....I am of the same persuasion in religion with this young hero, and I cannot say what the General Assembly could do for the Baptists in general, or the Ashfield brethren in particular, that they have not done...And I believe this is the opinion of the Baptists in general, and of all others but enthusiastical bigots.–A CATHOLIC BAPTIST.[27]

That was shameful stuff, but not the end of it, as a "minister from Deerfield" wrote to the *Gazette* on February 7, "It is a very common observation among us, that the people called Separate Baptist in these parts will not stick at any false representations to serve their purpose."[28]

What was the motive of the *standing order* of Massachusetts through this endless misinformation and run-around? James Manning told the truth about the whole matter in a letter to Samuel Stennett:

> I am told, some of our brethren are now in jail for ministerial rates, and... many are forcibly despoiled of their property for the same purpose. [They] ... are afraid if they relax the secular arm, their tenets have not merit enough and a sufficient foundation to stand.[29]

The Massachusetts General Assembly met at Cambridge in mid February, 1771 and summarily dismissed the memorial and prayer of the Baptists for relief from the religious tax. But the public debate had reached the ears of republican sympathizers and the shift in the thought of all the colonies was well underway.

Yea verily, those were not the only ears to hear the debate, for in October of that same year, a royal bomb was dropped on Massachusetts. King George III had disannulled the law that took the property of the

Baptists of Ashfield! Dr. Samuel Stennett, Baptist pastor from London, had taken a memorial to His Majesty's Commissioners for "disallowance of the said act," that is, the Ashfield tax act.[30] The Commissioners agreed with Stennett and the King granted the request. This unexpected blessing was a triumph for the Baptists but was an everlasting shame and embarrassment to the Massachusetts General Assembly; an embarrassment their members would not set aside. And revenge was in the air.

It has been said many times that the converts of the Great Awakening chose believer's baptism in great numbers due to their study and fidelity to the Bible, but there has been little discussion of divinely used human instruments in this work. May we then focus for a moment on a little lady named Rachel Thurber Scammon.

Rachel married a Massachusetts man in 1720 and settled with him on the Piscataqua River. She was a *baptized believer*, coming from Rehoboth. For 40 years she tried to convert others to Christ and to convince the saved of the scriptural truth of believer's baptism. In that 40 years she gained one convert. But she would often voice her belief and prayer that one day God would raise up a church of Christian Baptists in Stratham.

Somewhere along the timeline of her life, she happened upon a copy of the book *Plain Discourse upon Baptism* by Norcott. She had a burning desire to reprint the book, reasoning that if other people could read it they would turn to Christ; and the saved would follow Him in believer's baptism. She went to a printer in Boston to invest in the printing of it and behold, when she inquired she found the printer already had 110 copies of that very book!

Wasting no time, Mrs. Scammon purchased all of them and began to distribute them. They were scattered strategically by the Holy Ghost throughout Massachusetts. Then, Rachel Thurber Scammon died.

But a young physician named Samuel Shepard made a house call in Stratham. While there, he saw a book, "*Plain Discourse upon Baptism* by

Norcott. After reading it he became convinced that infant baptism was invalid and that believer's baptism was indeed Bible baptism. He did not know any Baptist people but he began to discuss the book with any who would care to listen and in so doing created a stir among the people of the Stratham, Brentwood and Nottingham areas. The distribution of the book also stirred the spirit of Eliphaleth Smith, who was the *standing order* minister of the Deerfield Congregational parish. Eliphaleth came under conviction as he preached on the need to follow Christ and believe, and be baptized.

In due time, Elder Hezekiah Smith, famed pastor of the Baptist church in Haverhill was called to Deerfield and in a monumental act of courage, the Congregational preacher Eliphaleth Smith and thirteen members of the Deerfield parish were buried in believer's baptism. Within the week, 24 more were immersed.

Among those baptized was Dr. Samuel Shepard, whom God called to the gospel ministry. The good doctor was ordained September 25, 1771, as pastor of the Baptist church at *Stratham* in answer to Rachel Thurber Scammon's 40 year prayer.

*　*　*

As Chileab Smith lay in his bed the morning of November 8, 1771, an officer of Hampshire County broke into his home and served him with a warrant for his arrest. Smith was charged with, of all things, *counterfeiting*. The authorities ransacked his house, shop, barn, fields, and belongings, looking for evidence. His small apple orchard, like his son's, was uprooted and burned and his dry goods stolen. Even though no evidence was found, Chileab Smith was shackled and transported to jail. It was clear that his real crime against Massachusetts was that he was a "principle member of the Baptist church," in Ashfield, in the County of Hampshire. After the Ashfield tax revolt and the illegal pilfering of the land owned by the church members, Massachusetts found their latest whipping boy and took the aged Smith into custody.

On February 14, 1772, from prison in Ashfield, Massachusetts, Chileab Smith wrote his testimony to Isaac Backus entitled, *The Sword of Oppression in the Land of Freedom.* He said, "I trust you have had some information how our substance has been forced from us, our lands sold at a out-cry, our apple trees torn up and cut to pieces...the slanderous reports that rang in our case like a storm...especially against our elder...and [they] would pull...him down."[31] Smith went to jail, losing much of his substance for the winter and much of his property sold off— all this in vengeance for pioneering the town and raising up the hated Baptist church, not to mention the hated Baptist preacher.

In the end the Ashfield oppression was stopped when Governor Hutchinson, in fear of alienating a growing Baptist constituency, investigated the matter. He sponsored new legislation that made reparations to the Baptists of Ashfield. That was finally accomplished in 1774.

Nathan Crosby of the Chelmsford Baptist church was arrested in Concord, Massachusetts on January 26, 1773 for refusing to pay ministerial taxes. He was sick in bed when they hauled him away. He eventually paid the tax but sued to get it back. The assessor was found at fault but not the collector so they could not receive their money back. This action finally caused some backlash in the community.[32]

Similar examples of state/church tyranny were being played out simultaneously throughout Massachusetts: in Haverhill in 1765, in Montague in 1769, in Berwick, and in Goreham. Of others oppressed by their Christian brothers in New England the list is legion. These are a sampling from the Backus papers of those suffering in New England:

William Hooper was imprisoned in 1749 for refusing to pay the minister taxes in Titicutt.

In 1750, the Baptist church in Thompson, and pastor Witman Jacobs were stripped of property for religious taxes.

1769, Samuel Harvey of Montague brought a test case before the state of Massachusetts, suing the tax assessors for "distraining" (confiscating or seizing) livestock. Not only did Harvey lose the case, the court called for the certificates of the rest of the church and fined and confiscated personal property for the payment of ministerial taxes.

Nathaniel Green Jr. had his livestock seized in 1771 to pay ministerial taxes.

In 1773 Simon Dakin was forced to move his church from Phillips Patent to Northeast Town, New York due to "mobs and riots."

The Massachusetts exempting law expired one more time in 1774. Another was made which required the Baptists to give a four-pence for a copy of it, in order to clear themselves. Four-pence was three-pence sterling, the same tax laid on a pound of tea. Many Americans gave their lives to be freed of the exact tax our Baptist forefathers were forced to pay.[33]

*   *   *

The word *excitement* is not strong enough to describe the mood of the patriots just prior to the meeting of the first Continental Congress. The Congress was slated for September 5 through October 26, 1774 in Philadelphia. The "Boston Tea Party" had taken place the previous year, and the English Parliament had passed what the colonists began to call the Intolerable Acts. In response, a convention of 56 delegates from 12 of the 13 colonies was gathered to organize fiscal and trade policy and form some kind of organized response to the tyranny of mother England.

John Gano and William Van Horne were in Providence in September for the 1774 commencement at Brown. Those two met with Hezekiah Smith and James Manning to discuss the idea of sending a delegation to Philadelphia to meet with some faction of the new national congress to address the plight of the Baptists suffering at the hand of the Massachusetts *standing order*. At their insistence, Isaac Backus was called upon to lead that delegation. The idea was approved unanimously at the Warren Association meeting on September 14, and the purpose was set "to see if something might not be done to obtain and secure our religious liberties beyond what we have yet enjoyed."[34]

Funds were gathered for Isaac to purchase a horse, and the hero of religious liberty set off for Philadelphia. Elders Gano and Manning, immediately departed for New York with their families to meet their father-in-law for a visit and later join Backus on his way.

Backus left on Monday, September 26, and was immediately joined by William Van Horne to begin a two-week ride. They preached nearly every night in different churches and gathered a small entourage as they progressed west and then south. In Norwich, Connecticut, old Chileab Smith, persecuted brother from Ashfield, joined them.[35]

When they arrived in Elizabethtown, New York, on October 3, they united with John Gano and Hezekiah Smith and on October 5, their delegation crossed the Delaware into Pennsylvania. Backus had a very refreshing time with his friend, Samuel Jones of Pennepek. Finally, an exhausted Backus rode into Philadelphia on October 8, 1774.

The city was flush with men and horses and peddlers replete with ideas and paraphernalia. The streets were busy with swiftly moving importance and underneath all of it, there was patriotism mingled with intrigue, for there were plenty of British loyalists in Philadelphia.

There was great care given to the delegates.

The Carpenters' Association, a group of well-known patriots, gave the use of their hall and, perhaps more importantly, their library. The directors of the Library Company of Philadelphia provided books. The citizens of Philadelphia welcomed the delegates with open arms and their diaries recorded the sumptuous food and hospitality.

On Tuesday October 11, the Baptist delegation met with Robert Settle Jones, Robert Moulder and the Quakers, Israel and James Pemberton and Joseph Fox. Backus wrote in his diary, "They advised us not to address the Congress as a body at present, but to seek for a conference with the Massachusetts delegates together with some other members who were known to be friends to religious liberty."[36] This was arranged. Meanwhile the Philadelphia Baptist Association assembled and Isaac Backus read the letter from the Warren Association. The report filled the minds of the Philadelphia brethren with sorrow. The Philadelphia Association then organized a grievance committee of their own.[37]

On Friday evening, October 14, the Baptist delegation met in Carpenters Hall with the delegates from Massachusetts to the Congress: Thomas Cushing, Samuel Adams, John Adams, and Robert Treat Paine. Also present were James Kinzie of New Jersey; Stephen Hopkins and Samuel Ward of Rhode Island; Joseph Galloway, and Thomas Miflin of Pennsylvania; and a few other members of Congress. Additionally, Mr. Rhodes, the mayor of Philadelphia and the Quaker, Israel Pemberton were in attendance. The conference began with James Manning reading the memorial grievance.* In part, he read:

> It may now be asked—What is the liberty desired? The answer is; as the kingdom of Christ is not of this world, and religion is a concern between God and the soul with which no human authority can intermeddle; consistently with the principles of Christianity, and according to the dictates of Protestantism, we claim and expect the liberty of worshipping God according to our consciences, not being obliged to support a ministry we cannot attend, whilst we deem ourselves as faithful subjects. These we have an undoubted right to, as men, as Christians, and by charter as inhabitants of Massachusetts Bay.[38]

What happened next we will allow Isaac Backus to narrate in his own words:

> In answer to [Mr. Manning] Mr. John Adams made a long speech, & Mr. Samuel another, both of whom said, "There is indeed an ecclesiastical establishment in our province, but a very slender one, hardly to called an establishment."
>
> And they exerted all their art for near an hour in trying to represent that we had no cause to complain of encroachment upon our religious liberties at all. As soon as they would permit we brought up facts to the contrary, which they tried to take off the edge of, but could not. Then they shifted their plea, and asserted that our general court was clear of blame, and had always been ready to hear our complaints and grant all reasonable help, whatever might be done by executive officers. Mr. S. Adams and Mr. Paine spent near an hour more upon this plea.
>
> When they stopped, I told them I was very sorry to have any accusation to bring against the government I belonged to, which I would gladly serve to the utmost of my power; but I must say that facts proved the contrary to their plea; and gave a short relation of our legislatures treatment of Ashfield, **which was very puzzling to them.***
>
> In their plea, Mr. S. Adams tried to represent that regular Baptists were easy among us, and more than once insinuated that these com-

---

* See Appendix E for the entire memorial.

* It was highly unlikely that the religious war in Massachusetts was "puzzling" to any of them.

plaints came from **enthusiasts** who made a merit of suffering persecution and also that enemies to these colonies had a hand therein. And Mr. Paine said there was nothing of conscience in the matter; **twas only a contention about paying a little money**, and also that we would not be neighborly to let them know who we were which was all they wanted, and then they would readily exempt us. In answer to which I told them, they might call it **enthusiasm** or what they please, but I freely own before all these gentlemen, that it is absolutely a point of conscience with me; for **I cannot give in the certificates they require, without implicitly acknowledging that power in man which I believe belongs only to God.**

This shocked them considerably and Mr. Cushing said it quite altered the state of the case, for if it was a point of conscience he had nothing to answer to that. And the conference of about four hours continuance closed with their promising to do what they could for our relief. Tho to deter us from thinking of their coming upon equal footing as to religion with us, Mr. John Adams once said, "We might as well expect a change in the solar system, as to expect they would give up their establishment;" and at another time said, "We might as soon expect that they would submit to the Port Bill, to the Regulating bill, and Murder bill as to give up that establishment." Which yet he and his friend in the beginning of their pleas called a very slender thing.[39]

Had Backus had the manuscript in front of him, he might have reminded Adams of his own words defending the soldiers of the Boston massacre, seeing now he was defending a government that had without hesitation punished a large number of innocent men. Backus concluded by commenting, "Such absurdities does religious tyranny produce in great men!"[40]

Here Isaac Backus was in his finest hour. However, New England would not get the true story of this pivot of history for quite some time. And what a tempest stirred after he returned to Massachusetts.

No sooner had Congress dismissed than Robert Treat Paine, who referred to the oppression of the Baptists as a contention about "paying a little money" started a rumor that "Mr. Backus went to Philadelphia in order to prevent the colonies from uniting in defense of their liberties." James Manning wrote a friend after the Philadelphia meeting that revealed the anger of Ezra Stiles' reaction to Backus and the Philadelphia and Warren association appeal for religious liberty.

Stiles had said:

The Baptists had made an application to the Congress against the Massachusetts Bay; the delegates of that Province expected only a private interview with some of the Baptists; but instead of that, when they came they found a house full, etc.; They were attacked and treated in the most rude and abusive manner;...the Baptists pretended they were oppressed, but, after all their endeavors, they could only complain of a poor fourpence; they were ashamed of their errand, and gave up their point, except one or two impudent fellows, who, with Israel Pemberton, abused them in a most scandalous manner; all the delegates present were surprised at and ashamed of them and thought they complained without the least foundation, etc. *When we have the power in our hands we will remember them.*[41]

Thus, a rumor was circulated that Backus went to Philadelphia to try to break the union of the colonies in their struggle to defend their privileges. This unveils the tremendous quandary that engulfed Isaac Backus. To be opposed to his government meant he must be attached to England. He fought long and hard to demonstrate otherwise. He resisted the option to petition the King of England and when it happened in the case of Ashfield, he was not the instigator.

The rumor of nonpatriotism persisted and Isaac Backus was forced to write a public remonstrance against the claims of Paine and Stiles.

A December 9, 1774 letter from Hezekiah Smith, to James Manning describes the attitude of the provincial congress toward Backus:

Will you believe that the old persecuting spirit remained in Massachusetts Bay? Mr. Joseph Haynes was one of the Provincial Congress, when Mr. Backus sent in a petition in behalf of the Baptists, to see if they would use their influence to free them from their oppressions, etc.; who gave me the following account in substance.—

Mr. Hancock, the President, informed the House that Mr. Backus had sent in a petition to them in behalf of the Baptists, etc., and with a smile, asked them whether it should be read, or not? One answered: No, we are no ecclesiastical court, and have no business with it. Another, another, and another agreed to the same. At last, one of the members got up and said, "This is very extraordinary, that we should pay no regard to a denomination who" in the place where he lived "were as good members of society as any, and were equally engaged with others in the defense of their civil liberties," and motioned to have it read. Another seconded the motion. Upon which it was read.

Then it was proposed to know whether they should act upon it or not. It was generally agreed not to do anything about it, but throw it out; when Mr. Adams got up and said, he was apprehensive, if they threw it out, it might cause a division among the provinces; and it was his advice to do something with it. Upon which, they chose a committee to sit upon it; who reported that they were no ecclesiastical court, and had no business with it. If Baptists were oppressed, they might apply to the General Court.[42]

Who hath believed our report? And so the tyranny marched on.

Backus' letter to the Congress of Massachusetts said among other things:

It seems that the two main rights which all America are contending for at this day, are—Not to be taxed where they are not represented, and—to have their causes tried by unbiased judges. And the Baptist churches in this province as heartily unite with their countrymen in this cause, as any denomination in the land; and are as ready to exert all their abilities to defend it. Yet only because they have thought it to be their duty to claim an equal title to these rights with their neighbors, they have repeatedly been accused of evil attempts against the general welfare of the colony; therefore, we have thought it expedient to lay a brief statement of the case before this assembly.

Those who ministered about holy things and at God's altar in the Jewish church, partook of and lived upon the things which were freely offered there; *Even so hath the Lord ordained that they who preach the Gospel, should live of the Gospel.* And such communications are called sacrifices to God more than once in the New Testament. And why may not civil rulers appoint and enforce with the sword, any other sacrifice as well as this?

Civil rulers ought undoubtedly to be nursing fathers to the church, by reproof, exhortation, and their own good and liberal example, as well as to protect and defend her against injustice and oppression; but the very notion of taxing all to support any religious denomination, tends to bias its professors against all such as dissent from it; and so to deprive them of having unbiased judges; for every man knows that so much money as he can get from a neighbor to support his minister, so much he saves to himself.

Backus then gave the reasons for the Baptist delegation and remonstrance to the Continental Congress in Philadelphia. Its purpose was not to divide the colonies, but to lay the foundation for "the future welfare of our country." He closed the letter by mentioning the ministerial tax and the three pence tax on the Baptists for the certificates. The certificate tax was the same amount that "all America are alarmed at," which of course, any American could avoid by not drinking tea, but that tax on the Baptists if avoided, would lead to arrest and fines. Backus ended by writing, "We dare not render that homage to any earthly power, we are determined not to pay, we cannot give in the certificates you require, we claim charter rights [and] **liberty** of conscience."[43] But the letter remained a dead file on the table of convenience.

*   *   *

Eight more Baptist churches were formed in New England just before the Revolutionary War and others were formed during the war. Backus wrote, "Neither could the ill treatment which the Baptists had met with, turn them against their country, who had oppressed them; for though they had received relief from the British court, several times, yet they saw that this was done for political ends, by men who now aimed to bring all America into bondage."[44]

*   *   *

On a tour of Pennsylvania and surrounding states, James Manning touched base in Virginia, and wrote to John Ryland, "Virginia is still in a flame, and hundreds are hopefully turning to God."[45]

Our narrative shall visit that flame presently.

Timeline for the Struggle for Liberty in Virginia

1768   June, the formal commencement of legal persecution against the Separate Baptists by the Virginia Courts.

1768   Elijah Craig imprisoned in Culpeper, Virginia

1769   Samuel Harriss ordained by Shubal Stearns

1769   December 2, the Lower Spotsylvania Church was constituted

1769   Ketockton, Virginia Association of Regular Baptists attempts union with the Sandy Creek Separate Association

1769   October, James Ireland baptized by Samuel Harriss

1769   November, James Ireland imprisoned in Culpeper, Virginia

1769   December 4, Blue Run Baptist Church was founded, Elijah Craig ordained pastor.

1770   John Picket imprisoned in Fauquier, Virginia

1770   November, Lewis Craig was ordained pastor of the Upper Spotsylvania Baptist Church

1771   The "Battle of Petitions" began in earnest in Virginia

1771   Goochland Baptist church was founded

The first Separate Baptist church, north of the James River was formed in 1767, the second in 1769. At the beginning of 1770, there were two Separate Baptist Churches in Virginia north of the James River, and about four, on the south side. Within 24 months, the Virginia Baptist churches had 1,355 members. By 1773, they had increased their numbers to 34 churches with 3,195 members. And more converts were about to be pressed into the kingdom of God.

CHAPTER TEN
Blood on the Walls in Old Virginia

If a creed of faith, established by law, was ever so short, and ever so true; if I believed the whole of it with all my heart—should I subscribe to it before a magistrate, in order to get indulgence, preferment, or even protection—I should be guilty of a species of idolatry, by acknowledging a power, that the Head of the Church, Jesus Christ, has never appointed.[1]*–John Leland.*

In 1765, Patrick Henry introduced his five Resolutions into the Virginia Assembly. These were introduced as a protest to the Stamp Act. Amidst cries of "Treason," "Treason," Henry said, "Tarquin and Caesar had each his Brutus, Charles I his Cromwell and George III may profit by their example." The Virginia assembly rejected Henry's doctrine of "no taxation without representation." Just ten years later, the assembly voted to sever her ties to Great Britain. What was the cause of Virginia's transformation? –J.R.B.

Unrighteous laws were conspiracies against God and the best interests of our race, plots of the Evil One, to be met by exposure and stern resistance, disobedience to which was loyalty to Jehovah.—William Cathcart

James Ireland rode north out of the woods from the church on Samuel Harriss' homestead. He was a commissioned man now, baptized by the "comet of Virginia," Harriss himself. Ireland was armed not only with the credentials of 11 Baptist preachers, but most importantly, with the power and approval of God Almighty.

As he approached Culpeper, he was drawn off the road into a meadow where the little jailhouse stood. He had done this one month earlier on his way to Sandy Creek, mesmerized by the familiarity of the place occasioned by a dream. In his dream Ireland was imprisoned for the cause of Christ. It was a dream with odd details of reality, with the Lord somehow speaking to his heart. All of that was to be fulfilled in short order.

Ireland was a Scotsman, brought to America as a very young man. He was an accomplished violinist and made his friends among the nonchalant sinners of Culpeper county. He came under violent conviction of the Holy Ghost through the preaching ministry of John Picket, the Separate Baptist, and was born again.

Picket preached publicly in Culpeper and raised the ire of Mr. Ireland's parson. This Anglican invited Bro. Picket to argue with him in the parish church, and in the course of the debate, James Ireland saw the arguments of the Baptists as more scriptural. He decided to unite with them.

We have previously related Ireland's baptism and subsequent ordination, now "Jamey" was called upon to suffer for the Gospel of Jesus.

Back at Smith's Creek, the little band of believers waited for the return of Jamey. That group of believers included Anderson Moffett. Moffet was evidently converted under the preaching of John Picket. He and Ireland and John Koontz were about to plant Smith's Creek Baptist Church. They were anticipating baptism which now could be performed by Samuel Harriss. They traveled with Ireland to unite with another number of the converts of John Picket.

On their journey Ireland preached in the home of Colonel Pugh and lodged at Colonel Tipton's. He was invited by Colonel Tipton to lodge on his way home to Smith's Creek, but Ireland declined saying with a smile, "I expect to be a prisoner in Culpeper jail by then." At the constitutional service, Harriss baptized 20-30 converts.

On the return trip to Carter's Run, James Ireland stopped at the home of Captain Thomas McClanahan to preach. The Anglican parson was there to greet him. He disputed with the parson, who steadfastly warned him he would be jailed if he preached the next day at the house of one Mr. Manifa.[2] That night Ireland wrestled with the Lord over the prospects of going to jail. He knew that other Baptist preachers were suffering in Virginia. He knew he would probably not escape the wrath of the magistrates, and he knew the consequences of imprisonment.

The next day as James Ireland was preparing to preach Mr. Manifa said, "Sir, you may expect to be taken up today. If you preach, a certain fine (I am told) will be imposed upon you, and so much upon each individual that will attend your preaching, as well as a fine of twenty pounds on me for granting you my house to preach in." If Ireland believed Mr. Manifa would now back pedal he was mistaken, for Mr. Manifa squared his shoulders and said, "DO NOT FLINCH YOUR DUTY."

No such flinching occurred as Ireland, with a large crowd gathering, directed some men to move a large wood table into the woods. When he had located the boundary line for Mr. Manifa's property, he had the table placed straddling the line. With a courageous and burning heart, he ascended onto the table and preached with power.

When he concluded and began a prayer, rustling was heard in the woods and voices, and as Mr. Ireland concluded his prayer he was yanked from the table by his collar and chained. The magistrates were breaking up the revival and demanded, "What are you doing with such a conventicle of people and who gave you authority?"

Ireland replied, "He that was the author of the Gospel, had a right to send forth whom he had qualified to dispense it." This answer was met with swearing and awful oaths from the persecutors. But the mood of that scene was changing. In their fury the magistrates did not realize the outrage in the crowd around them. For in the Culpeper woods, possibly for the first time in American history, the people—we the people— were tiring of tyranny. At once the crowd, who was the next target for either imprisonment or fines, began to speak out. In protest, many vehemently declared they would go to jail as well, "if a man could be incarcerated simply for preaching the Gospel."[3] Nevertheless Jamey Ireland was hauled away.

The hearing for Ireland was a farce. The court declared they would hear no more of his *"vile, pernicious, abhorrible, detestable, abominable, diabolical doctrines, for they were naucious to the whole court."*[4] He was led away to the Culpeper gaol.

It was a joyous occasion for the wicked crowd outside the jail that night as the enemies of James Ireland hurled rocks, sticks, and a variety of insults and curses at the window. In the night he began to waver, and to think of some way to escape the embarrassments and suffering of the blockhouse. Maybe he was wrong maybe his friends, who were now among his enemies, were right about the *baptized believers*, maybe he **was** *vile, pernicious, abhorrible, detestable,* even *abominable.* In his distress he began to read his Bible. As he read, the Holy Spirit of God gave him this verse:

> But rise, and stand upon thy feet: for I have appeared unto thee for this purpose, to make thee a minister and a witness both of these things which thou hast seen, and of those things in the which I will appear unto thee.—Acts 26:16

So James Ireland determined he would rise and minister, and witness. Repeating the example of his other Virginia brethren, he stood the next day to his feet and began to preach. He later recorded:

> When I would be preaching through the little iron grate, the wicked and persecutors would ride up at a gallop among my hearers, until I have seen persons of respectability under their horses feet; clubs have been shaken over the heads of other individuals, with threatenings if ever they attended there again; whilst the poor Negroes have been stripped and subjected to stripes, and myself threatened with being shut up in total darkness if ever I presumed to preach to the people again.[5]

Ireland was in Culpeper jail for five long months. One dreary night, gunpowder was placed under the jailhouse where he slept. It was detonated, and caused great damage to the jail but not to Ireland. While he preached or prayed, ungodly men "made their water in his face."[6] Sometime after he survived the gunpowder a fire was set to suffocate him. It failed. To these trials were added the obnoxious things of ridicule, inconvenience and scorn; the keeper of the prison even charged money for Ireland's friends to visit him. Yet after a period of time in testimony of that which God had evidently called him, he began to sign his letters, "from my Palace in Culpeper."

Some time during his imprisonment, a very large Irish man, Roman Catholic by birth, joined Ireland in the small prison. He was loud, profane, and a drunkard. Through a series of kind acts, first by offering his bed, then by giving him food, and then by prayers and supplications, this man became a friend. Mr. Ireland won him to Christ.

It became commonplace for Ireland's enemies to reach in and grab the preacher, choking him as he tried to preach. Inevitably, the big

Irishman could no longer stand that wicked behavior. When a ruffian reached in the big Irishman reached out and grabbed the man by the hair, pulling him in a most uncomfortable way against the grates. This happened a few times, with the big Irishman saying he should take care of the preacher if the preacher would not take care of himself. Not so miraculously, the attempts of the ruffians to grab the preacher ceased. God give us more big Irishmen![7]

When his trial date was officially set in March of 1770, James Ireland paid a bond and was released. With Elijah Craig, he rode to Williamsburg, with a petition signed by a number of distinguished citizens of Culpeper and Fredrick Counties. The petition was a request to Lord Bottetourt, governor of Virginia for permission to build a meeting-house and to preach the Gospel without molestation. A real miracle was required to win approval for the petition. The signature of an Anglican minister, in agreement with the request was required. By the grace of God the minister gave his approval and the petition for a BAPTIST MEETING-HOUSE was granted in writing, by the governor of Virginia!

James Ireland now had the ammunition he needed to win the day in Culpeper court. It happened that when the petition was presented to the court and Mr. Ireland's attorney pointed out that the conventicle acts in England had been repealed under William III, the bench began to evacuate, leaving Ireland without his accusers. Liberty was given James Ireland, and the door of **liberty** for the Baptists of Virginia began to open.

*　　*　　*

When the Separate Baptists began their ministry in earnest in Virginia they were met immediately with violent opposition. In the early days, they answered their opposition with eloquence and a calculated aggressiveness. It was written of Joseph Murphy of the famed Murphy boys, "He was not easily daunted by the opposition of his foes. When, on a certain occasion, he was apprehended and tried for daring to preach without a warrant from the establishment, he defended himself in the most manly and Christian-like style. Such was the impression produced on the minds of those who heard him, that he was at once acquitted and set at liberty."[8]

Dozens and then hundreds of men surrendered to preach the Gospel. Again, those preachers met their opposition with eloquence and aggressiveness.

James B. Taylor wrote about Richard Major:

> In Fauquier County, the officer with a warrant from Capt. Scott, attempted to take him, but providentially failed. At Bull Run there were warrants against him, and a mob, with clubs, rose to assist the execution of them; but here again they failed of their design, chiefly by means of **the Davises**, usually called the *giants*; those stout brothers had been prevailed on to oppose him; but after they had heard him preach, they became well affected toward him, and threatened to chastise any that should disturb him. In Fauquier, the mob was very outrageous, but did no mischief, though his friends feared they would have pulled him to pieces.
>
> A certain man, whose wife had been baptized by Mr. Major, determined to kill him on sight, and went to meeting for that purpose. He sat down in hearing, intending to catch at some obnoxious expression, which might fall from the preacher, and under that pretence, to attack him. But God produced a different result; for the man, instead of executing his design, became so convicted that he could not keep on his feet; and was afterwards baptized by the man he intended to murder.[9]

*   *   *

The scene of baptism in Virginia became as dramatic and convicting as it was in North Carolina. Samuel Harriss began to baptize in 1769. We have related his first baptisms, administered to James Ireland and then to some multitudes between the James and the Rappahannock rivers. 17-year-old John Taylor witnessed one such baptism taking place sometime in 1770:

> The first baptizing, in South River, the noted Samuel Harriss traveled two hundred miles to administer this solemn ordinance—and an awfully solemn thing it was indeed to thousands, who had never witnessed such a scene before. I think fifty-three were baptized on that day; several young ministers came with Harris—Elijah Craig, John Wal-

Waller, with a number of others. The rite of laying on of hands, on the newly baptized, was practiced by the Baptists in those days...about four ministers went together, each one laid his right hand on the head of the dedicated person...the prayers were with great solemnity and fervour.

On the same day, the church at South River was constituted under the style of a separate Baptist church. I was there the last two days, an ill grown boy about seventeen years old, and though I would not then have been a Baptist for all the world, was a close and serious observer of all that past. I happened to be near when their Church Covenant was read; I remember concluding no man on earth could comply with it.[10]

In 1770, elders William Webber and Joseph Anthony found themselves imprisoned in Chesterfield jail three months. It was probably at this time that Patrick Henry emerged on the scene in defense of the Baptist people, as Semple said, Henry, "being always the friend of liberty."[11]

There is an account of Patrick Henry defending Lewis and Joseph Craig and Aaron Bledsoe. It was recorded by the western pioneer preacher John Mason Peck, in his *Baptist Memorial of 1845*:

About the year 1770, when three Baptist ministers were to be tried at Fredericksburg, Virginia, Patrick Henry, the great orator, rode some sixty miles to attend the trial, and unexpectedly entered the court room as the indictment was being read. He listened as they were accused "of preaching the gospel of the Son of God," contrary to Virginia law. When the indictment had been read, and the prosecuting attorney opened the case, Patrick Henry, having glanced over the indictment, arose and addressed the court:

"May it please your worships, I think I heard read by the prosecutor, as I entered this house, the paper I hold in my hand. If I have rightly understood, the king's attorney of this colony has framed an indictment for the purpose of arraigning and punishing by imprisonment three inoffensive men, before the bar of this court, for a crime of great magnitude, as disturbers of the peace. May it please the court, what did I hear read? Did I hear it distinctly, or was it a mistake of my own? Did I hear an expression as if a crime, that these men are charged with? What! 'For preaching the gospel of the Son of God.'"

Swinging the indictment three times around his head, he exclaimed: "Great God! May it please your worships, in a day like this, when truth is about to burst its fetters, when mankind are about to be aroused to claim their natural and inalienable rights; when the yoke of oppression that has reached the wilderness of America, and the unnatural alliance of ecclesiastical and civil power are about to be dissolved — at such a period, when liberty — liberty of conscience is about to awake from her slumberings and inquire into the reason of such charges as I find exhibited here today in this indictment! If I am not deceived, according to the contents of this paper I now hold in my hand these men are accused of preaching the gospel of the Son of God! GREAT GOD!!" And with similar words, thrice repeated, he inquired: "What law have they violated?"

The judge could endure it no longer, and bade the sheriff dismiss those men.[12]

The above account has been questioned even though many reputable men such as Belcher, Little, and S. H. Ford have repeated it.

Even if Henry's speech did not happen, it was becoming apparent that Henry, James Madison, and especially Thomas Jefferson began to have a deep respect for the Baptists in Virginia. None of their suffering was done in a corner away from view, and these three American Patriots, destined for immortality in the American mind would witness this spectacle of tyranny and outrage. It would change their ideals of human government and turn the wheels of republicanism.

As Semple wrote, "persecution really promoted their cause: their preachers had now become numerous, and some of them were men of considerable talents. Many of the leading men favored them."[13]

Elsewhere in Virginia, William Marshall was holding forth the word of God. No relation to Daniel Marshall, William was a Regular Baptist, preaching at a struggling church at South River, Virginia. He was not yet ordained when he preached sometime in the winter of 1770 to a large crowd by the old meeting-house. In that crowd, in the snow, John Taylor heard the call of God:

The people were so numerous, that the preacher went to this stump about six feet from the end of the meeting-house, that all might hear; the vast concourse of people took their stand in the snow, and while I was amusing and diverting myself, ranging through the company to see the exercise of the people, I had got in near the stump, when this Thomas Buck broke out into a flood of tears and a loud cry for mercy; he being my old playmate, I stared at him for a while with awful wonder, and just at that time my eye and ear were caught by the preaching, the Minister was treating on the awful scene of judgment, and while he dropt these words; "Oh rocks, fall on me, Oh mountains cover me from the face of him that sitteth on the throne, and from the wrath of the Lamb, for the great day of his wrath is come, and who shall be able to stand." I felt the whole sentence dart through my whole soul, with as much sensibility as an electric shock could be felt.

With my mind instantly opened to understand and love all the preacher said afterwards, though every word condemned me. I loved the messenger that brought the awful tidings... From that moment, every thing belonging to religion bore an entire new aspect to me.[14]

John Taylor was baptized by James Ireland sometime in 1772.

The first meeting of the General Association of the Separate Baptists of Virginia was held at the Blue Run meeting-house in May of 1771. Virginia was now ablaze with the fervency of revival and the Regular Baptists were catching the heat from the Separate Baptist fire. Chappawamsic Baptist Church was constituted by David Thomas and became a mother church of several Virginia Baptist churches including the Potomach Baptist Church, which was constituted in Stafford County, March 26, 1771. Chappawamsic Church yielded some of the best preachers of the Virginia revival, men such as Jeremiah Moore, and Daniel and William Fristoe. These men were instrumental in forming the Ketockton Association of Virginia Baptists.

As David Thomas had suffered for the cause of Christ in Virginia, so did his spiritual sons William and Daniel Fristoe. The ruggedness of the Virginia Baptists became a thing of legend as the frontiersmen, new Christians, handled violent situations the only way they knew. Note this example concerning a preaching meeting of William Fristoe related by David Cummins:

One remarkable example of this involved a gang of around forty men led by Robert Ashby, who entered the meeting-house with the purpose of disrupting the meeting. Some stout fellows at the door took Ashby by the neck and heels and threw him out. This resulted in a melee involving the whole multitude in a knockdown-drag out battle. Soon after this incident, Ashby cut his knee, which became badly infected so that the joint opened and his leg hung only by the hamstrings. On his sickbed he would not let anyone touch him, and he desired preaching, but when the preacher began preaching, he would stop his ears and desire the preacher to stop because he could not stand to hear it. He died a horrible death of great suffering. So strongly did this impress the people that God had intervened that it put a damper on the mischievous designs of others to disrupt the Baptist meetings.[15]

Baptism was always an event. The young Daniel Fristoe, recently ordained as a "Regular" Baptist in the new Ketockton Association wrote this astounding testimony in his diary:

Saturday, June 15, 1771. This day I began to act as an ordained minister, and never before was such manifest appearances of God's working and devil's raging at one time and in one place. About 2,000 people came together. Many offered for baptism, 13 of which were judged worthy.

As we stood by the water the people were weeping and crying in a most extraordinary manner; and others cursing and swearing and acting like men possessed. In the midst of this, a tree tumbled down, being overloaded with people who had climbed up to see baptism administered; the coming down of that tree occasioned the adjacent trees to fall also being loaded in the same manner; but none were hurt.

When the ordinance was administered and I had laid hands on the parties baptized, we sang those charming words of Dr. Watts, "Come we that fear the Lord." The multitude sang and wept and smiled in tears, holding up their hands and countenances toward heaven in such a manner as I had not seen before.

In going home I turned to look at the people who remained by the water side and saw some screaming on the ground, some wringing their hands, and some in ecstasies of joy, some praying; others cursing and swearing and exceedingly outrageous. We have seen strange things today.[16]

*   *   *

When we left the Separate Baptist revival in chapter eight, the *baptized believers* had been routed and run out of North Carolina by Governor Tryon. The sons of thunder had laid their beloved father, Shubal Stearns to rest. Stearns was in heaven but his legacy was alive.

In old Virginia, Samuel Harriss was hard at the task. Now being referred to as the "Apostle of Virginia" the Episcopalian churchmen had lost their patience with him. One of their clergy wrote:

> The zealots for the old order were greatly embarrassed: "If'," say they, we permit them to go on, our Church must come to nothing, and yet, if we punish them, as far as can stretch the law, it seems not to deter them; for they preach through prison windows, in spite of our endeavours to prevent it.[17]

Harriss wielded a double-edged sword of love and hate wherever he went. We need not be confused by Colonel Harriss' brutal reception for our Saviour told us on many occasions that the cross would produce both sweet salvation and savage sword. While preaching in Orange County Harriss was pulled from the platform and dragged by his hair through the crowd by a man named Healey. A fight ensued with some of the Colonel's rugged converts defending him. Harris was dragged by one leg as his enemies kicked him. On one occasion his sermon so incited a man that he rushed to the place he was preaching and knocked Harriss down. Yes, pelting scorn was his lot as it was with Whitefield. Harris was jailed briefly in Hillsborough, North Carolina, apparently going there to preach to *the Regulators* in prison during the height of that crisis. But he was not jailed in Virginia which almost defied nature. Robert Semple speculated that Harriss was "tempered in some degree peculiar to himself, perhaps his bold, noble, yet humble manner, dismayed the ferocious spirits of the opposers of religion."[18]

There can be no doubt that this noble servant Samuel Harriss, was one of the greatest of all American evangelists with the possible exception of George Whitefield or Abraham Marshall. Harriss would preach to an individual as an audience or a crowd of thousands. His messages were consistent with the long line of American adherents to *experimental religion*, that is, he preached often "Ye must be Born Again." Note the zeal and compassion of Harriss and his disciple, James Ireland, in this testimony of Lynn Alderson:

> The party, consisting of Mary, Nellie, and Mr. Alderson, set out for the place of meeting. It was at a private house, and they were cordially welcomed.
>
> They were favorably impressed with the manners and appearance of Mr. Ireland and Col. Harriss. Mr. Ireland was still young and a man of handsome appearance, with a keen eye and a pleasant countenance. Col. Harriss moved with the air of one accustomed to the best society, and his manners were extremely engaging.
>
> The text on which the minister spoke was from John iii, 3. We will not attempt to give here a synopsis, but suffice it to say, that the speaker dwelt on the need of a new birth and pressed home upon his hearers the necessity of seeking this great change, if they were conscious it had never taken place within themselves. During the sermon, Lynn listened with deep attention. He felt his inmost being stirred by the preacher's words, and he longed for this great change, but how was it to be wrought in him?
>
> Near the close of the sermon, the minister affectionately and solemnly urged upon all who were not conscious of a renewed nature to begin that day; nay, that moment, to seek the Lord. Would any begin now? If so, let them kneel quietly at their places, and God's people would pray for them. The hymn was given out, "let me but hear my Savior say" and during the singing several knelt. Lynn's mind was in a turmoil. Thoughts and feelings, which he had alternately encouraged and suppressed, rushed upon him with overwhelming force. The hymn was ended. A solemn pause ensued. Col. Harriss arose. "Now is the accepted time; now is the day of salvation," he said in solemn, thrilling tones. Lynn felt that the words were addressed to him personally. Conscience stricken he rose slowly and knelt at his seat.
>
> "God be thanked," ejaculated good Mr. Ireland. "Let us pray," and Col. Harriss led the petitions of this humble little band with a beauty of diction, fervor, and a simplicity that Lynn thought he had never heard equaled.
>
> Mr. Ireland made his way to Lynn. "My dear friend, I pray God that you may have grace to persevere."[19]

John Weatherford, a convert of Samuel Harriss, was now called upon by God to suffer for Jesus' name. Introduced in chapter seven, Weatherford ought to be a revered memory to every American. He was born sometime near 1740 of Presbyterian parents. After the salvation of his soul he began a serious study of the scriptures in earnestness to grow in grace. He found in the New Testament a plain claim for believer's baptism. This surprised him. So much was his surprise that he believed perhaps, he may have had an inaccurate edition of the word of God.[20] But he found his copy to be accurate. In his confusion Weatherford sought out his family pastor, the great Presbyterian preacher David Rice, in an attempt to understand the reformed view of infant baptism. At the close of their conversation Rice said, "I perceive you will be a Baptist, go, and the Lord be with you." So at the age of 19, John Weatherford was immersed.

He had an immediate burden for souls for those without Christ in this world, and began to preach in meetings in the same fashion as his mentor Samuel Harriss. In 1773 his ministry took him to Chesterfield, Virginia where the long arm of Colonel Cary cast him into the Chesterfield jail for preaching without a license. J. B. Taylor recounts for us the now famous scene outside the gaol at Chesterfield:

> He preached at the door of the prison as long as allowed the privilege; when refused that, he preached through the grates of the window. But such determined opposition did he meet, that an effort was made by his enemies to put a stop to that also. For this purpose they built an outer wall, or fence, above the grate; but Weatherford devised means to overcome the obstacle. A handkerchief, by the congregation, was to be raised on a pole, above the wall, as a signal that the people were ready to hear. His voice being very strong, he could throw it beyond these impediments, and convey the words of life and salvation to the listening crowd.[21]

Weatherford's imprisonment wrote another testimony in *crimson red*. Angry men rode on horseback trying to disperse the crowd, other malcontents walked through the crowd beating on drums, trying to distract the crowd. But nothing could deter Weatherford from delivering his message and most frustrating to his enemies, any opposition to his sermon seemed to bring greater results in the hearts of his hearers. In a rage, **the constables lacerated his wrists with knives** as he beckoned to the crowd, and the blood of John Weatherford ran down the walls and even fell upon the congregation that came to hear him preach.[22]

Dozens were saved during his five-month imprisonment, and against horrid obstacles, nine were baptized in a night service, the fruit of his preaching from the prison. Then quite suddenly, his fine was paid and he was released. In his latter years, Providence would reveal who paid the fine.

There were other Baptist preachers who were incarcerated and used the Chesterfield jail as a pulpit: William Webber, Joseph Anthony, Augustine Easton, John Tanner, Jeremiah Walker and David Tinsley. Some of these men were whipped, all were fined, and none ceased to teach and preach Christ.[23]

"Swearing Jack" Waller was not silent during this great revival; indeed, one of the greatest threats to the Episcopalian establishment in Virginia at this time was John Waller. Waller was from the famous family of English Wallers, and displayed an early talent for speaking and quick wit. His early aim in life was to be an attorney, which led him to sit on juries and fraternize with the emerging Virginia political ranks. His salvation changed the course of his life. Waller suffered more for the cause of Christ and liberty than any other preacher of his generation. He spent more than 113 days in four different jails in Virginia during the great revival there. Lewis Peyton Little, relates this incident concerning Waller:

> While he was singing, the parson of the Parish would keep **running the end of his horse whip in his mouth**, laying his whip across the hymn book, etc. When done singing he proceeded to prayer. In it he was violently jerked off the stage; they caught him by the back part of his neck, beat his head against the ground, sometimes up, sometimes down, they carried him through a gate that stood some considerable distance, where a gentleman gave him something **not less than twenty lashes with his horse whip**. After they carried him through a long lane, they stopped in order for him to dispute with the parson. The parson came up, gave him abominable ill language, and away he went with his clerk and one more. Then Brother Waller was released, went

back singing praise to God, mounted the stage and preached with a great deal of liberty.[24]

In August 1771 in Middlesex County, elders John Waller, William Webber, with Mr. Wofford, Robert Ware, Richard Falkner, and James Greenwood, were arrested while preaching. They were dragged from the stand, and commandeered to the jail at Urbanna. Wofford was severely whipped, his blood staining the ground of Virginia. He was commanded to leave the county. Around the same time six other Baptists were apprehended and placed in the jail at Caroline—Lewis Craig, John Burns, John Young, Edward Herndon, James Goodrick, and Bartholomew Cheming. They also preached through the grated windows of their prisons to crowds who gathered around.[*]

On August 12, 1771, John Waller sent out a letter from Urbanna Prison, Middlesex County, Virginia to a friend. This letter testifies of the persecution of 12 Baptists in prison at one time, their response to the treatment they received from the jailers, and the ultimate triumph of their labours:

> Dear Brother in the Lord:
>
> At a meeting which was held at Brother McCain's, in this county, last Saturday, while William Webber was addressing the congregation from James 2:18, there came running toward him, in a most furious rage, Captain James Montague, a magistrate of the county, followed by the parson of the parish and several others who seemed greatly exasperated. The magistrate and another took hold of Brother Webber, and dragging him from the stage, delivered him with Brother Wafford, Robert Ware, Richard Falkner, James Greenwood, and myself, into custody, and commanded that we should be brought before him for trial.
>
> Brother Wafford was severely scourged, and Brother Henry Street received one lash from one of the persecutors, who was prevented from proceeding to further violence by his companions; to be short, I may inform you that we were carried before the above mentioned magistrate, who with the parson and some others, carried us one by

---

[*] The father of the great American statesman, Henry Clay, was also imprisoned, as a Baptist minister, in Virginia.

one into a room and examined our pockets and wallets for firearms, etc., charging us with carrying on a mutiny against the authority of the land. Finding none, we were asked if we had license to preach in this county; and learning we had not, it was required of us to give bond and security not to preach anymore in the county, which we modestly refused to do, whereupon after dismissing Brother Wafford, with a charge to make his escape out of the county by twelve o'clock the next day on pain of imprisonment, and dismissing Brother Falkner, the rest of us were delivered to the sheriff and sent to close jail, with a charge not to allow us to walk in the air until court day. Blessed be God, the sheriff and jailer have treated us with as much kindness as could be expected from strangers. May the Lord reward them for it! Yesterday we had a large number of people hear us preach; and, among others, many of the great ones of the land, who behaved well while one of us discoursed on the new birth. We find the Lord gracious and kind to us beyond expression in our afflictions. We cannot tell how long we shall be kept in bonds; we therefore beseech, dear brother, that you and the church supplicate night and day for us, our benefactors, and our persecutors.

I have also to inform you that six of our brethren are confined in Caroline jail, viz. Brethren Lewis Craig, John Burrus, John Young, Edward Herndon, James Goodrick, and Bartholomew Cheming. The most dreadful threatenings are raised in the neighboring counties against the Lord's faithful and humble followers. Excuse haste. Adieu. –John Waller [25]

Even in the midst of these storms the following churches were constituted: Lower King and Queen Baptist Church on October 17, 1772-Robert Ware, Pastor; Glebe Landing Baptist Church-James Greenwood, Pastor; Exol Baptist Church and Piscataway Baptist Churches. These were young churches pastored by very young men and their inspirational leader was John Waller.

The Episcopalians began to behave in desperate fashion with the parsons attending Baptist meetings trying to disrupt and cast doubt on the Baptist revival. The dilemma the *black hats* of Virginia faced was the uncanny way the Baptists increased when efforts were made to thwart them. There was simply an overwhelming tide of God's power in this heaven-sent awakening much like an unrelenting storm on a mission to destroy a coastline. Waller and his followers were decried as *wolves in sheep's clothing,* which Waller logically refuted by declaring, "wolves are not persecuted by sheep and no sheep ever destroyed wolves."[26] Robert Baylor Semple explained one reason for the Episcopalian decline:

> Their communion (Church of England) was often polluted by the admission of known drunkards, gaesters, swearers, and revelers: that even their clergy, learned as they were, had never learned the most essential doctrine of revelation, the indispensable necessity of the new birth, or being born again.[27]

Lewis P. Little, along with James B. Taylor, recorded the procession of these religious prisoners. In their biographies of the Virginia Baptist preachers were recorded details of at least 43 preachers deprived of liberty, property, dignity, and their blood. These brave voices fought manfully onward to astounding successes. Semple, giving a typical testimony of them, mentions "James Greenwood and William Loval, preached regularly while in prison, and to much purpose."[28]

By 1772 Baptist preachers had so often been imprisoned, fined, whipped and flogged that the political leaders of the emerging republican movement began to speak out against the persecution. James Madison said: That diabolical, hell-conceived principle of persecution rages among some, and, to their eternal infamy the clergy can furnish their quota of imps for such purposes."[29]

As the brethren in New England were sent on a demonic paper chase for *certificates,* Virginia Baptists were forced to obtain *licenses* from the state. The establishment of Congregationalism in New England was an American institution, that was evil enough, but the establishment in Virginia was British, and the founders of our nation began to realize that its power and authority on American soil had to go. With the Baptists and other dissenters, the *licenses* were granted to prove themselves worthy ministers in the eyes of the state. They insisted they did not need a *license* to preach the word of God. In the beginning they insisted they be treated as dissenters with the same privileges of their fellow sufferers in England. Now they began to make a case not just for toleration, but for LIBERTY, the freedom to worship and exercise their religion without state approval, licenses or tax.

To prove their cause was a matter of conviction, they continued to preach Christ no matter what pressure was placed upon them. Their judges, in the beginning, would find no ground to agree. To the time of the writings of Robert Baylor Semple in 1810, the Baptists could testify that the bigoted actions of Virginia judges and magistrates were "against the natural laws of liberty."[30] Semple, himself a Virginia lawyer, wrote:

> The Virginia statute books had no law which decreed imprisonment for unauthorized preaching, but there was a law requiring the licensing of dissenting preachers. Most Separate Baptist preachers, deriving their authority from God alone, rejected this law. They considered it no business of the state who should or should not preach and they would not apply for licenses.[31]

The patriots grew first to admire, and then gain strength from the Baptist rejection of the Episcopacy of England.

On Sunday March 13, 1774, Piscataway Baptist Church in Essex County, Virginia was constituted. Providence scheduled this church, just seven miles from Tappahannock, for a rough beginning. There were preachers from the Virginia Separate Baptist Association and a good crowd gathered for the reading of the covenant and the fellowship, and the food. No one knew that a warrant was issued to apprehend all the Baptist preachers that were in attendance at the constituting of the church![32] Arrested were John Waller, John Shackleford, Peter Ware and Evison Lewis.

Lewis was released because it could not be confirmed that he had actually preached inside the county's jurisdiction but the others were sent to prison. They commenced to preach during the week, give counsel, hold prayer meetings, and read the Bible constantly. David L. Cummins preserved the court record for us:

> The court record of Essex County, Virginia, records the proceedings of the twenty-first day of March. in the year of our Lord 1774: John Waller, Robert Ware, and John Shackleford, Anabaptist preachers being brought before this court by a warrant from under the hand of Archibald Ritchie, Gent., for preaching and expounding the Scriptures contrary to law, and confessing the fact, it is ordered that they

and each of them do give security in the sum of twenty pounds with two good and sufficient securities in the sum of ten pounds each for their behavior twelve months: And it is also ordered that they be forthwith committed to the gaol of this county there to remain the aforesaid term, unless they give such security.[33]

Ware had been here before, suffering wrongfully; he gave the security money and was released. Shackleford did the same and was also released. How can we fault these men, weary in the battle and longing for home and health? But John Waller just could not bring himself to accept bond. So he lay in an obnoxious cell, this time doubting himself, and tired of the harassment. As usual, loud, intoxicated Virginians were assigned as cellmates. He tolerated the gaol for 14 days and then, uncharacteristically, allowed bond to be paid. By the grace of God, "Swearing Jack" Waller never returned to prison.

The brick courthouse building still stands in ancient testimony along Route 17. Only now, instead of a stilted testimony of a sad past, the building has been born again. It is now the location of the Beal's Memorial Baptist Church. This is one of our favorite turns of poetic justice, and it is the author's prayer that we may preserve this sacred place to show and remind and instruct our children.

Shubal Stearns baptized Noah Alden in 1754, the same year John Leland was born. Leland came into this life on May 14, 1754, born in the village of Grafton, west of Boston, Massachusetts. After a mischievous and sinful adolescence Leland was convicted of his sin and brought to Christ in early 1774. 25 years after the "Apostle Paul of the Backcountry" had baptized Noah Alden, Alden baptized John Leland.[34] Leland immediately began to preach the gospel. He soon migrated to the middle of the Separate Baptist revival in Virginia and met John Waller.

Waller and Leland became friends, and Leland, (although not ordained by Waller until much later, in 1787) began an evangelistic preaching ministry not unlike the celebrated Samuel Harriss. "The summary of his labours during the fifteen years of his ministry in Virginia is thus recorded, "3009 sermons preached, 700 persons baptized, and two churches formed, one of 300 members, and another of 200."[35] The number of his accomplishments would more than double when he returned to Massachusetts. Before he journeyed home to Massachusetts, he performed one of the most extraordinary acts in the history of the American republic.

Every plan of the Episcopalian establishment to stop Baptist growth in Virginia failed. By the end of 1774, there were 30 Separate Baptist Churches on the south side of the General Association of Virginia, and 24 churches on the north side. Semple wrote, "So favorable did their prospects appear, that towards the close of the year 1774, they began to entertain serious hopes, not only of obtaining liberty of conscience, but, of actually overturning the church establishment, from whence, all their oppressions had arisen."[36]

This stupefying change in the make-up of the Old Dominion defies the explanation of most secular historians. They fumble at explaining the transformation of the state to liberty, both religious and political. But Robert Semple had the best handle on it, "The Baptist preachers were without learning, without patronage, generally very poor, very plain in their dress, unrefined in their manners, and awkward in their address; all of which, by their enterprising zeal and unwearied perseverance, they ...turned to advantage..."[37]

The War for Independence was about to begin, and as Semple wrote:

The British yoke had now galled to the quick: and the Virginians, as having the most tender necks, were among the first to wince. Republican principles had gained much ground, and were fast advancing to superiority; the leading men on that side, viewed the established clergy, and established religion, as inseparable appendages of Monarchy...the Baptists were republicans from interest as well as principle; it was known that their influence was great among the common people; and the common people of every country are, more or less, republicans.[38]

With the full history of Virginia in view, it is not all that remarkable that four out of the first five presidents were Virginians. They had an understanding of the republic that far out-distanced their colleagues north of Mason's and Dixon's line.

*　　*　　*

Before we leave our narrative of Old Virginia yet another example of heroic testimony should be noted. It involves John Corbley. An almost omnipresent force for God in Virginia, Corbley was instrumental in birthing over 30 churches in West Virginia, Pennsylvania and Kentucky.

Corbley came to America sometime before 1769 and was converted and baptized under the ministry of John Garrard. He too, spent time in the Culpeper jail and suffered gladly for the cause of Christ. Sometime before 1771 John Corbley moved his family to the rugged Pennsylvania backcountry of Redstone. There he planted the Goshen Baptist Church,* along with at least two other infant churches, which became a part of the Ketockton Association. It was in Pennsylvania that the Corbley family, on a walk to their church, left their testimony in *crimson red*. Corbley described the ordeal in a letter to William Rogers, pastor of the Baptist church in Philadelphia:

> Not suspecting any danger, I walked behind 200 yards, with my Bible in my hand, meditating. As I was thus employed, all of a sudden, I was greatly alarmed with the frightful shrieks of my dear family before me. I immediately ran with all the speed I could, vainly hunting a club as I

---

* The Goshen Baptist Church is now known as the John Corbley Memorial Baptist Church.

ran, till I got within forty yards of them; my poor wife seeing me, cried to me to make my escape. An Indian ran up to shoot me. I had to strip, and by doing so outran him. My wife had a suckling child in her arms; this little infant they killed and scalped. They then struck my wife several times, but not getting her down, the Indian who aimed to shoot me ran to her, shot her through the body, and scalped her. My little boy, an only son, about six years old, they sunk the hatchet into his brains, and thus dispatched him. A daughter, besides the infant, they also killed and scalped.

Amidst it all, for what purpose, Jehovah only knows. I was redeemed from surrounding death. Oh, may I spend my life to the praise and glory of his grace, who worketh all things after the council of His own will.[39]

Events Leading to the Independence
of the American Republic

1760   ENFORCEMENT OF NAVIGATION LAWS BY COMMISSIONING OFFICERS TO ENTER ANY HOUSE AT ANY TIME TO SEARCH FOR SMUGGLED GOODS.

1764   MAY, THE STAMP ACT, PASSED BY PARLIAMENT

1765   OCTOBER, THE STAMP ACT "CONGRESS" MET IN NEW YORK. THE TERM "AMERICAN" BEGAN TO BE USED INSTEAD OF "COLONIST"

1770   MARCH 5, BOSTON MASSACRE

1771   MAY 16, THE BATTLE OF ALAMANCE, N. CAROLINA

1772   JUNE 16, THE BURNING OF THE BRITISH GASPEE

1773   DECEMBER 16, BOSTON TEA PARTY

1774   DECEMBER 5, RHODE ISLAND GENERAL ASSEMBLY ORDERS ALL CANNON AND AMMUNITION REMOVED FROM FORT GEORGE FOR USE IN THE REVOLUTION

1774   DEC. 14, N. HAMPSHIRE CAPTURES FT. WM. AND MARY

1775   APRIL 19, BATTLES OF LEXINGTON AND CONCORD

1775   MAY, AMERICAN VICTORY AT FORT TICONDEROGA

1775   JUNE 17, BATTLE OF BUNKER (BREEDS) HILL

1775   DECEMBER, AMERICAN DEFEAT AT QUEBEC

1776   MAY 4, RHODE ISLAND SEVERS TIES WITH ENGLAND

1776   JUNE 12, VIRGINIA SEVERS TIES WITH ENGLAND

1776   JULY 4, DECLARATION OF INDEPENDENCE SIGNED

1776   JULY 4, TICONDEROGA FALLS TO THE BRITISH

1776   OCTOBER, TEN THOUSAND NAME PETITION, VA.

1776   AUGUST 27, BATTLE OF LONG ISLAND

1776   SEPT. 15, AMERICAN VICTORY AT WHITE PLAINS, N.Y.

1776   DEC. 25, WASHINGTON CROSSES THE DELAWARE

1776   DEC. 26, AMERICAN VICTORY AT TRENTON, N. J.

1777   OCTOBER 17, THE SURRENDER OF BURGOYNE

1777   WINTER AT VALLEY FORGE,

1778   DEC., THE FALL OF SAVANNA AND AUGUSTA, GA.

1779   AMERICAN ATTACK REPULSED AT SAVANNA

1779   THE VIRGINIA ACT FOR RELIGIOUS LIBERTY WAS WRITTEN AND INTRODUCED INTO THE VIRGINIA LEGISLATURE BY THOMAS JEFFERSON, BUT NOT PASSED.

CHAPTER ELEVEN
The Forging of Baptist Nation

In 1770 there were but 97 Baptist churches. The 34 churches in the Philadelphia Association averaged 69 and two-thirds members each. If the same average held throughout the 97 churches there were less than 6,800 members in the land. By 1784, there were 471 churches with 35,101 members.

Nothing is more plain, than that the Almighty has set up the government of the United States in answer to the prayers of all the saints, down from the first proclamation of the gospel. The earth, at last, has helped the woman.[1]
—John Leland

In 1774, according to Howison, the Baptists increased on every side; if one preacher was imprisoned, ten arose to take his place; if one congregation was dispersed, a larger assembled on the next opportunity. The influence of the denomination was strong among the common people, and was beginning to be felt in high places. In two points they were distinguished: first, in their love of freedom; and, secondly, in their hatred of the church establishment.
—William Cathcart.

In January of 2002, our research took us to Lexington, Massachusetts, to "the green," the sight of the supposed first battle of the American Revolution. As we were familiar with the story of the ringing of the bell to call out the men and gather the American militia in the church house, we desired to view those historic places. However, we soon discovered the church house had been destroyed years earlier, and the bell had been removed to a farm nearby, with no certain knowledge of its whereabouts.[2] Instead of a number of militia assembling from the meeting-house, as reported by Jonas Clark, pastor of the Congregational church at Lexington, we are now informed by official National Park publications that the first defenders of our liberty filed out of the local tavern (no doubt some did) to take their stand. The tavern on Lexington green is of course, well preserved.

It is commonly reported that the first shots fired in the Revolutionary War were lobbed at Lexington green. But as we have discovered, this was not the case. Liberty began as a tax revolt, not just about tea or stamps, but concerning *forced tithes*. What began as a protest in New England, escalated into an exchange of lead at Alamance, North Carolina. Hostilities would eventually break out at Lexington and Concord; but first, a naval ambush engineered by the sons of America's original *baptized believers* would be executed along the New England coast.

The summer of 1772 in Providence, Rhode Island was filled with an angry heat. The British government intended to keep in check the industrious Rhode Islanders from shipping their goods without the stringent tariffs imposed upon their trade.

Not much action was taken to thwart the sea merchants until Lieutenant Duddingston took command of the armed schooner "Gaspee." The *Gaspee* and Duddingston created fear and intimidation as they began raids up and down the Rhode Island coast. Benjamin Andrew wrote, "The behavior of the Gaspee officers in Narragansett Bay, their illegal seizures, plundering expeditions on shore, and wanton manners in stopping and searching boats, illustrate the spirit of the king's hirelings in America at this time. At last the Rhode Islanders could endure it no longer."[3]

The *Gaspee* fired shells at any craft that would not submit to their search, and more often than not, seized goods; confiscating them along with fines and jail time to the ship owners. That is why the heat intensified in Providence and simmered into a patriot broil at the business of the irascible John Brown.

This John Brown was the great, great, grandson of Chad Brown, the first pastor of the first Baptist church in Providence, Rhode Island, the remnant of the group that Roger Williams tried to organize into a church. Brown was the third of the famous four Brown brothers of Providence; he was the uncle of Nicolas Brown, for whom Brown University is named. John Brown was a Baptist of the Obadiah Holmes variety, and Holmes' ancestry and courage was in his bloodline. He was one of the first Americans to establish trade with China and the East Indies. With the British disrupting the shipping lines for no greater reason than punitive fees, all of the merchants of the New England coast, including Brown, were being run into the ground. Late spring and early summer he brooded over what opportunity may arise to stop the rude intrusion of the *Gaspee* into the free commerce of Rhode Island.

That opportunity came on June 9, 1772. Rhode Island captain Thomas Lindsay set out from Newport, sailing to Providence. Lindsey knew that the *Gaspee* would attempt to stop and search his vessel and this time, something in him would not allow that to happen. So when the warning shot came routinely from the deck of the *Gaspee*, Lindsey refused to stop. There would be no search, no seizure—not this time.

Lindsey managed to make it around Namquit Point[*] with the Gaspee and Lietuenent Duddingston making a daring attempt to cut Lindsey off by sailing over the shallows of the point. As Divine Providence would have it, the *Gaspee* stuck fast in the shallows, at the mercy of low tide, and without the promise of high tide until 3:00 a.m. the next morning.

Captain Lindsey pushed hard to the port of Providence and immediately broke the news of the stranded and helpless *Gaspee* to the men and merchants of the harbor. He went first to John Brown, about 5:00 p.m. By sundown, a large crowd of men gathered at James Sabin's Inn.[**] Shot was prepared at the hearth. At 10:00 p.m., eight long boats were launched with muffled oars, and the first American naval assault against British forces began.

The Rhode Island Patriot flotilla was under the command of Captain Abraham Whipple, a ship captain in John Brown's merchant fleet. Rowing past Fox Point and Field's Point, they quietly drew along side the hated schooner.

---

[*] Now named Gaspee Point.
[**] Present day South Main and Planet Streets.

The battle was quick work. The guard on deck of the *Gaspee* cried out as the men of Providence boarded her, bringing Duddingston to the surface. He was quickly wounded and apprehended. In the next few moments, a fierce hand-to-hand fight took place, but the tired crew of the *Gaspee* was no match for the Patriots. Her crewmen were taken from the ship to the shore at Warwick and with that accomplished, Captain Whipple's men set fire to the *Gaspee*. She burned until her own powder blew her to pieces in Narragansett Bay. Benjamin Andrews wrote, "There would be much propriety in dating the Revolution from this daring act." On this we would concur.[4]

Although a great reward was offered by the King to any who could find Whipple's men, no one gave any information and even the identify of Whipple was kept secret for 67 years.[5]

The burning of the Gaspee had far reaching effects, not the least of which was the rekindling of patriot fire in the heart of John Adams.[6] Page Smith wrote, "An Englishman in the company reprobated the action of the burners of the *Gaspee* and John discovered in himself 'the old warmth, heat, violence, acrimony, bitterness, sharpness of...temper and expression...'" How ironic, that the sons of the renegade Baptists, so misunderstood by Adams, should help him get his bearings, and secure his place in history.

The Revolution was fought in two stages. There was a military war for political independence; and there was a spiritual war for religious independence. Those two stages began in the same place—Rhode Island. They ended in the same place—Virginia.

In March of 1775, Virginia's Revolutionary Convention met in Richmond at St. John's Church. The fervent Patrick Henry set his countrymen on fire with his now famous "Give me Liberty or Give me Death" speech, in which he called for war. The next month fighting broke out at Lexington and Concord, Massachusetts. The British were humiliated at Bunker (Breeds) Hill.

Word among the Baptists in New Jersey spread rapidly. Hopewell Baptist Church, the home of the late Isaac Eaton was about to experience a mighty visit from God. Eaton had gone on to his reward and the old Hopewell Academy was now Rhode Island College. It would soon become known as Brown University. The Hopewell Church, through its pastor, had been instrumental in educating the majority of those men of renown among the baptized preachers of the Gospel. The Revolutionary War now visited the church. William Cathcart describes the scene:

> Colonel Houghton was in the Hopewell Baptist meeting-house, at worship, when he received the first information of Concord and Lexington, and of the retreat of the British to Boston with such heavy loss. Stilling the breathless messenger, he sat quietly through the services, and when they were ended, he passed out, and mounting the great stone block in front of the meeting-house he beckoned to the people to stop. Men and women paused to hear, curious to know what so unusual a sequel to the service of the day could mean. At the first words a silence, stern as death, fell over all. The Sabbath quiet of the hour and of the place was deepened into a terrible solemnity. He told them all the story of the cowardly murder at Lexington by the royal troops; the heroic vengeance following hard upon it; the retreat of Percy; the gathering of the children of the Pilgrims around the beleaguered hills of Boston; then pausing, and looking over the silent throng, he said slowly, "Men of New Jersey, the red coats are murdering our brethren of New England! Who follows me to Boston?"
>
> And every man of that audience stepped out into line, and answered "I." There was not a coward nor a traitor in old Hopewell Baptist meeting-house that day.[7]

*   *   *

The war in the north began in earnest. Ethan Allen led the "Green Mountain Boys" to surprise the British at Fort Ticonderoga. This victory, however, was followed by the folly of Benedict Arnold at Quebec, as noted in chapter six, and Canada was virtually lost to the British. In fact, Ticonderoga had to be abandoned.

In Virginia, in August of 1775, the Baptists of the Old Dominion made public their loyalty to the American cause in both stages of the war. In a letter to the Virginia Convention stating their desire to have Elijah and Lewis Craig, Jeremiah Walker and John Williams preach the gospel to Continental soldiers, the Virginia Baptist Association wrote:

> After we had determined 'that in some Cases it was lawful to go to War, and also for us to make a Military resistance against Great Britain', ...our people were all left to act at discretion with respect to enlisting, without falling under the censure of our Community. And as some have enlisted, and many more likely so to do, who will have earnest desires for their ministers to preach to them during the campaign, we therefore delegate and appoint our well-beloved brethren in the ministry, Elijah Craig, Lewis Craig, Jeremiah Walker and John Williams to present this address and to petition you that they may have free liberty to preach to the troops at convenient times without molestation or abuse; and as we are conscious of their strong attachment to American liberty, as well as their soundness in the principles of the Christian religion, and great usefulness in the work of the ministry, we are willing they may come under your examination in any matters you may think requisite.
>
> We conclude with our earnest prayers to Almighty God for His Divine Blessing on your patriotic and laudable resolves, for the good of mankind and American freedom, and for the success of our Armies in Defense of our lives, liberties and properties. Amen.
>
> Sign'd by order and in behalf of the Association the 14th August, 1775.
>
> Sam'l Harriss, Moderator
> John Waller, Clerk[8]

Their request was granted.

*   *   *

Concerning both stages of the war, military and spiritual, the *baptized believers* fought on both fronts. They enthusiastically fought with

their countrymen for liberty, knowing that spiritually they were still en-
cumbered by denominational establishment laws existing in most states.

Concerning the second stage of the war, the spiritual stage, the true
sentiments of the *standing order* religious establishment in New England
were clear.

In 1775 Asa Hunt, then pastor of third Baptist church in Middleborough, presented a letter to Isaac Backus with the written testimony of
80 church members who were refusing to pay minister tax rates. They
put themselves in peril for the cause of liberty.

At the Boston election sermon of 1776, the Rev. Mr. West declared,
"The primitive Christians did not oppose the cruel persecutions that
were inflicted upon them by the heathen magistrates; they were few
compared with the heathen world, and for them to have attempted to
resist their enemies by force, would have been like a small parcel of
sheep endeavouring to oppose a large number of ravening wolves and
savage beasts of prey; the wise and prudent advice of our Saviour to
them was, 'When they persecute you in this city, flee ye to another.'"[9]
Read the above quote again if you do not understand what the *standing
order* preacher was saying. Mr. West was communicating that if some
fellow American was being persecuted for his faith, then he should
LEAVE! Such was the sentiment in New England. The patience of Isaac
Backus was wearing thin.

*   *   *

A military victory would be required for our forefathers to sever
their ties to Great Britain. The man prepared by God for this task was
George Washington.

Washington was christened an Anglican, and grew up a planter in
northern Virginia. He became a surveyor. Concerning those days, L. C.
Barnes wrote:

> The young man left the ruts of an old Virginia plantation, and flung
> himself into the wilderness as a surveyor of land among the new set-
> tlements. His first extant writings are journals of that work. He de-

scribes vividly how he roughed it, living with the settlers as they lived. We simply know three things. First, Washington surveyed those woods. Secondly, those woods were full of Baptists. Thirdly, Baptists in those days did not hide their light under a bushel."[10]

George Washington became a major in the Virginia Militia at the tender age of 19 and rode with Braddock into Pennsylvania four years later. It was there at Fort Duquesne in July of 1755, that Washington began his legendary service. At the battle, which quickly became a massacre of Braddock's British and militia forces, Washington was miraculously spared death. *Four musket shots passed through his coat and two horses were shot from under him.* This miracle was common knowledge among the Indians who fought in the battle. In Loyd Collins' *God and American Independence*, the legendary story is related by an old Indian chief, present at Fort Duquesne, who had come to pay his last respects to Washington:

Seeing you were under the special guardianship of the Great Spirit, we immediately ceased to fire at you. I am old and soon shall be gathered to the great council fire of my fathers in the land of shades, but ere I go, there is something bids me speak in the voice of prophecy. Listen! The Great Spirit protects that man [pointing at Washington], and guides his destinies—he will become the chief of nations, and a people yet unborn will hail him as the founder of a mighty empire. I am come to pay homage to the man who is the particular favorite of Heaven, and who can never die in battle.[11]

It must be noted that while on the battlefield during the French and Indian War, he could see the contempt of the British regular army against the American militia.[12] It irritated him as an *American* commander. As the swell of support for American independence began to gain momentum, he was decidedly patriot.

When Washington returned to Mount Vernon, Virginia after Braddock's defeat, he crossed the Shenandoah Valley in time to view the spectacle of the Separate Baptist revival and ensuing struggle for liberty. For 15 years he remained in Virginia as revival fires flamed the patriot ideal. During those years he lived in Mt. Vernon and had the oversight of his mother's farm near Fredericksburg. In addition to these duties he often traveled to Williamsburg as a member of the House of Burgesses.

Then came the cyclone of the Separate Baptist revival. We know that they organized their first church in upper Virginia in November of 1767. Excitement, conviction, and outrageous activity followed the Separate Baptists as documented in this volume. The result was nothing less than the transformation of the colony, all of which Washington was an eyewitness.

Our reader may recall that the first instance of actual imprisonment of Baptists in Virginia took place in Spotsylvania County in the Fredericksburg jail. "On the 4th of June, 1768, John Waller, Lewis Craig and James Childs and others, were seized by the sheriff, and haled before three magistrates." Barnes, again wrote:

Three days after their arrest Washington's diary reads, "[June] 7. Went up to Alexandria to meet the Attorney-General and returned with him, his Lady and Daughter, Miss Corbin and Jennifer. 8. At home with above company. 9. The Attorney and [company] went away."[13] [14]

The above mentioned attorney was none other than John Blair, who endorsed the Baptist cause which led to the release of those preachers from the Fredericksburg jail.* George Washington's diary recorded:

1768, June, 28. Set out for and reached Fredricksburg. Began to cut the upper part of my Timothy Meadow. 29. Rid round and examined the wheat fields there, which were fine. 30.Went to Mr. Bouchers, dined there and left Jackey Curtis - returned to Fredericksburg in the aftern."

Barnes commented further, "Did Washington on any of those days, hear "Swearing Jack" Waller, as he stood reverently and earnestly preaching through the barred window of Fredricksburg jail? We know not. But we do know that four days later one of the prisoners was re-

---

* Barnes wrote, "Did the visit of the great landed proprietor, the already famous and influential Col. Washington have anything to do with that release? It is of course possible."

leased to go with a plea for his brethren to the Governor at Williams-burg.[15] [16]

There can be no doubt that Washington was repeatedly crossing the path of the Separate Baptist Revival at its beginning. Without contro-versy Washington was well aware of Baptist doctrine, polity and struggle as he entered into the most demanding and important time of his life. On June 15, 1775, the Continental Congress appointed Washington Commander-in-Chief of the American Army. He was 43 years of age.

His first assignment was Boston, sent to bolster and lead an army of just over 14,000 men to stand against a British force of 11,000. Eight months later, the British sailed out of Boston never to return to Massa-chusetts.

At this early stage of the war, the commander-in-chief made it plain that a well-paid staff of Bible believing chaplains should support the American Army. Some Protestant chaplains and their families were treated with devil-inspired hatred. Some were bayoneted, shot or muti-lated. An examination of Headley's *Chaplains of the American Revolution* would be in order for any patriotic American. Our attention will be di-rected to the Baptist chaplains the most hated group of all. One of the first to serve was David Jones.

David Jones was born in New Castle, County, Delaware. His grandmother was the sister of Enoch and Abel Morgan, first generation Wales immigrants who came to America as Baptist refugees. They were part of the famous Welsh Tract Baptist Church. Jones' cousin was the Revolutionary era Abel Morgan under whom he studied theology. He was among the stellar students of the venerated Isaac Eaton, the founder of the Hopewell Academy, the first educational center for the Baptists in America.

Jones was ordained as pastor of the Freehold Baptist church, Mon-mouth County, New Jersey. He journeyed twice on missions to the American Indians.

During his pastorate at Freehold, he began public proclamations of the cause of independence and liberty. For this he was rejected at Free-hold and in April of 1775, he began his ministry at Great Valley Baptist Church in Chester County, Pennsylvania.

When the Continental Congress met in 1775, one order of business was to proclaim a public fast in seeking the will of God for our nation. The cause of liberty was not universally accepted, but such days of fasting about what course to pursue caused many Americans to focus on the present need. God's men provided the issues to think upon. David Jones was one such man of God. In 1775, he was commissioned to preach before the regimental command of Colonel Dewees and delivered his famed "Defensive War in a Just Cause Sinless." This message was printed and spread abroad, making it another great source of fuel upon the burning fires of patriotism.

When the war began, he was appointed chaplain in Col. St. Claires' regiment. He was everywhere during the war—under Horatio Gates and Mad Anthony Wayne. He was at the suffering of the Paoli massacre and with the Army at Valley Forge.

Lemuel Call Barnes wrote:

> Washington insisted on having good Chaplains, on having them adequately paid, and on having them diligently attend to their religious work. In 1776 he wrote to Congress. His 'Orderly Book' shows the following order as issued July 9, 1776. "The honorable Continental Congress having been pleased to allow a chaplain to each regiment, with the pay of thirty-three dollars and one third per month, the colonels or commanding officers of each are directed to procure chaplains accordingly, persons of good character and exemplary lives, and to see that all inferior officers and soldiers pay them a suitable respect. The blessing and protection of Heaven are at all times necessary, but especially so in times of public distress and danger. The General hopes and trusts, that every officer and man will endeavor so to live and act as becomes a Christian soldier, defending the dearest liberties and rites of his country."[17]

*   *   *

America began to declare herself independent. Not surprisingly, Rhode Island was first, severing ties with mother England on May 4, 1776. Directly on her heels was Virginia, on June 12.

In sharp contrast with the declaration of Rhode Island the religious sentiment of many New Englanders was illustrated in Pepperell, Massachusetts. On June 26, 1776,[18] six persons were ready to be baptized publicly. Samuel Fletcher of Chelmsford, Massachusetts along with Elder Isaiah Parker of Harvard, Massachusetts, arrived to preach and baptize. A church was forming around these new converts and news spread that the *baptized believers* were going to do some "dipping."

The chief thugs met the group of believers and mocked them, threatening them with bodily harm. They baptized a dog in derision. Undaunted, Fletcher and Parker moved the meeting to a home of a friend. The thugs were equally undaunted and met them with two more poor dogs and dipped them, threatening the church and the preachers with *death*. They finally found a place of secrecy and six souls finally followed the Lord in beautiful believer's baptism. News of this was published in Boston to the shame of the town of Pepperell.

Just a few days later, the Congress of the United States, upon a motion made by Richard Henry Lee of Virginia, signed the Declaration of Independence.

At least one Episcopalian clergyman knew the ramifications. Thomas Barton, missionary for the Propagation of the Gospel in Foreign Parts (Church of England) wrote:

> The Church of England has now no longer an existence in the United Colonies of America. I look upon the King's supremacy and the constitution of the Church of England to be so intimately blended together that whenever the supremacy is either suspended or abrogated the fences of the Church are then broken down, and its visibility is destroyed. On the second day of July the Congress at Philadelphia were pleased to declare the Colonies "Free and independent states." Upon this Declaration it was judged incompatible with the present policy that his Majesty's authority within the new States should any longer be recognized.[19]

In July 1776, a large contingency of British soldiers landed at Staten Island. General Howe, bolstered by a powerful fleet commanded by his brother, Sir Richard Howe, also landed. That group of British soldiers was comprised of the number that had left Boston in the face of Washington's bayonets. Those British regulars, along with 2,500 English; 8,000 German Hessians; and other reinforcements, made the British force at New York close to 25,000. Washington countered by placing 10,000 Continentals at New York City.

The Northern Campaign now flared. Gentleman Johnny Burgoyne's pursuit of American troops through the thickets of New York ended in a series of defeats. Herkimer at Oriskany, Stark at Bennington, and the advance of Schuyler with his ever-increasing American reinforcements brought Burgoyne's mission to a halt. This coupled with the field heroics of Morgan and Arnold forced Burgoyne to retreat. On October 17, just three months and thirteen days after the signing of the Declaration of Independence, Burgoyne surrendered to the American General Horatio Gates at Saratoga. The first stage of the war in the north was essentially over.

The British plan of attack now was to isolate New England from the rest of the North and invade the middle states to split the North from the South.

As Washington began to fortify New York he assigned John Gano, pastor of the Baptist church in New York City, to be Chaplain of the Army. As the British drove the American army off of Long Island, Gano's church was abandoned and he took to his duties on the field of battle. Barnes describes the withdrawal and subsequent battle:

> The Americans were forced northward from point to point after they left the town. Finally the chief stand was made near White Plains, and a sharp battle was fought, the thickest of it being on a bluff, called Chattertons Hill. J. T. Headley, the historian of Generals and battles, thus describes this conflict and Chaplain Gano's part in it; "As soon as (the British General) got his twelve or fifteen pieces of artillery within range he fired on the American lines. The heavy thunder rolling over the heights carried consternation into the ranks of the militia, and as a round shot struck one of their number, mangling him frightfully, the whole turned and fled. Colonel Harlet tried in vain to induce them to drag forward the field pieces so as to sweep the ascending columns, but he was able to man only one, and that so poorly that he was compelled to seize the drag ropes himself. But he was denied the gratification of using even his one gun for as it was being slowly trundled to the front, a ball from the enemies batteries struck the carriage, scattering the shot in every direction, and setting fire to a wad of

tow. In an instant the piece was abandoned in terror. Only one man had the courage to remain and tread out the fire and collect the shot. After a little time McDougal found only six hundred of the fifteen hundred, with which he commenced the fight left to sustain the shock of the whole British army...it was on such a sight as this the fearless chaplain gazed with a bursting heart. As he saw more than half the army fleeing from the sound of cannon-others abandoning their pieces without firing a shot, and a brave band of only six hundred manfully sustaining the whole conflict, he forgot himself, and distressed at the cowardice of his countrymen, and filled with chivalrous and patriotic sympathy for the little band that scorned to fly, he could not resist the strong desire to share their perils, and eagerly yet involuntarily pushed forward to the front."

Gano himself describes the event very modestly almost deprecatingly. "My station, in time of action, I knew to be among the surgeons; but in this battle, I, somehow got in the front of the regiment; yet I durst not quit my place, for fear of dampening the spirits of the soldiers, or of bringing on me an imputation of cowardice. Rather than do either, I chose to risk my fate. This circumstance gave an opportunity to the young officers of talking; and I believe it had a good effect on some of them."[20]

The British had too much firepower for the Continentals in New York. Washington left Manhattan Island and escaped through New Jersey into Pennsylvania in early December 1776.

Being reinforced from there, Washington made his famous crossing of the Delaware back into New Jersey late on Christmas night and totally surprised the Hessians at Trenton. He took over 1,000 German prisoners. Washington and his army skirted the British columns under Lord Cornwallis and wintered in Morristown in 1776-77.

In 1777, Congress limited the number of chaplains, but elevated their importance and rank. The resolution of Congress, May 27, 1777, read:

Resolved, that for the future, there be only one chaplain allowed in each brigade of the army and that such chaplain be appointed by Congress; That each brigade chaplain be allowed the same pay, rations and forage allowed to a colonel in said corps; That each brigadier-general be requested to nominate and recommend to Congress a proper person for chaplain to his brigade; and that they recommend none but such as are clergymen of experience, and established public character for piety, virtue and learning.

Barnes remarked, "In that day of established churches in many of the States, we shall expect to see most of the chaplains drawn from the ranks of these churches. If any Baptist [was] chosen it must be because of such preeminent fitness to minister in the patriot army as to out-weigh every ordinary and lower consideration." [21] In a list of 21 Briga-dier-chaplains more were Baptist than any other denomination. Five were Congregationalists. Three were Presbyterians. Two were Episcopa-lians. Six were Baptists. Those Baptist brigade chaplains were: Hezekiah Smith, William Vanhorn, Charles Thompson, John Gano, David Jones, and William Rogers. [22]

Time and space do not permit us to even outline the great accom-plishments of other Baptist preachers during the war such as Samuel Stillman, pastor of the First Baptist Church of Boston; Dr. Samuel Jones; or Edmund Lily.

Not until August of 1777, did the army spring back into action and it was defeated at Philadelphia leading to a demoralizing retreat into Val-ley Forge, 21 miles west into Pennsylvania. They were encouraged there by the ministry of David Jones.

1778 found the Americans chasing the British back into New York avoiding the traitorous actions of General Charles Lee. They took posi-tions at White Plains.

The cause of the Revolution was suffering in Rhode Island. Charles Thompson became pastor of the Baptist church at Warren. This church became a particular target for the British, for Elder Thompson became a chaplain and served faithfully for three years. On May 25, 1778, British troops marched to Warren, burned the meeting-house, burned the parsonage, and burned several private homes around the church. They also took Thompson prisoner.[23] Through some miracle of God, Thompson was released one month later, but the British occupation of Rhode Island continued for several years.

The same year 1778, a new plan of government for Massachusetts was proposed. This plan had a provision to re-enact the old taxing laws for support of *standing order* ministers. At first the plan failed. The *standing order* mouthpiece, Charles Chauncy, said that the failure of the passage of the ministerial tax was the reason for the Continental Army's defeat in Rhode Island.[24]

Obviously the prejudices were still in place in Massachusetts and on one occasion a constable came to remove Hezekiah Smith from his preaching station. Even after three years of service as chaplain in the Continental Army, Smith was deprived the respect of a patriot. Guild relates:

> The constable of a neighboring town, to which Dr. Smith had gone to preach, was "a weak and inferior-looking person," but he was full of self-importance; and armed with the authority of the law. He came to warn the stranger out of the place. But when he saw the imposing appearance of the [preacher] he was confused and stammered out: "I warn you—off God's earth."
> Smith replied, "My good sir, where shall I go to?"
> "Go anywhere. Go to the Isle of Shoals."[25]

This left Elder Smith perplexed but he remained at his post.

*   *   *

The Ten-thousand Name Petition, was presented to the first Virginia General Assembly session on October 16, 1776. The document consisted of 125 pages joined together with wax seals, and was signed by an unprecedented 10,000 Virginia citizens. It boldly and specifically asked that sects be exempted from legal taxation for the support of a state church. It was so effective it resulted in the suspension of Episcopal clerical salaries.

The way was made for a bill of rights and a constitution for Virginia. The Virginia Declaration of Rights contained a revision by James Madison which said, **"All men are equally entitled to the free exercise of religion."** This phrase replaced George Mason's, "all men should enjoy the fullest **toleration**[*] in the exercise of religion." The marriage of church and state in Virginia was irreparably damaged. Yet, it would take nine more years of debate, petition and legislative action to insure an unequivocal separation.

The state of religion in the Virginia of 1776 was low, due to the distraction of the war. Help was on the way, however. In September, John Leland married Sally Devine and immediately set out for Virginia.

*   *   *

Sometime in 1778, Elijah Baker, a Baptist preacher from Lunenburg County, Virginia was imprisoned for *disturbing the peace*. Baker had been converted in 1769 and was baptized that same year by Samuel Harriss. Baker set out to do God's work with what little he had and soon became a firebrand for Jesus Christ. He preached throughout eastern Virginia. J. B. Taylor wrote of him: "It is doubtful whether any other man in the state has been as successful within the same length of time."[26]

After establishing a number of churches on the mainland in Virginia, Baker sailed to the Eastern Shore, becoming the first Baptist preacher on the peninsula. He preached at the Episcopal Church in Northampton causing no small stir. His converts in that county were formed into a church of which he took the charge in 1778. It was from there he was jailed in the Accomack County gaol.

Elijah Baker, like so many before him, preached through the jail windows. Thomas Batston, heard him gladly, and became burdened for his home state of Delaware. He pressed upon Baker to join him in

---

[*] We trust our readers will comprehend the difference between liberty and toleration.

Delaware to do a work in that place. Obviously, Baker was in no position to accept the invitation, so Batston returned to Delaware to pray and hope. Morgan Edwards wrote, "The rude Virginians (in order to silence [Baker]) took him out of jail and put him on board a privateer, with orders to land him on any coast out of America. Here he was compelled to work, and for his refusing and praying and preaching and singing was ill-used. The privateer put him on board another ship, ...that other ship put him on board a third, and the third put him ashore."[27] Not knowing where he was, Baker made inquiry, and to his astonishment, found himself in Delaware. He went to the home of an amazed Thomas Batston and soon began preaching. Philip Hughes from Virginia joined him in the work. Through their labor, *ten churches were formed.*

*   *   *

The northern part of Virginia, known as the "Northern Neck," exists by the intrusion of the Rappahannock River into the Virginia piedmont. In 1778, the Holy Ghost through the ministry of Lewis Lunsford visited it.

Lunsford began preaching at the tender age of 19. He was so successful so quickly, that the people of the Northern Neck took to calling him "the boy wonderful." He was baptized by William Fristoe and began his work as an itinerant evangelist. His preaching birthed the Moritico Church in 1778 and he joined them as their pastor. J. B. Taylor paints a vivid picture of revival in that place:

> Once when he had preached an evening sermon in a barn, many having eaten the spices of the garden of the Lord, they seemed unwilling to close the service. After they had remained awhile longer there, and it was concluded they must part, they commenced singing in a body, in the yard of the dwelling-house. When Mr. Lunsford was on the steps, going into the house, he discovered the people stood still in the yard, unwilling to depart, and turning, addressed them once more, by the light of the candle; and, as rain falls freely in a wet season, so from this after-cloud showers soon fell, not only of grace, but of tears. He said, "I must confess, this is more like enthusiasm than anything I

have lately seen, but whether we be beside ourselves it is to God, or whether we be sober, it is for your cause."[28]

Lunsford was typical of the Virginia Baptists—he was an untiring labourer for God. He was in great demand riding hour upon hour just to be at an appointment. He said of his own life, "My life is a continual chase through the world."[29] Indeed, it was a chase after souls. It was said of Lunsford:

> [His] zeal in the Redeemer's cause has been to me among the most pleasing qualities I saw in him. His Lord well knew what had been given him to do, and seemed, out of peculiar love, to hasten him in his work, quickly to ripen him for heavenly rest. Being thus quickened, he spared no pains in seeking the salvation of souls, and the prosperity of the churches, labouring more abundantly with the people, at all seasons, not in a confined set of forms, but accommodating his seasons and places of meeting, his subjects and methods; he thus hoisted and managed his sails, so as to receive the advantage from any heavenly wind that blew. One evening, preaching from the text, "As for me, God forbid that I should sin in ceasing to pray for you; but I will teach you the good and the right way." He said, he was at a loss to know whether to preach or pray, and wished the people to signify which they chose. A number of weeping souls were soon on their knees, and he turned his preaching into praying.[30]

To say Lunsford was "tireless" would be an understatement. He crossed the rivers of Northern Virginia countless times including once by paddling across a three mile stretch using a small pail.

Inevitably, Lunsford and the established church were on a collision course. Semple wrote:

> A constable was sent with a warrant to arrest him. The constable, with more politeness than is usual on such occasions, waited until Mr. Lunsford had preached. His fascinating powers palsied the constable's hand. He would not, he said, serve a warrant on so good a man.[31]

The next time Lunsford, preached a riot broke out similar to the type which visited the ministry of Samuel Harriss. But Lunsford escaped to preach again. Lunsford's preaching ability was noteworthy. J. B. Taylor wrote:

> In his best strains he was more like an angel than a man. His countenance, lighted up by an inward flame, seemed to shed beams of light wherever he turned. His voice, always harmonious, often seemed to be tuned by descending seraphs. His style and his manner were so sublime and so energetic that he was indeed like an ambassador of the skies, sent down to command all men everywhere to repent.[32]

John Taylor was now in the Northern Neck in 1779. He saw the results of Lunsford's ministry and the open hearts in that part of Virginia:

> It was more than a year before I paid my uncle, in the northern neck another visit; at which time I found a great revival of religion through the country, where he lived; himself with many others had been baptized: and [there was] Lewis Lunsford, now living in that part of the world. In every direction there was now such a call for preaching, day and night, that it required the best of lungs in the preacher, to bear the service; though the nights were short, the houses would often not hold the people, when I have known the preacher stand in the yard, by bright moon light, and the sand on which he stood in a manner, white as snow, and the light such, without a candle, that the preacher was capable to read, and hundreds, perhaps half a thousand, attentive to the sweet voice of the gospel, while their sighs, groans and cries for mercy would oblige every spectator to say that God is here of a truth.[33]

In case the reader would wonder if a few years of persecution should cool the warmth of their preaching, Taylor comments:

> [My uncle Carter] being very zealous in religion, my preaching passed better with him than might be expected for if nothing else attended it, there was plenty of noise; hence, after preaching one night in his hall, his [wife] remarked that before I came again, she must remove her great candle glass, lest the sound should break it to shivers.[34]

At this juncture of time, the work of God in the rest of Virginia, was slow. John Leland wrote of his efforts:

Now, for the first time, I knew what it was to travail in birth for the conversion of sinners. The words of Rachel to Jacob were the words of my heart to God: "Give me children or else I die." One night, as I lay on my bed weeping and praying, I thought if it was spring instead of autumn, I would spend all my time at the feet of Jesus in prayer, and at the feet of sinners, praying them to be reconciled to God; but winter was coming on, the summer was ended, and the opportunity past.[35]

Leland did see some fruit, albeit a bit dangerous:

In September, this year (1779), I was likewise returning from Bedford, and had an evening meeting at a place called the North Garden. After preaching was over, a Mrs. Bailey informed me that she had a desire to be baptized, but her husband had told her, if she was ever baptized he would whip her within an inch of her life, and kill the man that should baptize her. That he had once seen me, and liked me so well, that he said if Leland should come that way he might baptize her; and now she wished to embrace the opportunity. I asked her if she was willing to suffer, on supposition her husband should revolt to his first resolution. "Yes," said she, "if I am whipped, my Saviour had long furrows ploughed upon his back."

"Well," said I, "if you will venture your back, I will venture my head." Accordingly, the candles were lighted-we went to the water, and she was baptized. My engagements called me to start very early next morning. I heard afterwards that he whipped her, but the head of John the Baptist is not taken off yet.[36]

Like a rising sunlight began to break through for Leland and Virginia began once again to blossom as a rose:

For eight months after this, I had the spirit of prayer to a degree beyond what I ever had it in my life; and, if I mistake not, my preaching savored a little of the same spirit. My field of preaching was from Orange down to York, about one hundred and twenty miles. From November, 1779, to July, 1780, I baptized one hundred and thirty, the chiefest of whom professed to be the seals of my ministry. As this was the first time that ever such a work attended my ministry, it was refreshing **indeed; nor can I think of it now, without soft emotions of heart.**[37]

Wonderful works followed Leland. In York, he baptized the wife of Captain Robert Howard, who was an Episcopalian vestryman. Leland recalled what happened next:

> When [Captain Howard] heard of it, he called for his carriage, and took his cow-skin, and said he would lash me out of the county. His sister replied, "Brother Bobby, Mr. Leland is a large man, and will be too much for you."
>
> "I know it," said the Captain, "but he will not fight."
>
> His wife made answer, "Perhaps he may—he goes well armed; and if he should wound you in the heart, you would fall before him."
>
> "Ah!" said the Captain, "I know nothing about this heart-work." Afterwards he became serious, penitent, believing and was baptized.[38]

Leland recalled that the uncle of Captain Howard mocked the new convert saying, "Nephew Bobby, I pity you in my heart, to see you following that deluded people, and wasting your time so much, that you will raise no corn this year."

"My Uncle," said the captain, "I wish you had pitied me as much two years ago, when you cheated me out of my mill."[39]

It was time for Thomas Jefferson to introduce his masterpiece, *The Virginia Act for Religious Liberty* in 1779.[*] It was received under scrutiny and was widely debated but it did not pass into law. God's timetable was not in favor but it was approaching.

William Tryon was a veteran of intimidation and colonial scare tactics. As documented in chapter eight, his attack on the Baptist dissenters in North Carolina drove them over the mountains. He took his Episcopalian act to New York just in time for the Revolution. British General

---

[*] See Appendix F for the text of the act.

Clinton assigned him to scare tactic duty for the state of Connecticut. From July 5-11, 1779, he torched farms, villages, and generally inflamed hatred for the royal government. Clinton was not pleased with the surprising cruelty of Tryon. Washington pressed Tryon out of Connecticut and with swift action, Tryon was shipped back to England. Thus ended his infamous career. It was fortunate for him for his neck would have been in a noose if he had tarried much longer.

A convention was called on September 1, 1779 for the new Massachusetts government. On September 10 an article was discussed to give rulers power to support ministers by forced taxes. John Adams, reopening a can of bitter worms, accused the Baptists of sending an agent to the first national Congress in Philadelphia in 1774 to try to break the resolve of the union. It was the same lie.

On this occasion, Isaac Backus answered his accuser by publishing his account of the Philadelphia trip in the *Boston Chronicle* on December 2, 1779.

Even in the midst of accusations, the Baptist churches of New England had a powerful revival in 1779. The revival held sway for three years, and "greatly increased the old Baptist churches, and *more than thirty new ones were planted in one year* in New-England alone."[40]

Mr. Cooper preached the election sermon in Massachusetts on October 25, 1780. He pleaded for mutual candor and love among the dissenters. Whereupon, Isaac Backus rebuked in writing:

> But do any men plead conscience for violating their own promises? Or are any conscientious in denying *all* the country the liberty which they have long enjoyed in Boston? Yea, what do they do with their consciences in Boston, where the laws are made, since they are not enforced there? And if men call interest conscience, where is their religion?
>
> A just answer to these questions may be very serviceable. Paul says, "The weapons of our warfare are not carnal, but mighty through God to the pulling down of strong holds, casting down imaginations, and every high thing that exalteth itself against the knowledge of God, and bringing into captivity every thought to the obedience of Christ: 2Cor. 10:4-5."

Therefore, all use of carnal weapons to support religious ministers that ever has been in the world, has been a violation of the laws of Christ; for He is the only head of His church, and each church that supports her ministers in the name of any earthly head, is a harlot.[41]

Elder John Leland

Events Leading to Religious Liberty
and the Bill of Rights

1780   British General Clinton arrives in Charleston, South Carolina

1780   August 15, Americans defeated at Camden, South Carolina

1780   October 7, Battle of Kings Mountain, North Carolina

1781   January 17, Battle of Cowpens, South Carolina

1781   March, British victory at Eutaw Springs, North Carolina

1781   October 19, the Surrender of Cornwallis at Yorktown, Virginia.

1784   The Church of England disestablished, the Protestant Episcopalian has a brief "Incorporation"

1785   The *Great* Virginia Revival

1785   James Madison's Memorial and Remonstrance, a treatise against the General Assessment Bill published

1786   January 19, the Virginia Statute for Religious Liberty, written by Thomas Jefferson, became law in Virginia.

1786   "Incorporation" of the Protestant Episcopal Church in Virginia repealed, all religious properties are given into the hands of the churches individually, the State of Virginia to hold no ties to the Episcopal Church.

1791   December 15, Bill of Rights ratified.

1798   Official repeal of any vestry laws wedding the old established church to the state of Virginia leaving all religious "sects" on equal ground

CHAPTER TWELVE
Renouncing all Foreign Power

The Church [of England] doctrine of Baptismal Regeneration paralyses the ministry even of good and earnest men. For, since Justification accompanies Regeneration, Baptismal Regeneration is Baptismal Justification; infants, therefore, are justified as well as regenerated in Baptism; and, since **nearly the whole nation is baptized in infancy,** *nearly the whole nation is therefore justified in infancy by Baptism. Henceforth, therefore, they are no more dead in sin, or heirs of wrath, but "members of Christ, children of God, and inheritors of the kingdom of heaven:" the threatenings of the Gospel are addressed to them in vain. There is nothing left to arouse them from their insensibility.–Baptist Noel.*[1]

Of John Gano, L. C. Barnes wrote: "But patient examination, with occasional help from the minutes of the Association, show that he made not less than six missionary journeys to Virginia and North Carolina. Backus said of him in a general way, 'He has been the most extensive traveler to preach the gospel of any man now living in America.' Going and coming, between 1754 and 1758, Gano must have crossed Washington's fresh tracks in the Shenandoah region, not less than seven times. If they avoided meeting in those four years they must have almost taken pains to do so."[2]

The British were holding Rhode Island, but that was nearly all they had in the north. The middle states campaign had all but died with British troops lazily occupying Philadelphia with the help of the traitorous hands of Benedict Arnold. Washington was still there, waiting for any movement. In February of 1780, British General Clinton landed at Charleston, South Carolina with a plan to disrupt the south and sweep the remaining American resistance out of existence. The towns of Beaufort and Ninety-Six were sacked very quickly. What was worse, Clinton was able to field numbers of loyalists who entered his army as militia. The British army in South Carolina and Georgia had at least 7,000 men. Georgia was a lost cause.

Daniel Marshall, the great missionary, had extended his ministry into Georgia just before the beginning of the Revolution. He was imprisoned after establishing the Kiokee Baptist Church. He was active, even as an older man during the Revolution. Waldo P. Harris wrote of him:

> This church prospered greatly, till the country became involved in the horrors of the revolutionary war. Even these troubles were not sufficient to drive her faithful pastor from his post. Like John, he stood by his master, while all men forsook the province and fled. A friend of the American cause, he was once made a prisoner and put under strong guard; but, obtaining leave of the officers to have a religious service with the guard, he spoke with such power and demonstration of the Spirit, that the officers and guard were amazed and confounded, and he was safely and honorably discharged. When a part of Tories [loyalists] demanded of him where he had concealed his horses, he suddenly refused to utter a word, although reportedly threatened with death.[3]

Washington sent reinforcements under General Gates from New York and managed a meager number from Virginia to stand against the British regulars. Lord Cornwallis took command of the British army of the south. He immediately led the British to victory over Gates at Camden, South Carolina on August 15, 1780. But the further north the British pushed into the Carolinas the more difficult it became.

As Cornwallis moved his army through South Carolina he began to sense the influence of the Baptists of the backcountry and the residue of the Regulator movement. Did the Regulators become Loyalists, as some claim? "Though the Regulators had affection for their new British governor (Josiah Martin), Cornwallis said, 'I could not get one hundred men in all the Regulator's Country to stay with us even as militia.'[4] What Cornwallis could not accomplish could be attributed to the Regulator war, the Separate Baptist influence, and a young Baptist preacher named Richard Furman. Cornwallis would eventually meet with total frustration in Virginia, but before he got there, he sent a "posse" out into the wilderness in search of Furman, one of the biggest thorns in his side in the south.

Furman was found of Christ under the preaching of Joseph Reese, the venerable fireball of South Carolina. Reese had the fire of his Separate Baptist cultivation deep in his bones. Reese was a most powerful preacher, an associate of Daniel Marshall, whose organization and consecration he had followed.

Furman was born in New York in 1755. He proved to be one of those unusual individuals, reading very early in life. There are those who testified that Furman tried to hold the family Bible as a toddler, begging anyone who would care to listen to teach him to read God's word. He memorized parts of the "Iliad" by age seven and was converted in his early teens. Reese baptized him at 16 years of age.

He immediately began to preach and was ordained the pastor of High Hills Baptist Church in South Carolina. As a boy preacher, he attracted great crowds, but soon met with opposition. In Camden, South Carolina the sheriff forbade him from preaching in the courthouse because he had no license. But he took to the open air and so moved the people of Camden, that the sheriff forever opened the doors of the courthouse to him. Richard Furman was the embodiment of the scintillating fervor of the Separate Baptists, coupled with the sound doctrine of the Regular Baptists, and he put his zeal and balance into good use for God and his country. As the news of Alamance, the *Gaspee*, Lexington and Concord pieced together the foundation of patriotism, Furman flamed its cause in the south, especially in Virginia and South Carolina. Patrick Henry and his family were fascinated at his preaching. Henry presented him with a textbook on oratory, which became a family heirloom.[5]

*   *   *

Gates led his men to Hillsborough, North Carolina and attempted to reinforce his army. Amid news that Benedict Arnold had defected, Gates could not re-form his army, and Cornwallis was on the move.

As Morgan Edwards testified, 1500 families, or roughly 6,000 people "quit the province" of North Carolina after the battle of Alamance. They headed over the mountains into present-day Tennessee and Kentucky. Reminiscent of the Waldensian encampments of Europe, the majority of these pioneers were Separate Baptists, finding liberty and refuge in the rough terrain. The first settlement was called the Watauga and included land grants along Doe River, Roan Creek, Sinking Creek, Brush Creek, and Boone's Creek. Other settlements included Carters Valley, Shelby Fort and Nolichucky.[6]

The Watauga formed its own government in 1772, being out of the jurisdiction of any of the colonies and beyond the hated boundary placed upon them by the Proclamation of 1763.[7]

Tidence Lane, the first of the notable converts of Shubal Stearns was coming over the mountains into the Watauga. He presided over the execution of the will of Shubal Stearns and stayed at Sandy Creek until Sarah Stearns joined her husband, Shubal, in glory. Sometime in 1779, Lane made his way over the mountains. J. J. Burnett, testified, "Among the other emigrants there was a small body, which went out in something like a church capacity. They removed from an old church at Sandy Creek in North Carolina, which was planted by Shubal Stearns, and as a branch of the mother church they immigrated to the wilderness and settled on Boone's Creek. The church is now called Buffalo Ridge."[8] Several churches formed after his arrival.

These pioneers wanted no part of Great Britain. Indeed, "two sons of Tidence Lane, Isaac and Aquila, were in William Bean's company of militia, and engaged in chasing the Tories out of the country."[9]

When called upon to defend *America*, they responded.

It came to pass that a miracle army, a remnant of the *Regulators*, most of whom were *baptized believers*, came over the Alleghenies to lay siege on Cornwallis and his army. Known in history as the "Overmountain Men," these sharp-shooting frontiersmen were supplied by Baptist McNabb and mustered at various places including Three Springs, near Kingston and Sycamore Shoals near Johnson City in Tennessee.[10] Tidence Lane and his nine sons were among the patriots. The leadership of Lane cannot be ignored. This remnant army held up the British at King's Mountain, North Carolina. Benjamin Andrews wrote:

> There was now no organized American force in the Carolinas, and Cornwallis began a triumphant march northward. The brave mountaineers of North Carolina and Virginia rose in arms. October 7th, 1780, 1,000 riflemen fell upon a detachment of 1,100 British, strongly

posted on King's Mountain, N.C., and after a sharp struggle, killed
and wounded about 400, and took the rest prisoners.[11]

This forgotten piece of history makes one wonder why New York
and New England are reminded about their "Green Mountain Boys" but
Tennessee and the Carolinas, are not allowed to remember their
"Overmountain *Men*" in the history books.

It is a commonly stated fact however, that the victory at Kings
Mountain stirred the embers of liberty throughout the south. The
Americans faced long odds next at Cowpens. Washington replaced
Gage with General Nathaniel Green. With help from General Daniel
Morgan and an army of militia volunteers and American Continentals,
the Americans were victorious at Cowpens, South Carolina.

Cornwallis then made a stand at Guilford Court House and won at
Eutaw Springs, but nearly ruined his own army in the process. After
that, General Green chased the British out of North and South Carolina and onto the Virginia peninsula to Yorktown in September of
1781.

Lafayette's French troops caged Cornwallis in at Yorktown, while
the British commander waited to be evacuated by the navy. But a
French blockade prevented his plan. When Washington arrived at Yorktown with Rochambeau, artillery pulverized the trapped British army.
On October 19, 1781, Cornwallis surrendered.

Cornwallis' refused to surrender his sword to Washington. He ordered his assistant, Charles O'Hara, to deliver his battle sword to Rochambeau. Rochambeau, understanding the implications, sent O'Hara
to Washington, who promptly steered the British officer to his own second in command, Major General Benjamin Lincoln.

The British surrendered and a nation was born. But the second
stage of the Revolution was not yet over.

In New England, the religious stage of the war raged on.

John Leland wrote, "The clergy in New England, were champions in the revolution; but, to justify the separation from Great Britain, they were obliged to establish maxims, respecting the rights of men, which they are now loath to abide by."[12] From 1768-1798, Charles Chauncy, pastor of the Congregational church at Boston, lobbied, preached and argued publicly for a Congregational church establishment for Massachusetts and Connecticut. He was successful in those years, and the law established Congregationalism, until those laws were crushed by the Bill of Rights. And this, Charles Chauncy did in hypocrisy, for, as we have shown, Chauncy publicly opposed the establishment of the Episcopalians and exchanged heated arguments with them, which appeared in the Boston papers.[13] Of this hypocrisy, Backus reminded us that according to Deuteronomy 16:19, "a gift doth blind the eyes of the wise."

Chauncy held to infant baptism which Backus said, "lays bands upon children before they can choose for themselves."[14] Chauncy and the Congregationalists also believed that "support of religious teachers could be enforced by the magistrates," and believed in "installing and maintaining of ministers by the world, in whom the church could not remove." These were all tenets of the establishment of a national religion.

Isaac Backus continued to pray and lobby and write for relief in New England. He spent himself for the war of religious independence. He dutifully recorded the persecution of numbers of his Baptist brethren.

There was a 1778 petition to the General Court asking for the abolishment of religious taxes in the new constitution. It was ignored.

December 2, 1779, Elijah and Joseph Ames were charged with failure to pay ministerial taxes. James Hooper, Jr. refused to arrest them.

In 1780, Massachusetts adopted a new state constitution. Article three of the so-called "declaration of rights" was a clause to maintain public Protestant teachers "by taxation." Whereupon John Leland gave this opinion: "In the year 1780, when the constitution of Massachusetts was formed, the third article of the bill of rights occasioned a long and close debate. A gentleman, at the head of his party, said, 'We believe in our consciences that the best way to serve God, is to have religion protected and ministers of the gospel supported by law, and we hope that no gentlemen here will wish to wound our tender consciences.' The plain English of which is, Our consciences dictate that all the commonwealth of Massachusetts must submit to our judgments, and if they do not, they will wound our tender conscience."[15]

The physical attacks on conscience in New England had not ceased. On May 28, 1782, Richard Lee, a Baptist preacher came to Hingham, Massachusetts to preach the Gospel. Lee was about to commence in the home of David Farrars, when Captain Theophilas Wilder and Nathaniel Dammon entered the home with designs to stop Lee. An argument began. Wilder threatened Lee and ordered him out of the town, as he and Dammon were "a chosen committee sent to prevent any such fellows preaching in that town."[16] Mr. Lee pointedly asked, "...if they had any greater law than *that Holy Bible?*," and if they had such a law he would comply. Of course, he knew they did not, and so began to walk to the large room of the house to commence preaching to the crowd gathered. He reminded the people not to be afraid of these men that were attempting to halt their meeting, but to "fear him who can destroy both soul and body in Hell".

In disbelief that preacher Lee would defy their order, Captain Wilder gave an order and a large number of men came in to dispose of Lee. They forced him from the house and literally dragged him over the city limit line, striking him and cursing him. Someone knocked the *Holy Bible* out of his hands, stomped on it, even cursing the *Holy Bible* on the ground. To add insult, someone threw cow dung in his face.

Richard Lee preached in Scituate, Massachusetts later that night.

On December 17, 1781, Elijah Balkcom was arrested and prevailed upon to pay the ministerial tax. When Balkcom appealed the tax and fine he was defeated at Attleborough on February 22, 1781. But the principle was too important to allow neglect and Balkcom pressed the measure to the higher court at Taunton. He argued that since a new constitution was adopted in 1780, no new certification laws, so prejudiced to the Baptist cause, had been set up. If this was true, then what was the reason for requiring certificates and forcing payment of religious taxes? Balkcom won the case and Isaac Backus declared it a very important event, but in just four years, the victory proved meaningless.

In 1782 John Howard of Eaton was imprisoned for failing to pay the *standing order* minister Archibald Campbell.

In 1783, the Baptists of Cambridge, Massachusetts were taxed for ministerial rates. They appealed and lost their case. Thomas Green III was their pastor.

Gersham and Amos Cutter were arrested in Cambridge in 1784 also for refusing to pay the rates. When they came to trial in 1785, a Cambridge court ruled against Gershom. Even in the higher courts, the old certificate laws were found to wield their tyrannical effect.

As we have seen, *the real crucible of New England* was the realization that infant baptism was not scriptural and believer's baptism was not a re-baptism at all. In Connecticut, directly after the war there was reaction to the extremely large number of converts who sought and received believer's baptism. Infant baptism was weighed in the scriptural balances and found wanting. Therefore, rejection of infant baptism made the baptism of the *standing order* Protestants, passed down from Holy Mother church, "no baptism." Joseph Huntington, realizing this, and panicking, voiced the obvious concern that all Pedobaptist Protestants felt, "When you rebaptize those in adult years, which have been baptized in their infancy, you and they jointly renounce that Father, Son and Holy Ghost."[17] To them, believer's baptism was akin to blasphemy, or taking the Lord's name in vain.

George Eve was a native of Culpeper County, Virginia. He was ordained in 1778 and pastored the Blue Run church in Orange County for twelve years. Throughout the war, he "continued to preach with astonishing success and large numbers acknowledged him as the instrument of their conversion. George Eve, like so many of his fellow Baptist preachers, would migrate to Kentucky. While he finished out his ministry in Virginia, he performed an outstanding service to his new nation.

1784 was the year the Church of England was officially disestablished in Virginia. The Protestant Episcopalian Church had what was called a brief "Incorporation," which was repealed in less than two years.

In a sense, George Washington had begun to disestablish the Episcopalian Church. Washington was a member of the Episcopal Church at Williamsburg, Virginia. He began to refuse communion there, in fact, dismissing himself from the service when the commemoration would begin. L.C. Barnes wrote concerning this:

> It is interesting to note, however, whatever the significance may be, that, from the period of the war, Washington ceased to be an actual communicant in the Episcopal Church. On this point we have the undoubted testimony of a lady who lived twenty years in his family, his adopted daughter, the granddaughter of Mrs. Washington. She says, "My mother resided two years at Mount Vernon after her marriage with John Park Curtis, the only son of Mrs. Washington. I have heard her say, that General Washington always received the sacrament with my grandmother before the Revolution."
> Speaking of the time after the war, she says, "On communion Sunday he left the church with me after the blessing, and returned home, and we sent the carriage back for my grandmother."[18] [19]

Eventually, Washington excused himself from the entire church service on the Sundays he knew the ordinance would be observed.

The year 1784 also brought the history-changing vote on the "General Assessment," which would have "established a provision for the teachers of the Christian religion."[20] The assessment law was put to a public vote. The Virginia legislature distributed copies of the assessment bill throughout the state inviting the people to give their opinion of the bill. Many famous Virginians were for the general tax (which was in reality a forced tithe) including Patrick Henry and George Washington.

In response, James Madison wrote his famous "Memorial and Remonstrance."[*] He argued brilliantly against the assessment. Petitions ran three to one against the assessment bill and it was abandoned without being brought to a vote.

The time had come for Madison to bring Jefferson's "Virginia Statute for Religious Liberty" back for a vote. Even though Jefferson was out of the country at the time, it passed and became law early in 1786. So important was the "Statute for Religious Liberty" to Jefferson, that it was requested of him to be noted on his gravestone. Of all his accomplishments, only this and his authorship of the Declaration of Independence are etched on the stone. The battle over forced tithes and the licensing of Christian ministry was complete. With the passing of Jefferson's masterpiece, the religious stage of the war in Virginia was over.

In light of all our forefathers suffered, it may be easier for the reader to understand Jefferson's statement of a *"wall of seperation between church and state."* The statement was made in a letter to the Danbury BAPTIST Association. After reading our narrative, is there any question as to why he wrote it?

The reader may recall an attempt at union between the Regulars and Separates in Spotsylvania when David Thomas and John Garrard, the venerable veteran Regular Baptists collided with the young upstart Separate Baptists, James Read and Samuel Harris. The preachers were for the union but the crowd was divided, so no union took place. A second proposition for union was brought before the Sandy Creek Association by the Ketockton Regulars a few years later and caused a lengthy debate but no union took place. When the Separate Baptists divided in North Carolina, the Virginia brethren began the General Association of Separate Baptists in Virginia. We have witnessed their progress under God, that they grew exponentially. They divided their churches in 1782 into

---

[*] See Appendix G for this document.

North and South Districts. Then the next year, the association divided once again, Upper and Lower North and Upper and Lower South.

Finally in 1787, the Separate Baptists and the Regular Baptists of Virginia united. Robert Semple wrote "The committee appointed to consider the terms of union with our Regular brethren reported, that they conceive the manner in which the Regular Baptist confession of faith has been received by a former association, is the ground-work for such union."[21] Once this happened, a General Committee of the entire state was formed. The Baptists of Virginia were already a force to be reckoned with and yet, another revival broke out among them.

The United States Constitution and the Bill of Rights

The Articles of Confederation of the United States were considered weak and a new Constitution was deemed necessary. After much debate and rhetoric at the Constitutional convention, a new constitution was drawn up. In 1787 it was sent to the separate states for ratification.

The new constitution created a representative republic without an establishment of a national religion married to the state. But the liberty of conscience was still not a written guarantee. Rhode Island knew this and refused to ratify the document. Neither would Virginia. The Constitution needed Virginia, the most populous state, to ratify in order to have credibility. At the time, there were doubts as to whether the document would gain the approval of the nine states necessary, to make it the law of the land. Madison, Jefferson, Washington and Henry knew why Virginia hesitated.

It had not been so long ago, that Waller, the Craigs, Ireland, Weatherford, and a host of others were in prison for preaching without state approval. It had not been but a few years since the venerable Isaac Backus, recorder of American Baptist history had visited them. Backus published his volumes in 1777 and 1784. The sobering account of the *crimson red* blood of Obadiah Holmes, Thomas Painter, Mary Dyer, John Hazel, John Bolles and others cannot be underestimated. The oppression of their New England brethren, still occurring, must have been on their minds.

Although ignored by historians, a concern about a "regulated" militia must have been on their minds as well. "Regulated," not meaning "trained," but "restrained," as the *Regulators* desired in North Carolina. There was a concern about "the right of the people to bear arms," just in case the militia was not "regulated." Since Jefferson, *the Virginian* wrote the Declaration of Independence, it is more than just conjecture to consider these opinions. The Baptist contingency in Virginia, having their religious roots in North Carolina, would remember the need of an armed citizenry for protection against a tyrannical military; and the right to bear arms would be (and still is) a necessity.

James Madison, the *Virginian*, was the Father of the U. S. Constitution. The Constitutional Convention had embraced Madison's version of the federal document. But the Ratification Convention almost convened without Madison, and would have if it were not for the intervention of Almighty God.

The states ratified the Constitution by sending representatives approved by each county. Madison was not a sure winner in eight counties, especially Orange. The Baptist population, ever growing, by this time held sway in the election. The Baptists were not convinced of the reliability of the constitution due to the absence of guarantees of religious liberty. They did not fully trust Madison. But they did trust John Leland.

Madison received this letter in February of 1788 from James Gorden Jr:

> Dear Sir,
>   The sentiments of the people of Orange are much divided, the best men in my judgement are for the constitution but several of those who have much weight with the people are opposed, Parson Bledsoe & Leeland with Colo. Z. Burnley. Upon the whole sir I think it is incumbent on you with out delay, to repair to this state; as the loss of the constitution in this state may involve consequences the alarming to every citizen of America.
>
> ·Jas Gordon Jun[22]

John Leland's earnestness, work, and wit put him in great esteem with the people of Virginia. His words were weighty. Madison received word that Leland and the Baptists were wary of him and the new constitution. Patrick Henry's party was threatening to unseat Madison and the Baptists were siding with Henry and speaking out against the new constitution.[*]

Moving quickly, Madison arranged a meeting with Leland[* *] in which he promised the preacher that a definite declaration of liberty and rights would be added to the new constitution, to guarantee the religious liberty of all Americans.[23] Later in a stump speech, Leland threw his support to Madison.

To further insure his success, Madison informed George Eve, pastor of the Blue Run Baptist Church, "It is my sincere opinion that the constitution ought to be revised. It should contain all essential rights, particularly the rights of conscience in the fullest latitude, the freedom of press, trial by jury, security against general warrants, etc." On January 27, 1789, Eve defended Madison[24] in a public meeting in his church in Louisa County.

James Madison was elected to the Virginia Constitutional Ratification Convention on February 2, 1789 in a blinding snowstorm. Just before he left for Williamsburg, Leland wrote him:

> 15 February 1789
> Sir,
>   I congratulate you in your appointment, as a Representative to Congress; and if my Undertaking in the Cause conduced Nothing else towards it, it certainly gave Mr. Madison one Vote.
>   One Thing I shall expect; that if religious Liberty is anywise threatened, that I shall receive the earliest Intelligence.
>   I take the Liberty of writing thus to you, lest I should not be at Home when you pass by on your Way to Congress.
>
> John Leland"[25]

As every American surely knows, the Constitution, the product of the mind of James Madison, was eventually ratified.

---

[*] See Appendix H, *Excerpts from Letters in the Papers of James Madison* for quotes from ten letters documenting the relationship of Madison and Leland.

[* *] See Appendix I, Letter from Governor Briggs on the Leland-Madison Meeting.

After the ratification of the Constitution, another astounding revival took place in Virginia. It occurred in 1788-89 and was called the *Great* Revival. Because of this blessing, the Baptists became **the largest religious body in the state**. On December 15, 1791, under the leadership of a trustworthy James Madison, the Bill of Rights was ratified.

*   *   *

There was an incredible persistence of persecution in New England, even after the ratification of the Constitution and the Bill of Rights.

Jonathan Hallet was forced to pay the Cambridge tax in 1788.

Rehoboth, Massachusetts, the place of refuge first for Roger Williams and then for the Welsh Baptists under John Myles, became a place of tyranny in 1789. A large Baptist majority lived in the town. But the Congregational church minority still sought a way to tax the people of Rehoboth for the payment of the Congregational minister John Ellis. When this was demanded, the Baptists took over the parish meetinghouse and brought in preachers for the purpose of weekly sermons. Isaac Backus himself mounted the pulpit at Rehoboth and was surrounded by supporters ready to remove Ellis should he try to force his way into the pulpit. [26]

When it appeared that the lights of liberty would begin to shine over gloomy Massachusetts, a desperate John Lathrop in the western part of the state published a work defending Congregationalism. It passed through six editions from 1791-1793. The book alleged that the ministers of the *standing order* could claim apostolic succession, and even though it could not be proved, they had "a right to presume it."[27] To which Backus replied, "the bloody hands of Rome and England, could never convey just authority to any other ministers."[28]

Perhaps the most heartbreaking case was the persecution of Judah Eldridge of Harwich. He served as a private in Captain Small's ship, the *Hazard*. He was part of a company called upon to meet fifty British warships that threatened the Massachusetts coast. Eldridge served well and lost an eye during a six-month period as a prisoner of war in Halifax prison in Massachusetts. Years later, January 8, 1796, he, his wife, and his daughter were arrested and interrogated about delinquent religious taxes. Their livestock was confiscated. In reality, their livelihood was taken from them. They could not win their appeal. On January 31, Elder Abner Lewis and Eldridge visited Backus to tell him of 175 men who were taxed to pay ministerial rates. They brought forlorn tidings of five who were imprisoned. Our hearts can hardly imagine the injustice the patriot Eldridge sustained.

The tyranny of Massachusetts continued to the end of the 18th century. Backus had a record of Abner Chase, who had his crops seized at Harwich in 1799.

Even with the birth of Brown College, the educated Baptist preacher could not shake off the prejudices of the day. Lucius Bolles, the grandson of John Bolles, whose public flogging is mentioned in chapter nine, was degreed from Brown in 1801. Yet when he was ordained in Salem Connecticut, William Bentley wrote of him: "the day of Bolles' ordination was a dark one...we were afraid of the uncharitableness of his sect, which has been most illiterate in New England. All the ministers were invited. I did not attend. No right minister of the town was present."[29]

Isaac Backus left this present world on November 20, 1806, exactly 35 years after the death of Shubal Stearns. He died without seeing the completion of the second stage of the Revolution. He would have to witness it from Heaven. He died before his Massachusetts brethren were given relief from their oppression, which was the object of his splendid struggle.

Joshua Bradley was imprisoned in Wallingford in 1809. Bradley was falsely accused of forging the signature of the *standing order* minister in Mansfield, Massachusetts which was affixed to some kind of letter of recommendation. The prosecution never found the alleged letter, but it still took until 1812 to free Bradley from all charges. The real reason, however, for the false charges was found in the indictment of Bradley which stated he was "drawing away from their respective Pastors and Ecclesiastical Societies, to which they belonged, many of the citizens." The *no solicitation* rule had roots in 19th century New England. [30]

But the end of struggles came.

The New England states progressed from religious establishment of the Congregational church, to the toleration of "legal" dissenters, to the licensing of certain sects and "illegal" dissenters, to the final blessings of religious liberty. This progression was completed in 1833 when the Massachusetts State legislature finally repealed its religious establishment law.

The Baptism and the Sword of Washington

George Washington was keenly aware of his place in history and painstakingly used measures to insure his views were a part of his legacy. For written history, he was most attentive to detail. Other history would have to be remembered by the participants. To be sure, he did everything for effect, if just to give notice to following generations his intent and declarations.

According to tradition, towards the end of the war, General Washington began to contemplate following the Lord in believer's baptism. This persistent tradition is scoffed, mocked, and disregarded by many historians. But not all would so easily dismiss this stunning historic assertion, for some historians fully know the embarrassment of disbelieving an incident that is later proved to be true.[31] It was Washington himself who said in a letter to Noah Webster:

> Notwithstanding most of the papers, which may perhaps be deemed official, are preserved; yet the knowledge of innumerable things of a more delicate and secret nature is confined to the perishable remembrance of some few of the present generation.[32]

For insight on this "knowledge of innumerable things" Lemuel Call Barnes spent the greater part of thirty years. Imminent as a Baptist historian of the turn of the 20th century, Barnes interest in Washington's wartime walk with God came from his studies in preparing articles for the Washington bicentennial celebration. That event had launched the brightest thinkers in America to report on the Christian life of the beloved "Father of our Country". To Barnes' dismay, however, many historians dismissed Washington's Christianity and denied that he even prayed at Valley Forge.[33] Barnes then began to gather evidence demonstrating that Washington was a sincere Christian. In so doing, he discovered that the General had also requested and received immersion at the hands of a Baptist preacher. The first three years he gathered evidence. For the next thirty plus years, he tried in vain to publish his 180-page manuscript, *Was General George Washington Baptized by Chaplain John Gano?* [34]

According to Barnes, the documentation of this significant piece of history began with a letter to the *Boston Watchman* published on July 11, 1889. The letter was written by General Richard M. Gano, the great, grandson of John Gano, in which he testifies:

> General Washington on one occasion said to Chaplain Gano, "I am convinced that immersion is the baptism taught in the Scriptures, and I demand baptism at your hands."
>
> One of the witnesses, now living, talked with one of the witnesses, & also with John Gano, the administrator.[35]

Barnes immediately sent a letter to General Richard M. Gano, who was living in Dallas, Texas asking, "Would you have the kindness to give me the address of this 'one now living?'"[36]

General R. M. Gano answered Barnes, writing, "...there is now living a person who talked with some of the witnesses. There were only 42 witnesses at the baptism. The person living to whom I referred was Mrs. Margaret H. Ewing, of Georgetown Kentucky. She was [the] granddaughter of the Rev. John Gano. She is now past 90 years of age...but her mind is clear and memory good."[37]

Barnes began to gather evidence. He gathered the first two pieces from Georgetown, Kentucky:

> Georgetown, Ky, Aug. 16th, 1889.
>
> I am the grandson of Rev. John Gano, now in my eighty-third year and the brother of Mrs. Margaret Ewing. I was raised from my fifth

year to manhood by Mrs. Margaret Hubbell (nee Gano). I have heard her say that her father baptized (immersed), General Washington.

S. F. Gano, M. D.
Subscribed and sworn to in my presence this
16th day of August 1889
Stephen Gano Long, Notary Public,
State of Kentucky.

Georgetown, Ky., Aug. 16th, 1889
To whom it May Concern;

I, Margaret Ewing (nee Gano) age 90 years last May, being of sound mind and memory, make this statement; I have often heard my Aunt Margaret Hubbell (nee Gano), the eldest daughter of Rev. John Gano say that her father told her that he baptized General George Washington, at Valley Forge to the best of my recollection. She, Mrs. Hubbell, also said that General Washington, for prudent reasons, did not desire that his baptism should be made public. Rev. John Gano was a Chaplain in the revolutionary war, and an intimate personal friend of General Washington.

Margaret Ewing,
Subscribed and sworn to in my presence this
16th day of August 1889.

Stephen G. Long, Notary Public,
State of Kentucky

This written testimony certainly "seems to make it certain that Chaplain John Gano told his oldest daughter, that he had baptized General George Washington."[38] [39] These sworn affidavits were lost from the family for a period of time. But all of the nearly 200 pages of manuscript documentation including the original signed affidavits concerning Washington's baptism, which were gathered by L. C. Barnes, were found by the author in the archives of the Samuel Colgate Historical

Library, Rochester, New York. This letter from Jacob Creath, was also in the papers of L. C. Barnes:

> In 1810, Benedict, the author of the History of the American Baptists, stayed at my father's house in Mecklenburg County, Virginia some ten days, during which time I distributed his history, to which my father obtained a number of subscribers; and while he was at my father's house he gave my mother the life of Doctor John Gano, who, he told mother, was chaplain to General Washington's army during the Revolutionary War, and that he, Gano, immersed Washington during the war privately, and that Washington did not wish it known; and this statement he, Benedict, received from his father-in-law Stephen Gano of Rhode Island and he received it from his father...who moved from the Eastern states and settled in Town Fork, in Fayette County, Ky, near Lexington, and had the care of the Baptist church there; and my uncle, Jacob Creath, Sr., succeeded him in the pastorate of said church, as he told me and as I believe he did and as I heard others say.
>
> I saw and read the life of Gano, which Benedict gave to my mother and I heard her often relate what Benedict told her respecting the baptism of Washington by Doctor Gano, who died in Kentucky.

Jacob Creath
Palmyra, Mo., August 11, 1874.[40]

David Benedict was married to the daughter of John Gano. They had a daughter, Maria, who lived well into her 90's in Providence, Rhode Island. There was an exchange of letters between Mr. Barnes and Maria Benedict in which Miss Benedict said the account given of her father's statement by Creath seemed reasonable and trustworthy.[41]

Lemuel C. Barnes' gathering of evidence also included a sworn affidavit from General R. M. Gano and various newspaper clippings.[42] Yet for all of Barnes' documentation, he does not discuss the most logical reason the Father of our country would have had a Baptist chaplain immerse him.

For the logical reason, let us turn once again to the fabulous link to our patriot past, Isaac Backus. Backus wrote: "A minister of great note[*] said to their Legislature, 'The pastors are orderly and regularly set apart

---

[*] The minister was Ezra Stiles, D. D., the President of Yale College.

to the ministry, by the laying on of the hands of the presbytery, or of those who have regularly derived office power, in a lineal succession, from the apostles and Jesus Christ.'"[43]

It was ridiculous for Stiles to make such a claim and Backus wrote, "And though he knew that the first ministers in our country were ordained by their churches, and did not hold to such a succession, yet he said, 'These were all ordained before by the bishops in England.'"

To which an angered Backus opined, "**And they had theirs from Rome, the mother of harlots**, the great city which reigneth over the kings of the earth. Rev. xvii. 5, 18."[44]

This observation was punctuated by Backus stating, "Great Britain has lost all her power here, and **our rulers have sworn to renounce all foreign power over America**, and yet they compel the people to support ministers who claim a power of office from England. How shocking is this!"[45]

Think along with Isaac Backus as he explains the dilemma the *standing order* churches faced with the break from Mother England:

> There were many others in England, that held to a lineal succession of office, who wanted to have power in America; but...no bishop could be ordained in England, without swearing to the king's supremacy..."[46]

The importance of removing the obligation of infant baptism for all Americans cannot be emphasized too strongly. As Isaac Backus wrote:

> The Church of Rome, and the Church of England, have long held that ministers could regenerate persons by baptizing them. And they who renounced that practice have been called Anabaptists to this day.
>
> [There has been] an amazing attachment of ministers who thought they could save persons from hell by baptizing them; and from thence came the notion of the necessity of an external succession of ministerial ordinations, even through the corruptions of antichrist.[47]
>
> And though the fathers of the Massachusetts made laws to establish the government of the church over the world, yet **when that power was lost, Boston renounced the government of the world over the church**...And this practice cannot now be vindicated by Scripture, reason, nor by the example of any of the fathers of new-England, for sev-

enty years after it was planted. And it is also **contrary to the general government of these United States.**[48]

The victory of the Revolution militarily and spiritually, forged America into a Baptist nation. This was accomplished not by establishment, but by **dis-establishment**. In breaking off our ties with our mother country, we broke the succession of their state-church bishopric.

In the lobby of the John Gano Chapel on the campus of William Jewel College in Liberty, Missouri is a portrait depicting John Gano baptizing George Washington. E. T. Sanford of Manhattan's North church commissioned the portrait in 1908. A commemorative plaque reads:

CHAPLAIN JOHN GANO
ORDAINED TO THE GOSPEL MINISTRY MAY 1754
CHAPLAIN FOR GEORGE WASHINGTON IN THE CONTINENTAL ARMY
BELIEVED TO HAVE BAPTIZED GEORGE WASHINGTON
HISTORY RECORDS GANO "FIGHTING CHAPLAIN
OF THE REVOLUTION"
CHAPLAIN OF KENTUCKY STATE SENATE
ADVOCATE FOR EDUCATION
FOUNDER OF BROWN UNIVERSITY (THEN RHODE ISLAND COLLEGE)

THE PAINTING
IN 1908, REV. E.T. SANFORD OF MANHATTAN'S NORTH CHURCH IN NEW YORK COMMISSIONED A PAINTING OF WASHINGTON AND CHAPLAIN GANO WAIST-DEEP IN THE POTOMAC. IT WAS PRESENTED TO WILLIAM JEWELL COLLEGE BY CHAPLAIN GANO'S GREAT GRANDDAUGHTER, MRS. ELIZABETH PRICE JOHNSON, AT THE TIME OF THE DEDICATION OF THE JOHN GANO MEMORIAL CHAPEL IN 1926.

In the lobby, underneath the painting of the baptism is encased a sword. Sword? A commemorative plaque reads:

THE SWORD

IN 1996 MARGARET GANO REDPATH, THE GREAT, GREAT, GREAT, GREAT, GRANDDAUGHTER OF JOHN GANO OFFERED WILLIAM JEWELL COLLEGE THE FAMILY SWORD. GEORGE WASHINGTON HAD RECEIVED IT FROM THE MARQUIS DE LAFAYETTE; IN TURN, HE BESTOWED IT ON JOHN GANO, THE FIRST CHAPLAIN OF THE CONTINENTAL ARMY. HISTORY RECORDS GEORGE WASHINGTON GAVE THE SWORD TO JOHN GANO AFTER HE BAPTIZED WASHINGTON IN THE POTOMAC.

Giving gifts was a forte' of Lafayette and he was quite famous for it. But giving a battle sword was unique. Remember that Lord Cornwallis refused to give Washington his sword at the fall of Yorktown. Cornwallis' arrogance and pride would not permit him to yield such a symbol of submission to a mere American bumpkin. Of course, Cornwallis underestimated Washington, and of course it is he, Cornwallis, that appears now as the bumbling oaf, losing his dignity as well as the war. So, a sword from Lafayette would be given to Washington in honor, a symbol, no doubt, of humility and submission.

George Washington presented that battle sword, given to him by Lafayette, to his Baptist chaplain, John Gano. Let us not take this gesture of kindness too lightly, for a commanding officer knows exactly the ramifications of surrendering his sword. The sword now hangs in the lobby of the John Gano Chapel at William Jewel College in Liberty, Missouri. The author will leave the reader to ponder the full thrust of its meaning. However, "a word fitly spoken" is in order at this juncture of our narrative.

It is the contention of the author that Washington knew the symbols he was leaving to posterity: **He was breaking the baptism of the established church-state monstrosity**, by submitting to believer's baptism. He further demonstrated, to the best of his ability, his **deferment to the victor of the second stage of the war**, the spiritual stage. This deferment was not to John Gano personally, but to the Bible and the belief system he so profoundly represented. He placed **the symbol of victory and the final break with England, and in** essence, **Rome**, into the hands of a Bible believing *baptized* preacher of the Gospel.

For the Baptists, looking back through the leaves of history, the meaning of the baptism and the sword ought to be clear—America is not under the baptism of England, or Europe or Rome. America's baptism has no earthly headquarters.[*]

What followed after? Equal ground for *all* Christians in America. Now a new war was declared, not a war of musket and ball, canon and shot, or of death and blood, but a fabulous war for the souls of men.

---

[*]From that time until the present, antichrist has been attempting to put America back under Rome's baptism.

The First Baptist Associations in America

The Philadelphia Association, Pennsylvania 1707
The charleston Association, South Carolina, 1751
The Sandy Creek Association, North Carolina, 1758
The kehukee Association, North Carolina, 1765
The Ketockton Association, Virginia, 1766
The Warren Association, Rhode Island, 1767
The Congaree Association, South Carolina—1771
The General Association of Separate Baptists of Va.—1771
The Stonington Association, Connecticut, 1772
The Red Stone Association, Pennsylvania, 1776
The New Hampshire Association, 1776
The Shaftsbury Association, Vermont, 1781
The Woodstock Association, Vermont, 1783
The Georgia Association, 1784
The Elkhorn Association, Kentucky, 1785
The Holston Association, Tennessee, 1786
The Bowdoinham Association, Maine, 1787
The Vermont Association, 1787
The Danbury Association, Connecticut, 1790

CHAPTER THIRTEEN
A Sudden and Powerful Impulse

The Gospel into Georgia (1771), Tennessee (1779), Kentucky
(1781), Ohio (1790), Illinois (1798), Mississippi (1798),
and Indiana (1798)

*The emigration to that country is incredible. Its fruitful soil yielding
the most luxuriant abundance to all those who cultivate it; inviting
the poor and the wretched from the barren wastes of this continent,
and elsewhere, to fly to her fertile arms, that she may fill their
mouths with good and their hearts with gladness.*[1]—Lewis Lunsford
describing the new country of Kentucky.

T he law in Georgia forbade any worship contrary to "the rites of
the Church of England," and when Daniel Marshall invaded the
colony on January 1, 1771, he challenged it. He was a very
"young" old man, having served God from northern Virginia, and
throughout North and South Carolina. He had baptized a great company of believers.

Early in 1772 Marshall conducted a meeting near the run of Kiokee
Creek, just over the border from South Carolina. As a crowd gathered,
he commenced to pray. Before he could finish, a strong hand was laid
upon him and declared him under arrest for "preaching in the parish of
St. Paul." It is difficult to believe the Revolution was just a few years in
the future, but Episcopal rule would be in vogue in Georgia until the
victory of the American army would run it out. Before Marshall was led
away, his wife, the noble Martha Marshall, sister of the dearly departed
Shubal Stearns, quoted scripture in such a way that the constable began
to melt under conviction. Marshall appeared in court the next day. He
was ordered to leave Georgia. He simply replied, "Whether it be right to
obey God or man, judge ye," and did not cease to preach Christ.

The strong hand on Marshall's shoulder belonged to Constable Samuel Cartledge, who was converted and baptized in 1777. He went on to preach the gospel, finishing his course at age 93.[2]

As David Benedict[*] testified, Kiokee church "has been an important establishment, having been a nursery of a number of useful ministers, and the mother of many churches."[3] These men became preachers: Samuel Newton, Abraham Marshall, Alexander Scott, Sanders Walker, Charles Bussey, Loveless Savage, Samuel Cartledge, John and James Saunders, John Stanford, John Boyd, H. A. Boyd, James N. Brown, D. W. Marshall, Jabez Marshall, James Simms and Silas Mercer.[4] Silas' half brother, Thomas went to Mississippi to preach the gospel. It was a common saying with Daniel Marshall, "I would that all the Lord's servants were prophets."[5]

*　*　*

Edmund Botsford was converted at the First Baptist Church in Charleston, and on March 13, 1767, he was baptized. Oliver Hart ordained him in February of 1771. Equipped with a horse, saddle and his Bible, Botsford set out as an itinerant evangelist to the scattered believers in Georgia territory.[6]

---

[*] David Benedict, quoted often in our narrative, was born in Norwalk, Connecticut, October 10, 1779. He was born again at age 20 and entered Brown University to study for the Gospel ministry. He graduated in 1806. A great reader, he outlined sermons and wrote journals describing the early events of his ministry. He was ordained the pastor of the Baptist church in Pawtucket, Rhode Island, where he served 25 years with great distinction. He gathered materials from Isaac Backus, the remains of the papers of John Comer, and traveled extensively to gather information for his works. Benedict was one of the first historians to tie the Baptists of America to the ancient *baptized believers* of Europe. His *History of the Baptist Denomination* was published in 1813. Other works included, *Abridgment of Robinsons' History of Baptism*, 1817; *History of all Religions*, 1824; and *Fifty Years among the Baptists*, 1860. Just before his death he finished *The History of the Donatists*, which he compiled from the Latin texts, left by the enemies of those Baptist people. He translated the texts himself. Benedict flew safely into the presence of Jesus on December 5, 1874, very vigorous at age ninety-five.

Botsford, the Regular Baptist and Daniel Marshall, the Separate Baptist met in Georgia and their fellowship did much to improve the relationship between the two camps. In Georgia, the bridging of both groups combined to bring zeal and knowledge and a resultant revival.

On his way to preach at Kiokee, Mr. Botsford made a stop at the pioneer home of Loveless Savage. He was looking for directions, but God had His own purposes. Mr. Savage said, "I suppose you are the Baptist minister, who is to preach today at the Kiokee."

Mr. Botsford asked, "Will you go?"

Typical of the frontier at the time Savage said, "No, I am not fond of the Baptists; they think nobody is baptized but themselves."

Unfazed, Mr. Botsford retorted, "Have you ever been baptized?"

"Yes, to be sure," was his answer.

Botsford's logical question was, "How do you know?"

Savage answered, "How do I know? Why, my parents have told me I was."

"Then *you* do not know," answered Botsford, "only by information."

Botsford rode on to Kiokee, but the question, "How do you know?" permeated the mind of Loveless Savage. His relief was to come to the meeting and submit to believer's baptism at the hand of Daniel Marshall. Savage began to preach the Gospel the same day.[7]

The long pilgrimage of Daniel Marshall was coming to an end. Marshall founded the first Separate Baptist church in Virginia. He was responsible for the founding of six churches in South Carolina. In Georgia, after his *sixty-fifth birthday*, he planted six more churches and led in the establishment of the Georgia Association. This was his last act before his death. He left this life on November 2, 1784.

The Georgia Association was organized in 1784. It was the first in the state. In 1786 two years after it was formed, it contained these churches: Kiokee, Fishing Creek, Upton's Creek, Philip's Mill, Whatley's Mill, Long Creek of Ogechee, Providence on Rocky Comfort Creek, Powel's Creek, and Van's Creek.[8] In those ten churches, the number of baptized members was 518. The ministers of the Gospel included: Saunders Walker, Jephtha Vining, Dozier Thornton, Peter Smith, Abraham Marshall, Mark Cook, Silas Mercer, Thomas Mercer, and John Henry. Jeremiah Walker, David Tinsley, and Matthew Talbot joined them soon after 1786.

The Kiokee Baptist Church was now under the leadership of Daniel Marshall's son Abraham, a mighty man of God.

Abraham Marshall was born in Windsor, Connecticut on April 23, 1748. As we have witnessed his remarkable parents, Daniel and Martha Marshall were famous for their tireless work for God throughout Pennsylvania, Virginia, North and South Carolina and Georgia. Abraham was a brilliant child, but like so many of the pioneer evangelists, he had little classical education. He was converted in 1770 while his parents were still in South Carolina and baptized in the Savannah River. He began preaching the Gospel immediately.

He migrated with his parents to Kiokee Creek and assisted in the birthing of the first Baptist church in the state in 1772. He was ordained in 1775.[9]

"Shortly after his ordination, Mr. Marshall took a journey of six months to Virginia and traveled and preached from the seaboard to the mountains and as an itinerant exhorter throughout the southern states."[10] After his father's death, Abraham became the pastor of Kiokee Baptist Church.

For 13 years he made excursions from his home base and frequently revival followed in his wake. His most notable journey was in 1786 when he toured the entire nation, much like Whitefield, from Georgia to his native state of Connecticut. He kept a journal of his experiences on his northward journey:

1786, May 13, Being caught in a terrible storm of thunder, lightning, wind, rain and hail, he writes: If this small engagement of only a part of the elements was so alarming, good heavens! What an awful and tremendous scene will it be, when all, like contending armies in fierce array, display their power until they expire in the wreck of matter and the crush of worlds.

17.What rueful aspects have I seen these few days past (in South Carolina) People in huts, on sand-hills as barren as Arabia, at cards, games, etc.

31. Went four miles up, into the vicinity of the place where the traitor Arnold landed his seditious, refractory crew.

June 2. Rode twelve miles and arrived at Yorktown. This is the place the God of war wrought salvation for his American Israel.

June 12. Heard an Ethiopian preach from 'Ye cannot serve the Lord'. He first showed, who could not serve Him; second, why; third, who could and how. His reasoning was masterly. It was disputed whether a minister (under his disadvantages) at the Association could have exceeded him. Surely this is the Lord's doings and it is marvelous in our eyes.

Sunday 25. Made the most insipid declamation ever heard...calculated no more to awaken sinners than the report of a popgun would be to alarm the dead. "O wretched man that I am! who shall deliver me from the body of this death.?"

Monday 26. Traveled thirty-five miles. Asked a matron the way to the parson's. She answered, "You have left him behind...the parson is properly sent." By what could be learnt, the parson had been a schoolmaster, and was now clothed with authority by a bishop to shew the way to heaven. His talents were brilliant at ditties and gambling. The other was a pious man of God who had the hands of (ordination) of the presbytery. Yet one was a despicable preacher, and the other a venerable clergyman. "Oh Lord! how long shall superstitious ignorance make the people cry out, 'Great is Diana of the Episcopalians.'"

July 5. Rode 20 miles. Affectionately received by Oliver Hart in Hopewell. (New Jersey).

As Abraham entered Pennsylvania, the spiritual condition of his cousins, Joseph and Eliakim Marshall laid heavy upon his heart. Both were "Separate" Congregational preachers in Connecticut. Of this juncture in Marshall's journey, David Benedict wrote:

When Abraham was in Philadelphia on his way he fell in company with Mr. Winchester of whom he inquired about his relatives in New England. Mr. Winchester informed him...that Eliakim was a man of a sound judgment, strong memory and delicate conscience.

"Well," thought Abraham, 'if he has a sound judgment he will understand argument, if he has a strong memory he will retain it, and if he has a tender or delicate conscience, it will have an influence on his mind. And from these reasons I expect to baptize him before I leave him."[11]

His diary read:

July 8. Saturday. Called at the Sabbatarian meeting-house; invited to preach. The word appeared to be accompanied with the Divine Energy to hearts of almost all (three hundred in number) who were present.

9. Sunday, Rode ten miles to the Rev. Vanhorn's in the Scotch Plaines; preached to six-hundred. After service Mrs. Van horn and nine more submitted to the ordinance of baptism. Here is a very great revival of religion. Preached a second sermon, four miles below, to five hundred, in a large barn.

10. Visited the grave of Benjamin Miller.

11. Stayed with the Rev. John Gano, in company with Rev. Manning, D.D. President of the Baptist College in Rhode Island.

14. Entered into the land of my nativity, i.e. New England.

19. Came to the town of Windsor. Here kindly received by a cousin, Rev. Eliakim Marshall.[12]

He had come 1,100 miles and finally met his cousins, the established Presbyterian preachers, Joseph and Eliakim Marshall. Eliakim was a beloved and well-respected man, preaching the Gospel for 30 years. Their meeting was tender. Because of this connection, Abraham Marshall preached at the Pocomoke meeting-house in Windsor to 1,500 persons on August 6. Then he preached in the Broad Street meeting-house in Windsor, a place barred against the dissenters for 30 years. On August 8, he preached in Hartford, in the State house, to 1,500. That Sunday August 13, he preached in the Presbyterian meeting-house in Simbury to 2,400. While preaching, the gallery containing several hundred persons, cracked under the weight, and the crowd hysterically forced their way out through the windows and doors. Miraculously, no one was killed. Marshall calmly walked over into the field adjacent to the church house and stood on a wagon and preached.

There were large numbers of converts resulting from his preaching; moreover, his testimony on baptism was causing a stir. He had preached in 21 Presbyterian meeting-houses and had not compromised the truth of believer's baptism in one place. This tree of honesty began to produce fruit. A Presbyterian lady became convinced of her duty to be baptized as a believer by immersion. She did so before a crowd of 500 persons.

September 10, 1786, proved to be a day of great victory for Abraham Marshall. An unprecedented crowd for the state of Connecticut, consisting of 3,500 persons, gathered in a field to hear the youthful Georgia preacher. After the sermon, Eliakim Marshall stood on the stage. Eliakim had spent eight weeks with his venerable young cousin, disputing and conversing about the Bible doctrine of baptism. Benedict relates the wonderful scene:

> He informed them that he was awakened under the preaching of Whitefield. As if spoken to him with an audible voice this expression fastened on his mind, God is wisdom. His reflections were: "if God is wisdom He knows all my thoughts...all I am...and do." This followed him two of three days when he was impressed with the sentiment: "God is holiness and as such He must hate all in me which his wisdom sees is wrong." The third impression was God is power. "This," said he, "struck me like thunder and brought me to the ground." So saying, he burst into tears and for a moment the tears were flowing from near a thousand eyes.[13]

Eliakim then said to the stunned audience,

> [I] had been an advocate for infant sprinkling, in opposition to the primitive order and apostolic mode; [I am] now convinced that there is no warrant for it in the Bible, and am about to comply with the baptism of our Saviour, according to the manner it became Him and His followers.[14]

One would have thought the crowd would be angry, but instead, a large number retired to the river, and after listening to a sermon on the subject of baptism, observed the immersion of Eliakim Marshall.

The courage to stand before those religious crowds and proclaim the truths of baptism is almost incomprehensible and indicts the principles of so-called "union evangelism." Abraham left for his Georgia home the day following the immersion of his cousin.

After his return, the Lord blessed Abraham in 1787 with a notable revival. He baptized 100 in that corner of Georgia. The rest of Georgia was blessed as well. Marshall wrote, "In 1787 there was a glorious revival, thousands attended on the word. The Baptists have great influence, and are the most numerous of any denomination in this State. We are increased (that is, the Georgia Association) to upwards of 3,300 in about twenty years past."[15] Marshall married the daughter of John Waller in April of 1792.

The Kiokee church and her preachers transformed Georgia into a garden of harvest for Jesus. Eventually, Georgia overtook the state of Virginia in the number of Baptists within her borders.[*]

Franklin was one of those legendary places of America's past. It was a real place, a real haven for the adventurous and a European throwback as a place of escape for the persecuted. Situated mostly in what is now Tennessee, it was bordered on the east by Asheville, North Carolina and on the west by Knoxville, Tennessee.

Most significant was its religious sentiment. It was a haven of those misplaced souls from the war of the *Regulators*, a place for the western migration of the Separate Baptists. It would now serve as one of the launching pads for the Baptist assault on the American mainland.

Many of the emigrants from Sandy Creek came to settle on Boone's Creek in the Watauga area of what became known as Franklin. The preachers that made the journey were: William Murphy, James Kell, Thomas Murrell, Isaac Barton, Matthew Talbot, Joshua Kelly, and John Chastain.[16] They may have been preceded by Jonathan Mulkey, the son of Phillip Mulkey, the planter of Fairforest church in South Carolina and William Reno. J. J. Burnett, historian of the Tennessee Baptists mentions a claim that places Jonathan Mulkey "with three others, as pioneers in Carter's Valley, late in the fall of 1775."[17]

---

[*] Thomas Armitage, writing in 1877 said, "Their success has been astonishing, so that to-day they have the largest Baptist population of any state in the Union. They have 102 Associations, 1,601 ministers, 2,623 Churches, and 261, 314 members." Thomas Armitage, *History of the Baptists* (New York: Bryan, Taylor, & Co., 1887), P. 775.

Benedict reports, "There was a small body which went out in something like a church capacity. They removed from the old church at Sandy-creek, in North Carolina, which was planted by Shubal Stearns."[18] Tidence Lane and his large family traversed the mountains, apparently on a continual basis until Tidence settled at Buffalo Ridge and organized it in 1778 or 1779. Jonathan Mulkey eventually became their pastor.

In typical Separate Baptist fashion, five churches were formed in a few years.

In 1781 the Overmountain Men had secured their liberty. In the years that followed a great and effectual door was opened to the people of the colonies and a flood ran through it.

Franklin was an independent state from 1785-1787 and actually fought a border war for its independence, albeit it was a temporary independence.

In 1786, the Holston Association, the first Baptist association in Tennessee, was formed with the help of Tidence Lane. The first churches in this association were: Kendrick's Creek, Bent Creek, Beaver Creek, Greasy Cove, Cherokee, North Fork of Holston, and Lower French Broad. It is worth noting that once the Tennessee Baptists established their first association, their roots, either "Separate" or "Regular," did not seem to be a point of contention. As Benedict stated, "There was so little difference in their notions of doctrine and discipline, that these names were soon forgotten, and they went on together with great union and harmony."[19] So the union of the Separates and Regular Baptists was a point of fact in Virginia (see chapter 11) and now in Tennessee. The Holston Association adopted the Philadelphia Confession of Faith at the time of its constitution.

The immigration to "Franklin" or Tennessee continued. Churches such as Coors Creek in North Carolina moved half of their membership to Tennessee in 1791;[20] John Dillahunty, who described a "sudden and powerful impulse,"[21] also moved to Tennessee.[22]

From this "sudden and powerful impulse" the Holy Spirit then visited the western part of Tennessee. Benedict wrote, "A considerable number of families of the Baptist persuasion had settled in many parts of the Cumberland country, but it was not till the year 1790 that Baptist churches began to be established, or the denomination to flourish."

In 1790 John Gano, who could not seem to resist the frontier, came to the region of a little stream which runs near the borders of Kentucky and Tennessee called the Red River, and at one of its branches, named Sulphur Fork, gathered a small church. They were soon scattered by Indian raids, but in 1791 they re-gathered and sent a request to the Elkhorn Association in Kentucky for help to constitute a church.

In response to their request, John Taylor and Ambrose Dudley traveled on horseback to visit the little band. They constituted them into a "covenanted church of Christ, called Baptists," in the year 1791. It was called Tennessee Church and united with the Elkhorn Association.[23]

At the head of the Red River at Fort Station was a church which followed the "sudden and powerful impulse," and emigrated from Tar River, North Carolina. Other churches were soon gathered. In 1796, they were embodied into an Association called Mero District.[24] In 1797 the church on Mill creek near Nashville was organized and soon after that at Big Harpeth. Garner McConnico and James Whitsitt, were the pastors of these churches and were leaders for many years among the Baptists in Tennessee.[25]

From the Mero District Association sprang the Red River and Concord Associations. In 1825 and 1828 Forked Deer and Big Hatchie Assocations were organized in Tennessee.

The progress of the Baptists in Tennessee: In 1784, there were 370 members of Baptist churches. In 1792, there were 889 members of Baptist churches.

The powerful voice of Shubal Stearns was silent in the grave. Yet from 1772 to 1802, Stearns continued his ministry and in reality, *baptized the south* from his grave. (He, being dead, yet speaketh.) Stearns had ordained Daniel Marshall who went to South Carolina and Georgia. He had ordained Samuel Harriss who went to Virginia, and he ordained Tidence Lane, who ventured into Tennessee. He had ordained James Read, who baptized Lewis Craig, and Craig was about to perform an astounding feat of faith for the future state of Kentucky.

*   *   *

Kentucky became a gathering place for Virginia preachers. Historians sometimes referred to the country as that "dark and bloody ground," even though the Indian name probably meant "head of the river."[26] The first Baptist pioneer preachers in Kentucky were: Squire Boone—1770; Thomas Tinsley—1776; William Hickman—1776; George Stiles Smith, John Taylor and William Marshall—1779; and Joseph Barnett, John Whitaker, James Skaggs, Benjamin Lynn, and John Garrard—1780. Of these first 11 preachers, three disappeared: Tinsley, Barnett, and Garrard, presumed killed by the Indians; one went into sin; one defected to the errors of Alexander Campbell; and one slipped into a dead orthodoxy.

Despite these devilish setbacks, the *adversary* could not prevent the onslaught of the pious pioneer preachers. Entering the new country was certainly no "Sunday school picnic," it was a dangerous place and destitute of any civil pleasantries.

Thomas Tinsley was the first Baptist preacher to actually preach in Kentucky. In 1776, William Hickman, on a survey trip, met him there. Hickman described Tinsley thus:

> We went nearly every Sunday to town to hear Mr. Tinsley preach. I generally concluded his meetings. One Sunday morning, sitting at the head of a spring at this place, he laid his Bible on my thigh and said to me, "you must preach today." He said if I did not, he would not. I knew he would not draw back.
>
> I took the book and turned to the 23d chapter of Numbers, 10th verse: "Let me die the death of the righteous, and let my last end be like his." I suppose I spake fifteen or twenty minutes, a good deal scared, thinking if I had left any gaps down, he would put them up. He followed me with a good discourse, but never mentioned any blunders.[27]

Other preachers came to Kentucky. John Tanner, once an assistant to John Moore at Tar-River Falls Baptist Church in North Carolina, came to the wilderness after the close of the Revolutionary War. In June 1777, he was shot and nearly fatally wounded by a certain Mr. Dawson who resented the fact that Tanner had baptized his wife.[28]

In 1779 John Taylor, Joseph Redding, Lewis Lunsford, and several other ministers from Virginia visited Kentucky on a tour of observation. Only Mr. Redding stayed in the country at that time. William Marshall, the venerable veteran of Virginia revivals, moved to Shelby County, Kentucky in 1780.

The first church of any kind west of the Alleghenies was the Severns Valley Baptist Church founded on June 18, 1781, by John Garrard. The second Baptist church in Kentucky was at Cedar Creek, founded on July 4, 1781. The third Baptist church in the new country had an extraordinary beginning: The Travelling Church.

The Travelling Church 1781

In September of 1781 Lewis Craig led a group of Baptist pioneers and their acquaintances in a farewell service at Upper Spotsylvania Baptist Church. The area is now known as Craig's Station. They were about to embark on a daring mission—an attempt to remove their entire church from northern Virginia through the Blue Ridge and into the new country of Kentucky. There can be no doubt that news of the danger of that place had reached their ears, but a great calling was upon Craig and his brave church members. George Ranck describes the scene at Spotsylvania:

> Such a gathering of men, women and children, slaves, pack horses, cattle, dogs, and loaded wagons as had never been seen in the county before, but there was no unseemly disorder and but little noise except such as came from fretful infants and from the bells on the grazing stock. The crowd was too great for the house and most of the people were assembled under the trees in front of it where the women had been provided with seats. It could not be a camp meeting, there were no signs of either cheerfulness or enjoyment. It was not a funeral

though all were sad and many were deeply dejected. It was "farewell Sunday" at Upper Spotsylvania (Baptist) Church.[29]

The group consisted of over 600 souls. They were to make their way across Virginia southwest to the Cumberland Gap and then northwest into Kentucky country, a journey of over 600 miles. Ranck, wrote:

> Among them, according to tradition, was Elijah Craig, the bold exhorter of the Blue Run church who had lunched in jail more than once on rye bread and water for conscience sake; Ambrose Dudley, who had often labored with him; William E. Waller, pastor of County Line, and William Ellis, the aged shepherd of the Nottaway flock who had realized what "buffetings" meant long before the Revolution brought its blessed heritage of religious freedom. They had many relatives among the departing throng and all of them but the venerable Ellis soon followed them to the land of Boone.[30]

Tracing their route, they went along the old Catharpin road toward the west quite possibly stopping at the homestead of John Leland on their way west.[31] Their route turned into "the mountain road" past the hamlet of Gordonsville and thence to the cluster of houses known as Charlottesville. They found themselves in the midst of the noted Piedmont country and their road extended from Albemarle to the James. By this established route the travelers reached the James River and after they had slowly forded it, they advanced to the little knot of dwellings on its southern bank where Lynchburg was to be. There they camped.

Next, the old red road through the rolling tobacco lands of Bedford brought them to the village of Liberty where they saw the "everlasting hills" of the Blue Ridge and the Peaks of Otter. This was the beginning of a great succession of mountain barriers forever cutting them off from old Virginia.

From Buford's Gap on the crest of the winding way they saw the endless mountains and started a journey for old Fort Chriswell. After fording the Roanoke River, they climbed the rugged ascent of the Allegheny "divide." From there they descended down the mountain road and crossed New River. They arrived at Fort Chriswell, which was located about nine miles east of the present Wytheville. There they gave up their wagons for the journey's sake because the terrain and road would not allow it. The close of the third week of September found them safely encamped at the desired point—the "Wolf Hills" now known as Abingdon.

During the "halt at Abingdon" the glorious news came of the British surrender at Yorktown. A group of stranded pioneers also from Virginia had been in Abingdon for nearly a year. Lewis Craig formed them into a church, which was called Providence.

The "Travelling Church" was forced to stay in Abingdon for a month and built a group of primitive huts to live in. Those huts at Black's Fort at Abingdon were eventually left behind and a dash to the interior of Kentucky was begun.

Lewis Craig and his group of pioneers had determined before they ever left Virginia that they would strive to migrate to Gilbert's Creek, a tributary of the Dix River in central Kentucky territory. About the first of December, nearly three weeks after leaving Abingdon and the North Fork of the Holston River, the dauntless pioneers crossed the Cumberland Gap. They entered Kentucky, passing intimidating mountains and drop-offs, and in front of them an enormous wilderness.

Northward they went through what is now Bell County and over the Pine Mountains making their way in the snow. They passed the site of Barboursville in Knox, and following the old trace, passed through what is now the courthouse in London, Laurel County. Then they crossed Rockcastle River at the foot of Wild Cat Mountain.

Light was breaking through for them, and they moved on about five miles north of Rockcastle River where the buffalo path led toward the already famous Boonsborough. They followed this branch of the Wilderness Road to the place now known as Mt. Vernon. Within a short time, the emigrants were marching toward English Station which they reached without any added trouble. They then passed the cabins of "The Crab Orchard" and filing northwestwardly through the woods and canebrakes headed for Logan's Fort near the spot where Stanford was afterwards established.

The settlers of the area were ready for them. Some were friends and kindred from Virginia, and they gathered to meet them. When they appeared in sight of the stockade they were greeted with the firing of rifles and shouts of welcome. There were hearty hand-shakes, affectionate embraces, eager inquiries, tears of joy and repeated exclamations of delight.

They located on the little tributary of Gilbert's Creek, two and a half miles southeast of the then forest-covered site of the present town of Lancaster and in that part of the original County of Lincoln which now constitutes the County of Garrard.

Spurred on by cold weather and dire necessity, the Baptists quickly made a "clearing" in the woods at Gilbert's Creek and established "Craig's Station." There in that lonely outpost before the close of the second Sunday in December 1781, they gathered and worshipped around the same old Bible they had used in Spotsylvania. The word of God was preached by their pastor, Lewis Craig. So met the first church that ever assembled in central Kentucky, the Gilbert's Creek Church. They had traveled 600 miles in 4 months—an average of about 5 miles a day.

William Cathcart relates Lewis Craig's first actions in Kentucky:

> The next year he [Lewis Craig] gathered Forks of Dix River in the same county. In 1783 he and most of Gilbert's creek church moved to the north side of Kentucky River and **organized South Elkhorn church**, in Fayette County. Here he remained about nine years, laboring zealously in all the surrounding country.[32]

Lewis Craig had a profound effect on everyone, it was said of him:

> As an expositor of the Scriptures, [Lewis Craig] was not very skillful, but dealt closely with the heart. He was better acquainted with men than with books. He never dwelt much on doctrine, but mostly on experimental and practical godliness. Though he was not called a great preacher, perhaps there was never found in Kentucky so great a gift of exhortation as in Lewis Craig. The sound of his voice would make men tremble and rejoice. The first time I heard him preach, I seemed to hear the sound of his voice for many months.[33]

*   *   *

John Taylor was about to return to Kentucky and give the remaining 30 plus years of his life to the pursuit of souls. He was the epitome of the pioneer. He gave this testimony about his ordeal to keep a preaching engagement early in his ministry:

> I soon after came to a creek, over which a bridge had been made, I saw that the water was up to the planks...I pushed on but the [lead] horse first fell through and as the one I rode was going down, I sprang from him on the floating planks, with my saddle bags in my hand...both my horses [were] between the cills of the bridge, and barricaded with floating planks on each side. This stream was about eight steps across it, ...my plan was to stand on the cill of the bridge, up to my knees in water, and float the planks off till I got to my horses, and with mighty struggling with the poor animals, get them up the bank.
>
> [This being accomplished] My saddle was wet, the bridle caked with ice, and my hands so benumbed, that I could not draw on my gloves. I soon met with another creek, which ran over my horses, where I got a fresh dunking: when I came to the River, I found it was impossible to cross it except by swimming, which I had often done in similar cases; I concluded that it was not proper to tempt the Lord my God to work a miracle in my preservation...I...turned tail...riding on. I became so very cold in my wet freezing clothes, concluded a little walking would comfort me. But the beast I led...broke ground to run back, and both together ran off in full speed, I ran with all my might to keep in sight of them in hopes the water ahead of them would stop them which it did. I was now very wet with heat and sweat, what shall I do? I mounted my horse and swam the creek. (I had ten miles to go with the sun about two hours high, the road amazingly bad.) ...The water ran up around my middle and soon after my clothes froze. About dark I got to where I started from..., getting from my horse I could scarce keep my feet; I staggered on to the house, and soon went to bed, my hands were so swollen with cold that I could scarce use them, I slept sound for several days; I felt in a kind of listless stuper. About one month after this I was stricken with a prodigious sufait, a breaking out, from head to foot, in likeness of ringworm covered with white scales, ...and continues more or less to this day, which has been a good deal upwards of forty years.[34]

John Taylor was ordained in 1782 by Lewis Craig, John Picket, John Cunes, Joseph Redding and Theodoric Noel.[35] He arrived back in Kentucky to stay in 1783. He quickly joined the Gilbert's Creek Baptist Church, where he began his heroic ministry.

Taylor wasted no time in preaching the Gospel. In the winter of 1784-5, "We began," said Taylor:

> [We began] to hold night meetings at our little cabins in the woods. There seemed to be some heart-melting among the people. The first, I recollect, was at a night meeting, at my little cabin. Though the night was wet and dark, and scarcely a trace to get to my house, the little cabin was pretty well filled with people, and what was best of all, I have no doubt the Lord was there. Mrs. Cash, the wife of Warren Cash, was much affected and soon after was hopefully converted. Others were also touched by the heat, who afterwards obtained relief in the Lord." Mrs. Cash was, as far as we know, the first fruits unto the Lord in the far-famed Blue Grass Region of Kentucky.[36]

J. H. Spencer, Baptist historian of Kentucky wrote:

> Clear Creek Church was constituted of about thirty members, dismissed from South Elkhorn for that purpose, in April, 1785. A revival had commenced in the neighborhood the previous winter, which continued with but little interruption for about two years. During this period between eighty and one hundred were baptized. John Taylor was chosen pastor of this church which he had gathered in March 1786, and continued in that office about three years, when he resigned. The church then numbered about 150 members. In 1790 another refreshing from the Lord visited this church, and continued seven or eight months. About an hundred and fifty were added to Clear Creek church, which brought her number to upwards of three hundred.[37]

The churches formed in Kentucky up to the year 1784 in our narrative were: Severns Valley, Cedar Creek, Gilbert's Creek, Forks of Dix River, South Elkhorn, and Clear Creek.

In 1784 **William Hickman** returned to Kentucky to forevermore settle. He had been converted under the ministry of "Swearin' Jack" Waller, James Childs and Thomas Tinsley in Virginia in the early days of the Separate Baptist revival. He describes his travail of soul and conversion:

> The Lord sent these "new lights" near where we lived; curiosity led me to go some distance to hear these babblers; the two precious men were John Waller and James Childs. I thought they looked like angels; then each of them preached. God's power attended the word, numbers falling, some convulsed, others crying out for mercy. I went home heavy hearted, knowing myself in a wretched state; I told [my wife] I must see them "dipped."
>
> I went, and an awful day to me it was; one of those ministers preached before Baptism and then moved on to the water, near a quarter of a mile; the people moved in solemn order, singing, "Lord, what a wretched land is this, etc."...but my mind was in a foment, still striving under the law, still had little hope to get to heaven that way.
>
> There was a certain preacher of the name of David Tinsley, I disliked him in my heart, for no other reason than his faithfulness and candor. I could not pray, but sin and evil thoughts were in my best performance; considering that God was holy, and how I was to stand before Him. Condemnation seized my troubled soul; from that time I thought I grew worse and worse, for I saw sin enough in my best performance to sink me to Hell; when I heard the truth preached it all condemned me.
>
> I often wished I had never been born, or that I had been a brute, that had no soul to stand before the holy God; for months I tried to pray, but thought I grew worse and worse, till all hopes of happiness was almost gone; and when I heard preaching I was condemned.
>
> I often went to meeting to get converted, I heard the gospel was free, but not for me, I was such a wretch, and condemned. I went over to a rock to try to pray, my heart appeared to be hard as a rock; when I got to the place I put myself in every position of prayer, I must have been an hour in that dismal condition, it was so cold I had to return to the house. I got up...and went out...about the setting of daylight, all at once the heavy burden seemed to fall off, I felt the love of God flow into my poor soul; I had sweet supping at the throne of grace; my sins pardoned through the atoning blood of the blessed Saviour; I heard no voice, no particular scripture applied;[38]

Rueben Ford baptized Hickman.

William Hickman came to the new country of Kentucky with the fire and zeal of John the Baptist. In 1788 a group of Baptists at the Forks of Elkhorn experienced a visitation from God. A certain Mr. Nathaniel Sanders had heard that Hickman was preaching in those parts. He sent the old preacher John Major, another Virginia veteran, to call on Hickman to come to preach. It was harshly cold, but Hickman made the journey.

It may be helpful to point out, that at this time, pioneer preachers received no salary, but were oftimes given "presents" of goods and lands for becoming the settled minister. Hickman was offered 100 acres of land with a cabin—not an unusual gift. That this particular man, Mr. Sanders, would offer the gift was unusual. Hickman said to him, "Sir, you do not care about religion, I want to know why you want me to come."

Sanders replied, "If it never is any advantage to me, it may be to my family." This caused Hickman to weep, and the decision to stay at the Forks of Elkhorn was not difficult.

From here Hickman made his preaching excursions all over that part of Kentucky. It is said that he baptized more people than any other preacher of Kentucky and formed more churches than Lewis Craig. If that is true then he must have been singularly blessed of God. His first wife, who died in Kentucky, was the daughter of John Shackleford,[39] and bore him 13 children. Eight of those children died from the ravages of the frontier. A surviving son, William, became the pastor of the South Benson church where he served for many years. Another son, Paschal, was killed at the battle of the River Raisin. John Taylor wrote of Hickman:

> His whole deportment is solemn and grave, and is much like Caleb, the servant of the Lord, who at fourscore years of age was capable to render service in war as when young. This veteran can yet perform a good part in the Gospel vineyard. His style of preaching is plain and solemn, and the sound of it is like thunder in a distance, but when he becomes animated, it is like thunder at home, and operates with prodigious force on the consciences of his hearers.[40]

Turning our attention to Lewis Craig, it is evident Craig stayed busy in those early years in Kentucky. Cathcart stated, "A number of churches were founded, and Elkhorn Association was formed October, 1 1785."[41] This was under the direction of Craig.

The Elkhorn Baptist Association is a body of unparalleled historic significance. It was the first Baptist association in the state of Kentucky. It began in 1785 with three churches in fellowship: Tate's Creek, Clear Creek, and South Elkhorn; all of which were formed in 1785. It adopted the Philadelphia Baptist Confession of Faith.

The second Baptist association formed just three weeks later. Salem Baptist Association was organized at Cox's Creek Baptist Church on October 29, 1785. The founding churches were: Severn's Valley (1781); the first in Kentucky, Cedar Creek (1781); Bear Grass (1785); and Cox's Creek. Salem adopted the Philadelphia Confession without the modifications installed by the Elkhorn Association.[42]

There were other preachers who migrated to Kentucky, such as Elijah Craig who arrived in 1786. And significantly, the beloved John Gano after the death of his wife in New York, arrived in 1788. Gano was no doubt longing for the prospects of charting new fields for God even in his old age, just as he had done in North Carolina and New York. The move would prove to have adverse effects on his children.[43]

In seven short years, the Elkhorn Association had increased to 23 churches and 1,700 members.[44] We shall discover in chapter 15, how *the adversary* divided, confused, mutilated and plundered this early pioneer body of *baptized believers.*

The South Kentucky Association, or Separate Kentucky Association was formed in 1785, principally by the ministries of Robert Elkin, Joseph Bledsoe, and James Smith. These preachers were all emigrants from Virginia. In them the Separate Baptist loyalties were taken beyond the mountains. Unwilling to lose the distinctives, or the moniker "separate," these Baptists formed in contrast to the Elkhorn association north of them.

In 1789 there was an attempt made to abolish the names Regular and Separate and unify Elkhorn and the South Kentucky Separates. This had already been accomplished in Virginia and Tennessee. The attempt failed at this time.[45] Benedict wrote, "The Separates were afraid of being bound and hampered by articles and confessions." [46]

The union was attempted again in 1793. It was unsuccessful and resulted in the withdrawal of five churches from the South Kentucky Separates to form the Tate's Creek Association.

About 1792 the unflappable Lewis Craig moved to Bracken County, Kentucky. He formed several churches including the Washington church in 1785. Lewis Craig, in the words of William Cathcart, became "the father of Bracken Association."[47]

George Eve, the supporter of James Madison, also came to Kentucky, in 1794. He would suffer from a different kind of malady than that which struck John Gano and his children. Eve brought reproach upon himself and had to leave the ministry.

David Thomas, the respected veteran of the Revolution and persecution in Virginia, came to the new country in 1796. His age could not keep him from the call to the wilderness. He took charge of the Washington Baptist Church in the Bracken Association.

In 1790, there were in the state of Kentucky, three associations, 42 churches, and 3,105 members. At that date, the population of the State was 73,677. This gave one Baptist church, in round numbers, to every 1,754 of the population, and one Baptist to every 23 of the population.

Ohio 1790

The state of Ohio exploded in growth after 1790. In just 20 years the population grew from 3,500 to 230,760. This way was made by the conquest of the area north and west of the Ohio River by General George Rogers Clark and the civil government given to the area by Virginia. The first church of the *baptized believers* in Ohio was formed in 1790.

In the fall of 1788, a group of 23 men, 3 women and 2 children sailed down the Ohio River to a spot midway between Pittsburgh and the Falls of the Ohio (Louisville). On the 18th of November 1788, they landed at Duck Creek near the future spot of the city of Cincinnati. Most were from New Jersey, members of the Scotch Plains Baptist Church.[48] Scotch Plains had been the instrument for the formation of the first Baptist church in New York City, the church pastored by John Gano.

Stephen Gano, the son of John Gano, made a missionary sojourn to Fort Washington, near Duck Creek, and six miles from present day Cincinnati. There he baptized three believers and formed a church on the north side of the Ohio. This became the Columbia Baptist Church, later called the Duck Creek Church and still later, Cincinnati.[49] John Smith yet another Virginian, became their pastor.

In 1797 the Miami, Ohio Baptist Association was formed from four churches: Duck Creek, Staunton, King's Creek and Union.

Ohio became fertile ground for revival, but at Kirtland, it would become terrible ground for one of the most heinous heresies of modern times.[50]

Illinois 1798

A record of the Baptists into Illinois begins with the pioneer preacher James Smith. Smith was a native of Virginia and served in the 13th and the 7th Virginia regiments in the Revolution. He and other members of his family settled Smith's Station, Garrard County Kentucky in 1779.[51] Smith and John Whitaker formed the Bear Grass Creek Baptist Church in that settlement in January 1784. It was near Louisville.[52] Even though James Smith assisted in the organization of the South Kentucky Association of the Separate Baptists, he eventually united with the Forks of Dix River Baptist Church, a church in the Elkhorn Association. He was appointed as an itinerant evangelist.

The first group of settlers into Illinois settled in the Mississippi bottom just south of present day Waterloo. They had served with Colonel George Rogers Clark: James Moore; Shadrach Bond, Sr.; Robert Kidd; James Garretson; Larkin Rutherford; and James Piggott.[53] They arrived in 1781. In 1785, the Ogles, the Worleys and the Andrews, from Wheeling, West Virginia joined them. The next year, they were joined by James Lemen, Sr.; James McRoberts; George Atchision; and David Waddell and their families. The new settlement came to be known as "New Design."

In the summer of 1787, James Smith visited New Design and preached to the people. Several pioneers were converted including Joseph Ogle and James Lemen, Sr. Lemen's son James, just a child, never forgot that meeting. He later testified, "The influence of the Divine Spirit, descended, and some were converted. These were the first converts, and this **the first revival** ever known on the Father of Waters."[54] Little James Lemen became a faithful preacher of the Gospel. He labored for God in Missouri for over 60 years.

James Smith returned to New Design in 1790. As he traveled out of the settlement in the direction of Little Village, Indians ambushed his small company. A woman, Mrs. Huff, was killed and Smith was kidnapped. John Mason Peck wrote:

> Consultation was held by the Indians how they should dispose of their prisoner. Some proposed to kill him, fearing the white people would follow them, and pointed their guns at his breast. Knowing well the Indian character, he bared his breast, as though he dared them to shoot him, and then pointed upward, to signify the Great Spirit was his protector. Having caught him while in the attitude of prayer and hearing him sing hymns on his march, they concluded he was a 'great medicine' and held intercourse with the Great Spirit, and must not be killed. They took him to their town on the Wabash, from whence he obtained his freedom—the people of New Design paying one hundred and seventy dollar for his ransom.[55]

Absolutely unaffected by the ordeal, Smith later made a third trip to Illinois country.

The second preacher into Illinois country was Josiah Dodge. Dodge was from Connecticut and was visiting his brothers, John and Dr. Israel Dodge who were some of the first settlers to the Ste. Genevieve settlement in Missouri. Dodge baptized a number of converts in New Design—James Sr. and Catherine Lemen, John Gibbons and Isaac Enoch.

The time 1796 was ripe for the formation of the first Baptist church in Illinois. David Badgley gathered it. Badgley was a convert of Joseph Redding and John Taylor from their Virginia days who was baptized by William Marshall.[56] He came from Pendleton County, Virginia. He gathered a harvest of souls from his own work, the work of Josiah Dodge, and the work of James Smith into the Baptist church at New Design.

Badgley was also credited with preaching from a rock[*] into Missouri, as it was illegal to preach anything but Catholicism in the Louisiana Territory before 1804.

Mississippi 1798

The early arrival of the Baptists in Mississippi was on this wise: On the Pedee River in South Carolina, during the Revolutionary War, Richard and Phebe Curtis made no secret of their allegiance to the Patriot cause. They were Baptists who were forced into seeking a better country. They decided to pack their family and migrate to the Natchez country of Mississippi. In 1780 they left with 15 members of their family and a few friends. They journeyed first to the Holston River in Tennessee where they built three flatboats and prepared to sail to Mississippi.

While on the Tennessee River, they met with disaster, as this narrative explains:

> While descending the Tennessee River they were assailed by the Indians not far from the mouth of Clinch River. All hands on board commenced a vigorous defense, in which the women of the company took part. Mrs. Jones held up at thick poplar stool between her eldest son William (then twelve years old) and the bullets, while he steered the boat so as to enable his father to use his rifle. The stool was pierced with several bullets.
>
> Another lady took the steering oar from her husband that he might return the fire of the enemy, and with unfaltering courage guided the boat until disabled by a wound in the back. Hannah Curtis (Mrs. Courtney) was grazed on the head by a ball and Jonathan Curtis was slightly wounded. The two boats, which contained the Curtis and Ogden families, passed without the loss of any of the party. But the third boat, traveling in company with them, was captured and all on board killed except one woman who remained among them as a captive for many years.[57]

---

[*] John Clark, the Methodist, who became a Baptist, is believed to have preached from that famous rock, located close to present day Herculaneum.

They landed at the mouth of Cole's Creek about twenty miles above Natchez, and settled just southeast of there. They built a meeting-house and called Richard Curtis, Sr. to preach to them. They called their church, Salem. They then had a revival and some were converted and baptized by Curtis even though he was not ordained. Four other preachers soon joined them: Bailey Chaney, Mr. Harigail from Georgia, Barton Hannan, and William Owen.

Mississippi was still in Spanish hands at this time, and it was illegal to hold church services other than Roman Catholic; but lo, a Spaniard named Stephan Alvoy was converted, baptized and caused no small stir to the Catholic inhabitants of the territory.

Harigail began to preach with great zeal and irritated the Catholic authorities. They dedicated themselves to destroying Richard Curtis and Stephen Alvoy whom they rightly identified as their chief enemies. In 1794 the Spanish planned to kidnap Curtis and Alvoy and send them into the mines in Mexico as slave labour. This plan was made known to them and late one night, outfitted by their friends, the Mississippi duo escaped. They went east through the territories of Mississippi, Alabama and into the haven of South Carolina. It was an 18-month trek of terror through mostly uninhabited wilderness. They arrived in South Carolina in the fall of 1795.

Harigail was threatened and also escaped, and Bailey Chaney went into hiding. Then miraculous news came that the Natchez district was going from Spanish hands into American hands. A very courageous Barton Hannan sought permission from the Spanish authorities to preach in the camp in Natchez. He was allowed to preach on Sunday, June 4, 1797, but his sermon got him into trouble with "some Irish Romanists."[58] The Irishmen, showing more allegiance to Rome than America, beat the preacher mercilessly. Then Hannan was imprisoned. This outraged the already impatient Americans, and it seems Hannan had a wife that would not stand for her husband to suffer for conscience. Mrs. Hannan stirred the people of the settlement who had benefited from the ministry of her husband. W. E. Paxton wrote:

Hannan was also imprisoned and remained in the dungeon until his wife, a very resolute woman, demanded his release, with such assurance of the purpose of the people to back her demand with force, that the Governor deemed it prudent to comply.[59]

Col. Ellicott demanded that the Spaniards evacuate Fort Rosalie by the 30th of March 1798, and before daybreak that morning they marched out and surrendered the district to the Government of the United States.

A large brush arbor was erected at Natchez and Bailey Chaney was sent for. It was an immense crowd that heard the first religious service of any kind held in that country as a territory of the United States. Under the American flag he preached without harassment from the "minions of Rome." [60]

In a few months the stage was set for the return of Richard Curtis, Sr. to the Natchez country. He had not seen his wife or children for three years. As he approached the settlement at Coles Creek on Sunday evening, he was commandeered to the meeting-house and asked to preach. As it was in the throes of a great revival, the house was crowded and Curtis was confined to the front pulpit area. His wife arrived just before service and took her place toward the back. When the speaker for the night was announced the church was astonished to see their old preacher rise to address them but no one was more astonished than Mrs. Curtis, who fainted when her husband climbed into the pulpit. Phoebe had to be carried from the meeting. Elder Curtis knelt beside her and with calming words brought her to consciousness. No doubt in that churchyard was the happiest woman in all Mississippi.[61]

There seems to be some evidence that the Salem church was reconstituted or at least officially formed at this time with Richard Curtis, Sr. as the pastor.

In September of 1806, these five churches formed the Mississippi Association: Salem, New Hope, New Providence, Bethel and Ebenezer. They drew up a confession similar to the Philadelphia of their fathers. In the 20 years that followed they enjoyed a wonderful period of growth. In 1818 eight churches were dismissed to form the Union Association. By 1820, 36 churches and nearly 1,000 members were represented in the Mississippi Association. The most notable preachers were Richard Curtis, Sr., John Stampley, Moses Hadley, Ezra Courtney Dr. David

Cooper and Thomas Mercer, the venerable brother of Jessie Mercer. Thomas was considered "the revivalist of his day, the Boanerges of the Baptist Church."[62]

As John T. Buck describes, "On October 28, 1818, Richard Curtis, Sr. died at the house of a friend on Beaver Creek, in Amite County, where he had gone to seek medical relief from a cancer that occasioned his death. For a long time, his grave was unknown, but some years since it was identified and marked with a view to placing a monument over it, which the writer hopes to see done."[63]

Indiana 1798

The foothold for the Baptists in Indiana was begun with the formation of the "church of Christ on Owens Creek." (Now known as Silver Creek Church) It was located in the county of Knox and territory northwest of the Ohio River. It was constituted upon the principles of the Philadelphia Baptist Confession on November 22, 1798, by Isaac Edwards.[64] Soon other churches were formed around Fourteen Mile Creek. Theirs was a heroic struggle in the wilderness, with danger on all hands.

About that time:

Isaac McCoy and George Waller explored the wilderness of the Indian Territory as far as Vincennes, preaching wherever they could get a few gathered together, in the cabins or in the woods. Through their instrumentality a church was organized eight miles north of Vincennes in 1806, and the same year a church called Bethel, further down the Wabash. These were followed by the organization of the Patoka church, in what is now called Gibson county; and also Salem, Moriah, and Pigeon Creek. These six churches, with the same number of ministers, viz., Alexander Devens, James Martin, Isaac McCoy, and Stephen Strickland, were formed into an association called Wabash.[65]

The Maria Creek Church, which was named for the stream on which it is located, was organized in 1809. This was more than 100 miles northwest of the Silver Creek church.

Alexander Diven, of Columbia Church on the Patoka River, helped in the founding. Isaac McCoy of the Silver Creek Church was chosen as the first pastor. "At the ordination of Isaac McCoy, his father Elder William McCoy and Elder George Waller were present from Buck Creek church, Shelby County, Kentucky."[66]

In March of 1812, ten churches organized into the Silver Creek Baptist Association. That organization included the churches: Silver Creek, Mount Pleasant, Fourteen Mile, Knob Creek, Indian Creek, Upper Blue River, Camp Creek, Salem and White River.[67]

Jeremiah Vardeman

CHAPTER FOURTEEN
The Great Revival in the West
And the Birth of Foreign Missions

The Gospel into Missouri (1804), Alabama (1808), Louisiana
(1812), Arkansas (1818) and the Uttermost Parts.

There are several things that seem to me to argue, that the Sun of righteous-
ness, the Sun of the new heavens and new earth, when He rises—and comes
forth as the bridegroom of His church, ...shall rise in **the west,** *contrary to the*
course of things in the old heavens and earth. The movements of Providence
shall in the day be so wonderfully altered in many respects, that God will as it
were change the course of nature, in answer to the prayers of His church; as
He caused the sun to go from the west to the east, ... a deliverance out of the
hand of the king of Assyria. The Sun of righteousness has long been going down
from east to west; and probably when the time comes of the church's deliver-
ance from her enemies, so often typified by the Assyrians, the light will rise in
the west, till it shines through the world like the sun in its meridian brightness.
The same seems also to be represented by the course of the waters of the sanc-
tuary, Ezek. xlvii. Which was from west to east; which waters undoubtedly
represented the Holy Spirit, in the progress of His saving influences,
in the latter ages of the world.
—Jonathan Edwards.

Babylon hath been a golden cup
in the LORD's hand.—Jeremiah 51:7

The war for souls in America unofficially began with the formation
of the Sandy Creek Association in 1758. It was now in full engagement.

The preachers and people together took on the religious and the
heathen of the south with a vengeance. The Baptists of the north also
contended with the *standing order* and the citizens of the land of the *dying.* It was now a glorious war. Baptists, Congregationalists, Methodists
and Episcopalians debated, wrote pamphlets and tracts, held open fo-
rums, and challenged each other to public discussion. Rousing dialog

and argument was the order of the day. Baptist victories would often follow in their wake. For the first 35 years of this conflict, as we have seen, the Baptists waged war on the establishment.

In New England in 1758 the Baptists had roughly 30 churches. By the year 1793 there were at least 325 churches in New England representing over 25,000 persons.[1]

For the rest of the country it was another example of the "Book of Acts" kind of growth. According to the Asplund register of 1790 from the Eastern Shore of Virginia to the great river Mississippi, 879 Baptist churches were now flourishing with 1,171 preachers and 64,975 members, with a great new harvest about to commence. Here are just a few examples of God's visitation from 1758 to 1798:

> • 1780. There was a revival in the Six Principle Baptist Church in Tiverton, Rhode Island, under Peleg Burroughs and 91 were baptized in 13 months.
> • In 1780 Asa Hunt of the Third Baptist Church in Middleborough, Massachusetts, reported a remarkable revival even in the midst of tyranny in Massachusetts: There were 113 baptized in two years.
> • 1785. The Great Virginia Revival.
> • 1787. Another revival in Virginia under John Waller.
> • 1788. The Baptists of North Fork of Pamunkey in Virginia had a great revival. Their pastor was the Separate Baptist Aaron Bledsoe. They baptized several hundred so that by the end of 1792 they had 350 members in the Virginia wilderness.
> • 1798-99. At the church of Caleb Blood, the Fourth Baptist Church at Shaftsbury, Vermont, there were 175 persons converted and baptized in the winter season!
> • In 1800 a revival at the church of Jedidiah Hibard in New Hampshire resulted in the birthing of churches in Westford and Richford, Vermont.

With the establishment gone, all Christian denominations that believed and practiced *experimental religion* experienced unprecedented growth following the Revolutionary War. The Baptist churches in 1800 were gathered mostly in associations. They had general unions in several states including Virginia, Georgia, Tennessee and Kentucky.

Some unusual things were happening among them. David Cummins relates:

> Elijah Baker and Philip Hughes were challenged by two Methodist preachers to debate the subject of baptism during their labors, and Philip Hughes presented the Baptist case. He debated in Fowling Creek, Maryland, in 1782, and three Methodist 'class leaders' were later immersed by Hughes. Again in Virginia, in 1785 he was challenged to debate and 22 of the audience were immersed the next day.[2]

In 1805, Thomas Baldwin of Boston immersed Daniel Merrill, a Congregational minister of New Hampshire. Over 100 of his members followed his example and they established the Baptist Church at Sedgwick, Maine.[3]

In 1805, in Windham County, Connecticut, the *standing order* Congregational church built a meeting-house with tax money. They tried in vain to find a Congregational or Presbyterian to fill the pulpit. Nehemiah Dodge, a Baptist preacher was asked to preach there. He related the work of God in that place:

> After a meeting-house was erected, the people, who built it, made application to Presbyterian ministers, But these gentlemen replied, that they would not in conscience preach to them, nor fellowship those that would. Why? Because the people were immoral or scandalous in their lives? No. But because they said they had gone contrary to *law* in building their house.
>
> When it came to my turn according to appointment to visit this people for the first time (which was about a year ago), I perceived so much solemnity and candour among them, and such a spirit of inquiry after the apostolic truth and practice, as could not fail to interest my feelings in their behalf.
>
> Hence I appointed to visit them again in February, and continue with them eight or ten Sabbaths. Some, who had been members of the Presbyterian Church, obtained light upon Bible baptism, and the doctrine of the covenants. Many others began to inquire whether they had not taken that for granted, which ought first to have been provided, in supposing that baptism was appointed by God as a substitute for circumcision, and for a sign and seal of the same covenant. And whether in the case of infant sprinkling they had not acted without any positive or fairly implied

evidence. Our assemblies were large and solemn as they have ever since continued. And on Fast day, last spring, three persons were baptized, which, I conclude, were first ever baptized in this parish.

As my time of engagement was near expiring, the proprietors of the new house, with others, met and requested me to remove my family, and make my home with them.

Since I commenced my stated labours here, God has been pleased graciously to constitute his favour to the people. Some have been hopefully converted to God, and baptized. Several brethren and sisters from the Presbyterian Church have put into practice the light they have obtained upon this ordinance. Some backsliders have been waked up to purpose, and put on the Lord Jesus Christ.[4]

NEHEMIAH DODGE, LEBANON, DECEMBER 27, 1805.

A similar incident occurred at Canton, Massachusetts. During the ministry of the Reverend William Ritchie, the people of the Canton, Massachusetts *standing order* church began to seriously consider the claims of Baptists concerning believer's baptism. The formation of a Baptist church out of the *standing order* took place on May 29, 1814. That gathering was at the home of Ezra Tilden on the shores of Reservoir Pond, with a large number of souls buried in believer's baptism by Elder Joel Briggs.

The Printing of the "Common" Bible

The German Bible of Martin Luther was the first Bible printed in America. Christopher Saur in Germantown Pennsylvania, printed it. Printing was done in 1745, 1755, and 1763. In 1776, Saur had another 3,000 copies ready to be bound when the British army, for some satanic reason, overran Germantown and destroyed the entire issue. Their own Hessians could have used those Bibles.

The King James was called the "common" version. It had risen to supremacy in every English speaking country worldwide. America had imported her Bibles from England and Holland. Until the time of the Revolution no Bibles were printed here. There was a memorial received in Congress dated September 11, 1777, requesting Bibles in the "common" version. A committee reviewed the request and made a recommendation, which read in part, "The use of the Bible is so universal and its importance is so GREAT...the committee recommends that Congress will import 20,000 Bibles from Holland, Scotland or elsewhere into different parts of the states of the Union."[5] But they were never ordered.

Robert Aitken of Philadelphia took it upon himself to publish the New Testament in 1777. In 1781, just as the war was ending, he presented a petition to Congress seeking support for his endeavor. The Congress of the United States promptly adopted the following resolution:

> *Resolved*, That the United States in Congress assembled, highly approve the pious and laudable undertaking of Mr. Aitken, as subservient to the interest of religion as well as the progress of the arts in this country, and being satisfied from the above report of his care and accuracy in the execution of the work, they recommend this edition of the Bible to the inhabitants of the United States, and hereby authorize him to publish this recommendation in the manner he shall think proper.[6]

Dr. P. M. Simms wrote, "The Robert Aitken Bible, published in Philadelphia in 1782, was the King James Version and the first English Bible printed in America openly and with an American imprint."[7] It is the only Bible ever recommended by the U.S. Congress. God didn't seem to mind, as we shall shortly discover.

The publication of the "common" King James began in earnest. Most notable of the publishers was Isaiah Thomas of Worcester, Massachusetts. Thomas learned to print at the age of six, and as a young man he gave his influence as a newspaper publisher to the Revolution. In 1791 he published two editions of the King James. To those who were unable to pay all cash for the volume, he offered to accept "wheat, rye, Indian corn, butter or pork, if delivered to his store in Worcester."[8] Thomas took his responsibility of printing God's word seriously. Preachers from the area, comparing the copies with no less than eight other texts, examined every sheet of his editions.[9]

Isaac Collins did printing of the Bible at Trenton, New Jersey, in 1788 and 1791. In just a few years he had printed 10,000 Bibles, with his own children proofreading them 11 times. Only two errors were ever found—a broken letter and a misplaced punctuation mark.[10]

The Bible was printed in various other locations including Wilmington, Delaware, in 1797. In all, there were 20 editions of the entire Bible (representing over 100,000 copies) and 15 editions of the New Testament (representing over 90,000 copies) published in various places before the year 1800. That was astounding work for the primitive methods that were employed. The seed was now available to plant a vine. God now visited the vine, and Kentucky was first.

There was a lone bridal path that led to one of those old cabins in the woods of Kentucky. It led to the home of Judge Shreve. David Thomas, the silver haired patriarch of Virginia, was finishing his days there. In the year 1800, a young soldier in the war for souls, Jeremiah Vardeman, rode through the wilderness for a chance to speak and ask for the prayers of the unflappable warrior.[11] Vardemen had just returned to God from his miserable backslidings. He had preached for the first time in a house meeting in Pulaski County. He had not planned to speak, but being pressed into it, he began to beseech and weep with the people. The next week he was there again, and spoke testifying of what the grace of God had done for his soul. At the close of his message he was thronged with people, weeping and seeking rest for their souls. The Lord had confirmed His call upon his life.[12]

Vardeman was soon to be ordained and spend the rest of his life in the war for souls. So here in the woods he sought David Thomas to pray for him. Vardeman entered the home of Judge Shreve and requested prayer from Thomas. He knelt beside Thomas, who was now blind and near the door of death, and in pity the seasoned preacher placed his hand upon the head of the young preacher and prayed, "God bless him, and may he be blessed." Within a few months, David Thomas was honorably discharged to report to his Master, but the war for souls for Jeremiah Vardeman had just commenced.

*   *   *

The Great Revival in the West was a revival in reverse of nature as Jonathan Edwards predicted (see the short introduction to this chapter). It was a west to east national awakening and in two years it added *8,000 members* to the Kentucky Baptist churches alone. There were four "Christian" splinter groups that sprang from it: the Disciples of Christ or "Christian" Church (along with the various factions of the Church of Christ), the Cumberland Presbyterian Church, the Shakers, and surprisingly, the *Mormons*.

Before we draw back the curtain on the wonderful, awful, powerful religious explosion also known as the Great Revival of 1800 we should understand the spiritual state of things on the frontier just prior to this event.

John Taylor, the great evangelist and church planter of Kentucky, wrote about the days prior to 1800:

> I never had been so thoroughly cowed down by discouragement through the course of my ministry as now; though it had been in action for 25 years, and really thought I had better been dead than alive, for I felt as if Satan had gotten the mastery where I lived; So that I could say from my soul, "*Woe is me that I sojourn in Meseck, that I dwell in the tents of Keder!*"[13]

Samuel Howard Ford, preacher, editor and historical link to the Baptist push into the west, wrote:

> They preached as they always did, except with more earnestness and prayer; and not a landmark was removed or destroyed in their theology, or church polity, or usages. Among those unostentatious workers who claim no honor, and felt no ruinous inflation, were Baptists, who did more under God, in awakening and guiding the out-gush of religious sentiment that swept over Kentucky and the west than all the New Lights put together.[14]

The Methodists claim some credit for the start of the Great Revival in the West by citing the preaching of John McGee. The Presbyterians believe it began with their own James McGready. We say, after reading the accounts that the Holy Ghost is the reason for the revival and His antagonist, satan, is responsible for the counterfeit. The wise Christian will understand that for every mighty act of God, there is a reaction from the devil.

James McGready, the Presbyterian, was holding forth in southern Kentucky in Logan County. The scene at Red River was nearly beyond description. A fellow Presbyterian from Bourbon County, Barton Stone, came to view the work. He was convinced that it was of God. Stone took the experience back to his Presbyterian congregation at Cane Ridge and Concord in Bourbon County. Soon, as many as 20,000 people were swarming the hills at Cane Ridge. It was estimated that 3,000 souls were converted in one week.

"Father" Rice, the great Presbyterian leader of Kentucky said, "That we had a revival of the Spirit and power of Christianity among us, I did, do and ever shall believe, but we have dashed it down and broken it in pieces."[15] What did Rice mean?

At the Presbyterian Church at Walnut Hill, there "was a sacrament on the first Sabbath in September, 1801, when the following clergy-men were present and took part: Marshall, Blythe, Rice, Lyle, Crawford, Welch, Stuart, and Rannals."[16] Rice published the following account given to him by an eyewitness to the scene:

> Father Rice rose in the pulpit with his commanding form and silver locks, and in the most solemn manner began to repeat those words of scripture, "Holy, Holy, Holy is the Lord God Almighty!"
>
> There was an instantaneous hush throughout the house. Rice then tried to dissuade them from encouraging the bodily exercises. His efforts, for the time, were in vain. Even Mr. Lyle, who afterwards seconded his efforts, thought that Rice felt more concerned about his bodily affections than for lost souls. The excitement only rose the higher. Even Mr. Rice's plan for dividing the sexes during the hours allotted to sleep, was contemptuously rejected, and old Parson Rice denounced as standing in the way; as a deist at heart, as having no religion. The revival, with its strange accompaniments, went on.

Some talked, some sang. Some prayed, and others exhorted till the roof rang with deafening and reiterated peals of indistinct sound. Hundreds were praying and singing, and shaking hands, at the same time. Numbers were exhorting when nobody could hear; hallooing and screaming till hoarse and deliberated in constitution. The place was crowded, especially the larger aisle; but there was such a din from the intermingled exercise that a loud voice could be heard only a few inches. Mr. How was in one corner, Stuart and Lyle in another, while in another on the right of the pulpit, Mr. Steel, and Mr. Robinson up stairs, but none could get a hearing.[17]

S. H. Ford was surprised Mr. Rice published the account saying, "Such a description of a Presbyterian meeting, if penned by an enemy, would strike one as a misrepresentation; but penned by a worthy, old-fashioned Presbyterian preacher, an eye witness, what a strange picture it presents."[18]

The Baptists by and large did not participate at Cane Ridge or Walnut Hill. Some attended, but did not lead. Those that did attend kept their order, David Benedict noted:

In the course of the meeting the Lord's Supper was administered, and all Christians of every denomination were invited to partake of it. The Methodists and Presbyterians communed together, but the Baptists could not consistently unite with them.[19]

The revival among the Presbyterians and Methodists took on bizarre traits. The jerks, barking, and dancing, all strange phenomenon, were well documented. Barton Stone had a mix of Methodists, Presbyterians and a few Baptists and had a plan for them.[*] The Baptists, on the other hand, stayed in their own churches and associational meetings. William Hickman was still among them, as was George Eve and Lewis Craig–all of them old men, and the Lord visited them one last time.

*   *   *

---

[*] The rise of the "Christian" church in Kentucky is related in chapter 15.

For the Baptists, the revival seems to have had its beginning at Benjamin Craig's meeting-house with John Taylor. Taylor was used of God in the very first revival in Kentucky 20 years earlier and here he relates a meeting at the beginning stages of the Great Revival in the West, in Gallatin County along the Kentucky banks of the Ohio River:

> I had intended to be at his house (some 50 miles distant) the very night of the meeting, so that I deserve no credit for being at the meeting at Craig's. The house being much crowded, they invited me to preach. This I did with much reluctance. From the dull feelings of my heart, I took a text that suited my own feelings "Lord, help me." I continued but a short time, for I considered myself very worthless. After this they continued on in prayer, praise, and exhortation, with much noise at times, till late in the night. Some were rejoicing, having lately obtained deliverance; others groaning in tears, under a pensive load of guilt, while myself silently musing on what I saw or heard. My own heart so barren and hard, that I wished myself out of sight, or lying under the seats where the people sat, or trodden under their feet.[20]
>
> Many of the people tarried all night...one object with them was to converse with me; I never heard the question (What shall we do to be saved?) more prevalent.I felt unworthy to be in the company. About sunrise, I took my leave of this blessed company, I had one secret reason, which was to get by myself and mourn over my own barren soul.[21]

John Taylor traveled to his old church, Clear Creek; the church he had established many years earlier. The church had not had a single baptism for seven years! Richard Cave was the pastor and had Taylor return at the beginning of this revival season. Taylor wrote of the first sermon at Clear Creek:

> I preached from the text, "My heart's desire and prayer to God for Israel is, that they might be saved." Soon after I began, a sort of feeling overtook me that exceeded anything I ever felt in public speaking; they consisted in a profuse weeping that I could not suppress, while I made a comparison of the then state of Israel with my poor neighbors; and the whole assembly seemed to reciprocate the same feelings; perhaps there was not a dry eye in the house. What the Lord did at this meeting broke up all the dancing in the settlement.[22]

In that year 1800, a total of 326 souls were buried in believer's baptism and into the membership of the wilderness church at Clear Creek.

Taylor and Richard Cave began preaching excursions along the Ohio River. It short order, they baptized over 100 and began to realize the revival was "general." It was happening all over Kentucky and as they would later discover, across the south and into New England.

When they arrived in Bullitsburg, Kentucky, they baptized converts and formed them into a church, but they needed a preacher to "keep public worship." They met to discuss their need. Taylor described the tender scene:

> When they met, they had a very small, poor man among them. He was also decrepit, for he limped as he walked. His name was Moses Vickers. He was a good singer and a man of good religious fame. When they convened Vickers wept among them, and proposed to go to prayer; after which he exhorted them in tears to trust in the Lord. Several of them went to prayer. They had such a tender, weeping meeting, that they concluded to meet the next Sunday, and in fact, a revival took place among them.[23]

Moses Vickers became their pastor.

Of revival scenes, the list would fill many volumes. Our hearts are all ablaze as we read such as this:

> Ambrose Dudley preached to the Bryant Station Baptist Church. Here were no extra meetings, except prayer-meetings at private houses through the week. The bright cloud passed over them. Gently fell the soft showers on the long barren field. Monthly, people were buried with Christ in baptism, groups of rejoicing converts of every class. 367 were reported baptized into the church at Bryant's. At Great Crossings, the work was more extensive. The earnest and eloquent Redding preached day and night, and from house to house. Crowds thronged the meeting-house. From the Eagle Hills to Cane Runs, age and infancy, black and white, were aroused, were alarmed, were asking "what shall we do to be saved?" William Cave, James Suggett, and George Eve aided the pastor, and preached with new-felt power. God's presence and power was among them; like the lightening, like the thunder,

it shook, it prostrated, it killed to make alive again; and the beautiful waters of the Elkhorn were parted by the burial in baptism of hundreds who now tread the shores of immortality.[24]

From Clear Creek and the Crossings, the flame passed into the Forks of Elkhorn. Things proceeded in a solemn manner through the Baptist Churches of central Kentucky.

South Elkhorn was pastored by the Virginia veteran John Shackleford. Shackleford had wept over the deadness of his church. In the previous six years only six had been baptized into the church and this church, planted by the legendary Lewis Craig was nearly dead. When the time of refreshing came, 309 were baptized during the spring and summer of 1801 alone. The jerks and barking that were present in other places were kept in check here. But the warmth of their Separate Baptist roots was evident in the preaching from the pulpit and the weeping in the pews.

The Great Revival of 1800 finally brought the Regular and Separate Baptists into a more perfect "union" in Kentucky. Both Elkhorn and the South Kentucky Separates had become quite large with a combined 8,000 members between them. In October 1801 at Howard's Creek meeting-house in the county of Clash, they "agreed to lay aside the names of 'Regular' and 'Separate,' and to travel together in future communion and fellowship as united brethren."[25] This paved the way for a general union and a future statewide "convention."

Throughout the Elkhorn association the revival spread. Between the Forks and the Crossings, McConnell's Run Church, now known as Stamping Ground, received 156; at Marble Creek, now East Hickman, 133. To sum up all, there were 3,005 added to the association that year by baptism.[26]

The work of God extended up along the Ohio settlements through Boone, Bracken, and Mason counties. God did a work in Minerva under the labors of Lewis Craig and at Washington and Mayslick, where Donald Holmes labored. Hundreds were converted. Over 300 were added to the Church at Shawnee Run during the revival and a total of about 1,000 were added to the South District Association.

The Salem Association, begun just a few months after Elkhorn, had the largest percentage increase in the state of Kentucky from 1800 to 1802. The membership of Salem Association nearly quadrupled in those years. Its domain was from the Ohio River to the Green River to the territory west of the Kentucky River.

Salem Association divided in 1802, using the Salt River as the boundary line, with 23 churches north of the Salt forming the Long Run Association.[27] In 1817, Salem again divided creating the Goshen Association.

The Long Run Baptist Association of Kentucky held its first meeting in 1803 at the Long Run meeting-house in Jefferson County, Kentucky. There were 24 churches representing 1,619 members. John Taylor preached the first association meeting sermon using I Corinthians 15:58: "Therefore, my beloved brethren, be ye steadfast, unmovable, always abounding in the work of the Lord, forasmuch as ye know that your labour is not in vain in the Lord." Spencer complained, writing, "It would be well if the association, then about to be formed, would perpetually cherish that text as a motto."[28] This he said, for he knew that terrible dissention would tear at the Long Run Association. There would be divisions over antimission sentiments and the false doctrines of Alexander Campbell. For all of the strife, Long Run begat two great blessings to the American frontier west: Silver Creek Baptist Church, which was the first Baptist Church in Indiana; and Isaac McCoy, the "Apostle of the Great Plains," arguably the greatest missionary America has ever produced.

These are the numbers of church members in the Baptist associations in Kentucky from 1800 to 1802:

1800	1802
Elkhorn- 1,663	Elkhorn- 5,310
Bracken- 539	Bracken- 753
Green River- 400	Green River- 800
Tate's Creek- 600	Tate's Creek- 1,802
South Kentucky- 1,000	South Kentucky- 2,383
Salem- 564	Salem- 2,521
Total- 4,766	Total- 13,569

After the Great Revival of 1800, the shear numbers of converts gave increase to the number of Baptist associations in Kentucky.[29] Not only Long Run, from the Salem Association, but North Bend was formed from Elkhorn in 1803; Stockton Valley and Russell's Creek Associations came out of Green River Association in 1804.

*   *   *

Jeremiah Vardeman continued his ministry in Kentucky and throughout the south. Vardeman was born in Wythe County, Virginia, in 1775. In 1779, he and his family moved to Kentucky and settled in the wilds of the Crab Orchard in Lincoln County.

In the early days of his ministry, Elder Vardeman had the charge of four churches. In 1804, he preached in Lexington, Limestone, (Maysville), and several other places. From that period we find him connected with the South District Association. A gracious and extensive revival followed his ministry in David's Fork church. In 1810, 185 were converted and baptized there.[30] His preaching was described as "powerful, sonorous, and clear; his enunciation distinct, and he could be heard in the open air for a great distance."[31]

In 1816, we find him in Lexington, Kentucky, holding a series of meetings and the following year the First Baptist Church of Lexington appears in the minutes of the Elkhorn Association with 38 members.[32]

Vardeman also preached extensively in Louisville, Kentucky. S. H. Ford wrote of his influence there:

> In 1816 he commenced a series of meetings. Judge Rowan, a distinguished jurist and statesman, was a warm personal friend of Vardeman, and regarded him as the greatest pulpit orator he had ever heard. There were but few professors of religion in Louisville at that time.
>
> The Methodist meeting-house, was obtained through the influence of Judge Rowan and others, and Vardeman commenced a series of meetings. Col. McKay, who was present at these services, says. "His fame as a preacher brought out immense congregations of people for several successive days, to whom he preached with great effect; and from these meetings," continues Col. McKay, "the city of Louisville *is*

indebted in a great measure for its flourishing churches." Immediately after Mr. Vardeman's visit the First Presbyterian Church arose then the First Baptist, and so on.[33]

In 1817 in another revival at David's Fork, about 125 were added to the church by believer's baptism.

Of Vardeman, S. H. Ford wrote:

His success in the ministry of the gospel was perhaps unequalled by that of any other minister west of the Allegheny Mountains. This unusual success must by attributed in a great measure, under God, to the sympathy of his own heart with the unconverted. "Knowing the terror of the Lord" himself, he felt deeply for the poor sinner already condemned. He threw his soul into his sermons, while he would plead with and for them, as though he could take no denial. The earnestness of his manner was calculated to convince the sinner that the preacher felt, and felt deeply for him. When he perceived that his preaching had enlisted the feelings of the unconverted, he was in the habit of proposing to pray with and for them. All he would do was to make them the offer, that if they came forward for prayer they might regard it as a privilege.[34]

Early in the year 1810, a powerful revival commenced in the church at David's Fork and the other churches he labored. On the 4th of July there was a great barbecue at Montgomery's Springs, to which most of the respectable young people in the vicinity were invited. On hearing this, Elder Vardeman published that he would hold a meeting the same day at David's Fork meeting-house and invited all the parents to come and bring their children. He preached a pungent sermon from 1 Sam. vii: 12- "Then Samuel took a stone and set it between Mizpeh and Shen, and called the name of it Eben-Ezer, saying, Hitherto hath the Lord helped us." From that day the revival seemed to spread with more power, and then it was I first heard the Gospel, and first heard and saw him invite sinners forward for prayer.

Elder Vardeman either introduced or improved the Western practice of inviting awakened sinners to the altar of prayer, a practice that has had its friends and enemies; and still there are some who question the beneficial effect of such a practice. So far as my observation had extended, I am impressed with the belief that those (in general) who have publicly manifested themselves for the prayers of the church, have lived as pure and devoted Christians as others. And sure I am that many more have been added to Zion by this means than any other.[35]

Yet another revival took place at David's Fork in 1827-28, in which 250 were added to the church. In three consecutive years at Lulbegrud, there were 165 baptisms, and at Grassy Lick, 90.[36]

The progress of the Baptists in Kentucky: 1784–309 members, 1792–3,095 members, 1802–13,569 members, and 1812–22,694 members.

Tennessee and the Great Revival of 1800

Beginning in 1790, these preachers: Daniel Brown, Joshua White, Nathan Arnott and Patrick Moony gathered five churches: Mouth Sulphur Fork, Head Sulphur Fork, Middle Fork, West Fork and Station Camp. These churches were organized into the Mero District Association in Middle Tennessee. The union was not of long duration. Internal problems brought dissolution of this association in 1803 and the Cumberland Association was constituted in that same year to take its place. The Cumberland Association had 15 churches in the beginning. This is the mother of all the associations in Middle Tennessee.[37]

Three Associations were formed from the Cumberland: Elk River, Red River and Concord. Of all of these early associations, Cumberland (the mother), Elk River and Red River became "antimission" in sentiment. Concord Association became missionary minded and was formed from Cumberland in 1809 at Old Spring Creek Church, a few miles east of Lebanon, Wilson County.

In eastern Tennessee, the result of the Great Revival caused the Holston Association to divide. There were 36 churches at the time, with somewhere close to 3,000 members.[38] The southern association became known as the Tennessee Association. By 1809, Holston had 18 churches and Tennessee contained 30 churches and nearly 1,500 members. Tennessee Association did not adopt the Philadelphia Confession, but in a precedent which gained popularity among the Baptist churches of the south, they "professed to hold the substance and spirit" of the Philadelphia Confession, "with some modification of some of the articles which it contains."[39] In reality, this meant there was a reluctance to accept predestination, limited atonement and the harder tenets of election. Many of the churches in the Tennessee Association were in the neighborhood of Knoxville, and most were on the Holston, Clinch, and Tennessee Rivers.

Knoxville became known as "Baptist Town" reminiscent of Piscataway, New Jersey,[40] which had been dubbed "Anabaptist Town."

In the spring of 1820, Jeremiah Vardeman came to Nashville, Tennessee, to preach the Gospel. There were all but three Baptist people who lived in Nashville and they were members of Mill Creek church four miles away. Under Vardeman, a large number of people were saved and baptized and the Baptist Church of Nashville was organized on July 22, 1820. 35 members of Mill Creek Baptist Church came to help form the church. By the first of October, the church had 150 members and began building a meeting-house.[41]

The Baptist church at Chattanooga began in 1840 as a mission from the First Baptist Church of Nashville, Tennessee.

The progress of the Baptists in Tennessee: 1784–370 members, 1792–889 members, and 1812–11,325 members.

Georgia and the Great Revival of 1800

David Benedict wrote:

> The next remarkable ingathering here was about 1802, in the time of the great revival, which prevailed most powerfully at the time in many parts of Georgia. The religious attention at Kioka was very great; two or three camp-meetings were from necessity, held in the neighborhood, in which some of the most affecting scenes of joy and sorrow, of depression and transport were exhibited. In this revival, Mr. [Abraham] Marshall baptized about 100 more.[42]

Some account of the share, which Georgia had in the great revival in 1800 and onward, has already been given. Many thousands during the process of this revival were added to the Baptist churches. Jessie Mercer came to Georgia in 1775 when he was but 6 years of age. His father, Silas Mercer, had been a part of the marvelous revival at Kiokee led by Daniel Marshall. Jessie was singularly blessed of God in his preaching in the Georgia Association. During 1800-1801, Jessie baptized about 300 converts. Cathcart wrote of Jessie Mercer:

> To the graces of oratory, Mr. Mercer made no pretensions, but there was an unction from the Holy One that breathed from his spirit and beamed from his sweet and heavenly eye, which enchained and animated the hearer and thus more than supplied the absence of oratorical grace.[43]

In 1809 another revival began in the upper part of the State, in the bounds of the Georgia and Sarepta Associations and many hundreds were converted and united with the churches.

In 1812 there was a very extensive revival in many different parts of the state. By the four associations of Oakmulgee, Sarepta, Georgia, and Savannah it appears that 3,800 were added to them all in the course of the year. To the Savannah were added about 1,500 and to the Sarepta over 1,250.[44]

May we provide another example of faithfulness before we leave the fertile ground of Georgia?

The Kiokee Baptist Church was pastored first by Daniel Marshall, beginning in 1772. After Daniel's home going, his son Abraham pastored in his place until his death in the summer of 1819.

Abraham's oldest son Jabez, was resistant to salvation in his young years, but being convicted of his sins was born again soon after graduating from college. He began to preach the gospel and eventually in November of 1821, he was called to pastor the church at Kiokee just as his father and grandfather had done. Not only did he serve at Kiokee, but he preached for the Sharon Baptist Church at the same time. Jabez also served as clerk at the formation of the state convention in 1822. He also constituted the Salem Baptist Church in 1827.

Jabez Marshall died suddenly before his fortieth birthday on March 29, 1832, apparently of complications from measles.[45] The Marshalls had pastored the Kiokee Baptist Church from 1772 to 1832, 60 years of faithfulness.

South Carolina and the Great Revival of 1800

Richard Furman described a "union" meeting held in South Carolina in the summer of 1802 in a letter to Dr. Rippon of London, England, Furman wrote:

> Rev. and dear Sir,
>   It was appointed by the Presbyterian clergy in that part of the country, but clergymen of other denominations were invited to it; to be conducted on the same principles and plan with those held in Kentucky. The place is about 170 miles from Charleston. The numbers which assembled from various parts of the country, formed a very large congregation, to me there appeared to be 3,000, or perhaps 4,000 persons, some supposed there were 7,000 or 8,000.
>   The communion service was performed with much apparent devotion while I attended, which was at the serving of the first table. The Presbyterians and Methodists sat down together; but the Baptists, on the principle which has generally governed them on this subject, abstained.[46]

The practice of non-communion with Pedobaptists was in accordance with John Clarke, who refused to commune in Boston with the *standing order* (see chapter three), and Isaac Backus, who in 1756 concluded the Lord's Supper to be legitimate only among *baptized believers*.

The revival of 1800 was mighty among the Baptists of South Carolina. This letter was sent to the *Georgia Analytical Repository* from David Lilly, who described the happenings at a Baptist association meeting in South Carolina, dated August 23, 1802:

> Rev. and dear Sir,
>   I take my pen in hand to transmit to you good tidings, A great work of God is going on in the upper parts of this State. Multitudes are made to cry out, "What must I do to be saved?" A few days ago, I returned from our Association. We have had a truly refreshing season. A vast concourse of people assembled on Saturday, and considerable appearances of solemnity soon took place; but no uncommon effect till Sunday late in the evening. The lord was pleased to manifest his

power to many hearts. Numbers were powerfully exercised through the whole night, and some were thrown to the ground.

On Monday the work increased. The hearts of many were made to melt; and several men, noted for their impiety, were stricken and lay among the prostate. I must acknowledge it was a memorable time with my soul; the like I had not felt from many years before. Before sunrise, on Tuesday morning, the sacred flame began to burn afresh; several, who had been before unaffected, came to the earth. The association rose about 3 o'clock in the afternoon; and such a degree of brotherly affection as appeared among the ministers and messengers of the churches, I scarcely ever saw, It was enough to melt the heart of the greatest infidel living. So very intent were the people to hear, that they petitioned for preaching, after business was finished, and some of the ministers continued with them, in constant exercise, till midnight. During this time the work appeared to increase. About 20 persons came to the ground, several of whom were lusty strong men; and many more very deeply affected, were several officers of considerable rank, and others of equal respectability.

The hearts of sinners melt before the word of truth, like wax before the sun. Infidelity is almost ashamed to show its head. Several deists have been constrained, under a sense of their lost condition, to cry out aloud for mercy. A few, even of those who attributed the effects produced among us to infernal agency, have been reached, and overcome by an influence which they now acknowledge to be divine.

Ministers preach day and night; and when they make no appointments, are surrounded by distressed souls. These are daily obtaining the most satisfactory sense of peace with God, and pardon through the blood of Christ. After believing, they openly profess their faith, and crowd into our churches.

A few weeks past Mr. Shackleford baptized 36 at one time. Two were little girls; 12 and ten, yet they both gave satisfactory evidence of a gracious change. On this occasion, it was supposed that there were no less than 2,000 present; a third of whom, at least, were in tears at the same moment of time. Crowds came up to the ministers to be prayed for, and many fell helpless on the ground. This took place at Woodruff's meeting-house, in the district of Spartanburgh. The number baptized in our association since last year is 703.

My poor soul, some time ago much dejected and bowed down, is now rejoicing in God my Saviour. At this instant my eyes overflow with tears of gratitude and joy, while the flame of divine love burns in my heart.—Yours, David Lilly [47]

*   *   *

There was revival in Kentucky, Tennessee, Georgia, North and South Carolina, Virginia, and New England. The Baptists had gained a foothold in Ohio, Illinois, Mississippi and Indiana. Missouri, Alabama, and Arkansas were about to be visited for the first time.

*   *   *

Missouri 1804

The first Baptist preacher to set foot west of the mighty Mississippi River was the Separate Baptist William Murphy. Murphy had been converted under Shubal Stearns and he and his brother had been the primary agents in the conversion of Samuel Harriss, the great Virginia evangelist. Murphy migrated from North Carolina to Virginia and then Tennessee where he was instrumental in the formation of the Holston Association. According to David Benedict, he planted the Cherokee Church, one of the original churches of the Holston Association and formed the church at Bent Creek. In 1798 Murphy and Isaac Barton organized the "Church of Christ on Lick Creek." Benedict lost track of him at this point, probably because William Murphy was on his way to Missouri.

Murphy crossed the Mississippi sometime in 1798 with his sons Joseph, William and David. They passed through Ste. Genevieve and staked claims in St. Francois County near present day Farmington.[48] Based on the history of William Murphy, it is nearly certain that his intent was to begin a settlement and form the first Baptist church west of the Mississippi in Missouri territory. However, on the way back to the Holston area, William Murphy died at the home of his son John, a Baptist preacher who was holding forth in Kentucky.

William Murphy's widow, Sara Barton Murphy, made the treacherous 1,000-mile trip, up the Holston, down the Ohio, up the Mississippi and into St. Francois County to settle in the land her husband had claimed. She arrived in 1800 with her sons. While no Baptist church was formed at that time, Sara did organize the first Sunday School west of the Mississippi in 1805.

Thomas Johnson performed the first baptism in Missouri, according to the Missouri Baptist historian, R. S. Douglass. Johnson was on an excursion from Georgia and immersed Mrs. Agnes Blue in Randol Creek near Jackson. This occurred in 1799, but Thomas Johnson did not remain in the territory.

Another preacher that made excursions into Missouri was John Clark. As far as can be discovered, this John Clark was not related to Dr. John Clarke, the great leader of the first Baptist church in America, the hero of Rhode Island. This John Clark was a Methodist who renounced the bishopric of the Methodist church and came to Illinois around the time of the turn of the 19th century. John Mason Peck wrote a biography of him, *Father Clark*, and speaks of his conversion from Methodist beliefs to Baptist. Clark was baptized by one of his own church members, much like Roger Williams. We have no record of him gathering any Baptist churches except perhaps the Cold Water Church in northern St. Louis County, where he was the pastor for 20 years. He died in 1833.[*]

The first sermon preached by a Baptist in Missouri was by Thomas R. Musick of Kentucky sometime in 1801. Musick continued to preach, dodging the authorities.

We come now to the formation of the first Baptist church in Missouri.

In 1804 all of the Louisiana Territory including Missouri was transferred from France to the United States. The Louisiana Purchase opened the door for the Gospel. David Green, a Baptist preacher from Kentucky, came to Missouri. He arrived in Scott County and tried to organize a group of Baptists into a church, but it folded soon after.

When Green returned to Kentucky in the fall of 1805, he could not stay and so he returned to Missouri to finish what he had started. With the fragments of the old "church" in Scott County, and other converts

---

[*] Jeffrey Faggart, President of the Baptist History Preservation Society, and the author recently found Clark's memorial monument in Cold Water Cemetery. The marker declares him a "Methodist" preacher. One wonders how many other mistakes and outright lies find immortality in history books and cemeteries.

around Jackson he formed the Bethel Baptist Church, the first Baptist church in Missouri.[49] They met for the first time at the house of Thomas Bull on July 19, 1806.

Not long after, in 1807, the Fee Fee Baptist Church, with assistance from Thomas Musick was founded in St. Louis County.

In October of 1812, Bethel formed a sister church in St. Michael (Fredericktown). They also formed churches at St. Francois, Apple Creek and Turtle Creek. In 1818 Thomas Green became the pastor at Bethel Church and they continued the pioneering of new churches. From 1807 to 1824, they formed nine churches including Providence (now the First Baptist Church of Fredericktown) and Jackson Baptist Church.[50]

The Bethel Association was begun in 1816. It included churches mostly formed by Bethel church and some in Arkansas. The Missouri Association was formed in 1818.

Alabama 1808

John Nicholson formed the first Baptist church in Alabama on October 4, 1808. It was in Madison County and was known as the Flint River Baptist Church. They met in the home of Zadock Baker. Nicholson also led in the forming of Enon Baptist church (now the First Baptist Church of Huntsville), one year later.

On September 26, 1841, the Flint River and Enon churches helped in the organization of the Flint River association, the first in Alabama. Beckbee Association was formed next in 1816. Some believe this to be the first in Alabama. We doubt this. Beckbee became known as Bethlehem Association in 1827. Bethlehem grew and branched out to the Cahaba Association in 1818. This was a strong missionary association, overcoming the power of the "antimission" influence.

In 1819 the Alabama Association was formed in the southern portion of the state. From that, two more associations were formed: Bethel and Muscle Shoals, in 1820. The Tuscaloosa Association was founded out of the Cahaba. It was formed in 1834 and had Elder Joab Pratt as one of its preachers. Pratt later went west into Arkansas.

We may follow the influence of Sandy Creek Baptist Church and Association upon Alabama in this fashion: Shubal Stearns baptized Samuel Harriss, who baptized Joseph Redding, who formed the Turkey Creek Baptist Church in 1785. Turkey Creek founded the Poplar Springs Baptist Church in 1794 and had Benjamin Norcut as its pastor. Benjamin Norcut baptized David Andrews in December of 1823.

David Andrews became a great influence for Christ in Cahaba and Buttahatchie Associations in Alabama. His strong emphasis on Gospel preaching and missions kept much of Alabama from embracing "anti-mission" sentiments. In 1834 under Andrews, the North River United Baptist Association was formed.

Louisiana and Arkansas were the next states to receive the Baptist testimony.

Louisiana 1812

Entering the forbidden territory of Louisiana was no small task. Bailey Chaney delivered the first non-Catholic sermon west of the Mississippi in what is now the state of Louisiana. Bailey was the first preacher in the territory, moving his family into Eastern Louisiana, then called West Florida in 1798. He was imprisoned at Baton Rouge and when released, went to the Mississippi Natchez district. Ezra Courtney, who settled in Mississippi in 1802 also preached in Louisiana from time to time.

The preacher responsible for the first Baptist church in Louisiana was Joseph Willis. Here is William Cathcart's description of him:

> Soon after the cession of the French portion of the Territory, Joseph Willis, a mulatto, who was a licensed Baptist preacher, and who had been a co-laborer with Richard Curtis in Mississippi, boldly crossed the Mississippi River, and in 1804 preached at Vermillion and Plaquemine Brule. The following year he returned and settled on Bayou Chicot in St. Landry Parish, where he began to preach, and in 1812, with assistance from Mississippi, organized a church, of which he became pastor.

There were also churches formed along the Pearl River at Mount Nebo and Peniel, both constituted in 1813. Cathcart gives no indication of the identity of the preachers who founded them. Apparently, Ezra Courtney founded Hepzibah Church in 1814. In 1818 Benjamin Davis gathered a small church in New Orleans.

Joseph Willis remains obscure. He not only founded the church at St. Landry parish, but also formed churches at Cheneyville, Vermillion, Plaquemine Brule, and Hickory Flat. On October 31, 1818, the Louisiana Baptist Association the first in the state, was organized and Joseph Willis was the first moderator. He had by the grace of God, birthed five of the six churches in the first association in the state of Louisiana.

Arkansas 1818

Jesse James, the preacher, was born in the 1770's in North Carolina and arrived in Missouri Territory in 1815. In June 1816, the Missouri Bethel Baptist Association met in Cape Girardeau County, and sent Elders Jesse James, Benjamin Clark, and James Philip Edwards as missionaries to Lawrence County, then Missouri Territory. Their purpose was to establish the first Baptist Church in present day Arkansas.

The Bethel minutes of September 1818, state the church was constituted that year with 12 members and was represented by Elders Jesse James, Benjamin Clark and Richard Brazil. John Mason Peck, stated when he visited in 1818 that Elders Jesse James and Benjamin Clark were the ministers, the location of the church was on Fourche 'a Thomas, and the name of the church was Salem. According to the Bethel Minutes of 1819, Salem Church was constituted into another church named Union, also located in Lawrence County on Cypress Creek, with 14 members and represented by Jesse James and Richard Brazil. The Bethel Minutes of 1820 state that Union Church in Lawrence County was represented by Jesse James, Richard Brazil and Willis Wilson. James was again a messenger from Union in 1823, but was not mentioned in later minutes. David Orr, who was sent to Lawrence County by the Bethel Baptist Association in 1828, stated that when he arrived James was enfeebled and incapacitated for work.[51]

The "History of Bethel Association, Missouri" from the November 1856 issue of the *Christian Repository* has this version of the first Arkansas churches and association:

In 1822 Bethel Association [Missouri] appointed Elders Street, Clark and Edwards, to visit Arkansas Territory, and constitute therein two churches. They constituted two churches, Union and Little Flock, in Lawrence County, Arkansas Territory. These churches applied for membership at the next sessions of the association, September 1823, and were received. From these churches sprung others that were afterwards admitted into the association. In 1829 the following churches made application for dismission to organize an association in the Territory of Arkansas, viz: Spring River, New Hope, Little North Fork, and Richland.

The acceleration of Baptist churches and Associations between 1792 and 1812 cannot be totally accounted for in our narrative. Some statistics can give a picture, however inadequate, of the supernatural scope of the awakening of 1800. There were 892 Baptist churches in the United States in 1792 having 65,340 members. By 1812, there were 2,164 churches having 172,972 members.

American foreign missions had their beginning just after the Great Revival of 1800. An understanding of American foreign missionary endeavors must begin with an acquaintance with William Carey. Although our narrative is about American Baptists, William Carey, the Englishman, is worthy of note. Working within the English Northamptonshire Baptist Association, Carey began to voice the need to take the Gospel to the needy people in the foreign parts of the world. At a famous meeting John Ryland, marked with "antimission" leanings, made his infamous remark to Carey, "Sit down young man, when the Lord gets ready to convert the heathen, he will do it without your help or mine!" Thankfully, Carey did not give up and Ryland had a change of heart.

Carey issued a pamphlet entitled **An Inquiry into the Obligation of Christians to Use Means for the Conversion of the Heathen.** Mr. Carey became pastor of the church in Leicester in 1789. He labored with great zeal, constantly promoting the overwhelming need to organize and launch into foreign fields. His efforts brought to fruition the English **Baptist Missionary Society,** formally organized October 2, 1792.

William Carey sailed for India June 13, 1793. At Serampore, the missionaries set up a printing press and a large boarding school, and founded a college. Perhaps most importantly Carey and his associates studied the language and translated through painstaking labor, the Bible into the native tongues.

Missions became a concern worldwide in the 19th century. The Netherlands Missionary Society was formed in 1797, and the American Board of Commissioners for Foreign Missions was formed in 1810.

Carey's work influenced the American **Adoniram Judson.** Judson was born in Malden, Massachusetts, on August 9, 1788. When he was 16, he entered the sophomore class of Brown University, becoming a member of the institution on the 17th of August 1804. He graduated in 1807 with the highest honors of his class. The death of a classmate caused him to question his own salvation and led to his conversion. In 1809, he was admitted into the Andover Theological Institution and became a member of the Third Congregational Church in Plymouth, Massachusetts, of which his father was the pastor. In February 1810, Judson made a decision to follow the Lord in foreign missions. He sought out other young men at the Andover seminary who joined with him in praying for revival and missions at "Missionary Rock."

The young men prepared a paper to be presented to a general association of all the evangelical ministers of Massachusetts, which convened at Bradford in 1810, urging the leaders to attend to the great need of preaching Christ in foreign parts. They asked boldly for an appointment to the East. The result of this action was the formation of **the American Board of Commissioners for Foreign Missions.** Soon after his graduation, Judson was sent to England by the **American Board** to confer with the London Missionary Society on the matter of combining the efforts of the **American Board** and the **London Society** in the work of carrying the gospel to the heathen. These boards were both "Congregational" as Adoniram Judson had not yet come to his conviction of baptism.

Incredibly, he was kidnapped at sea by pirates but was quickly released and made it to England. The London Missionary Society appointed him and his fellow-students, Newell, Nott, and Hall, as missionaries to India. However, the American Board decided to send them without the aid of London.

Judson, with his wife, Ann Hasseltine Judson, Nott, Newell, Hall, and Rice sailed February 19, 1812, from Salem, Massachusetts. They reached Calcutta the 17th of the following June. By the time they reached India, Judson had come to see the truth of scriptural baptism and both he and his wife were immersed by William Ward[52] on September 6, 1812, in the Baptist chapel in Calcutta. His obedience to *believer's baptism*, of course, displeased the Congregational American Board of Commissioners for Foreign Missions and they immediately withdrew support from Judson. A local Baptist mission society was formed at Boston immediately, which took up some of the support for the Judsons. "Missionary Societies" began to spring up across the states.

On May 18, 1814, 33 delegates from several states met at the First Baptist Church in Philadelphia, Pennsylvania and organized **the General Missionary Convention of the Baptist Denomination in the United States of America for Foreign Missions**. It was organized to meet every three years to address the needs of foreign missions. Hence it became known as **the Triennial Convention**.[53] Richard Furman, the pastor of First Baptist Church in Charleston, South Carolina, with his fiery Separate Baptist background became the first president of the "Convention." Another shining light in this design was the great Boston pastor, Thomas Baldwin.

For many years, Dr. Judson devoted a part of his time to the translation of the Scriptures into the Burmese language and the compilation of a Burmese dictionary. He completed the Burmese Bible in 1834 but did not finish the dictionary. Anne Judson wrote this testimony about her husband's work:

> My mornings are busily employed in giving directions to the servants—providing food for the family, etc. At ten my teacher comes, when, were you present, you might see me in an Inner room, at one side of my study table and my teacher on the other, reading Burman, writing, talking, etc. I have many more interruptions than Mr. Judson, as I have the entire management of the family. This I took upon myself for the sake of Mr. Judson's attending more closely to the study of the

language; yet I have found by a year's experience that it is the most direct way I could have taken to acquire the language; as I am frequently obliged to speak Burman all day, I can talk and understand others better than Mr. Judson, though he knows more about the nature and constitution of the language.[54]

The General Missionary Convention also formed The Baptist Board of Foreign Missions for the United States. This board immediately appointed Luther Rice as "agent" to raise funds in America. This turn of events put Luther Rice into a ministry which had great and lasting effects and widespread opposition.

When The Baptist Board of Foreign Missions for the United States called upon Luther he responded. He rode thousands of miles, endured the slander and scorn of the "antimission" resistance and yet, without scandal, saw hundreds and thousands of dollars pass from his hands into the treasury of the board. When asked to raise funds for Columbian College he did so. The college became his great burden to provide a place to train Baptist preachers. The board in turn, mismanaged, misappropriated, and caused the school to dissolve. Columbian was resurrected with no Christian identity at all in the evolution of George Washington University.

There may be some that are unsure of the form of Rice's mission. But we are sure that Luther Rice was a true servant, a tireless, selfless man who, despite the incompetence of those around him, managed to do a wonderful amount of good; and did nothing but his best when called upon. For all of his critics, Rice never had an ill thing to say about any of his enemies, nor a bitter word to record in any of his letters or journals.

It became apparent that the Congregational East India Company was opposed to the work of Adoniram Judson. So he moved his mission to Burma and there made a stand for God. He arrived at Rangoon in July 1813.

Even after the Burmese king forbade Judson to preach, Mr. Judson continued his work and preached at his own peril. He devoted himself to the translation of the scriptures, and also prepared numbers of religious tracts to be circulated among the people.

After an extreme amount of government interference in which Judson was imprisoned, the harshness of travel and constant sickness caused Ann Judson to become violently ill. Mrs. Judson died at Amherst, Burma, on October 24, 1826, while her husband was away. A two-year-old daughter also died from fever a few months later. Dr. Judson removed to Maulmain November 14, 1827, and began again to preach the Gospel with power. He began works in Maulmain, Prome, Rangoon, and other places, becoming especially interested in the conversion of the Karens.

*　　*　　*

The "Bedford Plowboys"

Of the testimonies of the power of God unto salvation during the "war for souls," the list seems endless. One striking example is the story of the "Bedford Plowboys," J. B. Jeter and Daniel Witt.

Jeremiah Bell Jeter was born July 18, 1802, in Bedford County, Virginia. He was born again in 1821 and baptized by William Harris. After his baptism, he stood on the banks of the North Fork of the Otter River and preached his first sermon. Later that same year, he preached to a group of mountain men in the valley between Flat Top and Luck Mountains. He was 19 years of age.

Daniel Witt was also born in Bedford County in 1801. He was converted at an old-time "section meeting" at Hatcher's meeting-house in 1821, and baptized in December of that same year. It was there that Witt began his life-long affiliation and friendship with Jeter. Witt preached his first sermon just two months later.

Jeter and Witt were appointed missionaries at the same time at the Baptist General Association of 1823. They were referred to as the "Bedford Plowboys." Like two comets crossing the same sky, they lit up Virginia for Jesus. Their light brightened the counties of Henry, Patrick, Montgomery, Grayson, Giles, Wythe, Monroe, Greenbrier, Pocahontas, Alleghany, Bath, Rockbridge, and Botetourt. Their light stood in contrast to the "antimission" sentiment at the time.[55] Their ministries exemplified the office of a true evangelist.

In the early winter of 1824, Witt came to Charlotte, Virginia, to assist A. W. Clopton. Clopton became his mentor and taught him doctrine and theology, and gave him access to his wonderful library. Witt grew in grace in that place, and from there preached the Gospel with great blessing in Prince Edward County. He formed the Sharon Baptist Church at Sandy River, and stayed there serving God for 45 years. He pastored several churches at once, at Jamestown, Cumberland, Union, Prince Edward and Lebanon in Nottoway. He baptized 2,500 converts.[56]

J. B. Jeter baptized over 1,000 people in the first 12 years of his ministry, 1823-1835.

In the next 12 years, 1836-1849, Jeter pastored the First Baptist Church of Richmond, Virginia. He also made preaching excursions, and formed churches throughout Virginia. He baptized an additional 1,000 converts during that time. Jeter also formed the first African Baptist Church in Richmond, a church that began with nearly 2,000 members!

After the Civil War, Jeter edited the Baptist periodical, the *Religious Herald*. He also served as president of the Virginia Baptist Foreign Mission Society and was a part of the Board of Managers of the Triennial Convention of American Baptists.

The American Bible Society 1816 and
The American and Foreign Bible Society 1836

The British had formed the "British and Foreign Bible Society" in 1804. It was a national organization.

In America, the first Bible societies were local. The first was formed in Philadelphia in 1808. In eight years there were more than 100 such local and independent organizations across America. On May 8, 1816, 60 men representing 35 of those societies met in New York to organize the American Bible Society. They were from various denominations, but the Baptists spearheaded the organization. Their sole objective was "encouraging a wider circulation of the Holy Scriptures without note or comment."[57]

In 1823, Spencer Cone became pastor of the Oliver Street Baptist Church in New York. Eventually, he became the President of the

American Bible society. In 1841, Cone became pastor at the First Baptist Church of New York, in the legacy of John Gano.

At that time, William Carey, the British Baptist missionary was busy translating the scriptures into more than 25 dialects of the people of India and Ceylon. He was given $1,000.00 by the American Bible Society for help in the translating process; however, the Protestant/Pedobaptist faction of the American Bible Society, reading the translation carefully declared the translation "sectarian," that is, a *Baptist* version. Carey had "translated," rather than "transferred" the word "baptize" into the word "immerse." Additionally, upon closer examination, the American Bible Society discovered the Burmese Bible of Adoniram Judson was also an "immersion" version. Although both Carey and Judson drew their translation from the "common" King James and its underlying text, the American Bible Society withdrew support for their translations.

When this occurred, Spencer Cone believed he could no longer remain as President of the American Bible Society. He resigned in May of 1836, and before the ink was dry on his resignation, certain Baptist officers from the old society formed the *American and Foreign Bible Society*. The society would now finance and print Bibles "distributing of them in foreign languages, afforded to such only as are conformed as nearly as possible to the original text; it being understood that no words are to be transferred which are susceptible of being literally translated."[58] The new American and Foreign Bible Society would be at liberty to produce foreign language "immersion" versions. Another resolution of this new society was:

> Resolved, That in the distribution of the Scriptures in the English language, they (the Board) will use the commonly received version, until otherwise directed by the society.[59]

This resolution would be the cause for further controversy.

Passing of the Patriarchs

At the age of 56, **Elijah Baker** passed into the presence of his Lord on **November 6, 1798**. No one on Earth is sure where he is buried.

John Waller preached for 35 years, baptized more than 2,000 converts in sparsely populated areas, ordained 27 men to the Gospel ministry. He died on **July 4, 1802**. His last sermon was from Zechariah 2:4: "Run, speak to this young man."

John Corbley died **June 9, 1803**. This is recorded on his gravestone:

> Death, thou hast conquered me
> I by thy dart am slain;
> But Jesus Christ shall conquer thee,
> And I shall rise again.[60]

John Gano became a regent of the University of New York State in 1784. He was a trustee of King's College (now Columbia) in 1787. After the death of his wife in 1788, Gano traveled to Lexington, Kentucky. He finished his course as the pastor of Town Fork church. He died on **August 9, 1804**.

Hezekiah Smith, died January 22, 1805

Tidence Lane, died January 30, 1806

Isaac Backus after having served his generation by the will of God, died November 20, 1806.

James Ireland lost his daughter to a vicious act of poisoning by the hand of an enemy. He recovered from the chemicals. Ireland died **May 5, 1806**, and is buried somewhere in a cow pasture near the Buckmarsh Baptist Church in Virginia.

Abraham Marshall passed away on **August 15, 1819.** He was 72 years old. Marshall preached for over 50 years and baptized 2,000 converts, mostly in the wilderness of Georgia.

Time Line of the Rise of Campbellism, "Antimission" sentiments, Mormonism and the Baptist Revision

1801   The General Union of the Ky. State Baptists
1804   The first "Christian" Churches established by Barton Stone.
1808   Stone first voiced, "Baptism is administered to believing penitents in order to the remission of sins."
1809   Alexander Campbell arrived from Scotland, as an ordained Presbyterian preacher.
1810   "Antimission" sentiment in various places among the Baptists.
1812   Campbell immersed by Mathias Luce.
1813   Campbell received by the Redstone Baptist Association of Pennsylvania.
1820   The Presbyterians and Baptists of Meigs County, Ohio combine into "Christian Union"
1820   Campbell debate with John Walker
1823   Campbell debate with William McCalla
1823   Campbell began publishing the *Christian Baptist*.
1823-   Followers of Campbell began infiltration of
1830   Baptist associations.
1830   Campbell affirmed "immersion is the converting act."
1830   Silas Noel published his 39 articles exposing "Campbellism." Campbell's followers expelled from the Elkhorn Association in Kentucky.
1830   Campbell's followers split numerous Baptist churches and form their own organizations.
1830   Joseph Smith unearths and "translates" the golden plates in the Hill Cumorah
1830   Joseph Smith migrates west to Kirtland Ohio.
1830   Sidney Rigdon receives Mormon "baptism".
1836   Bible Revision movement is accelerated.
1850   The Bible Union, Baptist organization to Revise the "common" version is formed.

CHAPTER FIFTEEN
Satan's Plan for America

*We live in an extraordinary day—under the benign influence of
the gospel sun, that seems to be rising to his meridian height; no
nation or people, since government was first introduced into the
world, ever enjoyed equal privileges with us. We boast not
merely the enjoyment of civil, but of religious liberty, without
any check or control from the hand of oppression. How ought
every one to praise the Lord for his goodness and wonderful
works to the children of men! How ought we to wrestle with
God in prayer for grace equal to the day, that we may not, like
Jeshurun, grow wanton and abuse these glorious privileges!* [1]—
John Williams, Virginia Baptist Preacher

*I am not disposed to repent for sounding the gospel to perishing sin-
ners.*—John Gano, 1754, in response to the Hopewell church
on his "disorderly" preaching.

*For Satan mocks the Lord Jesus at every step
by matching His work with some
counterpart of evil.*—A. J. Gordon

*He staggered not at the promise of God through unbelief;
but was strong in faith, giving glory to God; And being
fully persuaded that, what he had promised, he was able
also to perform. And therefore* **it was imputed to him**
for righteousness. *Now it was not written for his sake
alone, that* **it was imputed** *to him; But for us also, to*
whom it shall be imputed, if we believe on him
that raised up Jesus our Lord from the dead.
—Romans 4:20-24

The churches of the state of Kentucky had nearly tripled in two
years. No wonder *the adversary* hated Kentucky. He brought an
assault on her that would drag on for 50 years.

There were three matters that divided what was called Christianity in the 19th century: The *Bible*, the *baptism* it reveals, and *imputation*. With the forward march of Christianity throughout America in the war for souls, satan stood up with all of his might to thwart the message of salvation.

The Baptist people as usual, would be his main target.[2] He would once again attempt to discredit the written word of God, corrupt baptism, and destroy the Gospel order.

During this time 1800-1850, the devil had his knife right at the heart of the gospel: *imputation*. This doctrine separates the Gospel of the grace of God from the false Gospel of works.

The first device used in obscuring *imputation* involved a corruption of the word of God by the infamous Augustine. From Titus 3:5 Augustine replaced the phrase "**washing** of regeneration," as it was preserved in the *Itala Biblia*, with the phrase "**laver** of regeneration." Augustine set in motion the heresy of baptismal regeneration by equating water baptism with regeneration. Water baptism became the "door to the church." The reformers borrowed this doctrine. Luther and Calvin claimed water baptism (the christening of an infant) was a "means to grace." And so water baptism became an initiation into the "church." This has always been the best device to cloud the issue of *imputation*.

In order for *the adversary* to destroy the tremendous work of God on the American frontier the confessions and creeds that stated the doctrine of *imputation* had to be called into question. A set of "anti-movements" would fulfill the task.

There were two "anti-movements:" "anticonfession" and "antimission." They both lead to divisions among the Baptists. How it happened may be outlined in this fashion:

- ♦ The Great Revival in the West from 1792-1801.
- ♦ The Controversy over Calvinism.
- ♦ The "anticonfession" movement with Barton Stone and the "Christians" in 1804.
- ♦ The "antimission" Baptist movement in reaction to mission societies from 1814 to 1842.

♦ The "reformation" of Alexander Campbell in reaction to both "anticonfession" and "antimission" movements which created divisions among the Baptists from 1820 to 1830.

The Controversy over Calvinism

That Baptists had always embraced Calvinism has been a subject of debate. What is not debatable is our forefathers' embracing of the grace of God for salvation. Ancient Baptists believed man was powerless to save himself long before Luther and Calvin. *Imputation*, or receiving Christ's righteousness apart from any work or sacrament, is the benefit of regeneration. That is a fact Baptists have always believed without controversy. *Imputation*, regeneration, and the new birth were expressed strongly in the Philadelphia Baptist Confession. These doctrines were not argued among American Baptists; however, election, predestination and the decrees of God in the Calvinist system have long been debated.[3]

It has always been the *extreme* of Calvinism that has caused controversy. It began with John Clarke at Boston in 1637. Clarke and the *opinionists* argued that a man can know he is regenerate by belief in the Bible promises and being born again. Clarke basically said that a person may know he is *elect*, but he cannot know that he is *reprobated*. This left the door open for the kind of preaching and evangelism that made the Newport church a mother of churches.

When the Philadelphia Baptist Association adopted their confession of faith it was based on the London Baptist Confession of 1689. Isaac Backus said this about the Philadelphia and London confessions:

> Some eminent ministers in England had also carried the doctrine of particular election so far, as to deny that any minister had a right to address the calls of the gospel to all sinners without distinction, and the Philadelphians had adopted this opinion; and they called themselves Regular Baptists, while those who went from Connecticut were called Separates.[4]

Backus understood that the call to sinners was consistent with the New Testament model and wrote:

We generally believe the doctrine of particular election, and the final perseverance of every true believer, while we proclaim a free salvation to all the children of men, and even to the chief of sinners; and we hold that God has appointed the means as well as the end, and the means in order to the end of every event.

But many men imagine that the choice and doings of men are the cause of it, and so would take the glory of it to themselves, instead of giving it to God alone. And free salvation by the Son of God is held forth to all men in the gospel as openly as the brazen serpent was to the camp of Israel; and the condemnation of all who do not receive him, is because they hate the light. (John iii. 14-20) Therefore the most moving methods ought to be taken with sinners in general to enlighten and turn them from sin to God. Light concerning these things gained gradually among the Baptists in Virginia, so as to unite them as one people in 1787, and they have increased much since.[5]

Apparently Backus' theology was much in agreement with John Leland, who wrote:

I conclude that the eternal purposes of God, and the freedom of the human will, are both truths; and it is a matter of fact, that the preaching that has been most blessed of God, and most profitable to men, is the doctrine of sovereign grace in the salvation of souls, mixed with a little of what is called Arminianism." [6]

John Gill was the ultimate Particular Baptist. He was an eminent Baptist scholar from England and his works were highly regarded in America. They were revered by Ephraim Bound, Samuel Stillman, Henry Plimpton, Nathan Plimpton, Hezekiah Smith, Phillip Freeman, Phillip Freeman, Jr., Ebenezer Moulton, Ebenezer Hinds and James Manning. However, Isaac Backus did not view Gill's Calvinism with as much respect. The two men exchanged several letters. In one telltale correspondance to Backus, Gill states, "few are the instances of conversion, and but seldom are there additions to our churches."[7]

Thomas Armitage wrote about John Gill:

And yet, with all his ability, he was so high a supralapsarian, that it is hard to distinguish him from an antinomian. For example, he could not invite sinners to the Savior, while he declared their guilt and condemnation, their need of the new birth; and held that God would convert such as He had elected to be saved, and so man must not interfere with His purposes by inviting men to Christ. Under this preaching his church steadily declined, and after half a century's work he left but a mere handful."[8]

Some Baptist churches rent in twain over "invitations" to Christ. Citing a typical example of the period, William G. McLoughlin wrote, "In 1769 the Baptist congregation at Weare split over whether or not it was proper to exhort sinners to come to Christ. Samuel Hovey led the group opposing the practice."[9]

Some Baptist preachers lost their zeal for souls. We bring to your attention one sad example, William Marshall. J. H. Spencer wrote of Marshall's early zeal:

> Some of the zealous Separate Baptists visited Fauquier county, and Mr. Marshall was converted and baptized. John Taylor, in his biography of William Marshall, speaks of him thus: "He soon began to preach, and a flaming zealot he was. His preaching was of the loud thunder-gust kind." [10]

Then according to John Taylor, in his later years, Marshall became tainted with what may be termed "hypercalvinism:"

> In the days of his success, he preached after the apostolic mode, strongly urging repentance toward God and faith in Christ Jesus, and with longing, heart-melting **invitations**, exhorting every sinner in his congregation to seek the salvation of his soul. He studied consistency, beginning with God's decrees. There he found eternal justification couched in the doctrine of election; and so on with the several links of his chain, till he was led to find out that the gospel address was only to certain characters, which, then explained, were already righteous, though they well deserved the name of sinners. But as for mere sinners, the law of Moses only was their portion. He found that a number of his Baptist Christians could not eat what they called his strong meat. This led him to doubt their Christianity, or at least, the soundness of their faith.[11]

The "Anticonfession" Movement

After the stunning success and subsequent confusion following the Great Revival of 1800, the need for preachers was tremendous. The Presbyterians, married to their system of education, could not meet the demand. The strict Calvinism of their creed was regarded as a hindrance to the sweeping revival if not for any other reason that it moved too slow. The pioneer Baptists on the other hand, had little or no formal education but were well versed in the Philadelphia Confession and the tenets of theology. As we have seen, associations argued over election and predestination.

These arguments were taking a toll. Some Baptists did not see the necessity of a creed or a confession. When Barton Stone began to expound his "no creed" concept it struck a chord. Alexander Campbell played the chord until the strings broke. The creeds and confessions began to fall into disuse, and the baby of *imputation* was thrown out with the proverbial bath water of the confession.

Barton Stone and his so-called "restoration" movement among the Presbyterians endeavored to create a unity without prejudice of "sect" or creed. He created new battlegrounds in the war for souls as large numbers of dissenters and downright traitors of the cause of Christ increased on every hand. In Kentucky it became a civil war for the control of the pulpit in every pioneer church birthed by the old warriors.

Barton Stone began the saga of the "anticonfession" movement with the Cane Ridge revival described in chapter 14. The result of the revival among Stone's followers was the establishment of the "Christian" Church. The first of these churches was formed in 1804. In 1808 Stone voiced for the first time, "baptism is administered to believing penitents **in order to** the remission of sins." Logic then would conclude there were no "Christians" in the "Christian" Church for the first four years of its existence.[12]

Along came Alexander Campbell. In 1809 Alexander, along with his father Thomas arrived in Pennsylvania from Scotland. They both were ordained Presbyterian preachers. Alexander soon established himself as a great orator and debater.

Even though Campbell had said, "At the age of 21, I discovered that the religion of the New Testament was one thing, and that of any sect that I knew was another,"[13] in 1812 he joined a "sect." He joined the Baptists. Matthias Luce immersed him and in 1813 he became a preacher in the Redstone Baptist Association of Pennsylvania. Redstone also had a rising Baptist preacher named Sidney Rigdon, but more about Sidney later.

The Redstone Association, sensing Campbell's powers of persuasion prevailed upon him to defend the Philadelphia Confession in writing. This Campbell did with remarkable skill. In the meantime, Barton Stone was decrying the confession and any other creed that any Christian should embrace. Moreover, Stone began to state publicly, "Baptism ought to be administered to believing penitents **for the remission** of sins."[14]

Then in 1820 in an unprecedented move, the Presbyterians and the Separate Baptists of Meigs County, Ohio, combined into "Christian Union." About this accomplishment Barton Stone wrote, "They agreed to cast away their formularies and creeds, and take the Bible alone for their rule of faith and practice—**to throw away their name Baptist**, and take the name Christian—and bury their association, and to become one with us in the great work of Christian union."

Quickly the Stone/Campbell juggernaut began to roll. In the same year 1820, Campbell won a great victory for believer's baptism in his debate with John Walker, a Presbyterian preacher from Mt. Pleasant, Ohio.[15] Next, in a showdown of grand proportions, Campbell was asked to debate the undisputed leader of the Presbyterians, William L. McCalla.

The "Antimission" Movement

At the time the Triennial Convention was making the Baptists a national denomination, the "antimission" movement began. It was also called "anti-effort," which was not an accurate description. John T. Christian refers to the movement thus, "One can hardly in this day, understand the rancor of speech which prevailed for years in many of the churches, and most of the early associations."[16]

We cannot concur with the wonderful J. T. Christian on this point. It may be **clearly** seen, that because pioneer "missionaries" had pierced the darkness of America for 75 years without one penny of financial help, the sudden need for raising funds was extremely distressing to the old pioneers.

The foreign missions movement had come on strong in America. The principle persons in that early movement were Adoniram Judson, Samuel Nott, Luther Rice and Samuel Mills.

In 1809 Samuel Mills, with another young man named Schermorhorn, made a journey through Ohio, Kentucky, Tennessee and Mississippi in an effort to raise mission support. While in Kentucky the young men traveled to see the venerable John Taylor. They did not make the greatest impression on the old warrior. Taylor said of this meeting:

> They became quite impatient with my indolence, assuring me that if I would only stir up the people to missions and Bible society matters, I should find a great change in money affairs in favor of the preachers; urging by questions like this: "Do you not know that when sponges are once opened they will always run?" Only, said they, get the people in the habit of giving their money for any religious use, and they will continue to appropriate for all sacred purposes.[17]

John Taylor wrote a treatise against the mission scheme in 1817. It contained a bitter denunciation against the methods of fund raising on the part of Luther Rice and John Mason Peck. John Taylor had written the following thoughts. We sense the bewilderment, the doubt and even the bitterness in his opinion:

> But my great doubt concerning them arises both from the scriptures and all the observation and experiences I have had for near fifty years. That far back I remember what kind of men of the Baptist name in Virginia were buffeted, imprisoned and counted the off scouring of all things. I remember their looks, their labors, and their success. Though not willing to make myself a standard, I recollect that far back, the anxiety of my soul for the prosperity of Zion, and the good of my fellow man, so that I could not rest, day nor night, for years together; and of what little moment in that case money appeared to me; so that from my soul I could say, I seek not yours, but you. And in that case, I

coveted no man's silver, gold or apparel; so that perhaps to a man, this temper attended all the Baptist preachers of that day.

Myself began to preach at about twenty years of age, and about five months after I was baptized by James Ireland, a faithful servant of Jesus Christ. My previous opportunity and my capacities, in my own esteem, were very small, and they must have appeared small in the esteem of others; but the church to which I belonged, treated me with all the tenderness of a mother. Their preachers also treated me as a son; for the church had three other preachers, to wit: James Ireland, their pastor, William Marshall, and the well known, laborious one of his day, Joseph Redding.

With the latter I traveled the most. He being an older man than myself, he was to me as a father, though he seemed to acknowledge me as his yoke fellow. We labored together in the wilds of Virginia about ten years before Kentucky came in vogue, to which place we both came in early times; and here he died a few years past. Our range of labor was from the Blue Ridge and Shenandoah River to the back of Virginia, on the branches of the Potomac and Ohio Rivers, a distance of about two hundred miles; and ofttimes among the dangerous rage of savage fury; though this circumstance took us out of the way of Virginia persecution below the Blue Ridge.

Neither of us was ever put in prison, though at times, either beaten or driven from our meetings by wicked mobs. We ofttimes traveled a whole day from one frontier settlement to another, through the rugged mountains without seeing a house, and our lives in danger every step we took, and when we could not reach a house, our lot was to camp in the woods. We went to many places where the Gospel had never sounded before, and so great was the effect, that ofttimes the cries of the people would drown our voices. We then hoped, that many experienced conversion, and some churches were built up where the Lord's name was not called on before, but to blaspheme it. Both of us having been raised to hardships, nothing appeared hard to surmount.[18]

In his book, *Thoughts on Missions*, John Taylor was perhaps too critical of Luther Rice and John Mason Peck. There are indications that he later regretted his attack.[19] Whatever the case, we may conclude the "antimission" division in the beginning was not about preaching to the lost, it was about how money was raised and the machinery created to spend it.[*]

One by one Baptist associations made declarations opposed to the mission scheme. Eventually the controversy evolved into whether conventions, Bible societies, benevolent societies, or mission agencies should exist at all.

Some associations, such as the Licking Association of Kentucky, declared itself out of the General Union of Kentucky in 1819 making a statement for limited atonement, calling itself "Particular" and opposing the forms of missionary societies.

Some of the "antimission" Baptists disintegrated into what may be termed "hypercalvinists," who opposed "human effort." One American "antimission" group adopted the philosophy of the British Warwick Association, who claimed, "All the preaching from John the Baptist until now, if made to bear on one unregenerate sinner, could no more quicken his poor dead soul than so much chattering of a crane or of a swallow."[20]

In 1835 the Chemung Association of New York and Pennsylvania "discontinued correspondence" with all associations supporting the "popular institutions of the day."

In May of 1836, the Baltimore Association passed a similar declaration which became the rallying document for "antimission" Baptists—the Black Rock declaration.[21]

Today, the "antimission" Baptists exist as the Primitive Baptists of America.[22]

Alexander Campbell and the "Current Reformation"

We left Alexander Campbell a few pages ago as he readied for his epic debate with William McCalla. The few newspapers in 1823 trumpeted the event. Word of mouth brought thousands of believers together in northeastern Kentucky at Washington on the Ohio. They met in the old Baptist meeting-house. Jeremiah Vardeman was the moderator and Sidney Rigdon was the secretary recording the event. Campbell

---

[*] The two preachers who drove "antimissions" into an actual break with the established associations were Joshua Lawrence in the east and Daniel Parker in the west.

won the debate in decisive fashion for believer's baptism by immersion thereby sealing his fame and influence among the Baptists of Kentucky. However, there was a problem among Campbell's arguments. Campbell, now infected with Barton Stone's opinions stated, "**the water of baptism formally washes away our sins.**"[23] That statement understandably caused suspicion among the old warriors.

Campbell became a celebrity and commenced a "march" through Kentucky preaching to huge crowds and leaving strange, lingering, question marks wherever he went.

In those days Jeremiah Vardeman and Old Jacob Creath were close friends. Creath embraced the "reforms" of Campbell immediately. Vardeman was tentative. Even when it appeared Campbell may be heretical, Vardeman hung on not wanting to give up on him and probably held on too long.

During his victorious tour through Kentucky, Campbell hinted at some doctrines that would eventually become part of the "Campbellite" dogma. He continually hurled his biggest criticisms toward the Philadelphia Confession of Faith. But he needed the old Baptist warriors to give credence to his views.

That summer of 1823, Campbell sought that support in Lexington at a huge preaching service. In the audience were Dr. James Fishback, John Taylor, Silas Noel, Jeremiah Vardeman and Old Jacob Creath. In the meeting, it became apparent that Alexander Campbell wanted to reform more than creeds. S. H. Ford wrote, "The result of that meeting was the surrender of Creath, the apparent acquiescence of Vardeman, and the hesitating neutrality of Fishbank."[24]

Ford also observed,

> But there were two men in that company, whose minds and whose principles Mr. Campbell's eloquence in public, or art in private, could not shake. They were Silas M. Noel and John Taylor. The former was, in mental power Mr. Campbell's equal; in learning, not far inferior to him; and in clearness of mental vision and logical consistency, far his superior.[25]

John Taylor, the old pioneer gave this startling account of their encounter with Alexander Campbell:

The night after preaching, we sat up very late, and had much conversation, as also next morning. Noel and myself exchanged thoughts about the new preacher. We strongly suspected he was deeply tinctured with Unitarianism, in which we became more confirmed by the friendship between him and Stone, and all of Stone's followers.

I heard a number of things from Campbell which made me stare; in some of which I withstood him. Elder Chilton was speaking of a good work going on–sinners weeping and crying for mercy. I saw Campbell raise his hand, and with a loud crack of his finger and a scornful look on Chilton, say: "I would not give that for it; if a sinner weeps when I preach, I know I have in some way deceived him."[26]

Taylor parted with Campbell near Frankfort, where the latter had an appointment to preach. He took hold of Taylor's hand and said, "May your last days be your best."

Whereupon Taylor replied, "May you preach and sinners weep, and when you preach use this text: 'Be afflicted, and mourn, and weep: let your laughter be turned to mourning, and your joy to heaviness.'"

To this Campbell could not reply. He may have gained Old Creath, but he could not ensnare John Taylor.[27]

In July of 1823 Alexander Campbell began his newspaper, the *Christian Baptist*.* With this publication he began dropping bombs on the Baptists in Kentucky, while his troops were busy finding weaknesses in the lines.

The war for souls now took on the tenor of "earnestly contending for the faith" as satan's plan for America became obvious–*distraction, division, derision and deception.*

No false doctrine or false "church" is effective unless it is "close" to the truth, just as the *Angel of Light* would have it. As many as four false religions would spin out of Kentucky all fueled by Baptist compromise and ignorance.

Old Jacob Creath had a nephew, Young Jacob Creath and this second Jacob Creath added up to trouble in central Kentucky.

---

* Later renamed the *Millennial Harbinger*.

In 1829 Old Creath immersed 100 at Nicholasville and convinced the church to drop its constitution. Next, both Creaths found another unstable congregation. It was of all places, Clear Creek Baptist Church, the scene of so much good under John Taylor.

In 1829 the Clear Creek church was without a pastor. Young Jacob Creath was asked to preach in the meeting-house once a month indefinitely. He was not a candidate to be the church pastor, but a small number asked him to fill the pulpit.

Ford testified, "He introduced Campbell's New Translation—would read from it in the pulpit. He continually attacked the principles held by the church as expressed in their articles of faith."[28] Young Creath, like his Uncle Old Creath, seemed to enjoy the controversy. Their arrogance speaks volumes of the followers of Alexander Campbell.

At Clear Creek contention in the church broke out. Young Jacob Creath had been given the pulpit, not to be the pastor, but to occupy once a month. Those who were against the action could not remove him. He claimed that if he were barred from the pulpit he would preach in the woods but he stayed in the church house anyway.

The old veterans of Clear Creek began to leave the church. A vote was taken and passed on the question "Shall we stick to and abide by our original constitution?"[29] But Young Creath declared, "the Philadelphia Confession of Faith was the abomination of desolation."[30]

Taylor reported, "He has since set up a church in THE SAME HOUSE, as they say, according to 'the ancient order of things.'"[31]

At the same time Young Creath was bringing strife and dissimulation in the Clear Creek church, his uncle, Old Creath held sway in the oldest Baptist church in northern Kentucky, the South Elkhorn. Even though John Shackleford, the Virginia veteran of persecution was the pastor, the church embraced Creath and "the current reformation." Shackleford's party excluded Old Creath and Old Creath's party excluded Shackleford. But the Creaths held the majority. The first item of business for the "South Elkhorn Church of Creath" was to "dispose with the Philadelphia Confession of Faith."[32]

In sorrow, we report that the old South Elkhorn Baptist Church, the mother of the Baptist churches north of the Kentucky River, dissolved. This occurred sometime after 1829 the year of the death of their old warrior pastor John Shackleford.[33]

The Campbellites then commandeered the Baptist church at Versailles. In 1828, old Creath debated at the church and won. The church was reconstituted upon the so-call "ancient order"; that is to say, "no creed."

When the Elkhorn Baptist Association met in 1829 in Lexington, Kentucky, "the current reformation" churches sought to take control of the old blessed association. They did not succeed in 1829, but set their sights on 1830.

*   *   *

Elsewhere, a small group of Baptist churches in Pennsylvania withdrew from the Mohoning Baptist Association, an Alexander Campbell stronghold, to form the Beaver Association. This courageous act was done in August of 1829 and was the first public repudiation of "Campbellism." According to the Beaver Association Alexander Campbell believed that:

1. There was no promise of salvation without baptism.
2. There is no direct operation of the Holy Spirit on the mind,   prior to baptism.
3. Baptism produces the remission of sins and the gift of the Holy Spirit.
4. No creed is necessary for the church but the Scriptures as they stand.[34]

*   *   *

Confusion reigned as the confession was dropped from many of the Baptist churches of Kentucky. At this time the views of Alexander Campbell concerning baptism reached their logical conclusion. In the July 5, 1830, issue of the *Millennial Harbinger* Campbell's claim that **"baptism formally washes away sin"**, became: **"immersion is the converting act"** and **"immersion and regeneration are two Bible names for the same act."** *Infusion* by *works* had now officially poisoned "the current reformation."[35]

In the course of the year 1830 such a campaign and battle for position had never been seen in Kentucky. The Creaths, John Smith, the
Stonites, the Campbellites, and a host of others set their goal to reform
old Elkhorn Association.[36] Victory here for "the current reformation"
could have meant the capitulation of the entire state to Campbell's doctrines. Given the influence of the Kentucky Baptists it could have meant
a recension of baptismal regeneration in *Baptist Nation*.

The association of Baptists south of Elkhorn was infiltrated as well.

William Hickman had constituted the South Benton Baptist
Church, in the Franklin Association, in 1801. They had settled John
Major as the pastor in 1828 and immediately had a revival resulting in
the church growing to 300 members. But they had problems and the
"Apostle of Division," Old Jacob Creath, and Joseph Hewlett paid them
a visit. Careful observation of these doings will recognize that satan
never builds anything himself—his aim is to take what some saints of
God have built and corrupt it. That certainly was the procedure for the
Campbellites.

Old Creath and Hewlett found Hickman's disgruntled son-in-law,
John Brown, and lobbied for him to be given opportunity to preach
once a month. Naïvely, the South Benson church consented, Brown
and Creath preached "the ancient order" and made converts.

When the church finally realized the "reformers" were attempting a
take over they called a meeting and asked the perpetrator to stop.
Caught in the act of dissimulation, Old Creath and company asked if
the records could be erased! They arrogantly asked if their man John
Brown could continue to preach once a month. This was rejected, and
Old Creath put on his hat and "dissolved the minority." But behold,
Young Creath, visiting from South Elkhorn, stood and said he would
"preach in the pulpit on the creed question." He proclaimed, "All in
favor of meeting here Monday to constitute on the book (holding up
either the King James or Campbell's translation, it is not known) say,
'Aye!'" A group of misled Baptists stood and agreed to meet that Monday.

The new South Benton church "of the ancient order" installed John
Brown as pastor. In true rebel fashion, Brown resigned and handed the

pulpit over to Young Jacob Creath. Eventually, the true South Benton Baptist Church expelled John Brown and 66 others.[37]

It must be noted that Young Jacob Creath, *during the entire South Benton fiasco*, was the *pastor* of the South Elkhorn Church.

Then incredibly, in the midst of the controversy, a revival broke out in Kentucky. And there was a battle over the converts, a battle over who was going to baptize them and what kind of baptism they would receive. It was a strange mix of Baptist baptism and Campbell immersion. A large number of Baptist people, confused about believer's baptism submitted to "another baptism" by Campbell's "reformers." John Smith, the most powerful preacher of the Campbellites admitted he "baptized 600 sinners and capsized 1,500 Baptists" in 1829-1830.[38]

During the surreal battle for baptism in Kentucky the most miserable tenet of the Campbell "reformers" came to light: They ridiculed the convicting power of the Holy Ghost. The strange remark of Alexander Campbell to John Taylor about sinners weeping was just a part of Campbell's apostate theology. Baptists were surprised that the Campbellites "even deny the special operation of the Spirit in quickening the dead sinner, and by way of ridicule, ask, 'where did the Spirit hit you?'"[39]

At last a great orator for the cause of the Baptists arrived on the scene. The Elkhorn association would have probably embraced the Campbell "reformation" if William Vaughan had not moved back to the Bracken district from Ohio. From 1827 forward, Vaughan moved among his Baptist preacher brethren exposing Campbellism for what it was: an attack on *imputation* and the convicting power of the Holy Ghost. He set Walter Warder and Jeremiah Vardeman straight and strengthened the center of Kentucky.

Vaughan was *the* thorn for Campbell, Smith and Creath. To thwart him, Young Creath went everywhere in Bracken or Elkhorn where Vaughn preached. Once at Millersburgh, William Vaughan and Walter Warder were to ordain John Holliday. Young Creath met them there to dispute, but was not allowed. That day, William Vaughan preached for *three and one half-hours* on the ills of "the current reformation." It kept

Campbellism out of the Millersburgh Church.[40] Warder became somewhat an assistant to Vaughan in this important work.

Finally, a frustrated Alexander Campbell met with Vaughan and Warder to ask them to cease and desist urging them to join with him in the advancement of the "ancient order" of baptismal necessity. They assured him they would do no such thing.

Now a faithful pen came to aid the Baptists. A call was made for an emergency meeting of the Franklin Baptist Association of Kentucky in July of 1830. It was a large gathering. At the meeting, the now famous circular letter of Silas Noel was distributed and read. It contained "39 Articles"* of the aberrant ideas of Alexander Campbell.[41]

This held in check the further advance of Campbellism, but damage had been done. The North District was all but lost to Campbell. There, as in most places, the point of contention was the Confession of Faith. The North District was basically absorbed into Campbell reform by the influence of John Smith.**

*   *   *

The stage was set for the Elkhorn Baptist Association meeting of 1830. On the side of the so-called reformers was John Smith and the Creaths. Joseph Hewlett parked himself at Providence church, just in time for the 1830 meeting of the Elkhorn Association.

The old Baptists had Silas Noel, George Waller, William Vaughan, Walter Warder and a now stable Jeremiah Vardeman.

As it happened, the circular letter from Noel and the preaching of William Vaughan had prepared the Elkhorn Association for what could have been a majority acquiescence to Campbell beliefs.

At the meeting at Silas, in Bourbon County, August 14, 1830, young Jacob Creath, who had control of the most famous and influential Baptist church in Kentucky, South Elkhorn, was not allowed a seat.

---

* The 39 articles are in Appendix J.
* * John Smith was from Tennessee and grew up under the influences of Tidence Lane and Jonathan Mulkey. He converted to Campbell ideas sometime in the early 1820's and became Alexander Campbell's most effective worker.

Neither was Joseph Hewlett. THEY WERE NOT BAPTISTS. The North District Association, under the leadership of Campbell's bright star John Smith, was rejected. Then Jeremiah Vardeman quickly accepted a motion to drop the Versailles church, of which Old Creath was a member, from correspondence.

Upon this resolution, Old Jacob Creath spoke for an hour against dropping Versailles. But by now, the Baptists of Elkhorn had had enough of Jacob. Versailles was dropped from the association. Thus Vardeman, who had moderated the meeting, cleaned the Elkhorn association of non-Baptists. Although the battle over baptismal regeneration, now in the mode of immersion, would wage on for many years, the Baptist churches were basically safe from infiltration.

There were however heavy losses to the "current reformation." The Baptists of Kentucky lost 9,580 members to the new sect from 1830 to 1833.[42]

The followers of Alexander Campbell went on to found the "Disciples of Christ" and various off shoots of the "Church of Christ."

The Campbellite spirit of arrogance that laid claim to church buildings, people, grounds, and assets of churches, was a fatal thread running through "the current reformation." Their cousins, the Church of Jesus Christ of Latter-day Saints, would inherit that spirit and the end would be violence in Missouri, Illinois, and Utah.

Latter-Day Saints (Mormons)

The Mahoning Baptist Association ordained Sidney Rigdon a Baptist preacher in Warren, Ohio. He worked with Adamson Bentley. About 1821 he and Bentley became enchanted with the teachings of Alexander Campbell. They followed his ministry carefully and believing the message of a new restoration and a new millennium began to expound some of the finer points of "the current reformation."

Rigdon followed Campbell to his debate with John Walker and became more than an acquaintance. When Campbell held his famous 1823 debate with William McCalla in Washington, Kentucky, Rigdon went along to be the secretary and record the event.

Through the influence of Alexander Campbell, who at that time was still active in the Redstone Association, Rigdon became the pastor of the First Baptist Church in Pittsburgh, Pennsylvania. But two years later in 1824, Rigdon was forced out because of his Campbellite views.[43]

Next we find Rigdon leading a Baptist congregation in Mentor, Ohio, near Kirtland. He steered the church into "the current reformation." But he argued with Alexander Campbell over "restoration." Rigdon believed in a kind of communal living and Campbell could not agree.

At this time in upper New York State, Joseph Smith claimed he had been visited by an angel named Moroni who led him to a stash of golden plates buried in the Hill Cumorah. He further claimed to have translated the writing on the plates into Elizabethan English to give to the world the book of Mormon. Their first "church" was in Fayette, New York, and was founded in 1830.*

The Mormon organization migrated by "revelation" to Kirtland, Ohio that same year. Their best convert was Parley Pratt, a former Campbellite preacher. Pratt was acquainted with Sidney Rigdon and came to see him in Mentor in 1830. Sidney was ready to hear anything that would give him more insight on "restoration." He was introduced to Joseph Smith who supposedly showed him the "Book of Mormon," God's new record given to men.

Pratt and Oliver Cowdery urged Rigdon to be baptized. Incredibly, he submitted to Mormon baptism. The arrogance and self-importance so vivid in Alexander Campbell and so evident in the haughtiness of his followers was in Rigdon. It was just what Joseph Smith and his "saints" needed.

Pratt quickly spread the news of Rigdon's "conversion" and declared, "the interest and excitement became general in Kirtland, and in all the region round about." Pratt and his companions were such a great success that in two or three weeks from their arrival in the neighborhood they had "baptized" 127 souls and this number soon increased to 1,000."[44] Rigdon's "conversion" and the ensuing "conversion" effort transformed Mormonism into "a major threat to Protestantism in the Western Reserve."[45]

---

* One of the saddest facts of history is the Mormon "conversion" of Joseph Wightman, the great grandson of Valentine Wightman. Joseph died in Kirtland, Ohio and is buried near the Mormon Temple.

The Mormons took to embezzlement and thievery in Ohio. They moved the church to the west plain of Missouri.

Joseph Smith began teaching the "saints" that gentile possessions belonged to them. He succeeded in converting his dazed followers into a kind of west plains highwaymen, something like American gypsies stealing from the Missourians. They were stealing not just grain and cattle, but women.

Sidney Rigdon in Far West, Caldwell County, Missouri made a famous speech on July 4, 1838. Rigdon managed to rouse the fury of the western frontiersmen by declaring:

> And that mob that comes on us to disturb us; it shall be between us and them a war of extermination, for we will follow them, till the last drop of their blood is spilled, or else they will have to exterminate us: for we will carry the seal of war to their own houses, and their own families, and one party or the other shall be utterly destroyed.[46]

Gunfights and bloodshed resulted and the Mormons were routed east out of the show-me state into central Illinois. There Joseph Smith, Sidney Rigdon and the Mormon leadership established the Mormon town of Nauvoo. Time and space do not permit an exhaustive narrative but the facts show that Sidney Rigdon was eventually excommunicated by the Mormons. But his ministry principles, gleaned from the Baptists; and his spirit, gleaned from the Campbellites, became a part of Mormonism. In addition, he may have been responsible for the initiation of Masonic practices into Mormonism.

It may be revealing to point out that the Separate Baptists at one time were convinced that God was *restoring the old order*. They even ordained "Apostles," over several areas. They later rejected the embarrassing idea. The Mormons, with the same mindset, recognized Joseph Smith as their "Prophet." Through the years the Mormon "Prophet" has been regarded as authoritative as any Pope that ever put on a miter cap.

When Joseph Smith and his brother were killed in a gun battle[47] at Nauvoo, the Mormons migrated to Utah. With Sidney Rigdon out of the way Brigham Young became the new leader of the Mormon organization. Brigham took the "saints" to their lowest level, instigating "blood atonement." It is historical Mormon doctrine that says a "gentile unbeliever" could have his *own blood shed* for the sake of his redemption. This history has been buried. The devils ran rampant in the west. If you are a member of the Latter-Day Saints, you are a victim of one of the biggest cover-ups in the history of civilization. May the Holy Spirit of God convince you of your sin and helplessness and may you turn to the Jesus of the Bible!

Bible Revision Movement of the Baptists

The national Bible societies progressed in this fashion:

The American Bible Society formed in 1816
American and Foreign Bible Society formed in 1836
American Bible Union was formed in 1850 and merged back with the American and Foreign Bible Society in 1887 which merged with the American Baptist Publication Society in 1887.

We now come to the time when many of the old "fathers" had fallen asleep that a new generation of Baptists decided to revise the Bible. Baptists were gradually taught to believe (1820-1850) that the Bible they read and preached was poor and untrustworthy. Those who began to clamor for a revision did so believing that the "common" Bible was weak. That belief leaves the mind flabbergasted. The "common" King James had produced in those years the greatest outpouring of revival the world had ever known.

When we examine the list of men who called for the Baptist revision we find some of the finest educators and pastors in America. We even find the name of Alexander Campbell, but we do not find *any* of the old time evangelist-church-planting preachers of the Gospel.

John Leland had his own opinion of Bible revision, protesting in 1836:

Words, sentences, aphorisms, and customs that were significant, and well understood in the days of King James, are now out of use and obscure. Should there be a new translation, according to modern diction, is it not probable that two or three centuries hence it would be as obscure?[48]

When Spencer Cone resigned the American Bible Society to form the Baptist led American and Foreign Bible Society it was understood that he did so in support of Carey and Judson's translations. That was true, but Cone and certain members of the leadership of the AFBS had designs to revise the "common" English Bible as well. Baptist preachers had debated "immersion" against infant christening for a generation in America. They were winning the argument. But some believed the King James so seriously in error that it had to be revised.

The American Baptist Publication Society referring to the revision movement of 1836-1865 claimed, "The whole English-speaking world came to the conclusion that we must have a revision of the English Bible."[49] However, a plain examination of history reveals that "the whole English-speaking world" did **not** want their Bible revised. It was not even what the entire executive committee of the American and Foreign Bible Society wanted.

Octavius Winslow, member of the board, expressed "in the strongest terms his deprecation of this new version measure."[50] In fact, Winslow stated that if he suspected "there was a lurking intention to introduce a new Baptist version, he would instantly sever the tie which now bound him so closely to those brethren."[51] Which is exactly what he was forced to do.

A number of Baptists *did* want to see the revision as a part of the work of the American and Foreign Bible Society. This would have made it a Baptist endeavor; however, there were other forces applying pressure for the revision. The November 17, 1853, edition of the *Western Watchman* carried this intriguing statement concerning Alexander Campbell and the revision:

> [The Campbellites] **gave more than one-third of the money for the getting up of the new version.** The Bishop of Bethany, Rev. Alexander Campbell, **one of the revisers,** said, "the Bible Revision will be, we hope, the greatest work of the age. I am sorry for the remarks made about our Baptist friends. We can afford to be liberal to them, for **they are doing our work for us.** We gave rise to this impulse for revision, we were foremost in it, nay, we began it years ago, and now we

will carry our cause by this translation. *Baptism for the remission of sins* is the great point of difference and this they must concede in the new version. They have to come to our ground.[52]

Campbell made that remarkable statement at a revision convention sponsored by his own followers, which took place in 1853.

In order for the American and Foreign Bible Society to revise the Bible the former principle of printing only the "common" King James had to be overthrown. At the annual meeting of the American and Foreign Bible Society held in May of 1849, a committee was formed to decide the question of printing English versions other than the "common" Bible. According to Thomas Armitage[53] the committee decided:

Resolved, That, in regard to the expediency of this board undertaking the correction of the English version, a decided difference of opinion exists, and, therefore, that it be judged most prudent to await the instructions of the Society.[54]

Behind the scenes Cone, aided by William H. Wyckoff and others, had already been putting together a revised "Baptist" version for some time. They had much of it ready to print but were deprived of making the revision an official part of the American and Foreign Bible Society. This was because of the opinion of the board "to await instructions from the Society."[55] Cone and his friends had a deep conviction that the issue needed to be pressed, so in February and March of 1850, they published their opinion in favor of revision in the *New York Chronicle*, making the surprising announcement:

A corrected edition of the English New Testament has been prepared by the subscribers, in connection with eminent scholars, who have kindly co-operated, and given their hearty approval to the proposed corrections. A copy of this will be sent gratuitously to the written order of each member of the Society who wishes to examine it.

William Colgate paid for the printing and plates for the revision.

So the revision had already been made without input from a large faction of the society. This did not sit well with a number of the brethren. It appears in retrospect that Mr. Cone and his associates, in their zeal gave the impression of forcing a new revision.

A pamphlet funded by William Colgate, was released by Cone and company about the revision and distributed nationwide. The pamphlet was an indictment of the old King James Version. It called into question the use of the words "baptize," "Holy Ghost," "master," and a host of other phrases. It also implied that the "common" version was a dishonest publication.

On March 28, 1850, a counter-revision group met in New York and organized a meeting. The meeting in support of the old Bible was held at Oliver Street Baptist Church on April 4, 1850. A large number of concerned Baptists met. Over 100 preachers signed a resolution in support of the old "common" Bible. Bartholomew T. Welch of Brooklyn was the chairman for the meeting and declared in his opening remarks:

> The Baptists have always planted themselves on the solid ground of Scripture. They have appealed directly to the laws and the testimony. In this way they have secured a vantage ground, which they should not rashly abandon. Their strength consists in adherence to the Sacred Word. With the old translation in their hands, they had gained distinguished triumphs. Would it not be unwise to give occasion to the taunt that they had found the old ground untenable, and were obliged to seek for another platform?[56]

At the Oliver Street meeting, J. L. Hodge said, "We ought not to change, we cannot change, one jot of one title in this blessed Book, except by the united action of the English-speaking world."[57]

Perhaps the most eloquent opposition to the revision came from William R. Williams, the respected pastor of Amity Street Baptist Church in New York City. Williams wrote the following pastoral letter to a number of concerned members of his church:

> If the book you and your fathers have so loved and quoted, trusted in, and argued from, consulting it amid the emergencies of life and the storms of temptation, and pillowing on it the languid head, as death was coming on, if this, the Oracle of the closet, the school and the

pulpit, be thus defective, and more than defective—dishonest, you have, my brethren, a right to turn sternly on your pastors, and ask how they justify it to their conscience and their God, that they have been using and commending such a volume, thus pandering to infidelity, and burdened with "palpable falsehoods" and "manifest blasphemy."[58]

Williams[59] argued that the printing of the Bible should be through separate mission boards. That is, independently without denominational control or interference. He also argued, as did John Leland, that if we seek to revise the scriptures to match the vulgar vernacular of each generation—we will never have a Bible.*

Protests against the revision poured in from all quarters.

On May 22, 1850, the American and Foreign Bible Society met in New York to settle the issue. Before the normal election of officers, Isaac Westcott moved: "That this Society, in the issues of circulation of the English Scriptures, be restricted to the commonly received version, without note or comment."[60] He further moved that the vote be taken without debate. A lively debate, however, did follow in the afternoon and each debater was given 15 minutes to speak.

The next day, Dr. Turnbull, of Connecticut, brought this resolution: "*Resolved*, that it is not the province and duty of the American and Foreign Bible Society to attempt, on their own part, or procure from others, a revision of the commonly received English version of the Scriptures." An overwhelming majority passed this resolution. A disappointed Spencer Cone was re-elected as president of the society, but he respectfully resigned.

---

* Williams wrote: "To the era of that illustrious sovereign (King James), to whom English laws, and freedom, as well as literature, owe so much...the word in question goes back. Its rights in the English language are older than Magna Carta—older than the Norman Conquest—coeval with the very birth of the language, properly so called. And yet it is proposed by some to repudiate and reject it, as an alien to our dialect. Are these brethren prepared to show as long a pedigree, and as unquestioned a possession, in favor of words they use, habitually and confidently, as being clearly and unquestionably English?"

Four days later on May 27, 1850, Spencer Cone, William Colgate, William Wykoff, and 20 others founded the American Bible Union. Thomas Armitage, in a rare misstatement, said that the meeting that led to the forming of the Bible Union, "was worthy to be compared with that of the few students behind the haystack near Williamstown, consecrating themselves to foreign missions."[61]

The founding of the American Bible Union was said to be "an important epoch," and articles promoting revision began appearing in Baptist periodicals such as the *Christian Repository* and *Christian Review*. S. W. Levy, principal of the Western Baptist Theological Institute, Covington, Kentucky, wrote the "Duty of Revising the Scriptures"[62] and David E. Thomas, preacher from Zanesville Ohio, wrote "Bible Revision" in the *Christian Repository* early in 1852.[63]

But there was an avalanche of those that saw no need for revision. O. B. Judd wrote, "Editors opposed to revision have exerted their combined influence against it. Ministers have concerted measures to prevent the people from taking and reading it. Advertisers have been appealed to, and in some instances persuaded, not to extend their patronage to it."[64]

Within a year, Cone and Wykoff published *The Commonly Received Version with Several Hundred Emendations*. Their helpers in this endeavor were A. C. Kendrick, J. C. Conant, and H. B. Hackett. Then in 1855, Spencer Cone passed from this life to the next.

As it was eventually revealed, the "Emendation" was not all the America Bible Union wanted. They wanted a completely new version, in reality, a new translation. They employed scholars, spent hundreds of thousands of dollars, lobbied and advertised. In later years, Thomas Armitage admitted, "This work of the Bible Union was cited in debate by high authorities, in the Convocation of Canterbury, as an incentive to immediate action in the proposed revision." Looking back at the infidelity that the so-called "revision" of Canterbury has produced in Christianity, would Armitage be boasting of a Baptist connection to the *Revised Version*? We doubt this.

The debate on revision dragged on until the time of the Civil War and beyond. In the final analysis we may judge the success of the efforts of the Bible Union of the Baptists with this simple analogy: A diligent book collector may procure a copy of *The Commonly Received Version with Several Hundred Emendations*, which would be a very expensive endeavor. Or, you may go to a nearby department store and purchase a copy of "King James's version" for about $2.00.

Passing of the Patriarchs

David Jones had gone into Ohio to be a Chaplain in the Northwest Territory. He served as Chaplain in the War of 1812. He left this earth for glory on **February 5, 1820.**

Lewis Craig: John Taylor said of Lewis Craig: "He was of middle statue, rather stoop shouldered, his hair black, thick set, and somewhat curled, a pleasant countenance, free spoken, and his company very interesting, a great peace maker among contending parties. William Cathcart wrote, "**About the year 1828,** he died suddenly, of which he was forewarned, saying, 'I am going to such a house to die,' and with solemn joy went on to the place, and with little pain left the world."[65]

By 1833, many of the old Baptists were gone. A reflection into the life of one of the last of these Baptist patriots, the ancient **John Weatherford,** is worth noting as we turn another page.

After the Revolution, Weatherford, whose blood stained the walls and the bodies of his congregation at Chesterfield prison, had grown old and infirm. He moved to a farm in Charlotte County Virginia, where he became a neighbor, befittingly, to Patrick Henry. One day as the two reminisced about their patriot days, John Weatherford learned for the first time who had paid his fine and argued his release from his bonds. It was none other than Patrick Henry.

On **January 23, 1833,** Weatherford left this earth to occupy the shores of Heaven. As he lay in state, a crowd came to pay their respects for a true American hero. Visible on his folded hands were the vivid scars from the vicious attack committed on him as he preached through the bars at Chesterfield jail.[66]

John Taylor, the ultimate pioneer evangelist, passed into the hands of Jesus in **January of 1836**. His body was laid to rest in the family cemetery in Franklin County.

In 1983 "his remains were moved to the Clear Creek Baptist Church cemetery in Woodford County. The inscription on his tombstone was visible in November of 1986."[67] Sometime in 2001, Jeffrey Faggart, the president of the Baptist History Preservation Society, searched for Taylor's grave. The cemetery, which including the graves of Taylor and his family, had been bulldozed to pave the way for a "family life" building addition to the church. The headstones had been piled behind the building.

The author of *America in Crimson Red* visited the John Taylor gravesite in early November 2002. The headstones had been moved to the left of the main auditorium building and placed at the head of a concrete slab. But this is not the place that holds the remains of John Taylor.

Mr. John Leland returned to his native Massachusetts, and lived the remainder of his life in Cheshire. Cathcart wrote of him:

> A sensational preacher he was not, nor a mere bundle of eccentricities. He was evidently 'a born preacher.' The life of a settled pastor would have been irksome to him. Everywhere he pleaded with all the energy of his soul for civil and religious liberty, and he had the satisfaction of seeing it at last come out of the conflict victorious over all foes. Among the class of ministers whom God raised up during the last century to do the special work which it was given the Baptist denomination to perform, John Leland occupies a conspicuous place. We doubt if his equal will ever be seen again. Mr. Leland Died **January 14, 1841**.[68]

John Leland is supposed to have baptized 1,500 in New England, as he said, "more than any in the country." It is said **that** John Waller baptized more converts than any other in Virginia, perhaps 2,000 souls. William Hickman baptized the most in Kentucky according to John Taylor. Now we come to the record of **Jeremiah Vardeman**.

Vardeman sold his farm and made a farewell excursion through Kentucky and Tennessee, and in October of 1830 he crossed over into

Missouri near Salt River in Ralls county. Several churches grew up under his immediate labors. In August of 1834 he led in the organization of the Missouri General Association for missions.

Vardeman became very feeble and unable to stand and so preached from a chair. Still, in this condition he preached with great power and pathos. Just two weeks prior to his death he visited the Sulphur Springs at Elk Lick, which appeared to give him some relief. Amazingly, he baptized his last five converts and constituted a church in that place.

On **May 28 1842**, Vardeman called his family around him, gave them some instructions, and said farewell. He died that same day. He had preached for over 30 years and baptized over *8,000 converts.*[69]

Adoniram Judson sailed for America in **April of 1850.** On April 12, he died aboard ship and was buried at sea.

Isaac McCoy

CHAPTER SIXTEEN
The Northwest, the Great West and Isaac McCoy

The Gospel into Florida (1825), Michigan (1822),
Oklahoma (1832), Texas (1834), Iowa (1834),
Wisconsin (1834), and Oregon (1844)

The influence of Adoniram Judson upon the minds of Christians during the 19th century was tremendous. One of those set on fire for God for the salvation of the Burmese people was George Dana Boardman. In 1828 Boardman arrived in Tavoy, a section of British Burmah. His intent was to establish a mission there and form churches. Not long after arriving, Boardman baptized three converts including Ko Thahbyu, who became a great missionary. An unusual thing happened at about this time:

> A curious story is told by Mr. Boardman in regard to a book delivered about twelve years before his arrival in Tavoy to these people, by a traveler, who told them that it was sacred and that they should worship it. It was put into the keeping of an old man of their tribe, who, though ignorant of its contents, carefully wrapped it in muslin and placed it in a basket made of reeds and covered it over with pitch. Ever since, it had been an object of worship and the old man had become a kind of sorcerer. Both he and the people fully believed that a teacher would come sometime and reveal to them the strange contents of the book.[1]

The book was an old English *Book of Common Prayer*. Boardman used it as an introduction to the Gospel and numbers of those in Tavoy were converted. But early in Boardman's ministry he grew gravely ill. A missionary was sent to relieve him and the first duty of the new missionary was to baptize. Boardman, at the point of death, was carried to the place of baptism:

> Never was there a more impressive scene in the history of Christianity; never a picture more worthy of the imagination of the poet, or the pencil of the painter. The new missionary, Mason, performing his first official act; the simple converts "buried with Christ in baptism;" the devoted wife directly to become a widow; the loving attendants; the dying missionary, his emaciated face lighted up with a glow of enthusiasm as he witnessed this glorious harvest home, the rocks, the mountains, the purling stream, the fresh foliage and the blue expanse encircling all—with the thought that this was to Boardman, "the last of earth," must have invented the whole scene with a moral sublimity not only touching, but overpowering. After baptism he seemed perfectly satisfied and had been heard to say during the day that if he could only witness the performance of this act he could gladly say, "Lord now lettest thou thy servant depart in peace, for mine eyes have seen thy salvation."
>
> As they were bearing him back to the mission house they looked to see if he needed anything, but his spirit had taken its flight far from the sphere of earthly comforts to the land where "there shall be no more death, neither sorrow, nor crying, neither shall there be any more pain."[2]

Not just in the life of Boardman, but Adoniram Judson made a difference that is felt to this day. His life has encouraged and inspired hundreds, perhaps thousands, to surrender to preach the Gospel on the mission field. However, the greatest influence of Judson may not have been on the so-called foreign field. It may well have been that his greatest hegemony was in America in the person of one of the greatest missionaries the American states ever produced: Isaac McCoy.

Isaac McCoy and the American Indian Mission Association

Like so many other forgotten heroes of our faith, Isaac McCoy is largely an unexamined man. Not until a recent biography by George M. Ella[3] has there been an attempt to examine all the documents about his remarkable life. Ella thankfully writes about McCoy from the view of a believer and understands and conveys the deep piety and motives of the man. Pity the Christian young person who knows nothing about this great American missionary. Pity and shame on Christians, young and old, who have more knowledge of athletic "stars" and Hollywood "stars" than of servants of Christ.

Isaac McCoy has been rightly called, the "Apostle of the Western Trail." He was the single most important friend the natives of America ever had. Spencer Cone said, "While the Elliots and Brainards are remembered, the name of Isaac McCoy, the red-man's benefactor, will not be forgotten."[4] Yet it has largely been forgotten. Our brief consideration of his life begins across the sea.

The McCoys, as one might suppose, came from Scotland. James McCoy, Isaac's grandfather, came to America sometime near 1700. He was a ten-year-old orphan who, according to family tradition, made his way across the Atlantic as a cabin boy.

In his youth, James moved to Pennsylvania and built a fort bearing his name, and there married a lady from the Bruce family of the Scotts. The family eventually settled in Uniontown. James and his wife had six children. One of these was William McCoy who was born at McCoy's fort in 1754. William was born again while living in Pennsylvania and married Eliza Royce in 1776. William and Eliza also had six children one of whom was Isaac McCoy, born June 13, 1784.

Isaac McCoy moved with his family to Kentucky in 1790. His father William, was a pioneer Baptist preacher. The McCoys homesteaded on the Ohio River some distance up from "the Falls" or present-day Louisville. Isaac's father William, eventually settled as the pastor of the Buck Creek Church. From there William McCoy and George Waller supplied the old Indiana church, Fourteen Mile Creek. This church removed to Silver Creek, five miles west of Charlestown in 1803. It took the name of Silver Creek from that time forward. William McCoy became the pastor of Silver Creek Baptist Church and tarried in that place to the end of his days. They built a little church building across from "the Falls."

Isaac was converted at age 16 and was baptized by Joshua Morris on March 6, 1801. He became a member of Buck Creek Church.

At the age of 18 he married 18-year-old Christiana Polk. The Ottawa Indians had kidnapped Christiana's mother and three of her siblings and held them for a period of three years, but this did not embitter her. Instead, it wrought in her a deep desire to take the Gospel to the Ottawas. She would do this and more as the wife of Isaac McCoy.

Isaac and Christiana McCoy arrived at Vincennes, Indiana in April of 1804, but did not stay long. They settled instead at Silver Creek under the leadership of William McCoy.

Isaac was busy immediately. He began preaching and organized a "mission society." He was licensed in July of 1807, and ordained to the Gospel ministry on October 12, 1810 by William McCoy and George Waller.

Isaac helped form the Maria Creek Baptist church. This church he pastored for eight fruitful years while doing the work of a pioneer evangelist, preaching all over the state of Indiana and Illinois. While off the field, he supported his family as a wheelwright, a skill he learned from his father and grandfather.

Isaac McCoy was a reserve soldier in the war of 1812. The Indians, especially the Shawnees under Tecumseh, were allied with the British. Isaac was asked to go deep into Indian Territory for raids. It was during this service that he saw the desperate need of the Indians. He saw the ravages of the introduction of alcohol or "fire-water," to the Indian way of life. He concluded that they needed the Bible in their own language and churches and schools of their own. Moreover, he realized that the Indians were facing extinction. He would be the first to voice the need of an Indian homeland to Congress. This would become his "splendid struggle."

God began to bless the churches he was pastoring.

Out of the wilderness came one Daniel Parker. Parker gained real power on the American frontier for his charismatic leadership and his persuasive power of argument concerning his strange "two-seed" doctrine.

Basically, Parker's "two-seed" doctrine stated that the human race was divided into two groups: the "seed of the serpent" and the "seed of the children of God." Since the seed of the serpent were assigned to Hell, no amount of preaching or persuasion could save them. Since the "seed of the children of God" were predestined to eternal life, no amount of preaching or persuasion would make a difference in their final destination. If the "two-seed" doctrine is true, then mission plans are vain and a waste of time and money.

Parker settled in southeastern Illinois in 1817 and began a campaign against the Baptist Board of Foreign Missions. His special target became the Maria Creek Baptist Church and Isaac McCoy. His other target was John Mason Peck. While Peck also came under fire from John Taylor, as we have seen, Taylor's real criticism was over the raising of funds and not of the need of preaching the Gospel to the lost. Parker, on the other hand, was a kind of "pseudo-hypercalvinist," who opposed preaching the Gospel to anyone except the "seed of the children of God."

In 1817 Isaac McCoy received what he longed for—his appointment as a missionary to the Indians of Indiana and Illinois. This appointment was made by the Baptist Board for Foreign Missions, or as it was called, the Triennial Convention. His appointment was for one year. After the first year was ended, McCoy continued his association with the Board, even though he had no formal contract with them.

He began by setting up a mission station at Raccoon Creek, Indiana. From there he contacted the federal government to explain his plans for the Indians for the first time. He now had his mission, his wife, and seven children. 1817 was also the year that he would lose the first of eleven children on the frontier. Mahale, at age 13, would die of Typhus Fever.

In 1818, McCoy wrote this letter to the Baptist Board, which graphically illustrates the results of his first eight years in the ministry, and the direction he was now contemplating:

Although I have travelled more than 1,900 miles since the 17th of last October, and besides attending church meetings, &c. have preached more than one hundred sermons, yet I have not been able to preach one sermon in Edwards, Davis, or Dubois counties, the last of which was formerly part of Pike county. In less than three weeks, I expect to have the sole charge of five churches, which are situated as follows: from White River church to High Bank is twenty miles, thence to Wabash twenty-four, thence to Maria twelve, thence to Prairie creek forty, from Prairie creek to White river church is seventy miles.

This extensive route lies through an immense population, all destitute of preaching by our ministers. There are also two or three places where I think churches might in a little time be formed, but there is none to blow the trumpet to assemble them. Now if I attend to preaching to these people, the Indians must be neglected, and if I attend to the Indians, "with whom shall I leave these few sheep in the wilderness?"

Should I be so happy as to embrace a brother in this work, it would be my wish to form a family establishment where, while one of us would be on a preaching tour, the other could be father to his children, and could attend closely to the ultimate object of the mission. I am very desirous to hear from the Board something on this subject.[5]

We see plainly the great burden placed upon the heart of Isaac McCoy. He asked the Baptist Board for a fellow laborer, for in his many miles of travelling he had developed a greater burden, the burden of caring for the souls of the American Indian.

Opposition was acute. In 1819 the Wabash Association withdrew support for the Baptist Board of Foreign Missions. In 1820 Daniel Parker wrote *A Public Address to the Baptist Society*, a book against the Baptist Board of Foreign Missions. In 1824 another book against the board and addressed specifically to Isaac McCoy's Maria Creek Baptist Church was published. Parker did not cease his pursuit of McCoy, even moving in the vicinity of Maria Creek and for a period of four years brought motions against the church and any association in correspondence with her.[6] This harangue continued until the "two-seed" promoter went to Texas.

McCoy did not get a straight answer from the Baptist Board as to whether they would renew support. Moreover, they chose not to give publicity of McCoy's substantial progress in his mission. The *Baptist Missionary Magazine* rarely mentioned McCoy's work. This kind of treatment went on for many years.

In 1820 McCoy moved his mission to Fort Wayne, Indiana. In this part of the frontier, the Indians were so scattered and so devastated by liquor, it was difficult to find a sober village. The lands of the Delaware Indians were completely gone and the rest of the tribes were nearly out of their minds with drunkenness. It was in Fort Wayne that McCoy began to realize the inevitable end of the Indians.

From the life of Isaac McCoy, we find three magnificent beliefs: First, the American Indians were not hopeless barbarians; Second, the American Indians were perishing only because nothing was being done to save them; Third, if a homeland for them was not created they would be annihilated as a race.

That Isaac McCoy gave himself to these beliefs, there can be no doubt.

*   *   *

Michigan 1822

The first of the *baptized believers* in Michigan were Orison Allen and his wife at a settlement where Pontiac now stands. This family was at the outpost in 1818. They were without a church until Elon Galusha came from the New York Baptist Convention to gather a church there in 1822. At the time the population of Michigan was about 9,000 with Detroit being a village of around 1500 souls. Nehemiah Lamb, missionary from New York gathered the second church with his sons. This was accomplished at Stoney Creek. In the summer of 1824 Elkanah Comstock, still another New York missionary, came to stay. Comstock became the pastor at Pontiac, and constituted a church at Troy in 1825. He also gathered a church at Farmington in 1826. Elkanah Comstock was a sailor early in life, from New London, Connecticut. He was converted and called to the Gospel ministry in 1800. He arrived in Michigan in 1824 and was yet another one of those obscure pivotal men that God used in the early days of His work in a great state.[7]

The first association in Michigan, appropriately named, the Michigan Baptist Association was organized in 1826 and consisted of the Pontiac, Stoney Creek, Troy and Farmington churches.

Florida 1825

On March 12, 1825, 20 hardy souls met at Campbellton, Florida to establish a Baptist church. The church constituted and the next day a preacher named Callaway was called to serve as the first pastor.

The Florida Baptist Association was organized in 1842 and originally covered the entire inhabited area of the Territory of Florida and a
portion of the southern part of Georgia.

The earliest churches to be organized were Bethlehem Baptist
Church, which was later called Campbellton Baptist Church, and Sardis
Baptist Church, which is no longer in existence. Both of the Jackson
County churches were organized in 1825.

By the time the association was organized in 1842, five churches
had been added: Ebenezer at Monticello in Jefferson County 1828, Indian Springs in Leon County 1829, Elizabeth 1834, Concord 1841, and
Monticello, 1841.

*   *   *

The Columbian College of Washington, D.C. opened in 1822. It
was approved by the Triennial Convention of 1817. It was to be an educational institution providing a "thorough knowledge of the Hebrew
and Greek languages of the original Old and New Testament Scriptures.
[As it was] indispensable for those who were to become foreign missionaries who would be called upon to translate the Scriptures into tongues
whose vocabulary was but ill-fitted to have incorporated...the great
truths of the Gospel."[8]

But the college was doomed from the start. Isaac McCoy's Fort
Wayne mission had grown to a group of helpers and students numbering over 50 souls and was in desperate need of support. Incredibly, the
Baptist Board of Foreign Missions had taken $10,000.00 from the mis-
sionary funds to assist in the construction of buildings at Columbian.[9]
As Etta wrote, "This was money which had been sent to the board especially earmarked for such work as McCoy was doing. It was built on the
empty stomachs of missionaries already on that field."[10]

McCoy sought financial help wherever he could find it. He cultivated friends in the government that were interested in his work in the
education of the Indians. There were monies available that he used.

He was ordered around and censured by the Baptist Board of Foreign Missions in ways that made them no different from any other ecclesiastical court or Romish hierarchy. William Staughton rebuked him
because his Indian students ate too much pork. He was chastised for

moving the mission from Raccoon Creek to Fort Wayne. However, he was patient with these things. His burden for preaching the gospel, education, and the creation of an Indian state was motivation to keep every door open for the tremendous financial investment that was needed. In the end, McCoy turned to individual churches and preachers for help.

The physical demands of riding thousands of miles every few months, and sleeping in the wet and cold of the trail, caused a reoccurring sickness which Isaac McCoy called his "putrid fever." From the accounts, it may be surmised that these were horrid migraines, or body fevers from frequent infections in the head and chest. Some of what McCoy describes reminds the author of bodily reaction to untreated diabetes. But it was the mental anguishes that took incalculable virtue from him. Most of the anguish came from lack of laborers or lack of common compassion on the part of Baptists in general. Two of the most outlandish of these examples we offer for our reader.

Just one year into his ministry at Fort Wayne, McCoy heard that a group of Potawatomi were seeking God. A young man led them whose name was Menominee. He was teaching reform and advocating moral values. It is not clear that this man Menominee was actually a saved man but he had gathered a large number of Indians to hear Isaac McCoy. Isaac spent several days among them but could not stay, having to return to the mission. He had no other preachers in his mission though he had written countless letters begging the Baptist Board to send him some. Of this open door among the Potawatomis and the agonizing result McCoy wrote:

> Here was an uncommonly favourable opening for doing good to these dear, artless people, who appeared ready to receive instruction in things relating both to this life and that which is to come; but it was impossible for a solitary missionary and his wife to improve the opening here. But among three or four hundred thousand of our denomination in the United States none manifested a willingness to make his home in the desert and teach these poor anxious inquirers the path to heaven. Within a year after the time of which we are writing, the party as such, began to dwindle, and long since it has ceased to exist as a religious party. We cannot now go back to atone for our **criminal neglect** of the party of poor Menominee.[11]

In 1822, the Wabash Association, because of "antimission" pressure, "struck off" Maria Creek Baptist Church from membership. But the good news from 1822 was the birth of the Carey mission, begun in the fall. It was located in what is presently Niles, Michigan. The Fort Wayne Mission remained intact and a Baptist church was established there. In 1823 the Thomas mission was begun, located up the Michigan peninsula at the present site of Grand Rapids. The Thomas mission was primarily to the Ottawa Indians. Niles and Grand Rapids grew up around these Baptist missions.

In July of 1825, McCoy applied to Dr. William Staughton at the Baptist Board for Foreign Missions for the admission of seven of his young Indian students into Columbian College. McCoy wrote several times, even to Luther Rice and Spencer Cone, but no real answer was forthcoming. Not knowing what else to do, McCoy took them east to Washington to enroll them in the college himself.

When he arrived at Columbian, to his amazement, the students were not accepted. This was a source of great grief knowing the college was supposed to be founded to train missionaries, and here were some natives in need of training to return to their own people. McCoy was urged to take the students to Kentucky for their education. But the students at Columbian, led by McCoy's own sons, Rice and Josephus, petitioned to have the Indian students accepted. For this effort, board member Lucius Bolles suggested McCoy withdraw his sons from the college.

In the end, Hamilton College in New York called for the seven students and they enrolled. Strangely, William Cathcart says, "They found a ready welcome at Hamilton, New York."[12] There was no mention of the fact that Columbian simply did not want Indians at the school. A confused Isaac McCoy headed back to his mission in Carey, Michigan.

In 1824 Secretary of War John C. Calhoun accepted Isaac McCoy's plan for an Indian homeland. The next year it became the government policy. Although some may believe the colonization of the American Indian was an inhumane insult, the purpose was plain. Far too many white Americans wanted annihilation of the Indians and this plan was the least of all evils.

Congress enacted a bill for the financing of Indian colonization west of the Mississippi. The Department of War then elected Isaac McCoy as a Commissioner and Treasurer of an expedition to the Indian Territory. The results of his tour were the location of another mission station at Sault de St. Marie, Michigan.

McCoy published his *Remarks on the Practicability of Indian Reform*. It outlined the plan of removal. The proposed territory for the Indian state stretched from the Red River in Texas to the Missouri and encompassed all of what became Nebraska, Kansas and Oklahoma. From 1830 to 1840 the Indians were removed from their present states, north and south into the territory.

The mission at Carey was eventually given up and sold. The Baptist Board for Foreign Missions received over $5,000 for the property.

Oklahoma 1832

The first Baptist church in Oklahoma was gathered in this fashion:

John Davis was a full blood Creek Indian (Muscogee) who had been converted in Alabama. He had been educated in the Withington Mission at Tucheebachee and answered God's call to preach the Gospel. When Isaac McCoy went to Georgia, Alabama and Mississippi to assist in the relocation of the Creeks to the Indian Territory, he met Davis and they became immediate friends. John Davis was relocated to Ebenezer Station, three miles north of the Arkansas River and fifteen miles west of Fort Gibson, in the present state of Oklahoma. The Baptist Board had sent an unaided missionary, David Lewis, to Ebenezer Station to assist in the education of the Creeks and Choctaws.

On September 9, 1832, Isaac McCoy constituted the Muscogee Baptist Church, Ebenezer Station, Indian Territory.

Within a year, the church had 80 members and John Davis had translated the Gospel of John and part of Matthew in the Creek language. Very quickly the number of people in Davis' congregation swelled to over 300.[13] With all of his success the Baptist Board or its paper, the *American Baptist Missionary Magazine* never recognized the great Indian pastor as the actual pastor of the church. He was simply referred to as "native assistant" or "native preacher."

The Board publicly announced in the June 1833 issue of the *American Baptist Missionary Magazine* that Isaac McCoy was "not in the service of the Board." This was said to be a mistake, but for all practical purposes, it was a reality. Later in 1833, the old Carey mission was officially reformed at the Kansas-Missouri border, now referred to as Shawnee Mission.

From this time until the start of the Civil War, a kind of "golden age" visited the Indians in the new territory. It was a time of good progress and revival among them. But there was a need for what was called "pan-Indian" law among them. In the wilderness the only law was revenge or reciprocation by theft, and the Osage, Kansa, Otoes, Omahas and Pawnees, who had long been at war with one another were living in the same territory. McCoy believed that the Choctaw model of a General Council among all tribes could work if the smaller tribes could be assured of their independence.

In 1840 McCoy published his *History of Indian Affairs*. It was a monumental achievement. This large work was filled with wonderful information and contained the heart of a sincere missionary. But tidings from the east would soon trouble him.

McCoy's final and official break with the American Board of Foreign Missions occurred in June of 1841 when the *American Baptist Magazine* reported that McCoy, since 1830, had been in the employment of the U.S. Government, and that he had not really since that time, been under the Board's patronage. It was a damaging article. Strange to view it now but obviously, a real enemy of McCoy was on the Board, or a two-face hypocrite was deciding policy. McCoy could never tell which were his true friends or enemies on the Board.

Protest of his official dismissal came to the Baptist Board of Foreign Missions from fellow laborers, missionaries, government officials, and most tellingly, from converted Indian chiefs. But the rift was permanent, and the result of this official severance was the immediate termination of governmental recognition. And with it, termination of monetary support from the government and from the churches for his educational enterprises.

In the year 1842, acting out of necessity and responding to his many acquired friends Isaac McCoy formed the **American Indian Mission Association**. J. H. Spencer wrote: "This [American Indian Mission Association] association was organized chiefly through the influence of Isaac McCoy, one of the most zealous and devoted philanthropists that have lived and died in Kentucky. This self-sacrificing Christian minister, and devoted missionary, deserves to be "held in everlasting remembrance," especially by all the friends of the American Indians."[14] But, he was not.

By now, readers and friends, the sleight of hand by our *adversary* in his continuing effort to divert the Baptist people from their own heritage ought to be expected.

Isaac McCoy left this world June 21, 1846. With his death, the death of the soul of the American Indian was on the horizon. With McCoy gone, treaty after treaty was broken, and encroachment on the Indian Territory made McCoy's dream a faded memory. Indeed, McCoy himself would become a faded memory. George Ella, writing of McCoy's missing legacy:

> Sometimes the omission of McCoy's name when portraying scenes in which he was obviously the driving force is most difficult to comprehend and one seeks in vain for a reason behind this silence. McCoy was one of the earliest campaigners for home Baptist missions, and Charles White in his *Century of Faith* argues conclusively that McCoy, along with Moses Merrill, was instrumental in founding the Baptist Home Mission. Yet, when Sidney Dyer, McCoy's successor as Corresponding Secretary of the A.I.M.A., composed the Home Mission's Jubilee Poem of 1882 to commemorate, among other things, the Baptists' work among the Indians, McCoy's name is conspicuous by its absence. On the other hand, Cone, Colgate, Going, Hill and Lincoln's names are mentioned in conjunction with the evangelizing of the Indians."[15]

With the closing of the life of McCoy we are in a sense, coming to the end of our narrative. We will end in similar fashion as we began. Roger Williams, a sidelight, though a great man, was not our founder and yet he is portrayed as such. John Clarke, the venerable leader of the church in the wilderness, Aquetneck, and Newport was the first preacher of our principles and founder of our first church. His life is obscure and we are diverted from his testimony. It was Clarke, as McCoy who could not stand idly by with what God had laid at his feet. Clarke picked up the *opinionists* at Boston and fled with them into the

New Hampshire wilderness. He located on Rhode Island, and birthed the first free government in the world, along with our first Baptist church. We end now with McCoy, his testimony from which our eyes have also been diverted. It was McCoy who could not bear to see the Indians die without Christ. It was McCoy who could not but agonize with them in their misery. McCoy as Clarke, could not neglect his duty to them. And Isaac McCoy, like so many of his fathers, was buried in the way. His grave was bulldozed and paved over in Western Cemetery, Louisville, Kentucky.

Our pitiful nation needs a new army of pioneer preachers. God give us some of those unknown servants of God, lying in unmarked graves, now dust, under streets, under paved parking lots and expansions of commerce! Give us preachers who will leave all behind, willing to carry no script, and no provision. Our fathers laboured under the bitterest of circumstances with no encouragement and in many cases no visible results.

Arresting thought! Ireland, Harris, Baker, Taylor, McCoy, et al., lie in unmarked graves, in the tomb of the *Unknown Soldier*, whose sacrifices far outdistance any decorated war hero. OH FOR THE DAY when God will "bring to light the hidden things of darkness, and will make manifest the counsels of the hearts: and then shall every man have praise of God"—1 Corinthians 4:5.

And so we begin our epilogue.

Texas 1834

The first colonization of Mexico was under Moses Austin in 1821. The second was by Green De Witt of Missouri in 1825. There were about 20,000 immigrants by 1830.

In 1830 the Mexican general assembly passed a law prohibiting further immigration into Texas from the United States. In fact, their Secretary of State, Lucas Alaman, said, "We find that, besides this territory having been occupied by colonists who never ought to have been admitted into it, there is not one among them in Texas, who is a Catholic."[16] That was quite a statement, indicative of the attitude of the Mexican authorities in regard to what was termed "anti-Catholic" activities. Activities such as the public preaching of the Gospel.

J. M. Carroll says that most historians assume the first Baptist church in Texas was at old Washington on the Brazos in 1837, but he gives evidence to the contrary.[17] The Baptist preacher Joseph Bays, and 32 other families migrated from Missouri to Camp Sabine on the Louisiana side of the Sabine River. They arrived on June 30, 1820. Bays was originally from North Carolina and his family migrated to Boonesboro, Kentucky, in 1794. He came to Missouri in 1814.

Camp Sabine was a clearing station for early pioneers into Texas. Bays took advantage of the opportunity at Camp Sabine and preached the Gospel to those who passed through. He caught the attention of Joseph Hinds who owned a large log house on the Texas side of the border. Bays began to have a monthly meeting at the house. This he shared with a Methodist preacher by the name of Billie Cook. Cook was an unconverted Universalist who was saved and baptized under the preaching of Bays. This was the first baptism in the state of Texas.

Moses Austin, who was trying to get the group of Missouri pioneers into Texas, died of pneumonia sometime before 1823. Moses' son, Stephen, succeeded in securing a place for the group of pioneers in San Felipe.

Immediately Bays began to preach. The Mexican authorities arrested him in 1823. But he escaped near the headwaters of the San Marcos River. He hid in the home of fellow Missourian, Joseph Kuykendall and then with his family headed back over the border to Camp Sabine. He would remain in Louisiana for 13 years until the independence of the state of Texas. His wife did not remain with him. In 1848 she fell spellbound with the Mormons and ran away with them to Utah.[18] Bays died in Matagorda County in 1854.

The second Baptist preacher in Texas was Freeman Smalley. He was born in Clinton County, Ohio. He ventured to Lamar County and

preached to a group of settlers there in 1822. But no church was constituted as of yet.

Carroll observes: "Daniel Parker, the principal leader on the antimissionary side, moved to Texas, entering on its eastern border. Freeman Smalley, one of the leaders on the missionary side, moved to Texas,
entering on its northern border, and became one the first resident Missionary Baptist preachers in central Texas."[19]

Of Stephen Austin's famous first 300 families, eleven were Baptists.
In the fall of 1828 a company of Baptists, 60 in number, sailed by river
through the southwest to Texas from New York. Among the travelers
was Thomas J. Pilgrim. Pilgrim organized the first Baptist Sunday School
in Texas.[20] Incredibly, the first Baptist church in Texas was actually organized as the Pilgrim church of Illinois, organized on July 26, 1833 by
Daniel Parker, that notorious "antimissionary" preacher. Astounding to
say, Parker brought the church as a body to circumvent Texas law prohibiting the organization of a Baptist church.[21] Under Mexican law, Article 3 of Mexico's 1824 constitution made the Roman Catholic Church
the religion of the Mexican nation.

Daniel Parker was born in Culpeper County, Virginia. As a child he
removed to Franklin County, Georgia. He was married in March of
1802. He was ordained at Turnbull Creek in Dixon County, Tennessee
on May 20, 1806 and began to pastor the Bledsoe Creek Baptist church.
He remained there for 10 years. In 1817 he journeyed to Illinois and
settled near Palestine in Crawford County. This is where he published
his book on the "Two Seed Doctrine."

He travelled to Texas in 1832 and upon investigating the Mexican
province; he reasoned that since a non-catholic church could not be
organized, then one already organized may migrate there. He organized
the latest edition of the travelling church by gathering a group of Baptist
pioneers into a church in motion. It was called the Pilgrim Church of
Predestinarian Regular Baptists. They eventually made their way to Austin's colony on January 20, 1834.[22] Of Parker's church, Carroll comes to
this conclusion:

> Through its pastor and others of its members, held official church ser-
> vices at different times throughout a territory embracing more than
> twenty East Texas counties—with Houston County as a center. It had

at different periods three regularly and officially established meeting places, which it designated as "Arms of the Church" and very many other meeting places where it held services more or less frequently. And as a result of these various services, over this large territory organized through its own efforts, nine new churches. How many churches in Texas, country or city, can show such a record?[23]

Texas declared itself independent on March 2, 1836. The declaration of independence was issued from the blacksmith shop of N. T. Byars, one of the few Baptists in the town of Washington, Texas. The moderator at the meeting in the blacksmith shop was a Baptist from Virginia, Judge Richard Ellis. The commander-in-chief of the Texas army was Sam Houston, as of yet unconverted, but destined to become a devout Baptist. Byars the blacksmith would become a great pastor, founding the church in which B. H. and J. M. Carroll would begin their ministries.[24] On March 6, 1836, the Alamo fell in San Antonio. And the war came on.

One of the shocking tragedies of the Texas War for Independence was the slaughter at Goliad. On the 19th of March a detachment of Texans was overtaken by the Mexican army and surrendered. But they were led to Goliad and brought out and systematically shot. The event was recorded by A.T. Myrth in his *Ambrosio De Letinez* and cited by J. M. Carroll as another testimony in *crimson red*:

> In the last lot came two Baptist preachers who went on exhorting their comrades. When they had reached the place where they were to suffer, the eldest called upon his companions to join him in prayer. Not one refused. Even many of the Mexicans, though unable to understand his language, fell on their knees in imitation of the Texans. Then with an enthusiasm of which it is impossible for any one who was not an eyewitness to form an idea, the elder called upon God, saying:
>
>> We return unto thee, O Almighty Being, who from high heaven directest all things for thy greatest glory. This body which thou gavest us is now a falling sacrifice because we have asserted the rights of freemen and the liberty of the Holy Gospel; but Oh! Vouchsafe thou to receive our spirits into thy bosom, and grant true freedom to this land, which has drunk the blood of our companions in arms. Deliver it from the

darkness that overshadows it, and inspire the people with repentance for their deeds of cruelty. Thy martyrs we are but we
lay it not to their charge. Let not our death be visited upon
them. We, who bleed beneath their knife, beg it of thee!

He was interrupted by the voice of the commander, who in a rage
called out, in Spanish, Fire! Fire! Finish with them! But yet, as the bul-
lets whistled, and his companions fell around him, the preacher lifted
up towards heaven his arms, now reddened with gore, and said, "We
come unto thee!"

He had no time to continue, for one of the dragoons (horsemen)
running up to him, cleft his head at one single stroke, and this assassin
was followed by his comrades, who frightfully hacking the dying and
the dead, soon achieved what their guns had left unfinished.[25]

Z. N. Morrell came to Texas just as they won their independence.
He was born in Tennessee in 1803. He was a great leader and preacher
in Tennessee. Morrell made a tour of Texas during 1835, and in January
of 1836 he rode to Nacogdoces. He described how the urgency to
preach Christ overwhelmed him. Morrell wrote:

There was a large crowd of Americans, Mexicans and Indians of various tribes. My mule was soon tied, and after consultation with my
great Master...I decided to preach, and began looking around for a
suitable place. Near by the vast crowd I saw the foundation timbers of
a large frame building already laid; No sooner discovered that I selected one corner of this for a pulpit—the sills and sleepers already laid
and well adjusted would answer for seats. I held up my watch in my
hand and cried, O yes, O yes, O yes. Everybody that wants to buy,
without money and without price, come this way and commenced to
sing the old battle song "Am I a Soldier of the Cross." Before I finished my song there was around me a large crowd of all sorts, and sizes
and colors.

As Morrell began to preach, a wagon pulled up and out stepped a
family he had baptized in Tennessee! He preached, illegally, for an hour
to good results.[26] In 1837 in Washington, the first Baptist church in free
Texas was established. In 50 years, there were over 400 churches and
pastors and 35 associations. Baylor College was organized in 1845.

Iowa 1834

The Baptist beginning in Iowa begins with Elder John Logan. Logan was born in Rockbridge County, Virginia on February 14, 1793. At the age of seven, his family moved to Garrard County, Kentucky. He was converted, along with his wife in October 1819. Both were baptized by Lee Allen in November of that same year into the New Hope Baptist Church in Simpson County Kentucky.

Very soon after, Logan began to preach the Gospel.

In the fall of 1828, Logan moved to Indiana to the Olive Church of Dubois County. He was ordained there by Charles Harper, John Graham and David Hornade. In just a matter of months he baptized more than 80 converts. One baptismal scene Logan describes:

> The next morning, by request of the pastor, we baptized four converts. Two were his eldest children; one a son of nine and a half years, the other a daughter of eleven years and six months. Each of these children told an "experience of grace," and gave substantial evidence of faith in Christ. We stood in a very narrow stream and took each of the children in our arms from the bank and gently laid them in the water as a symbol of their death to sin and resurrection to a new life, and their fellowship in the burial and resurrection of Jesus Christ. Both father and mother stood on the bank and with streaming eyes and joyful hearts, received them as "they arose out of the water."
>
> A large concourse of people stood on every side, to whom we exclaimed, "Baptists are always willing to baptize children on their own profession of faith but never that of their parents." Two others, a young man and a young women, were baptized at the same time.[27]

In May of 1828, John Logan settled in McDonough County, Illinois and united with Crane Creek Church, in the county of Schuyler. He preached often in the area for several years as an itinerant evangelist, helping feeble churches.

It was at this time that the Spoon River Association was formed in Illinois. The Crane Creek Church united with a few other churches in that district. Spoon River was an "antimission" association, however, participation in mission societies and benevolent agencies at that time was not considered a bar to fellowship, and no bar to fraternal cooperation between the ministers and churches.

In any event, John Logan preached as a missionary from Crane Creek into the "Black Hawk Purchase," now known as Iowa. His first sermon was "in a little rude cabin, the home of Noble Housley, Des Moines County, on the 19th of October, 1834."[28] Among the first settlers of this part of the Territory were a few Baptists from Illinois and Kentucky, who desiring to be organized into a church, had invited Elders Logan and Bartlett to visit them. Accordingly on the next day— October 20th—after another sermon by Elder Logan, the following names were enrolled and the pioneer Baptist church of Iowa was organized: Enoch Cyrus, Rebecca Cyrus, Anna Cyrus, Frank Cyrus, Rachel Dickens, Mary Ann Dickens, Nobel Housley, Naomi Housley, William Manly, Hspsibah Manly, Jane Lamb. The Articles of Faith adopted were those of the Brush Creek Baptist Church, Green County, Kentucky, which had been copied by William Manly.

"The organization was named the Regular Baptist Church at Long Creek, which later (1851) became known as Long Creek, though now known as the Danville Baptist Church, being located in the town of that name."[29] Two other churches, the Rock Spring and Pisgah were organized in 1838, and among the first three there were 90 members in Iowa.

In August of 1839, near Danville, the Iowa Baptist Association was organized. There were ten messengers present from the three churches, and their preachers were J. Todd, A. Evans, and H. Johnson. Elder Todd was chosen Moderator, and the nine other members of the association sat on a log while he conducted business.

In 1842 the Davenport Association was organized, later known as Des Moines. In 1859 Des Moines was divided into the Keokuk and Burlington Associations and by 1876 they numbered 40 churches with the membership of 2,663.

In June of 1842, the Iowa General Association was formed. The object of the organization was stated to be, "To Promote the Preaching of the Gospel, Ministerial Education, and all the General Objects of Benevolence throughout the Territory."[30]

Wisconsin 1834—The Brothertown Baptists

The first Baptist church in Wisconsin[31] actually had its beginning with the Presbyterian Preacher, the full blood Mohegan, Samson Occom. Occom was converted while listening to George Whitefield. The venerable Eleazar Wheelock, with whom the Indian preacher lived and labored from 1743 to 1747, educated him. Occom first went to Long Island where he preached the Gospel and set up a school for the Montauk Indians. He boarded with a Montauk named James Fowler. Occom married James' daughter Mary, and was instrumental in the salvation of Mary's brother, David.

David Fowler became known as the "Mercury of the Indian School." This was the name Wheelock gave to his enthusiastic pupil.

Samson Occom went preaching in England in 1776 and so excited the interest of Lord Dartmouth that the English nobleman took on the Indian school as his personal mission. Hence the school, when it moved to Hanover, New Hampshire became known as "Dartmouth."

When Occom returned to New England, he joined with other Indian leaders including David Fowler in moving the Indians from their desolate villages to Onieda, New York. The Onieda settlement was comprised of the remnants of six Indian tribes. These were the Narragansett, Pequot, Mohegan, Farmington, Niantic and Montauk. These together formed a township, which they named appropriately, Brothertown.

Sometime in these years, David Fowler became a Baptist, although the history of his changing his sentiments is missing. His wife was a member of the Baptist church of the Narragansetts in Charlestown, Rhode Island. This church was pastored by James Simons, and then Samuel Niles, one of the most eminent Indian preachers of his day. David Fowler gathered a group of believers at Brothertown into a Baptist church sometime near 1798.

In 1817 the Brothertown Indians were seeking other lands. They were granted a township on the east side of Winnebago Lake. In 1832 the first of the Brothertown Indians landed at the township. It was immediately named Brothertown in honour of their New York home.

In 1834 Elder Thomas Dick, a spiritual descendent of the Brother-town, New York church and its 80 year old Indian pastor, landed at the settlement. He immediately formed the first Baptist church in Wisconsin, the Brothertown Baptist Church.

Oregon 1844

"On May 25, 1844, the West Union Baptist church was formed on the Tualatin Plains, with eight members. It was the first Baptist church at that date in the United States west of the Rocky Mountains.[*] They met regularly for years to study the Bible and hear a sermon read by one of their number."[32] The church was organized in the home of David Lennox, who was part of the 1843 immigration to Oregon. He would not allow his company to travel on Sunday, as he set aside Sunday to read the word of God and hold services in their tent.

In February of 1845, Vincent Snelling preached the first sermon to the little flock and joined them along with his wife. He was also instrumental in organizing a number of pioneer Baptist churches in Oregon such as Yamhill near McMinnville (1846), Lacreole (Rickreall) (1846), Turner (1850), Eugene (1852), and Oregon City (1847). There were other early Baptist pioneers such as Hezekiah Johnson and Ezra Fisher from the American Baptist Home Missionary Society.[33] Others began to arrive and new churches were formed. By 1856 there were 26 churches in the Willamette Association, which was the first Baptist association on the Pacific Coast. There were 28 ordained preachers and 831 members and in the association. The mission to the Chinese was begun in 1874 and in 1877 at Cedar Mill, a German Baptist church was organized. By 1880 Oregon had nearly 80 churches, five associations, and a monthly paper: *The Beacon*. There were about 3,000 Baptist church members and a college, at McMinnville.[34]

Revivalists

---

[*] The original building is at the intersection of West Union and Dick roads located six miles from Hillsboro. It occupies a place on the roster of the National Register of Historic Places.

In closing out this chapter it may be appropriate to mention several Baptist evangelists, or revivalists. The pioneer evangelist-pastors blazed the trail through the first 50 years of the 19th century. During that time what might be termed "modern" evangelism emerged, including city-wide revival campaigns. These preachers were prominent among the Baptists:

William Cathcart wrote:

> **Elder Alfred Taylor,** a minister widely known and of great moral worth, was the son of Joseph Taylor, and was born in Warren, County, Kentucky, July 19, 1808. When three years of age he was taken by his parents to Butler County, where he grew up to manhood. He attended a school conducted by D. L. Mansfield, and was afterwards under the tutorship of the distinguished pastor, William Warder. He was for many years the intimate friend and fellow-laborer of Dr. J. M. Pendleton. He united with Sandy Creek Baptist Church, in Butler County, in 1829; was licensed to preach in 1831, and ordained in 1834. He soon became "pastor of four country churches." But his labor embraced a much larger field. He introduced into Gasper River Association in 1837 the practice of holding "protracted meetings."
>
> "Within less than six months," Dr. J. S. Coleman states, "he baptized over 800 persons." From this time he labored with indefatigable zeal for more than 20 years, and with a degree of success that few men have attained. Of the multitude baptized by him more than 30 became ministers of the gospel. He was active in all the benevolent enterprises of his denomination in the State. His sons, J. S. Taylor, J. P. Taylor, and W. C. Taylor, are excellent Baptist ministers. He died Oct. 9, 1855.[35]

Of Taylor, Samuel Ford wrote:

In 1842 David Burns crossed the Ohio to Ownsboro, Kentucky, to see about a situation as a stage-driver on the line from that place to Louisville. A meeting was in progress in the neighborhood. He attended it. It was conducted by Elder Alfred Taylor, a man of great simplicity and zeal and usefulness. From under his ministry more preachers have gone forth than from that of any man on the Ohio; among them: J. C. Coleman, Howard, Allen, Veatch, Bennett and now Burns. If we mistake not, Yeaman and Dawson.[36]

Thomas Jefferson Fisher, as Cathcart described him, was "a strangely gifted orator." He was born in Mount Sterling, Kentucky, April 9, 1812. At 16 years of age he professed religion and joined the Presbyterian church at Paris, Kentucky. Soon afterwards becoming interested in the subject of baptism, he was led to unite with David's Fork Baptist church, in Fayette County, where he was baptized in 1829, and in a short time licensed to preach. Having a great thirst for knowledge, he attended school at Middletown, Pennsylvania, and afterward at Pittsburgh, under the direction of S. Williams.

In 1833 he returned to Kentucky, and was ordained to the ministry, entering the pastoral office at Lawrenceburg. This was soon abandoned for the work of an evangelist, to which he devoted most of the remainder of his life. He made his home in Kentucky, but traveled and held meetings in the towns and cities of many of the Southern States. Vast crowds thronged to hear him, and it is estimated that 12,000 persons professed conversion under his ministry. "Whole congregations were frequently raised to their feet by the power of his eloquence."[37]

Samuel H. Ford describes Fisher in this fashion:

> He was holding one of those characteristic revivals of his at Hardingsburg, Kentucky...Fisher was in the height of all his peculiar glory—scattering "star-dust" in the eyes of the astonished hearers, or pouring streams of sulphurous flames into their ears. The wild beauties, the extravagant imagery, the resounding pomp of words and scraps of sublime poetry...[38]

Fisher was shot in the head in Louisville, Kentucky on January 8, 1866, and died three days later.

Jacob Knapp was born Dec. 7, 1799, in Otsego County, New York. He studied at Hamilton in 1821-25, and was ordained August 23 in the year last named. Entering the pastorate at Springfield, Otsego County, New York, he remained there five years; then removed to Watertown, New York, where he remained three years. Entering there upon the work of an "evangelist," he continued in that service during the remaining forty-two years of his public ministry. Fifteen years he resided at Hamilton, New York, twenty-five upon his farm near Rockford, Illinois. In his revivalist work he ranged widely over New York, New England, and the Western States, including California. "He preached about 16,000 sermons, led about 200 young men to preach the Gospel, and baptized 4000."[39] Cathcart wrote:

> Mr. Knapp's physique was in some sense a type of his mental and spiritual habit. He was of moderate height, strongly built, with broad shoulders and a muscular frame capable of great endurance. His conspicuous physical, like his mental, quality was that of robustness, while the business-like air with which he moved about in his ordinary avocations was typical of the serious, earnest, unflinching way in which he preached and toiled in the face of severe personal exposure and reproach. His preaching was doctrinal, direct, unsparing, even sometimes to the verge of coarseness; but his power over audiences was remarkable, and the fruits of his long toil in his chosen sphere, while not always genuine, were believed in many cases to be so, and always abundant. Among his last words, were, "Oh, I have come to the everlasting hill! On Christ the solid rock I stand, All other ground is sinking sand."[40]

Knapp died at Rockford, Illinois, March 3, 1874 and is buried there.

Jabez Smith Swan, the flaming evangelist of Connecticut, was the son of Joshua and Esther (Smith) Swan. He was born in Stonington on February 23, 1800. He was converted at age 22 and baptized by William Palmer. He studied for the ministry at Hamilton Literary and Theological Institution, New York and became pastor of the Stonington Borough Baptist Church. He was ordained June 20, 1827 and began immediate work as an evangelist eventually settling in Norwich, New York.

He was greatly used and prospered in revivals around, and returned to Connecticut in 1842. There he conducted remarkable meetings at Stonington Borough, Mystic Bridges, and New London; and also Albany, New York.

From 1843 to the time of his death, Swan preached with power in all of New England and New York. He was powerful in his sermons and in addresses, a mighty man in prayer, strong advocate of education and missions, the most powerful preacher as an evangelist ever known in Connecticut. A sketch of his life and labors was published in 1873. Swan baptized the notable Thomas Armitage. It was reported that more than 10,000 conversions occurred under his ministry.

William Evander Penn, the great Baptist evangelist, was born in Rutherford County, Tennessee, on August 11, 1832. He began his education at age ten and joined the Beachgrove Baptist Church on October 3, 1847. He attended one term each at the Male Academy, Trenton, Tennessee, and Union University, Murfreesboro, Tennessee. He studied and was admitted to the bar. Penn opened his law office in Lexington, Tennessee, about 1852. He married Corrilla Frances Sayle on April 30, 1856.

During the Civil War, Penn was assigned to Andrew N. Wilson's Regiment, Sixteenth Tennessee Cavalry in the Confederate Army, and was captured on February 18, 1864, in Hardiman County, Tennessee. He was in a group that was exchanged for captured Union soldiers on April 7, 1865, after which he was assigned to a regiment and promoted to major. After the Confederate surrender, Penn signed his parole at Shreveport, Louisiana, on June 21, 1865.

He and his family moved in January of 1866 to Jefferson, Texas, where he opened a law office. The Penns joined the Baptist Church at Jefferson and later he was ordained a deacon. Penn attended the Texas Baptist Sunday School and Colportage Convention and was elected president in 1873 and 1874. At a Sunday School institute in July 1875 James H. Stribling, pastor at the Baptist church at Tyler, Texas, asked Penn to preach a revival there. He was later licensed to preach by the Baptist church at Jefferson. He was ordained on December 4, 1880.

He wrote some hymns and published *Harvest Bells*, a hymnal with J. M. Hunt in 1881. A second edition was published in 1886, and H. M. Lincoln and Penn published a third in 1887.

Penn has been called the "Texas Evangelist," but he also led revivals in other states and in Scotland and England. The Penns moved to Eureka Springs, Arkansas, about 1887. He wrote the autobiographical *The Life and Labors of Major W. E. Penn* in 1892. He died at his home on April 29, 1895, and was buried in Eureka Springs Cemetery, Eureka Springs, Arkansas.[41]

Absalom Backus Earle was born in 1812 in Charlton, New York. He was converted at the age of 16 and began preaching the Gospel at age 18. He was ordained at Amsterdam, New York when he was 21. He pastored at Amsterdam for five years, and then resigned to enter the field of evangelism. For 58 years he held revivals, city-wide campaigns, and protracted meetings in the every state of the Union and Canada. It is estimated he conducted nearly 1,000 protracted meetings, and traveled over 350,000 miles. He had nearly 160,000 conversions and 400 called to the Gospel ministry. Earle also was the author of several books. He died at Newton, Massachusetts, on March 30, 1895, at the age of 83.

John Jasper

CHAPTER SEVENTEEN
Sabled Sons and the
Division of the Baptists

The Gospel into California (1849), Minnesota (1849),
Nebraska (1855), Kansas (1857), and Washington State (1863)

*A mysterious Providence has permitted a large portion of the sable sons of Af-
rica to be transported from their native country to this western world, and here
to be reduced to a state of absolute and perpetual slavery; but He who can
bring good of evil, has overruled this calamity for their spiritual advantage.*
—David Benedict.

Most Baptist historians such as Semple, Benedict, Sobel, Sid
Smith, and Walter H. Brooks have testified that African
Americans were converted and baptized into Baptist churches
as early as 1758. In 1813 David Benedict wrote:

Thousands of these poor, enslaved, and benighted people, we have
very satisfactory reason to believe, have found gospel liberty in the
midst of their temporal bondage, and are preparing to reign forever in
the kingdom of God.
There are multitudes of African communicants, in all the Baptist
churches in the southern and western States; and in Georgia there are
four churches, wholly composed of them.[1]

It is true that Baptist people "owned" slaves in America. A substantial number of Baptist preachers "owned" slaves as well. But there was
opposition to slavery among the Baptists long before the Civil War.

This query, submitted by Rolling Fork Baptist Church of Kentucky,
was brought before the Salem Association on October 31, 1789: "Is it
lawful for a member of Christ's Church to keep his fellow creature in
perpetual slavery?" Note their answer: "The association judge it improper to enter into so important and critical a matter at present."[2]

Joshua Carman and Josiah Dodge of Rolling Fork would not let the question rest and finally broke with Salem to form a separate "emancipation" church.

Opposition to slavery among the Baptists from the beginning days of the republic was scattered. Soon after the Revolutionary War John Murphy, son of the fabled William Murphy, wrote to his family in Missouri:

> As to religious matters there appears to be some considerable dissension among the Baptists and some among other sects about slave holding. For my own part I prefer to stand opposed to that system because I fully believe it to be contrary to the law of nature, contrary to sound reason, contrary to good policy, contrary to justice, contrary to republican principles, and, above all, because it is in direct opposition to the scripture directions.[3]

By 1793 approximately 19,000 of a total of 73,000 Baptists in America were black.

David Barrow[4] was the first Baptist preacher of note to oppose slavery in the south. He was born October 30, 1753, in Brunswick County, Virginia. He was converted at age 16, baptized by Zachariah Thompson, and studied under Jeremiah Walker. He was ordained in 1771. Barrow suffered persecution in 1778 as he preached at an outdoor meeting near the mouth of the James River. A group of ruffians attacked him and attempted to drown him.

Barrow became convinced that slavery was evil during the Revolutionary War. In 1798 he moved to Kentucky. He was active in the North District Association. He wrote a powerful pamphlet on the Trinity in 1803 that stopped the spread of Unitarianism in Kentucky. But the opposition he faced denouncing the practice of slave holding overshadowed the popularity brought on by his eloquence. He published *Involuntary, Unmerited, Perpetual, Absolute, Hereditary Slavery, Examined on the Principles of Nature, Reason, Justice, Policy, and Scripture*.[5] He had freed all of his own slaves and urged other Baptist preachers to do the same. He fell into disfavor among his brethren and even the wonderful Robert B. Semple criticized Barrow, writing:

It is questionable whether it was not in the end, productive of more harm than good. While it lessened his resources at home, for maintaining a large family, it rendered him suspicious among his acquaintances and probably in both ways limited his usefulness.[6]

The opposition resulted in David Barrow and his church being expelled from the North District Association, state of Kentucky in 1806. He was instrumental in forming the Licking-Locust Association and was a driving force in the Baptist emancipation society called the "Friends of Humanity." David Barrow died on November 14, 1819.

John Leland also had a great deal to say about slavery. His remarks alienated some of his southern brethren; nevertheless, he soundly criticized the practice:

The horrid work of bartering spirituous liquor for human souls, plundering the African coast, and kidnapping the people, brought the poor slaves into this state (Virginia); and, notwithstanding their usage is much better here than in the West Indies, yet human nature unbiased by education, shudders at the sight. The first republican assembly ever held in Virginia passed an act, utterly prohibiting the importance of any of them into the state.

In some things, they are viewed as human creatures, and in others, only as property; their true state then, is that of human property. The laws of Virginia, protect their lives and limbs, but do not protect their skin and flesh. The marriage of slaves is a subject not known in our code of laws. What promises soever they make their masters may and do part them at pleasure. If their marriages are as sacred as the marriages of freeman, the slaves are guilty of adultery, when they part voluntarily, and the masters are guilty of a sin as great, when they part them involuntarily.

Liberty of conscience, in matters of religion, is the right of slaves, beyond contradiction; and yet, many masters and overseers will whip and torture the poor creatures for going to meeting, even at night, when the labor of the day is over. No longer ago than November 1788, Mr.___ made a motion in the assembly, for leave to bring in a bill, not only to prevent the assembling of slaves together, but to fine the masters for allowing it; but to his great mortification, it was rejected with contempt.[7]

Leland's conclusion about slavery:

The whole scene of slavery is pregnant with enormous evils. On the master's side, pride, haughtiness, domination, cruelty, deceit and indolence; and on the side of the slave, ignorance, servility, fraud, perfidy and despair. If these and many other evils attend it, why not liberate them at once?[8]

Neither was Leland the only famous Baptist opposed to slavery. David Benedict gave this opinion:

In traveling to collect materials for this work, I set out with a determination to say nothing on the subject of slavery; but people would converse upon it. Some were very curious to learn the minds of the northern people respecting slavery; others wanted to know how we could do our work without Negroes; and many were anxious to clear themselves of the unjust aspersions, which, in their opinions, had been cast upon them.

There is a class of people, (though I am happy to say I do not find many in it who profess religion) that entrench themselves around with their laws, their customs, and their wealth, and spurn with indignity any scruple of the lawfulness of holding slaves.

There is another class who are so amazingly suspicious that you are about to censure them, that it seems really cruel to mention one word against the slave-holding policy. But by far the greater part of those brethren, who are concerned in slavery, converse upon the subject with much frankness, and the following are the principal reasons which they assign for their practice:

1st. They had no hand in bringing them in to the country; but since they are brought, somebody must take care of them.

2nd. They cost them much money, generally from three to five hundred dollars a piece, and sometimes more; if they set them free, all this must be sacrificed.

3rd. Others observed they had inherited their slaves as a part of their patrimonial estate: they came to them without their seeking, and now they know no better way than to find them employment, and make them as comfortable as their circumstances would permit.

4th. Some mentioned that the Romans and other nations had slaves; that they were numerous at the introduction of Christianity; that neither Christ nor the Apostles, nor any of the New-Testament writers said any thing against it; that if it were contrary to the spirit of the gospel, it is strange that it is no where prohibited.

The last of these arguments has just about as much weight as those which are brought in support of infant baptism; the others I shall leave without any comment.–David Benedict.[9]

The First Black Baptist Church in America
The Silver Bluff Church of South Carolina

Much of the early history of black Baptist churches involves George Leile, David George, Jessie Peter and Andrew Bryan.

George Leile was born in Virginia sometime in 1750. He was the slave of a British officer. He was converted and baptized under the ministry of Matthew Moore sometime in 1773.

Leile was permitted by his master to preach to the slaves all along the Savannah River in Aiken County, sometimes addressing the white congregations. He was God's instrument in the conversion of David George and he baptized Andrew Bryan.

Abraham Marshall gave these men much needed training. He not only trained Leile and George, but also another man, the eloquent "Brother Amos." God sent "Brother Amos" to Providence, Rhode Island sometime before 1791. By 1812 Amos' church had increased to 850 souls.[10]

The trials and works of David George are related in *Rippon's Register*. He was born a slave in Essex County Virginia, about 1742. His master was very severe with his people, which caused George to run away when he had grown to manhood. He went first to Pedee River in South Carolina, where he stayed just a few weeks. He next went towards the Savanna River where he worked for a Mr. Green about two years. But he was discovered and fled. David George then found himself among the Creek Indians who made him the slave of their king, *Blue Salt.*[11]

D. George found himself on the run once again and was captured by the Natchez Indians who promptly sold him to George Galphin, a man who lived on the Savannah River at Silver Bluff. Silver Bluff is a beautiful stretch of riverfront located 12 miles from Augusta on the north side of the Savannah.

Sometime around 1773, David George was converted under the preaching of George Leile. George described the meetings that took place there:

> Brother Palmer, who was pastor at some distance from Silver Bluff, came and preached to a large congregation at a mill of Mr. Galphin's. He was a very powerful preacher. Brother Palmer came again and wished us to beg Master to let him preach to us; and he came frequently.
>
> There were eight of us now, who had found the great blessing and mercy from the Lord, and my wife was one of them, and Brother Jesse Galphin. Brother Palmer appointed Saturday evening to hear what the Lord had done for us, and next day, he baptized us in the mill stream. Brother Palmer formed us into a church, and gave us the Lord's Supper at Silver Bluff.
>
> Then I began to exhort in the Church, and learned to sing hymns. Afterwards the church advised with Brother Palmer about my speaking to them, and keeping them together. So I was appointed to the office of an elder, and received instruction from Brother Palmer how to conduct myself. I proceeded in this way till the American War was coming on, when the Ministers were not allowed to come amongst us, lest they should furnish us with too much knowledge.
>
> I continued preaching at Silver Bluff, till the church, constituted with eight, increased to thirty or more, and 'till the British came to the city of Savannah and took it.[12]

Who was this "Brother Palmer" that baptized David George, his wife, Jesse Galphin and five others?

Pastor and historian Walter H. Brooks believes this was none other than Wait Palmer, the pioneer from Connecticut who baptized Shubal Stearns. The first Baptist church among American slaves was the church at Silver Bluff, South Carolina.[13] However, Silver Bluff, in the true legacy of the Baptists, found itself on the run. And David George found himself on the way to Nova-Scotia in 1778.

Silver Bluff Baptist Church in Exile

We shall let David George's testimony ring:

When the English were going to evacuate Charleston, they advised me to go to Halifax, in Nova-Scotia, and gave the few black people, and it may be as many as 500 white people, their passage for nothing. We were 22 days on the passage, and used very ill on board.

When we came off Halifax, I got leave to go ashore. On shewing my papers to General Patterson, he sent orders by a sergeant for my wife and children to follow me. This was before Christmas, and we staid there till June; but as no way was open for me to preach to my own colour, I got leave to go to Shelburne (150 miles, or more, I suppose, by sea) in the suite of General Patterson leaving my wife and children for awhile, behind.

Numbers of my own colour were here, but I found the white people were against me. I began to sing the first night, in the woods, at a camp, for there were no houses then built; they were just clearing and preparing to erect a town. The black people came far and near, it was so new to them; I kept on so every night in the week, and appointed a meeting for the first Lord's day, in a valley, between two hills close by the river, and a great number of white and black people came, and I was so overjoyed with having an opportunity once more of preaching the word of God, that after I had given out the hymn, I could not speak for tears.

In the afternoon we met again, in the same place, and I had great liberty from the Lord. We had a meeting now every evening, and those poor creatures who had never heard the gospel before, listened to me very attentively; but the white people, the justices and all, were in an uproar, and said that I might go out into the woods, for I should not stay there. I ought to, except one white man, who knew me at Savannah, and who said I should have his lot to live upon as long as I would, and build a house if I pleased. [We] then cut down poles, stripped bark, and made a smart hut and the people came flocking to the preaching every evening for a month, as though they had come for their supper.

Then Governor Parr came from Halifax, brought my wife and children, gave me six months provisions for my family, and a quarter of an acre of land to cultivate for our subsistence. It was a spot where there was plenty of water, and which I had before secretly wished for, as I knew it would be convenient for baptizing at any time. The weather being severe and the ground covered with snow, we raised a platform of poles for the hearers to stand upon, but there was nothing over their heads. Continuing to attend, they desired to have a meeting-house built. We had then a day of hearing what the Lord had done; and I and my wife heard their experiences, and I received four of my own colour; brother Sampson, brother John, sister Offee, and sister Dinah; these all were well at Sierra Leone, except brother Sampson, an excellent man, who died on his voyage to that place.

The first time I baptized here was a little before Christmas, in the creek, which ran though my lot. I preached to a great number of people on the occasion, who behaved very well. I now formed the church with us six, and administered the Lord's Supper in the meeting-house, before it was finished. They went on with the building, and we appointed a time every other week to hear experiences. A few months after, I baptized nine more, and the congregation very much increased. The worldly blacks, as well as the members of the church, assisted in cutting timber in the woods, and in getting shingles; and we used a few coppers to buy nails. We were increasing all the winter, and baptized almost every month, and administered the Lord's Supper.[14]

Canada was only a temporary home to David George, and to others from the States. He took a colony of blacks to Sierra Leone, British Central Africa, in 1792 and constituted a Baptist church.[15] This was a full decade before Adonirum Judson, making George the first Baptist foreign missionary sent from America.

Silver Bluff Baptist Church re-gathered in Georgia

As George Leile was a blessing in the beginning of the Silver Bluff, South Carolina church, he now became instrumental in re-gathering a portion of Silver Bluff and bringing it to Savannah, Georgia.

Out of the effort of George Leile, came the first black Baptist Church in the city of Savannah, which flourished during the British occupancy from 1779 to the year 1782.

Leile went to Jamaica in 1782 where he formed a church which quickly grew to over 500 members.[16]

From Leile's departure in 1782 until 1788, the little flock at Savannah, Georgia, was bitterly persecuted, but as Walter H. Brooks wrote, "its work of resuscitation, and progress, was wonderful—wonderful because of the moral heroism which characterized it."[17]

In the first year after the departure of Leile to Jamacia, Andrew Bryan, one of his converts began to preach at the church at Savannah. "Bryan and his associates were beaten unmercifully for their persistency in holding on to the work but they were prepared to yield their lives in martyrdom sooner than relinquish what Rev. George Liele had instituted, and it lived...amid the fires of persecution."[18]

Black Preachers in Crimson Red

Now Andrew Bryan was required to leave his testimony in *crimson red*.

Edward Davis permitted Bryan to erect a rough wooden building on his land at Yamacraw, outside the city of Savannah. Those meeting there were quickly routed, rounded up and **tortured**. Benedict wrote about their ordeal:

> It appears that these poor, defenseless slaves met with much opposition from the rude and merciless white people, who, under various pretences interrupted their worship and otherwise treated them in a barbarous manner. Andrew Bryan, and his brother Samson, were twice imprisoned and they, with about fifty others, without much ceremony *were severely whipped*. Andrew was inhumanly *cut*, and *bled abundantly*; but while under their lashes, he held up his hands and told his persecutors, that he rejoiced not only to be whipped, but *would freely suffer death for the cause of Jesus Christ*.[19]
>
> The design of these unrighteous proceedings against these poor innocent people was to stop their religious meetings. Their enemies pretended, that under a pretence of religion, they were plotting mischief and insurrections. But by *well doing* they at length silenced and shamed their persecutors, and acquired a number of very respectable and influential advocates and patrons, who not only rescued them from the

power of their enemies, but declared that such treatment as they had received would be condemned even among barbarians.[20]

After Andrew Bryan began his ministry and his converts began to increase, he was visited by an old Baptist preacher named Thomas Burton. Burton baptized 18 of Bryan's converts. In 1788, they were visited by Abraham Marshall, of Kiokee, who brought with him a young preacher of colour named Jesse Peter. Marshall baptized 45 more of the congregation in one day, formed them into a church, and ordained Andrew Bryan as their pastor. The church began with 80 members and in just four years had increased to 235.[21]

According to David Benedict, "Chief Justice Osbourne then gave them liberty to continue their worship any time between sun-rising and sun-set; and the benevolent Jonathan Bryan told the magistrates that he would give them the liberty of his own house or barn, at a place called Brampton, about three miles from Savannah."[22]

Andrew Bryan and his brother Samson set up meetings in their master's barn. By 1794, the first African church in Savannah contained 1,500 members and had become the mother of two other churches.[23]

Of Andrew Bryan, Joseph Cook of Ewhaw said, "His gifts are small; but he is clear in the grand doctrines of the gospel. I believe him to be truly pious; and he has been the instrument of doing more good among the poor slaves, than all the learned doctors in America."[24]

Andrew Bryan departed from this world in October of 1812 at the age of 90. 5,000 mourners followed the procession to his grave.

The Advance of Black Baptist Churches

The oldest black Baptist churches north of Mason and Dixon's Line, are the Independent or First African, of Boston, Massachusetts, planted in 1805; the Abyssinian, of New York City, planted in 1808; and the First African, of Philadelphia, Pennsylvania, planted in 1809.[25]

In the District of Columbia, Sampson White organized the first black Baptist church in 1839. It reached a place of prominence[26] some years later under William Williams, whose flock was the largest Baptist church in Washington, D.C. It could not be associated with the churches in the south, so it became a part of the Philadelphia Baptist Association.

The first black Baptist Church in Baltimore was organized in 1836 and made great progress under the direction of M. C. Clayton. They had a membership of 150 in 1846. A number of other Baptist churches in the city were soon gathered with several preachers among them. The most notable was Noah Davis of the Saratoga Street Baptist Church.

In the south, a steady rain of revival among the slaves began. There is evidence that there existed 20 African Baptist churches by 1813 in the state of Mississippi.[27] During the 1830's and 40's a number of African Baptist churches were established throughout the south, west and northwest.

The African Baptist Church of Richmond, Virginia, was established from the white church and placed in the care of Robert Ryland, a white preacher, who served at the same time as President of Richmond College. There was a black congregation in Portsmouth also.

The first African Baptist Church in Petersburg, Virginia, had 664 communicants, the largest membership in the Middle District Baptist Association. The largest Baptist Church in Manchester (now South Richmond) in 1846 was the African Baptist Church with a membership of 487. All of these black congregations were established in the early 1830's.

In South Carolina the blacks were not permitted to have churches separated from the whites; however, black church members greatly outnumbered their white brethren. In 1846, the year of the division of the Baptists north and south, there were 1,643 members of the First Baptist Church in Charleston and only 261 of them were white. The same was true of the Second Baptist Church; there were 312 black members and 200 white.

In other places in South Carolina the situation was more pronounced. Georgetown Baptist Church had 298 black members and only 33 white persons, and by 1846 the famous Welsh Neck Church had 477 black and 83 whites in their membership. In the membership of many churches of the south, blacks outnumbered whites two to one.

In the state of Alabama black membership in the Baptist churches was a little more than one-half of the number. In the city of Montgomery African-American membership was almost three to one. In Mobile there was such a revival among the slaves that in 1839 the First Baptist Church (white) became two congregations. They built a meeting-house and trained their own pioneer black preachers: Heard, Hunton, Hale, Stowe, Collins, Schroebel, and Grant.[28]

Jacksonville was the center of the Baptist advance among the black brethren in Florida. The First Bethel Baptist Church was organized in 1838 with four whites and two blacks as charter members. Woodson tells us that among these were: Rev. J. Jaudan and wife, Deacon James McDonald and wife, and two slaves belonging to Jaudan. The white members tried to separate sometime later and claim the church house, but the court decided it was the right of the black majority to possess the house.[29]

One-fourth of the Tennessee Baptists were black.

The membership in Kentucky had a much larger percentage. The African Baptist Church of Lexington under the leadership of L. Terrell was the largest in the Elkhorn Association in 1846. The First African Baptist Church of Louisville was also the largest in its association, having 644 members.[30]

The First African Baptist Church of St. Louis, Missouri was founded under the tremendous leadership of John Berry Meachum. After he had purchased his own freedom in Kentucky, Meachum immigrated to St. Louis, where he taught himself how to read and write. He established a school and preached to great crowds of black and white frontiersman. By 1846 his church was the largest in its association.[31]

Nearly all of the large cities of the north had some black Baptist churches. Philadelphia had the First African Church founded in 1809 with a membership of 257 under Richard Vaughn in 1846. The Union Colored Church had a membership of 200 under Daniel Scott. The pastor of the Third African Baptist Church was J. Henderson. They had a membership of 61. Another preacher was William Jackson, who preached to a small congregation at that time.[32]

Farther north the black Baptists were also making progress. New York City had the Abyssinian Baptist Church, which had a membership of 424 in 1846. In Boston the African Baptist Church had held its own, but the independent movement among the Baptists was not generally considered necessary in New England.

In the west independent black churches flourished. Pittsburgh, Buffalo, Cleveland, Columbus, Cincinnati, Detroit, and Chicago soon found black Baptists and churches among them. Some pioneer preachers were Richard DeBaptiste of Detroit and later of Chicago, and James Poindexter of Columbus.

The black Baptists of the Ohio plains established an independent association: the Providence Baptist Association. It was the first of its kind in the United States and was organized in Ohio in 1836.

The same thing happened in Illinois. In 1838 the African Baptist churches of St. Clair and Madison counties, along with Shawneetown, Vandalia, Jacksonville, Springfield, Galena, and Chicago organized the Wood River Baptist Association. In 1853 the churches of the Great Northwest organized the Western Colored Baptist Convention. Great progress was made in the west for several years.

Black churches had tremendous preachers such as John Jasper. Jasper was the son of a slave preacher. He was named for John the Baptist. He was born again on July 14, 1829. He began to preach at funerals and God's power upon his life was soon evident. He prayed that he might learn how to read and studied from an old spelling book with help from a friend. His master gave him a special dispensation to preach and the result of his ministry was the Sixth Mount Zion Baptist Church in Richmond, Virginia. The church began with nine members and grew to a membership of 2,000 at the time of Jasper's death in 1901.[33]

The Fugitive Slave Law of 1850 threw a satanic wrench into the works of many black preaching endeavors. Some black Americans who had escaped from the south and settled in these cities were forced to flee to Canada for safety.

The Division of the Baptists, North and South

The Baptists had a kind of national unity by 1835. The Triennial Convention held a denominational unity that was unlike any other Christian group in America. Each church was independent and each district association was independent. All parties were a part of a loose agreement of fellowship. With all of that independence the Triennial Convention conversely gave a sense of national unity. But truly, a good number of Baptists, perhaps even the majority of them, cared little for it. As long as the convention and the associations were mainly used as *conferences* and *not* hierarchy, they did good service to the churches.

An anti-national convention sentiment was a mind-set for many Baptists for very good reasons. The older preachers were not so far removed from the days of Congregational and Episcopalian control. The thought of Baptists forming a hierarchy of power or a synod system was unacceptable. Notwithstanding, most Baptists were putting up with the fundraising through the Triennial Convention for what was considered the greater good.

One can easily imagine how the *adversary*, as a roaring lion, could abuse the extra-Biblical structure of the convention system and thereby damage the churches of Jesus Christ. The Baptists of America were about to divide over a financial crisis. The financial crises would involve the ghastly realities of Baptist preachers owning other human beings.

The Demise of the Triennial Convention

The General Missionary Convention of the Baptist Denomination in the United States of America for Foreign Missions, or as it came to be called, **the Triennial Convention** was formed in 1814. It ceased to be a body in 1845.

The Board of the General Missionary Convention of the Baptist Denomination located in Boston passed a resolution stating they could no longer approve a slaveholder to be a missionary. This inevitable decision was a great grief and offense to the south. The south had furnished nearly all the Presidents, and many of the missionaries of the Convention. But northern opinions against trafficking and trading in human souls were too strong. Slavery could no longer be tolerated in the north. In 1844 in the Home Mission Department the "inexpedience of employing slaveholders as missionaries" was put in the form of a resolution. The leadership of the north including Francis Wayland, William Williams and Barnas Sears did not approve of the final resolution that forever divided the Baptists. Nevertheless, the resolution passed and financial support of slaveholding missionaries was forever revoked. The Triennial Convention of the Baptists was dissolved.

The northern brethren then organized the "American Baptist Missionary Union" in 1845. The south formed the "Southern Baptist Convention" on May 12, 1845 in Augusta, Georgia. For many years various churches held connections in both organizations, but the national unity among the Baptists was forever discarded.

California 1849

The first effort of the northern American Baptist Missionary Union took place in 1849. In November of 1848, O. C. Wheeler, pastor of the First Baptist Church of Jersey City, New Jersey, was asked by the American Baptist Home Missionary Society to leave New Jersey and sail to California. Somehow the Society knew California would fill with immigrants. After Wheeler set sail for the west coast, news of the discovery of gold in California hit the newspapers.

The voyage to California took three months and was executed by landing at the isthmus of Panama, going overland to the Pacific, and then sailing to the Golden Gate. By the time Wheeler and his wife reached Panama, five other vessels had overtaken them in the mad dash for California gold.[34]

They proceeded to the Pacific side of the isthmus by horseback and had to wait for the steamer *California* to pick them up. A large group waited on shore when the captain announced to the group, "I hope to God you haven't any missionaries for me to take." Needless to say, it was an interesting last leg of the trip.[35]

The Wheelers landed in San Francisco on February 28, 1849. California was a pure mission field; the only semblance of order was weak local government. The state was still in a superstitious stupor. Wheeler described the religious conditions of California in 1849:

> [A] far greater obstacle to our work was that all the religion in the country was Roman Catholicism in its most dilapidated stage and lowest forms of superstition and degradation. Only those who have lived in a country purely Catholic can have any idea how thick the darkness is. It is really a "darkness that may be felt," the dark pall of mildewed immorality that overspreads and enshrouds every human aspiration. In every attempt to promote virtue and elevate society it

confronts the gospel laborer at the threshold of his work, and recedes only as its powers are exhausted. It also awakens more promptly from its lowest depths of deepest slumber, and wages its warfare against all spiritual religion more vehemently and persistently than any other human organization.[36]

Perhaps the biggest obstacle to the work of God in California was the lack of labourers. Or shall we say, the lack of heart desire on the part of the "labourers." Wheeler described the unbelievable spiritual condition of the Baptists that came to California:

> Our want of laborers was not because they did not come to California, for between the 1st of April, 1849, and the 1st of August, 1850, I counted and registered forty-six men, all wearing the vestments and claiming the character of Baptist ministers in good standing, who arrived at San Francisco and **passed through to the mines**, not one of whom would stop for a single day to aid me in rolling to the top of the hill the ball that seemed ready to fall back upon and crush me—not an hour in the work of the Master.[37]

We cannot report this without weeping, and Wheeler ought to have the gratitude of the people of California as he pressed on amid the greed of his so-called brethren in the quest for souls.

The Lord in His gracious mercy sent some wonderful men who were not preachers but faithful in their work for God, including a merchant man who secured their monthly supplies, and a miner who gave from his findings financial support to the building of their first meetinghouse.

On July 6, 1849, O. C. Wheeler gathered a church consisting of six members in the home of Charles L. Ross. After reading the Articles of Faith, (which consisted of the New Hampshire Confession of Faith) and Covenant of the First Baptist Church of San Francisco, the church met for prayer.

Wheeler baptized Thomas Kellum, a miner, on October 21, 1849, in the San Francisco Bay. This was the first baptism on the Pacific coast and was widely attended.[38]

The first free public school in California was opened in the First Baptist Church in December of 1849. John C. Pelton and his wife conducted it and by April of 1850, there were 130 children enrolled. In September of 1850, the first ever session of the California Baptist Association met at the First Baptist Church of San Francisco. Churches represented were San Francisco, San Jose, and Sacramento.

Minnesota 1849

St. Paul was the place of the first Baptist church in Minnesota. The church was founded by John P. Parsons, who was appointed by the Baptist Home Mission Society. It was organized December 30, 1849. The Minnesota Baptist Association was organized in St. Paul, in September of 1852.[39]

Nebraska 1855

The First Baptist Church in Nebraska was at Nebraska City, and was organized August 18, 1855, at the old "frame meeting-house." The record of this important step in the new village was found in an old register, already yellow with age, lying in the archives of the church and reads as follows:

NEBRASKA CITY, N. T. August 18, 1855.

The following named brethren and sisters, to wit: B. B. Belcher, Samuel Findley, Edward Henry, Lucinda Nuckolls, Mary Ann Belcher, Lavison Cook and Caroline Toms met by appointment, at the frame meeting-house, and, after solemnly covenanting together, proceeded to organize the First Baptist Church of Nebraska City, and, as such, were recognized by Rev. J. C. Renfro, a minister of the Baptist denomination in regular standing.[40]

Kansas 1857

The Baptist church at Leavenworth, the first in the state, was organized in 1857 under the leadership of the Rev. Dennis Jones, father of attorney Dennis Jones Jr. It was known as the 6th and Miami Street Baptist Church.[41]

Washington State 1863

John Jay Clark was four years of age when his family moved to eastern Illinois and settled on the Wabash. In 1837, he enrolled at Shurtleff College in Alton, Illinois.

In August of 1863, John and his brother Alvin organized the Salmon Creek Baptist Church, located in what is now known as the Brush Prairie area of Washington State. John Jay Clark served as the pastor of the Brush Prairie Church for more than 25 years. He would often walk 10 to 15 miles to preach in various parts of the county.

The Brush Prairie Baptist Church, which has had a continuous existence since its organization, is the oldest Baptist Church in Washington State. In 1869 John Jay Clark was elected to the Territorial Legislature.

It is truly amazing how often the name "John Clark" occurs in American Baptist history.

CHAPTER EIGHTEEN
Education

*The striplings of genius, or striplings without genius, are sent to school
with the avowed purpose of preparing them for the ministry; as if the
preaching of the gospel was but the declension of nouns, or the conjuga-
tion of verbs, with the knowledge of a little Greek and Latin. Amos was a
rustic herdsman-John the Baptist was brought up in the wilderness-and the
apostles, for the most part, were ignorant Galileans, who followed the
trade of fishing; yet these were called by God, while the learned among
them were neglected.*[1]–John Leland

*In our colleges many learn corrupt principles, not only about what makes
a minister, but also about what makes a
Christian.*[2]–Isaac Backus

In 1720 Thomas Hollis, a Baptist man of means in England, established a professorship of theology at Harvard College. This was accomplished by granting 80 pounds per year to the school. The
money, with an additional 100 pounds, was to be given with the stipulation that ten pounds would be given to "ten scholars of good character,
four of whom should be Baptists, if any such there were."[3]

Even with this educational opportunity, the doctrines of Harvard
were against the Baptists. So in those early years Baptists educated themselves. One such self-educated man was William Bliss. On Christmas
Eve in 1780, Bliss became pastor of the third Baptist church in Newport, Rhode Island. He had no formal education, yet Ezra Stiles president of Yale, said of him, "[he] has a natural good sagacity; and was from
his youth addicted to books; I presume he surpasses three quarters of
the Protestant clergy educated in Universities—not for accuracy of language, but for knowledge of the scriptures, gift of prayer, and talent at
public instruction."[4]

Isaac Backus knew that a separate institute was needed for training
men for the Baptist ministry. The current educational opportunity was

hopelessly married to the Congregational system. He pointed out that Jesus did away with the church-state covenant. But New England tried to re-establish it by insisting that the new covenant was identical to the old. The educational system, fully entrenched, wholly supported the church-state establishment. Backus refuted this, writing:

> When our Saviour came, he fulfilled the law, both moral and ceremonial, and abolished those hereditary distinctions among mankind. But in the centuries following, deceitful philosophy took away the name which God has given to that covenant, (Acts vii.8)[*] and added the name *Grace* to it; from whence came the doctrine, that *dominion is founded in grace*. And although this latter name has been exploded by many, yet the root of it has been tenaciously held fast and **taught in all colleges and superior places of learning, as far as Christianity has extended, until the present time**; whereby natural affection, education, temporal interest and self-righteousness, the strongest prejudices in the world, have all conspired to bind people in that way, and to bar their minds against equal liberty and believer's baptism.[5]

To insure the education of Baptist preachers without the "temporal prejudices in the world," the Baptists began to make plans for an institution, or college of their own. That first college was Brown.

Brown University began as the Hopewell Academy. Situated near Philadelphia in the New Jersey flat land, Hopewell was to be a place for pastoral and theological studies.

Like most religious educational institutions, it started out *on-fire* for God. There was just as much concern for the heat of His power and the souls of men, as there was for the temporal benefits of academia. It was at Hopewell such giants for God as John Gano, Hezekiah Smith, and David Jones were trained. These men played key roles in the Revolution and established the Baptist churches as undisputed leaders of liberty and republicanism. The proprietor of Hopewell was the legendary Isaac Eaton.

We are incumbant to say that Isaac Eaton was one of the most influential men of his generation. Eaton was the son of Joseph Eaton, a preacher from Montgomery County, Pennsylvania. Isaac became the

---

[*] The covenant of circumcision.

pastor of the Hopewell Baptist Church on November 29, 1748 and became active in the Philadelphia Association. On October 5, 1756, the
Philadelphia Association allocated funds to begin the Hopewell Academy. They erected a building and opened the doors for Baptist ministerial students in 1757. The institution was the first of its kind and attracted the best and brightest of the sons of the *baptized believers.*

Was Backus pleased with the progress of Rhode Island College
(Brown)? Regarding Brown, Backus wrote:

> Dr. Manning was a faithful preacher of the gospel, and Presi-
> dent of our College (Brown), for twenty-five years, until he was
> called out of our world, July 29, 1791, in his fifty-third year. He
> was a good instructor in human learning, but **at every com-
> mencement he gave a solemn charge to his scholars, never to
> presume to enter into the work of the ministry, until they
> were taught of God, and had reason to conclude that they had
> experienced a saving change of heart.** And a tutor in the col-
> lege, who appeared to have met with such a change in October
> 1789, was instrumental in a revival of religion, both in the col-
> lege and in the town, and he was called into the ministry, and
> then was a President of the College eleven years. And then an-
> other tutor was hopefully converted, and called into the minis-
> try, and has been President ever since. And **I hope succeeding
> ages will follow these examples.**[6]

What did education at Brown College do for America's Baptist
preachers? Note the following testimony on preaching style. This is in
reference to Charles Thompson a graduate of Brown:

> He placed a high value upon time and improved all his hours to
> good purpose. In his family and in the church, he was a model
> of both kindness and firmness. As a preacher he held a very
> high rank. He had a voice of great depth and tenderness of feel-
> ing, and he often wept with his people, while he occasionally
> addressed them in a voice of thunder. His sermons were care-
> fully studied, and sometimes written, but his manuscript was

never seen in the pulpit, and his language was general such as was applied to him at the moment.[7]

About William Rogers another graduate of Brown, from a letter written by James Manning:

June 5, 1771

To Samuel Stennett,:

One of the youth [William Rogers] graduated at our first Commencement, who is thought to be savingly brought home by grace, has joined Mr. Thurston's church in Newport, and appears eminently pious. As soon as his age will admit, for he is quite a youth, he will be called to the work of the ministry...He bears the greatest resemblance to Mr. Hezekiah Smith of any person I know, and I hope will make another such **son of thunder**.[8]

Apparently James Manning, the first President of Brown, was seeking to produce such "sons of thunder." The historian of Brown said, "Brown University owes its origin to a desire on the part of members of the Philadelphia Association, to secure for the Baptist churches an educated ministry."[9]

Has Brown maintained the original purpose of Hopewell Academy? We trust the reader will judge.[10]

*   *   *

Christian people pioneered the educational system in America. In some cases the colleges were begun because of the increase in population. In other cases, colleges were begun to stem the tide of unbelief in the established colleges. In all cases, the sacrifice and investment were for the cause of Christ and His Gospel. The colleges and their affiliations are listed here:

1636 **Harvard** College, Congregational.
1693 College of **William and Mary** in Virginia, Anglican.
1701 **Yale** College, Congregational.

1746 College of New Jersey, which became **Princeton,** Presbyterian.
1751 Philadelphia Academy, which became the **Univ. of Pennsylvania,** Nonsectarian. (A large statue of George Whitefield adorns the campus.)
1754 King's College, which became **Columbia** Univ., Nonsectarian.
1764 Rhode Island College, which became **Brown** University, Baptist.
1766 Queen's College, which became **Rutgers** Univ., Dutch Reformed.
1769 **Dartmouth** College, founded to train Indian preachers, Congregational.

*   *   *

The Baptists were busy during the 19th century establishing colleges and theological institutions. For the Baptists there was a real need to defend and maintain Baptist principles and history. These needs remain to this day. In 1881 William Cathcart listed the following colleges and theological institutions as belonging to the Baptists:

College

Brown University	Providence, RI	1764
Madison University	Hamilton, NY	1819
Colby University	Waterville, ME	1820
Columbian University	Washington, DC	1821
Shurtleff College	Alton, IL	1827
Georgetown College	Georgetown, KY	1829
Denison University	Granville, OH	1831
Richmond College,	Richmond, VA	1832
Franklin College	Franklin, IN	1834
Wake Forest College	Wake Forest, NC	1834
Mercer University	Macon, GA	1838
Howard College	Marion, AL	1843
Baylor University	Independence, TX	1845
University at Lewisburgh	Lewisburg, PA	1846
William Jewell College	Liberty, MO	1849
University of Rochester	Rochester, NY	1850
Mississippi College	Clinton, MS	1850
Carson College	Mossy Creek, TN	1850
Furman College	Greenville, SC	1851
Central University	Pella, IA	1852
Kalamazoo College	Kalamazoo, MI	1855

Bethel College	Russellville, KY	1856
McMinnville Col	McMinnville, OR	1858
University of Chicago	Chicago, IL	1859
La Grange College	La Grange, MO	1859
Waco University	Waco, TX	1861
Vassar College	Poughkeepsie, NY	1861
University of Des Moines	Des Moines, IA	1865
Monongahela College	Jefferson, PA	1867
California College	Vacaville, CA	1871
Southwestern Baptist College	Jackson, TN	1874

Theological Institutes

Hamilton Theological Seminary	Hamilton, NY	1819
Newton Theological Institute	Newton Center, MA	1825
Rochester Theological Seminary	Rochester, NY	1851
Southern Baptist Theological Sem	Louisville, KY	1851
Shurtleff Theological Seminary	Alton, IL	1862
Baptist Union Theological Sem	Morgan Park, IL	1867
Crozer Theological Seminary	Upland, PA	1868
Vardeman School of Theology	Liberty, MO	1868

Concerning theological institutions Hamilton, the first of these, was founded by Nathaniel Kendrick in 1819. Until this time, Baptist preachers were trained in theology by other preachers. Kendrick placed himself under the tutelage of five other preachers including Thomas Baldwin and Samuel Stennett.[11] This was how the early American Baptists prepared for the theological battles of their ministry.[*]

The need for educating preachers became more acute when the revivals of the turn of the century produced young preachers in great numbers. Conversely, the loss of belief in *experimental religion* in older established colleges created a crisis of confidence. Those things along with the rapid expansion of the country, demanded the establishment of other colleges.

*　　*　　*

---

[*] For an example of this practice, see Appendix K, Pastoral Questions on Theology.

The following is the current state of things for the first 20 "Baptist" colleges established in America:

Brown University   Providence, RI   1764
Brown is no longer a ministerial training institution.

Madison University   Hamilton, NY   1819
Established as the Hamilton Literary and Theological Institution, later named Madison. Originally founded to educate ministers of the Gospel. After 1839, students "not having the ministry in view" were admitted. When the charter was changed to Madison in 1846 no mention in reference to training preachers was made. Madison is known today as **Colgate University**.

Colby University   Waterville, ME   1820
Founded as Maine Literary and Theological Institution, later Waterville College (1820), later Colby University (1867), and Colby **College** in 1899. There is no connection to the Baptists who founded Colby, nor any preparation for preachers into the Gospel ministry.

Columbian University   Washington, DC   1821
Founded as a training center for Baptist missionaries. Now known as **George Washington University**. There is no connection to its Baptist foundation.

Shurtleff College   Alton, IL   1827
Founded to train preachers for the task of preaching the Gospel in the west. Assimilated into Southern Illinois University. There is no connection to the Baptists today.

Georgetown College   Georgetown, KY   1829
Georgetown still has ties with the Kentucky Baptist Association and the Elkhorn Association. It has some ministerial students, but its original requirement for student behavior is nearly nonexistent.

Denison University   Granville, OH   1831
Of Denison, William Cathcart wrote, "It was incorporated in 1832 under the name of Granville Literary and Theological Institution."[12] Here are a few passages from their current college bulletin:

> Queer studies: An evolving and expanding discipline, Queer Studies encompasses theories and thinkers from numerous fields: cultural studies, gay and lesbian studies, race studies, women's studies, literature, film, media,

postmodernism, post-colonialism, psychoanalysis, and more. By engaging with this diverse range of fields, the work of Queer Studies distinguishes itself from the others in that it focuses on issues of sexuality and the way that the questions raised in these other arenas might be inflected through that central lens.

Here is what Denison currently says about its Religion Department:

> Religion is an essential part of the humanistic studies in a liberal arts education. The study of religion is one way to establish a view of reality, and more specifically a view of the meaning of human existence as individuals and as social beings in relation to ultimate reality.

Richmond College,   Richmond, VA   1832

The Virginia Baptists opened a seminary for men. The seminary soon added a program for literary studies and was incorporated as Richmond College in 1840. Now known as the **University of Richmond**, there is no tie to the Baptists. However, the Virginia Baptist Historical Society and archive is located on the campus.

Franklin College   Franklin, IN   1834

No ties, or even a hint that Franklin was founded by the Baptists of Indiana.

Wake Forest College   Wake Forest, NC   1834

The organizational meeting of the Baptist State Convention of North Carolina, held on March 26, 1830 proclaimed that the "primary objects of this Convention are, the enlargement and intellectual improvement of the Ministry, and the supplying of destitute Churches and sections of the country, within the limits of the State."

George Washington Paschal, historian at Wake Forest, writing in the 1940's said,

> Wake Forest College is a religious, a Christian, a denominational, and primarily a Baptist institution, established and maintained by the Baptists of North Carolina with the purpose of promoting the progress and acceptance throughout the world of the religion of the New Testament, its principles and ideals, and in particular to give its

students such education and training as will best enable them to aid in the accomplishment of THIS PURPOSE.[13]

In recent years, Wake Forest and the Baptists have severed all ties.
Mercer University   Macon, GA   1838
Spright Dowell, in his *History of Mercer University* wrote,

> Adiel Sherwood had drawn a resolution proposing the establishment of a manual labor school which he planned to offer at the annual meeting of the Convention in 1829, but withheld it in deference to the wishes of some of his brethren on the Executive Committee. At the annual Convention which met at Buckhead, Burke County, in 1831, he offered this resolution: "That as soon as the funds will justify it, this Convention will establish in some central part of the state a classical and theological school, which shall unite agricultural labor with study, and be open for those only who are preparing for the ministry."[14]
>
> The Convention met at Powelton in 1832, and passed this revised resolution: "That as soon as the funds will justify it, this Convention will establish, in some central part of the State, a literary and theological school, which shall unite manual labor with study; admitting others besides students in divinity under the direction of the Executive Committee."[15]

Mercer never was an adherent to its original intent.
Howard College   Marion, AL   1843
Founded by the Baptists for the purpose of ministerial studies, Howard was chartered in 1841 and opened its doors on January 3, 1842, in Marion Alabama. In 1887 it was relocated to Birmingham, and in 1957, the institution was moved to its present campus. It is now **Samford University**.

Samford claims to be a Christian College. The college in its early days kept a lively chapel preaching to the student body. It now has "Convocation." Here is the explanation of "Convocation" from their college information bulletin:

> The purpose of Convocation is to nurture students in faith, learning, and values from a distinctly Christian perspective. Students are made aware of the Christian worldview and are encouraged to develop sympathy with the

Christian mission in the world. Students are provided with opportunities to grow toward spiritual maturity. Convocation events help to cultivate the climate within which transcendent and teachable moments can occur in both formal and informal contexts at Samford.

Convocation offers nurture on an individual level, a corporate level, and a confessional level. First, Convocation offers activities which challenge persons to grow toward Christian maturity. Second, Convocation encourages persons to contribute to the Christian ethos of the University community. Third, Convocation offers formal means by which we, the University, can be who we say we are: a community committed to faith, learning, and values rooted in a Christian worldview.

What is Convocation 'not?'

Convocation is not an effort to coerce students to embrace a faith or belief system which they themselves do not accept. Rather, it invites students to share an understanding of what Samford University claims to be, a University committed to nurture within a Christian context. Requiring participation in functions which cultivate and underscore this unique context enables Samford to fulfill its unique mission.[16]

Baylor University   Independence, TX   1845

Still loosely affiliated with the Baptist General Convention of Texas.

Univ. at Lewisburgh   Lewisburg, PA   1846

Founded by Steven W. Taylor. Became **Bucknell** sometime after the Civil War. No trace of its Baptist roots can be found.

William Jewell Col.   Liberty, MO   1849

According to *History of William Jewell College*:

On Friday the 29th day of August, 1834 a number of Baptist ministers and laymen met at Providence Church in Callaway County. Of this meeting the Rev. Jeremiah Vardeman was elected Moderator; and the Rev. Robert S. Thomas was appointed Clerk. Article II of their constitution, was *to adopt means and execute plans to promote the preaching of the Gospel within the bounds of the State.* The first catalog of the College was issued in 1854, from which we learn that the number of students in attendance during the scholastic year of 1853-54 was 160, of whom 110 were in the Preparatory Department and 50 in the Collegiate classes. It is known that a number of these students were preparing for the ministry, but the catalog contains no reference to the fact.[17]

It was stated that one of the great objects of the Baptists in establishing William Jewell College was to provide an institution in which candidates for the ministry could receive such an education as would render them more competent for the great work to which they were called. This object had always been kept in view, but, up to the point at which we have now arrived in the history of the institution, no special provision, either in the way of theological instruction or in the way of pecuniary aid to those who were unable to meet their expenses, had been made for this class of students.[18]

They never did provide for their preachers. The college has recently dropped all ties to the Baptists.

Univ. of Rochester   Rochester, NY   1850
There is no trace of the Baptist founding of this institution.

Mississippi College   Clinton, MS   1850
The college maintains loose affiliation with the Mississippi State Baptist Convention.

Carson College   Mossy Creek, TN   1850
Began as the Mossy Creek Missionary Baptist Seminary.[19] It was founded by a group of Tennessee Baptist preachers, to train Baptist preachers for the Gospel ministry. Now known as **Carson-Newman College**, it has ties to the Southern Baptist Convention.

Furman College   Greenville, SC   1851
Named for Richard Furman. W. J. McGlothlin, author of A *History of Furman University*, wrote,

The organizers of the state convention put education as the first object to be fostered by that body. As set forth in their statement of principles at the first meeting—the increase of evangelical and useful knowledge, and of vital practical religion; the promotion of religious education, and particularly that of indigent, pious young men designed for the gospel ministry.(Constitution, Article II.)[20]

The proposed academy was intended primarily to train young ministers, preparing some to enter the Washington institution (Columbian University) where they could complete a thorough theological education, and giving to others who could not go on to Washington the most necessary elements in a theological education. Instruction for indigent young ministers was to be gratuitous.[21]

Central University   Pella, IA   1852

In 1916, Central University was transferred from Baptist affiliation to the Reformed Church in America. A passage from the current college handbook reads:

> Since its beginning Central College has identified itself with the Christian faith. Acknowledging that a liberal arts education requires diversity of thought and approaches to knowledge and that mature faith includes critical thought and inquiry, Central College maintains that academic freedom is essential to the development of mind and spirit.
>
> Non-Discrimination Policy
>
> Central College is committed to being an inclusive community whose members act with consideration for the physical, intellectual and spiritual well being of all persons. All members of the college community are responsible for creating an atmosphere that fosters openness, mutual respect and diversity. *(Board of trustees, 4/26/03)* The above nondiscrimination policy includes, but is not limited to, persons of every ethnicity, race, national origin, ancestry, color, socio-economic class, creed, religion, philosophical belief, marital status, disability, physical appearance, sex, age, **sexual orientation**, gender expression and identity, and organizational affiliation.

David Benedict

William Cathcart

Thomas Armitage

James Robinson Graves

CHAPTER NINETEEN
Of Hay Seeds and Lost Causes

It may well be said that the vast accumulated wealth of Rockefeller
and Carnegie may do more harm in its distribution than in its ac-
cumulation. . . twenty millions given to the Chicago University.
There is a fortified arsenal of unsound doctrine of all time to come.
You cannot dislodge it, for millions are behind it. They have
taken millions down into Oklahoma to buy up the lands and the in-
terest of that pours into the treasury until they do not know how to
invest their money and every dollar of it is against sound doctrine,
against the fundamentals of the faith that
Mr. Rockefeller himself professes.—B. H. Carroll

At the same time no little alarm was excited in Baptist circles by a
pamphlet in the interest of the Union Movement written by John D.
Rockefeller, Jr., and widely distributed, urging Baptists no longer to
require baptism as a condition of church membership.
—George W. Paschal[1]

Samuel Howard Ford was born in 1818 in Bristol, England. He was the son of the English Baptist, Thomas Howard Ford, whose ancestry was a part of the historic Broadmead Baptist Church. Samuel immigrated to America when his father came to Missouri in the late 1830's. After completing studies at the University of Missouri, Columbia, Ford was employed by John L. Waller, great-nephew to "Swearin' Jack" Waller of Virginia fame. Waller thought enough of young Ford's writing ability that he employed him in the inaugural year of the *Christian Repository*, a new Baptist magazine begun in Louisville, Kentucky in 1853.

From his pulpit in the East Baptist Church in Louisville and from his writer's chair at the *Repository*, Samuel Howard Ford became close friends with the aging Jeremiah Vardeman, Lewis Alexander, James Lemen, R. B. C. Howell, James Madison Pendleton, and B. H. Carroll. Ford saw the fascinating power of the simple Gospel in John Taylor and

James Suggett and experienced it himself. He recorded the following testimony from a 1841 pioneer revival on the Missouri frontier:

> While preaching in Missouri in a crowded house, and in a warm, hortatory manner, I saw a man of middle age sink on his knees at his seat with sobs and profuse weeping. Immediately a female, who had seen his agitation, rose and in piercing accents exclaimed, "*Jesus, Jesus, have mercy!*" She immediately fell, apparently lifeless.
>
> The scene alarmed and embarrassed me. I was but a youth, and had seen nothing of this character previously. I ceased preaching, and sat down. James Suggett, an aged man, formerly pastor at Great Crossings, Ky., who had passed through the Great Revival in Kentucky was with me in the pulpit. He immediately struck up a hymn, after which he invited mourners to come forward. Many came up and the meeting passed off as usual. Had we endeavored to excite further the deep state of feeling in the audience or encouraged its manifestation, perhaps scores might have fallen and wild extravagance followed.
>
> To the general effects of this revival, attention must now be directed. That great good resulted from it cannot be denied. Among the Baptists, I have given some of its results. "This revival," says an eminent writer, "was a death- blow to infidelity throughout this Valley. Not a few continued infidels and scoffers, but they were shorn of their strength. So many of their number had been converted, some of whom became efficient preachers of the gospel; that infidelity could no longer boast. It was a turning scale in public morals." A great and manifest change was wrought.
>
> We have once alluded to the wild and reckless habits of South Green River, in Kentucky. For more than a quarter of a century that part of the State has been distinguished for its moral and religious influence. But every part of the Mississippi Valley feels the effects. Numerous indeed, are the testimonies that might be here transcribed to the great and lasting effects of this revival.[2]

After the death of John L. Waller, Samuel H. Ford moved the *Christian Repository* to St. Louis, Missouri where he continued to record the history which David Benedict, Thomas Armitage and William Cathcart* had no access: the Baptist history of the west and southwest.

---

* William Cathcart was a native of Londonderry, Ireland, born November 8, 1826. He received his literary and theological education in the University of Glasgow, Scot-

*   *   *

Before 1845, all Baptist churches were independent, held together only by conferring ties of association and mission societies. After 1845, the advent of the various *conventions* created quite a mix of church affiliations among the brethren. We have seen how the north and the south divided (1845), leaving behind what eventually became the American Baptist Churches USA denomination. Today there are roughly 5,800 churches in the American Baptist Churches USA. Their Southern Baptist cousins have churches numbering somewhere close to 37,000. The National Baptist Convention also coming from the same Baptist stream number 3,700. The National Baptist Convention of America has approximately 2,500 churches. The Progressive National Baptist Convention has approximately 2,000 churches. There are also 1,700 churches belonging to the American Baptist Association; and the Baptist Missionary Association consists of at least 1,300 churches. Add to the mix the Baptist Bible Fellowship, which has 3,600 loosely affiliated churches and the General Association of Regular Baptists with about 1500 churches. There is the Conservative Baptist Association with roughly 1,000 churches. The Free Will Baptists number 2,500 churches and the General Baptists almost 1,000. In addition to all of these there is a sea of unassociated, unaffiliated, independent Baptist churches of which the author counts himself. That group may number as many as 15,000 churches. No one knows with any certainty. What brought this about?

---

land, and at Rawdon College, Yorkshire, England. His rearing was in the Presbyterian Church, but Cathcart was baptized into the Baptist church of Tubbermore in 1846. He was ordained pastor of the Baptist church of Barnsley, near Sheffield, England, early in 1850 but immigrated to America in 1853. In April 1857, he took charge of the Second Baptist church of Philadelphia, Pennsylvania, where he pastored for many years. In 1876, Cathcart was elected president of the American Baptist Historical Society, a position he held for many years. In the same year he published, *The Baptists in the American Revolution*. His greatest work without question was *The Baptist Encyclopedia*, a massive reference work that he compiled, edited and authored, publishing it in 1881. He died in 1908.

The 1858 Prayer Revival

The last great national revival occurred in 1858. It touched all Bible-believing denominations including the Baptists. The 1858 revival began as a prayer meeting on Fulton Street in New York City and blossomed into a time of great conviction and conversion across the county. Sometimes referred to as the "Second Great Awakening," the revival pressed an extraordinary number of souls into the kingdom of God. It gave salt to a nation on the brink of a satanic civil war.

Perhaps the most startling result of the 1858 Prayer Revival was the tendency of the converts from every denomination to desire believer's baptism.

The *Baptist Messenger* recorded, "Thousands are immersed who unite with other churches. This is so particularly with the Methodists. Their ministers, in order to keep them within their communion are obliged to immerse them. Nothing else will satisfy the people."[3]

The Methodists, Congregationalists and even some Episcopalians and Lutherans immersed some of their members during the 1858 revival. Even though some preachers among the Pedobaptists left their denomination to become Baptist, most simply immersed and remained in their own communion. Nearly half of the Methodist preachers in Boston, Massachusetts immersed converts who requested believer's baptism. The notable Henry Ward Beecher, the famous Congregationalist from Boston on one occasion immersed 56 converts. There was an astounding testimony of the baptism of 900 Lutheran converts in the state of Iowa. Another account reported the Methodists baptizing 30 converts in the Mississippi River at Natchez.[4] This practice would eventually cause a dilemma for the Baptists.

*   *   *

There were **six blows** that heavily damaged the Baptists in the mid-19th century. A combination of these blows led to the apostasy of the educational system and the assimilation of the Baptists into Protestantism. The **first** blow was the publishing of the *Origin of the Species* by Darwin. The **second** was the influence of German Rationalism on the educational system. The **third** blow was the Bible Revision Movement. The **fourth** blow was the Civil War. The **fifth** blow was the acceptance of the **1641 Theory** of baptism, and the **sixth** was the silencing of Baptist testimony.

*   *   *

R. B. C. Howell and James Robinson Graves

In Nashville, Tennessee the Baptists had suffered a number of setbacks including the loss of the First Baptist Church to the followers of Alexander Campbell. God raised up Robert Boyt C. Howell to help Nashville.

Howell came from Columbia College in Washington by way of North Carolina. He was one of the first graduates of the school which was at one time considered the hope of the south. Howell began his ministry at the Cumberland Church of Norfolk, Virginia in 1827 and then came to Nashville in 1832.

At that time J. B. McFerrin was a popular Methodist preacher and editor of *The Christian Advocate* paper of Nashville. The Methodists outnumbered the Baptists 5 to 1 in Nashville. *The Christian Advocate* became a very vocal opponent of R. B. C. Howell. The new pastor of the new First Baptist Church in Nashville was a force in the pulpit and a fierce worker in the field. Howell formed a strategy—in order to fend off the power of the Methodist *Christian Advocate*, he would immediately begin a paper of his own. He called it: *The Baptist*. The paper was the only one of its kind in the south, and met a desperate need in the battle with both Methodism and Campbellism. For over a decade, Howell held forth and withstood the arrows of McFerrin, his talented and able adversary. As the Lord would have it, the First Baptist Church of Nashville began to grow.

In 1845 James Robinson Graves came to Nashville and became the pastor of the Second Baptist Church.

The testimony of James Robinson Graves, so identified with the South, actually began in New England. He was born in Chester, Vermont, on April 10, 1820. His family was descendant from the French

Huguenots. He lost his father to sudden death before he was even a month old. Graves was converted and baptized at North Springfield Baptist Church in Springfield, Vermont. In 1839 at the age of 19, he moved to Kingsville, Ohio, to become the principal of an academy.

Not long after he took charge of the Clear Creek Academy in Nicholasville, Kentucky and joined Mt. Freedom Baptist Church. Mt. Freedom saw his ability and licensed him to preach and he began to fill the pulpit from time to time. Ryland Thompson Dillard ordained him.

In the fall of 1845, Graves became the pastor of the Second Baptist Church in Nashville, Tennessee, and began a friendship with R. B. C. Howell. In 1846 Howell, sensing the abilities and power of God upon Graves, asked the young preacher to become editor of *The Baptist*. He agreed and with a name change, *The Tennessee Baptist* was born. Graves commenced his life work.

James Robinson Graves, the young editor of the *Tennessee Baptist*, began a lifelong defense of Baptist principles. He became highly regarded for his concise, pointed, arguments in defense of believer's baptism and conversion. His series of letters arguing against infant christening to the Methodist Bishop Soule were unanswerable. Those arguments were put into book form and published as *The Great Iron Wheel*. "Wheel" was probably his greatest work. Later in life, Graves visited the aged David Benedict, who heartily greeted him as "the author of The *Great Iron Wheel*."[5]

Graves became a notable evangelist. Joseph Borum, writing for Cathcart's *Baptist Encyclopedia* said, he "was with him in Brownsville, Tennessee in 1849 where more than seventy persons, including the first men and women in the town, found the Savior. His argument, illustrations, and appeals were the most powerful I ever heard."[6] Before he was thirty, Graves had seen 1,300 conversions in revival meetings.

R. B. C. Howell was seeing the power of God as well. By the summer of 1850 the congregation at the First Baptist Church of Nashville had grown to over 500 souls, when Howell was called to Richmond, Virginia to the Second Baptist Church. Richmond was a Baptist stronghold. The climate for ministry was different there. The Pedobaptist influence was not as fierce, and the preachers were definitely more cordial.

But Howell was not to stay in Richmond. In an unusual turn of events, the people of the First Baptist Church of Nashville, prevailed upon Howell to return to be their pastor in 1857. By that time, J. R. Graves had resigned as pastor of the Second Baptist Church in Nashville to devote his time to revival work and editing the *Tennessee Baptist*. He was now a member of First Baptist Church and R. B. C. Howell became his pastor.

Nashville was still a battlefield and J. R. Graves and the *Tennessee Baptist* were in need of help. Reinforcements came in the persons of A. C. Dayton and James Madison Pendleton.

A. C. Dayton was from New Jersey, born in 1813. He was converted in a Presbyterian church at the age of 12. He studied medicine and became a doctor but became heavily involved in education and lecturing. He married and settled in Tennessee. In 1852 after a careful study of the scriptures, he concluded baptism must be for believers only and that by immersion. He quickly became an advocate for Baptist principles.

He met J. R. Graves in 1855 and began assisting him in the publication of the *Tennessee Baptist*. He also published the Christian novel, *Theodosia Ernst*, a widely popular book that emphasized the sacrifices made for scriptural baptism. Dayton's abilities brought credibility to the cause of the old time Baptists.

James Madison Pendleton was born in Virginia in 1811 and grew to a young adulthood in Kentucky. He was educated in one of those classic one-room schoolhouses on the prairie. He was born again and baptized at the Bethel Baptist Church in 1829 and began to preach immediately. He was ordained at Hopkinsville, Kentucky, on November 1, 1833 and took the charge of two churches, Hopkinsville and Bethel. After a ministry of four years he became pastor of Bowling Green Church where he continued for 20 years. In January of 1857, he took his great knowledge of the scriptures to Murfreesboro, Tennessee, to teach theology to the preacher boys in Union University. He also became pastor of the church there.

It was Pendleton who in 1854 wrote the doctrinal warning, *An Ancient Landmark Reset*. The book was a simple and straightforward message to Baptist churches, pointing out the inconsistency of having Pedobaptists preach in their pulpits. Since God's people have always had a

bad case of spiritual amnesia, Pendleton's warning served to remind the
Baptists of all they had suffered at the hands of non-Baptists. It questioned the validity of churches practicing infant christening, and
pointed out the invalid nature of Pedobaptist "immersion." The stand
against Pedobaptist pulpit affiliation and Pedobaptist immersion became known as "Landmarkism."

From the opposition that followed Pendleton, one would believe
that he had come up with some new-fangled doctrine, and that the
stand against Pedobaptist pulpit affiliation and Pedobaptist immersion
was heresy. Yet we cannot find that the statements of Pendleton concerning the named issues differed greatly from those of Isaac Backus,
Jessie Mercer, the Philadelphia Association, the Regular Baptists or the
Separate Baptists.

In 1858 J. M. Pendleton, still pastoring in Murfreesboro, joined A.
C. Dayton in assisting Graves at the *Tennessee Baptist.*

R. B. C. Howell returned to Nashville to pastor Graves and Dayton.
But Howell had already judged against so-called "Landmarkism." What
transpired next was similar to two freight trains colliding.

Dayton had become Corresponding Secretary to the Bible Board of
the Southern Baptist Convention. So he was employed by the Convention. He was a contributing editor of the *Tennessee Baptist,* so Graves
employed him. Graves had formed his own "Bible Union" publication
called Graves, Marks & Co. This he formed partly because of his vigorous opposition of J. C. Tustin, the Secretary of the Southern Baptist
Publication Society, who leaned so far toward the Pedobaptists that he
eventually became an Episcopalian.[7]

Sometime in 1857 and just prior to his return to Nashville, R. B. C.
Howell wrote this in a letter to the *Christian Index:*

But we are told by the newspapers that this very brother [Day-
ton] is himself rapidly preparing Sunday School books, and that
several will be ready, and actually presented to the "The Union"
in April next. Very well—let him prepare them if the Bible
Board will allow their Corresponding Secretary to devote nearly
ALL HIS time to writing books, and instead of presenting them

to "the Union" let him send them to the Southern Baptist Publication Society.[8]

Graves could not let the statement by R. B. C. Howell fall to the ground. In the February 13, 1858 issue of the *Tennessee Baptist* Graves wrote:

> There is manifestly a systematic attempt to cripple down the Secretary of the Bible Board, on the part of anti-landmark men, and editors. We allude to the allusion to brother Dayton in Elder Howell's letter to the *Index*, in which he virtually attaints brother Dayton for malfeasance in office by an insinuation.[9]

For three weeks, Graves called upon Howell to retract his insinuation that A. C. Dayton was neglecting his duties. We must candidly say at this point, that if J. R. Graves had a problem with his own pastor, he should have been more discreet. But a deeper problem was developing. There was a polarizing of views in the South; the old Baptist heritage of defending their distinct principles was separating from a newer more moderate stance.

In the fall of 1858, James Robinson Graves was accused of bringing upon "R. B. C. Howell, the Pastor of First Baptist Church of Nashville, reproach and injury." Among other things, the accusation said Graves was endeavoring to "distract and divide by means of a conflict between its pastor and four of its deacons," and that Graves had written "sundry foul and atrocious libels." Also among the crimes of Graves was that he "attacked, slandered and abused ministers and brethren of high character, belonging to our denomination." All of the crimes were said to have occurred as articles and writings in the *Tennessee Baptist* paper.[10]

There was an actual trial that took place during several sessions of the church between September 8 and October 13. Graves made a defense claiming the trial itself was unscriptural. He was no doubt disappointed when the church voted overwhelmingly to allow the trial. Graves withdrew his membership from First Baptist Church during the preliminaries. The church proceeded without him and he was expelled along with 70 other members who were his supporters.

Those expelled formed a church with Graves as the pastor. So popular was Graves that the Middle Tennessee Association recognized the Graves faction as the "original and regular First Baptist Church of Nashville." But after a time, they reconstituted[11] as the Central Baptist Church of Nashville.[*]

The Civil War put the Howell-Graves incident into oblivion.

J. M. Pendleton's stay at the *Tennessee Baptist* was short, for at the outbreak of the Civil War, he moved to Ohio. By the end of the hostilities, A. C. Dayton was dead and soon after so was R. B. C. Howell. The "Landmark" controversy however, still had plenty of life.

The Civil War devastated the South. Their economic and agricultural base was in shambles. Their industry was nearly non-existent and there was no money for rebuilding.

The Civil War had stopped the war for souls. It also stopped the educational system and for the most part, the church life of the South. The churches were especially decimated. The Baptist churches, which had a poor economic standing before the war; were afterwards well nigh helpless.

But the churches, which had always been rich spiritually, began to recover. One great instrument in their resurgence was James Robinson Graves. S. H. Ford testified that:

> None contributed more to this blessed and almost immediate result than Graves. Throughout Mississippi, Tennessee, Arkansas and Louisiana, he preached, lectured, held meetings, rallied the churches, gave unity to their aims, and expounded and illustrated, as few like him could do, the doctrines of Grace through faith in the Redeemer, against salvation through ordinances, or the church, or aught under

---

[*] By 1874, both First Baptist and Central Baptist Church were regular members of the Middle Tennessee Association.

the heavens but JESUS ONLY. The Lord seemed to endow him with extraordinary power, and showers of blessings followed his fervid ministrations.

He commenced at Memphis. A. B. Miller, now of Little Rock, was then pastor of the First Church in that city. The other church (Beal Street) had been broken up. Its house was destroyed and its membership scattered. It was rallied. Seventy-five prominent members of the First Church joined the remnant, and a new church was formed— the Central Church, whose magnificent building adorns the "Bluff City."

Graves became a burning, shining light in the South after the War. In Memphis, he held a revival that resulted in the conversion and baptism of over 200 in a matter of weeks. The church was resurrected.[12]

Graves restarted the *Tennessee Baptist,* reorganized the Southern Baptist Sunday School Union, and attempted to institute a book concern for the Baptists of the South. Somehow he found time to debate the Methodist leader, Jacob Ditzler. This celebrated and widely popular event was held in Carrollton, Missouri. Graves became the most widely used evangelist of the south.

Christian Union

Following the 1858 Prayer Revival was the advent of **union meetings**. The first of the modern union meetings was held in Philadelphia in 1858.[13] The effort at union died out during the Civil War, but renewed afterwards.

Some of the Baptist revivalists, mentioned in chapter 16, promoted union meetings at least in a practical sense without any observance of the ordinances. But some pressure came to the Baptists to observe the Lord's Supper with the Pedobaptists. In time, **Christian Union** associations sprang up around larger cities. These efforts became detrimental to Baptist principles and eventually led to the erosion of Baptist distinctives. Yet there was resistance.

The greatest example of resistance to "Christian Union" associations came from New York pastor and Baptist historian, Thomas Armitage.

Armitage immigrated to America at the age of 19. He was from the distinguished Armitages of Yorkshire in England. His family followed John Wesley and Armitage was the great grand son of a Methodist preacher. Converted as a young man, Armitage commenced to preach the Gospel from his youth. His first sermon was given at age 16, and as young man he was in constant demand in the pulpit.

Upon arriving in America, Armitage filled many pulpits in influential Methodist churches in New York. He eventually became the pastor of the Washington Street Methodist Church. But nagging doubts about falling from grace occupied his mind. And he doubted the validity of infant "baptism." He studied and eventually concluded infant christening to be error. The evangelist Jabez Swan baptized him in 1848. He was then given a gracious dismissal by the Methodists and was ordained to the Baptist ministry not long after. He became the pastor of the Fifth Avenue Baptist church in New York City on July 1, 1848. Two revival periods ensued, the first in 1853 when 140 persons were baptized, the second in 1857 when 152 followed the Lord in believer's baptism.

Armitage attended several union meetings and was not pleased with what he heard. The leaders of this movement, none of whom were Baptist, had publicly blamed the Baptists for the lack of unity among the denominations. Indeed, the Presbyterian preacher John Chambers, had said in his pulpit in Philadelphia, "The world can not be converted until the church is united, and the church can not be united until the Baptists renounce* close communion."[14]

In early 1866 in the city of New York, the Dutch Reformed pastor Dr. Vermilye, charged the Baptists with "bigotry and exclusiveness." His remarks became part of the public record.

---

* The Kentucky Baptist historian J. H. Spencer noted that Salem Association handled a question of order from the 1803 meeting. The question concerned the subject of "communing with other than Baptist societies, which was decided to be out of Gospel order." Spencer, A History of the Kentucky Baptists vol. 2: 52.

Meanwhile, because of his influence, Thomas Armitage was asked to speak at the next meeting of the Christian Union Association. This meeting was to be held at the Twenty-Ninth Street Dutch Reformed Church, the church pastored by Dr. Vermilye. Armitage, determined to answer both Dr. Vermilye and the accusations of the leadership of the Christian Union Association, agreed to speak. On March 25, 1866, he delivered his message, *Christian Union: Real and Unreal.* He delivered it no doubt, with the criticisms of Vermilye still ringing in his ears. Yet his answer resonated with charity, clarity, calmness, and incisive reasoning.

Armitage first tried to find the Christian Union Association definition of Christian union by saying, "As far as I can discover, my Pedobaptist brethren seem to think that [Christian union] consists very largely in a warm-hearted, loving feeling toward each other as regenerated men."[15] He said the effort at Christian union meant a setting aside of disagreement for the sake of worship and concluded that the association believed "disagreement, if you can agree about it, is unity!"[16] And to the Dutch Reformed, Congregational, Presbyterian and Methodist congregation he said, "That is, kneeling on the same floor, sitting on the same seat, singing the same hymn, uniting in the same prayer (when you have never been divided at all as to the floor, the bench, the hymn, or the prayer); and being as different as possible, in all other respects, constitute Christian union!"[17]

This "good feeling" Armitage said, "is looked upon, very generally, as good, fair, Bible Christian union. Well, it may be; but if it is, things have changed vastly since apostolic times. The truth is, that kindly feeling is not Christian union, and may exist where 'the unity of the faith,' is rent into a thousand shreds."[18]

The center of the problem of course, was Baptist belief about baptism. Armitage pointed out that Baptists and Pedobaptists were diametrically opposed on the issue of baptism, and therefore were in disagreement about church membership, and even what constituted a church. If Christian union called for Baptists to hold communion (the Lord's Supper) with Pedobaptists then the Baptists and the Pedobaptists would have to violate their own principles.

It certainly was absurd to call the Baptists bigoted for refusing Christian union based upon a conviction they were forced to maintain.

And in addition, Armitage argued correctly that "communion at the Lord's table is not at all a test of Christian union." The Bible never gave that ordinance such jurisdiction. The Lord's Supper, as Armitage said and as the Bible says, is "to show forth His death."

Armitage said,

> And our Pedobaptist brethren never gave it any other interpretation, except when, in an unhappy moment, they stand behind the cross of Christ to make their Baptist brethren appear unmitigated bigots. Is not this true? I appeal to my candid and honorable brethren of various denominations now present to say if this is not true.[19]

The truth of this matter is still with us. To receive infant sprinkling is no-baptism and proper baptism has always been required to take the Lord's supper in Methodist, Presbyterian, Congregational, Episcopalian and Baptist churches. In short, "Christian Union" is a non-possibility among the denominations if they are to remain consistent with their own principles. By their own principles, creeds and confessions, Pedobaptists have always counted the Baptists "hereticks." Thomas Armitage reminded what was left of *Baptist Nation*, of that undeniable fact.

*   *   *

As the population of the United States exploded in the cities, immigration brought more Europeans. For the most part, they brought their Catholicism or their Lutheranism and their alcohol. The challenge of taking the Gospel to the enormous ends of America became nearly insurmountable.

The Evangelical Alliance

Because of the epidemic of alcohol abuse, the temperance movement took deep roots. No longer ambivalent toward the evils of strong drink, the Bible-believing denominations took a united front against liquor.

Because of the incredible need for preaching in the cities they also took a united front in what became the era of the great revivalists. Such revivals spawned the "Evangelical Alliance." The Alliance was the off-spring of the mostly unsuccessful "Christian Union" movement. It was in particular a dream of the famed Congregational preacher of Boston, Henry Ward Beecher. Beecher's deep belief in the unification of all Protestant denominations was singularly revealed in his opposition to Presbyterian evangelist Charles Finney. Beecher had a fear that Finney's "new measures" would, "prevent the great evangelical assimilation, which is forming in the United States."[20]

There was at one time a "Plan of Union" between the Presbyterians and the Congregationalists. But Beecher had a wider dream of all Prot-estant denominations, including the Baptists, merging into one church organization. The spirit of antichrist campaigns for such to this day, may the Baptists have the discernment to resist it.

In the days following the Civil War, the dream of Beecher had promise in the growing power of the "Evangelical Alliance." The "Alli-ance" had a prestige about it during the citywide campaign revivals fol-lowing the war under D. L. Moody, D. W. Whittle and to a lesser extent Sam P. Jones.

Could a Baptist, knowing his heritage, sit at length under the minis-tries of Moody the Congregationalist, Sam Jones the Methodist, E. P. Hammond the Congregationalist, or Gipsy Smith the Calvinist-Methodist? Even though the revivalists were wonderful men and were widely successful, for which all believers should rejoice, many Baptists respectfully avoided the revival meetings and did not participate.

When Moody was in his fabulous four-month campaign in St. Louis in 1879, the *Christian Repository*, gave this editorial:

> If all the Christian effort now expended was confined to the proper channel—Gospel churches—far greater and more glorious results would attend the proclamation of the word.[21]

Baptist participation in that particular Moody campaign was small, and as plans for Mr. Moody's campaign in St. Louis were in the works, the Baptists brought in their own evangelist. The *Repository* observed:

Remarkable Conversions

> Perhaps in all the history of St. Louis there has never been a series of meetings in which the *power* of the gospel of the Lord Jesus Christ has been made more manifest than in the meetings now being held in the Third and Fourth Baptist churches by Bro. W. E. Penn, the Evangelist. Already there have been 380 conversions.[22]

We hope our reader, after travelling with us through 250 years of testimony in *crimson red*, can understand the stance of these Baptists still dissenting because of infant christening. We must ask, what has happened to that dissent? How could baptism, for which so many of our forefathers were martyred, maimed, and mutilated become no longer important? What does that say about our fidelity to the written words of Almighty God?

Sometime during this era 1865-1885, due to the influences of Christian union, the Evangelical Alliance, and the beginnings of Modernism, *Baptist Nation* ceased to exist. *Baptist Nation*, born in the wake of the Revolutionary War, lived for three score years and ten and then *gave up the ghost*.

Landmark Movement

James Robinson Graves continued to hold the position of the old Baptists on pulpit affiliation and Pedobaptist immersions (sometimes called *alien* immersion) in the *Tennessee Baptist*. There were of course, other assertions made by J. R. Graves, and we cannot say that we would agree with all of his findings. The two basic tenets of "Landmarkism" were in actuality, American Baptist practices since the days of John Clarke.

What followed Graves was protest by Pedobaptist and Baptist preachers alike challenging him to prove the existence of *succession*. In other words the opponents of Landmarkism demanded proof of the existence of Baptist churches throughout history and links in a Baptist chain of authority.

A particularly loud protest against Landmarkism came from A. M. Averill, pastor of the Prairie Valley Baptist Church in Lancaster Texas. Averill was accused of having an *alien* immersion and voiced his complaint in a discourse to his church in an effort to prove the Landmarkers wrong. We must say his protest demonstrated an intellectual arrogance arising among the educated preachers in Baptist ranks. Averill said of the old Baptist historians,

> Well, have you read, says one, what Baptist historians say about the longevity of the Baptist church? Again, I ask, who are your historians to whom you refer me? Why, Orchard, Benedict, Ford, Ray, Curtis, Graves. I have read the most of them, more or less, and besides them, histories that are histories from which those you have mentioned have borrowed about all they know. A historian is a man who has examined, through himself or assistants, all that has been written or printed and is accessible, in all languages, bearing on the subject on which he treats. Such historians were Gibbon, Neander, Giesseler, and to some extent, Milman and Mosheim.[23]

So according to Averill, the Baptist historians such as Orchard and Benedict, can not possibly compare to the Pedobaptist historians Gibbon, Neander and Mosheim. The simple and obvious reason for this opinion is that Averill, by this time (1880) had already thrown his heritage away and thought of himself as a Protestant. In the appendix of his book, *Baptist Landmarkism Tested*, Averill wrote, "the Baptists in the North have been wont to regard themselves as the most Protestant of the Protestant denominations and the least priestly of them all."[24]

Men like Averill demanded proof of a chain-link *succession* knowing the task was impossible. It was impossible because the records of our forefathers were destroyed in each generation. The only ancient record of our Baptist forefathers is the record left by their enemies. In fact, the first group of Baptists able to preserve their own history were the English and American Baptists from 1611 to the present time. God providentially allowed these groups of Baptists to survive, thrive, and record their sufferings. They helped formulate the American republic, and then evangelized the entire world.

While chain-link succession is impossible to prove, succession of the beliefs and distinctives of the Baptists to the candid observer is a fact of history. However, even that would come to be called in question.

*   *   *

In J. R. Graves the opponents of "Landmarkism" found someone to demonize. We cannot presently comprehend the vilification of his memory.[25] Graves may very well have been discredited so that his assertions on Baptist distinctives could be buried with him.

Yet many from his day had great admiration for him. The Honorable Joseph E. Brown, Governor of Georgia, said that Graves was the "one man who has done more that any fifty men now living to enable the Baptists of America to know their own history and their principles."[26] Several preachers such as J. B. Gambrell and B. H. Carroll regarded Graves as the greatest preacher of their generation.

Strangely, there are some who claim to this day, that Graves did not consider non-Baptists converted, yet, concerning Pedobaptist preachers, he wrote:

> Refusing to affiliate with them ministerially and ecclesiastically is not declaring by our act that we believe their ministers are unregenerate, but that they are not members of scriptural churches. Refusing to invite their ministers to preach for our churches, and to accept their immersions, is no more denying their Christian character than refusing to invite them to our communion table.
>
> We mean by our refusal, to emphasize our protest against their organizations as spiritual churches. Again all the teaching in God's Word where the plan of salvation is referred to or pointed to, even by a type, it is blood before water.[27]

In fact one of the highest estimation of Graves' worth came from a Methodist preacher, Dr. J. B. Searcy who wrote:

We never before saw the grace of God put in such clear light as he put it. Dr. Graves has been one of the worst misunderstood men of our day. I believe in one hundred years from today J. R. Graves will be quoted by the different denominations as the champion of salvation by grace and spiritual religion.[28]

In a conversation with the daughter of J. R. Graves, the leader of the Texas Baptists, B. H. Carroll said,

Your father was a great preacher and at one time the greatest Baptist evangelist preacher known. He not only made his audience understand what he said but he could make them see it. Let me tell you what I witnessed one time. He was preaching to a great audience on one occasion and he spoke of the blood of the martyrs. He began by picturing the blood that dripped from the thorn crowned brow of Christ as he hung there on the cross; of the blood that flowed upon the ground from his pierced side. It trickled on till met by the blood of James, of Stephen, of Paul, ever widening as it flowed on through the ages—mentioned the names of the great men who had given their life and blood for their faith in Christ. He made it so vivid that the audience craned their necks and looked over to the aisle where it seemed to flow and I actually saw a lady draw aside her skirts as though it was real.[29]

The evidence makes one wince when J. R. Graves is maligned with a false accusation. Consider this false statement about him by the former Southern Baptist Theological Seminary President, William H. Whitsitt:

Graves held that salvation is not possible outside a Baptist church. He places the church before Christ and the water before the blood.[30]

That was a very quaint statement by Whitsitt who no doubt spoke to create a proverbial criticism of Graves. Dr. Whitsitt's statement resulted in the following written protest by S. H. Ford:

In the *Christian Evangelist* is found an editorial, *Dr. Whitsitt on Baptist Succession.* The editor, makes prominent Whitsitt's reference to J. R.

Graves as holding and teaching that membership in a visible body is essential, to salvation — In other words, he held that salvation is not possible outside a Baptist church. "He places the church before Christ and the water before the blood."

I am truly sorry that Dr. Whitsitt ever made such a rash and unfounded statement, and as it has been published in your widely circulated journal I am sure you will permit me to show that it has no foundation in fact.[31]

Mr. Ford did in fact prove Whitsitt was wrong in his statements. J. R. Graves was nothing but a preacher of grace his entire ministry. That would not be the only time the famous William H. Whitsitt would be proven wrong.

William H. Whitsitt and the incredible "1641 Theory" of Baptism

The Baptists were now in every state and territory. Associations divided and then subdivided and churches were birthed—not near the rate of the old pioneers—but nevertheless, churches were being formed. The education of preachers became an extremely important issue. The most visible of the preacher-training institutions was the Southern Baptist Theological Seminary in Louisville, Kentucky. In 1872 William H. Whitsitt joined the staff of Southern Seminary. In 1895, he became President.

It is hard to criticize a soul such as William H. Whitsitt. His father, James Whitsitt, was a great pioneer preacher in Tennessee and William H. was a brave Civil War chaplain for the Confederate army.

William H. Whitsitt attended Juliet Academy and then studied for the ministry at Union University in Jackson Tennessee, under James Madison Pendleton, graduating in 1861. After the Civil War, he completed his studies at Southern Baptist Seminary in 1869.

Whitsitt chose to continue his studies at the *German Rationalism center of the universe* when he was accepted at the University of Leipzig and the University of Berlin. He completed his graduate studies in 1871. Returning to America, he accepted a pastorate in Albany, Georgia and remained there until he received the assignment he really wanted, that of teaching at Southern Baptist Seminary.

In 1880, a series of anonymous articles began to appear in the Congregational newspaper, the *New York Independent*, challenging the Baptists on immersion. The articles claimed that immersion was lost as the Gospel mode of baptism and not reinstated by the English Baptists until 1641. Note this from the *Independent*, New York, September 2, 1880:

> The *Congregationalist* speaks of the well-known immersion of Roger Williams by the unimmersed Ezekiel Holliman. To be sure, all the Baptists of America so assume, but the editor of the *Congregationalist* is more accurately acquainted with the origins of Baptist history than any of the Baptists themselves, and we expected that its statements would be more accurate. As we understand it, Roger Williams never was a Baptist in the modern sense—that is, never was immersed, and the ceremony referred to was anabaptism, rebaptism by sprinkling, and not 'Catabaptism,' or baptism by immersion.
>
> The baptism of Roger Williams is affirmed by Governor Winthrop to have taken place in March, 1639. This, however, was at least two years prior to the introduction of the practice of immersion among the Baptists. Up to the year 1641 all Baptists employed sprinkling and pouring as the mode of baptism. We are inclined to believe that no case of immersion took place among the American Baptists before the year 1644.
>
> It seems likely that Roger Williams, on his return from England in that year, brought the first reliable news concerning the change which had taken place in the practice of the English Baptists, three years before, and that it was then that the American Baptists first resolved to accept the innovation.

The editorial smacked of arrogance. By now it was apparent that among the more intelligent "doctors," the claim of ancient Baptist roots was an invention of unintelligent "hayseeds"—a claim made by the unscholarly grasping at a "lost cause" at best.

Another article followed the editorial in the *Independent* on September 9, 1880, from which we quote the following:

> It was not until the year 1644, three years after the invention of immersion, that any Baptist confession prescribes "dipping or plunging the body in water as the way and manner of dispensing the ordinance."[32]

The articles from the *Independent* were largely forgotten until 1896.

In the spring of 1896, Dr. William H. Whitsitt wrote an article about the Baptists for *Johnson's Encyclopedia*. The article stated his theory that the English Baptists did not begin to baptize by immersion until 1641, when a portion of the Anabaptists began immersing.

The "1641 Theory" set off a firestorm of opposition. Henry M. King of Rhode Island; Dr. J. H. Spencer, the Kentucky Baptist historian; and Dr. T. T. Eaton, editor of the *Western Recorder* immediately responded to Whitsitt. However, a certain Dr. H. M. Dexter exerted that the 1641 Theory was not new and claimed that he had held this position earlier than Whitsitt.

Mr. Whitsitt was not willing to give Mr. Dexter credit belonging to himself and so revealed that he, Dr. William H. Whitsitt, was the author of the infamous but now almost forgotten set of articles which appeared in the *New York Independent* in 1880.

John Taylor Christian,[*] a Baptist pastor in Mississippi, began to study the files of the *Independent* and found other editorials in which the Baptists were attacked. Now J. T. Christian and a host of other Baptist leaders began to question the integrity of Mr. Whitsitt. It was clear that Whitsitt undermined the principles of the Baptists while being employed by the sacrifices of Baptist people.

Mr. Whitsitt tried to explain his anonymous actions by claiming he "wrote from a Pedobaptist standpoint in order to provoke discussion and compel the Baptists to study their own history." In September of 1896 Whitsitt published *A Question in Baptist History*. He stated:

> During the autumn of 1877, shortly after I had been put in charge of the School of Church History at the Southern Baptist Theological Seminary, in preparing my lectures on Baptist History, I made the discovery that, prior to the year 1641 our Baptist people in England were in the practice or sprinkling and pouring for baptism. I kept it to myself until the year 1880, when I had the happiness to spend my sum-

---

[*] J. T. Christian later authored *A History of the Baptists*, released in 1926.

mer vacation at the British Museum. There I assured myself, largely by researches among the King George's pamphlets, that my discovery was genuine, and established it by many irrefutable proofs from contemporary documents.[33]

Whitsitt gained an ally in the "1641 Theory," Professor A. H. Newman of McMaster University in Toronto, Canada.

To his credit Mr. Whitsitt admitted that writing the editorials for the *Independent* was a mistake. He also regretted the offensiveness of the *Johnson Encyclopedia* entry. Whitsitt wrote, "...if in the future it shall ever be made to appear that I have erred in my conclusions, I would promptly and cheerfully say so. I am a searcher after truth, and will gladly hail every helper in my work."[34]

David Benedict had already proven Mr. Whitsitt to be inaccurate. William Cathcart, in his definitive *Baptist Encyclopedia*, included several articles, which proved Whitsitt to be in error. The brilliant Thomas Armitage, no doubt in response to the articles in the *Independent*, devoted much of his *Baptist History* of 1890 to prove that immersion was practiced throughout continental Europe and England in all ages.

In accordance to his request, Whitsitt's brethren set to work to show his errors. G. H. Orchard, in direct response to Whitsitt, wrote a compelling history of the Baptists. Most vigorously, John Taylor Christian, who made numerous trips to Europe in research, proved beyond question the errors in the assertions of Whitsitt. Publication after publication proved him to be in error. B. H. Carroll, S. H. Ford and W. W. Everts opposed the "1641 Theory." The response to his desire to be shown in error was thunderous.

Perhaps the most credible refutation of Whitsitt's "1641 Theory" came from England from the pen of Dr. Joseph Angus. In Ford's *Christian Repository*, in the January 1897 issue, Dr. Angus cited the existence of 26 Baptist churches practicing immersion before 1641. Perhaps most telling, he gave the names of at least 21 pamphlets which opposed the "dippers" (Baptists) and their manner of IMMERSION, all written *before* 1641. Angus wrote:

There is a great fluttering among our brethren in the United States and Canada on the question whether there were any real baptisms (immersions on a profession of faith) in England between 1509, the year of the accession of Henry VIII, and the year 1641. "Adult baptism by immersion," says Dr. Whitsitt, president of the largest Baptist theological school in the world, "was invented anew in England in 1641 under the light of God's Word."

"I am waiting patiently, but not very hopefully." says Dr. Newman "for proof that English Baptists practiced immersion before 1641."

So say the President of the Southern Seminary, Kentucky, and the Professor of Historical Theology in McMaster University, Toronto. Both are competent men and professors in Baptist Colleges. These statements are interpreted, as implying that English Baptist were sprinkled, not immersed, during 130 years between 1509 and 1641.

That there was no such delay in forming Baptist churches as our American friends have supposed is proved by the dates of the formation of a number of them. Churches were formed, chapels built, and doctrines defined long before 1641, and others, down to the end of that century, owed nothing probably to the discussions of that year.

The following churches formed in the years mentioned still remain: Braintree, Epthorne, Sutton, all in 1550; Warrington, 1522; Crowie and Epworth, both 1597; Bridgewater, Oxford, and Sadmore, 1600; Bristol (Broadmead), 1640; King Stanley, Newcastle, Kilmington (Devon), Bedford, Sutton, Cirencester, Commercial street (London), Lincoln, Dorchester, and Hamsterley, 1633; Lyme, Regis, Chipping, Sodbury, Upottery, Boston, etc., 1650 to 1658.

But there is another kind of evidence even more decisive showing that "the immersion of believers" was the common faith and practice of our fathers. I refer to the books published by them and against them in the century to which 1641 belongs.

I mention a few of the more important, giving the names in the briefest possible form. Most of them show clearly what the writers or their opponents, the Baptists, were supposed to hold.

Ærnstelodamus *Dissertation, Contra Anabaptist*. . . .	1535
Ærnstelodamus, *Baptimus Christianus*.	1539
Ampsing, J. A., *Disputationes, Contra Anabaptist*.	1619
Almsworth, H., *A seasonable Discourse on Anabaptism*	1623, 1644
Anabaptists, *Proclamations against*	1560
Articles of Visitation (Edw. VI., and Eliz.) 1547	1559
Apocalypsis of Anabaptists.	1640
Articles of Visitation.	1562, 1612
Barber, E. A., *A Treatise on Dipping*.	1641

Dr. Whitsitt was without question, in error, but he did *not* "promptly and cheerfully say so." He was forced to resign the presidency of the Southern Baptist Seminary in 1898.

The defeat of Whitsitt would lead one to believe that his 1641 Theory fell by the wayside and was dutifully rejected by Baptist educational institutions and the Baptist general public. Such was not the case. As always the *next* generation, which **does not pay a price** for its principles, begins to forsake them.

Southwestern Baptist Seminary was founded in 1908. B. H. Carroll the founder of the institution, wrestled with one of his professors, A. H. Newman, over "Whitsittism." Newman was dismissed, but his replacement W. W. Barnes, embraced Whitsittism. Barnes had been taught by Whitsitt's replacement at Southern Baptist Seminary, W. J. McGlothlin. Barnes wielded influence for several decades. McGlothlin moved on to Furman with Whitsittism in his agenda.

Whitsitt himself became President of Richmond College; probably happy that his 1641 Theory was becoming a false fact. Henry Vedder, a modernist historian from Crozer Theological Seminary in Pennsylvania, embraced Whitsittism and released his *Short History of the Baptists* in 1907. Vedder[*] was refuted by J. T. Christian, but still became the most widely read historian of the early 20th century. It was Vedder, the

---

[*] G. W. Paschal wrote of Vedder, "About the same time, Professor H. C. Vedder of Crozer Seminary published a paper in which it was argued that the Baptist position on baptism was untenable." Paschal Papers, PCMS 86 4/382 P. 12.

northern liberal,[36] who was honored by the Southern Baptist Convention when his *Short History* was distributed to the delegates of the convention in the early part of the 20th century.

The result was nothing less than the general acceptance of Whitsitt and the apparent sad "fact"?! that Baptists after all, did *not* exist until after the Reformation. The 1641 Theory and all of its ramifications became collectively known as the "English Separatist Descent Theory." Simply put, Whitsittism was the tool the *adversary* used to transform the Baptists of America into Protestants. This is not something that could have happened. It has already taken place.

The next generation of leaders acquiesced to a Whitsitt recension, and with it, modernist tendencies. Some Baptists withdrew, separated, and began new associations or affiliations. Some decided not to associate at all. The fallout of the 19th century among the Baptists produced an alphabet soup of Baptist affiliations.

The Fallout

The American Baptist Convention—what remained of the old "Triennial Convention" when the Baptists of the South formed their convention in 1845. Originally called the American Baptist Missionary Union, it was more of a society than a denomination. It was reorganized into the Northern Baptist Convention in 1907. Was renamed the American Baptist Convention in 1950 and then, the American Baptist Churches, USA in 1973. From the American Baptist Convention or American Baptist Church USA came:
1. The General Association of Regular Baptists—formed in 1932.
2. The Conservative Baptist Association—formed in 1943.

The Southern Baptist Convention—was formed in 1845. From the Southern Baptist Convention came:
1. The American Baptist Association—formed in 1905 from the churches and preachers clinging to the old Baptist "Landmark" position. From the American Baptist Association came:
     a) The Baptist Missionary Association of America—formed in 1950.

1. The Baptist Bible Fellowship—formed in 1950.

The National Baptist Convention—was formed in 1880, first as the Foreign Mission Convention for black Baptist associations. From them came:
1. The National Baptist Convention, USA.
2. The National Missionary Baptist Convention of America.
3. The Progressive National Baptist Convention.

The National Association of Free Will Baptists.

The General Baptists

The independent Baptist churches. These non affiliated, non associated churches came out of all the above groups, or formed independently.

The full story of what happened to the Baptists of America in the 20th century would require a large narrative volume.

The Modernist Movement and Fundamentalism

Not only did the Civil War totally destroy the Baptist educational centers of the South it also destroyed the warm spiritual influences the South had upon the North. From 1850-1870 numbers of Northern Baptist brethren had removed themselves to Europe for further education. This proved to have tragic consequences as these men were corrupted by German Rationalism and came back to America as advocates of Modernism.

This set the stage for a theological war in the South. As many Baptist colleges of the South reopened by the benevolent efforts of sympathetic Southerners, the intellectual content of the schools now came under the influence of Northern schools. Northern educated professors and administrators became the leaders in the colleges of the South. So both Northern and Southern educational centers became tinctured with German Rationalism and what became known as Modernism. Modernism touched all of the denominations. It infected the Evangelical Alliance.

The most vivid example of the corruption of modernism in the Baptist institutions of the South was the outrageous beliefs of Dr. Crawford Toy, the President of the Southern Baptist Theological Seminary. Toy stunned the Baptists of the south with his rejection of divine inspiration. Lottie Moon, the famed female missionary rejected Toy's proposal of marriage due to his infidelity to the Bible. Ford related the fiasco of Toy's unbelief in the *Christian Repository*:

> **The True and Real Inspiration of the Bible—Dr. Toy's Views.**
> In the address to the Trustees of the Southern Baptist Theological Seminary, accompanying his resignation, Dr. Toy says, in regard to the inspiration of the Scriptures: 'it is in the details of the subject that my divergence from the prevailing view of the denomination occurs.' He states with emphasis that, as the result of his examination, he believes "the Bible is wholly divine and wholly human."
>
> What is meant by "the details of the subject," and by "wholly human," it would probably be difficult for any one except himself to explain. Our own examination of the subject has led us to believe the Bible "is *wholly divine*," and in no sense human, except as human beings were the instruments though which it was communicated.
>
> The very term "inspired"– that is, to breathe into, and hence to inform to direct—is but a crystallization of what is expressed by II Peter 1:21: "Holy men of old spake as they were moved by the Holy Ghost." They were moved to speak, and the utterance, in all its import and characteristics, was the result of that divine movement upon the mind and faculties. It was God speaking through man.[37]

Crawford Toy was dismissed from the Southern Baptist Theological Seminary in 1879. He immediately moved north to work at Harvard.

That same year William Jewett Tucker began his teaching at Andover Seminary in Massachusetts. Andover began as a ministerial training ground founded to offset the corruption of Harvard. Tucker would be involved with four other professors in the "Andover Controversy" of 1886-1892, the erosion of belief in the Bible. In all probability, Toy and Tucker influenced a young Walter Rauschenbusch (1861-1918) of the Rochester, New York Seminary. Rauschenbusch is the father of the Social Gospel movement, and his liberalism paved the way for unbelieving professors like William Newton Clarke who in turn trained the infamous Harry Emerson Fosdick. (1878-1969)

It was Fosdick, the rank unbeliever masquerading as a Baptist preacher, who received financial support from J. D. Rockefeller, Jr.

Rockefeller offered Fosdick the pastorate of the Park Avenue Baptist Church in New York, the church of the Rockefeller family. He accepted only on the grounds that Rockefeller would build a new church building and that the church drop the Baptist distinctives for membership.

In 1890 Rockefeller decided to resuscitate the struggling University of Chicago. He did so with an endowment of 20 million dollars. Shailer Mathews was then hired as dean of the Divinity School. He quickly assembled a faculty of prominent liberal scholars, and the University of Chicago became the center of liberal theology in the country.

The Roots of the Fundamentalist Movement

In reaction to the *modernism* in the colleges and seminaries, Baptists began to attach themselves to a burgeoning movement: *fundamentalism*. Though the fundamentalist movement would peak in the 20th century its roots began in reaction to modernism, liberalism, and unbelief in the "Gilded Age."

In a real sense, fundamentalism could be viewed as an attempt to rescue the Evangelical Alliance from apostasy. Even though sincere, the Bible-believing Baptists, who had not given in to modernism and liberalism, were absorbed by "fundamentalism."

As a result and most astounding, Baptists for the most part do not have knowledge of their own history. How is this? When the fundamentalists began their own schools to train ministers of the Gospel, they were broad based and ecumenical in nature, to cover the spectrum of the movement. Eventually, fundamentalism evolved into a predominantly Baptist constituency. The educational centers for fundamentalism while training mostly Baptist ministers, educated them with the Evangelical Alliance as their heritage. The fruit of this mistake is the near total ignorance of Baptist testimony in the pulpits. Today, in a new era of birthing colleges exclusively for Baptists, the problem ought to be corrected. Educating an entire generation of Baptist people who know nothing about Isaac Backus, Shubal Stearns, Daniel Marshall, Samuel Harris, John Waller, John Leland, John Gano, James Ireland, the Craigs, the Murphys, the Fristoes, Lewis Lunceford, John Taylor, Jeremiah Vardeman, et al., must not be repeated.

Passing of the Patriarchs

A. C. Dayton died at his home in, Perry, Georgia, on June 11, 1865.[38]

R. B. C. Howell, passed from this life into the arms of Jesus April 5, 1868.

Daniel Witt passed on to his reward on November 15, 1871.

The venerable **David Benedict** aged 95, died at Pawtucket, Rhode Island on December 4, 1874.

J. B. Jeter died February 18, 1880.

In November of 1865, **James Madison Pendleton** took his place as the pastor of the Baptist church in Upland, Pennsylvania. This was the church home of the Crozer Theological Seminary. Pendleton enjoyed the blessings of God preaching in this place, and great and wonderful revivals. Once he baptized 200 converts in one meeting, at another, 40. He held forth for 18 years, during which time he taught with great influence at Crozer. His fascinating works not only were *An Old Landmark Reset*, but also included, *Three Reasons Why I Am a Baptist*, *The Atonement of Christ*, *Christianity Susceptible of Legal Proof*, *The Lord's Supper*, and *Christian Doctrines, a Compendium of Theology*. He resigned his office on June, 1883 and died March 4, 1891.[39]

James Robinson Graves departed this life on June 26, 1893. His last words to his son were, "Oh Willie Boy, what a change!"

Thomas Armitage remained at the Fifth Avenue Baptist Church until his death in 1897. Perhaps his most enduring legacy was his two-volume definitive *History of the Baptists*, which was published in 1890.

God took one of the greatest of the forgotten heroes of the 19th century **James Smith Coleman**, home on March 22, 1904. Coleman was ordained by Alfred Taylor and preached as a pastor and evangelist mainly in the state of Kentucky. He became known as the "Old Lion of the Pennyrile." Coleman saw over 10,000 converts and baptized 5,013.[40]

After writing more Baptist biographies than any other writer of his time, and laboring for over 50 years to make the testimony of the old Baptist fathers known, **Samuel Howard Ford** left the confines of this present world. He died on July 5, 1905 at age 87. He was carried to Bellefontaine Cemetery from his home in Jennings, just outside of St. Louis, Missouri. Several preachers were supposed to be in attendance, but in the end, one preacher officiated and his wife and two children witnessed.[41] It was just as well, for all that was his world had gone on before him.

CHAPTER TWENTY
Baptist Nation's Greatest Need

*Return, we beseech thee, O God of hosts: look down from heaven,
and behold, and visit this vine; And the vineyard which thy right
hand hath planted, and the branch that thou madest strong for
thyself.*—Psalm 80:14-15

Page Smith, in the *Life of John Adams* said, "Life was led, on the highest plateau of self-consciousness and led moreover with an intensity that modern man cannot imagine." It may be said then, if you can find that intensity God will find you, and He will use you in an extraordinary way.

May some young man launch out with holy desire to preach Jesus to a needy place like John Clarke did at Seekonk, or Isaac McCoy to the Indians. May some middle-aged man with zeal and the power of God preach and turn a community upside down like Shubal Stearns and Daniel Marshall. May some old man dream a dream like David Thomas and John Gano, and head for a needy place knowing that the time is short. May God grant a Rachel Thurber Scammon or a Sara Barton Murphy to do what is needed while the time is at hand. With consecration such as this, perhaps God would visit this vine.

We have attempted to preserve the record of power and passion, which consumed our forefathers in their fervent quest for souls. No warm-hearted person can read of such exploits in a dull drone.

We have seen the suffering and sacrifice made by our forefathers. We have witnessed them defending believer's baptism by immersion. We have reported the monumental effort to birth churches and save the country. May embers be stirred, may flames wave over us, pressing us to do something about our country's current course of destruction and cataclysmic catastrophe.

It is evident that we Baptists have had little regard for our own heritage. Is it not because we are stupefied, yea, even deceived? Are we not leaving the doorway open for antichrist to once again dominate, control, and hunt down the *baptized churches* of Jesus Christ? It is imperative that we keep our heritage intact, restate our principles, and raise memorials to our heroic brethren.

From the time of the founding of the colonial Baptists and the immersion of George Washington, God has had a nation to use, divorced from the baptism of Rome. Since 1850 there has been a concerted effort to re-unite American with Europe. *Baptist Nation* has degenerated into "Humanist Nation" and will degenerate into "Antichrist Nation" in the future. May God have mercy on us. May He once again visit this vine.

Let us visit one last scene for our edification.

"Swearin' Jack" Waller had a nephew, Absalom Waller, who became the pastor of the Lower Spotsylvania Baptist Church in Virginia. The church became known as "Wallers" church. Waller had enjoyed many seasons of revival in the church. However, in 1817 coldness arrested the congregation and indifference set in among the people. Absalom invited Elder G. Hodgen and William Warder to address his church. When they did revival broke, something for which Absalom was not prepared. He wrote, "From this period I began to entertain an humble hope that the set time to favor our Zion was at hand."[1] When it became evident that God was going to "visit this vine," Waller recorded his thoughts in his journal:

> I was in the frequent habit of retiring into a grove of pines, where are deposited the remains of many of my relatives, together with two of my own children, for the purpose of prayer; and having, one cloudy morning, felt more than common distress in mind concerning my own situation, as to my unwillingness to forsake all for Christ. I entered my usual retreat, for the solemn purpose of seeking communion

with God. The lowering clouds, the thick cluster of pines, and also the graves of the sleeping dust, seemed greatly to increase the spirit of devotion; my very soul was lifted in strongest cries to the throne of mercy, for Divine instruction concerning the way of duty.

While I was thus engaged the thought struck me with great force indeed, that the souls of my dear departed children near whose graves I was then kneeling were at that moment in glory, singing the praises of the Lamb of God, who died for the redemption of lost sinners! And that I was surely a most ungrateful wretch, to feel unwilling to spend and be spent in the cause of Christ! I am unable to describe my feelings at that moment; I wept, under a sense of God's goodness and my own ingratitude—nay more, I fell on my face and cried out, O Lord! send me, and I will go; I will forsake all for Christ, and try to spend my last breath in exhorting sinners to repent and turn to God.[2]

The Holy Ghost then visited Absalom Waller. For nearly a year a steady stream of hungry people came to his ministry. He wrote,

The constant inquiry, "What shall we do?" and my uniform answer, was, "Believe on the Lord Jesus Christ, and you shall be saved." The ordinance of baptism was regularly administered.

After church-meeting we repaired to the river; the place was vastly convenient for the proper arrangement of the spectators; and while I beheld the multitude standing in solemn order on the banks of the river, many of whom were in tears, I was reminded of the banks of Jordan, where thousands attended the ministry of the first Baptist that ever was in the world. The service was introduced by solemn prayer and praise, and then commenced a most heavenly scene. The candidates marched down into the water in pairs, singing as they went the high praises of God; so soon as they were baptized they returned in the same order; and to behold a pair of lovely children newly baptized meeting the welcome embrace of their weeping and pious parents on the bank, afforded a feast to the enraptured minds of God's people which I am unable to describe.

The revival had now become general in three churches and having none to help me I was almost exhausted in the labors of the vineyard, as well as in continual watchings by night and by day. But the Great Head in Zion was with me and supported my feeble frame.[3]

While researching *America in Crimson Red*, my wife and I visited the Old South Presbyterian Church in Newburyport, Massachusetts. This church holds the remains of George Whitefield. Marsha Pike Landford, a member of the church for over 30 years, graciously led us to the site. It was a holy moment as we stepped down the stairs to view the crypt. The site had recently been restored by the work of the Baptist History Preservation Society. The final resting-place under the pulpit area was in need of reinforcing. The plaque also had been updated by the society because it did not contain the correct message as desired by Whitefield himself.[4] The new marker, placed beside the vault, according to Whitefield's instruction, now read:

> I AM CONTENT TO WAIT TILL THE DAY OF JUDGE-
> MENT FOR THE CLEARING
> UP OF MY CHARACTER: AND AFTER I AM
> DEAD I DESIRE NO OTHER EPITAPH
> THAN THIS, "HERE LIES G.W. WHAT
> SORT OF MAN HE WAS THE GREAT
> DAY WILL DISCOVER."

After a few moments of solemn silence, we ascended the stairs and sat in the ancient auditorium and tried to picture the scenes of the Great Awakening and the sight of Whitefield preaching in that place.

As we headed out the door, we thanked Marsha for her kindness. She asked me about my interest in George Whitefield. I simply told her that I was a grateful Baptist pastor who owed a great debt to Mr. Whitefield. She then said, "There is a lot of rich church history here in Newburyport. Except for the Baptists. The last two Baptist churches in our town have changed their names to 'community' church, or whatever." She paused and concluded, "Very strange."

All we could do was nod our heads as we turned to begin our long journey back to Missouri.

APPENDIX A

Mr. Marshall and Mr. Manuel: have you no Shame?

AN OPEN LETTER FROM JAMES BELLER TO THE
AUTHORS OF
"THE LIGHT AND THE GLORY"

The widely popular historic narrative *The Light and the Glory* is now nearly 30 years old. It continues to be a bestseller among Baptist Christian schools and home schools.

Dear Mr. Marshall and Mr. Manuel:

I am not of the belief that this letter will trouble you. But if I do not write this I will be troubled with myself. I have developed quite a controversy with you and I am anxious to remove this weight I feel is on my back, and place it squarely (in Christian love) on yours. I do not doubt for one minute you are Christian brothers, but I know from experience and history that being a Christian never exempts someone from being wrong, sometimes even cruel. I hope I will not come across as cruel, but one of my aims is to share the outrage that has come upon me as I studied and re-studied the facts of history.

I do not pretend to be a historian in the professional sort of way. I am a pastor and church planter and a lover of books. I admire with profound awe what our forefathers of the faith have accomplished. You are a part of my passion. You fueled the beginning stages of my desire to know real American history.

As a new Christian I came across your material, and although nearly a quarter of a century has passed since the publishing of your book, *The Light and the Glory*, its illustrations and thoughts are fresh as spring rain in my mind. It is well written, compelling, and enjoyable to read. Who could have imagined the impact your work would have on our generation?

It was not until I began my own journey of discovery in the ocean of history that I began to sink into a certain disillusionment toward your work. I am talking about your treatment of Roger Williams, Isaac Backus, Henry Dun-

ster, John Leland and a host of the Separate Baptists who were pillars of America's quest for independence and liberty.

While it is true that historians have rewritten history in the 20th century and much of our Christian heritage has been ignored, what gives you the right to assassinate a man of the caliber of Roger Williams and then ignore colonial America's greatest Christian patriots? I shall ask about your malignity towards Mr. Williams in a moment, but here are some pertinent questions:

When you wrote of the "Covenant Way" did you realize that most Americans would not comprehend that you were speaking of a kind of church-state relationship that had its zenith in Massachusetts in the mid 17th century? In your second volume of *The Light and Glory* you made no correction and were clearly identifiable as what I would call "Covenant Theocrats." Am I correct in saying that Covenant Theology produces the "Reformed Theological Way"—entangled in the national governments of nations where it reigns supreme? In New England, the record shows that Reformed Theological "Covenanters" tried to control the population by subjecting them to a *system*, which had infant baptism as the door of entrance.

Consider this:

The blood of Obadiah Holmes flowed from Boston Square in September of 1651. The site of his suffering was the same site of the Boston Massacre, which took place over one hundred years later. Yet the blood shed at both events was for the same cause—liberty.

Holmes was beaten at the Boston marketplace for the crime of holding an unauthorized church service.[1] He was a *baptized believer* who defied the *standing order* of the "New Israel" by visiting and preaching in the home of a Baptist. Holmes' blood along with the blood and suffering of a large number of those with "dangerous opinions" was later brought to the attention of patriots in Connecticut and Virginia. Their testimony would

---

[1] Alvah Hovey, D. D., *The Life and Times of Isaac Backus* (1858, reprint ed., Harrisonville: Gano Books, 1991), P. 162.

be a deciding factor in the establishment of true liberty in the emerging American republic. Why is there no treatment given the brave Obadiah Holmes in *The Light and the Glory*?

Consider this:

Isaac Backus of Middleborough, Massachusetts was the first Baptist historian in American history. His rejection of the laws of Massachusetts, set down by the "People of the Covenant Way," resulted in the imprisonment of his own mother. She refused to support the *standing order* church (Congregational) with tithes levied by taxation. Her resistance was no different than the patriot motto of "NO TAXATION WITHOUT REPRESENTATION." Forced taxation without representation was tyranny on the part of England and forced tithing by the *standing order* was tyranny on the part of the "Puritans." The record shows that hundreds of Baptist people lost their homes, property, and blood because of their conscientious resistance to the laws of the "Covenanted Peoples of New England."[2]

Isaac Backus faced imprisonment for refusing to support the state Congregational Church of Massachusetts. He testified before some members of the Continental Congress on behalf of religious liberty. His testimony in December of 1774 was monumental. He further petitioned the Massachusetts Assembly on behalf of the Baptists. The renowned John Hancock answered the petition in this fashion:

Resolved, that the establishment of civil and religious liberty to each denomination in the province, is the sincere wish of this Congress.[3]

How is it that in your 360-page book on our "American Christian Heritage" there is no mention of Backus?

Time does not permit similar queries about Elijah Craig, Samuel Harriss, Jack Waller, James Ireland, and John Weatherford. A total of 43 Baptist preachers were jailed in the state

of Virginia for unlicensed preaching. This was in the years just prior to the sacrifice and tears of the Revolution.

It is a fact that the great Separate Baptist revival, led by church planters trained by Shubal Stearns, resulted in a large number of Baptist converts and churches in the state of Virginia. They became the largest religious body in the state and influenced the "Old Dominion" to embrace the patriot movement.

Consider this:

John Leland, the fabulous Baptist pastor and patriot from New England was providentially transplanted to Virginia at the time of the ratification of the United State Constitution. The policy of the Episcopal Church of Virginia and the old provincial government was to jail Baptist preachers. James Madison feared the new constitution would not be approved in Virginia due to the lack of protection of her preachers. Madison met with John Leland and promised the preacher a written "Bill of Rights" attached to the constitution that would guarantee full religious liberty and the distinct prohibition of the establishment of a state church. This was tantamount in the emergence of the Christian nation we became.[4]

This man Leland, whom history insists "brokered the Bill of Rights" for all Americans, is a non-entry in *The Light and the Glory*. How is it that you found space in your 360-page book to give us the run down on the "great work" of Jesuit missionaries, yet Leland is not mentioned in your narrative? In addition, I would really be interested in an explanation of your pro-Romish leanings which betray the fact that you are Presbyterians with a Reformed theological slant.

Most importantly consider this:

I speak of your treatment of Roger Williams and your opinion of him. In turning to page 191 of *The Light and the Glory*, I find this amazing statement:

---

[2] William Cathcart, D. D., *The Baptists and the American Revolution* (Philadelphia: S.A. George and Company, 1876), P. 10-18.

[3] Hovey, *Life of Backus*, 222-223.

[4] E. Wayne Thompson and David L. Cummins, *This Day in Baptist History* (Greenville: Bob Jones University Press, 1993), P. 66.

The most amazing part of this ongoing miracle in God's new Israel was that it involved so many individuals, **each of whom had his own free-will choice to either be actively committed or remain passively rebellious.** God was planting a new vineyard, and many chose to be rooted into it as living vines.

No doubt you were banking on weak scholarship and fearful Baptist historians to get away with this totally false statement about free will choice. THERE WAS NO SUCH FREE WILL CHOICE, BAPTISTS WERE BANISHED, AND QUAKERS WERE HANGED. Of this you must have been aware. But because you think like Augustine, Zwingli and the Inquisition it is much easier to cover or ignore the truth.

Marshall and Manuel wrote:

Williams is tragic, self-righteous, impossible, arrogant, judgmental...From the moment he stepped off the boat, he brought anguish to the hearts of all who came to know him. Because to know him was to like him, no matter how impossible were the tenets he insisted upon. And they *were* impossible. Williams insistence upon absolute purity in the Church, beyond all normal extremes, grew out of his own personal obsession with having to be right—in doctrine, in conduct, in church associations—in short, in every area of life. This need to be right colored everything he did or thought; indeed, it drove him into one untenable position after another.[5]

I suppose that you wanted Mr. Williams to violate scripture in order to fit in, but he was governed by 1 Thessalonians 5:21: *Prove all things; hold fast that which is good.* Of course we are to assume you believe the *Congregationalists* of New England were not concerned with being right. Right?

You continued your assault on Williams thus:

For the alternative—facing up to one's self-righteousness and repenting of it on a continuing basis—was more than he could bring himself to accept.[6]

In this statement you show your Augustinian arrogance by chastising Mr. Williams the same way Augustine chastised the Donatists. Augustine condemned (to death) the Donatists for being self-righteous and for RE-BAPTIZING former Catholics.

Historians such as Isaac Backus, James Ernst and Emily Easton paint a different picture of Williams. In their view, he was eloquent, fair, brave and selfless. He frankly forgave a greedy brother who cheated him out of his inheritance.[7] He willingly uprooted his family and moved to Rhode Island where his efforts with the Native Americans saved hundreds of English lives.[8] His formulated plans to evangelize the Native Americans. He was the first to learn their language and the first to demand fairness in dealing with their land.

All equitable historians agree that Williams found fault with 1.) *The Law of Patents* and 2.) The punishment of *First Table* violations by human government.

We understand the *Law of Patents* being the Divine right of Kings to confiscate foreign lands from natives. This was Williams's first argument with John Cotton. We further understand that Williams believed that the government should not enforce the *First Table* (the first four commandments—man's responsibility to God.) His preaching on these subjects lead to his banishment to Rhode Island.[9]

Your most disturbing indictment of Mr. Williams has to do with your opinion on his refusal to assume preaching duties at the Boston Church. You correctly say that John Winthrop invited him. But you imply that his Separatist ways were a shock and surprise to Winthrop. You side with the *standing order* in repeating the "new and dangerous" or "strange opinions" mantras of William Brad-

---

[5] Peter Marshall and David Manuel, *The Light and the Glory* (Tarrytown: Fleming H. Revell, 1977), P. 193.

[6] *Ibid.*

[7] James Ernst, *Roger Williams* (New York: MacMillan Co., 1932), P. 191-192.

[8] Isaac Backus, *An Abridgement to the Church History of New England* (1804; reprint ed., Boston: Harvard University, 1935), 34-35.

[9] Backus, *Abridgement*, P. 31.

ford. The truth is that his opinions were neither new, nor dangerous, nor strange.

As you should know, dissenters in old England at the turn of the 17th included the Puritans, who wanted to reform the Anglican Church; the Separatists and Independents, who wanted to break completely with the Anglican Church; and the Baptists, who rejected infant baptism. Rivers of tracts and pamphlets flooded old England long before the plans for the Massachusetts Bay Colony were formulated at John Cotton's St. Batolph Church.[10] In fact, Cotton's church was a think tank of opinion for Puritan and Separatist alike before 1630.

The astonishing truth is that Williams was friends with his future enemies while they were formulating their opinions in Old England. Mr. Williams never hid his opinions. They were anything but new, and they were anything but strange. The historian Ernst relates the record of Williams, John Cotton, and Thomas Hooker's discussions, which took place on the way to Cotton's St. Batolph's Church in Old England:

> The famous meeting brought together a goodly company of godly men at Sempringham. Even the Bishop of Lincoln aided his brethren to escape the persecutions of Laud's party. They discussed the plans for settling, financing, and governing the projected colony, and talked a great deal of Indian conversion. Here Mr. Williams met his future New England persecutors–all seeking an escape for "tender consciences."

During their ride to and from Sempringham, the three men of God carried on a lively discussion about theology and church reform, making the trip a memorable one. "Possibly, Master Cotton may call to mind that the discusser," recounts Mr. Williams, "riding with himself and one other person of precious memory, Master Hooker, to and from Sempringham, presented his arguments from Scripture why

he durst not join with them in their use of Common Prayer."[11]

I ask now, are we to believe the *standing order* was surprised at Roger Williams and his love for liberty and the freedom of dissent? Can we agree that the *standing order* was forming a new tyranny?

Probably not.

Mr. Marshall and Mr. Manuel, I take exception to your definition of the *Liberty of Conscience*. On page 193–194 of *The Light and the Glory* you define the *Liberty of Conscience* by saying:

> "Nobody is going to tell me what I should do or believe." Taken out of balance and pursued to its extremes (which is where Williams, ever the purist, invariably pursed everything), it becomes a license to disregard all authority with which we do not happen to agree at the time.[12]

Do you mean for instance, disregarding the authority of the government of England at the time of the War of Independence? I mean really, is that your true opinion of the *liberty of conscience*?

In Conclusion:

I for one, do not have "sorrow" for Mr. Williams as you have asked your naïve readers on page 199. I have nothing but admiration and respect for him.

In William Cathcart's definitive *The Baptists and the American Revolution* the Baptists of the formative years of the American republic were given proper respect. Several patriots gave favorable opinions of an entire faction of the American revolutionary movement that you completely ignore.

Thomas Jefferson

Jefferson was well known for his affection for the Baptist churches. On November 21st, 1808, in an address to the General Meeting of the Baptist of Virginia at Chesterfield, Jefferson said:

> In reviewing the history of the times through which we have passed, no portion of it gives greater satisfaction than that

---

[10] *Tracts on the Liberty of Conscience* (London: The Hanserd Knollys Society, 1846)

[11] James Ernst, *Roger Williams* (New York: MacMillan Co., 1932), P. 55.

[12] Marshall and Manuel, *The Light and the Glory*, P. 193.

which presents the efforts of the friends of religious freedom and the success with which they were crowned. And we have experienced the quiet as well as the comfort which results from leaving one to profess freely and openly those principles of religion which are the inductions of his own reason.[13]

President Washington's Sentiments about the Baptists:

Washington wrote:

I recollect with satisfaction, that the religious society, [the Baptist church] of which you are a member has been throughout America, uniformly and almost unanimously the firm friends of civil liberty, and the persevering promoters of our glorious Revolution.[14]

If the father of our country held these "dangerous" people in such high esteem why are they dung in your eyes?

Submitted passionately and respectfully,
Pastor James Beller, Arnold, Missouri.

---

[13] Cathcart, *Baptists in the Revolution*, 66-67.
[14] *Ibid.*, 69.

APPENDIX B

Which church was the first Baptist church in America?

by James R. Beller

This we read from the *Western Watchman* September 22, 1853:

The Oldest Baptist Church in America
A correspondent of the Christian Chronicle, writing from Newport, R. I., says of the First Baptist church in that city: "Though usually bearing the date of 1644, it was really constituted in 1638, and is the oldest Baptist church in America. It stands as a monument of the preserving care of God; for it is the only church in all New England that has existed for over two hundred and fifteen years, that has not departed from its original faith; every other church in New England of the same age having gone to Unitarianism. Its founder and first pastor was the distinguished Dr. John Clark, the original projector of the settlement on the island; the man who, in 1651, with Obadiah Holmes, and John Crandall, was imprisoned in Boston, and condemned to a fine, or to be whipped, for preaching Baptist sentiments in Massachusetts. It was he too, by his own unaided but preserving efforts, who obtained that distinguished character of Rhode Island, the root of our American liberties—securing perfect liberty of conscience to all. Though this church has existed two hundred and fifteen years, it has had but thirteen pastors, including Rev. S. Adlam; its present successful incumbent; and a large proportion of its present members are descended form those who first constituted the church.

Isaac Backus states on page 45 of his *Abridgement to the Church History of New England*, that Roger Williams "formed the first Baptist church in America March 1639." He further states on page 48 that the Newport church

under John Clark began in 1644. In his unabridged *History of New England, with Particular Reference to the Baptists*, Vol. 1 page 123, he says, "about the year 1644."

Backus, justifying the actions of Williams in baptizing without so-called apostolic succession (also known derisively as "se-baptism") quoted Mr. Williams' apology to John Cotton:

> As sacrifices and other acts of worship were omitted by the people of God, while his temple lay in ruins; and that they were restored again by immediate direction from Heaven, so that some such direction was necessary to restore the ordinances of baptism and the supper, since the desolation of the church in mystical Babylon.[15]

According to Isaac Backus, Roger Williams church in Providence disbanded after he could not defend his own baptism. Backus states: "In March, 1639, he was baptized by one of his brethren, and then he baptized about ten more."[16] Williams then abandoned "such administrations among them."

Thomas Crosby in his *History of the English Baptists*, said "Roger Williams' church came to nothing."[17] Evidence shows that Thomas Olney picked up the pieces and re-gathered the church at Providence. This occurred in July of 1639.

About the year 1653, the First Baptist Church of Providence experienced a church split over the controversy of "laying on of hands." Thomas Olney remained the pastor of the "Six-principled" First Baptist Church while Wickenden, Dexter and Browne began the "Five-principled" new First Baptist Church of Providence somewhere around 1652. Thomas Olney pastored the old church until his death about 1682.

The old Olney church disbanded according to Callender's discourse on page 61, and the

---

[15] Isaac Backus, *An Abridgement of the Church History of New England* (1804, reprint ed., Harvard: Harvard Library, 1935), P. 45
[16] *Ibid.*
[17] Thomas Crosby, *History of the English Baptists*, Vol. 1 (London: sp, 1734), P. 17.

Wickenden, Dexter and Browne congregation lived on as the First Baptist Church of Providence. This is the church that David Benedict testified became a prolific mother of many Baptist communities.

John Comer's papers, the most ancient record of the Baptists in America, may have indicated that the Newport church was the first in America. Unfortunately, as James Willmarth wrote, "the two manuscript volumes [of his diary] of the Rhode Island Historical Society are but a small portion of his writings, for through the centuries lay vandal hands upon manuscripts and unbound memoranda."[18]

It is evident that Callender, and then Isaac Backus, had Comer's papers when he wrote. Backus' *Abridgement* indicates this on page 156. But we do not know how much remained.

In Barrows' notes on Comer's diary, page 35, concerning the Newport church he writes:

> The organization of the First Church was effected probably early in 1638, the year of the settlement of the colony. Mr. Clarke began his ministry as soon as the colonists arrived. John Winthrop, the governor of Massachusetts, assures us of this fact in a written statement made that very year; in 1638 he affirmed that Mr. Clarke was "preacher to those of the Island."

The most obvious argument for the Newport church as the first Baptist church in America has to do with the banishment of the *Opinionists* in the winter of 1637-38. This of necessity, made them a church in the wilderness. We cannot believe that such devout people would not have formed themselves into a church in 1637. They certainly would have not waited until "about 1644," which is the date that Isaac Backus assumes. I admit it is difficult to disagree with the findings of Isaac Backus who I admire with unfeigned

respect. But surrounded by the excitements of persecution and the imposing testimony of the men of Providence and Brown University, Backus may have regarded their opinions as correct. Or, Backus simply recorded the plain fact that the Newport *version* of the 1637 wilderness church was finally and officially organized in about 1644.

John Callender became the sixth pastor of the First Baptist church in Newport, beginning his ministry in 1730. He made this footnote in his *Historical Discourse*:

> Since this was transcribed for the Press, I find some Reasons to suspect, that Mr. Williams did not form a Church of the Anabaptists, and that he never join'd with the Baptist Church there. Only, that he allowed them to be nearest the Scripture Rule, and true primitive Practice, as to the Mode and Subject of Baptism. But that he himself waited for new Apostles, etc. The most ancient inhabitants now alive, some of them above eighty Years old, who personally knew Mr. Williams, and were well acquainted with many of the original Settlers, never heard that Mr. Williams formed the Baptist Church there, but always understood that Mr. Browne, Mr. Wickenden, Mr. Dexter, Mr. Olney, Mr. Tillingast, etc, were the first Founders of that Church."[19]

If Callender is correct, then the first Baptist church in Providence began in 1639.

Callender also wrote:

> The people who came to Rhode-Island, who were Puritans of the highest Form, had desired and depended on the Assistance of Mr. Wheelwright, a famous Congregational Minister aforementioned. But he chose to go to Long-Island, where he continued some Years. In the mean Time Mr. John Clark, who was a Man of Letters,

---

[18] James W. Willmarth, Supplementary notes, *John Comer's Diary* (Providence: Published by the Rhode Island Historical Society, Edited by C. Edwin Barrows, D. D., 1893), P. 125.

[19] John Callender, *Historical Discourse on the Civil and Religious Affairs of Rhode Island* (Boston: Kneeland and Green, 1734), P. 56.

carried on a publick Worship at the first coming."[20]

Which means they had church services in 1638. I believe they were simply carrying over what they had begun in the New Hampshire wilderness the previous winter.

Callender, having already confirmed the 1638 ministry of John Clarke on the Island, makes this statement, "It is *said*, that in 1644, Mr. John Clarke, and some others, formed a Church on the Scheme and Principle of the Baptists." The meaning is clear, that the church had already commenced in 1638, and the official forming may have been 1644. He continues by saying, "It is *certain* that in 1648 there were fifteen Members in full Communion." The meaning here is also clear, that the first official record of any kind does not appear until 1648.[21]

Dr. S. Adlam became the pastor of the First Baptist Church of Newport, Rhode Island in 1850. He soon discovered that the Warren Association, of which the Newport church belonged, had recently examined the confusion concerning the first Baptist church in Rhode Island and the first Baptist church in America. The Warren Association concluded that the Newport church had formed first. This caused Adlam to set forth his arguments that John Clarke and the church at Newport formed the first Baptist church. At the conclusion of his booklet, *The First Church in Providence, not the Oldest Baptist Church in America*, the clerk of the Newport church, Asa Hildreth, wrote the following:

The matter of the formation of the First Baptist Church was brought before the Warren Association at its meeting in 1847, and at the annual meeting of the association in 1848 the following votes were passed by that body:

First—That the date of 1638, inserted under the name of the First Baptist Church in Newport, contained in the tabular estimate in the minutes of last year, be stricken out and the date (1644) be inserted, as in the minutes of the years preceding.

Second—That a committee, consisting of T. C. Jameson, J. P. Tustin, and Levi Hale, be appointed to inquire into the evidence as to the date of the First Baptist Church in Newport, with instructions to report at the next session of the association.

This committee reported in 1849, that they are of the opinion that this church was formed certainly before the 1st of May, 1639, and probably on the 7th of March, 1638.

This called out a review of the fore-named report by a committee of the First Baptist Church in Providence, whose report is dated August 22, 1850, which led Rev. S. Adlam, who had just settled over the first Church in Newport, to make a thorough investigation of the matter which resulted in his book upon the First Baptist Church in Providence.

It was expected that this book would call out a reply from some one of the First Church in Providence, as there were several very able members of that church [who were] professors in Brown University, but as no reply came, Mr Adlam asked one of their ablest men (I am reliably informed) when his little book was to be answered? He replied: "**It is unanswerable**."[22]

The above finding was either ignored or overlooked by the historians Thomas Armitage and William Cathcart. Those historians copied from David Benedict, who copied from Isaac Backus. A host of others have followed suit. The Baptists of America are continually pointed to the First Baptist Church of Providence as the first in America. It is high time to stop.

---

[20] John Callender, *Historical Discourse on the Civil and Religious Affairs of Rhode Island* (Boston: Kneeland and Green, 1734), P. 62.

[21] Callender, *Discourse*, P. 62.

[22] S. Adlam, D. D., *The First Church in Providence not the Oldest Baptist Church in America*, (Texarkana: Baptist Sunday School Committee, 1939).

The truth is, Roger Williams baptized no one legitimately, trained no preachers, and birthed no churches. First Baptist of Providence presently accepts any mode of baptism from any denomination as legitimate, and no longer insists on the new birth as a prerequisite for membership.

APPENDIX C

The Confession of Dr. John Clarke

The decree of God is that whereby he hath from eternity set down with himself what shall come to pass in time, Eph. 1:11. All things, with their cases, effects, circumstances, and manner of being, are decreed by God, Acts 2:23.

This decree is most wise, Rom. 11:33; Most just, Rom 9:13-14; Eternal, Eph. 1:4-5, IIThess. 2:13; Necessary, Psalm 33:11, Prov. 19:21; Unchangeable, Heb 6:17; Most free, Rom 9:18; And the cause of all good, James 1:17; But not of any sin, I John 1:5.

The special decree of God concerning angels and men is called predestination, Rom. 8:30. Of the former, viz. angels, little is spoken in the Holy Scriptures; of the latter more is revealed, not unprofitable to be known. It may be defined the wise, free, just, eternal and unchangeable sentence or decree of God, determining to create and govern men for his special glory, viz. the praise of his glorious mercy and justice, Rom. 9:17-18 and 11:36.

Election is the decree of God, of His free love, grace and mercy, choosing some men to faith, holiness, and eternal life, for the praise of his glorious mercy, IThess. 1:4, IIThess. 2:13, Rom. 8:29-30. The cause which moved the Lord to elect them who are chosen was none other but his mere good will and pleasure, Luke 12:32. The end is the manifestation of the riches and of His grace and mercy, Rom 9:23, Eph. 1:6.

The sending of Christ, faith, holiness and eternal life, are the effects of his love, by which He manifesteth the infinite riches of His grace. In the same order God doth execute this decree in time, he did decree it in his eternal counsel, IThess 5:9, IIThess 2:13. Sin is the effect of man's free will, and condemnation is an effect of justice inflicted upon man for sin and disobedience. A man in this life may be sure of his election, IIPeter 1:10, IThess. 1:4. Yea, of his eternal happiness, but not of his eternal reprobation; for he that is now profane, may be called hereafter.[23]

Author's note From his confession we may conclude that John Clarke was mildly Calvinistic without some of the absurdities of supralapsarianism. His was not a creed of "antimissionary" sentiment. According to Clarke, a man can know he is elect but cannot know he is reprobated. Therefore room is left in his life for "experimental religion," the experience of a new birth from on high. As Dr. Clarke wrote, "he may be called hereafter."

---

[23] Isaac Backus, *An Abridgement of the Church History of New England* (1804, reprint ed., Harvard: Harvard Library, 1935) P. 114-115.

APPENDIX D

The First Statement of the Rhode Island Charter Granted by King Charles II,

Secured by Dr. John Clarke on July 8, 1663. The charter was in force until the constitution, which was adopted in November 1842, became operative the first Tuesday of May 1843.

CHARLES the Second, by the Grace of God, King of England, Scotland, France and Ireland, Defender of the Faith, &c., to all to whom these presents shall come, greeting: Whereas, we have been informed, by the petition of our trusty and well-beloved subject, John Clarke, on the behalf of Benjamin Arnold, William Brenton, William Codington, Nicholas Easton, William Boulston, John Porter, John Smith, Samuel Gorton, John Weeks, Roger Williams, Thomas Olney, Gregory Dexter, John Coggeshall, Joseph Clarke, Randall Holden, John Greene, John Roome, Samuel Wildbore, William Field, James Barker, Richard Tew, Thomas Harris, and William Dyre, and the rest of the purchasers and free inhabitants of our island, called Rhode Island, and the rest of the colony of Providence Plantations, in the Narragansett Bay, in New England, in America, that they, pursuing, with peaceable and loyal minds, their sober, serious, and religious intentions, of godly edifying themselves, and one another, in the holy Christian faith and worship, as they were persuaded; together with the gaining over and conversion of the poor ignorant Indian natives, in those parts of America, to the sincere profession and obedience of the same faith and worship, did, not only by the consent and good encouragement of our royal progenitors, transport themselves out of this kingdom of England into America, but also, since their arrival there, after their first settlement amongst other our subjects in those parts, for the avoiding of discord, and those many evils which were likely to ensure upon some of those subjects not being able to bear, in these remote parts, their different

apprehensions in religious concernments, and in pursuance of the aforesaid ends, did once again leave their desirable stations and habitations, and with excessive labor and travel, hazard and charge did transplant themselves into the midst of the Indian natives, who as we are informed, are the most potent princes and people of all that country; where, by the good Providence of God, from whom the Plantations have taken their name, upon their labor and industry, they have not only been preserved to admiration, but have increased and prospered, and are seized and possessed, by purchase and consent of the said natives, to their full content, of such lands, islands, rivers, harbors and roads, as are very convenient, both for plantations, and also for building of ships, supply of pipe-staves, and other merchandise; and which lie very commodius, in many respects, for commerce, and to accommodate our southern plantations, and may much advance the trade of this our realm, and greatly enlarge the territories thereof; they having by near neighborhood to and friendly society with the great body of the Narragansett Indians, given them encouragement of their own accord, to subject themselves, their people and lands, unto us; whereby, as is hoped, there may, in time, by the blessing of God upon their endeavors be laid a sure foundation of happiness to all America: And whereas, in their humble address, they have freely declared, that it is much on their hearts (if they may be permitted) to hold forth a lively experiment, that a most flourishing civil state may stand and best be maintained, and that among our English subjects, with a full liberty in religious concernments; and that true piety rightly grounded upon gospel principles, will give the best and greatest security to sovereignty, and will lay in the hearts of men the strongest obligations to true loyalty: Now, know ye, that we, being willing to encourage the hopeful undertaking of our said loyal and loving subjects, and to secure them in the free exercise and enjoyment of all their civil and religious rights, appertaining to them, as our loving subjects; and to preserve unto them that liberty in the true Christian faith and worship of God, which they have sought with so much travail, and with peaceable minds, and loyal subjection to our royal progenitors and ourselves, to enjoy; and because some of the people and inhabitants of the same colony cannot, in their private opinions, conform to the public exercise of religion, according to the liturgy, forms and ceremonies of the Church of England, or take or subscribe the oaths and articles made and established in that behalf; and for that the same, by reason of the remote distances of those places will (as we hope) be no breach of the unity and uniformity established in this nation: Have therefore thought fit, and do hereby publish, grant, ordain and declare, That our royal will and pleasure is, that no person within the said colony, at any time hereafter shall be any wise molested, punished, disquieted, or called in question, for any differences in opinion in matters of religion, and do not actually disturb the civil peace of our said colony; but that all and every person and persons may, from time to time, and at all times hereafter, freely and fully have and enjoy his and their own judgments and consciences, in matters of religious concernments, throughout the tract of land hereafter mentioned, they behaving themselves peaceable and quietly, and not using this liberty to licentiousness and profaneness, nor to the civil injury or outward disturbance of others, any law, statute, or clause therein contained, or to be contained, usage or custom of this realm, to the contrary hereof, in any wise notwithstanding. And that they may be in the better capacity to defend themselves, in their just rights and liberties, against all the enemies of the Christian faith, and others, in all respects, we have further thought fit, and at the humble petition of the persons aforesaid are graciously pleased to declare, That they shall have and enjoy the benefit of our late act of indemnity and free pardon, as the rest of our subjects in other our dominions and territories have; and to create and make them a body politic or corporate, with the powers and privileges hereinafter mentioned.

APPENDIX E

James Manning's Memorial

This address was delivered to the Massachusetts delegation to the Continental Congress on October 14, 1774. The grievance committee of the Philadelphia Association drew up the memorial and James Manning read it.

It has been said by a celebrated writer in politics that but two things were worth contending for—Religion and Liberty. For the latter we are at present nobly exerting ourselves through all this extensive continent; and surely no one whose bosom feels the patriot glow in behalf of civil liberty, can torpid to the more ennobling flame of RELIGIOUS FREEDOM.

The free exercise of private judgment, and the unalienable rights of conscience, are of too high a rank and dignity to be subjected to the decrees of councils, or the imperfect laws of fallible legislators, The merciful Father of mankind is the alone Lord of conscience. Establishments may be enabled to confer worldly distinctions and secular importance. They may make hypocrites, but cannot create Christians. They have been reared by craft of power, but liberty never flourished perfectly under their control. That liberty, virtue, and public happiness can be supported without them, this flourishing province (Pennsylvania) is a glorious testimony; and a view of it would be sufficient to invalidate all the most elaborate arguments ever adduced in support of them. Happy in the enjoyment of these undoubted rights, and conscious of their high import, every lover of mankind must be desirous, as far as opportunity offers, of extending and securing the enjoyment of these inestimable blessings.

These reflections have arisen from considering the unhappy situation of our brethren the Baptists, in the province of Massachusetts Bay, for whom we now appear as advocates; and from the important light in which liberty in general is now beheld, we trust our representation will be effectual. The province of the Massachusetts Bay, being settled by persons who fled from civil and religious oppression, it would be natural to imagine them deeply impressed with the value of liberty, and boldly scorning a domination over conscience. But such was the complexion of the times, they fell from the unhappy state of being oppressed, to the more deplorable and ignoble one of becoming oppressors.

But these things being passed over, we intend to begin with the charter obtained at the happy restoration. This charter grants, "that there shall be liberty of conscience allowed in the worship of God, to all Christians except Papists, inhabiting or which shall inhabit or be resident within this province or territory;" or in the words of the late Governor Hutchinson, "We find nothing in the new charter, of an ecclesiastical constitution, Liberty of conscience is granted to all except Papists."

The first General Court that met under this charter, returned their thanks for the following sentiments delivered before them; "That the magistrate is most properly the officer of human society; that a Christian by non-conformity to this or that imposed way of worship, does not break the terms upon which he is to enjoy the benefits of human society; and that a man has a right to his estate, his liberty, and his family, notwithstanding his non-conformity." And on this declaration the historian who mentions it, plumes himself, as if the whole future system of an impartial administration was to begin. By laws made during the first charter, such persons only were entitled to vote for civil rulers as were church-members.

This might be thought by some to give a shadow of ecclesiastical power; but by the present [charter] "Every freeholder of thirty pounds sterling per annum, and every other inhabitant who has forty pounds personal estate, are voters for representatives." So that there seems an evident foundation to presume they are only elected for the preservation of civil rights, and the management of temporal concernments. Nevertheless they soon began to assume the power of establishing Congregational worship, and taxed all the inhabitants towards its support; and no Act was passed to exempt other denominations from   1692 to

1727, when the Episcopalians were permitted to enjoy their rights.

The first Act for the relief of the Baptists was in 1728, when their polls only were exempted from taxation, and not their estates; and then only of such as lived within five miles of a Baptist meeting-house. The next year 1729, thirty persons were apprehended and confined in Bristol jail; some churchmen, some Friends, but most of the Baptist denomination. Roused by these oppressions, the Baptists and Quakers petitioned the General Court; being determined if they could not obtain redress, to apply to his Majesty in council. Wherefore the same year, a law was passed exempting their estates and polls; but clogged however with a limitation, for less than five years. At the expiration of this act, in 1733, our brethren were obliged again to apply to the General Assembly; upon which a third Act was passed in 1734, exempting Baptists from paying ministerial taxes. This third Act was more clear, accurate and better drawn than any of the former; but for want of a penalty on the returning officer, badly executed, subjecting our brethren to many hardships and oppressions. This Act expired in 1740, and another was made for seven years; but still liable to the same defects. In 1747, the Baptists and Friends, wearied with fruitless applications to the assemblies, once more proposed applying at home for relief, when the laws exempting them were reenacted for ten years, the longest space ever granted.

To show what the liberty was that these unhappy people enjoyed, it will be necessary, though we aim as much as possible at brevity, just to mention that if at any time a Baptist sued a collector for the breach of these laws, any damages he recovered were laid on the town, and the Baptists residing therein were thereby obliged to pay their proportionable part towards his indemnification. At this time such as instance occurred in the case of Sturbridge, when Jonathan Perry sued the collector, Jonathan Mason, and the damages were sustained by the town, though the Baptists in town meeting dissented. And here it may not be improper to observe that the judges and jury are under the strongest bias to determine for the defendants.

In the beginning of the year 1753 an act was passed, breaking in upon the time limited, enacting that "no minister or member of an Anabaptist church shall be esteemed qualified to give certificates, other than such as shall have obtained, from three other churches commonly called Anabaptist, in this or the neighboring Provinces, certificate from each respectively, that they esteem such church of their denomination, and that the conscientiously believe them to be Anabaptists."

But not to take too much of your time, we would here just observe that all the laws have been made temporary, and without any penalty on the collector or assessor for the breach of the law, and come more particularly to speak of the law passed at the last June session; as it has been generally understood to be so framed as to take away complaint and establish a general liberty of conscience. This act is like all the others, temporary, and indeed limited to a shorter duration than most of them, being only for three years. It is without any penalty on the breach of it, and an additional trouble and expense is enjoined by recording the certificates every year, (though in some others obtaining one certificate during the existence of the law was sufficient) and concludes thus; "That nothing in this act shall be construed to exempt any proprietor of any new township from paying his part and portion with the major part of the other proprietors of such new township, in settling a minister and building a meeting-house, which hath been or shall be required as a condition of their grant."

And here we would just add a few words relative to the affairs of Ashfield.

On the 26th day of December next, three lots of land belonging to people of our denomination, will be exposed for sale; one of them for the payment of so small a sum as ten shillings eleven pence. Although we have given but two instance of oppression under the above laws, yet a great number can be produced, well attested, when called for.

Upon this short statement of facts we would observe, that the charter must be looked upon by every impartial eye to be infringed, so soon as any law was passed for the establishment of any particular mode of worship. All Protestants are placed upon the same footing; and no law whatever could disannul so essential a part of a charter intended to communicate the blessings of a free government to his majesty's subjects. Under the first charter, as was hinted, church-membership conferred the rights of a free-man; but by the second, the possession of property was the foundation. Therefore, how could it be supposed that the collective body of the people intended to confer any other power upon their representatives that that of making laws relative to property and the concerns of this life?

Men unite in society, according to the great Mr. Locke, "with an intention in every one the better to preserve himself, his liberty and property. The power of the society, of Legisla-ture constituted by them, can never be supposed to extend any further that the common good, but is obliged to secure every one's property." To give laws, to receive obedience, to compel with the sword, belong to none but the civil magistrate; and on this ground *we affirm* that the magistrate's power extends not to the establishing of any articles of faith or forms of worship, by force of laws; for laws are of no force without penalties. The care of souls cannot belong to the civil magistrate, because his power consists only in outward force; but pure and saving religion consists in the inward persuasion of the mind, without which nothing can be acceptable to God.

It is a just position, and cannot be too firmly established, that we can have no property in that which another may take, when he pleased, to himself; neither can we have the proper enjoyment of our religious liberties, (which must be acknowledged to be of greater value) if held by the same unjust and capri-cious tenure; and this must appear to be the case when temporary laws pretend to grant relief so very inadequate.

It may now be asked—What is the liberty desired? The answer is; as the kingdom of Christ is not of this world, and religion is a concern between God and the soul with which no human authority can intermeddle; consistently with the principles of Christian-ity, and according to the dictates of Protes-tantism, we claim and expect the liberty of worshipping God according to our con-sciences, not being obliged to support a minis-try we cannot attend, whilst we deem our-selves as faithful subjects. These we have an undoubted right to, as men, as Christians, and by charter as inhabitants of Massachusetts Bay.[24]

---

[24] Alvah Hovey, *The Life and Times of Isaac Backus* (1858; reprint ed., Gano Books, 1991), P. 204-210.

APPENDIX F

The Virginia Act for Religious Liberty

by Thomas Jefferson

Progression of Virginia religious law:

1623 Law of Tithes to the Church of England Clergy

1633 Law of Tithes repealed

1643 Church of England officially established in Virginia.

1659-1660 Quakers imprisoned or banished

1661 Law for the construction of church buildings in each parish and vestries appointed.

1776 October. Ten-thousand name petition, Episcopal clergy tax revoked in Virginia

1779 **The Virginia Act for Religious Liberty was written and introduced by Thomas Jefferson, but was not passed.**

1784 The Church of England disestablished, the Protestant Episcopalian has a brief "Incorporation"

1785 James Madison's Memorial and Remonstrance, a treatise against the General Assessment Bill published

1786 January 19. **The Virginia Statute for Religious Liberty, written by Thomas Jefferson, becomes law in Virginia.**

1786 "Incorporation" of the Protestant Episcopal Church in Virginia repealed, all religious properties are given into the hands of the churches individually, the state of Virginia to hold no ties to the Episcopal church.

1788-9 The *Great* Virginia Revival

1798 Official repeal of any vestry laws wedding the old established church to the state of Virginia leaving all religious "sects" on equal ground

1791, December 15, Bill of Rights ratified.

The Virginia Act for Religious Liberty[25]

Well assured that the opinions and belief of men depend not on their own will, but follow involuntarily the evidence proposed to their minds; that Almighty God hath created the mind free, and manifested his supreme will that free it shall remain by making it altogether insusceptible of restraint; that all attempts to influence it by temporal punishments, or burthens, or by civil incapacitations, tend only to beget habits of hypocrisy and meanness, and are a departure from the plan of the holy author of our religion, who being Lord both of body and mind, yet chose not to propagate it by coercions on either, as was in His Almighty power to do, *but to extend it by its influence on reason alone;* that the impious presumption of legislators and rulers, civil as well as ecclesiastical, who, being themselves but fallible and uninspired men, have assumed dominion over the faith of others, setting up their own opinions and modes of thinking as the only true and infallible, and as such endeavoring to impose them on others, hath established and maintained false religions over the greatest part of the world and through all time: That to compel a man to furnish contributions of money for the propagation of opinions which he disbelieves *and abhors,* is sinful and tyrannical; that even the forcing him to support this or that teacher of his own religious persuasion, is depriving him of the comfortable liberty of giving his contributions to the particular pastor whose morals he would make his pattern, and whose powers he feels most persuasive to righteousness; and is withdrawing from the ministry those temporary rewards, which proceeding from an approbation of their personal conduct, are an additional incitement to earnest and unremitting labours for the instruction of mankind; that our civil rights have no dependence on our religious opinions, any more than our opinions in physics or geometry; that therefore the proscribing any citizen as unworthy

---

[25] Edwin S. Gaustad, *A Documentary History of Religion in America* (Grand Rapids: William B. Eerdmans Publishing Company, 1982), P. 259.

the public confidence by laying upon him an incapacity of being called to offices of trust and emolument, unless he profess or renounce this or that religious opinion is depriving him injuriously of those privileges and advantages to which, in common with his fellow citizens, he has a natural right; that it tends also to corrupt the principles of that *very* religion it is meant to encourage, by bribing, with a monopoly of world honours and emoluments, those who will externally profess and conform it; that though indeed these are criminal who do not withstand such temptation, yet neither are those innocent who lay the bait in their way; that the opinions of men are not the object of civil government, nor under its jurisdiction; that to suffer the civil magistrate to intrude his powers into the field of opinion and to restrain the profession or propagation of principles on supposition of their ill tendency is a dangerous fallacy, which at once destroys all religious liberty, because he being of course judge of that tendency will make his opinions the rule of judgment, and approve or condemn the sentiments of others only as they shall square with or differ from his own; that it is time enough for the rightful purposes of civil government for its officers to interfere when principles break out into overt acts against peace and good order; and finally, that truth is great and will prevail if left to herself; that she is the proper and sufficient antagonist to error, and has nothing to fear from the conflict unless by human interposition disarmed of her natural weapons, free argument and debate; errors ceasing to be dangerous when it is permitted freely to contradict them.

We the General Assembly of Virginia do enact that no man shall be compelled to frequent or support any religious worship, place, or ministry whatsoever, nor shall be enforced, restrained, molested, or burthened in his body or goods, nor shall otherwise suffer, on account of his religious opinions or belief; but that all men shall be free to profess, and by argument to maintain, their opinions in matters of religion, and that the same shall in no wise diminish, enlarge, or affect their civil capacities.

And though we well know that this Assembly, elected by the people for the ordinary purposes of legislation only, have no power to restrain the acts of succeeding Assemblies, constituted with powers equal to our own, and that therefore to declare this act irrevocable would be of no effect in law; yet we are free to declare, and do declare, that the rights hereby asserted are of the natural rights of mankind, and that if any act shall be hereafter passed to repeal the present or to narrow its operation, such act will be an infringement of natural right.

APPENDIX G

James Madison's
Memorial and Remonstrance

We the subscribers, citizens of the said Commonwealth, having taken into serious consideration a bill, printed by order of the last session of General Assembly, entitled, "A bill establishing a provision for teachers of the Christian Religion;" and conceiving, that the same, if finally armed with the sanction of a law, will be a dangerous abuse of power; are bound, as faithful members of a free State, to remonstrate against it, and to declare the reasons by which we are determined. We remonstrate against the said bill.

Because we hold it for a fundamental and unalienable truth, "that religion, or the duty which we owe to the Creator, and the manner of discharging it, can be directed only by reason and conviction, not by force or violence." The religion, then, of every man, must be left to the conviction and conscience of every man; and it is the right of every man to exercise it as these may dictate. This right is, in its nature, an unalienable right. It is unalienable, because the opinions of men depending only on the evidence contemplated by their own minds, cannot follow the dictates of other men. It is unalienable, also, because what is here a right towards man, is a duty towards the Creator. It is the duty of every man to render to the Creator such homage, and such only, as he believes to be acceptable to him. This duty is precedent both in order and time, and in degree of obligation, to the claims of civil society, he must be considered as a subject of the Governor of the Universe. And if a member of civil society, who enters into any subordinate association, must always do it with a reservation of his duty to the general authority; much more must every man, who becomes a member of any particular civil society, do it with a saving of his allegiance to the Universal Sovereign. We maintain, therefore, that in matters of religion, no man's rights is abridged by the institution of civil society; and that religion is wholly exempt from its cognizance. True it us, that

no other rule exists, by which any question, which may divide society, can be ultimately determined, but by the will of a majority; but it is also true, that the majority may trespass on the rights of the minority.

Because if religion be exempt from the authority of the society at large, still less can it be subject to that of the legislative body. The latter are but the creatures and vicegerents of the former. Their jurisdiction is both derivative and limited. It is limited with regard to the co-ordinate departments; more necessarily, it is limited with regard to the constituents. The preservation of a free government requires, not merely that the metes and bounds which separate each department of power, be invariably maintained; but more especially that neither of them be suffered to overleap the great barrier which defends the rights of the people. The rulers, who are guilty of such an encroachment, exceed the commission from which they derive their authority, and are tyrants. The people who submit to it, are governed by laws made neither by themselves, nor by an authority derived from them, and are slaves.

Because it is proper to take alarm at the first experiment on our liberties, we hold this prudent jealousy to be first duty of citizens, and one of the noblest characteristics of the late revolution. The freemen of America did not wait until usurped power had strengthened itself by exercise, and entangled the question in precedents. They saw all the consequences in the principle, and they avoided the consequences by denying the principle. We revere this lesson too much, soon to forget it. Who does not see that the same authority, which can establish Christianity in exclusion of all other religions, may establish, with the same ease, any particular sect of Christians, in exclusion of all other sects; that the same authority, which can force a citizen to contribute three pence only of his property, for the support of any one establishment, may force him to conform to any other establishment, in all cases whatsoever?

Because the bill violates that equality which ought to be the basis of every law; and which is more indispensable, in proportion as the validity or expediency of any law is more liable to be impeached. "If all men are, by nature, equally free and independent," all men are to be considered as entering into society on equal conditions, as relinquishing no more, and, therefore, retaining no less, one than another, of their natural rights; above all, are they to be considered as retaining an "equal title to the free exercise of religion according to the dictates of conscience." Whilst we assert for ourselves a freedom to embrace, to profess, and observe the religion which we believe to be of divine origin, we cannot deny an equal freedom to those, whose minds have not yet yielded to the evidence which has convinced us. If this freedom be abused, it is an offense against God, not against man. To God, therefore, and not to man, must be account of it be rendered.

As the bill violates equality, by subjecting some to peculiar burdens; so it violates the same principle, by granting to others peculiar exemptions. Are the Quakers and Menonists the only sects who think a compulsive support of their religions unnecessary and unwarrantable? Can their piety alone be entrusted with the care of publick worship? Ought their religions to be endowed, above all others, with extraordinary privileges, by which proselytes may be entitled from all others? We think too favourably of the justice and good sense of these denominations, to believe, that they either covet pre-eminences over their fellow-citizens, or that they will be seduced by them from the common opposition to the measure.

Because the bill implies, either that the civil magistrate is a competent judge of religious truths, or that he may employ religion as an engine of civil policy. The first is an arrogant pretension, falsified by the extraordinary opinion of rulers, in all ages, and throughout the world; the second, an unhallowed perversion of the means of salvation.

Because the establishment proposed by the bill, is not requisite for the support of the Christian religion itself; for every page of it disavows a dependence on the power of this world; it is a contradiction to fact, for it is known that this religion both existed and flourished, not only without the support of human laws, but in spite of every opposition from them; and not only during the period of

miraculous aid, but long after it had been left to its own evidence and the ordinary care of Providence: nay, it is a contradiction in terms; for a religion not invented by human policy, must have pre-existed and been supported, before it was established by human policy: it is, moreover, to weaken in those, who profess this religion, a pious confidence in its innate excellence, and the patronage of its Author; and to foster in those, who still reject it, a suspicion that its friends are too conscious of its faculties, to trust it to its own merits.

Because experience witnesses that ecclesiastical establishments, instead of maintaining the purity and efficacy of religion, have had a contrary operation. During almost fifteen centuries has the legal establishment of Christianity been on trial. What have been its fruits? More or less in all places, pride and indolence in the clergy; ignorance and servility in the laity; in both, superstition, bigotry, and persecution. Inquire of the teachers of Christianity for the ages in which it appeared in its greatest lustre; those of every sect point to the ages prior to its incorporation with civil policy. Propose a restoration of this primitive state, in which its teachers depended on the voluntary rewards of their flocks, many of them predict its downfall. On which side ought their testimony to have the greatest weight, when for, or when against their interest?

Because the establishment in question is not necessary for the support of civil government. If it be urged as necessary for the support of civil government, only as it is a means of supporting religion, and it be not necessary for the latter purpose, it cannot be necessary for the former. If religion be not within the cognizance of civil government, how can its legal establishment be said to be necessary to civil government? What influence, in fact, have ecclesiastical establishments had on civil society? In some instances, they have been seen to erect a spiritual tyranny on the ruins of the civil authority; in more instances, have they been seen upholding the thrones of political tyranny; in no instance have they been seen the guardians of the liberties of the people. Rulers who wished to subvert the publick liberty, may have found on established clergy convenient auxiliaries. A just government instituted to secure and perpetuate it needs them not. Such a government will be best supported by protecting every citizen in the enjoyment of his religion, with the same equal hand which protects his person and property; by neither invading the equal hand which protects his person and property; by neither invading the equal rights of any sect, nor suffering any sect to invade those of another.

Because the proposed establishment is a departure from that generous policy, which, offering an asylum to the persecuted and oppressed of every nation and religion, promised a lustre to our country, and an accession to the number of its citizens. What a melancholy mark is the bill, of sudden degeneracy? Instead of holding forth an asylum to the persecuted, it is itself a signal of persecution. It degrades from the equal rank of citizens, all of those whose opinions in religion do not bend to those of the legislative authority. Distant as it may be, in its present form, from the inquisition, it differs from it only in degree: the one is the first step, the other the last, in the career of intolerance. The magnanimous sufferer under the cruel scourge in foreign regions, must view the bill as a beacon on our coast, warning him to seek some other haven, where liberty and philanthropy in their due extent may offer a more certain repose for his troubles.

Because it will have a like tendency to banish our citizens. The allurements presented by other situations are every day thinning their number. To superadd a fresh motive to emigration, by revoking the liberty which they now enjoy, would be the same species of folly, which has dishonoured and depopulated flourishing kingdoms.

Because it will destroy that moderation and harmony, which the forbearance of our laws to intermeddle with religion has produced among its several sects. Torrents of blood have been spilt in the old world, by vain attempts of the secular arm to extinguish religious discord, by proscribing all differences in religious opinion. Time has at length revealed the true remedy. Every relaxation of narrow and rigorous policy, wherever it has been tried, had been found to assuage the disease. The American theatre had exhibited proofs, that equal and complete liberty, if it does not wholly eradicate it, sufficiently destroys its malignant influence on the health and prosperity of the State. If, with the salutary effects of this system under our own eyes, we begin to contrast the bounds of religious freedom, we know no name that will too severely reproach our folly. At least, let warning be taken at the first fruits of the threatened innovation. The very appearance of the bill has transformed that "Christian forbearance, love, and charity," which of late mutually prevailed, into animosities and jealousies, which may not soon be appeased. What mischiefs may not be dreaded, should this enemy to the publick quiet be armed with the force of law?

Because the policy of the bill is adverse to the diffusion of the light of Christianity. The first wish of those, who ought to enjoy this precious gift, ought to be, that it may be imparted to the whole race of mankind. Compare the number of those, who have as yet received it, with the number still remaining under the dominion of false religions, and how small is the former? Does the policy of the bill tend to lessen the disproportion? No; it at once discourages those who are strangers to the light of truth, from coming into the regions of it; and countenances, by example, the nations who continue in darkness, in shutting out those who might convey it to them. Instead of leveling, as far as possible, every obstacle to the victorious progress of truth, the bill, with an ignoble and unchristian timidity, would circumscribe it, with a wall of defence against the encroachments of error.

Because an attempt to enforce by legal sanctions, acts, obnoxious to so great a portion of citizens, tends to enervate the laws in general, and to slacken the bands of society. If it is difficult to execute any law, which is not generally deemed necessary nor salutary, what must be the case when it is deemed invalid and dangerous? And what may be the effect of so striking an example of impotency in the government on its general authority?

Because a measure of such singular magnitude and delicacy, ought not to be imposed without the clearest evidence that it is called for by a majority of citizens; and no satisfactory method is yet proposed, by which the voice of the majority n this case may be determined, or its influence secured. "The people of the respective counties are, indeed, requested to signify their opinion, resecting the adoption of the bill, to the next session of Assembly." But the representation must be made equal, before the voice, either of the representatives or of the counties, will be that of the people. Our hope is, that neither of the former will, after due consideration, espouse the dangerous principle of the bill. Should the event disappoint us, it will still leave us in full confidence that a fair appeal to the latter will reverse the sentence against our liberties.

Because, finally, "the equal right of every citizen to the free exercise of his religion according to the dictates of his conscience," is held by the same tenure with all our other rights. If we recur to its origin, it is equally the gift of nature; if we consult the "Declaration of those rights which pertain to the good people of Virginia, as the basis and foundation of government," it is enumerated with equal solemnity, or rather with studied emphasis. Either then we must say, that the will of the Legislature is the only measure of their authority; and that in the plentitude of this authority, they may sweep away all our fundamental rights; or, that they are bound to leave this particular right untouched and sacred: either we must say, that they may control the freedom of the press; may abolish the trial by jury; may swallow up the executive and judiciary powers of the State; nay, that they have no authority our very right of suffrage, and erect themselves into an independent and hereditary assembly; or we must say that they have no authority to enact into a law, the bill under consideration. We the subscribers say, that the General Assembly of this Commonwealth have no such authority; and that no effort may be omitted on our part, against so dangerous an usurpation, we oppose to it this Remonstrance, earnestly praying, as we are in duty bound, that the

Supreme Lawgiver of the Universe, by illuminating those to whom it is addressed, may, on the one hand, turn their councils from every act, which would affront his holy prerogative, or violate the trust committed to them; and, on the other, guide them into every measure which may be worthy of His blessing, may redound to their own praise, and may establish more firmly the liberties, the property, and the happiness of this Commonwealth.

APPENDIX H

Excerpts from Letters in the Papers of James Madison, showing Madison's connection with Elder John Leland.

****

From James Gordon, Jr to James Madison

February 17th, 1788

Dear Sir,

Being favd. by Colo. Monroe with a sight of your letter of the 27 January and finding no mention therein of your being in our county in a short time, [I] take the Liberty as yr. Friend to solicit your attendance at March Orange court. I am induced to make such a request as I believe it will give the county in general great satisfaction to hear your sentiments on the new Constitution.

The sentiments of the people of Orange are much divided, the best men in my judgement are for the constitution but several of those who have much weight with the people are opposed, Parson Bledsoe & Leeland with Colo. Z. Burnley. Upon the whole sir I think it is incumbent on you with out delay, to repair to this state; as the loss of the constitution in this state may involve consequences the alarming to every citizen of America.

Jas Gordon Jun[26]

****

---

[26] R.A. Rutland and others, editors, *The Papers of James Madison*, (Richmond: University of Virginia, 1977), 10: 515

From John Spencer to James Madison

Orange County Febry. 28th 1788

D Sir:

Col. Thos. Barber offers as a Candedit for our March Election...amoungs his Friends appears, in a General way the Baptus's the Prechers of that Society are much alarm's fearing Relegious liberty is not sufficiently secur'd.

Several of your Connections in Orange Joines me in opinion, thinking it would Answer a Valuable purpus for I am Cartain that pople Relye much on your integerity & Candure, Mr. [John] Leeland & Mr. [Aaron] Bledsoe and [Nathaniel] Sanders are the most public men of that Society in Orange, therefore as Mr. Leeland Lyes in your Way home from Fredricksburg to Orange would advise you'l call on him & Spend a few Howers in his Company, in Clos'd youl Receive his Objections which was Sent by me to, Barber, a Coppy I tooke.

Joseph Spencer[27]

Joseph Spencer noted this:
Rev'd Joh Leeland's Objections to the Federal Constitution Sent to Col. Thos. Barber by his Request, a Coppy taken by Jos.Spencer, entended for the Consideration of Capt. Jas. Walker Culpeper.

Leland's Objections are printed in *Documentary History of the Constitution*, IV, 526-529.

****

---

[27] *Ibid.*, 540-541

From Edmund Randolph to James
Madison

Richmond Feby 29, 1788

My Dear Friend,
     The Baptist interest and the
Counties on the So. Side of Jas,
river from Isle of Wight, upwards,
are highly incensed by Henry's
opinions, and public speeches,
whensoever occasion has presented.

Edmund Randolph[28]

****

From James Madison, Jr. to James
Madison

July 1, 1788
Hond. Sir,
     I send herewith 2 copies of the
Federalist, one for Mr. Leland—the
other for Mr. Bledsoe.

Your dutiful son
Js. Madison Jr.[29]

****

From Burgess Ball

Fredericksburg, 8th of Dec. 1788

     This county, I'm in hopes, will
be at least as much for you as
against you, the principle Men
havg. declar'd themselves for you,
W-l-s & Waller excepted. [John
Whitaker Willis "Waller" was
possibly John Waller]

For the interest of our county,
you must take some trouble however disagreeable it may be to
you...anxious indeed that you wd.
come in without delay.
     Upon the whole, the Baptist
Interest seems every where to prevail. Bletcher and Leland in the
Counties above, and the Wallers
below. [The identity of "Blec-
tcher" is uncertain. Ball may have
referred to Aaron Bledsoe. John
Waller was pastor of Lower Spotsylvania Church, subsequently
known as "Waller's."]
     I think upon such an Occa-
sion, I wd. even solicit their Interest...[30]

****

From James Madison Jr. to George
Eve

2 January 1789.

Sir,
     Being informed that reports
prevail not only that I am opposed
to any amendments whatever to
the new federal Constitution; but
that I have cased to be a friend to
the rights of Conscience; and in-
ferring from a conversation with
my brother William, that you are
disposed to contradict such reports
as far as your knowledge of my
sentiments may justify, I am led to
trouble you with this communication of them. [George Eve (birth.
1748), a native of Culpeper
County, was ordained a Baptist
minister in 1778. At the time of
the election he was serving as pastor of Blue Run Church in Orange
County.]
     I freely own that I have never
seen in the Constitution as it now
stands those serious dangers which

---

[28] Ibid.,10: 542.
[29] R.A. Rutland and others, editors, The Papers of
James Madison, (Richmond: University of Virginia,
1977), 11: 185.

[30] Ibid., 385.

have alarmed many respectable Citizens. I opposed all previous alterations as calculated to throw the States into dangerous contentions. The Constitution is established on the ratifications of eleven States and a very great majority of the people of America; and amendments, if pursued with a proper moderation and in proper mode, will be not only safe, but may serve the double purpose of satisfying the minds of well meaning opponents, and of providing additional guards in favour in liberty. Under this change of circumstances, it is my sincere opinion that the Constitution ought to be revised, and that the first Congress meeting under it, ought to prepare and recommend to the States for ratification, the most satisfactory provision for all essential rights, particularly the rights of Conscience in the fullest latitude, the freedom of the press, trials by jury, security against general warrants &c.

I have intimated that the amendments ought to be proposed by the first Congress. [31]

****

From George Nicholas To James Madison

2 January 1789

Dear Sir,

I apprehend greater danger of the event than those gentn. you mention in your letter. Goochland [has] a majority against you; you should write to [Rueben]Ford the preacher in the county whom you know.

Your county man Leland has great influence in Louis and

Goochland cannot he be prevailed on to exert himself. Culpeper and Spotsylvania are most to be dreaded and the greatest efforts made in that quarter. [32]

****

From Benjamin Johnson to James Madison

12th, Jany. 1789

Sir,

On my way to Fredbg. on Friday, I called on Mr. Leeland, who was from home, attending Meetings which he had apptd. for Friday, Saturday, & Sunday; his Circuit was through Culpr. His wife informed me he did not see Mr. Waller when in Spotsylvania; Several Gentlemen in this district, appointed to be held in Louisa...

I was informed by Mr. Patton that Mr. Malone would most undoubtedly attend the Said Meeting; I favr. of him to notify you of the time & place of the meeting in Louisa. [33]

****

From Benjamin Johnson To James Madison

19th Jany. 1789
Sir,

I went yesterday to Mr. Eve's Meeting, where I was informed, that on Saturday night, in their Church Meeting, Mr. Adam Banks made a Motion, Seconded by Early, that they should then go into the business of the approaching Election, and endeavour to

---

[31] Ibid., 404-405

[32] Ibid., 406-408.
[33] Ibid., 414-415.

unite on the Occasion, when Mr. Early took the Opportunity of displaying his vanity and falsehood to the utmost. He there Continued Publickly to affirm, that you Said in Convention, the Constitution had no defects, and that it was the nearest to Perfection of any thing that Could be obtained;

In this he was supported by Mr. Hollon, after this Mr. Eve took a very Spirited and decided Part in your favour, he Spoke Long on the Subject, and reminded them of the many important Services which you had rendered their Society, in particular the Act for establishing Religious Liberty, also the bill for a general Assessment; which was averted by your Particular efforts; Mr. Eve urged that he thought they were under Obligations to you, and had much more reason to place their Confidence in you, than Mr. [James] Monroe;

I went with them from the Meeting-house to the River, which gave me an opportunity of Speakg to many of the people, and I think Mr. Eve has given a great wound to Mr. Early's Cause.

Benjamin Johnson[34]

****

From John Leland to James Madison

15 February 1789 [JM set out from Orange on 18 Feb. 1789] Sir,

I congratulate you in your appointment, as a Representative to Congress; and if my Undertaking in the Cause conduced Nothing else towards it, it certainly gave Mr. Madison one Vote.

It would give me further Satisfaction to know whether the Duties arising from Commerce are sufficient (without a direct Tax) for supporting the federal Government, and the payment of our Interest upon debts.

One Thing I shall expect; that if religious Liberty is anywise threatened, that I shall receive the earliest Intelligence.

I take the Liberty of writing thus to you, lest I should not be at Home when you pass by on your Way to Congress.

John Leland[35]

****

Rutland wrote concerning the time period, October 1788-February 1789, on Madison's election to the Constitutional Ratification Convention:

With the election a scant few weeks away, JM faced the problem of communicating his views to a widely scattered and sometimes hostile constituency. In addition to Orange his district included Amherst, Albemarle, Fluvanna, Louisa, Goochland, Culpeper, and Spotsylvania. Only two counties in this gropup, Orange and Albemarle, had voted for ratification. Friends advised JM to speak to the freeholders on the various county court days, to write to influential county leaders, and to publish a formal address to the people.

In three [existing letters] he carefully explained his attitude toward amendments and his preference for the congressional method of submitting them. (JM to George Eve, 2 Jan. 1789, JM to Thomas Mann Randolph, 13 Jan. 1789, JM to a Resident of Spotsylvania County, 27 Jan. 1789)

Everyone agreed that Culpeper, which had a considerably larger voting popula-

---

[34] *Ibid.*, 423-424.

[35] *Ibid.*, 442-443.

tion than any other county in the district,
was crucial to the outcome. He denied
rumors of his reported opposition to a bill
of rights, lest the gossip cost him the support of the dissenting religious sects, notably the Baptists, who were politically active
not only in Culpeper but throughout the
district. Soon after returning home JM
wrote Baptist preacher George Eve to reas-
sure him that his devotion to the cause of
religious liberty had not abated and that
he now favored adding to the Constitution a declaration of fundamental rights,
including "the rights of Conscience in the
fullest latitude." Pastor Eve responded by
actively promoting JM's candidacy among
his flock, as did the Reverend John
Leland, the leader of the Virginia Baptists
and a resident of the district (JM to Eve, 2
Jan. 1789; Leland to JM, ca. 15 Feb.
1789.)

On election day, 2 Feb. 1789, JM defeated
Monroe by 336 votes out of 2,280 cast in the
eight counties combined—ten inches of snow
and sub-zero temperatures doubtless dept
many freeholders home by their firesides. JM
lost decisively only in Spotsylvania, Monroe's
home and Amherst, stronghold of the Anti-
federalist Cabells. But he did much better in
Spotsylvania than Monroe did in Orange,
which was virtually unanimous for JM; and a
smashing victory in Culpeper more than
offset the loss of Amherst. The visit to Louisa
also had proved highly beneficial. Six out of
the state's ten representatives were "firm and
known friends to the Constitution," a result
that "exceeded the hopes" of most of the
federalists.[36]

---

[36] *Ibid.*, 303.

APPENDIX I

A Letter from Governor Briggs on the meeting of Leland and Madison

To B. Sprague editor, *Annals of the American Pulpit, Vol. VI*, W., (Philadelphia: Arno Press, 1969), P. 177-184.

Pittsfield, Mass., April 15, 1857.

Dear Sir:

The first personal recollection I have of Elder John Leland dates back to 1803 or 1804.

Three or four years before he died, Mrs. Briggs and myself spent an afternoon with him, and his aged and worthy wife.

In the course of the afternoon, I told him that I had recently seen in the public prints an extract from an Eulogy delivered by J. S. Barbour, of Virginia, upon the character of James Madison; that Barbour had said that the credit of adopting the Constitution of the United States properly belonged to a Baptist clergyman, formerly of Virginia, by the name of Leland; and he reached his conclusion in this way—he said that if Madison had not been in the Virginia Convention, the Constitution would not have been ratified by that State; and that it was by Elder Leland's influence that Madison was elected to that Convention.

He replied that Barbour had given him too much credit; but he supposed he knew to what he referred. Soon after the Convention which framed the Constitution of the U.S. had finished their work, and submitted it to the people for their action, two strong and active parties were formed in the State of Virginia, on the subject of its adoption. The state was nearly equally divided. One part was opposed to its adoption...At the head of this great party stood Patrick Henry. The other party agreed with what their opponents said...but they contended that the people would have the power, and could as well incorporate the amendments into the Constitution after its adoption as before; at the head of this party stood James Madison. The

strength of the two parties was to be tested at the by the election of county delegates to the State Convention. Elder Leland and his sympathies were with Henry and his party. He was named as the candidate opposed to Mr. Madison. Orange was a strong Baptist County; and his friends had an undoubting confidence in his election. Though reluctant to be a candidate, he yielded to the solicitations of the opponents of the Constitution, and accepted the nomination.

For three months after the members of the Convention at Philadelphia had completed their labours, and returned to their homes, Mr. Madison with John Jay and Alexander Hamilton, had remained in that city for the purpose of preparing those political articles that now constitute *The Federalist*. This gave the party opposed to Madison, with Henry at their head, the start of him, in canvassing the State in his absence. At length, when Mr. Madison was about ready to return to Virginia, a public meeting was appointed in the County of Orange, at which the candidates for the Convention on the one side, and Leland on the other, were to address the people from the stump. On his way home from Philadelphia, Mr. Madison went some distance out of his direct road to call upon him. "I know your errand here," said [Leland], "it is to talk with me about the Constitution. I am glad to see you, and to have an opportunity of learning your view on the subject." Mr. Madison spent half a day with him, and fully and unreservedly communicated to him his opinion upon the great matters, which were then agitating the people of the State.

The day came and they met, and with them nearly all the voters in the County of Orange, to hear their candidates respectively discuss the important questions upon which the people of Virginia were so soon to act. "Mr. Madison first took the stump, [said Leland] which was a hogshead of tobacco, standing on one end...for two hours he addressed his fellow citizens...and my friends called for me. I took it and went in for Mr. Madison. This is, I suppose, what Mr. Barbour alluded to.

APPENDIX J

Silas Noel's 39 Articles on Campellism

To the churches composing the Franklin Association:

Dear Brethren:

You will learn from our minutes, the result of this called session of our Associations. Before Alexander Campbell visited Kentucky, you were in harmony and peace; you heard but the one gospel, and knew only the one Lord, one faith and one baptism. Your church constitutions were regarded, and their principles expounded and enforced, by those who occupied your pulpits. Thus you were respected by other denominations, as a religious community. Often were you favored with refreshing seasons from on high, and many of your neighbors and of your families were brought to a knowledge of the truth. How delightful were your morning and evening interviews, cheered by the songs, prayers and exhortations of brethren, and by the presence of Him who has promised that where two or three are gathered together in his name, to be in their midst. Have not these happy days gone by? In place of preaching, you now may hear your church covenants ridiculed, your faith, as registered upon your church books denounced, and yourselves traduced; while the more heedless and unstable abjure the faith, and join with the wicked in scenes of strife, schism and tumult. The fell spirit of discord stalks in open day though families, neighborhoods and churches. If you would protect yourselves as churches, make no compromise with error, mark them who cause divisions; divest yourselves of the last vestige of Cambellism.

As an association, we shall deem it our duty to drop correspondence with any and every association or church, where this heresy is tolerated. Those who say they are not Campbellites, yet countenance and circulate his *little pamphlets* are insincere; they are to be avoided. When they say they are persecuted, because they will not swallow the Philadelphia Confession of Faith," you are not to believe it, for no church has called one of them in question on that point so far as we know. It is not so much their objection to this book, but rather our objections to their Confession of Faith, that makes the difference. When they tell you that the Holy Spirit begins the work of salvation, that he carries it on, and that he perfects it, they may only mean that all this done, by the words of the Holy Spirit, that is, by the Testament read or heard, and not be the quickening energies of God's Spirit, directly. All supernatural, immediate influences are discarded by them, as mere physical operations. All that we have esteemed religion, the work of God's grace in the soul, directly, is rejected. Mr. Campbell calls I a whim—a metaphysical whim! And that you may know the full extent of our objections, we herewith send you several articles gathered from the *Christian Baptist*, and *Millennial Harbinger*, with a reference to the pamphlet and to the page, where you can read.

When reference is made to the Millennial Harbinger, in the thirty-nine Articles, the first Volume of that periodical is meant. C. B. stands for *Christian Baptist*, and M. H. for *Millennial Harbinger*.

Judge whether they are, or are not, the reformation tenets. It may be said that these scraps are garbles from many volumes. Verily, they are but scraps; but each scrap embodies an opinion easily understood; so that this may with some propriety, be called a *confession of opinions*. We are not obliged to republish his pamphlets. Were we, however, to do it, the nature and bearing of these opinions would not be changed.

THE THIRTY NINE ARTICLES;
or, A NEW EDITION OF OLD ERRORS,
EXGTRACTED FROM ALEXANDER CAMPBELL'S
CHRISTIAN BAPTIST AND *MILLENNIAL HARBIN-
GER.*

HERE ARE 39 OF CAMPBELL'S ERRORS:

1. That there has been no preaching of the gospel since the days of the apostles.

2. That the people have been preached to from texts of Scripture until they have been literally preached out of their senses.

3. That all public speaking now necessary, is to undo what has already been done.

4. That John Calvin taught as pure Deism as was ever taught by Voltaire or Tom Paine; and that this Deism is taught in all the colleges in Christendom.

5. That all the faith that men can have in Christ, is historical.

6. That the words "little children," in the phrase, "I write unto you, little children," (in the epistle of John) are to be understood literally. [M.H. page 100 compared with pages 104-5.]

7. That faith is only an historical belief of facts stated in the Bible.

8. That Baptism, which is synonymous with immersion and for which every such believer is a proper subject, actually washes away sin, and is regeneration. [For last two articles, see M.H., pages 117, 119.]

9. That in the moral fitness of things, in the evangelical economy; baptism or immersion is made the first act of a Christian's life, or rather the *regenerating act itself*, in which the person is properly born again—born of water and spirit—without which, into the kingdom of heaven he cannot enter. [C.B. Vol. V. page 223.]

☞No prayers, no songs of praise, no acts of devotion, in the new economy, are enjoined on the unbaptized.

10. Most certainly, where a man is born of water, there is the bath of regeneration. Jesus gave himself for his bride, the church, and that she might be worthy of his affection, he cleansed her with a bath of water and with the word, etc. [C.B. Vol. page 123.]

11. That there is but one action ordained or commanded in the Testament, to which God has promised or testified, that he will forgive our sins. This action is Christian immersion. [C.B. Vol. VI. page 158.]

12. That by the mere act of a believing immersion into the name of the Father, Son and Holy Spirit, we are born again, have all our sins remitted, receive the Holy Spirit, and are filled with joy and peace. [C. B. Vol. V. page 213.]

QUERY. Is a believer in Christ not actually in a pardoned state before he is baptised?

ANSWER. Is not a man clean before he is washed!! Where there is only an imaginary line between Virginia and Pennsylvania, I can not often tell with ease whether I am in Virginia or Pennsylvania; but I can always tell when I am in Ohio, however near the line; for I have crossed the Ohio river. And blessed be God! He has not drawn a mere artificial line between the plantations of nature and of grace. No man has any proof that he is pardoned until he is baptized. And if men are conscious that their sins are forgiven, and that they are pardoned before they are immersed, I advise them not to go into the water, for they have no need of it. [C.B. Vol. VI. page 188.]

13. That Christian immersion is the gospel in water. "The Lord's Supper is the gospel in bread and wine." [C.B. Vol. V. page 158.] "As water saved Noah, so baptism saves us. He had faith in the resurrection of the earth; and we have faith in the resurrection of Jesus. He believed in God's promise of bringing him out of the water, and we his promise of raising from the dead. We leave our sins where Noah's baptism left the ungodly. [C. B. Vol. VII. page 123.] "As in the natural world a child cannot be said to be born of his father until he is first born of his mother, so in the spiritual world, no one can be said to be born of the spirit until he is born of the water." [M.H. Vol. I. page 206.]

14. Can men, just as they are fund when they hear the gospel, believe? We answer boldly, yes; just as easily as we can believe the well attested facts concerning the person and the achievements of General George Washington." [C.B., Vol. 6, page 187.]

15. We rejoice to know that it is just as easy to believe and be saved as it is to hear or see. [C. B., Vol. 5, page. 221.]

16. All the sons of men cannot show that there is another faith, but the belief of facts

either written in the form of history or orally delivered. Angels, men or demons cannot define anything under the term faith, but the belief of facts or of history; except they change it into confidence. While men are talking and dreaming and quarreling about a metaphysical *whim*, wrought in the heart, do you arise and obey the Captain of Salvation. And my word—nay more, the word of all the apostles for it, and of the Lord himself, you will find peace and joy, and eternal salvation, springing from the obedience of faith. [C. B., Vol. 6, page. 186.]

17. That to be born children of wrath means only to be born Gentile. [Same page.]

18. Millions have been tantalized by a mock gospel, which places them as the fable places Tantalus, standing in a stream, parched with thirst, and the water running to his chin, and so circumstanced that he could not taste it. There is a sleight-of-hand or religious legerdemain in getting around the matter. To call any thing grace, or favor, or gospel, not adapted to man, as it finds him, is the climax of misnomers. To bring the cup of salvation to the lips of a dying sinner, and then tell him for his soul he cannot taste it without some sovereign aid beyond human control, is to mock his misery and torment him more and more. [C.B., Vol. 6, page 187.]

19. That baptism is the only medium, divinely appointed, through which the efficacy of the blood of Christ is communicated to the conscience. Without knowing and believing this, immersion is as empty as a blasted nut. The shell is there, but the kernel is wanting. [C.B., vol. 6, page 160.]

20. No person on earth believed that the Messiah would die a sin offering or rise from the dead, from Eve to Mary Magdalene. If we do not make this assertion good before we finish the essays on the Jewish and Christian dispensations, we shall eat it up. [C.B., vol. 6, page 217.]

21. The election taught by the college men contemplated all the righteous, from Abel to the resurrection of the dead, as standing in the relation of elect persons to God; than which nothing can be more opposed to fact and scripture; for though Abel, Enoch and Noah were worshipers of the true God, they were not elect men; nay, though Melchisedec himself, King of Salem, was at once priest of the most high God, and the most illustrious type of the Messiah; though he received tithes of Abraham, blessed him, and, as Paul informs us, was greater than he; yet neither Melchisedec nor any of the numerous worshipers for whom he officiated in the quality of God's priest, did ever stand in the relation of elect worshipers in the scripture sense of the word elect. Abraham was the first elect man; and it remains for those who assert the contrary of this to prove their proposition—a thing they never can do by scripture. [C.B., Vol. 6, page 228-9.]

22. Abraham, Isaac and Jacob, were not chosen of God, for the mean, partial purpose of being dragged into heaven, will or no will, on the principle of final perseverance. [C.B., Vol. 6, page 230.]

23. Whether a man can believe, *i.e.* imbibe the electing principle, is never answered in the Holy Scriptures, for this substantial reason. It is never asked. This is an unlearned question of modern divinity, *i.e.* (deviltry, if such a word or thing there be) and could be agitated only by fools and philosophers; all the world knowing that we must believe what is provided. [C.B., Vol. 6, page 231.] (Query—Does he believe there is a Devil?)

24. The "moral law" or decalogue, is usually plead as the rule of life to believers in Christ; and it is said that it ought to be preached "as a means of conviction of sin." The scriptures never divide the law of Moses into moral, ceremonial and judicial. This is the work of schoolmen, who have also *divided* the invisible world into heaven, hell and purgatory. [C.B., Vol. I, page 147.]

25. ☞ Look at this. The spirit of God insulted, and his word deceitfully handled, in glossing away the force and meaning of another text, proving the inhabitation of the spirit and his direct agency upon the souls of believers. "Likewise the spirit also helpeth our infirmities; for we know not what we should pray for as we ought; but the spirit itself maketh intercession for us, with groanings which can not be uttered." Rom. viii. 26. Look now at the glossing:

The spirit referred to in this text is the spirit of man, and not the spirit of God; or rather, it is the spirit of patience; for there is no adjunct or epithet attached to the term spirit, which would authorize the conclusion that the spirit of God is referred to; and why should the spirit of God use groans which can not be expressed in words? Does this weakness belong to that divine agent. [M. H., Vol. I, page 115.]

26. I have never spent, perhaps, an hour in ten years in thinking about the trinity. It is no term of mine. It is a word which belongs not to the Bible, in any translation of it I ever saw. I teach nothing, I say nothing, I think nothing about it, save that it is not a scriptural term, and consequently, can have no scriptural ideas attached to it. [C.B. Vol. 7, page 208.]

27. "*Trinity.* This is one of these untaught questions which I do not discuss, and in the discussion of which I feel no interest. I neither affirm not deny anything about it. I only affirm that the whole controversy is about scholastic distinctions and unprofitable speculations."

28. Come Holy Spirit, Heavenly Dove,
With all thy quick'ning powers!
Kindle a flame of sacred love,
In these cold hearts of ours.'

In the singing this hymn, which is very ingeniously adapted to your sermon and prayer, you have very unfortunately fallen into two errors. First—you are singing to the Holy Spirit, as you prayed to it, without any example from any one of the old saints, either in the Old or New Testament; and without the possibility of ever receiving an answer to you prayer. The second error into which have fallen, is this: You acknowledge your church to be the church of Christ; and if the church of Christ, its members of course have the spirit of Christ." [C. B., Vol. 7, page 129.]

29. Does the preacher preach up Sinai instead of Calvary, Moses instead of Christ, to convince or convict his audience? Then he sings—
Awak'd by Sinai's awful sound,
My soul in awful guilt I found,

And knew not where to go;
O'erwhelm'd with sin, with anguish slain,
The sinner must be *born again*;
Or sink to endless woe.
&c., &c., &c.

I know of nothing more anti-evangelical than the above verses; but they suit one of our law convincing sermons, and the whole congregation must sing, suit or non-suit the one-half of them. But to finish the climax, the exercise is called *praising God.* [C.B. Vol. 5, page 105-6.]

When I can read my title clear
To mansions in the skies,
I'll bid fare well to every fear,
And wipe my weeping eyes.

Queries for the Thoughtful. 1.What title is this? 2.What would make it more clear? 3.Who issued this title? 4.Where is it filed? 5.Why does its dubiety forbid to part with every fear, and to banish tears? 6. Could you not make it more clear by instituting a new action, or course of action?

Without being prolix, or irksome in filing objections to all these specimens of hymn singing, I shall mention but two or three: They are, in toto, contrary to the spirit and genius—of the Christian religion . . . . They are an essential part of the corrupt systems of this day, and a decisive characteristic of the grand apostasy. [C.B., Vol. 5., page. 107.]

30. To separate and distinguish the spirit from its own word, is the radix of unhallowed speculation. What the gospel, written or spoken, does, in regenerating or purifying the heart, the spirit of God does, and what the spirit of God does, the gospel spoken or written does. Those who reject the gospel proclamation, resist the spirit of God; and those who resist the spirit of God, resist and reject the gospel proclamation." [C.B., Vol. 4, page 282.]

☞Whoever, then, hears a verse or chapter of the New Testament read, hears the spirit's voice. Such is Mr. C's creed, in regard to the Holy Spirit's energies—that spirit which he imagines is nothing else than the word of Revelation!

31. The ancient gospel reads thus: "Unless ye believe, ye cannot receive the Holy Spirit." . . . "When ye believe ye receive the Holy Spirit" . . . What does the expression Holy Spirit mean? *Ans.* In scripture, it stands first, for God the Holy Spirit; and secondly, for the holy mind or spirit of the believer. For illustration: "Why has Satan tempted you to lie unto the Holy Spirit; ye have not lied unto men, but unto God." And the Savior says, "How much more will your heavenly father give a Holy Spirit (as it should be translated), to those that ask him." Again, "Praying in a Holy Spirit." [C.B., Vol. 4, page 249.]

32. THE BELIEF OF ONE FACT, and that upon the best evidence in the world, is all that is requisite as far as faith goes, to salvation. The belief of this one FACT, and submission to ONE INSTITUTION, expressive of it, is all that is required of Heaven to admission into the church. The one fact is, that Jesus, the Nazarene is the Messiah: The evidence upon which it is to be believed, is the testimony of twelve men, confirmed by prophecy, miracles, and spiritual gifts. The one institution is, baptism into the name of the Father, and of the Son, and of the Holy Spirit. Every such person is a Christian, in the fullest sense of the word. [C.B., Vol. I., page 221.]

33. *Revivals.* Enthusiasm flourishes, blooms, under the popular system. This man was regenerated when asleep by a vision of the night. That man heard a voice in the woods, saying, "Thy sins are forgiven thee." A third saw his Savior descending to the tops of the trees at noonday. A thousand form a band, and sit up all night to take Heaven by surprise. Ten thousand are waiting for a power from on high, to descend upon their souls; they frequent meetings for the purpose of obtaining this power. [C.B., Vol. I, page 187.]

34. To show Mr. Campbell's utter contempt for Christian experiences, it is enough to notice the following narrative written and published by him in the C.B. Vol. 7, page. 191:

Campbell wrote:

Relating experiences. A good old Virginia Negro, and a very regular and orthodox professor, of more than ordinary attainments among the sable brotherhood, was accustomed to prepare "*experiences*" for such of his friends as wished to join the church. He disclosed to them, how they ought to feel in order to make good converts, and how they ought to relate their feelings in order to make a good confession. His usual fee was a good fat chicken, for each convert that passed the ordeal of the church. But as he insured his converts for a chicken a piece, if any one was rejected, he got nothing. *No cure, no pay,* was his motto. Once, a Negro, more stupid than the others, was rejected; he tried a second and a third time, but was rejected. Sambo then declared he would not insure him, unless he would promise him three chickens. To this he acceded; and by great exertions, he got him able to repeat how he felt, how dark it was with his soul, how a great light broke into his mind, how happy he was, and how much he loved Jesus. He was received and Sambo eat his chickens with joy and a good conscience. [C.B. Vol. 7, page 191.]

35. Some look for another call, a more powerful call than the written gospel presents. They talk of an inward call, of hearing the voice of God in their souls. This special call is either a lie or it makes the general call a lie. This is where the system ends. The voice of God, and the only voice of God which you will hear, till he calls you home, is his written gospel. [M.H., Vol. I, page 126-7.]

36. Did humanity die, and divinity leave the Son of God? To this the scriptures do not respond. It has arisen from the dissecting knife of theological anatomists. They are as skillful to separate and treat of humanity and divinity in the Son of God, as is Col. Symmes in forming this globe into so many hollow spheres, each having its own properties and inhabitants. [C.B., Vol. 2, page 287.] Is Jesus Christ the very and eternal God?

Ans. If men could debate such a question upon their knees it would be scarcely admissible. It is an untaught question, a scholastic one in its form, and terms, and tends to perpetuate a controversy, and a peculiar style of speaking, which, the sooner it could be forgotten, the better for both saint and sinner." [C.B., Vol. VI. 282.] We pray to the same God and Father, through the same Lord and Saviour, and by the same Holy Spirit. [M.H., Vol. I., page 175.]

☞Thus, it seems, he will not pray directly either to Christ or the Holy Spirit.

37. The Holy Spirit begins, carries on, and consummates the salvation of men." [M.H., Vol. I, page 139.

38. ☞ In the natural order of the evangelical economy, the items stand thus: 1st, Faith; 2d, Reformation; 3d, Immersion; 4th, Remission of sins; 5th, Holy Ghost; 6th, Eternal life." [C.B., vol. 6, p. 66.] There are three kingdoms; the Kingdom of Law, the Kingdom of Favor, and the Kingdom of Glory; each has a different constitution, different subjects, privileges, and terms of admission. The blood of Abraham brought a man into the Kingdom of Law, and gave him an inheritance in Canaan. Being born, not of blood, but through water and the spirit of God, brings a person into the Kingdom of favor; which is righteousness, peace, joy, and a Holy Spirit, with a future inheritance in prospect. But if the justified draw back, or the washed return to the mire, or if faith die and bring forth no fruits, into the Kingdom of Glory he cannot enter. Hence good works through faith in Jesus, gives a right to enter into the holy city. [C.B., Vol. VI, page 255.]

☞ By this, can we understand any thing else, than the entire rejection of the doctrine of the final perseverance of saints, and justification by the righteousness of Christ, imputed to the believer?

39. There is no democracy or aristocracy in the governmental arrangements of the church of Jesus Christ. The citizens are all volunteers when they enlist under the banners of the great King, and as soon as they place themselves in the ranks, they are bound to implicit obedience in all the institutes and laws of their sovereign. So that there is no putting the question to vote, whether they shall obey any particular law or injunction. Their rulers and bishops have to give an account of their administration, and have only to see that the laws are known and obeyed. [C.B. Vol. V, page 121.]

☞ Truly, this is not democracy; nor is it a moderate aristocracy. What is it, short of Episcopacy or Papacy?!

Brethren: Can you read this, and say or think that it is not, even now, high time to "march out of Babylon?" Doubtless, you can not hesitate. In February 1825, Mr. Campbell denounced reformation. "The very name," said he, "has become as offensive as the term 'Revolution,' in France." He is now a paroxysm about reformation. In all the extravagance on unbridled fanaticism, he fancies that he has already introduced the millennium, as far as his tenets have prevailed. The millennium, he dreams, has bursted in upon South Benson, Versailles, Clear Creek, David's Fork and Shawnee Run. Who besides himself, (and those who have sold their birth right have, who have committed their heads and hearts for reformation pottage) can indulge in a conceit so silly and ridiculous. From such frenzy and quackery, and above all from such a millennium, may a kind Providence deliver us.

Amen.

-From J. H. Spencer, A History of the Kentucky Baptists from 1769-1885, V. I, II (Cincinnati: By the Author, 1885), P. 624-635.

APPENDIX K

Pastoral Questions on Theology

Nathaniel Kendrick had been tutored by the great Baptist pastors Samuel Stennett and Thomas Baldwin. In 1802 Kendrick placed himself under the tutelage of Asa Burton, the *standing order* minister of the Congregational church of Thetford, Vermont. Burton challenged the young preacher on his stand on baptism. S. W. Adams relates the experience:

With this theologian Mr. Kendrick commenced his course in divinity, July 5th, 1802, and continued under his instruction till near the close of the ensuing October. That his time and opportunities were improved in a manner creditable to himself, and promotive of his cherished objects, is evident from the fruits of his investigations. In his brief pupilage under this excellent divine, he surveyed the leading subjects embraced in the ordinary field of theological study. These were taken up in logical order, and the sentiments adopted, and the reasons in their support, were embodied in dissertations, lucidly expressed and carefully written. These papers all evince thoroughness, and a mastery of the subjects under examination, such as may well surprise us. They are, in style, concise, and full in argument; none of them shrinking into more skeletons. They are liberal in length, and comprehensive, some even to prolixity, in their range of discussion. Though more than half a century has stamped its traces upon the manuscripts, they still give occular proof that the author of these essays elaborated them with genuine enthusiasm. He manifestly took pleasure in writing upon such themes, and executed his labor with a zest which took from it entirely the character of a drudgery. Hence a recurrence to these essays, in after years, must have awakened satisfaction, since the sterling manner in which they were cast would not demand a reconstruction. They are fine models for students now, who can command stationary far superior to that produced a half a century since.

The merits of teacher and pupil are still farther disclosed in the questions put by the former, and the ingenuity and skill with which they are treated by the latter. On the doctrine of church membership, and gospel order, it must be borne in mind they were at issue. It may have been, and doubtless it was, singularly fortunate, that he who, in subsequent years, was to act as a guide to students in divinity, who would themselves be guides to many, should have the privilege of sitting at the fact of no second-rate man, but a champion of the ecclesiastical order to which he belonged: the Congregationalists of New England.

The gist of the difference in their opposing views was elicited by the following questions:

1st. What warrant had Abraham to circumcise himself and his house?

2d. What was the design of circumcision?

3d. What is meant by one thing's coming in the room in stead of another?

4th. Did not God command Abraham's seed to circumcise their male children?

5th. Has Abraham a seed among the Gentiles, if he has, who are they?

6th. Are not God's commands binding till revoked by Himself; and is not a revelation of God's will necessary to revoke a command?

7th. What is the design of baptism?

On the supposition that *Infant Baptism* is not valid, how are the following questions to be answered:

1st. Infants were the subject of a religious rite under the Old Testament. What reasons can be assigned why they should not be the subjects of a religious rite under the New Testament, such as baptism?

2d. If it was the design of God that they should not be the subjects of a religious rite of baptism under the *New*, as they were of circumcision under the Old

Testament, what reason can be given why God has not given express information on this subject in the New Testament?

3d. As the Jews in the apostolic days warmly opposed the omission of ancient rites, among which washing or baptising infants, as well as adults, with water, was one, what reason can be given for their silence, when they saw that this rite was omitted, by the Apostles, towards the infants of adult parents whom they had proselyted?

4th. If there be no arguments sufficient to destroy the validity of infant baptism, and no argument sufficient to establish its validity, in what light must we view infants, and why should they be more neglected under the New than under the Old Testament? How are we to understand 2 Cor., vii., 14, "For the unbelieving husband is sanctified by the wife, &c." And Acts ii. 38 ?

Thus it will be seen that the main parts of the Pedobaptist doctrine were set before Mr. Kendrick, and the essays written at that time furnish convincing proof that he did not evade the questions pressed upon him, but with his clear and penetrating views gave an easy and scriptural solution of them. Those pertaining to this subject far exceed in length others produced at that time.[37]

In 1819, Kendrick founded Hamilton Seminary, Hamilton, New York, the first Baptist Theological Seminary in America.

---

[37] S. W. Adams, *Memoirs of Rev. Nathaniel Kendrick, D. D.* (Philadelphia: American Baptist Publication Society, 1860), P. 29-35.

BIBLIOGRAPHY

Books

Adams, S. W. *Memoirs of Rev. Nathaniel Kendrick*. Philadelphia, PA: American Baptist Publication Society, 1860.

Adlam, S., and Graves, James Robinson. *The First Baptist Church in America*. Texarkana, TX: Baptist Sunday School Committee, 1939.

Alderman, Pat. *The Overmountain Men*. Johnson City, TN: The Overmountain Press, 1986.

Allen, I. M. *The Triennial Baptist Register. No. 2*. Philadelphia, PA: Baptist General Tract Society, 1836.

An Appeal to the Friends of the Bible, and of Equal Rights. New York, NY: J. R. Bigelow, 1845.

An Argument Sustaining the Common English Version of the Bible. New York, NY: Proceedings of a Meeting held in the Oliver St. Baptist Church, Printed by J. A. Gray 1850.

Anderson, S. E. *Baptists Unshackled*. Elgin, IL: S. E. Anderson, 1971.

Andrews, E. Benjamin. *History of the United States, vol. II*. New York, NY: Charles Scribner's Sons, 1903.

Armitage, Thomas. *A History of the Baptists*. New York, NY: Bryan, Taylor & Co., 1887.

Armitage, Thomas; Rose, A. T., and others. *Addresses and Other Matter*. New York, NY: American and Foreign Bible Society, 1882.

Ashcraft, Robert, General Editor. *History of the American Baptist Association*. Little Rock, AR: History and Archives Committee, 2000.

Asher, Louis Franklin. *John Clarke (1609-1676), Pioneer in American Medicine & Liberty*. Pittsburgh, PA: Dozrance Publishing Co., 1999.

Averill, A. M. *Baptist Landmarkism Tested*. Dallas, TX: Carter Gibson Printers, 1880.

Backus, Isaac. *An Abridgement to the Church History of New England*. 1804; reprint ed., Boston, MA: Harvard University. 1935.

_____. *Papers and Remains*. Providence, RI: n.p. John Hay Library, Brown University, n.d.

_____. *History of New England, with Particular Reference To the Baptists, 2nd Ed. vol. 1, 2*. Paris, AR: 1871. Reprint. The Baptist Standard Bearer. n.d..

Barker, W. M. *Memoirs of Elder J. N. Hall*. Fulton, KY: Baptist Flag Print, 1907.

Barnes, L. C., and Mary Clark. *Pioneers of Light, the First Century of the American Baptist Publication Society*. Philadelphia, PA: The American Baptist Publication Society, n.d.

Belcher, Joseph. *George Whitefield: A Biography*. New York, NY: American Tract Society, n.d.

_____. *The Religious Denominations in the United States*. Philadelphia, PA: John E. Potter, 1856.

Beller, James R. *The Soul of St. Louis*. St. Louis, MO: Prairie Fire Press, 1998.

Benedict, David. *A General History of the Baptist Denomination, vol. 1 and 2*. 1813; reprint ed., Dayton, OH: Church History Research and Archives. 1985.

_____. *History of the Donatists*. Pawtucket, RI: Nickerson, Sibley and Company, 1875.

Bicknell, Thomas W., A.M. *The Story of Dr. John Clarke*. Providence, RI: By the Author, 1915.

Borum, Joseph H. *Biographical Sketches of Tennessee Baptist Ministers.* Memphis, TN: Rogers and Co. Publishers, 1880.

Brooks, Elder James P. *The Biography of Eld. Jacob Locke.* Glasgow, KY: Times Print, 1881.

Brooks, Walter H. *The Silver Bluff Church.* Washington, DC: Press of R.L. Pendleton, 1910.

Burgess, W. J. *Baptist Faith and Martyrs' Fires.* Little Rock, AR: Baptist Publications Committee, 1964.

Burgess, Walter H. *Smith, The Se-Baptist and the Pilgrim Fathers, Helwys and Baptist Origins.* London, England: James Clarke & Co. 1911.

Burnett, J. J., *Sketches of Tennessee's Pioneer Baptist Preachers.* Nashville, TN: Press of Marshall & Bruce Co., 1919.

Callender, John. *Historical Discourse on the Civil and Religious Affairs of Rhode Island.* Boston, MA: Kneeland and Green, 1739.

Cammack, Melvin Macye. *John Wyclif and the English Bible.* New York, NY: American Tract Society, 1938.

Carroll, J. M. *A History of Texas Baptists.* Dallas, TX: Baptist Standard Publishing Co., 1923.

Cashdollar, Charles D. *The Transformation of Theology 1830-1890.* Princeton, NJ: Princeton University Press, 1989.

Cathcart, William, *The Baptist Encyclopedia, vol. I, II.* Philadelphia, PA: Louis H. Everts, 1883.

_____. *The Baptists in the American Revolution.* Philadelphia, PA: By the author, 1876.

Chapin, Howard M. *Our Rhode Island Ancestors.* Providence, RI: Rhode Island Historical Society, nd.

Christian, John T. *Close Communion.* Louisville, KY: Baptist Book Concern, 1892.

_____. *History of the Baptists Together with some Account of Their Principles and Practices.* Nashville, TN: Sunday School Board of the Southern Baptist Convention, 1926.

Church Heritage, Double Springs Independent Missionary Baptist Church. Kingsport, TN: n.p., n.d.

Clark, James G. History *of William Jewell College.* St. Louis, MO: Central Baptist Press, 1893.

Clarke, John. *Ille Newes from Newe England.* Boston, MA: Collections of the Massachusetts Historical Society VII, 4th Series, 1854.

Coalter, Milton J. Jr. *Gilbert Tennent, Son of Thunder.* Westport, CT: Greenwood Press for the Presbyterian Historical Society, 1986.

Comer, John. *Diary.* Providence, RI: Rhode Island Historical Society, edited by C. Edwin Barrows, 1893.

Confessions of Faith, and Other Public Documents. London, England: Hanserd Knollys Society, 1854.

Cramp, J. M. *Baptist History: From the Foundation of the Christian Church.* Philadelphia, PA: American Baptist Publication Society, 1888.

Crosby, Thomas. *The History of the English Baptists, vol. I, II.* London, England: 1738.

Dallimore, Arnold A. *George Whitefield, The Life and Times of the Great Evangelist, vol. 1, 2.* London, England: The Banner of Truth Trust, 1970.

Day, Richard Elsworth. *Rhapsody in Black.* Valley Forge, PA: Judson Press, 1953.

Devin, Robert I. *A History of Grassy Creek Baptist Church from it's Foundation to 1880.* Raleigh, NC: Edwards, Broughten & Co., Printers and Binders, 1880.

Dillow, Myron D. *James Smith, Baptist Trailblazer in Illinois.* Nashville, TN: Historical Committee of the Illinois Baptist State Association, 1987.

Doctrinal and Practical Tracts. New York, NY: Thomas Holman, 1884.

Douglass, R.S. *History of Missouri Baptists.* Kansas City, MO: Western Baptist Publishing Company, 1934.

Dowell, Spright. *A History of Mercer University.* Macon, GA: Mercer University, 1953.

Dwight, Sereno E. *Memoirs of Jonathan Edwards, from the Works of Jonathan Edwards.* Edinburgh, Scotland: Banner of Truth Trust, 1998.

Easton, Emily. *Roger Williams Prophet and Pioneer.* Freeport, NY: Books for Libraries Press, 1930.

Edwards, Jonathan. *The Works of Jonathan Edwards, vol. I & II.* London, England: William Tegg, 1860.

Edwards, Morgan. *Materials towards a History of the Baptists, vol. 2.* Danielsville, GA: Heritage Papers, Prepared for Publication by Eve B. Weeks and Mary B. Warren, 1984.

Ella, George M., *Isaac McCoy, Apostle of the Western Trail.* Springfield, MO: Particular Baptist Press, 2003.

Ernst, James. *Roger Williams, New England Firebrand.* New York, NY: The MacMillan Company, 1932.

Evans, B. *The Early English Baptists.* London, England: Bunyan Library Publication, 1864.

Faber, George Stanley. *An Inquiry into the History and Theology.* London, England: R. B. Seeley and W. Burnside, 1838.

Fletcher, Joseph. *History of Revival and Independency in England.* London, England: J. Snow, 1843.

Ford, S. H. *Ecclesiastical History, Condensed from the Apostles to the Reformation.* St. Louis, MO: Christian Repository, 1889.

Fries, Adelaide L., M.A. *Records of the Moravians in North Carolina.* Raleigh, NC: Edwards & Broughton Printing, 1925.

Gaustad, Edwin S. *A Documentary History of Religion in America.* Grand Rapids, MI: William B. Eerdmans Publishing, 1982.

_____. *Baptist Piety.* Grand Rapids, MI: Christian University Press, 1978.

Gillette, A.D., Editor. *Minutes of the Philadelphia Baptist Association.* Philadelphia, PA: American Baptist Publication Society, 1851.

Gillies, John. *Memoirs of George Whitefield.* New Haven, CT: Horace Mansfield, 1834.

Goadby, J. Jackson. *Bye-Paths in Baptist History.* London, England: Elliot Stock, 1871.

Goen, C. C. *Revivalism and Separateness in New England. 1740-1800.* New Haven, CT: Yale University Press, 1962.

Grady, William P. *What Hath God Wrought?* Schererville, IN: Grady Publications, 1996.

Graves, J. R., and Ditzler, Jacob. *The Great Carrollton Debate.* Memphis, TN: Southern Baptist Publication Society, 1876.

Guild, Reuben Aldridge. *Early History of Brown University.* Providence, RI: By the Author, 1896.

Hailey, O. L. *J. R. Graves: Life, Times and Teachings.* Nashville, TN: By the Author, 1929.

Harrelson, Ralph S. *Pioneer Baptist Ministers, Voices in the Wilderness of the Illinois Country.* n.a. By the Author, 1987.

Hatcher, Eldridge B. *William E. Hatcher.* Richmond, VA: W.C. Hill Printing, 1915.

Hendricks, Garland A. *Saints and Sinners at Jersey Settlement.* Thomasville, NC: Charity and Children, John E. Roberts, Editor, Revised Ed. by Delmar Co. 1964, 1988.

Hickman, William. *A Short Account of my Life and Travels.* 1828; reprint ed., Louisville, KY: The Kentucky Baptist Historical Commission. 1969.

Holmes, Col. J. T. *The American Family of Obadiah Holmes.* Columbus, OH: Published by the Author, 1915.

Hovey, Alvah. *The Life and Times of Isaac Backus.* 1858; reprint ed., Harrisonburg, VA: Gano Books, 1991.

Hunt, Gaillard. *James Madison and Religious Liberty.* Washington, DC: Annual Report of the American Historical Association, vol.1, 1902.

Ireland, James. *The Life of the Rev. James Ireland.* Winchester, VA: J. Foster, 1819.

James, Charles. *A Documentary History of the Struggle for Religious Liberty in Virginia.* New York, NY: Da Cape Press, 1971.

John Taylor. *A History of Ten Baptist Churches.* Bloomfield, KY: William H. Holmes, 1827.

Judd, O. B. *Revision or no Revision, and Address before the Philadelphia Bible Union.* New York, NY: Pamphlet in the Partee Center Archives, William Jewel College, Liberty, MO, 1853.

King, Henry M. *A Summer Visit of Three Rhode Islanders.* Providence, RI: Rhode Island Historical Society, 1896.

_____. *Early Baptists Defended, A Review.* Boston, MA: Howard Gannett, Publisher, for the Rhode Island Historical Society, 1880.

King, Joe M. *A History of South Carolina Baptists.* Columbia, SC: South Carolina General Board of South Carolina Baptist Convention, 1964.

Leckie, Robert. *George Washington's War.* New York, NY: Harper Collins Publishers, 1992.

Leland, Elder John. *The Writings of Elder John Leland, Including Some Events in his Life.* New York, NY: G. W. Wood, 1845.

Lewis, John A. *A Biographical Sketch of Rev. Cadwallader Lewis.* Georgetown, KY: By the Author, n.d.

Ludlow, William L. *The Story of Bible Translations.* New York, NY: Vantage Press, 1990.

Lumpkin, William. *Baptist Inroads in the South.* Shelbyville, TN: Bible and Literature Missionary Foundation, n.d.

Marshall, Peter and Manuel, David. *The Light and the Glory.* Tarrytown, NY: Fleming H. Revell Co., 1977.

Massey, George Valentine II. *Ancestory of Elizabeth du Pont Bayard.* Providence, RI: By the Author, 1953.

McClellan, Graydon E. *Rev. George Whitefield.* Newburyport, MA: n.p. Pamphlet given at Old South Presbyterian Church, n.d.

McGlothlin, W. J. *A History of Furman University.* Nashville, TN: Sunday School Board of the Southern Baptist Convention, n.d.

_____. *Baptist Beginnings in Education.* Nashville, TN: Sunday School Board of the Southern Baptist Convention, n.d.

McLoughlin, William G. *Isaac Backus on Church, State, and Calvinism.* Cambridge, MA: Belknap Press, Harvard University, 1968.

_____. *Modern Revivalism.* Providence, RI: Ronald Press Co., 1959.

_____. *New England Dissent 1630-1833.* Cambridge, MA: Harvard University Press, 1971.

McTyeire, Holland N. *History of Methodism.* Nashville, TN: M. E. Church, South Publishing House, 1910.

Mead, Frank S. *Handbook of Denominations.* Nashville, TN: Abingdon Press, 1990.

Muir, William. *Our Grand Old Bible.* London, England: Morgan and Scott, Ld. 1911.

Murray, Iain H. *Jonathan Edwards, A New Biography.* Edinburgh, Scotland: Banner of Truth Trust, 1987.

Norton, Herman. *The United States Army Chaplaincy, vol. II.* Washington, DC: Office of the Chief of Chaplains, Dept. of the Army, 1977.

Nowlin, William Dudley. *Kentucky Baptist History, 1770 - 1922.* Louisville, KY: Baptist Book Concern, 1922.

Orr, J. Edwin. *The Event of the Century, The 1857-1858 Awankening.* Wheaton, IL: International Awakening Press, 1989.

Paschal, G. W. *History of North Carolina Baptists vol. 1, 2.* Raleigh, NC: Edwards & Broughton Co., 1955.

Peck, John Mason. *Father Clark, the Pioneer Preacher.* New York, NY: Sheldon, Lamport and Blakeman, 1855.

Penn, W. E. *The Life and Labors of Major W. E. Penn.* St. Louis, MO: Woodward, 1896.

Pope, John F. *History of First Baptist Church of San Francisco.* San Francisco, CA: John H. Carmany and Co., 1874.

Proceedings of the Bible Revision Convention. Louisville, KY: Hull and Brother, 1852.

Ranck, George W. *The Travelling Church.* Louisville, KY: Press of Baptist Book Concern, 1891.

Riley, B. F. The *Baptists in the Building of the Nation.* Louisville, KY: Baptist Book Concern, 1922.

Rogers, Horatio. *Mary Dyer of Rhode Island, Quaker Martyr.* Providence, RI: Reston and Rounds, 1896.

Rosenthal, Bernard. *Salem Story–Reading the Witch Trials of 1692.* Boston, MA: Cambridge University Press, 1993,

Russell, W. B. *A Short History of the Evangelical Movement.* London, England: A. R. Mowbray & Co., 1915.

Rutland, R. A. and others. *The Papers of James Madison, vol. 10, 11.* Richmond, VA: The University of Virginia, 1977.

Salley, Alexander S. Jr.. *Narratives of Early Carolina.* New York, NY: Barnes & Nobles, INC., 1911.

Schaff, Phillip. *History of the Christian Church, vol. VII, VIII.* Grand Rapids, MI: William B. Eerdmans Publishing Company, 1977.

Semple, Robert Baylor. *The Rise and Progress of the Baptists in Virginia.* Richmond, VA: By the Author, 1810.

Sermon on the Death of General George Washington. Providence, RI: Collections of the Rhode Island Historical Society, printed by John Carter, 1800.

Shurden, Walter B. *Crises in Baptist Life.* Nashville, TN: The Historical Commission of the Southern Baptist Convention, 1979.

Simms, James M. *The First Colored Baptist Church in North America.* Philadelphia, PA: J. B. Lippincott, 1888.

Simms, P. Marion. The *Bible in America.* New York, NY: Wilson: Erickson Inc., 1936.

Simpson, William S. *Virginia Baptist Ministers, 1760-1790: A Biographical Survey, vol. 1-4.* Richmond, VA: By the Author, 1990-2002.

Smith, Page. *John Adams.* Garden City, NY: Doubleday and Company, Inc. 1962.

Spencer, J. H. *A History of Kentucky Baptists from 1769-1885, vol. I, II.* Cincinnati, OH: By the Author, 1885.

Sprague, William B., ed. *Annals of the American Pulpit, vol. VI, VIII.* Philadelphia, PA: Arno Press, Reprint of the 1865 series by Robert Carter and Brothers, New York, N.Y., 1969.

Stott, William T. *Indiana Baptist History.* Franklin, IN: By the Author, 1908.

Sturgess, Alice Murphy. *History of William Murphy and His Descendants.* St. Louis, MO: Nixon-Jones Printing Co., 1918.

Taylor, James B. *Virginia Baptist Ministers, Series I and II.* Richmond, VA: Lippincott & Co., 1859.

Taylor, John. *The History of Ten Baptist Churches.* Bloomfield, KY: William H. Holmes, 1826.

Thawer, Cpt. Simeon. *Journal of the Invasion of Canada in 1775*. Providence, RI: Collections of the Rhode Island Historical Society, vol. 6, 1867

The Baptist Library, vol. 1. New York, NY: Lewis Colby and Co. 1846.

The Trial of J. R. Graves, Nashville, TN: Archives of Southern Baptist Theological Seminary Library, 1858.

Thompson, E. Wayne and Cummins, David L. *This Day in Baptist History*. Greenville, SC: Bob Jones University Press, 1993.

Thompson, Parker C. *The United States Army Chaplaincy, vol. 1*. Washington, DC: Office of the Chief of Chaplains, Dept. of the Army, 1978.

Torrey, Joseph. *General History of the Christian Religion and Church*. Boston, MA: Crocker and Brewster, 1875.

Tracts on Liberty of Conscience and Persecution. London, England: Hanserd Knollys Society, 1844.

Vedder, Henry. *A Short History of the Baptists*. Valley Forge, PA: American Baptist Publishing Society, 1907.

Wheeler, O. C. *The Story of Early Baptist History in California*. Sacramento, CA: California Baptist Historical Society, 1888.

Williams, Roger. *The Complete Writings of Roger Williams vol. I, II, III*. New York, NY: Russell & Russell, 1963.

Williams, Samuel C., and Tindell, Samuel W. *The Baptists of Tennessee*. Kingsport, TN: Kingsport Press, 1930.

Woodson, Carter. *A History of the Negro Church*. Washington, DC: Associated Publishers, 1921.

Manuscripts

Backus, Isaac. Papers in the John Hay Library, Brown University, Providence, Rhode Island.

Barnes, Lemuel Call. Papers in the Archives of the American Baptist Samuel Colgate Historical Library, Rochester, New York.

_____. *Was General George Washington Baptized by Chaplain John Gano?* Papers of Lemuel Call Barnes. In the Archives of the American Baptist Samuel Colgate Historical Library, Rochester, New York.

Benedict, David. Manuscripts in the Rhode Island Historical Society, Providence, Rhode Island.

Dunster, Henry. Papers. In the Archive of the Pusey Library, Harvard University, Cambridge, Massachusetts

Edwards, Morgan. Materials towards a History of the Baptists in America. Microfilm in the American Baptist Historical Society, Rochester, New York.

McLoughlin, William G. Data Sheets on the Isaac Backus Papers. John Hay Library, Brown University, Providence, Rhode Island.

Papers on the *Gaspee*. In the Archives of the Rhode Island Historical Society, Providence, Rhode Island.

Paschal, George Washington. Papers in the Z. Smith Reynolds Library at Wake Forest University, Winston-Salem, North Carolina.

_____. "The Board's Declaration on Union Work." George Washington Paschal Papers, PCMS 86 4/382, n.d. Z. Smith Reynolds Library, Wake Forest University, Winston-Salem, North Carolina.

Periodicals

"Aged Baptist Minister Buried in Bellefontaine." St. Louis Daily Globe-Democrat. 5, 9 July 1905. P. 1.
Angus, Joseph. "Early English Baptists." Christian Repository, Jan 1897.

Buck, John T. "Historical Sketches of the Baptists in the State of Mississippi." Christian Repository, Jan, Mar, Jun, Nov 1883.

Carroll, B. H. "The Whitsitt Case at Wilmington." Christian Repository, July 1897. P. 441-444.
"Celebrate Centennial of Brothertown Baptist Church." Chilton Wisconsin Times-Journal, 9 Aug 1934. P. 1.
Christian Repository. Dec 1856, P. 339-340.
Christian Repository. Aug, Dec 1871.

Edwards, Morgan. "Materials Toward a History of the Baptists in North Carolina." N. C. Review Vol. VII no. 3, 1930. P. 370-383.
_____. "Materials for a History of the Baptists in Rhode Island." Collections of the Massachusetts Historical Society I, 4th Series, 1854. P. 302-348.
"English Bible." Western Watchman, 22 Sep 1853. P. 1.

Ford, Sallie Rochester. "America's Pioneer Female Missionary." Christian Repository, Nov 1883, P. 390-393.
Ford, Samuel H. "Baptist Triennial Convention." Christian Repository, Jan 1876, P. 28-34.
_____. "David Thomas, The Old Blind Preacher." Christian Repository, Mar 1857. P. 162-170.
_____. "Dr. Whitsitt's Statement In Regard To Dr. J. R. Graves—A Protest." Christian Repository, Jan 1900. P. 169-170.
_____. "Life, Times and Teachings of J. R. Graves." Christian Repository, Mar 1900, P. 162-169.
_____. "Planting and Progress of the Baptist Cause in Tennessee." Christian Repository, Jan 1876, P. 40-49.
_____. "Rise and Progress of the Baptist Cause in Indiana." Christian Repository, Feb 1876, P. 48-53.
_____. "Rise of the Current Reformation." Christian Repository, Jan 1860, P. 20-33.
_____. "Rise of the Current Reformation." Christian Repository, Aug 1860, P. 561-573.
_____. "The True and Real Inspiration of the Bible." Christian Repository, Feb 1880. P. 102-103.
_____. "The Vardemans." Christian Repository, July 1876, P. 72-80.

Grime, J. H. "History of Middle Tennessee Baptists." Baptist and Reflector, 1902.

Hackley, W. B. "The Well across the Road." Virginia Baptist Historical Society, Number Three, 1964.
Harvey, William P. "Baptist Work in Kentucky for Ninety-nine Years." Christian Repository, Nov 1875, P. 342-355.

Inman, W. G. "The Graves Trial." Christian *Repository*, Apr 1900. P. 232-250.

"Lynn Alderson." *The Baptist Sentinel*. Vol. 2, No.2, 1871. P. 54-59.

"Memoir of the late Elder John Logan, of McDonough County, Ill." *Western Watchman*, 3 July 1851. P. 1.

"New Version of the Scriptures." Western *Watchman*, 5 Jan 1854. P. 1.

Nowlin, William Dudley. "A Pioneer Baptist Hero." *Christian Repository*, Oct 1905. P. 607-610.
_____. *N.C. Historical Review Vol. VII Number 3*. Raleigh, NC: North Carolina Historical Commission, 1930.

Paxton, W. E. "Early Baptists of Mississippi." *Christian Repository*, July 1876. P. 9-14.
Peck, John Mason. " Jeremiah Vardeman." *Christian Repository*, Aug 1854. P. 458-479.
_____. "Did Patrick Henry Make that Speech?" *Christian Repository*, Oct 1890, P. 272-276.
Periodical Paper, Extra of the American and Foreign Bible Society. No. 32, May 1852.
Phillips, Georgie Dees. "Incidents in the Missionary Life of Rev. George Dana Boardman." Christian *Repository*, Sep 1881, P. 201-203.
"Pioneer Preachers of the West." *Christian Repository*, Dec 1871, P. 520-526.
Polk, William. "History of the Bethel Association, Missouri." *Christian Repository*, Nov 1856.

"Remarkable Conversions." Christian *Repository*, Jun 1879. P. 297.
Robey, George W. "Planting and Progress of the Baptist Cause in Iowa." *Christian Repository*, Aug 1876. P. 410-414.

"The Amended Version." *The Examiner*, 9 Feb 1865.
"The Campbellites and the New Version." *Western Watchman*, 17 Nov 1853.
"The Oldest Baptist Church in America." *Western Watchman*, 22 Sep 1853.
The Providence Gazette. 6-13 Oct 1770.

Western Recorder vs. the Western Watchman." *Western Watchman*, 3 Nov 1853.
Western Watchman. 24 Apr, 3 July 1851.
Western Watchman. 8 July 1852.
Western Watchman. 17 Nov 1853.
Western Watchman. 5 Jan 1854.
Whilden, B. W. "Rev. Abraham Marshall, of Georgia." *Christian Repository*, Apr 1874. P. 274-283.
Word and Way. 20 April 1922.

INDEX

Holliman, Ezekiel, 13, 14, 479
Hollis, Thomas, 445
Holmes, Obadiah, xvii, xiv, 38, 39, 43, 44, 45, 47, 49, 51, 52, 57, 61, 64, 72, 74, 78, 87, 92, 180, 204, 215, 255, 289, 495, 496, 500
Holmes, Susannah, 87
Holston Baptist Association, 311
Holy Commonwealth, 25, 42, 61
Hooker, Thomas, 6, 59, 60, 77, 500
Hooper, William, 220
Hopewell Academy, 140, 210, 257, 262, 446, 447, 448
Hopewell Baptist meeting-house, 257
House of Burgesses, 260
Howard, John, 286
Howell, R. B. C., 459, 463-468, 488
Hunt, Asa, 259, 334
Hunter, Ezekiel, 155, 156, 159, 160
Husbands, Herman, 187
Hutchinson, Anne, 23- 29, 39, 64, 91, 507
Hutchinson, William, 23, 39

imputation, 266, 370, 374, 384
incendiaries, 36, 44, 61, 204
Independent Baptist churches, 461, 485
infant baptism, 7, 10, 36, 41, 46, 47, 49, 57-63, 69, 72, 132, 133, 145, 150, 184, 195, 203, 211, 219, 241, 284, 286, 298, 431, 495, 498, 529, 531
invitations, 118, 373
Involuntary, Unmerited, Perpetual, Absolute, Hereditary Slavery, Examined on the Principles of Nature, Reason, Justice, Policy, and Scripture, 428

Ireland, James, xvii, 175, 176, 189, 191, 193, 228, 230-240, 365, 377, 496
Ireland's imprisonment, 231
Isle of Rhodes, 23, 24, 30

Jacobs, Witman, 220
Jefferson, Thomas, xx, 166, 182, 236, 252, 274, 278, 498, 510
Jersey Settlement church, 153, 196
Jessy, Henry, 37
Jesus Christ, 23, 27, 50, 58, 102, 119, 120, 191, 199, 229, 269, 298, 336, 365, 377, 417, 435, 440, 474, 492, 493, 527, 530, 531, 534, 535
Jeter, J. B., 362, 363, 488
John Eliot, 12, 77
Johnes, Samuel, 65
Johnson, Hezekiah, 420
Johnson's *History of New England*, 56, 96, 205
Jones, David, 262, 263, 267, 395, 446
Jones, Griffith, 113
Jones, Robert Settle, 222
Jones, Samuel, 88, 90, 222, 267
Judson, Adoniram, 359, 361, 364, 376, 397, 399, 400
Judson, Anne, 360

Kansa Indians, 410
Keach, Benjamin, 88
Keach, Elias, 88
Kendrick, A. C., 394
Kendrick, Nathaniel, 450, 528, 529, 537
Ketockton Baptist Association, 190, 237, 238, 249, 302
Kimball, Martha, 211
King James Bible, 57
King Phillip's War, 75, 76
King, Henry M., 482
Kiokee Baptist Church, 280, 305, 306, 350

Knapp, Jacob, 423
Knollys, Hanserd, 37, 498, 538, 542
Knoxville, 310, 349

Lafayette, 283, 300
Land for Preacher Deal, 10
Landford, Marsha Pike, 494
Landmarkism, 466, 474, 475, 476, 537
Lane, Dutton, 143, 156, 157, 160, 161
Lane, Tidence, 138, 143, 150, 156, 179, 198, 282, 311, 313, 365, 385
Laud, William, 5-7, 21, 22, 25, 38, 39, 498
Law of Patents, 8
laying on of hands, 94, 95, 153, 235, 500
Leach, Phebe, 206
Ledoyt, Biel, 208
Lee, Richard, 285
Legalists, 27
Leile, George, 431, 432, 434, 435
Leland, John, xvii, xx, 229, 247, 253, 270, 272, 277, 284, 290, 291, 315, 372, 389, 393, 396, 429, 445, 495, 496, 516, 521, 540
Lemen, Sr, James, 324
Leverette, John, 73
Lewis, Evison, 246
Lexington green, 253
Leyden, 3, 4, 19
liberty, xv, 1, 3, 13, 15, 20, 23, 24, 35, 37, 40, 41, 49, 58, 59, 65, 69, 74, 77, 79, 81, 86, 92, 108, 129, 135, 159, 166, 181, 182, 196, 198, 203, 204, 209, 210, 213, 223, 227, 233, 234, 235, 236, 242, 243, 245, 246, 248, 253, 258, 259, 260, 262, 263, 269, 275, 282, 283, 291, 292, 311, 364, 415, 427, 433, 436, 446, 495, 496, 498, 499, 500, 505, 507, 508, 509, 510, 514, 516, 518

ENDNOTES

CHAPTER ONE
The Hand of Kind Providence

[1] Isaac Backus, *An Abridgement to the Church History of New England* (Boston: Reprint of 1804 work by Harvard University, 1935), P. 25-35.

[2] *Ibid.*, 27.

[3] Emily Easton, *Roger Williams, Prophet and Pioneer* (Freeport: Books for Libraries Press, 1930).

[4] James Ernst, *Roger Williams, New England Firebrand* (NewYork: MacMillan Co., 1932), 15.

[5] Foiled attempt in 1605 by Jesuit agents to murder James I.

[6] Coke was arrested and placed in the prisoners tower of London by King James in 1623. He was instrumental in the protestation against the King's rebuke of the House of Commons. King James had rebuked the House for criticizing his attempts at attracting a Spanish maiden for his son, Prince Charles. Coke was imprisoned for two years. Easton, *Roger Williams*, P. 94-99.

[7] See Appendix A, *Mr. Marshall and Mr. Manuel, Have You No Shame?*

[8] John Callender, *Historical Discourse on the Civil and Religious Affairs of Rhode Island* (Boston: Kneeland and Green, 1734), 7-8. Callender wrote:

> The Puritans, it seems, had few or no objections, to the Articles of Faith, but they chiefly objected against the Liturgy, the Ceremonies, and the Constitution and Discipline. But however, they were not perfectly agreed among themselves; while the much larger part of them, Fathers of those since called Presbyterians, generally strove to keep their places in the Church, without conforming to some of the most offensive Ceremonies, and by voluntary Agreement among themselves, sought to remedy, and supply what they thought was amiss or wanting in the parliamentary Establishment, other of them, Father of those since called Independents and Congregationalists separated wholly from the publick Worship, in the Parish Churches, and sought a thorough alteration, in the whole Form and Constitution of the Church, and to lay aside the Liturgy, and all the Ceremonies together.

[9] Debatable.

[10] Ernst, *Roger Williams*, 37-40.

[11] Easton, *Roger Williams*, 134.

[12] **Those guys in the black hats**. This is our first set of *black hats*. Boston in the 1630's had a court of deputies that were chosen each spring and each fall. The house of deputies usually consisted of 25-30 members chosen from the *standing order* church. They made laws, decrees and exacted punishment upon evildoers.

[13] Concerning William Laud, Dr. David L. Cummins, wrote:

William Laud (1573 1645) Archbishop of Canterbury, born at Reading, Berkshire, England. Studied at Oxford. In 1601 he was ordained and in 1603 he became a chaplain. Advancement was rapid, and by 1611 he was elected the head of the St John's College. In 1621 he was appointed bishop of St. David's. He increased in royal promotions and favor. With the ascension of Charles 1 in 1625 real power in the Church of England began. He believed in the divine right of kings, and the divine right of bishops and exercised authority accordingly. In 1626 he became Bishop of Bath and Wells, and in 1628, he became the Bishop of London. In 1629 he was made chancellor of the University of Oxford where he pursued a program of scholarly reform, founded a school of Arabic which is still in existence. In 1633 he was made Archbishop of Canterbury and began work as head of the church [of England] with great zeal and determination. In his first year there he attempted to force ritualism on the Scottish Presbyterian Church. This led to riot in the churches, and a flare of rebellion in the entire land of Scotland. When the king endeavored to squelch the rebellion, trouble broke out at home, and the Civil War of 1642 to 1649 followed. Laud's severe program against the Puritans incurred their bitter hostility; his dealings with the Queen, who was a Roman Catholic, stirred her to enmity. In 1640 he was impeached for treason. He was confined and sent to the Tower in 1641. He was tried, and in 1643, with great firmness, he met his death on the scaffold of the Tower. He was narrow, cruel, and an enemy of the Baptists.

[14] Roger Williams, *The Bloody Tenet Yet More Bloody*, N.C.P., vol. IV, 65.

[15] Easton, *Roger Williams*, 119.

[16] *Ibid.*

[17] The Oath of a Freeman:

I, A.B. being by God's providence an inhabitant and freeman in this Commonweal, do freely acknowledge myself to be subject to the government thereof, and therefore do here swear by the great and dreadful name of the everliving God, that I will be true and faithful to the same, and will accordingly yield assistance and support hereunto with my person and estate as in equity I am bound, and will also truly endeavour to maintain and preserve all the liberties and privileges thereof; submitting myself to the wholesome laws and orders made and established by the same. And further, that I will not plot nor practise any evil against it, nor consent to any that shall so do; but will truly discover and reveal the same to lawful authority now here established, for the speedy preventing thereof. Moreover I do solemnly bind myself in the sight of God, that when I shall be called to give my voice touching any such matters of this state wherein freemen are to deal, I will give my vote and suffrage as I shall judge in mine own conscience may best conduce and tend to the public weal of the body, without respect of persons or favour of any man; so help me God in the Lord Jesus Christ.

[18] Isaac Backus, *An Abridgement to the Church History of New England* (1804; reprint ed., Boston: Harvard University, 1935), P. 30.

[19] Williams great observation is recorded in *the Bloody Tenet*:

Henry the seventh leaves England under the slavish bondage of the Pope's yoke. Henry the eight reforms all England to a new fashion, half papist, half protestant. King Edward the sixth turns about the wheels of state, and words the whole land to absolute Protestantism. Queen Mary succeeding to the helm, steers a direct contrary course, breaks in pieces all that Edward wrought, and brings forth an old edition of England's reformation, all popish. Mary not living out half her days (as the prophet speaks of bloody persons) Elizabeth (like Joseph) is advanced from the prison to the palace, and from the irons to the crown; she pluck up all her sister Mary plants, and sounds a trumpet, all protestant. What sober man is not amazed at these revolutions! Backus, *Abridgement*, 69.

[20] David Benedict, *A General History of the Baptist Denomination* (1813; reprint ed., Dayton: Church History Research and Archives, 1985), P. 453.

[21] Backus, *Abridgement*, 72.

[22] *Ibid.*, 30-31.

[23] Isaac Backus, *History of New England, with Particular Reference To the Baptists, vol. 1* (1871; Paris: reprint ed., The Baptist Standard Bearer, n.d.), P. 57.

[24] Backus, *Abridgement*, 36.

[25] The Providence Compact is the first of four documents showing the progression of liberty in America. The second document we mention in our narrative is the Mayflower Compact, and the third the Portsmouth Compact. The fourth, the Rhode Island Charter written in 1663 by John Clarke, was in spirit, a combination of the first three great documents and was the basis of the U. S. Constitution.

[26] Backus, *History of New England, vol. 1:* 74.

[27] *Ibid.*, 86.

[28] *Ibid.*, 86-87.

[29] John Callender suspected that Roger Williams did not form a church. Callender wrote:

Since this (the discourse) was transcribed for the press, I find some reasons to suspect that Mr. Williams did not form a church of the Anabaptists, and that he never joined with the Baptist Church there. Only, that he allowed [believed] them to be nearest the scripture rule, and true primitive practice, as to the mode and subject of Baptism. But that he himself waited for new Apostles, & etc. The most ancient inhabitants now alive, some of them above eighty years old, who personally knew Mr. Williams, and were well acquainted with many of the original Settlers, never heard that Mr. Williams formed the Baptist Church there, but always understood that Mr. Browne, Mr. Wickenden or Wiginten, Mr. Dexter, Mr. Olney, Mr. Tillinghast, & etc., were the first founders of that church. Callender, *Historical Discourse,* 56.

[30] Cotton Mather, *The Great Works of Christ in America,* (Carlisle: Banner of Truth Trust, vol. 7, 1979), P. 9.

[31] Backus, *History of New England, vol. 1:* 90.

[32] *Ibid.,* 89.

[33] Consider the words of John Spilbury, the pastor of the first Baptist church in London:

Because some think to shut up the ordinance of God in such a strait, that none can come by it but through the authority of the popedom of Rome; let the reader consider who baptized John the Baptist before he baptized others, and if no man did, then whether he did not baptize others, he himself being unbaptized. We are taught by this what to do on the like occasions. I fear men put more than is of right due to it, that so prefer it above the church, and all other ordinances; for they can assume and erect a church, take in and cast out members, elect and ordain officers, and administer the supper, and all anew, without looking after succession, any further than the scriptures; but as for baptism, they must have that successively from the apostles, though it comes through the hands of Pope Joan. What is the cause of this, that men can do all from the Word but only baptism? Thomas Crosby, *The History of the English Baptists,* vol. 1 (London: By the Author, 1738), P. 104, 105.

Or consider the words of John Callender:

Surely the disciples of Jesus Christ, must of necessity have an inherent right, to revive, or rectify, any of His ordinances that have been misused. The Protestants in general have done so, by both sacraments, which they have all of them rescued from some or other of the corruptions of Popery. And why they may not be as well rescued from every corruption, as from some, and why Christians may not revive the true form of administering Baptism as well as the Supper, is hard to tell, unless we make a Charm of the institution. So long as we have the New Testament, wherein the original commission and instructions are contained, we can want no immediate warrant, to obey the general laws of Christ, any more than new revelation, and new miracles to justify our believing the old facts and doctrines of the Gospel. Callender, *Historical Discourse,* 58.

[34] Peter Marshall and David Manuel, *The Light and the Glory* (Tarrytown: Fleming H. Revell, 1977), 192-199.

[35] *Ibid.,* 192-193.

[36] *Ibid.,* 193-194.

[37] Ernst, *Roger Williams,* 17-20.

[38] John Callender was the sixth pastor (1730-1748) of the first Baptist church at Newport, Rhode Island.

CHAPTER TWO
Banned in Boston

[1] Isaac Backus, *An Abridgement to the Church History of New England* (1804; reprint ed., Boston: Harvard University, 1935), P. 40.

[2] John Callender, *Historical Discourse on the Civil and Religious Affairs of Rhode Island* (Boston: Kneeland and Green, 1734), P. 7-9

[3] *Ibid.*, 7-8.

[4] *Ibid.*, 8.

[5] From 1628 to 1643 21,200 persons came to New England, and Backus reports that "very few had separated from the Church of England."

[6] Edward Wightman was condemned for his religious opinions at Litchfield, England, December 14, 1611 and burned April 11, 1612.

[7] Attributed to Joseph Hall, *A Common Apology against the Brownists* (Printed: 1610), sec. 11.

[8] Callender, *Historical Discourse*, 15.

[9] The Mayflower Compact:

> In ye name of God, Amen. We whose names are underwritten, the loyall subjects of our dread soveraigne Lord, King James, by the grace of God, of Great Britaine, Franc, and Ireland king, defender of the faith, etc.
>
> Haveing undertaken, for ye glorie of God, and advancemente of ye Christian faith, and honour of our king & countrie, a voyage to plant ye first colonie in ye Northerne parts of Virginia, doe by these presents solemnly & mutualy in ye presence of God, and one of another, covenant & combine our selves togeather into a civill body politick, for our better ordering & preservation & furtherance of ye ends aforesaid; and by vertue hearof to enacte lawes, ordinances, acts constitutions, & offices, from time to time, as shall be thought most meet & convenient for ye generall good of ye Colonie, unto which we promise all due submission and obedience. In witnes wherof we have hereunder subscribed our names at Cap-Codd ye 11th. of November, in ye year of ye raigne of our soveraigne lord, King James, of England, France, & Ireland ye eighteenth, and of Scotland, ye fiftie fourth. Ano: Dom. 1620.
>
> Signed by: John Carver, Edward Tilly, Digery Priest, William Bradford, John Tilly, Thomas Williams, Edward Winslow, Francis Cooke, Gilbert Winslow, William Brewster, Thomas Rogers, Edmund Margeson, Isaac Allerton, Thomas Tinker, Peter Brown,

Miles Standish, John Rigdale, Richard Bitteridge, John Alden, Edward Fuller, George Soule, Samuel Fuller, John Turner, Richard Clark, Christopher Martin, Francis Eaton, Richard Clark, William Mullins, James Chilton, John Allerton, William White, John Craxton, Thomas English, Richard Warren, John Billington, Edward Doten, John Howland, Moses Fletcher, Edward Leister, Stephen Hopkins John Goodman

[10]There are three documents that blazed the trail for liberty and the establishment of the American republic. The first was drawn together inside the bowels of the Mayflower, and it was the first document of separation from mother England. The second was Providence Compact, penned in Providence, Rhode Island (noted in chapter one) and was the first document of government order giving power only from the consent of the governed. The third document was the Portsmouth Compact. Rarely given the credit it deserves, the compact at Portsmouth was uniquely powerful because of its implications of liberty. It has been often copied in principle in each ensuing generation.

[11] All historians record Clarke's history as scant. However his writings and actions tell us much about his beliefs and character.

[12] On March 3, 1636 the Boston court enacted this:

This court doth not nor will hereafter approve any such companies of men, as shall henceforth join in any way of church fellowship without they shall first acquaint the magistrates, and the elders of the greater part of the churches of this jurisdiction, and have their approbation herein. And further it is ordered, that no person being an elder of any church which shall hereafter be gathered without the approbation of the magistrates and greater part of the said churches shall be admitted to the freedom of the Commonwealth. Backus, *Abridgement*, 39.

[13] The Massachusetts Bay Colony elected their governor every year.

[14] Callender, *Historical Discourse*, 20.

[15] Election held on May 25, 1636.

[16]Isaac Backus, *History of New England, with Particular Reference To the Baptists, vol. 1* (1871; reprint ed., Paris: The Baptist Standard Bearer, n.d.), P. 62.

[17] Backus, *History of New England, vol. 1*: 63.

[18] Callender, *Historical Discourse*, 25.

[19] *Ibid.*, 22.

[20] Thomas Bicknell, *The Story of Dr. John Clarke*, (Providence: By the Author, 1915), 39-41

[21] Callender, *Historical Discourse*, 24-25.

[22] Bicknell, *Dr. John Clarke*, 63.

[23] Backus, *History of New England, vol. 1*: 65.

[24] "Mr. Winthrop, being rechosen Governour, with a great struggle, he strenuously exerted himself, to crush and exterminate the Opinions he disapproved." Callender, *Historical Discourse*, 20-21.

[25] Callender, *Historical Discourse*, 28.

[26] Backus, *History of New England, vol. 1*: 66.

[27] According to the old Massachusetts Bay law, disfranchised meant: No person being a member of any church which shall be gathered without the approbation of the magistrate and the said (other congregations of the immediate area) churches shall be admitted to the freedom of the commonwealth.

[28] Backus, *History of New England, vol. 1*: 68.

[29] The "Ann Hutchinson Thing" is a result of historical re-write designed to give Mrs. Hutchinson more credit than she is due. The historians on the side of the Boston synod such as Cotton Mather, and Neal in his *History of the Puritans* distort the place of Mrs. Hutchinson to make it appear that she was the ringleader in a seditious movement. Modern historians use this distortion (without consulting the Baptist accounts) to build a case that her civil rights were violated and she was the center of the controversy.

[30] Callender, *Historical Discourse*, 62.

[31] Backus, *History of New England, vol. 1*: 125.

[32] Winthrop's *Journal, vol. 1*, P. 297.

[33] Callender, *Historical Discourse*, 56.

[34] For more details on the first Baptist church in America, see Appendix B.

[35] Some studies make a case that the first bona fide preacher in America who practiced believer's baptism was Gregory Dexter, Baptist minister from London, England who came to Providence, Rhode Island in 1644. Dexter immediately joined himself to what was left of Roger Williams' church and most probably brought believer's baptism with him from England. He lived to the age of 90.

[36] John Comer, *Diary* (Providence: Published by the Rhode Island Historical Society, Edited by C. Edwin Barrows, D. D., 1893), P. 88.

[37] Callender wrote:

As the pious people, who first planted this island and colony were so concerned about **the best way of evidencing a man's good estate**, methinks there is no more proper remark for us to finish with than the duty, the wisdom, and the necessity of every one to get into a good estate as to God and the future world and to seek after sufficient and satisfactory evidence thereof. Dr. Cotton Mather later reported that the controversy that led to the Boston banning was "briefly...the Points whereon depend, the Grounds of our Assurance for Blessedness in another and better World. Callender, *Historical Discourse*, 25, 118-119.

CHAPTER THREE
The Devil's Post

[1] Isaac Backus, *History of New England, with Particular Reference To the Baptists*, vol. 1 (1871; reprint ed., Paris: The Baptist Standard Bearer, n.d.), P. 117.

[2] Backus, *History of New England*, vol. 1: 127.

[3] *Ibid.*

[4] Edwin S. Gaustad, *Baptist Piety* (Grand Rapids: Christian University Press, 1978), P. 16.

[5] *Ibid.*, 126.

[6] Backus, *History of New England*, vol. 1: 82. In the footnotes by David Weston.

[7] *Ibid.*

[8] Gaustad, *Baptist Piety*, 8-9.

[9] *Ibid.*, 9.

[10] Backus, *History of New England*, vol. 1: 58-59.

[11] Isaac Backus, *An Abridgement to the Church History of New England* (1804; reprint ed., Boston: Harvard University, 1935), P. 63-64.

[12] *Ibid.*

[13] Backus quotes the early New England historian Johnson on the seven sectaries to be shunned, or banished from Massachusetts: The Gortonists, the Papists, the Familisits, the Seekers, the Antinomians, the Anabaptists, and the Prelacy. These and the 80 errors condemned at the 1637 synod at Boston became the foundation for the "Cambridge Platform." Backus, *Abridgement*, 33.

[14] Gaustad, *Baptist Piety*, 17.

[15] *Ibid.*, 15.

[16] John Russell Bartlett, *Letters of Roger Williams*, VI (Providence: Narragansett Club, 1874), P. 187-88. See also the Massachusetts Colony Records, III. 173.

[17] Gaustad, *Baptist Piety*, 19.

[18] *Ibid.*

[19] *Ibid.*

[20] Backus, *History of New England*, vol. 1: 177.

[21] Henry M. King, *Early Baptists Defended*, (Boston: Howard Gannett, Publisher, for the Rhode Island Historical Society, 1880) P. 18. See also the works of John Gorham Palfrey, *History of New England*, and Henry Martyn Dexter, *As to Roger Williams*. Mr. King said that Dexter's book was an attempt at "nothing less than the reversal of the judgment of history."

[22] Commissioners from New Hampshire, Connecticut, Plymouth & Massachusetts met in Boston 1643 and signed articles of confederation for mutual protection and defense. Rhode Island was not included. It was New England's punishment of Rhode Island for harboring the likes of Williams, Clarke and Gorton.

[23] Backus, *History of New England*, vol. 1: 178.

[24] William Cathcart, *The Baptist Encyclopedia* (Philadelphia: Louis H. Everts, 1883), P. 539.

[25] King, *Early Baptists*, 28-30.

[26] [Online] http://www.usgennet.org/usa/ma/state/main/essex_court.html PRE-SENTMENT'S. 11 mo. 1641. See also John Taylor Christian, *A History of the Baptists, Vol. 2* (Nashville: Sunday School Board of the Southern Baptist Convention, 1926), P. 52.

[27] King, *Early Baptists*, 30.

[28] It is possible that their demeanor disarmed their captors and they simply walked away to finish their business with Witter.

[29] King, *Early Baptists*, 33.

[30] Gaustad, *Baptist Piety*, 19.

[31] King, *Early Baptists*, 38.

[32] Backus, *History of New England, vol. 1*: 181.

[33] John Comer, Diary (Providence: Rhode Island Historical Society, edited by C. Edwin Barrows, D. D., 1893), P. 75-76.

[34] Sent the next morning Thursday August 1. Backus, *History of New England, vol. 1*: 181.

[35] *Ibid.*

[36] Backus, *History of New England, vol. 1*: 181.

[37] *Ibid.*,182-184.

[38] Backus, *History of New England, vol. 1*: 192.

[39] King, *Early Baptists*, 41.

[40] King, *Early Baptists*, 47.

[41] Backus, *History of New England, vol. 1*: 193.

CHAPTER FOUR
A Yankee Defector in Harvard Yards

[1] George Parker Winship, London Biographical Society, found in the Henry Dunster Papers. In the Archive of the Pusey Library, Harvard University, Cambridge, Massachusetts.

[2] Dunster Papers.

[3] William Cathcart, *The Baptist Encyclopedia*, (Philadelphia: Louis H. Everts, 1883), P. 350.

[4] Isaac Backus, *An Abridgement to the Church History of New England* (1804; reprint ed., Boston: Harvard University, 1935), P. 84.

[5] Thomas Armitage, *A History of the Baptists*, (New York: Bryan, Taylor and Co., 1887) P. 438. Armitage wrote:

> At the very time of these public disputations the Westminster Assembly met, by order of Parliament, and was in session from 1643 to 1649, and its discussions were sorely disturbed on this question of 'dipping.' Yet, according to Neal, there was not one Baptist in that body. Dr. Lightfoot, one of its leading members, kept a journal of its proceedings, and his entry for August 7, 1644,

tells us of 'a great heat; in the debate of that day, when they were framing the 'Directory' for baptism, as to whether dipping should be reserved or excluded, or whether 'it was lawful and sufficient to besprinkle.' Coleman, called 'Rabi Coleman' because of his great Hebrew learning, contended with Lightfoot that *tauveleh*, the Hebrew word for dipping, demanded immersion 'over head;' and Marshall, a famous pulpit orator, stood firmly by him in the debate, both contending that dipping was essential 'in the first institution.' Lightfoot says that when they came to the vote, 'So many were unwilling to have dipping excluded that the vote came to an equality within one, for the one side was twenty-four, the other twenty-five; the twenty-four for the reserving of dipping, and twenty-five against it.' The business was recommitted, and next day, after another warm dispute, it was voted that 'pouring or sprinkling water on the face' was sufficient and most expedient. How did this Presbyterian body, without a Baptist in it, came to such 'a great heat' on dipping if it were a novelty and an innovation amongst them in England?

[6] According to official U.S. Government web site [Online] http://www.loc.gov/exhibits/religion/rel01.html Dec 2003.

[7] An examination of the writings of Roger Williams, John Clarke, and John Comer show overwhelming evidence of the King James as being the version of choice.

[8] Isaac Backus, *History of New England, with Particular Reference To the Baptists*, vol. 1 (1871; reprint ed., Paris: The Baptist Standard Bearer, n.d.), P. 228.

[9] Both John Cleaveland of Ipswich (in 1684) and Cotton Mather (in 1702) repeated this devil thing while defending infant baptism.

[10] Cathcart, *Baptist Encyclopedia*, 350.

[11] *Ibid.*

[12] Dunster Papers.

[13] Backus, *Abridgement*, 27.

[14] *Ibid.*, 37.

[15] *Ibid.*, 42.

[16] *Ibid.*, 27-28.

[17] Backus, *History of New England*, vol. 1: 216.

[18] There seems to be no question in Isaac Backus' mind that Henry Dunster influenced Thomas Gould in his "scruple" against infant baptism. William G. McLoughlin seems to have problems with it, though the author of *America in Crimson Red* cannot find a warrant for his problems. According to Henry Herbert Edes: "Upon leaving Cambridge, Dunster went first to Charleston, where he was hospitably entertained at the house of Thomas Gould, subsequently minister of the First Baptist Church in Boston, who was an intimate acquaintance of Benanuel Bowers, also of Charlestown and a fellow-Baptist, whom he named in his will as one of his overseers." Henry Herbert Edes, *The Colonial Society of Massachusetts Vol. III* (Cambridge: University Press, 1897), P. 13.

[19] Backus, *History of New England*, vol. 1: 291.

[20] *Ibid.*

[21] *Ibid.*

[22] Horatio Rogers, *Mary Dyer of Rhode Island, The Quaker Martyr that was hanged on Boston Common* (Providence: Preston and Rounds, 1896), P. 31

[23] *Ibid.*

[24] Backus, *Abridgement,* 92.

[25] *Ibid.,* 93.

[26] *Ibid.,* 95.

[27] Armitage, *History,* 670.

[28] This is the fourth and most important political document written before the U. S. Constitution. The majority of historians agree that the Constitution is based upon the patterns and principles found in the Rhode Island Charter. John Clarke was the author

[29] Appendix D contains the first portion of the Rhode Island Charter.

[30] Armitage, *History,* 678.

[31] McLoughlin calls Roger Williams and Ann Hutchinson "eccentric prophets," and Henry Dunster an "intellectual savant". William G. McLoughlin, *New England Dissent 1630-1833* (Cambridge: Harvard University Press, 1971), P. 50.

[32] McLoughlin, *Dissent,* 49.

[33] Not as severe as excommunication.

[34] Backus, *Abridgement,* 96.

[35] Backus, *History of New England, vol. 1:* 297.

[36] *Ibid.,* 298.

[37] King Charles II had sent a letter to the Boston Court in support of the Church of England planting churches in Massachusetts. Charles II cited the original patent of the colony which, he says, "And since the principle and foundation of that charter was and is the freedom of liberty of conscience, Wee do hereby charge and require you that that freedom and liberty be duely admitted and allowed."

[38] Thomas Hutchinson, *A Collection of Original Papers Relating to the History of Massachusetts Bay* (Boston: By the Author, 1769), P. 378.

[39] McLoughlin, *Dissent,* 60.

[40] Backus, *History of New England, vol. 1:* 300.

[41] *Ibid.*

[42] *Ibid.*

[43] Bellingham was educated as a lawyer. Served as city recorder for Boston, Lincolnshire, England from 1625 to 1633. Immigrated to Massachusetts in the American Colonies in 1634. Elected Deputy Governor of the Massachusetts Bay colony in 1635. Elected Governor in 1644. Re-elected several times including continuously from 1665 to 1672 until his death. He is well known as a character in the famous classic novel, *The Scarlet Letter.* He was infamous for creating a legal crisis in 1641 when he married and performed the cere-

mony himself. In spite of his eccentricities, he was well respected, even among his opponents for his knowledge of the law. He was also renown for having a sister, Anne (Bellingham) Hibbins who was one of those accused and burned as a witch in the Salem Witch Trials.

[44] William Bradford, *History of Plymouth Plantation* (Cambridge: Collections of Massachusetts Historical Society, Fourth Series, III. n.d.), P. 386, 387.

[45] McLoughlin, *Dissent*, 63.

[46] *Ibid.*, 70.

[47] Backus, *Abridgement*, 103-104.

[48] McLoughlin, *Dissent*, 71.

[49] Backus, *History of New England, vol. 1:* 308.

[50] McLoughlin, *Dissent*, 73.

[51] Alice Morse Earle, Curious Punishments of Bygone Days, 1896. [Online] http://www.getchwood.com/punishments/curious/index.html May 2003.

[52] McLoughlin, *Dissent*, 49.

[53] Backus, *Abridgement*, 128.

[54] *Ibid.*, 53

[55] Backus, *History of New England, vol. 1:* 103.

[56] Backus, *Abridgement*, 124.

[57] *Life of John Clarke* (Newport: First Baptist Clarke Memorial Baptist Church, 1983), P. 15.

[58] The exact date is unknown.

[59] Jonathan Edwards, George Whitefield, Isaac Backus and Shubal Stearns.

CHAPTER FIVE
New England Lost

[1] John Callender, *Historical Discourse on the Civil and Religious Affairs of Rhode Island* (Boston: Published by the Author, 1739), p. 41.

[2] C. Edwin Barrows wrote:

Increase Mather: Son of Richard Mather and Catharine Hoult, was born at Dorchester, June 21, 1639. At the age of twelve, he entered Harvard College, and was graduated in the class of 1656. In July of the following year he sailed for England in response to an invitation from his brother Samuel, who was then a minister in Dublin, Ireland. He enrolled himself as a student in Trinity College, and when but nineteen year of age received the Master's Degree. Returning home he married, March 6, 1662 Maria Cotton, daughter of John Cotton. In 1664, he was pastor of North Church (Congregational) in Boston. President of Harvard from 1684 till 1701. The original "Doctor of Divinity" bestowed by Harvard in 1692. d August 23, 1723. C. Edwin Barrows, *The Di-*

ary of John Comer (Providence: Rhode Island Historical Society, Edited by C. Edwin Barrows, D. D., 1893), P. 43.

[3] Isaac Backus, An *Abridgement to the Church History of New England* (1804; reprint ed., Boston: Harvard University, 1935), P. 134.

[4] Backus, *Abridgement*, 136.

[5] Bernard Rosenthal, *Salem Story–Reading the Witch Trials of 1692* (Boston: Cambridge University Press, 1993), P. 183.

[6] Backus, *Abridgement*, 144.

[7] Before Thomas Hooker, the founder of Connecticut died, he had written; "Children as children have no right to baptism so that it belongs non to any predecessors, either nearer or further off, removed from the next parents, to give right of this privilege to their children." Connecticut would reject his sentiments under the Saybrook Platform. Backus, *Abridgement*, 68.

[8] E. Wayne Thompson, David L. Cummins, *This Day in Baptist History* (Greenville: Bob Jones University Press, 1993), P. 491.

[9] *Ibid.*

[10] *Ibid.*

[11] Thomas Armitage, *A History of the Baptists* (New York: Bryan, Taylor and Co., 1887), P. 708.

[12] Armitage wrote:

The father of the noted Dr. Benjamin Rush, a signer of the Declaration of Independence, was a member of his Church at Cold Spring. William Penn, it is supposed, caught his liberal views from Algernon Sidney; he had suffered much for Christ's sake, and had adopted quite broad views of religious liberty; for at the very inception of legislation in Pennsylvania, the Assembly had passed the 'Great Law,' the first section of which provides that in that jurisdiction no person shall 'At any time be compelled to frequent or maintain any religious worship, place or ministry whatever, contrary to his or her mind, but shall freely and fully enjoy his or her Christian liberty in that respect, without any interruption or reflection; and, if any person shall abuse or deride any other for his or her different persuasion and practice, in matter of religion, such shall be looked upon as a disturber of the peace, and be punished accordingly. Armitage, *History*, 706.

[13] *Ibid.*

[14] *Ibid.*

[15] *Ibid.*

[16] *Ibid.*

[17] *Ibid.*

[18] *Ibid.*

[19] *Ibid.*

[20] Thomas Armitage wrote:

A most interesting Church was organized in 1689 at Piscataqua. This settlement was named after a settlement in New Hampshire (now Dover), which at that time was in the Province of Maine. We have seen that Hanserd Knollys preached there in 1638-41, and had his controversy with Larkham respecting receiving all into the Church (Congregational), and the baptizing of any infants offered. Although Knollys was not a Baptist at that time, his discussions on these subjects proved to be the seed which yielded fruit after many years.

In 1648, ten years after he began his ministry at Dover, under date of October 18th, the authorities of the day were informed that the profession of 'Anabaptistry' there by Edward Starbuck had excited much trouble, and they appointed Thomas Wiggin and George Smith to try his case. Starbuck was one of the assistants in the Congregational Church there, possibly the same people to whom Knollys had preached; but the results of the trial, if he had one, are not given. The Colonial records of Massachusetts make the authorities say (iii, p. 173): "We have heard heretofore of divers Anabaptists risen up in your jurisdiction and connived at. Being but few, we well hoped that it might have pleased God, by the endeavors of yourselves and the faithful elders with you, to have reduced such erring men again into the right way. But now, to our great grief, we are credibly informed that your patient bearing with such men hath produced another effect, namely, the multiplying and increasing of the same errors, and we fear may be of other errors also if timely care be not taken to suppress the same. Particularly we understand that within these few weeks there have been at Seckonk thirteen or fourteen persons rebaptized (a swift progress in one town), yet we hear not if any effectual restriction is intended thereabouts."

When Knollys left, in 1641, a number of those who sympathized with his Baptist tendencies left with him, and when he returned to London they settled on Long Island, and remained there until that territory fell under the power of English Episcopacy, when they removed to the vicinity of New Brunswick, N. J. There they formed the settlement of Piscataqua (afterward **Piscataway, near Stelton) and organized a Baptist** Church, which has exerted a powerful influence down to this time, being now under the pastoral care of John Wesley Sarles, D.D.

The constituent members of this Church form an interesting study. It is certain that amongst the original patentees, in 1666 Hugh Dunn and John Martin were Baptists, and amongst their associates admitted in 1668 the Drakes, Dunhams, Smalleys, Bonhams, Fitz Randolphs, Mannings, Runyons, Stelles and others were of the same faith. About the time of organizing the Baptist Church at "New Piscataqua," as they called the place, the township confined about 80 families, embodying a, population of about 400 persons. From the earliest information this settlement was popularly known as the "Anabaptist Town," and from 1675 downward the names of members of the Baptist Church are found amongst the law-makers and other public officials, both in the town and the colony, showing that they were prominent and influential citizens.

Their connection with Pennepek was slight, yet some of the families of the old Church may have been in the new. Amongst them were John Drake, Hugh Dunn and Edmund Dunham, unordained ministers, who had labored for several years in that region as itinerants. About six years before the formation of the Church—1685-90—a company of Irish Baptists, members of a Church in Tipperary, had landed at Perth Amboy and made a settlement at Cohansey, some of whom went farther into the interior. It is quite probable that Dunn and Dunham—were both of that company, and quite as likely that Mr. Drake was from Dover, N. H., where it is believed that his father had settled many years before from Devonshire, England. Thomas Killingsworth also was present at the organization of this Church, but John Drake, whose family claims kindred with Sir Francis Drake, the great navigator, was ordained its pastor at its constitution, and served it in that capacity for about fifty years.

Another Church was established at COHANSEY. The records of this Church for the first hundred years of its existence were burned, but, according to Asplund's Register, the Church was organized in 1691. Keach had baptized three persons there in 1688, and the Church was served for many years by Thomas Killingsworth, who was also a judge on the bench. He was an ordained minister from Norfolk, England, of much literary ability, eminent for his gravity and sound judgment, and so was deemed fit to serve as Judge of the County Court of Salem. About 1687 a company had come from John Myles's Church, at Swansea, near Providence, which for twenty-three years kept themselves as a separate Church, on the questions of laying on of hands, singing of psalms and predestination, until, with Timothy Brooks, their pastor they united with their brethren at Cohansey.

It was meet that before this remarkable century closed the nucleus of Baptist principles should be formed in the great Quaker city of Philadelphia, and this was done in 1696. John Fanner and his wife, from Knolly's Church in London, landed there in that year, and were joined in 1697 by John Todd and Rebecca Woosencroft, from the Church at Leamington, England. A little congregation was held in Philadelphia by the preaching of Keach and Killingsworth and slowly increased. The meetings were held irregularly in a store-house on what was known as the "Barbadoes Lot," at the corner of what are now called Second and Chestnut Streets, and formed a sort of out-station to Pennepek. In 1697 John Watts baptized four persons, who, with five others, amongst them John Hohne, formed a Church on the second Sabbath in December, 1698. They continued to meet in the store-house till 1707, when they were compelled to leave under protest, and then they worshiped, according to Edwards, at a place "near the draw-bridge, known by the name of Anthony Morris's New House."

They were not entirely independent of Pennepek till 1723, when they had a dispute with the Church there about certain legacies, in which the old Church wanted to share; May 15th, 1746, this contest resulted in the formation of an entirely independent Church of 56 members in Philadelphia. This rapid review of the Baptist sentiment which had shaped into organization in these colonies at the close of the seventeenth century, together with a few small bodies in Rhode Island, besides the Churches at Providence and Newport, Swansea, South Carolina and New Jersey, give us the results of more than half a century's struggle for a foothold in the New World.

The new century, however, opened with the emigration of 16 Baptists, from the counties of Pembroke and Carmarthen, Wales, under the leadership of Rev. Thomas Griffith, whose coming introduced a new era in Pennsylvania and the region round about. They had organized themselves into what Morgan Edwards calls "a Church emigrant and sailant" at Milford, June, 1701, and landed in Philadelphia in September following. They repaired immediately to the vicinity of Pennepek and settled there for a time.

They insisted on the rite of laying on of hands as a matter of vital importance, and fell into sharp contention on the subject, both amongst themselves and with the Pennepek Church. In 1703 the greater part of them purchased lands containing about 30,000 acres from William Penn, in Newcastle County, Delaware. This they named the Welsh Tract and removed thither.

There they prospered greatly from year to year, adding to their numbers both by emigration and conversion. But they say: "We could not be in fellowship (at the Lord's table) with our brethren of Pennepek and Philadelphia, because they did not hold to the laying on of hands; true, some of them believed in the ordinance, but neither preached it up nor practiced it, and when we moved to Welsh Tract, and left twenty-two of our members at Pennepek, and took some of theirs with us, the difficulty increased." For about seventy years their ministers were Welshmen, some of them of eminence, and six Churches in Pennsylvania and Delaware trace their lineage to this Church.

As early as 1736 it dismissed forty-eight members to emigrate to South Carolina, where they made a settlement on the Peedee River, and organized the Welsh Neck Church there, which during the next century became the center from which thirty-eight Baptist Churches sprang, in the immediate vicinity. Armitage, *History*, 710-713.

[21] The London Baptist Confession of Faith of 1689 has an appendix which became a source of controversy. Cathcart cleared up the controversy by writing:

The Appendix has this statement: The known principle and state of the consciences of divers of us that have agreed in this Confession is such that *we cannot hold church communion with any other than baptized believers, and churches constituted of such*; yet some others of us have a greater libery and freedom in our spirits that way." This refers to the admission of unbaptized persons to the Lord's Table by some churches, and their rejection by others.

Within a few years, an effort has been made in this country to prove that
our Baptist fathers of the Philadelphia, and other early Associations, practiced
"open communion" because of this item in the Appendix of the London Confession. The learned "strict communion" author of "Historical Vindications"
has contributed to this error, by making the grave mistake that the Appendix
was Article XXXIII of the Philadelphia Confession of Faith. And he gives as
his authorities for this extraordinary statement the Hanserd Knollys Society's
copy of the Confession of 1689, and the Pittsburgh edition of The Philadelphia Confession of Faith. In the former, it is not placed as an Article, but as
an Appendix. In the latter, it is *not to be found in ay form*. It never appeared in
any edition of the Philadelphia Confession of Faith, from Benjamin Franklin's
first issue down to the last copy sent forth from the press. And this could have
been easily learned from the title page. In the end of the title in the Hanserd
Knolly's Society's copy of the Confession of 1689 are the words, "With an
Appendix concerning Baptism." The portion of the title covering the Appendix, and the Appendix itself, cannot be found in any copy of our oldest
American Baptist creed. That the honored writer acted in good faith in this
part of this valuable work, I have no doubt; but that he was held astray himself, and that he has drawn others into a grave mistake, I am absolutely certain. William Cathcart, *The Baptist Encyclopedia*, (Philadelphia: Louis H.
Everts, 1883), P. 264-265.

[22] Armitage, *History*, 713.

[23] Thomas Crosby, rescued those documents from Neal and wrote the *History of the
English Baptists*, which was published in 1740.

[24] Backus, *Abridgement*, 159.

[25] John Comer, Diary (Providence: Rhode Island Historical Society, edited by C.
Edwin Barrows, D. D., 1893), P. 17-19.

[26] *Ibid.*, 20.

[27] C. Edwin Barrows wrote:
Joseph Stennet, son of Edward Stennett, a minister of some distinction during
the Parliamentary war, was born in Berks County, England, in 1663, and or-
dained March 4, 1690, pastor of the Sabbatarian church, meeting in Pinner's
Hall, London, in which office he remained till his death, which occurred July
11, 1713. On Sundays he ministered to other Baptist churches. He was a fine
Hebrew scholar, and composed many beautiful hymns, which are still used in
the church. In 1702 he published an admirable defense of baptism in reply to
Mr. David Russen's book, entitled *Fundamentals without a Foundation*. Comer,
Diary, 26-27.

[28] *Ibid.*

[29] *Ibid.*, 27.

[30] "Laying on of Hands" was a practice brought to America by the early Baptist
settlers in which hands were laid upon a believer at his baptism in accordance
to Acts 8:17, Hebrews 6:2, and others. Those that practiced this ordinance

were called "6 Principle Baptists." They based their principles on Hebrews 6:1-3 and were "general" in their outlook on the atonement.

[31] This was the beginning of the Calvinist/Arminian controversy in America. It is evident that the first churches along the Atlantic seaboard south of Rhode Island were "general" in their outlook of the atonement.

[32] C. Edwin Barrows wrote:

Ephraim Wheaton was born in 1653. He served the Swanzey Church for thirty years, first as associate pastor with Mr. Luther from 1704 till the death of the latter in 1717, then as sole pastor till his own death, April 26, 1734. The meeting-house, though in Swanzey, stood near the borders of Rehoboth, and he and many of his people who lived therein were taxed to [support] Pedobaptist ministers of that town. He occasionally corresponded with friends in London. Mr. Backus has preserved letters, which passed between him and the munificent London merchant, Thomas Hollis. Letters of his are recorded in the books of the First Church in Newport. Wheaton appears to have been a valued friend of John Comer; they died within a month of each other, and were buried side by side. Comer, *Diary*, 43.

[33] *Ibid.*, 94.

[34] Cathcart's *Baptist Encyclopedia*, 255.

[35] Willmarth wrote of Comer:

The local historians tell us that Mr. Comer was curious in noting all the remarkable events that came within his knowledge, and the two manuscript volumes [of his diary] of the Rhode Island Historical Society are but a small portion of his writings, for the centuries lay vandal hands upon manuscripts and unbound memoranda. Comer, *Diary*, 125.

[36] Backus, *Abridgement*, 160.

[37] Alvah Hovey, D.D., *The Life and Times of Isaac Backus* (1858, reprint ed., Harrisonville: Gano Books, 1991), P. 34.

[38] Sereno E. Dwight, *Memoirs of Jonathan Edwards* (reprinted, Edinburgh: Banner of Truth Trust, 1998), P. xxviii.

[39] *Ibid.*, xxviii

[40] *Ibid.*, xxxix.

[41] *Ibid.*

[42] *Ibid.*, xxii

[43] Comer, *Diary*, 46.

[44] *Ibid.*, 47.

[45] *Ibid.*, 48.

[46] *Ibid.*, 54.

[47] *Ibid.*, 55.

[48] *Ibid.*, 65.

[49] *Ibid.*, 57.

[50] *Ibid.*, 62.

[51] *Ibid.*

[52] *Ibid.,* 91.

[53] *Ibid.,* 100.

[54] *Ibid.,* 101.

[55] Callender, *Historical Discourse,* 16.

[56] *Ibid.,* 11.

[57] Here is the list of the Six Principle Baptists in New England as recorded by Comer in 1729:

In Newport: James Clarke (nephew of Dr. John Clarke), Daniel Wightman, John Comer.

In Providence: James Brown (grandson of Obadiah Holmes), Jonathan Sprague. At the second Baptist church in Providence: Peter Place and Samuel Fisk.

In New York: Nicholas Eyres;

In Connecticut: Groton, Valentine Wightman; Dartmouth, Phillip Tabor; New London, Stephen Gorton.

In Massachusetts: South Kingston, Daniel Everett; Swanzey, Joseph Mason; Warwick, Manassah Martin; North Kingston: Richard Sweet;

Those of the Particular redemption view according to Comer in 1729: Rhode Island: Newport, Willam Peckcom (1st church); Massachusetts: Swanzey, Ephraim Wheaton; Boston, Elisha Callender (1st Church).

[58] Comer, *Diary,* 79.

[59] George Whitefield said this.

CHAPTER SIX
The Great Awakening

[1] Isaac Backus, *An Abridgement to the Church History of New England* (1804; reprint ed., Boston: Harvard University, 1935), P. 174.

[2] Arnold Dallimore, *George Whitefield, The Life and Times of the Great Evangelist, vol. 1* (London: The Banner of Truth Trust, 1970), P. 242.

[3] James H. Hutson observes of this episode, "The distribution of the great amulets showed in its eerie way that men facing stress and anxiety wanted links to a preacher of a living God. One need look no farther for the reason evangelicalism demolished deism." *George Whitefield: British Calvinist in America* [Online] http://capo.org/Whitefield.htm Aug 2002.

[4] James Kirby Martin, *Benedict Arnold Revolutionary Hero, An American Warrior Reconsidered* (New York: New York University Press, 1997).

[5] *Ibid.*

[6] September 9, 1708. 16 delegates: 12 ministers and 4 laymen adopted the articles of discipline known as the Saybrook Platform.

[7] Arnold Dallimore *George Whitefield, The Life and Times of the Great Evangelist, Vol. 1, 2* (London: The Banner of Truth Trust, 1970).

[8] Dallimore, *Whitefield*, vol. 1: 259-260.

[9] *Ibid.*, 240.

[10] *Ibid.*

[11] *Ibid.*, 435.

[12] *Ibid.*, 439.

[13] *Ibid.*

[14] *Ibid.*, 441.

[15] *Ibid.*, 528.

[16] *Ibid.*, 530.

[17] Arnold Dallimore wrote:

Whitefield's whole outlook, both theological and in relationship to the daily Christian life, was affected by this deeper understanding of Divine grace. In his letters he began to tell forth the truths he had thus experienced and, in so doing, enunciated the basic tenets of a theological system—the system which is known as Calvinism. Dallimore, *Whitefield*, vol. 1: 404.

[18] *Ibid.*, 406.

[19] *Ibid.*, 407.

[20] *Ibid.*, 408.

[21] *Ibid.*, 409.

[22] Alvah Hovey, *The Life and Times of Isaac Backus* (1858; reprint ed., Gano Books, 1991) P. 55.

[23] Hovey, *Life of Backus*, 56.

[24] Backus, *Abridgement*, 164.

[25] *Ibid.*, 165.

[26] Jonathan Edwards, *The Works of Jonathan Edwards, vol. I* (London: William Tegg, 1860), P.115.

[27] Backus, *Abridgement*, 166.

[28] Ibid., 169.

[29] Hovey, *Life of Backus*, 38.

[30] *Ibid.*, 39.

[31] *Ibid.*, 40.

[32] *Ibid.*, 43.

[33] *Ibid.*

[34] James Kirby Martin, *An American Warrior Reconsidered* (New York: New York University Press, 1997). Introduction.

[35] Hovey, *Life of Backus*, 59.

[36] *Ibid.*, 63.

[37] *Ibid.*, 64.

[38] Backus, *Abridgement*, 184.

[39] *Ibid.*, 177.

[40] *Ibid.*, 175-185.

[41] Dallimore, *Whitefield, vol. 1*: 241.

[42] E. Wayne Thompson, David L. Cummins, *This Day in Baptist History vol. 1* (Greenville: Bob Jones University Press, 1993), P. 158.

[43] Hovey, *Life of Backus*, 87.

[44] On November 8, 1753, 40 churches of the "Separate" constitution met to discuss baptism, and mixed communion. Solomon Paine the unofficial leader of the "Separate" Congregationalists, recanted an earlier stance of acceptance of communion with "Separate" Baptists. He now publicly announced his rejection of mixed communion with Baptists.

[45] Stephen Drown, Stephen Babcock, Nathaniel Draper and Peter Werden remained mixed communionists. Hovey, *Life of Backus*, 114.

[46] C. C. Goen, *Revivalism and Separatism in New England, 1740-1800* (New Haven: Yale University Press, 1962), P. 208.

[47] Backus, *Abridgement*, 178.

[48] William Lumpkin, *Baptist Inroads in the South* (Shelbyville: Bible and Literature Missionary Foundation, n.d.) P. 20. Mr. Lumpkin gives no source for the quote.

[49] See the author's book, *The Soul of St. Louis* for a summary of the events leading to the apostasy of the Congregational Church.

[50] Dallimore, *Whitefield, vol. 2*: 303e.

[51] *Ibid.*, 504.

CHAPTER SEVEN
God's Power out of North Carolina

[1] George Washington Paschal, *History of North Carolina Baptists vol. 1* (Raleigh: Edwards & Broughton Co., 1930), P. 240.

[2] David Benedict, *History of the Baptist Denomination, vol. 2* (1813; Reprint ed., Dayton: Church History Research and Archives, 1985), P. 24.

[3] Benedict, *History vol. 2*: 24.

[4] Of David Thomas, William Cathcart wrote:
R. B. Semple says, 'There were few such men in the world in his day, [he] was born at London Tract, Pa., Aug. 16, 1732. He was educated at Hopewell, N. J., under the famous Isaac Eaton, and received the degree of A.M. from Rhode Island College (now Brown University). He was ordained to the ministry at about the age of eighteen years. In 1751, he went with John Gano and James Miller as a missionary from the Philadelphia Baptist Association to Virginia. During a preaching tour in Fauquier County he formed the Broad Run church, and became its pastor about 1762. Immense crowds were attracted by his ministry, and people traveled from fifty to a hundred miles to hear him. In 1763, he went to Culpeper County to preach, but the mob anticipated and prevented him. He, however, entered Orange County, and was more success-

ful. This was the first time any Baptists had preached in that part of Virginia, and he met with much rude treatment, at one time being dragged from the pulpit and treated in a brutal manner. In spite of opposition he continued his labors with unabated zeal, until many churches were formed in Northern Virginia. During the Revolutionary war, he gave his influence and the power of his great eloquence to the cause of the colonies. A poem of his, denouncing the union between the Episcopal church and the state in Virginia, had much to do with the destruction of the unholy relation. Thomas Jefferson held him in high esteem, and Patrick Henry cherished a warm regard for him. In 1788 he removed to Berkeley County, and took charge of Mill Creek church, to which he ministered about eight years. In 1796, he removed to Kentucky, and was settled over Washington church in Mason County. After a short time he located in Jessamine County, and united with East Hickman church. He died about 1801. William Cathcart, *The Baptist Encyclopedia* (Philadelphia: Louis H. Everts, 1883), P. 1147-1148.

[5] Of John Garrard, James B. Taylor wrote:

Garrard was among the earliest and most successful Baptist ministers of Virginia. Nothing is known of his parentage, the circumstances of his conversion, or his entrance into the ministry, He migrated from the State of Pennsylvania to the County of Berkeley, Virginia, in the year 1754, and there labored for some time as a preacher of the gospel. That part of the country was then sparsely inhabited, and subject to the assaults of the Indians. Having been frequently annoyed by them, most of the church, with Mr. Garrard, removed below the Blue Ridge, and settled for a while in the County of Loudon. During his stay there, he was instrumental in the conversion of many sinners. From house to house he went, warning men to flee the wrath to come, and preaching Christ and him crucified.

Thus, what seemed at the time a heavy trial, was made to eventuate in good. Such was his success that it was deemed expedient to constitute another church, which was called Ketockton. When the Ketockton Association was formed, consisting only of four churches, he was one of the delegates, and assisted in the deliberations of the meeting. This was after his return to Berkeley. He continued to serve the Mill Creek Church until his death. For some time he was also employed in supplying Buck Marsh Church, in the County of Frederick. In addition to these efforts in his own immediate vicinity, he delighted to spend as much time as possible in carrying abroad the blessed gospel. Like the Apostle of the Gentiles, he cherished a holy ambition to preach Christ where he had not been named. In the journeys of that devoted man, David Thomas, he was frequently accompanied by Elder Garrard, and proved a most faithful and successful coadjutor.

His talents were by no means inconsiderable. Such was the estimation in which he was held by his brethren, that for several years in succession he was chosen Moderator of the Association. He was a speaker of lively address. In his whole ministerial course, he was distinguished by a glowing and persevering zeal. James B. Taylor, *Virginia Baptist Ministers vol. 1* (Richmond: Lippincott & Co., 1859), P. 26.

[6] According to John Comer's Diary entry on September 17, 1729.

[7] Of Paul Palmer, George W. Paschal wrote:

Paul Palmer was a native of Maryland, was baptized at Welsh Tract in Delaware, and ordained in Connecticut. After serving churches in New Jersey and Maryland he came to North Carolina. The year of his coming is not known, but in 1720 he was at Edenton and married Joanna Peterson, widow of Thomas Terterson, a man of prominence in colonial affairs, who had been church warden of St. Paul's Parish, and had given the land on which the town of Edenton was built. Palmer and his wife were brought into court on the charge of stealing a Negro, but the case was never tried and was probably malicious, since the chief witness "absconded the court," and Palmer was soon after a grand juror in the very court in which the charge against him had been made. Soon after his marriage he moved with his wife to her estate in Perquimans, and lived there the remainder of his life, dying probably about 1743. He gathered his first church in Chowan in 1727; his name is found on the petition for the registration of the church now called Shiloh in Camden County, which is dated September 5, 1729. Edwards says that he gathered a church on New River, Onslow County, about the year 1743. Palmer was in correspondence with Baptist ministers in the Northern Provinces, among them John Comer of Newport, R.I., who in his Diary often refers to Palmer's letters, and speaks of him as a man of worth. G. W. Paschal, *N. C. Review Vol. VII* Number 3, 1930, P. 370.

[8] Morgan Edwards gave these details on these churches:

CHOWAN (1727)

PASQUOTANK (Shiloh) (1736) General Baptist in the beginning—William Burgess

KEHUKEE (1742) originally General Baptist, 1st pastor William Sojornier

TAR RIVER FALLS (1744) founded by John Moore as a General Baptist Church

FISHING CREEK (1745) General William Walker, founder–from Kehukee; Gave rise to Tar River and Coosawhatchee. [Josiah Hart: Ordained John Moore in 1748 who became the pastor at Tar-River Falls. Hart also ordained William Walker, and baptized John Thomas. Hart, along with Henry Ledbetter baptized Charles Daniel. p. 375.]

LOWER FISHING CREEK (1748) a church plant from Kehukee.

TAR RIVER (1749) Began as a General Baptist church, William Washington was the first pastor.

GREAT COHARA (1749) Began as a General Baptist church.

REDBANKS This church was constituted as a General Baptist church in 1750's, "reconstituted" as a Particular Baptist church in 1758.

TOSNEOT (1756)started as General Baptist John Thomas was the founding pastor.

BEAR CREEK (1756)

SWIFTS-CREEK (unknown date) General Baptist Church; founded with help from William Burgess of Pasquotank NC (Shiloh); Joseph Willis was 1st pastor. Morgan Edwards, "Material Towards a Baptist History of North Carolina," *N. C. Historical Review vol. VII Number 3*, 1930, P. 383.

[9] Edwards, "Materials N. C.," 370.

[10] These were the Regular Baptist churches in existence in North Carolina, after the transformation from "General" and before the New Light Separate Baptists arrived in 1755:

PASQUOTANK (Shiloh) William Burgess, his son John Burgess "embraced the Regular (Particular) scheme in 1757—John's son William was his assistant. John Burgess died in 1763 (age 38)—church grew from 12 to 192 in 13 years. After John Burgess died, the church was without a pastor for 6 years.

KEHUKEE changed to Regular (Particular) by the ministry of Benjamin Miller & P.P. Van Horn (1755) followed by Thomas Pope. (till 1762) And then (to 1749) John Meglanor. Until 1772 when he left for Nottaway and was followed by William Burgess.

FISHING CREEK became Regular (Particular) in 1755 under Miller & Van Horn.

LOWER FISHING CREEK In 1756, a new constitution was drawn along Regular (Particular) Baptist lines.

TAR RIVER Reconstituted as a "Calvinistic" Regular (Particular) Baptist church in 1761. Henry Ledbetter became the pastor in 1761, sometime after he had assisted Shubal Stearns in the ordination of Daniel Marshall.

GREAT COHARA Became a Regular (Particular) Baptist church in 1759. The church was decimated by the war of the Regulators as Morgan Edwards writes:

They began by means of [Edward Brown's] preaching in 1749, and when a considerable number was baptized sent for Rev. Mess. Thos. Pope, Jonathan Thomas and Stephen Hollingsworth to form them into a church, which was effected October 15, 1759. The constituents were 12. They increased exceedingly until the troubles of the Regulation compelled them to quit the province except the 8 persons before mentioned.—Ibid., 370-371.

REDBANKS "reconstituted" as a Regular (Particular) Baptist church in 1758.

TOSNEOT Came to Regular (Particular) sentiments in 1758.

BLADEN CO (Beaver Dam) (1756) by Stephen Hollingsworth joined the Charleston Association in 1758.

BEAR CREEK was reorganized a Regular (Particular) Baptist church in 1759.

THREE CREEKS (1758) Became a member of the Charleston Association.

SWIFTS-CREEK (unknown date) became a Regular (Particular) Baptist church in 1756. Pg 383

HITCHCOCK (1772). *Ibid.*, 370-371.

[11] George Whitefield, *George Whitefield's Journals* (Guildford and London: Banner of Trust, Billing and Sons, Ltd., 1960), 379.

[12] Paschal, *History of N. C. Baptists vol. 1:* 244.

[13] James Ireland, *The Life of the Rev. James Ireland* (Winchester: J. Foster, 1819), P. 72.

[14] Edwards, "Materials N. C.," 387.

[15] William Lumpkin, *Baptist Inroads in the South*, (Shelbyville: Bible and Literature Missionary Foundation, n.d.), P. 10.

[16] Robert Baylor Semple, *The Rise and Progress of the Baptists in Virginia* (Richmond, By the Author, 1810), P. 2.

[17] *Ibid.*, 5.

[18] *Ibid.*, 3.

[19] Lumpkin, *Baptist Inroads*, 22.

[20] *Ibid.*

[21] *Ibid.*

[22] *Ibid.*, 23

[23] Semple, *Baptists in Va.*, 4.

[24] Lumpkin, *Baptist Inroads*, 27.

[25] Part of the criticism had to do with Martha Stearns' prayers and "exhortations." William Lumpkin tries to claim Mrs. Marshall was "exhorting" as early as the Virginia encampment of the Separate Baptists. But we doubt she did anything other then testify or be actively involved winning the lost. It is evident that she prayed and testified publicly on occasion and her prayers would often move a congregation to tears. Paschal, *History of N. C. Baptists vol. 1:* 289.

[26] Semple, *Baptists in Va.*, 370

[27] Some of Daniel Marshall's most notable converts: James Read, William and Joseph Murphy, John Waller, and Joseph Reese. After establishing himself with Shubal Stearns at Sandy Creek, North Carolina, Marshall was ordained in 1756 and brought into existence Baptist churches at Abbots Creek, N.C., Stephens Creek, S.C. and Kiokee, Georgia. His preaching ministry was legendary and the fruit of his ministry in Georgia single-handedly resulted in the supremacy of the Baptist denomination in that state. Semple, *Baptists in Va.*, 394.

[28] Isaac Backus, *An Abridgement to the Church History of New England* (1804; reprint ed., Boston: Harvard University, 1935), 227.

[29] Backus, *Abridgement*, 250.

[30] Some credit should be due the General Baptists for breaking up the fallow ground of North Carolina. Hugh McAlden, Pedobaptist preacher from New England was in N. C. from 1753 to 1756 and said the people were eager to

hear the gospel. Paschal, *History of N. C. Baptists vol. 1:* 323. This is a different testimony from that of Whitefield. What happened? Edward Brown, the General Baptist, had preached in those parts and had a number of the pioneers converted. They lacked church organization, however. When the Separate Baptists arrived in 1755, a revival ensued.

[31] Lumpkin, *Baptist Inroads*, 30.

[32] Semple, *Baptists in Va.*, 1.

[33] Paschal, *History of N. C. Baptists vol. 1*, footnote P. 288.

[34] Edwards, "Materials N. C.," 387.

[35] Semple, *Baptists in Va.*, 4.

[36] On page 24, of *Baptist Inroads in the South*, William Lumpkin refers to the Separate Baptists as part of the "history of Christian enthusiasm." He repeats the critical comments of the Episcopalians who opposed the Separate Baptists. If Mr. Lumpkin considered the history of the Separate Baptists part of "the history of Christian enthusiasm," then he ought to include in his criticism the early Christian Baptists of the book of Acts. So successful were they at being "enthusiastic," they turned the world upside down. Ah yes, and to this day, the critics of aggressive Christianity say, "believe, but do not 'proselytize.'"

[37] Semple, *Baptists in Va.*, 4.

[38] Dr. David L. Cummins in a non-published article given to the author.

[39] They were accused of being "roundheads," the party of Oliver Cromwell who trimmed their hair around their ears.

[40] Edwards, "Materials N. C.," 391.

[41] Elnathan Davis was called at the Haw River Church in 1764, but was not officially ordained until Nov. 13, 1770. This means Shubal Stearns, Daniel Marshall, Phillip Mulkey, or Joseph or William Murphy baptized for him. He was there for 34 years until 1798, when he left for South Carolina and the Saluda Association.

[42] Paschal, *History of N. C. Baptists vol. 1:* 300.

[43] Morgan Edwards, "Materials Towards a History of the Baptists in South Carolina," Microfilm at the American Baptist Historical Society, Rochester, New York.

[44] Paschal, *History of N. C. Baptists vol. 1:* 290.

[45] Benjamin Miller, who helped reconstitute the old General Baptist churches of North Carolina into Regular churches with nearly irresistible results was pastor at Jersey Settlement. He left in January of 1756. The church was probably without a pastor until John Gano settled there in 1758.

[46] Semple, *Baptists in Va.*, 5.

[47] James B. Taylor records that Ledbetter was brother in law to both Daniel Marshall and Shubal Stearns. Taylor, *Va. Baptist Ministers vol. 1:* 20.

[48] Robert I. Devin, *A History of the Grassy Creek Baptist Church* (Raleigh: Edwars, Broughten and Co., 1880), P. 92.

[49] This is the human explanation for the birthing of 42 churches in 15 years, and the birthing of over 1,000 within 30 years. Would to God preachers would plan to birth other works by "sitting as a church!"

[50] Paschal, *History of N. C. Baptists vol.* 1: 292.

[51] *Ibid.*, 325.

[52] *Ibid.*, 311.

[53] *Ibid.*, 311-318.

[54] *Ibid.*, 317.

[55] *Ibid.*

[56] *Ibid.*

[57] *Ibid.*, 318.

[58] *Ibid.*, 307.

[59] Hunter was succeeded by Robert Nixon. Nixon was no less zealous and effective for the cause of Christ. Nixon pastored New River church for 20 years. He had the care of Lockwood's Folly. During his pastorate, New River branched to White Oak River in Jones County, North Carolina. In 1785, Nixon helped found Muddy Creek Baptist church in Duplin county North Carolina. In 1793, Nixon, Dillahunty and Oliver Hart ordained Job Thigpen pastor of Muddy Creek Baptist church. Nixon worked with Samuel Newton, who organized the Old Bull Tail Baptist church. Newton died during the Revolutionary War. *Ibid.*, 320.

[60] Dillahunty went on to pastor this church from 1781 until 1796 when he migrated west to Tennessee. A great victory for the Baptists in Eastern N. C. occurred when Dillahunty was given the church building of the right Rev. Mr. Reed and the majority of that Anglican flock became Baptist! Paschal, *History of N. C. Baptists vol.* 1: 315.

[61] Morgan Edwards, *Materials Towards a History of the Baptists, vol.* 2 (Danielsville: Heritage Papers, Prepared for Publication by Eve B. Weeks and Mary B. Warren, 1984), P. 48.

[62] Taylor, *Va. Baptist Ministers vol.* 1: 34.

[63] Semple, *Baptists in Va.*, 377.

[64] *Ibid.* 4.

[65] Churches were considered "arms" or "branches" with an "exhorter" who led them until an ordained preacher would come among them and be their pastor.

[66] Charles A. Johnson, *The Frontier Camp-Meeting: Religion's Harvest Time* (Dallas: Southern Methodist University Press, 1955), P. 27-28.

[67] Paschal, *History of N. C. Baptists vol.* 1: 324.

[68] Paschal, *vol.* 1: 317.

[69] Lumpkin, *Baptist Inroads*, 109.

[70] Of the first Separate Baptist Church in Virginia, Robert Baylor Semple said:

They endured much persecution, but God prospered them, and delivered them out the hands of all their enemies. Semple, *Baptists in Va.*, 5.

[71] *Ibid.*, 380.

John Taylor, *The History of Ten Baptist Churches* (Bloomfield: William H. Holmes, 1826), P. 278.

[73] Semple, *Baptists in Va.*, 10.

[74] Robert Semple said it was "grog" and John Taylor said it was "a large bowl of rich toddy." At this point, some Baptists had not taken a strong stand against social drinking.

[75] J. Taylor, *History of Ten Baptist Churches*, 279.

[76] David Benedict, *History of the Baptist Denomination, vol. 1* (1813; Reprint ed., Dayton: Church History Research and Archives, 1985), P. 394.

[77] "Swearing Jack" was ordained to the Gospel ministry on June 20, 1770. Waller's imprisonments and influence will be noted in chapter ten. *Ibid.*, 395.

[78] Semple, *Baptists in Va.*, 12.

[79] William G. McLoughlin, Biographical Sheets on the Isaac Backus Papers, Hay Library, Brown University, Providence, Rhode Island.

[80] Semple, *Baptists in Va.*, 15.

[81] J. H. Spencer, *A History of the Kentucky Baptists from 1769-1885 vol. 1* (Cincinnati: By the Author, 1885), P. 29.

[82] It is interesting to note that Spotsylvania was the most devilish of all places during the Civil War.

[83] Semple, *Baptists in Va.*, 16.

[84] *Ibid.*

[85] *Ibid.*

[86] *Ibid.*, 11.

[87] *Ibid.*, 13.

[88] *Ibid.*

[89] *Ibid.*, 14.

[90] *Ibid.*, 17

[91] *Ibid.*

[92] *Ibid.*, 18.

[93] *Ibid.*, 19.

[94] *Ibid.*

[95] Paschal, *History of N. C. Baptists vol. 1*: 322.

[96] Cathcart, *Baptist Encyclopedia*, 1100.

[97] Backus, *Abridgement*, 251.

CHAPTER EIGHT
A Corn of Wheat

[1] George Washington Paschal, *History of North Carolina Baptists vol. 1* (Raleigh: Edwards & Broughton Co., 1930), P. 333.

[2] The request said, "The bearers of this letter can acquaint you with the design of writing it. Their errand is peace, and their business is a reconciliation between us, if there is any difference subsisting. If we are all Christians, all Baptists, all New-lights, why are we divided? Must the little appellative names, Regular and Separate, break the golden band of charity, and set the sons and daughters of Zion at variance? "Behold how good and how pleasant it is for brethren to dwell together in unity," but how bad and how bitter it is for them to live asunder in discord. To indulge ourselves in prejudice, with a witness. O, our dear brethren, endeavor to prevent this calamity in the future." *Ibid.,* 400.

[3] James Ireland, *The Life of the Rev. James Ireland* (Winchester: J. Foster, 1819), P. 130-131.

[4] Paschal, *History of N. C. Baptists vol. 1*: 400.

[5] Of Richard Major, J. B. Taylor wrote:
In 1768, [Major] was ordained as the pastor of Little River Church. Little River Church was formed of individuals who had been converted under the ministry of D. Thomas. In this work, however, he was powerfully aided by Rev. Richard Major, their first pastor; for although the first seed was sown by Mr. Thomas, yet Mr. Major watered and nourished the plants, until he brought them to perfection. So rapidly did the gospel spread in this church, that just two years after they were constituted, they were the most numerous church in the association, having two hundred and seventy-two members. Her branches, however, extended into the neighboring parts. When any of these branches became sufficiently numerous, they were constituted into new churches, by which the mother church was reduced in members. In regard to his influence in another church, called Bull Run, Elder Semple states, "When the gospel was carried there by the amiable Richard Major, a great revival of religion arose, so that in a little time a church was constituted, having one hundred and twenty-six members. From the constitution of new churches, etc. their number had become somewhat reduced, until, about 1792, they had the smiles of heaven, and large additions were made. Not many less than a hundred were baptized; Six or eight churches were originated principally through his instrumentality. James B. Taylor, *Virginia Baptist Ministers vol. 1* (Richmond: Lippincott & Co., 1859), P. 61.

[6] Ireland, *Life*, 145.

[7] Morgan Edwards, "Materials Towards a Baptist History of North Carolina." *N. C. Historical Review vol. VII Number 3*, 1930, P. 386.

[8] Robert Baylor Semple, *The Rise and Progress of the Baptists in Virginia* (Richmond, By the Author, 1810), P. 6.

[9] Where did Stearns envision the type of association he established? It could not have been Philadelphia. Philadelphia was not like Sandy Creek. The only

Baptist Association of which he was acquainted was the old Six Principle Baptist meetings in New England under the influence of Valentine Wightman and Timothy Wightman. During Stearns' lifetime, the only case of censure at Sandy Creek Association involved John Newton and Joseph Reese. The association at Sandy Creek was basically a revival conference. It was out of its character when it tried to act in any other way.

[10] Semple, *Baptists in Va.*, 6.

[11] *Ibid.*, 7.

[12] Robert I. Devin, *A History of the Grassy Creek Baptist Church* (Raleigh: Edwars, Broughten and Co., 1880), P. 53.

[13] The emergence of the Baptist association as typified by the Sandy Creek association, was first; an advisory association with a presbytery of preachers for the purpose of ordination; and secondly, never intended to control churches, only to aid in their birth and act as an encouraging agency. The "advisory" association became a denominational hierarchy by 1845.

[14] Edwards, "Materials N. C.," 387.

[15] Semple, *Baptists in Va.*, 1.

[16] Paschal repeatedly insists that the "War of the *Regulators*" was a war on the Separate Baptists of North Carolina. Paschal, *History of N. C. Baptists vol. 1*: 361.

[17] William Lumpkin, *Baptist Inroads in the South*, (Shelbyville: Bible and Literature Missionary Foundation, n.d.), P. 34.

[18] Paschal, *History of N. C. Baptists vol. 1*: 358.

[19] *Ibid.* See Col. Rec., VII, 102.

[20] *Ibid., vol. 2*: 42.

[21] *Ibid.*, 307. According to Paschal see Col. Rec. VI 562 For other Episcopalian complaints see: Col. Rec. VI 565,594-95, *Col. Rec. VI 316,562, VII 705,IX 23,326.

[22] *Ibid., vol. 1*: 308.

[23] *Ibid.*

[24] *Ibid.*, 310.

[25] *Ibid.*

[26] Adelaide L. Fries, M.A., *Notices of the Records of the Moravians in North Carolina* (Raleigh: Edwards and Broughton Printing Co. 1925), P. 321.

[27] Paschal, *History of N. C. Baptists vol. 1*: 311.

[28] *Ibid.*, 312. See Col. Rec. VI 316, 729, IX 326.

[29] *Ibid.*, See Col. Rec. VI 223.

[30] *Ibid., vol. 1*: 335.

[31] *Ibid.*, See Col. Rec. VII, 283-88.

[32] *Ibid., vol. 1*: 362.

[33] *Ibid.*, 331.

[34] Eventually, the Presbyterians began to realize the unfair practice of the marriage fee. Of the 30 lbs. silver they collected for marriages only 5 shillings was

given to the officiating minister. One-half of the fee went to Tryon, and the rest to the Anglican/Episcopalian church.

[35] Paschal, *History of N. C. Baptists vol. 1:* 352.

[36] *Ibid.* See Col. Rec. VII, 432.

[37] *Ibid., vol.* 1: 362.

[38] *Ibid. See Col.* Rec. VII 813f.

[39] *Ibid., vol. 1:* 333. See Col. Rec. VI 223, 1039f. 7mon, 7 eacl. VII, 41f.

[40] *Ibid.,* 333.

[41] *Ibid.,* 334.

[42] *Ibid.,* 354-355. See Col. Rec. VII, 805.

[43] There was a paper called "Regulator Advertisement No. 9" which listed the names of many Baptists in the Sandy Creek, Abbott's Creek, and Yadkin area. *Ibid.,* 366.

[44] *Ibid.,* 366.

[45] *Ibid.* See Col. Rec. VIII, 19f.

[46] *Ibid.,* 371.

[47] *Ibid.,* 373.

[48] *Ibid..*

[49] Of the 47 sections of the North Carolina State Constitution adopted in 1776, 13 were the result of reforms sought by the *Regulators.* Paschal, *History of N. C. Baptists vol. 1:* 377.

[50] *Ibid.,* 322.

[51] Semple, *Baptists in Va.,* 46.

[52] Ireland, *Life,* 137.

[53] Semple, *Baptists in Va.,* 45.

[54] Paschal, *History of N. C. Baptists vol. 1:* 364.

[55] Lumpkin says that there was an invasion of the Sandy Creek associational meeting by two men named Hunter and Butler. He then says that Shubal Stearns called for the formation of a milder form of protest through a group he would call, "the Associators." No source is given for this information. Lumpkin, *Baptist Inroads,* 80.

[56]"This checked the design much; and the author of the *Impartial Relation* (Edwards here is referring to the book by Herman Husbands, one of the leaders of the Regulators) is obliged to own, p. 16, "There (in Sandy Creek) the scheme met with some opposition on account that it was too hot and rash, and in some thing not legal...." Edwards, Materials Toward the History of the Baptists in North Carolina. On this point, G. W. Paschal corrects Morgan Edwards by noting, "Morgan Edward was in error in supposing that Husband meant that the opposition spoken of was from Baptist people or Association. The reference is to the opposition of the earlier and more moderate Regulators of which Husband himself was leader." In other words, Husbands, quoted

by Edwards was not referring to the incident at the associational meeting of 1769. Paschal, *History of N. C. Baptists vol. 1:* 364.

[57] Semple, *Baptists in Va.,* 46-47.

[58] Paschal, *History of N. C. Baptists vol. 1:* 376.

[59] William Edwards Fitch, *Some Neglected History of North Carolina* (New York: Neale Publishing Company), 1905. Preface.

[60] Morgan Edwards badly blunders in his assessment of the Regulator problem he stated, "Governor Tryon is said to "have represented the regulators as a faction of Quakers and Baptists who aimed at oversetting the Church of England. The same insinuation has also appeared in a newspaper. If the governor did as here suggested, he must be misinformed." But how could Tryon be misinformed since he was the source of the information?

[61] Paschal, *History of N. C. Baptists vol. 1:* 364.

[62] Colonial Records, VIII, 639. Merrill's speech according to G. W. Paschal: "I stand here exposed to the world as a criminal; my life will soon be a change; God is my comforter and supporter...I am condemned to die for opposing the government. All you that are present take warning by my miserable end when I shall be hung up as a spectacle before you. My first seducers were Hunter and Gelaspie; they had often solicited me, telling that a settlement only was contended for with regard to public officers: who, they said, had oppressed the people; and that unless those measures were taken, there could be no remedy or duress hereafter. Thus they pressed me on by assuring me the dispute (as they called them) then existing, might be settled without the shedding of blood. I considered this unhappy affair and thought, possibly, the contentions of the country might be brought to some determination without injury to any; and in this mind I joined the regulation. After I had listed under the banner of the Regulators I was ever after pressed to be made a leading man among them; and was one of the number who opposed Col. Waddell with his troop; information prevailing that the governor was in his march to lay waste this country and destroy its inhabitant; which I now find to be false, and propagated to screen old offenders from justice. As to my private life I do not know of any particular charge against me. I received by the grace of God a change fifteen years ago; but have since that time been a backslider, yet providence, in which is my chief security, had been pleased to give me comfort under these evils in my last hour; and although' the halter is round my neck, believe me, I would not change station with any man on the ground. All you who think you stand take heed lest ye fall. I would be glad to say a few words more before I die...In a few moments I shall leave a widow and ten children; I entreat that no reflection be cast on them on my account; and if possible, shall deem it a bounty should you, Gentlemen, petition the governor and council that some part of my estate may be spared for the widow and the fatherless; It will be an act of charity, for I have forfeited the whole by the laws of God and man.

Paschal wrote, "Baptist historians have questioned the accuracy of Edward's account, who was classed as a Tory, and was set on clearing the Baptists of what he considered a heinous crime." That Merrill spoke as Edwards says is hard to believe. *Ibid.*, 365.

[63] *Ibid.*, 367.

[64] *Ibid.*, 299.

[65] Edwards, "Materials N. C.," 385.

CHAPTER NINE
Who Hath Believed our Report?

[1] Isaac Backus, *An Abridgement to the Church History of New England* (1804; reprint ed., Boston: Harvard University, 1935), P. 234.

[2] Mather's own grandson became a Baptist preacher according to William G. McLoughlin, Data Sheets on the Isaac Backus Papers, Hay Library, Brown University, Providence, Rhode Island.

[3] Backus, *Abridgement*, 225.

[4] *Ibid.*, 48.

[5] *Ibid.*, 149.

[6] William G. McLoughlin, Biographical Sheets on the Isaac Backus Papers, Hay Library, Brown University, Providence, Rhode Island.

[7] Information on the Acts of Exemption:

1728-First act of Exemption for the Baptists "An Act to exempt persons commonly called Anabaptists, and those called Quakers, within this Province, from being taxed for and towards the support of ministers." This exemption did not include land and if you attended church at a distance of more than 5 miles you could not be exempted. Alvah Hovey, *The Life and Times of Isaac Backus* (1858; reprint ed., Gano Books, 1991), P. 168.

1729- The Second act of Exemption made the first one better by allowing exemption of your land. This was a real relief for approximately five years.

1734- The Third Act of Exemption for Baptists provided "assessors", who would gather the names of those who "frequently and usually attend their meeting, for the worship of God." This failed miserably because the assessors, would often on purpose, neglect their duty.

1740- The Fourth Act of Exemption was identical to the Third and the results were the same vexations upon our Baptist forefathers. It expired in seven years.

1747- The Fifth Act of Exemption was to last 10 years. It was more lenient than the rest and it seemed real relief was upon the Baptists.

[8] Isaac Backus, *History of New England, with Particular Reference To the Baptists*, vol. 1 (1871; reprint ed., Paris: The Baptist Standard Bearer, n.d.), P. 134.

[9] McLoughlin, Data sheets. See Jeremiah Barstow.

[10] Isaac Backus documented two men who served in the Revolution even after the mistreatment at Sturbridge. They were: Thomas Cheney, member of the Sturbridge Massachusetts Baptist church who had charge of the minutemen of Dudley; and Henry Fiske, who with his brother Daniel, who served in the Continental Army as Lieutenant. *Ibid.*

[11] Backus, *History of New England*, vol. 2: 134.

[12] *Ibid.*, 135.

[13] It would be a mistake to speak about the founding fathers of our nation and not examine the tenor and fervency of their home churches.

[14] Page Smith, *John Adams*, vol. 1 (Garden City: Doubleday and Company, Inc., 1962), P. 33.

[15] *Ibid.*

[16] Rueben Aldridge Guild, *Early History of Brown University* (Providence: Guild, 1896), P. 174.

[17] Backus, *History of New England*, vol. 2: 138.

[18] *Ibid.*

[19] *Ibid.*

[20] *Ibid.*, 146.

[21] *Ibid.*

[22] The law was that the first settled minister was allotted land and exempted.

[23] Backus, *History of New England*, vol. 2: 152.

[24] *Ibid.*, 154.

[25] Smith, *John Adams*, vol. 1: 124.

[26] Backus, *History of New England*, vol. 2: 157.

[27] *Ibid.*

[28] *Ibid.*

[29] Guild, *Brown University*, 191.

[30] *Ibid.*, 169.

[31] McLoughlin, Data sheets.

[32] *Ibid.*

[33] Some of the obnoxious establishment laws were not repealed in New England until 1834.

[34] Isaac Backus, *Journey to Philadelphia*, manuscript diary, Isaac Backus Papers, Hay Library, Brown University, Providence, Rhode Island.

[35] Here in Norwich, Backus' brother Elijah, still a member of Mr. Lord's standing order church, somehow convinced Mr. Lord to allow Isaac Backus to preach in his pulpit!

[36] Backus, *Journey to Philadelphia*.

[37] The committee included Robert Strettle Jones as President, Samuel Davis, Stephen Shewell, Thomas Shields, George Wescot, Alexander Edwards, Benjamen Bartholomew, William Rogers, John Evens, John Mayhew, Edward

Keasby, Samuel Jones, Morgan Edwards, William Van Horne, Abraham Beak-
ley, Abel Evans, Secretary, Samuel Miles, James Morgan and John Jarman.

[38] Hovey, *Life of Backus*, 204-210.

[39] Backus, *Journey to Philadelphia*.

[40] *Ibid.*

[41] Guild, *Brown University*, 280.

[42] Hovey, *Life of Backus*, 220.

[43] *Ibid.*, 215-220

[44] *Ibid.*, 206.

[45] Guild, *Brown University*, 191.

CHAPTER TEN
Blood on the Walls in Old Virginia

[1] Elder John Leland, *The Writings of Elder John Leland Including Some Events In His Life* (New York: G. W. Wood, 1845), P. 106.

[2] James Ireland, *The Life of the Rev. James Ireland* (Winchester: J. Foster, 1819), P. 157.

[3] We may face the same decision in our generation. May God give us the courage to not sit idly by in silence.

[4] *Ibid.*

[5] *Ibid.*, 165.

[6] *Ibid.*

[7] *Ibid.*, 172.

[8] James B. Taylor, *Virginia Baptist Ministers vol. 1* (Richmond: Lippincott & Co., 1859), P. 29.

[9] Taylor also wrote:
Another actually attacked him with a club, in a violent manner. Mr. Major, being remarkable for great presence of mind, turned to him, and, in a solemn manner, said, "Satan, I command thee to come out of the man." His club immediately began to fall, and the lion became as quiet as a lamb. These are a few of the many occurrences of this kind that took place in the long life of this valuable man. *Ibid.*, 62.

[10] John Taylor, *The History of the Ten Baptist Churches* (Bloomfield: William H. Holmes, 1826), P. 9-11.

[11] Robert Baylor Semple, *The Rise and Progress of the Baptists in Virginia* (Richmond, By the Author, 1810), P. 22.

[12] In the beginning of his ministry John Mason Peck, one of the first missionaries west of the Mississippi, accepted this incident as fact and included it in his *Baptist Memorial of 1845*. On June 17, 1857, Peck wrote the *Christian Repository* and said that he received the evidence for the speech of Patrick Henry

from Thomas Hinde of Mount Carmel, Illinois. Hinde got his information from two old saints of God, Bartlett Bennett and William Ficklin. These men were in the court house and heard Henry make the speech. But since no one in the Waller or Craig family had any record of the incident, and it was not a tradition in any of their family records, Peck in the end doubted the testimony of Bennett and Ficklin. The *Christian Repository* of October 1890 contains the doubts of Peck. Samuel Howard Ford, the editor of the *Christian Repository* from 1870-1905, also gave the story in his book *Baptist Origins*, written in 1860. Lewis Peyton Little gives the incident in *Imprisoned Preachers of Virginia*. Frankly, the author of *America in Crimson Red* cannot see why the testimony of Bennett and Ficklin should be discarded.

[13] Semple, *Baptists in Va.*, 24.

[14] Taylor, *History of the Ten Baptist Churches*, 16-17.

[15] E. Wayne Thompson and David L. Cummins, *This Day in Baptist History* (Greenville: Bob Jones University Press, 1993), P. 123.

[16] Lewis Peyton Little, *Imprisoned Preachers and Religious Liberty in Virginia* (Lynchburg: J. P. Bell Co., 1938), P. 243-244.

[17] Semple, *Baptists in Va.*, 20.

[18] *Ibid.*, 383.

[19] "Lynn Alderson, A Leaf from Baptist History," *The Baptist Sentinel*, February 1871, p. 54.

[20] Taylor, *Va. Baptist Ministers vol. 1*: 51.

[21] *Ibid.*, P. 52.

[22] Thompson and Cummins, *This Day in Baptist History*, 31.

[23] For a concise overview of the suffering of the Virginia Baptists, see William S. Simpson, Jr., *Virginia Baptist Ministers, 1760-1790, a Biographical Survey* (Richmond: By the Author, 1990-2000).

[24] Little, *Imprisoned Preachers*, 30-31.

[25] *Ibid.*, 275-76.

[26] Semple, *Baptists in Va.*, 22.

[27] *Ibid.*

[28] *Ibid.*, 22.

[29] Charles F. James, *A Documentary History of the Struggle for Religious Liberty in Virginia* (1900; reprint ed., New York: Da Cape Press, 1971), P. 36.

[30] Semple, *Baptists in Va.*, 24.

[31] *Ibid.*, 110.

[32] *Ibid.*, 23.

[33] Thompson and Cummins, *This Day in Baptist History*, 103.

[34] Leland's testimony about baptism:

When my father was a young man, he was convinced (as he has told me) by reading the Bible, that believers were the only proper subjects of baptism, and immersion the only gospel mode; but when he broke his mind to his mother, she gave him an alarming warning against heresy; and as there was no preachers thereabout but pedobaptists, he sunk from his conviction, and concluded that his mother and the ministers were right. Accordingly, after he was married, and had a son born unto him, he presented his child for baptism: but after the rite was performed, his mind was solemnly arrested with the text, "Who hath required this at your hand ?" that it was with difficulty he held his son from falling out of his arms; nor did he get over the shock until he had six more children born. He then got his scruples so far removed, that he invited the minister of the town to come to his house on a certain Sunday, after public service was over, and baptize all of them. At this time I was something more than three years old. When I found out what the object of the meeting was, I was greatly terrified, and betook myself to flight. As I was running fast down a little hill, I fell upon my nose, which made the blood flow freely. My flight was in vain; I was pursued, overtaken, picked up and had the blood scrubbed off my face, and so was prepared for the baptismal water.

All the merit of this transaction, I must give to the maid who caught me, my father and the minister; for I was not a voluntary candidate, but a reluctant subject, forced against my will. Leland, *Writings of John Leland,* 570.

[35] Cathcart, *Baptist Encyclopedia,* 683.

[36] Semple, *Baptists in Va.,* 25.

[37] In another one of those classic understatements Semple wrote, "The great success and rapid increase of the Baptists in Virginia, must be ascribed primarily, to the power of God." *Ibid.,* 25-26.

[38] *Ibid.*

[39] Thompson and Cummins, *This Day in Baptist History,* 238.

CHAPTER ELEVEN
The Forging of Baptist Nation

[1] Elder John Leland, *The Writings of Elder John Leland Including Some Events In His Life* (New York: G. W. Wood, 1845), P. 410.

[2] According to the testimony of a local merchant.

[3] E. Benjamin Andrews, *History of the United States, vol. 2* (New York: Charles Scribner's Sons, 1903), P. 58.

[4] *Ibid.,* 58.

[5] Papers on the *Gaspee,* in the Archives of the Rhode Island Historical Society, Providence, Rhode Island.

[6] Page Smith, *John Adams, vol. 1* (Garden City: Doubleday and Company, Inc., 1962), P. 140.

[7] William Cathcart, *The Baptists in the American Revolution* (Philadelphia: By the Author, 1876), P. 11, 12.

[8] Robert B. Semple, *History of the Baptists in Virginia, rev. ed.* (Lafayette. Tenn.: Church History Research and Archives, 1976), P. 493-94.

[9] Isaac Backus, *An Abridgement to the Church History of New England* (1804; reprint ed., Boston: Harvard University, 1935), P. 216.

[10] Lemuel Call Barnes, Papers. In the Archives of the American Baptist Samuel Colgate Historical Library, Rochester, New York.

[11] William P. Grady, *What Hath God Wrought?* (Schererville: Grady Publications, 1996), P. 145.

[12] Robert Leckie, *George Washington's War* (New York: Harper Collins Publishers, 1992) P. 21.

[13] Lemuel Call Barnes, *Was General George Washington Baptized by Chaplain John Gano?* Papers of Lemuel Call Barnes. In the Archives of the American Baptist Samuel Colgate Historical Library, Rochester, New York.

[14] Barnes, Papers.

[15] Barnes, *Was General George Washington Baptized?*

[16] Barnes, Papers.

[17] Barnes, *Was General George Washington Baptized?*

[18] McLoughlin says it was 1778, we will assume Backus' date is correct.

[19] Edwin S. Gaustad, *A Documentary History of Religion in America* (Grand Rapids: William B. Eerdmans Publishing Company, 1982), P. 240-250.

[20] Barnes, *Was General George Washington Baptized?*

[21] *Ibid.*

[22] These Baptist pastors also served in the Revolution:

Nicholas Folson, Baptist pastor of Meredith, New Hampshire, fought in the Continental Army at the battle of Bennington. Later pastored until 1825. Stephen Gano, son of John Gano served as a surgeon.

Stephen Gano was converted in 1783 and in 1793 he became pastor of the First Baptist Church of Providence, Rhode Island. He married the daughter of Joseph Brown. He went on to help organize the Baptist Triennial Convention in 1814. One of his daughters, Maria, married David Benedict.

David Barrow fought in the Army. He was from Brunswick County, Virginia. He went on to become the first anti-slavery preacher in the South. Cathcart said of him, "David Barrow: a brother of spotless character, and of extensive usefulness, held in universal esteem, not only commended patriotism to others, but when danger pressed he shouldered his musket and performed good service against the common foe, and he obtained the same reputation in the camp and in the field which he enjoyed in the happy scenes of ministerial toil elsewhere."

Silas Burrows, served as an unofficial chaplain in the Continental Army. On September 6, 1781 when Ft. Griswold was captured by the British, he ministered to the sick and dying, watched sixty of his neighbors die, many of them his own church members. Burrows "saw in that struggle not only the political enfranchisement of the land, but...freedom to worship independent of the civil power." John Courtney, Sr., past or of the Upper College Baptist Church in King William County, Virginia, fought as a soldier in the Revolutionary War.

Ebenezer David, Baptist evangelist from Westerly, Rhode Island died near Philadelphia while serving as a chaplain.

Jedidiah Hibard was baptized by Isaac Backus, on June 7, 1771. He served under Colonel Jonathan Chase at Ticonderoga and Saratoga. Pastored several Baptist churches in Connecticut and New Hampshire till his death in 1809.

Dr. William Rogers of Philadelphia, was the first student of Brown, then known as Rhode Island College. He was a close friend to George Washington. Cathcart wrote: "When Pennsylvania raised three battalions of foot, the legislature appointed Dr. Rogers their chaplain. He was afterwards a brigade-chaplain in the Continental army. For five years this distinguished man followed the fortunes of the Revolutionary army as an unwearied and beloved chaplain." Cathcart, *Baptists in the Revolution*, 38.

Other Baptist preachers active in the Revolution would include Abraham Marshall, William Hickman and Tidence Lane.

[23] Rueben Aldridge Guild, *Early History of Brown University* (Providence: Guild, 1896), P. 100.

[24] Backus, *Abridgement*, 214.

[25] Cathcart, *Baptists in the Revolution*, 37.

[26] John Taylor, *The History of the Ten Baptist Churches* (Bloomfield: William H. Holmes, 1826), P. 112.

[27] Morgan Edwards, *Materials Towards a History of the Baptists, Vol. 2.*, (Danielsville: Heritage Papers, Prepared for Publication by Eve B. Weeks and Mary B. Warren, 1984), P. 11.

[28] Taylor, *History of the Ten Baptist Churches*, 140.

[29] *Ibid.*

[30] *Ibid.*

[31] Semple, *Baptists in Va.*, 418.

[32] In complete surprise, Lunsford died in 1793. He was 40 years old. Taylor, *History of the Ten Baptist Churches*, 144.

[33] *Ibid.*, 39.

[34] *Ibid.*, 40.

[35] Leland, *Writings of John Leland*, 20.

[36] *Ibid.*, 20.

[37] *Ibid.*, 21.

[38] *Ibid.*

[39] *Ibid.*, 22.

[40] Backus, *Abridgement*, 216.

[41] *Ibid.*, 216.

CHAPTER TWELVE
Renouncing all Foreign Power

[1] George W. E. Russell, *A Short History of the Evangelical Movement* (London: A. R. Mowbray & Co. LTD., 1915), P. 16-17.

[2] Lemuel Call Barnes, *Was General George Washington Baptized by Chaplain John Gano?* Papers of Lemuel Call Barnes. In the Archives of the American Baptist Samuel Colgate Historical Library, Rochester, New York.

[3] E. Wayne Thompson and David L. Cummins, *This Day in Baptist History*, vol. 2 (Greenville: Bob Jones University Press, 1993), P. 640.

[4] George Washington Paschal, *History of North Carolina Baptists vol. 1* (Raleigh: Edwards & Broughton Co., 1930), P. 379. State Records, XVII, 1011.

[5] William Cathcart, *The Baptist Encyclopedia* (Philadelphia: Louis H. Everts, 1883), P. 426.

[6] Pat Alderman, *The Overmountain Men* (Johnson City: The Overmountain Press, 1986), P. 17.

[7] *Ibid.*, 22.

[8] J. J. Burnett, D. D., *Sketches of Tennessee's Pioneer Baptist Preachers* (Nashville: Press of Marshall & Bruce Co., 1919), P. 321.

[9] Samuel C. Williams, *The Baptists of Tennessee* (Kingsport: Kingsport Press, 1930), P. 11.

[10] *Church Heritage, Double Springs Independent Missionary Baptist Church* (Kingsport: n.p., n.d.). P. 2.

[11] E. Benjamin Andrews, *History of the United States, vol. 2* (New York: Charles Scribner's Sons, 1903), P.108.

[12] Elder John Leland, *The Writings of Elder John Leland Including Some Events In His Life* (New York: G.W. Wood, 1845), P. 410.

[13] Isaac Backus, *An Abridgement to the Church History of New England* (1804; reprint ed., Boston: Harvard University, 1935), P. 202.

[14] *Ibid.*

[15] Leland, *Writings of John Leland*, 295.

[16] William G. McLoughlin, Data Sheets on the Isaac Backus Papers, Hay Library, Brown University, Providence, Rhode Island.

[17] Backus, *Abridgement*, 217.

[18] Barnes, *Was General George Washington Baptized?*

[19] Lemuel Call Barnes, Papers. In the Archives of the American Baptist Samuel Colgate Historical Library, Rochester, New York.

[20] Robert Baylor Semple, *The Rise and Progress of the Baptists in Virginia* (Richmond, By the Author, 1810), P. 33.

[21] *Ibid.*, 75.

[22] R. A. Rutland and others, editors, *The Papers of James Madison, vol. 10, 11* (Richmond: The University of Virginia, 1977), 10: 515.

[23] William Sprague, *Annals of the American Pulpit, The Baptists vol. VI* (1846; reprint ed. Philadelphia: Arno Press, 1969) P. 177-180.

[24] Rutland, *The Papers of James Madison*, vol 11: 404-405. See also Garland Tyree, "County Scene of Religious Freedom Fight," *Orange Review*, 12 July 1984.

[25] *Ibid.*, 11: 442-443.

[26] McLoughlin, *Data Sheets on the Isaac Backus Papers.*

[27] Backus, *Abridgement*, 230.

[28] *Ibid.*

[29] McLoughlin, *Data Sheets on Backus Papers.* See January 9, 1805.

[30] *Ibid.*

[31] Personal conversation with Willard Sterne Randall, Visiting Professor of History at Champlain College, Burlington, Vermont.

[32] Barnes, Papers.

[33] "Prayer Stamp for Washington Called Baseless," *New York Herald-Tribune*, 5 February 1930. P. 1.

[34] Barnes wrote in the front sheet of his manuscript:
Paper by Lemuel C. Barnes prepared for the Backus Historical Society.
First read to the "C.C." May 4, 1891
Pittsburgh Baptist Ministers Conference, Sept. 25, 1893
Fourth Avenue Church, Feb. 21, 1897 a.m. (In part) First Church Worcester, Feb. 22, 1903 (In part) First Church Milwaukee, Feb. 21, 1926 (In part)

Promised to Prof. English, President Backus Historical Society for the Society.
After that promised to 'The Standard' of Chicago for publication but never handed over to them.

A revision submitted to the presidents of all Baptist Theological seminaries in 1922. All approved of having it published, several quite warmly. One, Dr. Horr, with a misgiving. Plan not pursued.

Another recension was given as a dedication address of the Gano Memorial Chapel, William Jewel College, Liberty, Mo. Sept. 26, 1926. Published, (without proof reading!) in the College Bulletin.

Two pages are given to the baptism tradition in the thirty-three page discussion of "George Washington and Freedom of Conscience" in the "JOURNAL OF RELIGION" quarterly, Oct. 1932." Barnes, Papers.

[35] Letter of Gen. Richard M. Gano, published in the *Witness of the Spirit*, P. 205. Barnes, Papers.

[36] *Ibid.*

[37] *Ibid.*

[38] Barnes, *Was General George Washington Baptized?*

[39] Barnes, Papers.

[40] *The Watchman*, Boston 1889. Quoted by L. C. Barnes in his unpublished manuscript, *Was General George Washington Baptized by Chaplain John Gano?*

[41] Barnes, Papers.

[42] Barnes also had a note in his papers which stated:

The *Examiner*, Feb 20, 1908. Cut of oil painting of Gano baptizing Washington, made by order of Rev. E. T. Sanford of North Church, Manhattan. He "employed French and German artists to paint picture representing baptism of G.W. in the Potomac River." Desk of G[ano] in home of C.V. Sanford, Mrs. Mary Forbes Gano, Bryan Cobb of New London, Indiana, d[aughter] of Daniel G[ano], John G[ano]'s son, said, (97 yrs old June 11, 1901), that her father was a witness of the baptism of G.W.—Barnes, Papers.

[43] Backus, *Abridgement*, 217.

[44] *Ibid.*

[45] *Ibid.*

[46] *Ibid.*, 219-220.

[47] *Ibid.*, 263.

[48] *Ibid.*, 262.

CHAPTER THIRTEEN
A Sudden and Powerful Impulse

[1] James B. Taylor, *Virginia Baptist Ministers vol. 1* (Richmond: Lippincott & Co., 1859), P. 142

[2] Joe M. King, *A History of South Carolina Baptists* (Columbia: South Carolina General Board of South Carolina Baptist Convention, 1964), P. 340.

[3] David Benedict, *History of the Baptist Denomination, vol. 2* (1813; Reprint ed., Dayton: Church History Research and Archives, 1985), P. 174.

[4] *Ibid.*

[5] *Ibid.*, 174.

[6] *Ibid.*, 180.

[7] James Donovan Mosteller, *A History of the Kiokee Baptist Church in Georgia* (Ann Arbor: Edwards Brothers, 1952), P. 232.

[8] Benedict, *History of the Baptist Denomination, vol. 2*: 174.

[9] B.W. Whilden, "Rev. Abraham Marshall." *Christian Repository*, April 1874, P. 274.

[10] David Benedict, "Biography of Abraham Marshall." Manuscript in the Papers of David Benedict, Rhode Island Historical Society, Providence, Rhode Island.

[11] Benedict, "Abraham Marshall."

[12] Whilden, "Abraham Marshall."

[13] Benedict, "Abraham Marshall."

[14] Whilden, "Abraham Marshall."

[15] Benedict, *History of the Baptist Denomination*, vol. 2: 188.

[16] *Ibid.*, 215.

[17] J. J. Burnett, D.D., *Sketches of Tennessee's Pioneer Baptist Preachers* (Nashville: Press of Marshall & Bruce Co., 1919), P. 389.

[18] Benedict, *History of the Baptist Denomination*, vol. 2: 215.

[19] *Ibid.*, 216.

[20] George Washington Paschal, *History of North Carolina Baptists vol. 1* (Raleigh: Edwards & Broughton Co., 1930), P. 317

[21] Paschal, *History of N. C. Baptists vol. 1*: 315.

[22] Benedict wrote:

At the annual meeting of the Association in 1797, the churches on Richland Creek, Mill Creek, and the Head of Red River, were admitted as members of the infant establishment. That on Richland Creek was the first Baptist church that was gathered on the south side of the Cumberland River. The Rev. John Dillahunty took the care of this church at its commencement, and still continues their much-respected pastor. He emigrated from the Neuse Association an eminent and successful Baptist preacher for fifty-five years. Benedict, *History of the Baptist Denomination*, vol. 2: 220.

[23] S. H. Ford, "Planting and Progress of the Baptist Cause in Tennessee." *Christian Repository*, January 1876, P. 41.

[24] Benedict, *History of the Baptist Denomination*, vol. 2: 219.

[25] Ford, *"Planting and Progress in Tennessee*, 41.

[26] John Mason Peck, "Jeremiah Vardeman." *Christian Repository*, August 1854. P. 458.

[27] J. H. Spencer, *A History of the Kentucky Baptists from 1769-1885 vol. 1* (Cincinnati: By the Author, 1885), P. 13.

[28] George W. Pascal, *North Carolina Historical Review vol. VII, No. 3*, July 1930.

[29] George Ranck, *The Travelling Church* (Louisville: Press of the Baptist Book Concern, 1891), P. 6.

[30] *Ibid.*

[31] W. B. Hackley, "The Well Across the Road," *Virginia Baptist Historical Society, Number Three*, 1964, P. 135.

[32] William Cathcart, *The Baptist Encyclopedia* (Philadelphia: Louis H. Everts, 1883), P. 285.

[33] Spencer, *History of Ky. Baptists*, vol. 1: 31-32.

[34] John Taylor, *The History of the Ten Baptist Churches* (Bloomfield: William H. Holmes, 1826), P. 34.

[35] *Ibid.*, 29.

[36] Spencer, *History of Ky. Baptists*, vol. 1: 58-59.

[37] *Ibid.*, 63.

[38] William Hickman, *A Short Account of my Life and Travels* (1828; reprint ed., Louisville: The Kentucky Baptist Historical Commision, 1969), P. 5.

[39] *Ibid.* 20.

[40] William P. Harvey, "Baptist Work in Kentucky for Ninety-nine Years." *Christian Repository*, November 1875, P. 347.

[41] Cathcart, *Baptist Encyclopedia*, 285.

[42] J. H. Spencer, *A History of the Kentucky Baptists from 1769-1885 vol. 2* (Cincinnati: By the Author, 1885), P. 47.

[43] Gano's son and grandson became entangled with the Campbellite heresy.

[44] Benedict, *History of the Baptist Denomination, vol. 2:* 229.

[45] The Separates were distinctive in their manner, demeanor, and way of life. There can be no doubt that the distinctives of the Separates were kept at a price and with certain sacrifices. We cannot help but believe something special was lost when those distinctives, along with their name, began to vanish.

[46] Benedict, *History of the Baptist Denomination, vol. 2:* 238.

[47] The Bracken Association was formed out of Elkhorn in 1798. Cathcart, *Baptist Encyclopedia*, 285.

[48] John Taylor Christian, *A History of the Baptists* (Nashville: The Sunday School Board, 1926) P. 306.

[49] Cathcart, *Baptist Encyclopedia*, 867.

[50] See chapter 15 for information on the Church of Jesus Christ of Latter-Day Saints.

[51] Ralph S. Harrelson, *Pioneer Baptist Ministers, Voices in the Wilderness of the Illinois Country* (By the Author, 1987), P. 4.

[52] Myron D. Dillow, *James Smith, Baptist Trailblazer in Illinois* (Nashville: Historical Committee, Illinois Baptist State Association, 1987), P. 8.

[53] Harrelson, *Pioneer Baptist Ministers*, 5.

[54] "Pioneer Preachers of the West." *Christian Repository*, December 1871. P. 522.

[55] John Reynolds, *Pioneer History of Illinois* (Chicago: Fergus printing company, 1887), P. 256.

[56] Taylor, *History of the Ten Baptist Churches*, 19.

[57] W. E. Paxton, "Early Baptists of Mississippi." *Christian Repository*, July 1876, P. 9-15.

[58] John T. Buck, "Historical Sketches of the Baptists in the State of Mississippi." *Ford's Christian Repository*, March 1883, P. 184.

[59] Paxton, "Early Baptists of Mississippi," P. 12.

[60] *Ibid.*,13.

[61] Buck, "Baptists in Mississippi," 184.

[62] *Ibid.*, 276.

[63] *Ibid.*, 186.

[64] William T. Stott, *Indiana Baptist History* (Franklin: By the Author, 1908), 37.

[65] Samuel H. Ford, "Rise and Progress of the Baptist Cause in Indiana" *Christian Repository*, January 1876, P. 50.

[66] Stott, *Indiana Baptist History*, 51.

[67] *Ibid.*, 42.

CHAPTER FOURTEEN
The Great Revival and the Birth of Foreign Missions

[1] William Lumpkin, *Baptist Inroads in the South* (Shelbyville: Bible and Literature Missionary Foundation, n.d.), P. 20.

[2] E. Wayne Thompson and David L. Cummins, *This Day in Baptist History* (Greenville: Bob Jones University Press, 1993), P. 496.

[3] "The Baptist Triennial Convention" *Christian Repository*, January, 1876, P. 30.

[4] David Benedict, *History of the Baptist Denomination*, vol. 1 (1813; reprint ed., Dayton: Church History Research and Archives, 1985), P. 524-526.

[5] P. Marion Simms, *The Bible in America* (New York: Wilson Erickson Co., 1936), P. 126.

[6] *Ibid.*

[7] *Ibid.*, P. 126-127.

[8] *Ibid.*, P. 128.

[9] *Ibid.*

[10] *Ibid.*

[11] John Mason Peck, "Jeremiah Vardeman." *Christian Repository*, August 1854, P. 464.

[12] Samuel H. Ford, "David Thomas, the Old Blind Preacher." *Christian Repository*, March 1857, P. 162.

[13] John Taylor, *The History of Ten Baptist Churches* (Bloomfield: William H. Holmes, 1826), P. 135.

[14] *Christian Repository*, December 1856, P. 339.

[15] *Ibid.*

[16] *Ibid.*

[17] *Ibid.*

[18] *Ibid.*

[19] Benedict, *History of the Baptist Denomination*, 2: 253.

[20] Taylor, *History of Ten Baptist Churches*, 131.

[21] *Ibid.*, 132.

[22] *Christian Repository*, December 1856, P. 340.

[23] Taylor, *History of Ten Baptist Churches*, 142.

[24] *Christian Repository*, December 1856, P. 342.

[25] J. H. Spencer, *A History of the Kentucky Baptists from 1769-1885 vol. 1* (Cincinnati: By the Author, 1885), P. 547.

[26] *Christian Repository*, December 1856, P. 341.

[27] Spencer, *History of Ky. Baptists, vol.1*: 51.

[28] J. H. Spencer, *A History of the Kentucky Baptists from 1769-1885 vol. 2* (Cincinnati: By the Author, 1885), P. 150.

[29] With such progress, *the adversary* brought distraction to the Kentucky Baptists. Just as the Great Revival in Kentucky was coming to a close, John Garrard, Baptist preacher and sometime governor of Kentucky and Augustine Eastin, also a preacher, became entangled with "Arianism." This heresy renders Jesus inferior to His Father. Garrard and Eastin were probably infected with this by their contact with Harry Toulmin, the Secretary of State.

Cooper's Run Baptist Church embraced Garrard and Eastin and was expelled from the Elkhorn Association in 1802. The Spiritual condition of the association was much improved by a sound pamphlet on the Trinity written by David Barrow.

In the South District John Bailey apparently embraced the sentiments of the Universalists. This occurred in 1791. For whatever reason, South District restored Bailey in 1801. In 1803 John Bailey was elected moderator of the South District.

Here, John Rice and a very young Jeremiah Vardeman withdrew from the South District to form their own South District Association without the tincture of Universalism from Bailey. Rice and Vardeman's new association was the one recognized by the other Baptists. *Ibid.*, 552.

[30] "Jeremiah Vardeman." 470.

[31] S. H. Ford, "The Vardemans." *Christian Repository*, July 1876, P. 73.

[32] "Jeremiah Vardeman," 471.

[33] Ford, "The Vardemans," 73.

[34] "Jeremiah Vardeman."

[35] *Ibid.*

[36] *Ibid.*

[37] J. H. Grime, *History of Middle Tennessee Baptists* (Nashville: Baptist and Reflector, 1902), P. 34-35.

[38] Benedict, *History of the Baptist Denomination, vol. 2*: 216.

[39] *Ibid.* 217.

[40] See endnotes from chapter five.

[41] "Jeremiah Vardeman." 472.

[42] Benedict, *History of the Baptist Denomination, vol. 2*: 174.

[43] William Cathcart, *The Baptist Encyclopedia* (Philadelphia: Louis H. Everts, 1883), 780.

[44] Benedict, *History of the Baptist Denomination, vol. 2*: 188.

[45] Thompson and Cummins, *This Day, vol. 1*: 128.

[46] Benedict, *History of the Baptist Denomination, vol. 2*: 169.

[47] *Ibid.*, 165-67.

[48] Alice Murphy Sturgess, *The History of William Murphy and His Descendants* (St. Louis: Nixon-Jones Printing Co., 1918), P. 9.

[49] R. S. Douglass, *History of Missouri Baptists* (Kansas City: Western Baptist Publishing Company, 1934), P. 22.

[50] *Ibid.*

[51] Cathcart, *Baptist Encyclopedia*, 38.

[52] William Ward baptized Adoniram and Ann Judson. William Cathcart originally recorded that William Carey baptized them at Serampore, September 6th, 1812. Cathcart later corrected the error. Sallie Rochester Ford, "America's Pioneer Female Misssionary," *Christian Repository*, November 1883, P. 391.

[53] Cathcart, *Baptist Encyclopedia*, 1165.

[54] S. Ford, "Pioneer Female Misssionary," 391.

[55] Cathcart, *Baptist Encyclopedia*, 1267.

[56] *Ibid.*, 1267.

[57] Thomas Armitage, *Addresses and Other Matter* (New York: American and Foreign Bible Society, 1882), P. 5.

[58] *Proceedings of a meeting held in the Oliver Street Baptist Church* (New York: J. A. Gray, Printer, 1850), P. 15.

[59] *Ibid.*

[60] Thompson and Cummins, *This Day in Baptist History*, 238.

CHAPTER FIFTEEN
Satan's Plan for America

[1] James B. Taylor, *Virginia Baptist Ministers vol. 1* (Richmond: Lippincott & Co., 1859), P. 131

[2] Consider the following incident. Although it seems trivial, it had far-reaching consequences: Around 1809, Old Jacob Creath, pastor and Thomas Lewis, member of Town Fork Church in Lexington, Kentucky, exchanged slave girls. The poor girl that was given to Old Jacob Creath died. So the preacher refused to pay(!) a difference owed on her. This neglect of payment was brought before the church!! The church said Creath did not have to pay. The obnoxious nature of all of this is bile to our taste and bickering over bartering of human beings is repugnant to say the least.

We shall come to discover, in the latter career of Old Jacob Creath, a better understanding of the immense distraction caused by his actions. Something about him miffed the old Kentucky preachers. Elijah Craig wrote a tract indicting Creath of odd charges. Baptist people in that part of Kentucky took sides on the ridiculous issues. Town Fork Baptist Church called a council from 16 churches to investigate!!! The pressing of the issue by Thomas Lewis and Elijah Craig should not have occurred. But, we may well see the power of Creath, because he won the approval of the council, yet made himself odious to the older pioneer preachers.

Creath's aquittal angered the churches at Bryants Creek, Boons Creek, East Hickman, Elk Lick, Ravens's Creek, Mountain Island, Silas, Rock Bridge, Mill Creek and Flat Creek. So much did they resent Creath, they attempted to dissolve Elkhorn Association and create a new association at Bryant's Creek. When the "new" association and the old association met separately in August of 1810, the old Elkhorn sent an appeal for unity. The new association refused their invitation and withdrew to form the Licking Association. There must have been deeper reasons for avoiding Jacob Creath than what was generally broadcast. The leadership of Licking Association included John Price, Ambrose Dudley, Joseph Redding, Lewis Corbin and Absolom Bainbridge. J. H. Spencer, *A History of the Kentucky Baptists from 1769-1885 vol. 2* (Cincinnati: By the Author, 1885), P. 552

[3] Whitefield had a "modified" Calvinism. According to William Lumpkin, Whitefield often quoted Isaac Watts: "We should first go to grammar-school of faith and repentance, before we go to the university of predestination." William Lumpkin, *Baptist Inroads in the South* (Shelbyville: Bible and Literature Missionary Foundation, n.d.), P 60.

[4] Isaac Backus, *An Abridgement to the Church History of New England* (1804; reprint ed., Boston: Harvard University, 1935), P. 254.

[5] *Ibid.*, 254-255.

[6] Elder John Leland, *The Writings of Elder John Leland Including Some Events in His Life* (New York: G. W. Wood, 1845), P. 172.

[7] William G. McLoughlin, Data Sheets on the Isaac Backus Papers, Hay Library, Brown University, Providence, Rhode Island.

[8] Thomas Armitage, *The History of the Baptists, vol. 2* (1890; reprint ed., Watertown: Maranatha Baptist Press, 1976), P. 561.

[9] McLoughlin, Data sheets.

[10] J. H. Spencer, *A History of the Kentucky Baptists from 1769-1885 vol. 1* (Cincinnati: By the Author, 1885), P. 15.

[11] *Ibid.*, 16.

[12] S. H. Ford, "Rise of the Current Reformation." *Christian Repository*, January 1860, P. 22.

[13] *Ibid.*

[14] Ford, "Current Reformation," Jan (1860): 24.

[15] John T. Christian, *A History of the Baptists in the United States* (Nashville: Sunday School Board, 1926), P. 424.

[16] *Ibid.*, 404.

[17] *Ibid.*, 413.

[18] John Taylor, *Some Thoughts on Missions* [Online] http://www.carthage.lib.il.us/community/churches/primbap/Thoughts2.html, Jan 2004.

[19] Spencer, *History of Ky. Baptists vol. 1:* 575.

[20] William Cathcart, *The Baptist Encyclopedia* (Philadelphia: Louis H. Everts, 1883), P. 78.

[21] *Ibid.*

[22] William Cathcart wrote in 1883: "The record of 1844 reported 184 Old School Associations, 1622 churches, 900 ordained ministers, 2374 baptized in the year preceding, and 61,162 members. The year book for 1880 returns 900 Old School churches, 400 ordained ministers, and 40,000 members—a loss of one third in thirty-six years. *Ibid.*

[23] Ford, "Current Reformation," Jan (1860): 24.

[24] *Ibid.*

[25] *Ibid.*

[26] *Ibid.*

[27] *Ibid.*, 28-29

[28] S. H. Ford, "Rise of the Current Reformation." *Christian Repository*, August 1860, P. 567.

[29] *Ibid.*, 570.

[30] John Taylor, *The History of Ten Baptist Churches* (Bloomfield: William H. Holmes, 1826), P. 14-18.

[31] *Ibid.*

[32] Ford, "Current Reformation," Aug (1860): 570.

[33] Spencer, *History of Ky. Baptists, vol. 1:*43.

[34] Ford, "Current Reformation," Aug (1860): 610.

[35] This is precisely what happened to the legacy of Charles Finney at Oberlin College in Ohio. It will happen to every Baptist college that has no real articles of faith regarding man's powerlessness to save himself, therefore needing the imputed righteousness of Christ. While the author is not a "Calvinist" Baptist, we affirm "justification by the imputed righteousness of Jesus Christ." (Romans 4:20-24)

[36] Ford, "Current Reformation," Aug (1860): 172.

[37] The actual expulsion took place in January of 1831. *Ibid.*

[38] Spencer, *History of Ky. Baptists, vol. 2:* 599.

[39] The deniers of *experimental religion* will always have a hatred for those that preach the religion of the heart, the conversion of the sinner evidenced by an affected soul. Spencer, *History of Ky. Baptists, vol. 1:* 618.

[40] *Ibid.*, 620.

[41] *Ibid.*, 624-635.

[42] *Ibid.*, 642.

[43][Online]
http://www.christianchronicler.com/History2/delusions_of_sidney_rigdon.html   Jan 2004.

[44] F. Mark McKiernan, *The Voice of Sidney Rigdon* (Lawrence, KS: Coronado Press, 1972, 79), P. 36.

[45] *Ibid.*

[46] Sidney Rigdon, *Oration on the 4ᵗʰ of July 1838* (Far West: Printed at the Journal Office, 1838), P. 12.

[47] The Mormons claim he was martyred.

[48] Leland, *Writings of John Leland*, 685-687.

[49] Lemuel Call Barnes, *Pioneers of Light, The First Century of The American Baptist Publication Society 1824-1924* (Philadelphia: The American Baptist Publication Society, n.d.), P. 70.

[50] "An Argument Sustaining the Common English Version of the Bible," *Proceedings of a Meeting held in the Oliver St. Baptist Church* (New York: J. A. Gray, 1850), P. 15.

[51] "The Amended Version." *The Examiner,* 9 February 1865.

[52] "The Campbellites and the New Version." *Western Watchman,* 17 November 1853.

[53] The full text of Armitage' report:
The American and Foreign Bible Society held its annual meeting in New York May 11th, 1849, and, on the motion of Hon. Isaac Davis, of Massachusetts, after considerable discussion, it was "Resolved, That the restriction laid by the Society upon the Board of Managers in 1838, to use only the commonly received version in the distribution of the Scriptures in the English language, be removed."

This restriction being removed, the new board referred the question of revision to a committee of five. After long consideration that committee presented three reports: one with three signatures and two minority reports. The third, from the pen of Warren Carter, Esq., was long and labored as an argument against altering the common version at all. In January 1850, the majority report was unanimously adopted in these words:

"Resolved, that, in regard to the expediency of this board undertaking the correction of the English version, a decided difference of opinion exists, and, therefore, that it be judged most prudent to await the instructions of the Society." Armitage, *History,* 900-901.

[54] *Ibid.*

[55] "An Argument," 1.

[56] *Ibid.,* 11.

[57] *Ibid.,* 37.

[58] William R. Williams, "Letter to the Members of Amity Street Baptist Church." *An Argument Sustaining the Common English Version of the Bible* (New York: J. A. Gray, 1850), P. 44.

[59] *Ibid.*, 48.

[60] Armitage, *History*, 902.

[61] Barnes, *Pioneers of Light*, 70-71.

[62] *Christian Repository*, vol. 1, 1852, P. 272.

[63] *Ibid.*, 417.

[64] O. B. Judd, "Revision or no Revision, An address given to the Philadelphia Bible Union." *New York Chronicle*, 26 January 1853.

[65] Cathcart, *Baptist Encyclopedia* , 285.

[66] Lewis Peyton Little, *Imprisoned Preachers and Religious Liberty in Virginia* (Lynchburg: J. P. Bell Co., 1938), P. 338-58.

[67] William S. Simpson, Jr., *Virginia Baptist Ministers, 1760-1790: A Biographical Survey*, vol. 1 (Richmond: By the Author, 1990), P. 37.

[68] Cathcart, *Baptist Encyclopedia*, 682.

[69] John Mason Peck, "Jeremiah Vardeman." *Christian Repository, August* 1854, P. 474.

CHAPTER SIXTEEN
The Great West

[1] "Incidents in the Missionary Life of Rev. George Dana Boardman." *Christian Repository*, September 1881, P. 201.

[2] *Ibid.*

[3] George M. Ella, *Isaac McCoy, Apostle of the Western Trail* (Springfield: Particular Baptist Press, 2003).

[4] *Ibid.*, 9.

[5] *Ibid.*, 48.

[6] *Ibid.*, 53.

[7] William Cathcart, *The Baptist Encyclopedia*, (Philadelphia: Louis H. Everts, 1883), P. 787.

[8] *Ibid.*, 252.

[9] Ella, *Isaac McCoy*, 91.

[10] *Ibid.*, 91.

[11] *Ibid.*, 112.

[12] Cathcart, *Baptist Encyclopedia*, 766.

[13] Ella, *Isaac McCoy*, 375.

[14] *Ibid.*, 7.

[15] *Ibid.*, 21.

[16] J. M.Carroll, *A History of Texas Baptists* (Dallas: Baptist Standard Publishing Co., 1923), P. 13.

[17] *Ibid.*, 17.

[18] *Ibid.*, 22.

[19] *Ibid.*, 27.

[20] *Ibid.*, 42.

[21] *Ibid.*, 8.

[22] *Ibid.*, 46.

[23] *Ibid.*, 50.

[24] *Ibid.*, 55.

[25] *Ibid.*, 58-59.

[26] Joseph H. Borum, *Biographical Sketches of Tennessee Baptist Ministers* (Memphis: Rogers and Co. Publishers, 1880), P. 487.

[27] "Memoir of the late Elder John Logan, of McDonough County, Ill." *Western Watchman*, 3 July 1851.

[28] George W. Robey, "Planting and Progress of the Baptist Cause in Iowa." *Christian Repository*, August 1876, P. 410.

[29] *Ibid.*, 411.

[30] *Ibid.*, 410.

[31] "Celebrate Centennial of Brothertown Baptist Church." Chilton, *Wisconsin Times-Journal*, 9 August 1934.

[32] Cathcart, *Baptist Encyclopedia*, 873.

[33] [Online] http://www.worldstar.com/~carltown/porthis2.htm

[34] Cathcart, *Baptist Encyclopedia*, 873.

[35] *Ibid.*, 1132.

[36] Samuel H. Ford, *Christian Repository*, August 1871, P. 103.

[37] Cathcart, *Baptist Encyclopedia*, 396-7.

[38] Ford, *Christian Repository*, Aug (1871): 104.

[39] Cathcart, *Baptist Encyclopedia*, 662-3

[40] *Ibid.*

[41] W. E. Penn, *The Life and Labors of Major W. E. Penn* (St. Louis: Woodward, 1896).

CHAPTER SEVENTEEN
Sabled Sons and the Division of the Baptists

[1] David Benedict, *History of the Baptist Denomination, vol. 2* (1813; reprint ed., Dayton: Church History Research and Archives, 1985), P. 189.

[2] J. H. Spencer, *A History of the Kentucky Baptists from 1769-1885, vol. 2* (Cincinnati: Spencer, 1885), P. 47.

[3] Alice Murphy Sturgess, *The History of William Murphy and His Descendants* (St. Louis: Nixon-Jones Printing Co., 1918), P. 15.

[4] Spencer, *History of Ky. Baptists*, 2: 48.

[5] Carter Woodson, *A History of the Negro Church* (Washington, D.C.: Associated Publishers, 1921), P. 33.

[6] J. H. Spencer, *A History of the Kentucky Baptists from 1769-1885, vol. 1* (Cincinnati: Spencer, 1885), P. 195.

[7] John Leland, *The Writings of Elder John Leland* (New York: G. W. Wood, 1845), P. 94-95.

[8] *Ibid.*

[9] Benedict, *History of the Baptist Denomination*, 2: 208-9.

[10] *Ibid.*, 206.

[11] Benedict, *History of the Baptist Denomination*, 1: 287.

[12] Walter H. Brooks, *The Silver Bluff Church* (Washington: Press of R. L. Pendleton, 1910), P. 7-9.

[13] *Ibid.*, 16.

[14] Benedict, *History of the Baptist Denomination*, 1: 288-290.

[15] Brooks, *The Silver Bluff Church*, 23.

[16] Woodson, *History of the Negro Church*, 46.

[17] Brooks, *The Silver Bluff Church*, 29.

[18] *Ibid.*

[19] Benedict, *History of the Baptist Denomination*, 2: 190.

[20] *Ibid.*, 190-1.

[21] *Ibid.*, 191.

[22] *Ibid.*

[23] *Ibid.*

[24] *Ibid.*, 192.

[25] Brooks, *The Silver Bluff Church*, 4.

[26] Woodson, *History of the Negro Church*, 111-120.

[27] John T. Buck, "Historical Sketches of the Baptists in the State of Mississippi." *Ford's Christian Repository*, March 1883, P. 186.

[28] Woodson, *History of the Negro Church*, 112-119.

[29] *Ibid.*, 119.

[30] *Ibid.*, 120.

[31] *Ibid.*

[32] *Ibid.*, 121.

[33] Richard Elsworth Day, *Rhapsody in Black* (Valley Forge: Judson Press, 1953), P. 40.

[34] O. C. Wheeler, *The Story of Early Baptist History in California* (Sacramento: California Baptist Historical Society, 1888), P. 13.

[35] *Ibid.*, 14.

[36] *Ibid.*, 16.

[37] *Ibid.*, 19.

[38] John F. Pope, *History of First Baptist Church of San Francisco* (San Francisco: John H. Carmany and Co., 1874), P. 4.

[39] William Cathcart, *The Baptist Encyclopedia* (Philadelphia: Louis H. Everts, 1883), P. 799.

[40] [Online] http://www.kancoll.org/books/andreas_ne/otoe/otoe-p6.html Jan 2004.

[41] From the collections at the Leavenworth County Historical Society and Museum. [Online] http://skyways.lib.ks.us/genweb/leavenwo/library/ Feb 2004.

CHAPTER EIGHTEEN
Education

[1] Elder John Leland, *The Writings of Elder John Leland Including Some Events in His Life* (New York: G. W. Wood, 1845), P. 311-312.

[2] Alvah Hovey, *The Life and Times of Isaac Backus* (1858; reprint ed., Gano Books, 1991), P. 63.

[3] Isaac Backus, *An Abridgement to the Church History of New England* (1804; reprint ed., Boston: Harvard University, 1935), P. 128.

[4] William G. McLoughlin, Data Sheets on the Isaac Backus Papers, Hay Library, Brown University, Providence, Rhode Island.

[5] Backus, *Abridgement*, 136.

[6] *Ibid.*, 229.

[7] Reuben Guild, *Early History of Brown University* (Providence: By the Author, 1897), P. 101.

[8] *Ibid.*, 175.

[9] *Ibid.*, 7.

[10] Isaac Backus, *History of New England, with Particular Reference To the Baptists, vol. 2* (1871; reprint ed., Paris: The Baptist Standard Bearer, n.d.), P. 137.

[11] S. W. Adams, *Memoirs of Rev. Nathaniel Kendrick, D.D.* (Philadelphia: American Baptist Publication Society, 1860), P. 25-26.

[12] William Cathcart, *The Baptist Encyclopedia* (Philadelphia: Louis H. Everts, 1883), P. 327.

[13] George Washington Paschal Papers, Z. Smith Reynolds Library, Wake Forest University, Winston-Salem, North Carolina.

[14] Spright Dowell, *A History of Mercer University 1833-1953* (Macon, Georgia, Mercer University 1953), P. 41.

[15] *Ibid.*, 42.

[16] [Online] http://www.samford.edu/ groups/ministries/convoques.html Feb 2004.

[17] James G. Clark, L.L. D., *History of William Jewell College* (St. Louis: Central Baptist Press, 1893), P. 17-18.

[18] *Ibid.*, 18.

[19] J. J. Burnett, D.D., *Sketches of Tennessee's Pioneer Baptist Preachers* (Nashville: Press of Marshall & Bruce Co., 1919), P. 78.

[20] W. J. McGlothlin, *A History of Furman University* (Nashville: Sunday School Board of the Southern Baptist Convention, n.d.), P. 50.

[21] *Ibid.*, 52.

CHAPTER NINETEEN
Of Hayseeds and Lost Causes

[1] George Washington Paschal, "The Board's Declaration on Union Work." George Washington Paschal Papers, PCMS 86 4/382, Z. Smith Reynolds Library, Wake Forest University, Winston-Salem, North Carolina, P. 12.

[2] Samuel H. Ford, *Christian Repository*, January 1857.

[3] J. Edwin Orr, *The Event of the Century* (Wheaton: International Awakening Press, 1989), P. 267.

[4] *Ibid.*

[5] S. Adlam and J. R. Graves, *The First Baptist Church in America* (Texarkana: Baptist Sunday School Committee, 1939), P. 21.

[6] William Cathcart, *The Baptist Encyclopedia* (Philadelphia: Louis H. Everts, 1883), P. 466.

[7] S. H. Ford, "Life, Times and Teachings of J. R. Graves." *Ford's Christian Repository*, March 1900, P. 163.

[8] *The Trial of J. R. Graves*, Archives of the Southern Baptist Theological Seminary Library, Louisville, Kentucky, 1858, P. 25.

[9] *Ibid.*

[10] The "reproach and injury" came from these issues of the *Tennessee Baptist*: No. 23, Feb. 13, 1858; No. 24, Feb. 20, 1858; No. 26, March 6, 1858; No. 33, April 24, 1858; and July 17, 1858. *Ibid.*, 2.

[11] W. G. Inman, "The Graves Trial." *Ford's Christian Repository*, April 1900, P. 233-234.

[12] Ford, "Life of Graves," 226.

[13] "Christian Union, Baptist Exclusiveness," *Doctrinal and Practical Tracts* (New York: Thomas Holman, 1884), P. 32.

[14] Thomas Armitage, "Christian Union, Real and Unreal," *Doctrinal and Practical Tracts* (New York: Thomas Holman, 1884), P. 5.

[15] *Ibid.*, 4.

[16] *Ibid.*

[17] *Ibid.*

[18] Armitage, "Christian Union," 4.

[19] *Ibid.*, 7.

[20] William McGloughlin Jr., *Modern Revivalism* (Providence: Ronald Press Co., 1959), P. 37.

[21] *Christian Repository*, April 1880, P. 312.

[22] "Remarkable Conversions." *Christian Repository*, June 1879, P. 297.

[23] A. M. Averill, *Baptist Landmarkism Tested* (Dallas: Carter Gibson Printers, 1880), P. 14.

[24] *Ibid.*, Appendix.

[25] Walter B. Shurden called Graves, "the founder and high priest of Landmarkism." We find Graves certainly was *not* the founder of Landmarkism. The "high priest" remark is bizzare. Shurden, in typical modern historical tones wrote, "A 'landmark' was, therefore, an ancient Baptist principle. The problem was that certain 'landmarks' were not as ancient as Landmarkers suggested." Walter B. Shurden, *Crises in Baptist Life*, (Nashville: The Historical Commission of the Southern Baptist Convention, Pamphlet series, 1979).

[26] O. L. Hailey, *J. R. Graves: Life, Times and Teachings*, (Nashville: By the Author, 1929), P. 14.

[27] Ford, "Life of Graves." 170.

[28] Hailey, *Graves: Life*, 64.

[29] *Ibid.*

[30] Samuel H. Ford, "Dr. Whitsitt's Statement In Regard To Dr. J. R. Graves—A Protest." *Christian Repository*, January 1900, P. 169.

[31] *Ibid.*

[32] William Dudley Nowlin, *Kentucky Baptist History, 1770 - 1922* (Louisville: Baptist Book Concern, 1922), P. 142-154.

[33] *Ibid.*

[34] *Ibid.*

[35] Joseph Angus, "Early English Baptists." *Christian Repository*, January 1897.

[36] Vedder, Professor of Church History in Crozer Theological Seminary wrote: "The greatest error of historic Christianity, and error so grave in results as to be both tragic and pathetic, has been its agelong effort to substitute for the ever ripening expression of the inner life of Christians of all ages the Christian experience of a single age, as an unchanging, authoritative, infallible norm of the Christian life for all time to come. Instead of something dynamic, the attempt has been made to make theology static. The bane of religion is the dogmatist's search for authority, and his insistence that he has found authority where none exists. For, in the usual sense of the word, there is no authority in religion, nothing fixed, unalterable, infallible; because religion is life, and life is growth, and growth is change." Henry C. Vedder, *Fundamentals of Christianity* (New York: The Macmillan Company, 1923), P. 215

[37] S. H. Ford, "The True and Real Inspiration of the Bible." *Christian Repository*, February 1880, P. 102-103.

[38] J. J. Burnett, D.D., *Sketches of Tennessee's Pioneer Baptist Preachers* (Nashville: Press of Marshall & Bruce Co., 1919), P. 136-138.

[39] *Ibid.*, 400-408.

[40] William Dudley Nowlin, "A Pioneer Baptist Hero." *Christian Repository*, October 1905, P. 607.

[41] "Aged Baptist Minister Buried in Bellefontaine." *St. Louis Daily Globe-Democrat*, 5 July 1905, P. 1.

CHAPTER TWENTY
Baptist Nation's Greatest Need

[1] James B. Taylor, *Virginia Baptist Ministers vol. 1* (Richmond: Lippincott & Co., 1859), P 286.

[2] *Ibid.*, 288.

[3] *Ibid.*, 289.

[4] Joseph Belcher, *George Whitefield: A Biography* (New York: American Tract Society, n.d.), P. 318.